Naval Blockades in Peace

This book examines a number of major blockades, inc
in the Napoleonic Wars, the War of 1812, the American Civil War, and World Wars I
and II, in addition to the increased use of peacetime blockades and sanctions with
the hope of avoiding war. The impact of new technology and organizational changes
on the nature of blockades and their effectiveness as military measures are discussed.
Legal, economic, and political questions are explored to understand the various
constraints on belligerent behavior. The analyses draw on the extensive amount of
quantitative material available from military publications.

Lance E. Davis is Mary Stillman Harkness Professor of Social Science, Emeritus, at
the California Institute of Technology. He is author or editor of many books, includ-
ing *Institutional Change and American Economic Growth* (1971, with Douglass North),
Mammon and the Pursuit of Empire: The Political Economy of British Imperialism (1986,
with Robert Huttenback; revised and abridged edition, 1988), *International Capital
Markets and American Economic Growth, 1820–1914* (1994, with Robert Cull), and
*Evolving Financial Markets and International Capital Flows: Britain, the Americas, and
Australia, 1865–1914* (2001, with Robert E. Gallman), all published by Cambridge
University Press.

Stanley L. Engerman is John H. Munro Professor of Economics and Professor of
History at the University of Rochester. Among his co-authored and co-edited
volumes are *Time on the Cross: The Economics of American Negro Slavery* (1974, with
Robert W. Fogel), *The Cambridge Economic History of the United States* (1996, 2000,
with Robert E. Gallman), *A Historical Guide to World Slavery* (1998, with Seymour
Drescher), and *Finance, Intermediaries, and Economic Development* (Essays in Honor
of Lance E. Davis; 2003; with Philip T. Hoffman, Jean-Laurent Rosenthal, and
Kenneth L. Sokoloff).

Naval Blockades in Peace and War

AN ECONOMIC HISTORY SINCE 1750

LANCE E. DAVIS
California Institute of Technology

STANLEY L. ENGERMAN
University of Rochester

CAMBRIDGE UNIVERSITY PRESS
Cambridge, New York, Melbourne, Madrid, Cape Town,
Singapore, São Paulo, Delhi, Mexico City

Cambridge University Press
The Edinburgh Building, Cambridge CB2 8RU, UK

Published in the United States of America by Cambridge University Press, New York

www.cambridge.org
Information on this title: www.cambridge.org/9781107406155

First published 2006
First paperback edition 2012

A catalogue record for this publication is available from the British Library

Library of Congress Cataloguing in Publication Data
Davis, Lance Edwin.
Naval blockades in peace and war : an economic history since 1750 / Lance E. Davis,
Stanley L. Engerman.
p.   cm.
Includes bibliographical references and index.
ISBN 0-521-85749-X (hardcover)
1. Blockade – History.   2. Blockade – Economic aspects.   3. Naval strategy.   4. Sea-power.
5. Economic sanctions.   6. Naval history, Modern.   I. Engerman, Stanley L.   II. Title.
V180.D38   2006
359.4'409–dc22   2006016306

ISBN 978-0-521-85749-9 Hardback
ISBN 978-1-107-40615-5 Paperback

To our children

Maili Davis Kessler
David, Mark, and Jeffrey Engerman

Contents

Preface

Our interest in the subject of blockades came about when we were both asked to discuss the work of David Surdam on the American Civil War blockade imposed by the Northern states on the Confederacy. Surdam's analysis of this case was thorough and his general conclusions were quite interesting. What we became curious about was whether other of the notable blockades of the past two centuries had similar outcomes, and if not, why not. As we began to examine other blockades, we found that there was a considerable body of international law that had some influence on the outcomes but whose changes over time reflected changing political, economic, and military factors. The blockades of interest were not just those for military purposes in wartime but also Pacific blockades, or sanctions, presumably imposed in the attempt to prevent warfare.

The study of blockades posed many interesting economic issues and there were available considerable amounts of quantitative data to permit much statistical analysis. This aspect of the study fits well with our professional background. There were two possible problems that we do not believe seriously weaken the analyses in the book. First, we had no formal training as military historians, nor did we seek to utilize naval archives to obtain primary material. Nevertheless, there have been ample amounts of material collected in secondary sources, and there is an extremely rich body of important work by military historians for us to utilize for quantitative and qualitative information. Second, we have rather limited abilities in languages other than English but could, with the help of colleagues, learn from foreign-language publications. Given the time that has passed since the blockades on which we focused, much of the key foreign language material has been translated into English, in full or in part, so that we have been able to benefit from many of the works first published in other languages. Although there may be some difficulties due to these two problems, we do feel that they had little impact on our analysis and conclusions.

We have benefited from the comments received at presentations at the 2000 meeting of the Economic History Association, the 2001 meeting of the American Economic Association, at Eli F. Heckscher: A Celebratory Symposium held at the Stockholm School of Economics in May 2003, and at a public lecture at Colby College.

We also have benefited from comments by François Crouzet, three readers for Cambridge University Press, David Surdam, Richard Patard, Gregory A. Caldeira, John Nye, Mary McKinnon, and Hugh Rockoff. A shortened version of Chapter 8 was published in the *Journal of Economic Perspectives*, Spring 2003, which contains the relevant acknowledgments for that essay.

Secretarial and other logistical support were supplied by the Division of Humanities and Social Sciences, California Institute of Technology (particularly by Heather Guyett), and by the Department of Economics, University of Rochester. Excellent research assistance was provided by Ozgur Yilmaz and Maria E. Canon at the University of Rochester. The final typescript was prepared by Ken Maher. We also wish to thank, for extensive help and guidance, Frank Smith at Cambridge University Press, Richard Shrout and associates for indexing, and Kenneth Karpinski at Techbooks for guidance through the production process.

1

Introduction

"Thou Shalt Not Pass"

1. ECONOMIC WARFARE

During a war there are a number of alternative military and naval strategies that a belligerent power can pursue in that country's efforts to defeat its enemies. Obviously, one such strategy is conquest by force of arms in direct combat. Such a strategy involves the siege or the invasion of an enemy's territory, and it is aimed at the destruction, capture, or surrender of the enemy's armed forces and, perhaps, the permanent occupation of its territory. Economic warfare, by weakening the enemy's ability to pursue military action, can substitute for or complement a strategy of direct combat. Such an economic strategy is designed to sever the trading links between the enemy and his allies or with neutral powers, and, in so doing, to reduce the level of military and civilian goods that are available to support his military ventures. Historically, the blockade, usually sea-based but occasionally land-based, has been the most common form of economic warfare; however, in the more recent past, other forms of economic warfare have been utilized. They include the imposition of higher tariffs, nontariff exclusions, restrictions on capital movements, and policies aimed at encouraging the production of substitutes by the targeting and neutral nations – all tactics designed to reduce enemy exports as well as their imports. In addition, the scope of direct economic warfare has been expanded to include the aerial bombardment of economic objectives, sanctions designed to restrict trade to neutral countries, sabotage of economic targets, preemptive purchases of strategic material, and, more generally, psychological warfare. Although naval blockades remained their major concern, this widening of scope was mirrored in the British government's decision to change the name of the department charged with implementing that county's economic warfare efforts from the Ministry of Blockade during World War I to the Ministry of Economic Warfare during World War II.[1]

For centuries, land and sea blockades have been initiated unilaterally by belligerent powers for military or commercial motives. Some early naval blockades were mainly extensions of land blockades, part of the siege of a fortress or city located on the sea. It was, however, only in early modern Europe that the rules and laws of blockade, like the laws of war, were formalized and enshrined in a series of international agreements. Although such agreements date back to at least 1689, from the point of view of the past century, the most important were the treaty that emerged from the Congress of Paris of 1856 and the never ratified end product of the Conference of London of 1909. Both spelled out a set of rules that were, formally or informally, accepted by most developed nations. Nevertheless, as with most rules of law, their acceptability and applicability varied with the intensity of the conflict and with changes in the technology and organization of warfare.

In simple terms, a naval blockade can be viewed as an attempt by one belligerent, through the "interception by sea of the approaches to the coasts or ports of an enemy," to cut "off all his overseas communications."[2] The general aim is to reduce the enemy's ability to effectively carry out military operations. Blockades designed to starve or weaken the enemy's civilian and military population by reducing imports of food supplies have received the most attention; however, blockades also have been aimed at the importation of munitions, other war supplies, and critical raw materials – petroleum and minerals, in particular. In addition to reducing imports, blockades frequently have also been directed at a country's exports. In this latter case, the goal is usually to reduce the enemy's ability to obtain the wherewithal to pay for imported resources. In a somewhat parallel fashion, the blockading power

1 W. N. Medlicott, *The Economic Blockade*, 2 vols. (London: His Majesty's Stationary Office, 1952) vol. 1, xi, 1–3.
2 C. John Colombos, *The International Law of the Sea*, 4th rev. ed. (London: Longmans, 1959), 649–687. Von Heinegg, writing on "Naval Blockade" in 2000, uses the "widely accepted definition" of a blockade as "a belligerent operation to prevent vessels and/or aircraft of all nations, enemy as well as neutral, from entering or exiting specified ports, airfields, or coastal areas belonging to, occupied by, or under the control of enemy nations," citing the U.S. Department of the Navy, *The Commander's Handbook on the Law of Naval Operations*. (Note the addition of aircraft to the customary list of vessels in the definition of a blockade.) Von Heinegg claims that most blockades are for military purposes, not for economic ends. See Wolff Heintschel von Heinegg, "Naval Blockade," in *International Law Across the Spectrum of Conflict: Essays in Honor of Professor L. C. Green on the Occasion of his Eightieth Birthday*, ed. Michael N. Schmitt (Newport: Naval War College, 2000), 203–230. For this distinction, see also Julian S. Corbett, *Some Principles of Maritime Strategy* (London: Longmans, Green, 1911) and Charles H. Stockton, *Outlines of International Law* (New York: Charles Scribner's Sons, 1914), both of whom distinguish blockades to restrict military vessels from blockades to stop the flows of trade.

may attempt to use political pressure or military threat against neutrals to limit the enemy's ability to acquire loans and capital from neutral nations. It is this diversity of ends and of means that makes evaluation of the success of any blockade difficult.

Strictly speaking, a legal blockade entails the right to stop all merchant vessels seeking to enter a previously designated area. The legal right to seize contraband, by contrast, applies only to a limited and specific list of war materials; but these materials can be seized anywhere in the world.

A country's decision to deploy a blockade designed to limit enemy exports and imports has a counterpart in the use of embargoes to limit that country's own exports to foes and neutrals. The aim of such embargoes often appears to be less economic than political – by creating a shortage of specific goods, the nation or coalition adopting the embargo hopes to influence a third country's behavior toward the other belligerent. Although there have been some notable, if not particularly effective, embargoes – Jefferson's early-nineteenth-century embargo of all American exports and the South's embargo of cotton exports during the Civil War, to cite two examples – the relative importance of blockades and embargoes in history can be effectively proxied by the coverage given to the two strategies in the standard works on international law. In those publications, embargoes received less than 10 percent of the coverage given to blockades.

Although most blockades are deployed by belligerent powers in wartime, there have been some that involved neither war nor belligerent powers. For example, blockades have been used to deter war by weakening a potential enemy before an official declaration of war. The legal status of such Pacific blockades is rather uncertain; but, in recent years, under the newly coined rubric of "economic sanctions," they have been deployed by both individual countries and by international organizations (the United Nations [UN] and the North Atlantic Treaty Organization [NATO], for example). Nor are all blockades deployed for political or for purely economic reasons. For example, during the years following its political decision to halt the transatlantic slave trade, Britain mounted a blockade of the African coast. The British government drew on existing antipiracy laws to justify its decision, and their naval squadron actually engaged in military skirmishes with vessels from France and other powers. Earlier, during the long series of eighteenth-century wars between Britain and France, the British maintained a mainly military blockade of French ports on the Atlantic. That blockade was designed to keep the French fleet bottled up in port and to prevent it from supporting an invasion of the British Isles, although it did have an impact on French trade with the West Indies.

The major legal and political problems engendered by blockades arise not only from the impact of the intervention on enemies but also from their effect on neutral "third" countries. Neutrals often represent potential alternative sources of supply; and, given that goods from anywhere can be routed through those neutrals, a blockade that does not restrict neutral trade with the enemy may well prove ineffective. Neutrals are, however, not belligerents; and as nonbelligerents they often believe that their commercial activities should not be constrained. Attempts to limit their exports and imports can bring them into direct conflict with the blockading power, and attempts to resolve those disputes have generated an extensive body of international law. Moreover, the issues involving neutral rights go beyond those raised by a naval blockade – such blockades are relevant only to controversies arising from contacts at sea. For a blockade to be effective, it must be extended to cover neutrals contiguous to or connected by land with the enemy; and, therefore, international laws must be extended to cover the myriad of political policies designed to deal with neutral overland trade.

The expected benefit of a successful blockade seems clear – a loss of enough of the enemy's military power to shift the probability of victory in a favorable direction. But these benefits are not pure profits; there also are costs involved in any decision to deploy a blockade. These costs include the direct expenditures on vessels and manpower that are needed to mount the blockade, the opportunity costs of diverting resources from alternative employment, the potential costs (in men and vessels) from damage or destruction by enemy action, and the possible costs that might result should the blockade induce a neutral to enter the war on the side of the enemy. Any military planner who sets out to design an "optimum naval blockade" must take into account geography (the length of the relevant shoreline), the available technology (ships, aircraft, equipment), and the level of military organization, economic power, and the probable response of neutral countries.

The planner, however, must always assess the likely enemy responses. Those responses can have a major impact on the blockade's costs and effectiveness. Such reactions will depend, in part, on the enemy's technology (again, ships, aircraft, and equipment), its economic power, and the level of its military organization. The planner will, in addition, also be forced to estimate the enemy's willingness to use what has proved to be the most effective weapon against a "distant" blockade – the convoy. A convoy is simply a group of merchant ships sailing together escorted by a number of armed vessels whose officers are charged with neutralizing any attacks by the blockading fleet.[3] Convoys, of course, are not free and they cannot be used unless the country has sufficient naval power to implement this policy. Their use imposes costs. By bunching the merchant vessels in the same small area of the ocean, the convoy presents an attractive target for the blockading force; and the time needed to gather together the convoy's vessels and the need to limit the convoy's pace to the top speed of the slowest ship are costly in terms of both time and resources. These have been used by naval officers to argue against the introduction of convoys, although in most cases it seems that the benefits exceeded the cost.

Nor does this list of direct costs represent a complete description of the economic burdens imposed by the blockade or by other similar strategies. The additional costs that must be borne by the belligerent powers or neutral powers include losses related to the decline of imports from, and exports to, the enemy, plus whatever indirect costs that arise through the reduction of trade between neutrals and the enemy (unless of course those reductions are offset by trade diversion), as well as the additional costs imposed by the use of the more roundabout routes that are necessary to circumvent the blockade. Because of the loss of access to goods and resources, a blockade imposes economic and military costs on the blockaded power. It is, however, not only the belligerent powers who are forced to bear a portion of the costs of economic warfare. The evidence indicates that, because of reduced levels of, and more expensive, trade, neutral powers also are required to pay a part of the cost of the economic war – third parties are not exempt. The magnitude of the costs that are actually imposed on each of the parties will, of course, depend on the relevant elasticities of supply and demand, as well as on the effectiveness of blockade-runners and the productivity of any other innovations designed to weaken the blockade's impact. To the extent that alternative sources of supply – sources not affected by the blockade – are available at relatively low prices, costs to the blockaded belligerent powers and the benefits accruing to the blockading power are both reduced. Similarly, the buildup of a large stockpile of goods before the imposition of the blockade, although certainly not free, will, in the short run, reduce the costs imposed on the blockaded country and lengthen the time before the blockade will have a major impact on their war effort. Such lengthening will, in turn, increase the costs of imposing the blockade.

3 For some definitions and discussion of the convoy, see Samuel Eliot Morison, *The Battle of the Atlantic, September 1939–May 1943* (Boston: Little, Brown, 1947), 17–26. See also Colombos, *International Law*, 694–700. There will be discussions of convoys in specific wars later.

2. INTERNATIONAL LAW BEFORE WORLD WAR I

The examination of the nature of changes in the international law regarding blockades and embargos could be discounted as an exercise in futility if it were expected that these laws will be binding on belligerents and neutrals. Even though these laws provide some constraint, however limited, on feasible behavior in wartime, in times of wartime emergencies belligerents will not be limited in their behavior by previously accepted peacetime agreements. The study of legal aspects of blockades has, however, provided useful insights into what people believed, and how they responded to actual and anticipated economic, military, and technological developments.[4]

Blockades – interdictions the primary purpose of which "is to prevent the enemy from receiving goods which may be used in warfare and which are designated as contraband" and to limit the ability of a neutral to trade with the enemy by making it legal to capture and condemn all neutral vessels sailing for enemy ports – thus not only directly involving the belligerent powers but, obviously, also neutral third countries. Such blockades have long raised major issues of international legal concern.[5] Beginning at least as far back as the late sixteenth century, in a long series of proclamations and international treaties, the concept of a "legal" blockade has been defined and its rules formally specified.

(a) To the Eighteenth Century

The modern discussion of blockades customarily begins with the 1584 Dutch operation against Spanish-held ports in Flanders. The leading nation in defining conditions of naval transportation during periods of wartime were the Dutch, who had treaties that stated that the fate of the cargo was determined by the flag of the vessel, so that neutral goods on enemy ships were considered to be good prize, whereas they claimed that free ships make free goods. A Dutch Proclamation of 1630 laid out some basic principles, in allowing the confiscation of neutral ships that had broken the blockade, that were later regarded as the core of blockade laws. Provisions of immunity of

---

4 The literature on international law and naval blockades has been expanding at a rapid rate. Many of the most important works are contained in the ongoing series on International Law Studies, now published by the Naval War College.

5 For an early, but still useful, discussion, see Maurice Parmelee, "Blockade," in *Encyclopedia of the Social Sciences*, ed., Edwin R. A. Seligman (New York: Macmillan, 1930), vol. 2: 594–596. See also his *Blockade and Sea Power: The Blockade, 1914–1919, and its Significance for a World State* (New York: Thomas Y. Crowell, 1924). Among the land blockades of interest, much attention has been given to Mohammad's successful blockade of Mecca in the seventh century. See, for example, Uri Rubin, "Muhammad's Curse of Mudar and the Blockade of Mecca," *Journal of the Economic and Social History of the Orient* 31 (1988), 249–264.

goods in neutral vessels were included in several other international treaties, such as the Treaty of Pyrenees (1659), a treaty between France and Spain that restricted the definition of contraband to "arms and munitions of war," whereas various treaties made by the Dutch with other European powers were to provide for "free ships, free goods." The Anglo-Dutch Treaty of Whitehall (1689), however, effectively did mean that neutral ships were not recognized. England, generally, maintained the view that confiscation of enemy goods in neutral vessels was acceptable. A French ordinance of 1681, continuing earlier ordinances, was modified in 1744 and, again, in 1788, to permit the immunity of goods in neutral vessels. Between 1674 and 1679, a series of treaties among Holland, France, Sweden, and England, recognized blockades as long as they could be regarded as effective, based on real investment in the blockade.[6]

In defining the terms of which goods could be confiscated, a provision was made by the British, called the Rule of the War of 1756 – a rule that was to prevent the French from using the Dutch trade to its colonies in order to circumvent the British blockade. This provision was to be carried forward into future years, with the argument that "a neutral is not entitled to carry on a trade which is closed to him in time of peace."[7]

In 1780, during what would be the more than century-long war between England and France, Russia enunciated several principles, "which were directed primarily against the maritime pretensions of England." These included: free navigation for neutral vessels; the principle of "free ships, free goods" for neutral vessels, except for contraband; the only goods to be considered contraband were munitions of war; and the definition of an effective blockade.

In the years after 1780, Russia, Denmark, Prussia, Portugal, Sweden, Holland, Austria, the United Provinces, and the Two Sicilies joined to form the League of Armed Neutrality – an organization based on advocating these principles. Two decades later, a second League was organized by Russia, Denmark, Sweden, and Prussia. The basis of the institution's structure was, again, the original four principles, but this time a fifth, the neutral right of convoy, was added.[8]

---

6 On this legal background, see Colombos, *International Law*, 503–505, 556–557, 610–615, 649–651, and George B. Davis, *The Elements of International Law* (New York: Harper and Brothers, 1900), 376–383.
7 Colombos, *International Law*, 613–614. This rule was extended by the United States in the Civil War as the theory of continuous voyage to preclude shipments of goods from neutral ports to a belligerent, thus circumventing a blockade.
8 Parmelee, *Blockade*, 19–20. Most of the subsequent citations to Parmelee are to his quotations from laws, documents, and conference reports, not to his interpretations of specific events. See also Colombos, *International Law*, 568–569, and Chapter 3.

These principles, however, were not universally recognized. In the case of Britain, even before 1815, prize courts had recognized a similar but different set of rules – rules that were less focused on the rights of neutrals: (1) "a blockade to be binding must be effective"; (2) "only a belligerent can establish a blockade"; (3) "to be valid a blockade must be duly declared and notified; the declaration must state the exact geographical limits of the blockaded area and the days of grace allowed to neutral vessels to enable them to come out of the blockaded port"; and (4) "the blockade must be limited to the ports and coasts of the enemy."[9] Thus, there was room for differences concerning the legal basis of a blockade and sufficient ambiguities to leave substantial room for both judicial and military conflict. Such ambiguities led, as described in Chapter 3, to disagreements over neutral rights that arose between the United States and Great Britain; and that disagreement, as well as other issues relating to the control of the American West and the expansion into Canada, ultimately led to the War of 1812.

(b) The Nineteenth Century

The Crimean War (1853–1856) again raised issues of the legality of blockades, and the first international declaration of the fundamental principles of international law on the subject was the product of the resulting 1856 Congress of Paris. That declaration provided a basic set of legal rules that were to govern the operation of naval blockades. It included four major provisions, in part a trade-off of desired goals, particularly on the part of France and Britain, that were, in large measure, to define the interests of both belligerents and neutrals:

1) "Privateering is and remains abolished."
2) "The neutral flag covers enemy's goods, with the exception of contraband of war. ('Free ships' make 'free goods'.)"
3) "Neutral flags, with the exception of contraband of war, are not liable to capture under an enemy's flag."
4) "Blockades, in order to be binding, must be effective; that is to say, maintained by a force sufficient really to prevent access to the coast of an enemy."

Initially, the declaration was signed by seven nations (England, France, Austria, Russia, Sardinia, Turkey, and Prussia). Over the course of the rest of the century, it was signed by most other nations; and, at the turn of the

---

9 Medlicott, *Economic Blockade*, vol. 1, 4.

century, international lawyers argued that it "has been generally recognized as binding by the civilized world."[10]

As early as 1859, the legal position of neutrals was again clouded, when the American Secretary of State argued against any commercial blockade during time of war. He wished to restrict military actions to those aimed at men, not trade.[11] However, his position was to be undercut by his own government during both the U.S. Civil War and, again, after the entry of the United States into World War I. During the Civil War, despite the Treaty of Paris, the Northern government enunciated, and the blockading fleet implemented, a rule that was known as the principle of the "continuous voyage."[12] The Northern courts held that no longer did "neutral ships mean neutral goods," and, with the court's decision in hand, the government "took the position that a voyage from the European or other original ports of departure to the ultimate destination in the blockaded Confederate port formed one continuous voyage, and that the United States had the right to seize contraband articles obviously intended for an ultimate Confederate destination even though consigned to an intervening neutral port."[13] The blockading fleet enforced that decision for the remainder of the war. Not surprisingly, many European authorities severely, but ineffectively, criticized this decision as a violation of international law.[14]

---

10 Parmelee, *Blockade*, 20–21. See also Colombos, *International Law*, 417–418.

11 Over most of the years from 1860 to 1920, the United States was an aggressive advocate of a neutral's right to trade freely with all belligerents. The government's position, however, was quickly reversed (in an equally aggressive manner) each time the country found itself in the role of a belligerent.

12 The doctrine was originated by Lord Stowell during the wars arising out of the French Revolution. Parmelee, *Blockade*, 24. H. A. Smith notes an earlier discussion of the issue of continuous voyage "during the Anglo-Dutch wars of the seventeenth century, when the geographical situation made it possible for cargoes consigned to the Spanish Netherlands to be sent on to Holland over inland waterways of the Low Countries." The issue was discussed again in 1756. H. A. Smith, *The Law and Custom of the Sea*, 2nd ed. (London: Stevens and Sons, 1950), 122.

13 Stephen R. Wise, *Lifeline of the Confederacy: Blockade Running During the Civil War* (Columbia: University of South Carolina Press, 1989), 66–73; Parmelee, *Blockade*, 63–67.

14 For example, see the remarks of the members of the Maritime Prize Commission of the Institute of International Law: "The unanimous opinion of the Maritime Commission was as follows: 'That the theory of continuous voyage as we find it enunciated and applied in the judgment of the Supreme Court of America, which condemned as good prize of war the entire cargo of the British bark *Springbok* (1867), a neutral vessel on its way to a neutral port, is subversive of an established rule of the law of maritime warfare, according to which neutral property on board a vessel under a neutral flag, whilst on its way to another neutral port, is not liable to capture or confiscation by a belligerent as a lawful prize of war; that such trade when carried on between neutral ports has, according to the law of nations, ever been held to be absolutely free, and that the novel theory, as above propounded, whereby it is presumed that the cargo after having been unladen in a neutral port, will have an ulterior destination to some enemy port, would aggravate the hindrances to which the trade of neutral is already exposed, and would, to use the word of Bluntschli, '*annihilate*' such trade, by subjecting their property to confiscation, not upon *proof* of an actual voyage of the vessel and cargo to an enemy port, but upon *suspicion* that cargo, after having been unladen at the neutral port to which the vessel is

"In 1885, in the course of her war with China, France declared that rice would be treated as absolute contraband when destined for ports situated north of Canton." The British government protested, arguing that "food-stuffs could not in general be treated as contraband"; the French "replied that its action was justified by 'the importance of rice in the feeding of the Chinese population.'[15] Again, during the Russo-Japanese War (1904–1905), even before the widespread innovation of submarines, the belligerent powers introduced certain innovations "which disregarded neutral rights and frequently endangered the lives of neutrals and non-combatants." The war-ring powers defined strategic areas "on the high seas from which neutral shipping was excluded under the threat of sinking." "Neutral prizes were frequently sunk," instead of being escorted to port. "Mines were sown indis-criminately in the strategic areas, thus endangering merchant vessels, their cargoes, and the human beings on board, not only during the hostilities but for a long time thereafter"; and the definition of contraband was extended well beyond munitions. The Russians, for example, declared raw cotton to be legal contraband.[16] Moreover, by 1914, and almost certainly earlier, it had become clear that the existing rules – "definitions, which presupposed naval action close to an enemy's coasts, had little relevance to a war in which modern artillery, mines, and submarines made such action impossible, and in which the enemy was so placed geographically that he could use adjacent neutral ports as a channel for supplies."[17]

(c) The Twentieth Century to World War I

As a result of the problems raised both by the unilateral amendments to the Declaration of Paris and the changes in military technology, a new convention was signed at the second Hague peace conference in 1907 (the

bound, may be transshipped into some other vessel and carried to some effectively blockaded enemy port.

"That the theory above propounded tends to contravene the efforts of European powers to establish a uniform doctrine respecting the immunity from capture of all property under neutral flag, contraband of war alone excepted.

"That the theory in question must be regarded as a serious inroad upon the rights of neutral nations, inasmuch as the fact of the destination of a neutral vessel to a neutral port would no longer suffice of itself to prevent the capture of goods noncontraband on board.

"That, furthermore, the result would be that as regards blockades, every neutral port to which a neutral vessel might be carrying a neutral cargo would become *constructively* a blockaded port if there were the slightest ground for *suspecting* that the cargo, after being unladen in such neutral port was *intended* to be forwarded in some other vessels to some port actually blockaded." Quoted in Parmelee, *Blockade*, 65–66.

15 D. T. Jack, *Studies in Economic Warfare* (New York: Chemical Publishing House, 1941), 71. See Albert E. Hogan, *Pacific Blockades* (Oxford: Clarendon Press, 1908), 122–126.

16 Parmelee, *Blockade*, 22.   17 Medlicott, *Economic Blockade*, vol. 1, 4.

first was in 1899 and primarily discussed land war). The twenty-six articles of the "Hague Convention XIII of 1907," although dealing with a variety of issues, such as the treatment of interned troops and wounded persons, focused on the rights and duties of neutral powers; and it concludes with the provision that "Should any member of the League resort to war in disregard of its Covenants . . . it shall *ipso facto* be deemed to have committed an act of war against all members of the League."[18]

Many of the changes were readily accepted by the representatives of the signatory countries; however, the Convention also called for the establishment of an international prize court to which cases could be appealed from the national courts. The court was to act in the following manner (Article 7): "If a question of law to be decided is covered by a treaty in force between the belligerent captor and a power which is itself or whose subject or citizen is a party to the proceedings, the court is governed by provisions of the said treaty. In the absence of such provisions, the court shall apply the rules of international law. If no generally recognized rule exists, the court shall give judgment in accordance with the general principles of justice and equity."[19]

The new rules were, however, not without the problems. The court was instructed to apply the rule of international law relating to prizes, but that law had never been codified nor clearly stated by any international authority; and there were major differences between the past rulings of individual national courts.

The British representatives concluded that they would be unable to secure their government's approval of the international court unless the powers of the court were strictly defined.[20] As a result, the British government invited the major naval powers to a conference to establish the rules of law that were to govern the international court's decisions before the court began to operate. The discussion would include issues such as:

a) The nature of contraband "including the circumstances under which particular articles can be considered as contraband; the penalties for their carriage; the immunity of a ship from search when under convoy; and the rules with regard to compensation where vessels have been seized, but have been found in fact only to be carrying innocent cargo."

b) The nature of a legal blockade, "including the question as to the locality where seizure can be effected, and the notice that is necessary before a ship can be seized."

18 For a summary of the Convention, see Jack, *Studies*, 53–58.
19 Parmalee, *Blockade*, 27.
20 Louis Guichard, *The Naval Blockade, 1914–1918* (New York: D. Appleton, 1930), 9.

c) "The doctrine of continuous voyage in respect both of contraband and of blockade."

d) "The legality of the destruction of neutral vessels prior to their condemnation by a prize court."

e) "The rules as to neutral ships or persons rendering 'unneutral services' ('assistance hostile')."

f) "The legality of the conversion of a merchant vessel into a warship on the high seas."

g) "The rules as to the transfer of merchant vessels from a belligerent to a neutral flag during or in contemplation of hostilities."

h) "The questions whether the nationality or the domicile of the owner should be adopted as the dominant factor in deciding whether property is enemy property."[21]

Ten governments were invited and sent delegates to the conference that met in London from December 1908 to February 1909.[22] The outcome was the adoption of a "Declaration Concerning the Laws of Naval Warfare," commonly known as the 1909 Declaration of London.[23] The Declaration was long (consisting of seventy-one articles) and covered most of the questions raised over the course of the past century and a half. In addition to questions involving the rules of governing the international prize court and the repeal of the doctrine of continuous voyage, the Declaration attempted to spell out and define the nature of "contraband," a definition that had become increasingly fuzzy as the nature of war had changed. At the Hague Convention, the powers had been unable to agree on the British proposal to suppress contraband entirely on the grounds that "the attempt to deprive an enemy of war supplies had not succeeded to an extent which was sufficient to justify the inconvenience which was created to neutral traders."[24] Two years later, by recognizing a threefold distinction – absolute contraband, conditional contraband, and free goods – the delegates moved in the opposite direction. Given that the nature of war was changing, and with it the nature of what might be considered absolute and conditional contraband, to say nothing of the nature of free goods, the definitions were never internationally operationalized – even had the Declaration been signed by all the major powers "it was admitted that as a war proceeded a belligerent would

---

21 Parmalee, *Blockade*, 28.

22 The ten were: Great Britain, United States, Germany, France, Russia, Italy, Japan, Austria-Hungary, Spain, and Holland.

23 Parmelee, *Blockade*, 26–29. See also Stockton, *Outlines*, 57–59, who was an American delegate to the conference and had helped draft the U.S. proposal.

24 Jack, *Studies*, 76–79; Guichard, *Naval Blockade*, 10.

have the right to add further articles to the list [of absolute contraband] provided that these articles also were 'susceptible exclusively of military use' and that neutrals were notified thereof."[25] As it was, each country continued to make its own decisions. For example, when the war began, Britain revised and extended the list; and, as the war progressed, that process was continued until, by 1917, "the list of articles liable to seizure in neutral ships covered almost anything of strategic value."[26]

The Declaration of London was, however, never ratified. Although Great Britain had both initiated and hosted the meeting and was largely responsible for the agenda, the Declaration induced a violent reaction against its adoption throughout that country. There were three major complaints. First, there would be only one British representative on the eight-member prize court; and, thus, it was believed that there was a substantial probability that the Court's decisions might undercut existing British maritime law. Second, it was thought that Article 34, dealing with conditional contraband, would permit a "belligerent at war with Great Britain to stop all foodstuffs consigned to the United Kingdom." Finally, it was argued that Article 49 – an article that "allowed the destruction of neutral prizes if the captor's safety would be endangered by bringing them into port" – could put vessels, seamen, and passengers at risk before any prize court had made a decision. The Declaration was passed by the House of Parliament; on December 13, 1913; however, "the House of Lords threw out the essential part of the Declaration, which thus became a dead letter owing to the failure of Great Britain to ratify."[27] It should be noted, however, that despite the failure of

25 Guichard, *Naval Blockade*, 10–13. "The position as it then was, and continued to be could best be described in Lord Reay's words as 'a custom established by international law'. Each belligerent could specify its own list of contraband, whereupon it became a matter of negotiation with neutral traders to determine the extent to which the inconveniences of search could be reduced." See also Jack, *Studies*, 78–79.

26 "A proclamation of August 4 [1914] placed all aircraft and its component parts on the list of absolute contraband. An order of October 29, 1914 added iron-ore, nickel, ferrochrome, copper, lead, aluminum, motor vehicles of all kinds, and mineral oils and motor spirit (except lubricating ores) within the category of absolute contraband. A few days earlier, an order of September 21, 1914 added copper, lead, glycerin, ferrochrome, iron-ore, rubber, hides, and skins to the list of conditional contraband." In 1915, cotton was added. Jack, *Studies*, 85. See also D. P. O'Connell, *The Influence of Law on Sea Power* (Annapolis: Naval Institute Press, 1975), 20.

27 There still remains the question of why, given the Navy's position on economic warfare, the British naval delegates were central to negotiating the Declaration and then actively supported its acceptance by the British government. Although the issue is still unsettled, Avner Offer suggests that, although it may have been a case of benign neglect, it is also possible that there may be a more Machiavelian explanation – namely that Fisher, and therefore the Admiralty, believed that the rules would be adhered to only when it was to Britain's advantage to do so. Offer notes that "Fisher was no respecter of the laws of war" ("Fisher repeatedly asserted that any talk of restraint in war was dangerous nonsense, and told both friend and foe that might was always right"). Offer cites a 1908 Admiralty document that appears to support the Machiavellian interpretation: "When Great Britain is belligerent, she

the major powers to ratify the Declaration, the instructions given by France, Germany, and Great Britain to their navies at the outbreak of the war closely followed its terms.[28]

3. INTERNATIONAL LAW – THE TWENTIETH CENTURY

There were important changes made in the law regarding blockades in the twentieth century reflecting economic, technological, and military developments, including the submarine and the airplane. As before, these changes reflected adjustments people believed necessary to keep the moral basis underlying the laws up to the technological developments that had occurred.

It is clear, however, that by the end of World War I, the policies adopted by Britain, Germany, and the United States had made a shambles of that part of international law that dealt with naval blockades. Given the British refusal to ratify the Declaration of London, and despite the fact that the major belligerents gave lip service to those amended rules, the Declaration was a "dead letter" at the start of the War. On the question of contraband, there was no agreed definition; and "on October the 30th, by an Order in Council, the British Government asserted the right to intercept conditional contraband if consigned 'to order', that is, in blank. The shipper must prove innocence of intent by showing the name of a genuine consignee." Four days later, the British declared the entire North Sea a "military area"; and, despite the fact that they had not formally declared a blockade, their naval vessels began "diverting merchant vessels to port for purposes of search."[29]

In February 1915, the Germans, arguing that noncontraband articles bound for Germany had been seized on neutral vessels, declared an all-out submarine war. "Allied merchantmen in a 'war area' comprising the coasts of the British Isles and northern France were liable to be destroyed without warning and without consideration for the lives of crews or passengers.

can be safely trusted to look after her own interests, but the dangerous time for her is when she is neutral and does not wish to take such a strong line as to render herself liable to be drawn into war. At such a time, the existence of a well reasoned-out classification of goods will be of enormous advantage, not only to Britain, but to all other commercial communities." ['Notes on Contraband', ADM 116/1073]. Avner Offer, *The First World War, An Agrarian Interpretation* (Oxford: Clarendon Press, 1989), 270–279. See also Guichard, *Naval Blockade*, 13–15.

28 "The French instructions drawn up in 1912 contained the principal articles of the Declaration *verbatim*, as did the German instructions of 1909 – which were in force when the war broke out." And during the War the Germans did use Article 49 as an excuse for the "behaviour of her submarines," although that outcome had not been anticipated by the delegates at the conference. Guichard, *Naval Blockade*, 14–15.

29 Frank P. Chambers, *The War Behind the War, 1914–1918: A History of the Political and Civilian Fronts* (New York: Harcourt, Brace, 1939), 134–135.

Neutral ships in the same waters would be exposed to danger, for the *ruse-de-guerre*, which allowed the ships of a belligerent to fly a neutral flag, made it impossible to distinguish the nationality. The German government officially maintained that its action had been forced upon it by the Allies' disregard of the law of contraband and in particular of the Declaration of Paris."[30]

The next month, "the British and French Governments retaliated with the so-called Reprisals Order of March 1915." They announced that they would, in the future, seize "any goods at sea whose 'destination, owner-ship, or origin' were presumed to be hostile." The Order, for all intents and purposes, "gave the Allies complete freedom to apply the doctrine of continuous voyage to whatever articles they wished, whether absolute or conditional contraband, or whether consigned to a known or unknown importer."[31]

Nor was the United States exempt from the popular game of adding new additions to the list of "infractions" of international law. With the exception of its innovation of the continuous voyage during the Civil War, it can be argued that, "up to the time of its entrance into the European War in 1917, the United States had invariably advocated the freedom from seizure at sea of all private property, belligerent as well as neutral with the exception of contraband of war." "During the years 1914 to 1917, the American government protested repeatedly "against violations of international law by both sides." It protested against the belligerent powers "floating mines in the North Sea"; "it protested against the British use of the American flag"; it protested against the Central Powers "sinking of American ships and the killing of American citizens"; and, in 1915, "it denounced the British blockade as illegal."[32] No sooner, however, had the United States entered the war than the government deployed naval units to help enforce the "illegal" British blockade; and, in addition, it innovated a number of policies of its own – many of them policies that it, alone, had the financial power to implement. The history of the American attitude toward blockades, both in the Civil War and again during World War I, "furnishes a good illustration of the manner in which nations are prone to act in accordance with their interests of the moment, even though such actions are inconsistent with their previous policy," to say nothing of violating international laws.[33]

---

30 Chambers, *War Behind the War*, 135. It should be noted that the German deportation of Belgian citizens to Germany to augment that country's labor force "contravened any normal interpretations of international law; and [those deportations] were carried out with extreme brutality." Chambers, *War Behind the War*, 215.

31 Chambers, *War Behind the War*, 135–136.   32 Parmalee, *Blockade*, 63–67.

33 Parmelee, *Blockade*, 65–66.

By the end of the war, scholars spoke of the uncertain state of international law. The British (and American) economic "blockade" was certainly a major attempt to control world industry and commerce. It not only affected imports and exports but also involved attempts to stimulate production of certain commodities by subsidies and the fixing of minimum prices, to limit the production of other commodities by fiat, to monopolize the sources of many raw materials, and to alter "trade routes by control of shipping." Given the "state" of international law, historians were hesitant to charge the Allies with imposing "illegal" embargoes on particular neutral countries; but Parmelee did acknowledge that "the blockade demonstrated the feasibility of such regulation and control on a large scale"; and recognized that, in the future, if there were another major war, there would likely be attempts to implement such measures again.[34]

Thus, although in 1914 the international laws governing blockades were in a state of flux, it was generally recognized that the major features of the law in the case of belligerent powers were roughly as follows:

1) Blockades were legal, but only if they were effective – that is, they must be enforced in large part by naval means and "every port of the blockaded country must be effectually blocked by the blockading fleet." No longer, however, was it necessary to maintain a "close" blockade – the blockading force could be stationed outside of the range of artillery, aircraft, mines, and, hopefully, submarines.

2) The blockading belligerents could legally confiscate contraband; and the definition of contraband had been expanded to include both absolute and conditional contraband ("goods which might eventually be used for war purposes, though not consigned directly to the government of the blockaded nation"). Prize courts were empowered to examine and confiscate commodities and to decide what shall be done with them. Goods, if condemned in such a proceeding, were ordinarily sold; "and the proceeds are paid to the owners of the goods, either at the time or after the end of the war."

3) The belligerent had a legal right to visit and search belligerent and neutral "vessels and other conveyances carrying commodities which are, or may be, destined for the enemy." The rules governing visit and search "had been extended

---

34 Parmelee, *Blockade*, 16, 331, 383–390. He, however, went on to suggest that the solution for "imperialism of all kinds and the wars which arise therefrom is the World State." He is, however, not optimistic about achieving this, since "The present world crisis demands international statesmanship of the highest order and furnishes an almost unexampled opportunity to establish an international state based on the principle of world-wide human cooperation in the place of the conflicting nations of today. But it is likely that owing to the passions which permeate the masses, the petty intriguing of diplomats, and the short-sighted policies of statesmen governed primarily by temporary expediency, this opportunity will be lost, and mankind will again plunge for a series of generations into the maelstrom of rivalry and conflict based on brute force."

by the doctrine of the continuous voyage. Contraband goods consigned to a neutral country, but which are eventually destined for use by the government of the blockaded country, are regarded as subject to seizure, on the ground that the passage through the neutral country is merely a part of a continuous voyage into the blockaded country."

4) The belligerent right of angary "authorizes belligerents to confiscate and use for war purposes neutral property on belligerent territory."

In the case of neutral powers:

1) Neutral territory and territorial waters within three miles of the neutral coast, must be respected by belligerents – "there can be no fighting upon neutral territory." "Combatants who enter neutral territory can be interned for the duration of the war"; "belligerent vessels may, however, pass through territorial waters and enter neutral ports in order to take shelter from the weather, or in order to obtain provisions or make necessary repairs."

2) Citizens of neutral countries have the right to trade with, including the right to sell munitions to, the citizens of belligerent countries.

3) "Neutral public ships, mail steamers, and neutral ships under convoy of neutral war vessels are sometimes exempted from the belligerent rights of visit and search and capture and confiscation."[35]

The years of World War I were to witness major amendments to the *de facto*, if not the *de jure*, rules of "legal" blockades. The problem was twofold. On the one hand, no one on either side had yet come to recognize the possibility of total war. On the other hand, there had been no generally ratified international agreement since the Declaration of Paris in 1856 (and the United States had not been a signator to that accord). The intervening half century had seen both a technical and institutional revolution in the nature of warfare. Thus, the unanswered question remained "whether the new practices demanded by the changed conditions of economic warfare were in accordance with the spirit of international law as it concerned the relations of belligerents and neutrals." "The outbreak of war on a continental scale in August 1914 soon convinced the belligerents that an unprecedented effort was needed." The belligerent powers then moved in ways that also trespassed greatly on the rights of neutral powers. "They insisted upon regulating the trade of neutral nations to a degree almost unparalleled in the history of the world. Neutral territory and territorial waters were frequently violated, neutral citizens were greatly restricted in their rights of trade and intercourse with belligerent citizens. Neutral mail steamers were held up

---

35 Parmelee, *Blockade*, 23–26.

and searched, and the right of convoy by neutral war vessels was seriously questioned and sometimes denied." "The belligerent right of blockade was carried to the uttermost limit in applying the rights of visit and search and of the capture and confiscation of contraband of war." However, "the neutral, who by the very fact of neutrality was in large measure untouched by the sense of danger, anger, and exhilaration of the combatants" continued to cling to their earlier views of the nature of war.[36]

There were obvious grounds for conflict, and both the Allies and the Central Powers were to innovate policies that would have been unthinkable only a few years before. For Germany, it was to be a blockade of England mounted by submarines, with all the potential costs to neutral vessels and civilians that such a policy entailed. The German policy of unrestricted submarine warfare aimed at the British that was announced in February 1915, stated that German submarines could attack merchant ships of enemies and neutrals without the warning and aids to crew specified in international codes.[37] For the British, although they never formally declared a blockade, it was to involve not only a distant blockade of Germany but the innovation of policies that, by applying both indirect pressure and import quotas on neutral nations, were designed to keep those neutrals from supplying the Central powers.[38] The latter policy had been discussed in the spring of 1915, and it was adopted at the Conference of London in October 1915. Although a severe break with the existing prewar definition of a legal blockade, in September 1915 it was granted legal sanction by the decision of the British Prize Court in the case of the Denmark-bound Norwegian vessel *Kim*.[39] Finally, international law had never denied a nation or an individual

---

36 Medlicott, *Economic Blockade*, vol. 1, 5, 7; Parmelee, *Blockade*, 10–11.
37 Roger Chickering, *Imperial Germany and the Great War*, 1914–1918 (Cambridge: Cambridge University Press, 1998), 88–94.
38 The British never formally declared a blockade. "British war vessels could not enter the Baltic, because the sound between Denmark and Sweden, through which vessels must pass, is very narrow at one point and is, therefore, neutral territory. Hence it was impossible for the British fleet to blockade the German Baltic ports, and thus prevent overseas trade between Germany and Sweden, Denmark, and Norway. The British blockade, therefore, could not be effective within the meaning of the Declaration of Paris of 1856, which was reiterated in Article 2 of the Declaration of London, namely, that a blockade, in order to be binding, must be maintained by a force sufficient really to prevent access to the enemy coastline." Parmelee, *Blockade*, 38. See also Guichard, *Naval Blockade*, 6–8.
39 The *Kim*, with three other steamers, had been stopped by the British fleet in November 1914 because they were carrying nineteen million pounds of lard from New York to Copenhagen. Now Denmark had only imported 1,459,000 pounds of lard in previous years and lard was included in the list of conditional contraband. "The court began by declaring that it had the right and the duty to find out if the consignment of these goods to the port of Copenhagen was not a fictitious one. It held then that it ought to be told whether these goods were destined for Denmark in order to be 'incorporated in the general stocks of the country,' and it agreed that an introduction of such a quantity of lard into Denmark, which was an exporter of food products, made it a practical certainty that the major portion was destined ultimately for Germany. By the judgment of the court, which was very ably

the right of selling munitions to a belligerent. Thus, after 1914, and increasingly as the war went on, the British signed huge contracts for munitions with American firms. Those contracts were often signed by American businessmen – Charles M. Schwab, to name only one – and the purchases were coordinated (and sometime underwritten) by American investment banking houses such as J. P. Morgan.[40] At the same time, the British fleet prevented the Germans from exploiting the same market.[41]

4. THE SUBMARINE

Given the absence of any military deployment of submarines in the wars of the late nineteenth and the first decade of the twentieth centuries, there was no discussion of the rules regarding submarine warfare until the onset of World War I. Even though several countries had begun to add U-boats to their fleets, neither The Hague Conference of 1907 nor the London Conference of 1909 had any special laws regarding submarines. With the onset of war, the principle issue dealt with the question of whether or not the rules that applied to submarines were to be the same as those applied to all other vessels, or if new weapons meant new rules. The fear that because of its difficult to defend against quality of traveling under water, and, because it could always be converted into a fighting vessel of the most formidable kind, the submarine would become a decisive new weapon, led the British Secretary of State of Foreign Affairs to call for exceptional treatment. Rather ironically, in 1916, the U.S. Department of State argued that there was nothing that would render the existing rules of international law inapplicable to submarines, and, in 1917, the government of the neutral Netherlands also took this position. Yet another argument for the special treatment of submarines rested on the sudden recognition of the fact that the existing rules on warning and on providing safety to those aboard captured vessels would, in effect, make it impossible for U-boats to be used in a war against enemy commerce at sea.

After the experience with submarine warfare in World War I, during which time there were still no specific provision in international law regarding their operation, several issues were raised about the rules of submarine

---

stated, the *Kim's* cargo was confiscated 'on account of the extreme probability of its being destined for the enemy.'" Guichard, *Naval Blockade*, 53–56.

40 Chambers, *War Behind the War*, 48–53, 197–200; see also Parmelee, *Blockade*, 282–284.

41 The Germans did, in 1916, manage to send one cargo submarine to Baltimore; and it returned with a load of American supplies of metals. After the United States entered the war, this ship was converted from "an unarmed commercial submarine freighter into a warship." John Terraine, *Business in Great Waters: The U-Boat Wars, 1916–1945* (London: Leo Cooper, 1989), 90–91, 683.

warfare during the postwar period.[42] There were some attempts made by the British to abolish submarines as a tool of war; but this position, raised at the Washington Conference of 1922, attracted no support. It was subsequently reintroduced in 1930, but again to no effect. The major debate in the postwar period followed earlier lines: did new weapons require new rules, as the Germans advocated, or were submarines to be regarded as any other vessel, with the same rules to be applied to them as to the surface vessels – rules that required the giving of warning and the provision of safety for the crew and passengers of the vessels under attack? Although those rules would be in accord with the earlier provisions of naval warfare, the requirement that a submarine must surface would eliminate one of that vessel's major military advantages; and it would greatly limit its effectiveness.

There were two major naval conferences in the interwar period – conferences that, in addition to issues involving submarines, dealt with overall fleet size, the ability to construct new vessels, and allowed ship tonnage. In addition, in 1936, there was an agreement on a protocol regarding submarine warfare – an agreement that set the terms of international law, and an agreement that was still in effect at the onset of World War II. The first, and the most important, of the two conferences was held in Washington in 1922; it was attended by the United States, Great Britain, France, Italy, and Japan. In addition to setting out a general limitation on the nature and size of the fleets of the five attendees, a treaty relating to the use of Submarines and Noxious Gases in Warfare was signed. That treaty declared that submarines were to be regarded as if they were surface vessels.[43] Thus, submarines could not attack merchant ships without giving full warning, and they were not to be used "as 'commerce destroyers.'"[44] Because the Naval Treaty was due to expire at the end of 1936, further conferences would then be required, if the agreement was to remain in force.

The 1930 London Conference was attended by the same five nations as the 1922 conference in Washington. The British received some support for their attempt to abolish submarines; but, because of strong opposition

---

42 In preparing the Treaty of Versailles, there was some discussion of prohibiting the building of new submarines, and destroying and dismantling those that existed. This was not implemented, and although the Treaty contained a provision to prevent Germany from acquiring any submarines, this was not part of the Covenant of the League of Nations. See Howard S. Levie, "Submarine Warfare: With Emphasis on the 1936 London Protocol," in Richard J. Grunawalt, ed., *International Law Studies 1993: Targeting Enemy Merchant Shipping* (Newport: Naval War College, 1993), 28–71.

43 See Yamato Ichihashi, *The Washington Conference and After. A Historical Survey* (Stanford: Stanford University Press, 1928), 72–82. Raymond and Leslie Buell, *The Washington Conference* (New York: D. Appleton, 1922), 215–239.

44 Buell and Buell, *Washington Conference*, 219–221. Colombos, *International Law*, 23–25, 447–448.

from the French and the Japanese, and in exchange for some limitations on submarine warfare, this proposal was dropped. All five powers signed a treaty that included in Article 22 the same terms that were to appear in the 1936 protocol – terms that basically treated submarines as subject to the same rules as surface vessels. These terms included:

1) "In their action with regard to merchant ships, submarines must conform to the rules of International Law, to which surface vessels are subject."

2) "In particular, except in the case of persistent refusal to stop on being duly summoned, or of active resistance to visit or search, a warship, whether surface vessel or submarine, may not sink or render incapable of navigation a merchant vessel without having first placed passengers, crew and ship's papers in a place of safety. For this purpose the ship's boats are not regarded as a place of safety unless the safety of the passengers and crew is assured, in the existing sea and weather conditions, by the proximity of land, or the presence of another vessel which is in position to take them on board."[45]

The treaty's terms regarding submarines were to be in force indefinitely, but the remainder of the treaty also was to expire at the end of 1936. After the expiration of this treaty, Japan and Italy decided to pursue their separate interests. In November 1936, the United States, Australia, Canada, France, the United Kingdom, India, Ireland, Italy, Japan, New Zealand, and South Africa agreed to a protocol based on Article 22 of the 1930 London Treaty; and, by 1939, it had been signed by thirty-seven other states, including Germany. This protocol was in force at the beginning of World War II; but Germany, claiming that the protocol would limit the usefulness of its submarines, soon violated the terms of the agreement. Both Doenitz and his predecessor, Raeder, were charged at Nuremberg with violation of the protocol, as well as other war crimes. Doenitz defended himself on the charge of carrying out unrestricted submarines warfare by arguing that the British had either armed their merchant ships or else had used them for intelligence purposes. This argument, however, was not accepted by the Tribunal.[46]

At the end of both world wars, international organizations were organized in an attempt to maintain world peace through the collective action of member States. Both the Covenant of the League of Nations and the Charter of the United Nations allowed the imposition of sanctions to discourage warlike actions, and such sanctions were to be collectively imposed and enforced. No basic changes in the law of blockades were introduced, but

---

45 Colombos, *International Law*, 429, 447.   46 Colombos, *International Law*, 439–442.

the pursuit of collective action by international organizations simplified a process that had previously required more consultation and discussion.

5. COUNTERVAILING POLICIES

Although blockades have been affected by technical and political changes, it has been the shifting efficiency of blockades relative to what has become the most effective antiblockade weapon – the convoy – that probably represents the single most important recent chapter in the history of the blockade. The role of convoys was both defensive, in limiting losses of merchant ships, and offensive, in attacking and destroying submarines.[47] Naval convoys were hardly a new innovation. In fact, convoys antedated the first effective naval blockades. In the ninth, tenth, and eleventh centuries, the Venetians employed convoys for protection of their river trade with the inland cities of what had been the Holy Roman Empire.[48] By the middle of the thirteenth century, they were conducting convoys up the Po as far as its junction with the Mincio and up the Adige as far as Legnago.[49] However, then, as now, convoys, although highly effective in reducing losses, were not costless. As early as the seventeenth century, Venetian "shipowners protested that convoys used eight to fourteen months for a voyage that could be made in three or four, required excessive escort fees, and that made markets always unfavorable because of the competition of the many ships arriving at once."[50] Similar complaints were voiced in America and Britain in the years between 1939 and 1945. The costs in time of gathering together a convoy and the slow sailing speed enforced often were used as arguments in debates among naval officers about whether or not to introduce convoys.

Even a cursory glance at history suggests that, to a large extent, the relative efficiency of naval blockades vis-à-vis countering strategies – and in the recent past those strategies have almost all involved convoys – has, in large

---

47 The effectiveness of convoys in World War I is indicated by the British losses of sailings in overseas trade from August 1917 to October 1918 of 4.79 percent for nonconvoyed ships compared to 0.53 percent for those in convoys. In World War II, from September 1939 to May 1945, loss rates for nonconvoyed vessels were more than twice those of convoyed ships, Eric J. Grove, ed., *The Defeat of the Enemy Attack on Shipping, 1939–1945* (Aldershot: Ashgate, 1997), 300–310.

48 Frederic C. Lane, *Venice: A Maritime Republic* (Baltimore: Johns Hopkins University Press, 1973), 6.

49 Lane, *Venice*, 62.

50 Lane, *Venice*, 418. Some background on the British use of convoys from the thirteenth to the twentieth century can be found in John B. Hattendorf et al., eds., *British Naval Documents, 1204–1960* (Brookfield: Scolar Press, 1993). See, for example, p. 232, for an eighteenth-century example of problems of enforcing discipline. The editors state that the initial convoys were composed of merchant ships sailing together for "mutual protection," but these soon acquired military escorts (p. 17).

part, depended on the nature and responses to five major regime changes. First were technological changes. In the fifteenth century, changes in vessel design finally permitted the development of effective blockades, and, centuries later, steam and steel replaced wind and wood in both the convoying and the blockading force. Later, telegraph and radio replaced visual signals, radar greatly increased the range of effective search, and submarines, aircraft, mines, and aircraft carriers greatly changed the nature of the opposing forces. The second change was related to the increasing size and scope of major conflicts – it remains a question whether the American Civil War or the Franco-Prussian War of 1871 can be viewed as the earliest example of "total war," but there is no question that the first and second world wars qualify for that dubious distinction. Total war, as its name implies, tends to infer a willingness on the part of the belligerent powers to do anything required to win. Third, as trade expanded and nations attempted to pursue their competitive advantage, they became more dependent on international trade. As a result, they faced greater costs, should a blockade prove effective. Fourth, at least in the West, as nations grew economically and their governmental structures became more solidly emplaced, those governments were better able to control the actions of their own military forces. Finally, the size and power of both the belligerents (individual states, grand coalitions, international organizations) and the neutral powers altered the political infrastructure that supported the blockading fleets and the naval forces deployed in attempts to break that economic stranglehold.

2

Britain, France, and Napoleon's Continental System, 1793–1815

1. FRANCE VERSUS ENGLAND, SEVENTEENTH TO NINETEENTH CENTURY

From the late seventeenth century until the final ending of the Napoleonic Wars in 1815, France and Britain were at war more than 50 percent of the time, in addition to their frequent and quite visible manifestations of commercial rivalry (see Table 2.1).[1] Other European nations were involved in some of these wars; for example, in the War of the Spanish Succession (1701–1714) and the War of the Austrian Succession (1740–1748). In others, such as the Seven Years' War (1754–1763), the French and British were the sole or primary antagonists in North America, but with many nations involved in Europe. In the American Revolution (1775–1783), despite the possible importance of their contribution to the final outcome, the French role was probably relatively small. But, for the years between 1793 and 1815, with a small pause with the Peace of Amiens, from March 1802 until May 1803, the major fight for dominance in Europe was between France and England, with both nations seeking as many political and military allies as

---

1 Michael Clodfelter, *Warfare and Armed Conflicts: A Statistical Reference to Casualty and Other Figures, 1618–1991* (2 vols.) (Philadelphia: McFarland & Company, 1992). See also Quincy A. Wright, *A Study of War*, 2nd ed., "With a Commentary on War since 1942" (Chicago: University of Chicago Press, 1965), 643–644 and inserts. The dates in the text are from R. Ernest Dupuy and Trevor N. Dupuy, *The Encyclopedia of Military History from 3500 B.C. to the Present* (Revised Edition) (London: Jane's, 1980), and differ for some wars by one year from the dates given by Wright. Of the twelve conflicts, in three Britain and France were on the same side, none after 1720. For a survey of the naval aspects of the conflicts, see Robin Ranger, "The Anglo–French Wars, 1689–1815," in Colin S. Gray and Roger W. Barnett, eds., *Seapower and Strategy* (Annapolis: Naval Institute Press, 1989), 157–185. The most complete works on the Continental System are still Frank Edgar Melvin, *Napoleon's Navigation System: A Study of Trade Control during the Continental Blockade* (New York: D. Appleton, 1919); and Eli F. Heckscher, *The Continental System: An Economic Interpretation* (Oxford: Clarendon Press, 1922). For a brief summary of the latter, see Eli F. Heckscher, "Continental System," in *Encyclopedia of the Social Sciences*, ed. Edwin R. A. Seligman (New York: Macmillian, 1930), vol. 4, 310–311.

Table 2.1. *Wars Involving Britain and France, 1665–1815*

Second Anglo-Dutch War	1665–1667
War of the Devolution	1667–1668
Third Anglo-Dutch War*	1672–1674
Dutch War (First Coalition vs. Louis XIV)*	1672–1679
War of the Grand Alliance (Nine Years' War)	1688–1697
War of the Spanish Succession	1701–1714
War of the Quadruple Alliance*	1718–1720
War of the Austrian Succession	1740–1748
Seven Years' War (French and Indian War)	1754–1763
American Revolution	1775–1783
French Revolutionary Wars	1789–1802
Napoleonic Wars	1803–1815

* As allies

Source: Michael Clodfelter, *Warfare and Armed Conflicts: A Statistical Reference to Casualty and Other Figures, 1618–1991*, 2 vols. (Philadelphia: McFarland and Company, 1992). For slightly different dates within one year of those given, see Quincy A. Wright, *A Study of War* (Chicago: University of Chicago Press, 1965), 643–644 and inserts; John J. McCusker and Russell R. Menard, *The Economy of British America, 1607–1789* (Chapel Hill: University of North Carolina Press, 1985), 366; Linda Colley, *Britons: Forging the Nation, 1707–1837* (New Haven: Yale University Press, 1992), 1.

they could acquire, whether by military force (France) or by cash subsidy (Britain).[2]

During periods of warfare, as well as during the intervals of peace, restrictions on trade, including tariffs and blockades were deployed by these nations against each other, as well as in their involvement with other nations, belligerent or neutral. These constraints were designed to affect the European power balance and also to encourage domestic economic development. Both Britain and France actively pursued mercantilistic policies; and, as a result, international economic and military rivalries characterized Europe from at least the late seventeenth century. There was a brief pause in these rivalries after the Eden Treaty, between England and France, of 1786.[3] This treaty eliminated prohibitions of imports and lowered customs duties; these policies were, however, widely believed to be beneficial to the British; and were

2 On the role of British subsides paid to continental nations, see John M. Sherwig, *Guineas and Gunpowder: British Foreign Aid in the Wars with France, 1793–1815* (Cambridge, MA: Harvard University Press, 1969), 345–356; Heckscher, *Continental System*, 67, 253; Clive Emsley, *British Society and the French Wars, 1793–1815* (London: Macmillan, 1979), 22, 80–81, 150–151, 169.

3 See Heckscher, *Continental System*, 18–25; also David Kaiser, *Politics and War: European Conflict from Phillip II to Hitler* (Cambridge, MA: Harvard University Press, 1990), 250–251.

opposed by the French. The treaty was in force for only a limited time, as, in February 1793 war again broke out between the French and the British. Both nations soon reverted to their earlier policies of trade control – policies that included prohibitions on specific manufactured imports, a policy particularly desired by French industry, and attempts to limit all of the carrying trade of their opponent.[4] In 1796, the French law was extended from prohibition on British goods to exclude all goods acquired by British trade. These provisions were extended in the Nivôse Law of 1798, which was, however, nullified in 1799.[5] Moreover, both nations introduced measures designed to restrict the trade of neutral nations with their rival. In particular, laws were placed restricting trade in various foodstuffs, the French (1793) capturing any neutral vessels that were carrying food that belonged to Britain or were carrying British goods, a policy similar to that of the British at the time.[6]

From 1793 until the end of the first part of the war with France, Britain had implemented a rather traditional type of naval blockade, a close blockade of the major French port of Brest as a means of observing and limiting the movement of the French fleet.[7] During the second part of the war between the French and the British, from 1803 to 1815, both nations imposed blockades designed to limit trade and to control warships: and both met with some mixed success.[8] By 1800, the British had more than twice the number of warships than did the French, reflecting a dramatic change in the military environment since the beginning of the eighteenth century, when the two navies were of roughly equivalent size, with a sharp relative growth in the number of English warships between 1740 and 1800 (see Table 2.2).[9] The French navy suffered a severe setback with Nelson's victory

---

4 See Heckscher, *Continental System*, 25, 27, 43. In June 1793, Britain forbade all food imports into France, but this lasted only a few months.
5 See Heckscher, *Continental System*, 27, 77, 91.
6 See Heckscher, *Continental System*, 42, 43, 47. See also J. Holland Rose, "Napoleon and English Commerce," *English Historical Review* 8 (October 1893), 704–725. For a detailed description of the issue of neutrality during the "Napoleonic Period" (c. 1793–1815), see W. Alison Phillips and Arthur H. Reede, *Neutrality: Its History, Economics, and Law*, vol. II, *The Napoleonic Period* (New York: Columbia University Press, 1936).
7 Roger Morriss, ed., *The Channel Fleet and the Blockage of Brest, 1793–1801* (Burlington: Ashgate, 2001), 1–21, particularly 13–15. For earlier discussions, see Captain A. T. Mahan, *The Influence of Sea Power upon the French Revolution and Empire 1793–1812*, 9th ed., 2 vols. (Boston: Little, Brown, 1898), vol. 1, 335–380.
8 D. T. Jack, *Studies in Economic Warfare* (New York: Chemical Publishing House, 1941).
9 George Modelski and William R. Thompson, *Seapower in Global Politics, 1494–1993* (Seattle: University of Washington Press, 1988), 68–71. At this time, the total for France and Spain equaled that of the British. See also Richard Harding, *The Evolution of the Sailing Navy, 1509–1815* (New York: St. Martin's, 1995), 102, 118, 126, 131, 136; Jan Glete, *Navies and Nations: Warships, Navies, and State Building in Europe and America, 1500–1860*, two vols. (Stockholm: Almqvist and Wicksell, 1993), 173–443, who shows the same patterns for sailing-ship navies and for Atlantic navies.

Table 2.2. *Size of Sailing Ship Navies,*
England and France, 1700–1820

Year	England	France
1700	196	195
1720	174	48
1740	195	91
1760	375	156
1780	372	271
1790	473 (459)	324 (314)
1800	546	204
1810	673	194
1815	616 (609)	228
1820	498	221

Source: Jan Glete, *Navies and Nations; Warships,*
Navies and State Building in Europe and America,
1500–1860, 2 vols. (Stockholm: Almqvist &
Wiksell, 1993) 241, 311, 376, 422. Numbers in
parentheses are based on counts given for start
of years presented. See also George Modelski and
William R. Thompson, *Seapower in Global Politics,*
1494–1993 (Seattle: University of Washington
Press, 1988), 68–71 for related estimates of global
power warships.

at Trafalgar (1805). And, although the French added warships after the start
of the nineteenth century, the British navy increased by a greater amount
to 1815. It is this difference in the size of the two fleets that was to influence both the nature of the two blockades and their relative successes. The
difference also underscored the importance of France's need to induce the
other continental nations to impose trade restrictions and blockades against
the British. The attempt to control the continent and its external trade was
the basis of Napoleon's Continental System, and was central to his wartime
efforts.

Within fourteen months of the failure of the Peace of Amiens, a number
of military and commercial actions were undertaken by the British and by
the French. The British seized all French and Dutch vessels in British ports
(May 1803), regulated the neutral trade with the enemy colonies (June
1803), and proclaimed a blockade of the Elbe and Weser rivers (June–July
1803) – a blockade that limited the trade from German cities. In August
1804, the blockade was extended to all French ports on both the English
Channel and the North Sea; however, the effects of these blockades gradually

eroded in the years before 1810.[10] France, for its part, employed policies that were designed to limit British trade with the continent. Those policies involved military occupation as well as political coalitions with continental nations; and, in part, they were directed at raising tariffs and imposing other types of prohibitions on the import of British goods. Napoleon was initially successful militarily on the continent, but the British dominated the war at sea.[11]

Although it is believed that Napoleon's Decree had been planned earlier, meaning that the British Order was used as a pretext, his dramatic political and military activities came after a British Order in Council of May 1806 – an order that included the placement of two military blockades of the European coast; one from Brest to the Elbe River, the other from Ostend to the mouth of the Seine.[12] In November 1806, Napoleon responded by issuing the so-called Berlin Decree; and it was followed, in November and December 1807, by the two Milan decrees. These three decrees provided the basic structure for the Continental System. The provisions of the Berlin Decree included: (1) prohibition of all trade with the British; (2) all British subjects in French-occupied areas were prisoners of war and their property was "fair prize"; (3) all trade in British goods was prohibited and all goods from England and her colonies were fair prize (and one-half their value was to be used to indemnify French merchants for loses to the British); and (4) no ships coming from the ports of Britain or its colonies would be permitted to use any port on the Continent.[13] The Second Milan Decree extended these regulations to cover all vessels from all nations, and it made any vessel that had called at or was on its way to any British port a fair prize. Given

---

10 See Heckscher, *Continental System*, 81–83.

11 On the patterns of war and diplomatic issues, see. J. Holland Rose, "The Continental System, 1809–1814," in A. W. Ward, E. W. Prothero, and Stanley Leathes, eds., *The Cambridge Modern History, Volume IX: Napoleon* (Cambridge: Cambridge University Press, 1906), 361–389; H. W. Wilson, "The Command of the Sea 1803–1815," in *Cambridge Modern History: Napoleon*, 208–243; J. Holland Rose, *Man and the Sea: Stages in Maritime and Human Progress* (Boston: Houghton Mifflin, 1936), 219, 239; Michael Duffy, "British Diplomacy and the French Wars, 1789–1815," and Piers Mackesy. "Strategic Problems of the British War Effort," both in H. T. Dickinson, ed., *Britain and the French Revolution, 1789–1815* (New York: St. Martin's Press, 1989), 127–145 and 147–164, respectively.

On the relative importance of land and sea control, see C. C. Lloyd, "Armed Forces and the Art of War. B. Navies," in C. W. Crawley, ed., *The New Cambridge Modern History Volume X, War and Peace in an Age of Upheaval, 1793–1820* (Cambridge: Cambridge University Press; 1965), 76–90; Colin S. Gray, "Seapower and Landpower," in C. Gray and R. Barnett, eds., *Seapower and Strategy*, 3–26. For the discussion of the naval losses of the French and British, see Michael Glover, *Warfare in the Age of Bonaparte* (London: Cassell, 1980), 181–184, 197, 200; F. W. Hirst, *The Political Economy of War* (London: J. M. Dent, 1915), 58, 67; and Jack, *Studies*, 36–37.

12 See Heckscher, *Continental System*, 81; Melvin, *Napoleon's Navigation System*; Mahan, *Influence of Sea Power*, vol. 2, 269–274.

13 See Heckscher, *Continental System*, 90, 96.

the weaknesses of the French navy and its inability to impose heavy costs on the British, the declaration of these blockades and the subsequent actions at sea were, as Heckscher points out, rather a "theatrical gesture." Heckscher describes the French action as the imposition of a "self-blockade" – that by cutting off imports to the continent the blockade was aimed at restricting the sales of British and British colonial goods and, in this way, damaging Britain's economic power.[14]

In 1807 in reaction to the Berlin and Milan decrees, the British responded with several related Orders in Council – proclaiming policies that were basically aimed at tightening the blockade of France, restricting the direct trade of Britain's enemies with their colonies, and limiting French maritime trade with neutrals. The first Order required that neutral vessels call at a British port before proceeding to the continent, hitting at neutrals such as the United States, as well as France. Thus, "all direct intercourse between the enemy countries and other ports is prohibited, except when the 'other ports' are either European British ports or ports in the vessel's own country."[15] Taken together, the orders imposed economic and political costs on the trade of both enemies and of neutral nations. The regulation of neutral trade by both the British and the French was to be the source of continuing international conflict with the United States, then the major neutral trader in Europe's overseas commerce. By the end of 1807, the basic contours of the Continental System, the British blockade, and the United States' policies that were to provide that country's reaction to these measures were all set in place. Although their duration was to be only a few years, these new policies did have a dramatic effect on the shape of the European and American economies.

2. THE NATURE OF THE FRENCH BLOCKADE

Although dictated by the relative military balance-of-power between the British and the French, Napoleon's aims in the deployment of the Continental System were somewhat unusual among the historical rationales for blockades.[16] France was the strong military power on the European continent, at least until war with Spain and Russia weakened its capabilities; but, relative to the British navy, it was very weak at sea. Thus France

---

14 See Heckscher, *Continental System*, 90–93, 96, 114–124, 389–407.
15 See Heckscher, *Continental System*, 16, 113, 116–117; William Smart, *Economic Annals of the Nineteenth Century, 1801–1820* (London: Macmillan, 1910), 154–161.
16 See Rose, *Man and the Sea*; Kaiser, *Politics and War*, 237–263.

could not really impose a blockade aimed at halting British shipping or stopping imports from elsewhere into the British Isles. Nor could it easily stop exports from Britain to the continental nations, unless the continental nations would refuse to purchase them. That, indeed, was Napoleon's continental strategy: to control, directly or indirectly, the imports of the continental nations from Britain and its colonies, and it was the strategy that underlay the concept of a "self-blockade" – a blockade designed to restrict British exports.[17] This "self-blockade" resembled more closely a system of tariff and quota restrictions than the customary naval blockade; and the policy was aimed both at harming the British economy, and, as tariffs also are designed to do, to encourage the production of the French and continental industries.

Because of naval weakness, and because of his firm mercantilist beliefs, Napoleon's Continental System sought ends unlike those of most other blockades. Whereas most blockades were intended to reduce the enemy's military and economic power by depriving them of certain critical commodities, particularly weapons and foodstuffs, Napoleon's aim was to weaken the British economy by adversely affecting its financial capabilities, by leading to unbalanced trade in addition to reducing British military expenditures on the continent.[18] This strategy would not only aim to limit Britain's exports – exports that would provide them with foreign earnings – but it also was intended to encourage British imports. Imports meant British expenditures for foreign goods; and, thus, if foreign transactions were sufficiently unbalanced, to specie outflows. Reducing British revenues and specie reserves would not only reduce Britain's wealth and power and, presumably, weaken that country's credit and ability to borrow; but it also would have a more direct impact. It would greatly lessen Britain's ability to subsidize continental nations – a subsidy that was a part of the British attempt to lure those nations away from France and to redirect their trade toward Britain. Although both customary blockades and Napoleon's Continental System were aimed at reducing enemy exports, the specific reason for deploying such measures – measures designed to limit their revenues – were somewhat different. In one case, it was to reduce the ability to purchase imports; in the

---

17 See Michael Lewis, *The History of the British Navy* (London: George Allen and Unwin, 1959), 180–181, 205–207, for his description of the Continental System as "the first full–scale experiment in economic warfare, a bold attempt to blockade Britain without warships."

18 Mahan, *Influence of Sea Power*, vol. 2, 197–200, describes the French system after 1793 as concerned with "commerce-destroying," pursuing "warfare against commerce," rather than with maritime warfare. His chapters covering 1793 to 1813 are entitled "The Warfare against Commerce." See also O'Brien, "Public Finance."

other, it was to increase the balance-of-payments deficits and cause specie outflows.

The peculiar nature of the French blockade is indicated by France's rather paradoxical behavior during the British grain crises of 1810.[19] Rather than seeking to impose costs on Britain by forcing a reduction in British grain imports at a time of domestic shortage, Napoleon encouraged exports to Britain from France and its allies on the continent, particularly Holland, as a means of generating an increased trade deficit at this fortuitous time of high grain prices, as well as giving aid to French farmers.[20] Grain exports from France stopped the following year, not because of a desire to try to starve the British, but because France was now suffering from poor harvests. Thus, in evaluating the success (or not) of the Continental System, it should be noted that Napoleon's aim was to reduce Britain's specie supply (a goal he was successful in achieving in the years of the blockade, because bullion at the Bank of England fell from £6.9 million in 1808 to £2.2 million in 1814), rather than to limit the British acquisition of resources that could be used for consumption and production (Figure 2.1).[21] Furthermore, the blockade was designed to contribute not only to a hoped-for military victory but also to an increase in French industrialization – which would further limit English exports of manufactures, and thus its economic power.

Because both Britain and France introduced restraints on neutral nations, there were significant effects of commercial warfare. Neither nation was able to substantially offset the effects of the blockades by obtaining needed goods through trade with neutral powers. More important, by making neutral vessels fair prize, the blockades engineered a significant response by the biggest of the neutral powers, the United States. That response led, in 1807, to an Embargo Act directed against trade with both belligerent powers, then to the Non-Intercourse Act of 1809, and finally to a war between the United States and Britain – a war that began in 1812 in some part over

---

19 See Melvin, *Napoleon's Navigation System*, 88–89; Macksey, "Strategic Problems of the British War Effort"; W. Freeman Galpin, *The Grain Supply of England during the Napoleonic Period* (New York: Macmillan, 1925), 168–188; Lewis, *History of the British Navy*, 205–207; Robert A. Doughty and Harold E. Raugh Jr., "Embargoes in Historical Perspective," *Parameters* 21 (Spring 1991), 21–30; Heckscher; *Continental System*, 336–347; and B. R. Mitchell and Phyllis Deane, *Abstract of British Historical Statistics* (Cambridge: Cambridge University Press, 1962), 441–443.

20 For discussions of whether it would have been possible that France starve out England, see Galpin, *Grain Supply*, 109–122, 168–201; Mancur Olson Jr., *The Economics of Wartime Shortage: A History of British Food Supplies in the Napoleonic War and in World Wars I and II* (Durham: Duke University Press, 1963), 49–72; Rose, *Man and the Sea*.

21 See Mitchell and Deane, *Abstract*, 441–443.

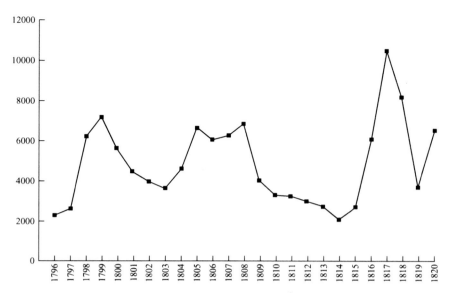

Figure 2.1. Bullion at The Bank of England – 1796–1820 (£000). *Source:* B. R. Mitchell and Phyllis Deane, *Abstract of British Historical Statistics* (Cambridge: Cambridge University Press, 1962), 441–443.

neutral rights.[22] Previously, in 1810, the United States had passed a law that stated that if one of the belligerent powers revoked their trade regulations (and the other did not follow suit within three months), the United States would use the Non-Intercourse Act to reduce trade with the nonrevoking nation. Napoleon adopted policies that appeared to meet these terms, and the United States narrowed its use of trade restrictions to the British. Soon, however, the restrictions proved ineffective; and the United States declared war. Although the British had rescinded the offending Orders in Council, the American declaration of war was not withdrawn; and for three years Britain and the United States remained at war. It is not clear which of the belligerent powers suffered the most because of these extensive sets of rules restricting neutral trade. It is, however, clear that the British triumphed militarily, against both France and the United States. And, although disputes over neutral rights frequently arose during the course of many blockades, such as those deployed during the American Civil War and both World Wars, the Napoleonic Wars represent one of the few cases of such a dispute

22 See Chapter 3. See also François Crouzet. "America and the Crisis of the British Imperial Economy, 1803–1807," in John J. McCusker and Kenneth Morgan, eds., *The Early Modern Atlantic Economy*, (Cambridge: Cambridge University Press, 2002), 278–315.

between a belligerent power and a neutral power playing an important role in leading to outright war.

3. NAVAL AND MILITARY PRACTICES

In the nine years between the Berlin Decree and the French surrender, there were numerous changes in policy and in behavior on the part of both France and Britain and of their allies. Some of these changes in policy reflected shifts in internal economic and social conditions, whereas others reflected changing military circumstances and shifting alliances among the continental nations. Although the Continental System existed for the entire period, it was not always effectively implemented; and, as a result, it is difficult to evaluate its success or failure. It is generally argued that the Continental System was effectively used to control trade only from mid-1807 to mid-1808 and from mid-1810 to mid-1812, or a total of three years, one-third of the period in question.[23] Such a short period in a world with economies marked by long lags in both shipping and production, as well as lags in trading responses, means that any attempt to measure the effectiveness of the Continental System is difficult.

Both belligerents were not just seeking to implement successful blockades; they also were pursuing other goals. The French wished to maintain continental alliances, by military force or by commercial agreement, but they also were concerned with the expansion of French industry and commercial power. The British wished to maintain their commercial and military power; and, to that end, they attempted, both by paying subsidies and through other political and economic policies, to draw continental nations away from the French.

In discussing the changes and reactions of the two nations during the blockade years, it is important to remember that there were many other events that influenced the economies and the societies of the belligerent powers.[24] The blockade was not the only component of the economic and political policies that changed, and any attempt to measure the ex-ante

---

23 See Heckscher, *Continental System*, 320–323, 348–352, on limits to French success. See also Kaiser, *Politics and War*, 252–253; Crouzet, "The Impact of the French Wars"; Markham, "The Napoleonic Adventure," 329–336; Rose, "The Continental System," 368–370.

24 See Gaston Bodart, *Losses of Life in Modern Wars: Austria-Hungary and France* (Oxford: Clarendon Press, 1916), 116–138, who lists the sequence of wars with the other continental nations that Napoleon fought, ultimately fighting with all but Turkey and Denmark. The importance of land activities is seen in the comparison of 7 naval battles, with 221 land battles, and 81 sieges.

or ex-post profitability of the blockades needs to take these other factors into account. There were changes in military fortunes on land and at sea, fluctuations in the size of the harvest because of weather conditions, and the customary fluctuations that reflected the impact of economic conditions on business activity – conditions that influenced both domestic and foreign demands. Even more important, perhaps, were the variations in Napoleon's political and military relations with other nations. Some countries were added to his alliance but, as with Spain and Russia, some managed to successfully withdraw, by military measures, from French domination and ally themselves with Britain. Thus, there were numerous other forces that affected the success or failure of the blockades, and, as a result, any simple evaluation is problematic.

4. CHANGING POLICIES, 1809–1815

In 1809, among the many political factors that affected the extent of the British blockade was the desire to attract nations away from France by providing them with more favorable trading conditions. An Order in Council of April of that year ended the blockade of all European countries except France, Holland (then ruled by France), Northern Italy, and Northern Germany.[25] By this time, Spain had succeeded in breaking away from French domination; and that country had shifted much of its trade to Britain. It was not only Spain but also the Spanish colonies of Central and South America that increased their trade with Britain; and that increase helped to offset the reduction in British trade with the continent.[26] In response, in 1810, France undertook several new measures to increase economic pressure on the British. The Trianon tariff of August 1810 greatly increased the taxes on imports from foreign and colonial areas; however, this meant increasing the prices of foreign goods in the home market. It did represent a marked shift in French goals, away from the exclusion of colonial goods

---

25 See François Crouzet, *Britain, France and International Commerce, from Louis XIV to Victoria* (Aldershot: Ashgate, 1996).
26 See Mitchell and Deane, *Abstract*, 311; Arthur D. Gayer, W. W. Rostow and Anna Jacobson Schwartz, *The Growth and Fluctuation of the British Economy, 1790–1850: An Historical, Statistical and Theoretical Study of Britain's Economic Development*, two vols. (Oxford: Clarendon Press, 1953), vol. 1, 89; Heckscher, *Continental System*, 245. The amount of exports to Latin America and the foreign West Indies rose from an average of £315,500 in 1804–1805 to an average of £6,176,000 in 1809–1810, and remained above at least £3,000,000 for the remainder of the war and afterward. Exports to Spain also rose, from an average of £40,000 in 1805–1806 to an average of £1,890,000 in 1809–1810.

to a more customary reduction of foreign trade by use of tariffs.[27] The Fontainebleau decree of October 1810 "prescribed the destruction of all English goods throughout the Continent," a measure that was clearly aimed at halting all imports from British manufacturers. Even more important in influencing French policy and in limiting the impact of the blockade was the Licensing Decree of July 1810. Licensing was a practice that the British had innovated. The British government, at its discretion, had been granting licenses to shippers wishing to trade with foreign nations. The aim of the British policy was not to restrict, but to expand, British trade with the continent. The French adoption of the licensing system meant that traders could obtain licenses to trade with the British; however, as the British still prohibited imports from France, the French attempt to use these to increase their exports did not succeed. Nevertheless, this policy did lead to more trade between the belligerents, particularly during the British grain shortage of 1810; and it marked an apparent policy shift from trade limitation by naval blockade to the use of tariffs and direct regulation of trade to reduce imports. In administering licenses, there was a conflict between their use as a regulatory measure and their role of a means of raising revenue. Most of the continental nations did not follow France in large tariff increases; they raised tariffs slightly, if at all. They did, however, allow for licensing to regulate trade.[28] Despite these important changes in foreign trade relations, there were, perhaps, more important matters in late 1810 that were to lead to France's ultimate loss to Britain. These were not, however, the direct impact of blockade-related matters. Rather, in reaction to various French pressures, Russia severed relations with France. This led to a shift in Russia's trade allegiance from France to Britain, giving rise to Napoleon's ill-fated invasion and subsequent military defeat by the Russians and various other European nations in 1814.[29]

In late 1811, even during the war between the two countries, Britain did attempt to allow some trade reciprocity with France, but this new opening led to no effective changes in policy. In June 1812, Britain did, however, repeal the Orders in Council that had influenced their trade with the United States and other neutral nations. These had angered American merchants and politicians, but this repeal occurred a few days *after* the United States had declared war on Britain; and, thus, it did not prevent the War of 1812.[30] Not

27 See Melvin, *Napoleon's Navigation System*, 223–234.
28 See Melvin, *Napoleon's Navigation System*, 235–310; Heckscher, *Continental System*, 153, 205–220.
29 See Duffy, "British Diplomacy."
30 See Melvin, *Napoleon's Navigation System*, 256–283, 289–291.

surprisingly, the war caused a massive decline in Anglo-American trade; but, with the war's end, the decline was quickly reversed.[31] In 1812, Napoleon's policy again shifted; the new policy was to encourage French imports – preferably imports of raw materials – from other nations, including Britain, as long as they were balanced by an equivalent amount of French exports, preferably exports of manufactured goods. This change led to some increase in total French trade.

The period between 1810 and 1812 was one of economic difficulties in Britain, France, and Europe in general. Output declined; and, initially in Britain, there were grain shortages and limited food supplies. Britain benefited from grain surpluses in Spain; but, in addition, from imports from France, Holland, and Flanders, countries that also had grain surpluses in 1810 but that were still at war with Britain. The French aim, an aim consistent with the overall goal of its blockade policy, was to both take advantage of the opportunity to sell at high prices in order to drain Britain of specie, and to provide expanded markets for those French farmers with surplus production. The next year, however, grain shortages led to the need of France to import grain. In response to the grain shortages, the French imposed embargos against corn exports but, as sales under licenses were permitted, this policy was never fully enforced. The history of the years 1810 to 1812 indicates both the unusual nature of the Continental System and the somewhat strange French expectations of what the system could accomplish. The defeat of Napoleon in Russia in 1812 effectively ended any trade war with Britain; and, in 1814, with Napoleon's defeat at the hands of several continental nations and his abdication, the Continental System came to an end.

5. FRENCH AND BRITISH TRADE

In discussing the success or failure of both the Continental System and of the British blockade it is necessary to remember the goals that the two sets of policies were intended to achieve, and also that by the start of the nineteenth century Britain had command of the seas, such that it could apply the blockade not only against the French but also the rest of Europe as well. The British blockade was more traditional; an attempt to restrict French exports and the imports by France and its other continental allies

---

31 See Mitchell and Deane, *Abstract*, 311; G. R. Porter, *Progress of the Nation: In Its Various Social and Economic Relations, from the Beginning of the Nineteenth Century* (London: John Murray, 1847[1836–1843]), 359–360, 380–381, 400.

from neutral nations.[32] For the French, one goal was the familiar one of achieving military victory by reducing the economic power of an adversary. The policies adopted were, however, not so much aimed at reducing British imports of foodstuffs and other goods, as they were at lowering British foreign earnings by reducing that country's exports and increasing its financial outflows by having them increase their imports of necessary items. The hope was to create a balance-of-payments deficit for Britain; a deficit that would lead to an outflow of specie, thus, reducing British wealth and productive capacity.[33] The second goal of the French policy was to use the Continental System to attack British economic power by raising tariffs, and, it was hoped, increasing the costs and decreasing the availability of British manufacturers, in order to encourage the development of French industry.[34] The Continental System was, however, a rather expensive means of deploying tariffs and trade exclusions. In regard to this second French aim, it is difficult to present a full evaluation of benefits and costs; there were clearly some positive effects – it spurred the growth of some industries, such as cotton textiles, chemicals, and beet sugar.[35] But there also were some negative effects. The trade limitations increased the price of imports, including those of raw materials needed for manufacturing; and, thus, it actually reduced production in some sectors. In addition, with the implementation of tariffs and the introduction of loans for industrial establishments, the industrial policy involved an increased role of government. The Continental System and the blockades had an impact on industry in the other continental nations similar to the impact on France, being both mixed and relatively minor.[36]

Both within the war period and in the longer term, there is a need to distinguish between military and economic benefits. The fact that France lost the war is suggestive of the failure of the Continental System, but it may be argued that the war served to prolong and make closer a war in which the French were, initially, in a less than powerful position. Whatever may have

32 See Heckscher, *Continental System*, 98–100.
33 See O'Brien, "Public Finance"; Larry Neal, *The Rise of Financial Capitalism: International Capital Markets in the Age of Reason* (Cambridge: Cambridge University Press, 1990), 201–222.
34 See Melvin, *Napoleon's Navigation System*, xii–xiii; Rose, "The Continental System."
35 See François Crouzet, "Wars, Blockade, and Economic Change in Europe, 1792–1815," *Journal of Economic History* 24 (December 1964), 567–588; Geoffrey Ellis, *Napoleon's Continental Blockade: The Case of Alsace* (Oxford: Clarendon Press, 1981), 159–160; W. O. Henderson, *Britain and Industrial Europe, 1750–1870: Studies in British Influence and the Industrial Revolution in Western Europe, 1750–1870*, 3rd ed. (Leicester. Leicester University Press, 1972), 24–34, 46–48.
36 See Crouzet, "Wars, Blockade, and Economic Change"; Henderson; *Britain and Industrial Europe*; Heckscher, *Continental System*, 266, 295–323.

been the relative power of the belligerents before 1789, the internal turmoil generated by the French Revolution initially weakened the capability of the French military. By the time the Continental System was introduced, the French strength was on land, whereas the British clearly had superior power at sea. As a result, the French were probably not in a strong position to achieve success with a naval blockade of the standard type. There was little prospect that a French blockade designed to bring down England would be successful, but the introduction of the Continental System probably had a somewhat positive effect from the French point of view.

Taken together, the Continental System and the British blockade did have an impact on the magnitude of international commerce, as well as on the geographic pattern and the commodity composition of trade.[37] In the case of the British, during the early nineteenth century, the size of the official values of total imports and total exports fluctuated, with little trend and few extreme changes[38] (see Table 2.3). The largest deviation from the average was in the high level of imports in 1810, the year of grain shortage, but this was followed by a sharp decline in 1811.[39] Although there were no dramatic changes during the war period, there was a slowing down of the rates of growth of exports from the levels that had been reached over the preceding two decades. The rate of growth of British exports during the years 1802–1814 fell to 3.1 from the 6.4 percent per annum that had marked the years 1781–1802, and the rate of growth of imports declined from 5.4 percent to 1.2 percent.[40] These declines are suggestive of some impact of the war, if not of the blockade itself. The Continental System also led to some shifts in British export markets, and the same is true for the conflict with the United States (see Table 2.4). There was a relatively small decline in the share of goods going to continental Europe, particularly after 1805, but there were some increases in trade with Spain and Portugal after those countries

---

37 For discussions, see François Crouzet, *L'Économie Britannique et Le Blocus Continental (1806–1813)*, two vols. (Paris: Presses Universitares de France, 1958); François Crouzet, "Great Britain's Response to the French Revolution and to Napoleon," in François Crouzet, *Britain Ascendant: Comparative Studies in Franco-British Economic History* (Cambridge: Cambridge University Press, 1990 [1975]), 262–294; Mitchell and Deane, *Abstract*, 281–282, 289–290, 295, 311; A. Chabert, *Essai sur les Mouvements des Revenues et de L'activité Economique en France de 1798 à 1820*, 2 vols. (Paris: Librairie de Médicis, 1945–1949), 321–328. Albert H. Imlah, *Economic Elements in the Pax Britannica: Studies in British Foreign Trade in the Nineteenth Century* (Cambridge, MA: Harvard University Press, 1958).
38 See Mitchell and Deane, *Abstract*, 281–282.
39 See Mitchell and Deane, *Abstract*, 281–282. See also Galpin, *Grain Supply*; Heckscher, *Continental System*; Porter, *Progress*, 359–360.
40 See François Crouzet, "The Impact of the French Wars on the British Economy," in Dickinson, ed., *Britain and the French Revolution*, 189–209 (see p. 191).

Table 2.3. *United Kingdom, Overseas Trade, Official Values and Values at Current Prices, 1796–1820 (£ Million)*

	Computed or Declared Values			Official Values		
		Domestic			Domestic	
Year	Imports	Exports	Re-exports	Imports	Exports	Re-exports
1796	39.6	30.1	8.5	23.2	19.1	11.4
1797	34.4	27.5	9.3	21.0	16.9	12.0
1798	49.6	32.2	11.3	27.9	19.7	13.9
1799	50.9	36.8	9.4	26.8	24.1	11.9
1800	62.3	37.7	14.7	30.6	24.3	18.8
1801	68.7	40.6	12.9	31.8	24.9	10.4
1802	54.7	45.9	12.9	29.8	25.6	12.8
1803	53.9	36.9	9.1	26.6	20.5	8.1
1804	57.3	38.2	11.0	27.8	22.7	9.0
1805	61.0	38.1	10.0	28.6	23.4	7.7
1806	53.8	40.9	9.2	26.9	25.9	7.8
1807	53.8	37.2	8.3	26.7	23.4	7.7
1808	51.5	37.3	6.5	26.8	24.6	5.8
1809	73.7	47.4	14.3	31.8	33.5	12.8
1810	88.5	48.4	12.5	39.3	34.1	9.5
1811	50.7	32.9	6.7	26.5	22.7	6.2
1812	56.0	41.7	9.1	26.2	29.5	9.7
1814	80.8	45.5	24.8	33.8	34.2	19.4
1815	71.3	51.6	16.8	33.0	42.9	15.7
1816	50.0	41.7	12.6	27.4	35.7	13.5
1817	61.0	41.8	10.1	30.8	40.1	10.3
1818	80.7	46.5	12.3	36.9	42.7	10.9
1819	56.0	35.2	10.2	30.8	33.5	9.9
1820	54.2	36.4	10.4	32.4	38.4	10.6

Source: B. R. Mitchell and Phyllis Deane, *Abstract of British Historical Statistics* (Cambridge: Cambridge University Press, 1962), 281–282. There are no entries for 1813.

had freed themselves from Napoleon's rule. The major shift in the pattern of British trade was triggered by the growth in South American market. In several years between 1808 and 1814, exports to South and Central American markets were equal to the average level of exports to the United States.[41] Moreover, the enhanced Latin American market continued to draw high levels of British exports after the war ended. In the postwar period, there was increased trade with almost all markets – a set of markets that included

41 See Mitchell and Deane, *Abstract*, 311; Gayer, Rostow, and Schwartz, *Growth and Fluctuation*, vol. 1, 83–109.

Table 2.4. *Great Britain, Geographic Composition of Exports and Imports, Official Values, 1796–1820 (£000)*

	Northern Europe		Southern Europe		Asia		Africa		British N. Amer.		U.S.		British W. Indies		Foreign W. Indies & S. America	
	Imports	Exports	Imports	Exports	Imports	Exports	Imports	Exports	Imports	Exports	Imports	Exports	Imports	Exports	Imports	Exports
1796	6,805	8,317	2,072	2,457	3,373	2,377	120	614	204	815	2,081	6,054	3,967	3,223	877	1,041
1797	4,897	9,185	1,277	1,587	3,942	2,288	54	887	213	845	1,176	5,057	4,309	3,144	1,078	665
1798	6,528	10,139	1,303	1,405	7,627	1,146	70	1,291	220	1,054	1,783	5,580	5,419	5,198	1,159	1,264
1799	7,292	7,939	1,842	2,099	4,285	2,436	113	1,622	170	1,092	1,819	7,057	6,162	5,947	1,390	1,048
1800	7,026	14,325	2,403	3,404	4,942	2,860	97	1,099	393	976	2,358	7,886	7,369	4,087	1,497	479
1801	7,235	14,442	2,274	3,545	5,424	2,946	139	1,124	456	1,017	2,707	7,518	8,436	4,386	2,577	589
1802	5,916	15,015	3,242	7,752	5,795	2,930	169	1,161	368	1,351	1,924	5,329	8,531	3,926	1,658	285
1803	5,346	11,372	3,527	3,968	6,349	2,733	94	819	328	1,082	1,914	5,273	6,132	2,380	355	193
1804	6,435	12,716	2,217	3,033	5,215	1,766	164	1,173	378	1,056	1,651	6,398	7,682	4,282	346	312
1805	7,137	13,026	2,872	2,440	6,073	1,669	107	991	294	865	1,767	7,147	6,720	3,832	736	319
1806	5,805	10,533	2,392	2,678	3,755	1,937	116	1,433	330	951	2,000	8,613	8,815	4,734	1,227	1,796
1807	5,154	9,412	2,819	3,278	3,402	1,884	122	798	450	1,061	2,848	7,921	7,980	4,579	1,341	1,326
1808	2,120	4,734	2,091	6,547	3,858	1,933	143	533	827	1,125	836	3,992	8,778	5,929	2,838	4,830
1809	5,660	13,666	3,935	10,055	3,366	1,648	185	706	678	1,748	2,205	5,188	7,703	5,975	5,090	6,382
1810	7,480	11,221	4,996	8,385	4,710	1,717	257	484	885	1,845	2,614	7,813	8,258	4,790	6,961	5,970
1811	2,652	2,358	1,685	12,606	4,106	1,665	189	317	802	1,910	2,309	1,432	8,452	4,123	3,831	3,047
1812	3,213	5,460	2,952	15,528	5,602	1,779	172	444	720	1,419	1,294	4,136	7,487	4,767	2,471	4,115
1814	6,399	22,922	3,443	12,348	6,304	1,698	269	422	323	4,093	23	7	8,497	6,315	6,220	4,302
1815	4,986	19,860	3,244	9,071	8,042	2,093	325	393	369	3,099	2,370	1,193	8,527	6,916	3,371	3,786
1816	2,784	18,493	2,068	9,000	8,313	2,205	240	380	493	2,208	2,386	7,800	7,547	4,608	1,974	3,284
1817	4,897	16,988	3,100	9,529	7,688	2,795	348	506	615	1,396	3,057	6,377	8,021	6,762	1,702	4,882
1818	7,875	17,181	4,944	10,141	7,343	3,196	285	479	690	1,795	3,427	8,383	8,347	5,785	2,331	5,552
1819	4,819	16,016	3,175	9,441	7,344	2,422	254	423	751	2,001	2,688	4,302	7,888	4,490	2,017	3,472
1820	4,799	18,982	3,453	10,693	7,568	3,391	174	566	841	1,676	3,651	3,921	8,011	4,353	2,326	4,450

Source: Mitchell and Deane, *Abstract*, 311. There are no entries for 1813.

Table 2.5. *Great Britain, Commodity Composition, Exports, Official Values, 1796–1820 (£000)*

Year	Coal	Iron & Steel	Hardwares & Cutlery	Nonferrous Metals & Manufactures	Cotton Yarn & Manufactures	Woolen & Worsted Yarn & Manufactures	Linen Yarn & Manufactures	Silk yarn & Manufactures
1796	522	1,277	–	1,243	3,061	5,677	955	373
1797	453	1,152	–	1,011	2,464	4,625	757	296
1798	455	1,145	–	1,079	3,622	6,177	1,103	225
1799	467	1,596	–	1,346	5,859	6,435	1,115	306
1800	510	1,605	–	1,414	5,851	6,918	808	297
1801	465	1,466	–	1,349	6,941	7,321	1,009	280
1802	521	1,610	–	1,557	7,667	6,687	895	232
1803	511	1,197	–	1,185	7,143	5,303	561	155
1804	514	1,102	–	874	8,792	5,694	727	187
1805	509	1,008	–	842	9,653	6,006	657	200
1806	543	1,260	–	693	10,482	6,248	800	218
1807	471	1,394	–	818	10,287	5,373	766	198
1808	527	1,193	–	682	13,411	4,854	874	129
1809	406	1,392	–	700	19,732	5,416	1,157	190
1810	510	1,578	–	717	19,109	5,774	1,018	190
1811	524	1,245	–	491	12,261	4,376	703	137
1812	617	1,446	–	737	16,939	5,085	840	166
1814	675	1,095	355	750	17,869	5,629	1,543	219
1815	698	1,127	871	1,150	22,555	7,480	1,619	258
1816	200	938	740	1,212	17,564	5,586	1,559	162
1817	214	1,065	439	1,343	21,259	5,675	1,943	153
1818	230	1,288	580	1,231	22,589	6,344	2,158	168
1819	201	961	443	959	18,282	4,602	1,547	127
1820	213	1,025	343	1,135	22,532	4,364	1,935	118

Source: Mitchell and Deane, *Abstract*, 295. There are no entries for 1813.

the United States and continental Europe. There was, however, only a small change in the level of trade with France. With the exception of the higher postwar level of imports (but not exports) coming from the British West Indies, the list of nations from which imports to Britain increased looked very much the same as the list of countries that had recovered increased levels of exports.

Despite the French policies designed to limit the expansion of British manufacturing industries, particularly the rapidly developing cotton textile sector, British exports of cotton textiles increased rapidly during the era of the Continental System[42] (see Table 2.5). Much of the increase in exports

42 See Michael M. Edwards, *The Growth of the British Cotton Trade, 1780–1815* (Manchester: Manchester University Press, 1967), 51–64; 243–247; Mitchell and Deane, *Abstract*, 295, 311.

Table 2.6. *Great Britain, Commodity Composition, Imports, Official Values, 1796–1820 (£000)*

Year	Tobacco	Iron	Flax	Hemp	Linen Yarn	Oils, Seeds, Nuts for Expressing Oil, Gums & Tallow	Hides & Skins	Dyewoods & Dyestuffs
1796	224	526	640	526	404			
1797	255	363	410	415	360			
1798	389	510	766	551	441			
1799	354	480	828	640	525			
1800	357	375	795	507	506			
1801	423	331	530	636	423			
1802	254	531	530	415	418			
1803	346	429	575	620	375			
1804	217	222	714	618	463			
1805	173	268	914	519	540	992	630	1,316
1806	228	317	699	620	501	1,127	499	798
1807	244	233	830	643	325	941	401	1,355
1808	78	205	403	219	35	644	406	1,155
1809	276	240	968	722	234	941	507	673
1810	499	197	945	752	287	1,195	943	1,762
1811	321	273	431	388	12	852	751	1,322
1812	146	171	675	629	12	907	272	1,155
1814	54	214	948	464	273	1,542	576	1,833
1815	416	208	633	620	251	1,272	581	1,413
1816	290	83	435	313	52	1,036	411	1,609
1817	186	99	818	389	127	1,020	305	1,047
1818	419	162	844	561	256	1,516	564	1,945
1819	259	137	795	402	130	1,323	434	1,011
1820	342	96	763	355	111	1,676	454	1,226

Year	Corn	Coffee	Sugar	Tea	Wine	Timber	Raw Cotton	Raw Wool	Raw, Thrown & Waste Silk
1796	2,174	2,302	3,057	617	535	690	1,027	207	684
1797	1,175	2,297	2,885	1,624	371	552	768	280	599
1798	1,215	2,748	3,663	4,487	541	431	1,049	144	801
1799	1,108	2,678	4,637	1,508	803	433	1,430	307	1,123
1800	2,673	3,988	4,301	1,510	732	582	1,848	500	739
1801	3,031	4,608	5,436	2,980	932	682	1,629	417	653
1802	1,401	3,169	5,878	2,736	735	527	2,088	423	756
1803	935	1,498	4,356	3,085	914	626	1,871	317	824
1804	1,201	3,513	4,440	2,668	459	627	2,156	460	981
1805	1,835	2,394	4,337	2,854	795	674	2,081	463	1,010
1806	814	3,608	5,205	2,216	854	511	2,034	382	987

(continued)

Table 2.6 *(continued)*

Year	Corn	Coffee	Sugar	Tea	Wine	Timber	Raw Cotton	Raw Wool	Raw, Thrown & Waste Silk
1807	1,124	2,821	4,972	1,260	952	714	2,610	666	743
1808	146	4,899	5,128	3,568	1,122	410	1,471	128	246
1809	1,137	4,711	5,451	2,164	1,174	484	3,117	350	947
1810	2,701	5,330	6,558	1,961	1,130	808	4,555	564	1,175
1811	466	3,765	5,346	2,121	499	799	3,148	271	266
1812	379	2,574	5,033	1,826	839	578	2,131	412	1,288
1814	1,210	6,448	5,493	2,611	766	338	2,031	745	1,478
1815	396	5,340	5,440	2,560	768	602	3,336	655	1,031
1816	406	3,325	5,141	3,623	445	439	3,152	316	596
1817	2,196	3,520	5,189	3,147	680	457	4,158	617	693
1818	3,914	2,804	5,418	2,007	892	565	5,764	1,017	1,249
1819	1,613	2,451	5,568	2,375	576	652	4,869	692	967
1820	1,388	2,974	5,553	3,015	558	591	4,934	375	1,384

Source: Mitchell and Deane, *Abstract,* 289–290. There are no entries for 1813.

went to continental Europe, and that pattern continued after the war. Raw cotton imports increased, but, otherwise, there was little change in the level of imports from its former American colonies. And, as in the case of geographic patterns, there were no major long-term shifts in the commodity composition of British imports (see Table 2.6).

French foreign exports during the war period fluctuated, but generally within a range of about 15 percent above and below the mean level in the period[43] (see Table 2.7). Exports to (and imports from) England declined very sharply between 1803 and 1809; but, after 1810, they rose again to above late-eighteenth-century levels (see Table 2.8). Thus, there appears to have been a minimal long-term impact of the interruption of trade between the two nations. In part because of the British capture of several of the French West Indian colonies, in part because of the independence of Haiti, and in part because of the effectiveness of the blockade, French exports to their colonies fell to almost zero between 1798 and 1814. There were some variations in the level of trade with continental nations – nations that were dependent on their alliance with France – as well as some differences in the level of trade with the United States – differences that were largely due to the then current interpretation of neutrality codes. France suffered a sharp

43 See Chabert, *Essai.* See also Maurice Levy–Leboyer, "La Croissance économique en France au XIXIe siécle: Résulatats Prelimininarres," *Annales* 23(1968), 788–807.

Table 2.7. *France, External Trade, 1798–1820 (francs)*

Years	Exports	Imports
1798	253,801,000	309,235,000
1799	300,690,375	289,656,000
1800	271,575,604	351,330,394
1801	305,245,000	434,472,177
1802	339,120,607	492,692,856
1803	373,468,506	500,040,592
1804	411,067,287	510,538,773
1805	400,783,338	548,422,457
1806	464,810,280	531,558,442
1807	384,639,709	418,284,811
1808	341,386,672	421,382,663
1809	340,605,400	357,803,500
1810	376,619,600	384,776,700
1811	327,905,800	298,561,600
1812	418,648,200	307,987,000
1813	354,257,300	251,085,500
1814	346,052,900	238,955,900
1815	432,625,000	295,703,900
1816	443,631,000	333,588,000
1817	380,062,000	426,747,000
1818	428,084,000	443,970,200
1819	382,748,500	387,355,800
1820	373,238,400	360,126,300

Source: A. Chabert, *Essai sur les Mouvements des Revenues et de L'activité Économique en France de 1798 à 1820*, 2 vols. (Paris: Librarie de Médicis, 1945–1949), vol. 2, 321.

decline in imports from 1811 to 1814, a decline that affected its trade with many of European and American nations, particularly the German states (see Table 2.9). The movements of French exports were similar to those for imports. French exports included both foodstuffs and industrial products, and, the value of manufactured goods increased both relatively and absolutely over time (see Table 2.10). Imports of cotton textiles declined somewhat during the war period, as did imports of colonial products and foodstuffs; these declines were due to both the British blockade and the weakness of French shipping (see Table 2.11). After the war, there were recoveries in the level of imports of most commodities; and there was a return to the prewar sources of supply for these goods.

The Continental System was in effect, a variant of a protectionist tariff that, by precluding imports of British manufactures, was designed to spur

Table 2.8. *France, Regional Composition, Exports, 1798–1820 (francs)*

Years	Prussia	Austria	Hanseatic Cities	Denmark	Sweden	Russia	United States	Ottoman Empire	French Colonies
1798	3,806,000	324,000	20,430,000	6,628,000	723,000	82,000	10,913,000	6,505,000	
1799	11,091,300	40,509	33,215,900	12,973,419	551,800	288	2,557,500	1,390,800	
1800	9,373,993	102,461	12,107,500	11,105,641	382,560	154,414	357,665	692,650	
1801	13,270,000	26,000	25,575,000	9,192,000	900,000	353,000	9,379,000	1,479,000	
1802	7,245,772	465,449	17,583,145	3,879,545	1,212,992	2,876,739	15,096,696	13,515,598	
1803	13,487,923	6,402,062	22,204,050	6,612,793	1,188,241	3,753,924	17,199,426	14,412,817	
1804	22,508,888	1,603,807	12,011,567	14,667,803	2,959,744	4,283,351	39,943,799	7,655,373	
1805	33,747,408	257,596	13,356,992	22,153,761	662,391	3,573,128	32,226,546	4,345,787	
1806	18,718,470	1,436,696	24,119,925	30,806,213	243,190	1,558,567	45,923,932	5,826,611	
1807	1,207,001	505,555	3,376,867	35,556,768	–	383,490	43,159,886	2,445,409	
1808	1,122,006	591,105	5,797,086	2,652,060	–	802,266	1,825,872	395,462	
1809	2,005,900	785,000	3,717,400	28,435,500	42,900	4,030,600	1,384,600	6,633,300	
1810	728,500	3,441,300	1,967,700	779,000	167,000	817,800	4,411,200	5,367,700	327,900
1811	1,130,600	1,894,400	3,128,600	9,401,800	167,900	207,300	14,655,700	6,055,400	179,600
1812	2,125,300	1,146,900	24,534,100	30,145,200	582,900	145,100	24,799,800	3,928,200	
1813	859,900	281,000	–	9,349,200	605,100	8	31,622,200	5,624,600	
1814	2,028,800	1,805,500	4,972,700	1,466,400	1,154,200	4,252,500	56,113,900	4,488,600	17,260,000
1815	10,365,600	667,600	3,195,600	3,380,000	3,298,200	4,674,400	4,498,000	3,132,100	40,334,000
1816	10,177,100	1,453,300	2,912,400	4,909,900	3,216,200	4,677,800	43,145,600	2,587,600	14,572,500
1817	10,027,200	544,800	2,423,900	3,729,600	2,448,300	5,790,800	41,783,100	2,934,100	22,584,000
1818	10,042,600	1,049,900	2,321,700	4,651,000	1,513,800	6,769,800	53,430,100	9,408,000	22,508,000
1819	14,528,300	1,479,900	3,063,500	5,793,600	5,166,400	12,341,900	21,539,100	8,092,900	20,524,300
1820	14,164,700	1,115,200	3,703,500	5,112,600	3,150,800	15,151,800	24,509,300	9,214,000	26,246,000

Years	Spain and Colonies	Portugal and Colonies	Sardinia	Italy	Naples and Sicily	Rome	England	Low Countries and Colonies	German States	Switzerland
1798	51,231,000	777,000	7,814,000	–	489,000	–	–	34,074,000	54,560,000	31,375,000
1799	65,403,477	503,900	5,859,900	–	14,169	3,053	476,920	40,413,000	78,803,500	29,023,600
1800	62,441,389	1,283,311	3,477,792	–	1,718	630	94,581	37,751,585	70,165,417	38,809,141
1801	54,366,000	2,265,000	8,987,000	–	431,000	–	461,000	41,632,000	73,896,000	35,188,000
1802	74,779,688	5,633,435	11,059,823	697,751	2,683,806	285,443	15,560,315	49,701,986	76,269,556	27,480,540
1803	70,211,340	5,462,754	504,140	8,971,505	2,697,070	412,077	17,199,426	54,572,994	74,068,023	29,807,755
1804	89,908,410	3,860,591	561,522	12,894,302	1,556,257	216,371	192,915	53,014,509	104,107,777	23,336,945
1805	64,196,156	10,441,349	329,410	18,032,358	2,167,381	313,683	127,481	50,246,062	108,330,402	20,112,959
1806	65,311,998	9,280,315	3,222,410	40,059,277	1,661,059	1,669,986	–	56,446,389	126,132,876	25,673,182
1807	65,614,563	6,946,021	2,817,033	40,607,655	1,397,655	–	–	45,123,015	99,465,993	23,577,247
1808	33,202,221	91,966	16,812	44,310,509	2,538,608	944,443	–	80,217,934	131,838,310	23,331,811
1809	33,907,500	–	–	43,840,300	3,861,100	4,042,800	–	66,667,200	115,618,700	18,615,000
1810	38,343,200	–	179,800	51,646,700	12,014,700	1,097,400	38,918,100	44,574,400	143,391,700	21,217,100
1811	40,427,500	–	933,600	52,563,700	19,011,800	–	29,987,300	16,432,600	110,544,300	20,706,400
1812	38,183,300	–	2,635,700	56,906,300	28,627,800	–	76,973,000	–	111,034,800	16,877,800
1813	22,168,100	–	–	47,944,000	16,262,900	–	114,632,200	9,564,300	72,514,000	22,829,800
1814	61,774,000	10,541,800	11,607,000	30,622,900	4,042,600	351,700	53,369,700	53,549,200	65,300,900	21,122,600
1815	54,337,800	10,805,600	32,279,800	20,427,800	2,900,500	100,600	38,624,600	64,664,200	81,178,000	26,871,600
1816	56,642,000	13,532,700	16,287,600	1,882,700	10,563,300	176,500	26,563,500	72,891,000	73,037,700	24,927,900
1817	50,094,900	6,789,600	14,729,700	15,103,700	3,008,100	221,100	41,562,100	48,259,600	52,211,800	19,158,800
1818	56,909,900	13,543,800	12,465,000	15,794,000	6,302,500	499,000	50,719,100	60,905,300	70,397,900	23,346,300
1819	46,342,500	11,834,400	16,238,000	21,428,100	6,937,200	614,600	35,991,800	59,760,700	60,099,800	26,356,500
1820	52,294,200	9,621,600	22,310,200	18,008,500	5,276,100	551,000	34,532,900	56,778,900	59,797,100	28,307,500

Source: Chabert, *Essai*, 325–326.

47

Table 2.9. *France, Regional Composition, Imports, 1798–1820 (francs)*

Years	Spain	Holland	Prussia	Germany	Switzerland	America	Hanseatic Cities	Denmark	Sweden	Tuscany
1798	44,545,000	51,456,000	3,611,000	23,820,000	31,350,000	19,748,000	8,492,000	7,587,000	1,691,000	11,091,000
1799	64,017,100	71,568,200	2,624,000	31,604,400	18,018,100	3,610,400	6,753,900	2,611,700	1,371,300	7,029,400
1800	64,446,479	80,788,312	24,819,957	41,072,785	17,008,573	10,950,129	18,994,547	37,764,147	1,234,543	–
1801	71,422,000	103,151,000	35,283,000	47,013,000	21,558,000	22,788,000	33,042,000	20,828,000	2,149,000	–
1802	73,890,764	85,266,717	38,981,707	45,297,629	20,930,612	55,355,884	26,810,148	22,362,384	4,806,433	6,773,116
1803	121,871,798	66,878,216	64,183,458	39,107,259	26,337,267	44,769,083	6,443,902	14,718,602	5,922,552	5,717,805
1804	122,987,284	95,123,777	19,066,190	66,639,963	28,548,732	70,717,762	11,558,131	7,701,307	7,031,850	5,650,300
1805	90,223,490	121,714,763	11,038,848	80,994,003	22,770,358	107,751,504	2,602,750	10,512,633	2,624,108	5,706,030
1806	63,651,607	126,504,982	2,530,858	75,869,048	17,997,056	113,208,686	2,489,053	7,988,086	1,558,184	26,983,284
1807	39,756,454	98,464,459	539,211	54,905,792	12,152,501	98,744,358	70,286	5,367,009	–	23,065,980
1808	55,825,892	151,813,750	11,068	78,118,008	12,249,906	29,851,874	821,695	1,406,281	38,873	15,239,958
1809	38,985,900	93,775,300	27,800	90,666,500	18,462,300	6,573,700	550,200	191,100	–	18,046,200
1810	40,743,700	58,556,000	107,700	70,832,300	10,672,700	2,089,700	819,300	818,300	2,800	12,149,900
1811	22,150,800	10,615,200	2,599,900	78,504,400	10,746,600	8,247,500	2,876,200	8,633,100	921,600	6,321,200
1812	21,316,200	–	6,580,800	110,889,300	9,917,600	15,375,100	5,214,800	18,272,700	1,734,000	–
1813	12,091,900	–	140,400	76,648,500	10,280,500	13,310,800	5,347,800	4,574,400	770,600	–
1814	26,735,700	35,577,500	2,171,800	16,165,300	4,257,900	6,381,900	1,097,100	800,100	2,908,500	–
1815	21,249,800	46,341,500	1,841,800	13,507,800	5,001,600	44,359,700	2,057,500	639,200	5,133,200	–
1816	24,161,700	71,662,800	5,729,700	25,958,600	7,534,400	26,992,100	2,193,000	786,000	5,006,400	–
1817	28,012,100	69,000,400	8,975,000	19,483,300	7,292,100	29,109,500	1,969,900	1,088,800	5,492,200	–
1818	37,710,800	57,711,500	9,408,900	16,517,400	7,876,100	36,814,800	3,096,800	1,195,600	4,412,900	–
1819	26,970,300	42,115,700	7,383,300	14,860,600	7,860,900	40,882,700	2,449,000	1,703,700	4,149,700	–
1820	41,523,000	53,429,500	9,065,700	13,586,600	7,800,700	40,362,300	2,099,300	1,454,100	4,325,800	–

	Italy	Ottoman Empire	Kingdom of Naples	Sardinia	Austria	Russia	Portugal	Rome	England
1798	–	8,030,000	4,565,000	4,939,000	84,000	1,624,000	3,721,000	73,000	–
1799	–	2,627,500	1,641,800	3,817,200	56,000	180,800	2,288,900	59,700	–
1800	–	263,611	25,447	1,732,732	300,735	220,885	4,008,498	27,984	–
1801	–	2,082,000	1,502,000	11,776,000	2,177	767,000	12,842,000	–	–
1802	400,684	12,527,379	18,085,719	8,411,060	3,036,439	4,344,441	23,327,656	278,630	6,738,725
1803	5,644,920	26,275,708	13,868,981	256,129	2,760,286	10,577,280	15,207,278	319,237	2,163,996
1804	5,325,579	19,914,946	3,160,635	548,871	2,410,626	3,237,050	22,433,802	88,774	–
1805	6,381,941	17,124,854	11,826,943	569,191	841,940	4,251,878	29,009,592	961,288	–
1806	21,029,345	10,484,941	6,528,877	2,712,507	720,530	1,384,353	40,857,134	791,904	–
1807	15,537,807	9,895,675	4,085,152	2,867,141	24,215	29,409	40,085,792	2,061,728	–
1808	27,096,315	3,751,563	3,424,638	240,571	16,324	10,917	2,074,330	1,147,072	–
1809	41,731,400	9,881,400	5,557,600	52,200	2,100	864,400	286,000	5,212,900	–
1810	42,807,500	17,603,200	13,725,300	207,200	177,100	650,100	–	2,321,000	41,117,900
1811	43,625,300	12,530,400	10,061,000	1,063,100	1,010,800	644,000	–	46,400	32,428,700
1812	60,191,000	5,812,100	10,422,506	1,010,700	2,174,100	526,800	–	–	26,437,200
1813	49,377,600	10,109,100	11,701,100	–	1,323,700	103,900	–	–	44,552,700
1814	13,844,200	9,355,300	5,951,000	10,022,700	587,400	2,336,000	15,416,000	223,600	77,000,600
1815	9,114,400	9,155,700	3,639,900	37,890,400	722,000	2,465,900	16,218,300	96,300	50,753,000
1816	5,086,600	7,349,400	5,586,900	23,592,400	115,500	3,422,400	13,998,000	244,400	45,845,700
1817	16,972,900	14,795,100	7,255,300	37,719,400	613,500	13,368,300	13,723,300	141,400	47,024,700
1818	17,506,000	6,549,800	19,700,800	43,409,400	1,067,900	11,877,300	19,406,100	1,442,800	42,834,300
1819	12,178,000	23,311,500	9,280,300	37,133,800	1,440,200	13,505,600	18,579,400	447,000	35,581,100
1820	18,266,000	20,975,100	11,671,800	47,658,600	1,180,800	16,336,800	20,455,100	225,100	37,902,000

Source: Chabert, *Essai,* 324–325.

Table 2.10. France, Commodity Composition, Exports, 1798–1820 (francs)

Years	Subsistence	Raw Materials	Industrial Products	Manufactured Objects	Wheat	Colonial Products	Textile Fibers	Cotton	Wool	Fish	Metal
1798	73,388,000	26,252,000	30,679,000	114,207,000	326,000	11,959,000	4,091,000	661,000	1,074,000	179,000	3,819,000
1799	108,246,338	27,948,781	27,406,618	126,132,868	5,983,689	5,057,906	4,141,603	1,674,393	397,223	60,277	5,250,644
1800	86,834,900	32,804,908	25,107,833	117,707,927	3,659,700	2,037,700	3,985,900	2,015,500	197,500	23,300	4,050,800
1801	110,127,000	36,516,000	30,586,000	115,390,000	2,232,000	2,824,000	4,052,000	1,625,000	138,000	49,000	5,881,000
1802	90,495,006	34,299,395	39,971,919	147,154,140	–	3,034,373	3,659,547	1,281,333	95,899	41,634	7,183,718
1803	120,603,219	40,670,716	38,270,747	135,013,247	–	9,353,726	7,587,508	1,354,614	90,201	3,918,623	5,535,981
1804	126,668,194	35,506,465	39,370,154	165,266,479	1,904,025	3,976,556	5,906,364	1,526,968	58,496	2,160,629	5,711,970
1805	152,349,237	34,243,171	41,273,644	133,339,386	16,360,726	2,759,521	7,491,087	2,807,978	72,383	2,990,330	6,695,914
1806	168,589,837	53,624,682	51,540,498	168,305,120	7,290,177	2,418,010	12,634,718	1,731,758	156,281	8,311,304	7,499,605
1807	118,755,635	44,076,545	44,140,308	156,305,499	33,431,928	776,797	7,617,516	561,373	118,427	4,680,406	5,172,963
1808	112,606,632	37,877,970	39,281,542	131,625,302	10,895,530	484,044	5,809,091	995,982	–	3,673,352	3,911,861
1809	134,781,100	37,763,000	30,929,800	120,319,700	3,393,800	1,852,600	5,066,400	117,300	66,300	3,748,100	3,285,200
1810	128,910,600	41,260,100	41,355,300	163,382,200	20,559,700	1,510,800	4,406,200	92,700	99,900	2,033,000	3,757,300
1811	90,886,600	46,356,700	41,434,000	137,755,200	209,200	8,225,700	7,408,100	1,159,600	679,800	3,346,400	3,657,400
1812	103,787,900	63,396,000	52,281,300	184,352,900	227,000	5,429,100	18,405,900	1,178,100	503,400	11,465,000	5,461,600
1813	85,300,500	37,296,200	69,019,500	150,985,600	–	3,393,900	8,204,400	637,300	446,800	4,623,800	4,342,400
1814	132,050,800	34,118,100	35,588,700	133,407,100	25,407,100	1,138,600	11,496,100	5,133,800	3,153,500	2,061,400	2,205,100
1815	146,606,000	45,325,700	44,890,200	182,652,700	12,973,900	802,900	20,111,600	13,479,100	7,779,500	432,800	2,616,000
1816	124,456,200	40,665,500	83,118,200	121,703,900	82,600	1,124,200	10,203,500	3,683,900	3,776,400	644,600	3,918,500
1817	88,574,400	36,497,600	80,618,500	158,654,500	39,000	439,200	11,294,300	1,731,700	6,348,000	684,900	4,167,000
1818	115,383,800	47,552,500	74,682,600	172,837,800	–	1,170,600	15,937,400	1,034,600	11,558,600	734,400	2,905,200
1819	134,048,000	42,064,900	67,620,200	125,165,800	3,040,800	3,452,200	11,932,700	1,032,200	8,695,000	448,900	1,771,900
1820	137,313,100	37,483,100	67,303,800	141,638,500	3,736,000	3,697,300	9,280,800	999,700	5,609,200	869,800	2,082,000

Source: Chabert, Essai, 323.

50

Table 2.11. *France, Commodity Composition, Imports, 1798–1820 (francs)*

Years	Subsistence	Raw Materials	Industrial Products	Manufactures Textiles	Wheat	Colonial Products	Fibers	Cotton	Wool	Fish	Metal
1798	116,768,000	114,038,000	15,738,000	40,059,000	6,258,000	59,409,000	45,096,000	23,161,000	15,594,000	2,684,000	6,214,000
1799	95,028,400	106,419,000	12,890,300	26,038,400	1,043,600	61,911,600	44,219,700	20,883,500	16,338,000	1,789,500	7,398,000
1800	125,851,400	144,153,300	9,837,700	32,548,700	356,800	98,580,100	63,095,400	41,601,900	15,014,800	2,368,000	5,273,700
1801	131,358,000	197,570,000	13,812,000	51,279,000	273,000	106,546,000	98,481,000	51,809,000	28,949,000	13,627,000	9,274,000
1802	165,686,592	210,015,532	16,900,852	47,520,289	9,016,650	107,620,879	88,264,725	39,079,958	27,843,776	11,008,632	12,252,613
1803	194,170,077	222,637,116	18,866,851	68,931,296	3,298,625	49,318,377	90,847,546	40,736,298	35,710,614	3,022,948	15,064,412
1804	117,048,921	214,232,883	16,116,270	65,710,536	570,036	71,603,169	94,595,478	46,665,514	31,406,239	4,583,014	18,169,810
1805	167,038,846	223,255,102	15,437,867	65,179,913	557,768	120,485,661	110,308,521	59,168,190	37,854,638	4,599,618	10,924,733
1806	168,968,544	227,823,380	21,273,649	31,086,348	181,051	123,937,871	112,403,945	63,395,052	31,956,295	5,971,460	11,518,006
1807	134,894,792	202,584,988	19,987,468	11,373,335	700,058	98,798,044	99,376,851	62,802,154	24,470,316	5,313,958	11,601,404
1808	85,193,116	151,085,371	19,885,236	14,503,205	133,662	51,474,152	86,109,163	45,549,170	26,416,833	5,915,316	14,113,706
1809	56,633,600	177,572,600	16,811,500	12,749,700	269,200	26,256,900	126,255,900	72,249,800	32,424,500	8,888,800	10,794,300
1810	60,519,800	206,280,700	21,279,600	19,050,100	911,500	28,834,800	109,856,900	40,374,500	40,113,000	12,359,000	15,565,400
1811	70,687,200	169,945,500	19,747,700	19,056,300	7,227,900	26,602,700	87,802,400	29,094,100	31,191,500	8,454,200	12,782,500
1812	66,853,100	167,322,100	21,267,500	24,714,400	9,870,000	26,310,000	98,700,700	19,743,000	36,073,300	20,146,000	15,642,100
1813	50,235,300	137,716,800	19,512,100	20,853,400	3,302,900	19,675,500	85,881,200	30,755,100	24,357,400	14,839,200	9,532,200
1814	90,228,700	106,782,600	10,200,000	16,242,500	167,700	64,784,000	49,670,000	28,811,300	10,073,800	5,085,600	10,048,600
1815	84,759,400	162,321,900	13,592,800	16,644,600	1,933,500	42,252,000	81,737,400	56,413,200	9,737,900	9,569,600	11,672,200
1816	108,249,300	158,724,200	22,340,700	20,213,400	14,537,200	51,976,800	77,961,600	33,373,500	23,442,900	11,358,100	13,690,300
1817	163,699,800	179,224,500	38,491,400	19,367,600	42,670,200	65,305,700	90,770,400	35,140,700	28,350,600	14,589,600	16,577,900
1818	145,233,100	230,768,600	19,031,000	16,426,600	34,739,200	63,386,300	130,491,300	55,700,200	43,168,600	17,585,600	16,426,600
1819	140,506,800	185,268,700	22,752,600	14,529,200	21,690,100	77,226,000	110,270,700	64,938,700	17,201,600	16,229,300	16,158,700
1820	153,458,600	382,932,400	21,978,700	16,712,700	11,447,500	95,385,200	115,581,300	61,102,700	21,414,700	19,487,100	23,265,300

Source: Chabert, *Essai,* 322.

51

French industry, but one that led to severe dislocations when introduced. There was some growth in certain French industries, cotton textiles for example, and the French began to produce beet sugar; but, given the short period of time that this tariff was effective, there was neither dramatic growth during the war, nor did growth continue in these industries in any major way once the war had ended and the blockade was lifted. Although both the French and the British saw more rapid growth and higher levels of trade with the return of peace, as a policy for generating import substitution, the French policy was expensive and not effective.[44]

44 See Melvin, *Napoleon's Navigation System*, 330–346; W. Cunningham, *The Growth of English Industry and Commerce in Modern Times*, two vols., *Part II, Laissez Faire*, 6th ed. (Cambridge: University Press, 1917; first published 1882), 676–695; Silvia Marzagalli, "Roundtable: Reviews of Silvia Marzagalli, 'Les boulevards de la Fraude: Le negoce maritime et le Blocus continental, 1806–1813: Bordeaux, Hambourg, Livourne,'" *International Journal of Maritime History* (2002), 151–194, particularly 176, 189–194; Heckscher, *Continental System*, 364–374.

3

The United States versus Great Britain, 1776–1815

Although a state of formal war between the United States and Great Britain existed for only 126 of the 477 months between April 17, 1775, and December 24, 1814, a state of near war, including both American embargos and British blockades of the American coast, encompassed much of that thirty-eight and one-half year period that began with the American Declaration of Independence and ended shortly after the signing of the Treaty of Ghent.[1] Given the nature of the period and the interest of this study in the role of international law, it seems most reasonable to temporally divide this chapter into three parts. The first covers the years of the American Revolution (April 17, 1775, to April 15, 1783). The second span the years of "neither war nor peace" (April 1783 to June 19, 1812), when the young republic, because of the maritime focus of its economy, found itself involved as a "neutral" in the ongoing conflict between Britain and France. Finally, the last section will cover the years of the disastrous (at least from the American point of view) War of 1812 – June 1812 until the middle of January 1815.

The roots of the major issue that underlay U.S.-British relations during the entire period rested in a series of British laws – the first of which predated the Declaration of Independence by more than a century and a half. Those laws initially were designed to protect British shipping from Dutch competition; over time, they helped make the British merchant marine the largest in the world; and, later, they helped England defend that position from the threat of American competition. Early laws regulating trade – that

---

1 The only major American military victory – the Battle of New Orleans – was fought in December 1814 and January 1815, culminating with the major battle of January 8, 1815. The war had officially ended with the signing of the Treaty of Ghent on December 24, 1814.

Virginia send her tobacco and sugar exports to England and that they be sent only in English ships, and that England restrict imports of Spanish tobacco and domestically grow no tobacco – were passed in 1621 and 1624. A dozen laws – laws that are most often grouped under the general heading of the "Navigation Acts" – were passed between 1650 and 1766; and most were designed to strengthen the restrictions on foreign shipping. For example, "the Navigation Act of 1651 provided that no products of Asia, Africa, or America could be imported into England, or English possessions, except in vessels owned in England or the colonies and of which the master and most of the crew were English subjects; the products of European countries could be imported only in such vessels or in those of the country in which they were produced or from which they were usually of necessity first shipped."[2] Over time, additional legislation further tightened those restrictions. However, in general, and, although they imposed substantial costs on continental powers, the impact of the Navigation Acts on the American colonies was probably relatively slight. Although historians have stressed both the costs and the benefits of those laws to the thirteen colonies, on net it appears that, given the importance of agricultural production for internal consumption, they most likely imposed a relatively small cost on the American economy.[3] The Navigation Acts were, however, soon to prove to impose enormous costs on the economy of the newly independent country.

The years leading up to the American Declaration of Independence on July 4, 1776, had found the thirteen colonies linked in an involuntary partnership with England, in that country's more than century-long war with France.[4] The Seven Years' War had given England hegemony in America,

---

2 Chester W. Wright, *Economic History of the United States* (New York: McGraw-Hill Book Company, 1941), 142. See also Lawrence Harper, *The English Navigation Laws* (New York: Columbia University Press, 1939) and Lewis Cecil Gray, *History of Agriculture in the Southern United States to 1860*, 2 vols. (Washington, DC: Carnegie Institution, 1933), vol. 1, 213–258.

3 A bevy of historians have long argued about the costs imposed by the Navigation Acts on the American colonial economy. For example, George Bancroft, Lawrence Harper, and Curtis P. Nettels have concluded that the costs were substantial, whereas George L. Beer and Oliver Dickerson have argued that the costs were negligible. In an important article written over forty years ago, Robert Paul Thomas calculated the costs and revenues to the colonies and concluded that, at most, the net costs imposed on the colonists amounted to less than one percent of national income. Among the writers on the topic, see Lawrence Harper, "Mercantilism and the American Revolution," *Canadian Historical Review*, 23 (March 1942), 1–15; Oliver Dickerson, *The Navigation Acts and the American Revolution* (Philadelphia: University of Pennsylvania Press, 1951), 55; Curtis P. Nettels, "British Mercantilism and the Development of the Thirteen Colonies," *Journal of Economic History*, 12 (Spring 1952), 114; and Robert Paul Thomas, "A Quantitative Approach to the Study of the Effects of British Imperial Policy upon Colonial Welfare: Some Preliminary Findings," *Journal of Economic History*, 25 (December 1965), 615–638. Subsequent work has not markedly altered Thomas' conclusions. See the discussion in Jeremy Atack and Peter Passell, *A New Economic View of American History from Colonial Times to 1940*, Second ed. (New York: W. W. Norton, 1994), 54–80.

4 With only some interruption, England and France were at war frequently between 1714 and 1815: See Table 2.1.

but the 1763 Peace of Paris, the treaty that ended the war, left both principal parties unsatisfied. "The same terms of peace which were condemned by Pitt as a betrayal of British interests, were regarded by French statesmen as so severe that they necessitated a policy of revenge."[5] Thus, the conflict continued. But the war had an indirect impact – an impact that was to effect the relations between England and her American colonies. In the case of the Seven Years' War, the French had not lost – and many said they had won – in most parts of the world where the two nations had been militarily engaged (for example, the Caribbean and India) – but the exception was mainland North America. And there, it was the men of the milita forces – men who had most often been drawn from New England – who were largely responsible for the victory. "Their success encouraged in them that inordinate sense of their superiority," and that perception struck at the heart of their mental and emotional links to Great Britain.[6]

The years leading up to 1776 also saw changes in the rules of international law, but those years also underscored the difficulty of enforcing such laws during time of war. For example, in the British Rule of 1756 "the belligerent claimed that the neutral, by covering with his flag a trade previously the monopoly of the enemy, not only inflicted a grave injury by snatching from him a lawful prey, but was guilty likewise of a breach of neutrality; the neutral contended that the enemy had a right to change his commercial regulations, in war as well as in peace." The law, however, "cannot prevent the interests of belligerents and neutrals from clashing, nor speak with perfect clearness in all cases where they do."[7] Thus, although the 1766 treaty between Great Britain and Russia excluded horses from the list of contraband goods, it said nothing about the status of naval stores. This article, however, was later interpreted to mean that the only articles of contraband were "arms, equipments and munitions of war." That interpretation "ruled out naval stores and provisions, unless belonging to the Government of a belligerent."[8]

Finally, in 1780, the Empress of Russia drew up a document that has become known as the "Declaration of Armed Neutrality." That

5 Hugh Edward Egerton, *British Foreign Policy in Europe to the End of the Nineteenth Century: A Rough Outline* (London: Macmillan, 1917), 6. For a more recent discussion of Anglo-French naval issues after the Seven Years' War, see Nicolas Tracy, *Navies, Deterrence, and American Independence: Britain and Seapower in the 1760s and 1770s* (Vancouver: University of British Columbia Press, 1988); on reactions to the Treaty of Paris, see pages 1–4.
6 Egerton, *British Foreign Policy*, 63.
7 Egerton, *British Foreign Policy*, 389. On the Rule of 1756, see Chapter 1, and for a thorough discussion of the laws regarding neutral rights before 1763, see Richard Pares, *Colonial Blockade and Neutral Rights, 1739–1763* (Oxford: Clarendon Press, 1938).
8 Egerton, *British Foreign Policy*, 369.

declaration – a declaration that focused on the protection of neutral rights, mainly against Great Britain – became the basis of an international league formed by most of the nations of northern Europe. The declaration contained four rules:

1. "That all neutral vessels may freely navigate from port to port and on the coasts of nations at war."
2. "That the goods belonging to the subjects of the Powers at war shall be free in neutral vessels, except contraband articles."
3. "That the Empress, as to the specification of the above-mentioned goods, holds to what is mentioned in the 10th and 11th articles of her treaty of commerce with Great Britain, extending these obligations to all the Power at war."[9]
4. "That to determine what is meant by a blockaded port, this denomination is only to be given to that where there is, by the arrangements of the Power which attacks it with vessels, stationed sufficiently near, an evident danger in attempting to enter it."

It was "evident that no great maritime State, situated as England then was, would submit to the first and third [provisions] as a matter of right."[10] Both contemporaries and historians have treated the formation of the League of Armed Neutrality as an "effort to bridle the aggressions of England, and as investing the principles expressed in the Russian declaration with the authority of such doctrines as are accepted by the body of civilized nations." However, history has shown that all those who signed the Declaration would, at one time or another, violate at least one of the four rules when they were next at war.[11]

It was in this political, military, and legal environment that the thirteen colonies found themselves during the crucial months between July 4, 1776, and September 3, 1783.

2. THE AMERICAN REVOLUTION

Following Richard Henry Lee's Resolution for Independence of June 7, the Declaration of Independence was passed by the Continental Congress

---

9   "Article 10, restricts contraband to 'munitions of war'"; and the 11th article lists the items included as 'munitions of war'; Henry Wheaton, "History of the Law of Nations in Europe and America from the Earliest Times to the Treaty of Washington, 1842," in James Brown Scott, ed., *The Armed Neutralities of 1780 and 1800: A Collection of Official Documents Preceded by the Views of Representative Publicists* (New York: Oxford University Press, 1918), 245–266, particularly page 247. See Chapter 1.

10 The quotation is from Captain A. T. Mahan, *The Influence of Sea Power upon History, 1660–1783,* 5th ed. (Boston: Little, Brown, 1894), 406.

11 Egerton, *British Foreign Policy,* 370, 371, quoting W. E. Hall, *International Law,* 641.

on July 4, 1776; however, the colonies and the mother country had been engaged in what, although undeclared, could best be viewed as a commercial war since, at least, October 1770.[12] On October 24, 1774, the Continental Congress passed what the historian Vernon Setser has called "the first complete piece of national commercial legislation." Although the congressmen still professed loyalty to the English king, the act prohibited the importation into the colonies of goods from Britain and Ireland and of East Indian tea. The purpose of the congressional action was clearly expressed in both the debate and in the act itself – "to force Parliament to repeal all the objectionable legislation enacted since 1763."[13]

The British government's response was, if not swift, at least forceful. On March 30, 1775, they enacted legislation that "prohibited the participation of the New England colonies in the Newfoundland fisheries," and prohibited those residents from trading with any part of the world except Britain, Ireland, and the British West Indies. Even stronger action was to follow. On December 22, 1775, Parliament enacted a law "prohibiting completely all commercial intercourse with the thirteen colonies, and making colonial merchandise good prize when captured."[14]

During the pre-Revolutionary years, the colonies had pursued a policy of "passive denial of the advantages of the [American] trade to Great Britain." "This policy had proved highly successful in securing the repeal of the Stamp Act and the Townshend legislation." Not surprisingly, it played an important, although less successful, role in the new nation's Revolutionary diplomacy. As the undeclared conflict heated up, and word of the passage of British prohibitory laws reached the colonies, Congress added another commercial weapon to its arsenal – the opening of American "commerce to foreign nations in exchange for assistance in the use of more deadly weapons." This latter strategy was "tantamount to a declaration of independence, and was made a considerable time prior to the official declaration."[15]

Although the data on commerce for the entire thirteen colonies are, at best, sketchy, those for Philadelphia provide an insight into the impact of the Prohibitory Act. During the six months between September 6, 1775, and March 1, 1776, a total of 8,866 tons of shipping entered that port. That figure amounts to only slightly more than one-third of the normal

---

12 One of Lee's resolutions stated that the "Colonies are, and of right ought to be, free and independent States." See Henry Steele Commager, ed., *Documents of American History*, 6th ed. (New York: Appleton-Century-Croft, 1958), 100.
13 Vernon G. Setser, *The Commercial Reciprocity of the United States, 1774–1829* (Philadelphia: University of Pennsylvania Press, 1937), 6.
14 Setser, *Commercial Reciprocity*, 7.   15 Setser, *Commercial Reciprocity*, 5–6.

peacetime entries over comparable earlier periods. Nor was the period of decline over; during the next six months only 2,586 tons of shipping entered Philadelphia. However, the same evidence indicates that it was not only British policy that was proving successful. Over the five months between April 26 and August 27, 1776, about 70 percent of the vessels that entered Philadelphia "had cleared from non-British ports." Apparently, the decision by Congress to open American ports was beginning to have its intended effect.[16]

As Philadelphia became the focal point of international and coastal commerce, the British were, at first, rewarded. Until 1782, they had confronted an enemy that had no strategic center; but, with Robert Morris's 1781 appointment as financier general of the Confederation and, because of his attempts to centralize trade in the Pennsylvania city, they found themselves better placed to interdict such commerce. However, despite Morris's objections, the Americans were largely able to offset the pressure of the British navy by dispersing their resources. The growth of Baltimore as an alternative to Philadelphia provides evidence of the American resiliency.[17]

In December 1775, the English King had branded the Americans as rebels; and, in response, Parliament passed legislation outlawing all American commerce. The colonial response was to "open the ports to foreign nations, nullify the navigation laws, and institute a commercial system peculiarly American." On January 17, 1776, the American Congress set in motion plans to accomplish those ends by the following March.[18] On April 6, Congress adopted a number of resolutions – resolutions that might well be termed "the declaration of commercial independence" – that established the American commercial system that was, in the absence of British interference, to govern trade throughout the war.[19]

Legislation is one thing but enforcement is quite another. Even during the war, many Americans failed to support the legal ban on British trade. Several alternative routes channeled the "illegal" imports into the colonies. There was "overland trade between the towns occupied by British troops," and those held by the Americans; there were collusive capture agreements between British and American captains; some imports piggybacked on the legal trade with Bermuda; and, as the government sometimes gave permission to individuals to bring in personal effects, such imports were

---

16 Richard Buel Jr., *In Irons: Britain's Naval Supremacy and the American Revolutionary Economy* (New Haven: Yale University Press, 1998), 37–40.

17 Buel, *In Irons*, 234–239.   18 Setser, *Commercial Reciprocity*, 10–11.

19 Setser, *Commercial Reciprocity*, 11.

Table 3.1. *Estimates of Tonnage Libeled in Selected Admiralty Courts, 1776–1782*

Court	1776	1777	1778	1779	1780	1781	1782
Massachusetts Bay	23,492	23,491	19,838	26,270	17,303	16,382	14,186
New London	1,241	1,295	1,957	5,280	1,980	7,725	2,515
TOTAL	24,733	24,786	21,795	31,550	19,283	24,107	16,701

Source: Richard Buel Jr., *In Irons: Britain's Naval Supremacy and the American Revolutionary Economy* (New Haven: Yale University Press, 1998), 117, 169. See also 117–118.

at times used as a cover for the import of British manufactures. In response, in December 1781, Congress passed an ordinance that provided for the "seizure and condemnation of all produce of Great Britain and its dependencies, even in neutral bottoms, when taken within three miles of the American coast." Later, Congress encouraged the states to enact legislation that would permit "the seizure of such merchandise when found on land."[20] "Most of the states complied with Congress's recommendation, but neither the measures of the states nor of Congress made much headway against market forces."[21]

Not surprisingly, given her position as the world's leading naval power, the British response was a naval blockade – a blockade designed not only to cut off the colonies from Europe and the Caribbean but also to sever intercolonial commerce. Given the existing state of overland transport technology, almost all such commerce between colonies depended on coastal shipping. The British were, however, never able to fully stop either the international or the coastal trade. In the latter case, "the inland water route between Philadelphia and the northern Chesapeake remained open" and "comparatively safe." In the cases of the lower Delaware and the eastern seacoast, the blockade was, however, more effective.[22] Over the years 1776 through 1782, the tonnage libeled by the British navy in the admiralty courts of Massachusetts Bay and New London averaged about 23,280 tons – a figure that was equal to the equivalent of the tonnage of over two hundred commercial ships arriving in Philadelphia "from beyond the Delaware", 1779–81 (see Table 3.1).

Because of the blockade and the British occupation of Philadelphia – an occupation that lasted from September 1777 to June 1778 – that port lost its position as the colonies' major international commercial center to

20 Setser, *Commercial Reciprocity*, 33–34.   21 Buel, *In Irons*, 227.
22 Buel, *In Irons*, 113–114.

Table 3.2. *Estimates of Philadelphia Arrivals from "Beyond the Delaware," 1779–1781*

	1779		1780		1781	
	Number	Tons	Number	Tons	Number	Tons
Prizes	42	3,545	47	4,520	44	4,235
Commercial Arrivals	70	5,870	98	9,940	139	14,290
TOTAL	112	9,415	145	14,460	183	18,525

Source: Buel, *In Irons,* 177.

Baltimore; but it continued to draw a not insignificant tonnage. As Tables 3.2 and 3.3 indicate, commercial arrivals to Philadelphia from "beyond the Delaware" totaled 70 vessels (5,870 tons) in 1779, 98 vessels (9,940 tons) in 1780, and 139 vessels (14,290 tons) in 1781, before declining to 55 vessels (6,020 tons) in 1782.[23]

It is generally agreed that the Revolution would not have ended (at least not in 1782) in American independence if it had not been for the French. Still, at least two questions remain. The answer to the first – why give secret aid to the Americans – is fairly obvious. In 1776, the French, following the policy of their foreign minister, the Viscomte de Vergennes, and nearly two-thirds of the way through that country's off-again–on-again, century-long war with the British, were more than willing, despite the rules of international law regarding the duties of a neutral, to approach the Continental Congress and to encourage that body to accredit envoys to France and to send the colonies' privateers into French ports with their prizes, and, later, to provide money and credit to the new government.[24]

The answer to the second – "why did the French government, already overwhelmed with debt, abandon the policy of secret aid to the Americans which had been so rich in results, which had cost so little, and which seemed to be so entirely successful, for a policy which meant certain war, and probable financial ruin, even if the war were won" – is less obvious. Again, however, the answer lies in the relations between France and England. In December 1777, Vergennes wrote, "The question which we have to solve is to know whether it is more expedient to have war against England and America united or with America for us against England."[25]

---

23 Buel, *In Irons,* 173–174, 223. In contrast, in 1782, Baltimore drew 129 vessels of 9,760 tons from "beyond the Delaware."

24 C. H. Van Tyne, "Influences which Determined the French Government to make the Treaty with America, 1778," *American Historical Review,* 21 (April 1916), 528–544.

25 Van Tyne, "Influences," 528, 531, 539–541.

Table 3.3. *Number and Estimated Tonnage of Commercial Vessels Entering Baltimore and Philadelphia, 1782*

	Baltimore		Philadelphia	
	Vessels	Tons	Vessels	Tons
Overseas Entries	95	9,265	46	5,180
European	*8*	*1,060*	*11*	*1,470*
Islands	*87*	*8,205*	*35*	*3,710*
Coastal Entries	34	495	9	840
Local Entries	352	14,255	257	4,825
Total Entries[a]	482	24,135	312	10,845

[a] Includes one with unknown port of origin.

Notes: European Entries include the Atlantic Islands. Coastal Entries are from "beyond the the Delaware" (Philadelphia) and Chesapeake (Baltimore). All but four of the coastal entries for Baltimore are from North Carolina. Local entries include all New Jersey and Delaware entries for Philadelphia and all Chesapeake entries for Baltimore. For Baltimore one entering brig's port of origin is unknown.
Source: Buel, *In Irons,* 223.

To him, the answer was obvious. Early in 1778, he repeated the words of Beaumarchais – "We must not forget that the power which recognizes the independence of the Americans first will gather all the fruits of this war." Vergennes, speaking for the king and the French government, first recognized the colonies' independence, and, then, entered into two treaties – the Treaty of Alliance with France and the Treaty of Amity and Commerce – that together cemented a commercial and military alliance with the United States, and, finally, declared war on Britain.[26]

The Americans were not, however, entirely innocent bystanders in the game between Britain and France. By the end of 1777, the American Congress's representatives, Benjamin Franklin and Arthur Deane, who had been sent to France to buy munitions, were soon telling their host's "that America might have to make peace with England, and even to turn on France, because the United States got so little support in Europe." Similarly, one of the American commissioners provided the French with a memoir that suggested that, if France "lets England triumph, this force in America which united to France might put England where it could do no harm, will

---

26 See Van Tyne, "Influences," 540–541; Commager, *Documents,* 105; J. H. Plumb, *England in the Eighteenth Century: 1714–1815* (Harmondsworth: Penguin, 1950), 130–131. W. Cunningham, *The Growth of English Industry and Commerce in Modern Times, two vols., Part II, Laissez Faire* (Cambridge: University Press, 1917; first published 1882), 669–673.

be directed against France. In America the love of conquest might replace that of patriotism."[27]

The British were not slow to respond to the French commercial intervention, doing so in the fall of 1777, even before the declaration of war. In their attempt to prevent contraband from reaching America, "the Royal Navy began routinely searching French vessels in European waters for contraband and seizing those that appeared off the North American coast. And to the extent that their resources permitted, they attempted to strengthen the blockade of the American coast." Early in 1778, several British line-of-battle ships joined the customary frigates in patrolling key entry points such as the Delaware and Chesapeake.[28] Overall, by mid-June 1778, even before the commencement of hostilities, the records indicate that the British had seized at least 134 French vessels on the high seas and another 21 while they were docked in British ports. However, as that enumeration does not include the loss of any vessels sailing from La Rochelle (one of France's major ports of departure for vessels plying trade with the French Caribbean) or those sailing "from almost all of the less prominent Atlantic ports," the total actually may have been substantially higher.[29]

The French responded to the increasing effectiveness of the British blockade by initiating, despite its costs − costs both in terms of military expenditures and in terms of the increase in the average time of voyages − a convoy system; but the response was slow, hesitant, and not always effective.[30] Initially, in April 1778, they instituted limited convoys − convoys operating within "forty leagues off shore in both Europe and the West Indies." In the fall, however, "British privateers seized a fleet of sixty West Indian vessels and three East Indiamen on their way home just after the merchantmen had parted from their naval escorts." In early 1779, the French response was the deployment of *convois obligatoires*; again, however, the results were mixed. During the next year, in one case, "all eleven vessels of one outgoing convoy escorted by several armed merchantmen were seized"; and, in another, fourteen of forty-eight vessels were lost when the convoy encountered two seventy-four-gun line-of-battle ships. Thereafter, convoys were better protected; "but rarely was a French vessel of force

---

27 Van Tyne, "Influences," 538.   28 Buel, *In Irons*, 55.
29 Buel, *In Irons*, 57.
30 As we will show in our analysis of the costs of convoys in both World Wars (Chapters 5 and 6), not only did they incur the cost of naval escort vessels, but ships lost time as they awaited the assemblage of the convoy, and they all had to adjust their speed to that of the slowest vessel. See also Chapter 1.

available to protect ships sailing directly from the islands or from France to North America."[31]

Because of its physical location – a location marked by narrow channels and frequent fog – Boston and the surrounding waters proved most difficult for the British to blockade effectively. In addition, after 1778, Britain was committed to operations in the South – operations that drew vessels from the Northern blockade. Taken together, Massachusetts Bay continued, throughout the war, as the safest port for entry; and, despite French and American efforts to redirect traffic to ports that were closer to their military operations, a large proportion of French imports were routed through New England. Many such imports ultimately went to the middle states, but the additional cost of land transport increased their delivered prices.[32]

During the late summer and fall of 1778 and the early winter of 1779, as loyalist privateers joined the pursuit of vessels attempting to reach American ports, the British naval blockade became more effective. The privateers were particularly active in such areas as the Capes of the Chesapeake. "In late August, the navy's share of libels filed in the New York Vice-Admiralty Court fell to two-thirds of the total"; and by the end of the year, that fraction had declined to one-third. As the blockade became more effective, the businessmen who were underwriting the blockade-runners were forced to begin to arm their merchant vessels, again increasing the costs; and, in late 1778, local governments, in an attempt to harness the privateers, began to issues letters of marque.[33] Those attempts were only partially successful, and American losses continued to rise. The British occupied St. Eustatius in 1781, and that occupation closed what had, heretofore, been a major center for the redistribution of commercial imports. In 1782, losses were particularly heavy as the new Southern deployment of the Royal Navy began to seize American vessels that were trading with the Caribbean. "British naval action was much more intensive in the last year of the war," and it increased the risk of blockade running – and, not surprisingly, insurance costs reached an all-time high. Accordingly, the "wartime flow of goods in and out of the colonies probably peaked before 1782."[34]

The blockade was effective in reducing the tonnage deployed in the Atlantic trade; however, that reduction meant that, despite the rising costs – costs that, because of the absence of domestic substitutes, could be readily

31 Buel, *In Irons*, 61–62.   32 Buel, *In Irons*, 73–74.
33 Buel, *In Irons*, 134–137.
34 James F. Shepherd and Gary M. Walton, "Economic Change, After the American Revolution: Pre- and Post-War Comparisons of Maritime Shipping and Trade," *Explorations in Economic History*, 13 (October 1976), 398.

passed on – the profits of those entrepreneurs who were willing to take the risk soared. Freight rates rose, particularly for bulky commodities: flour brought transport charges of 25 to 33 percent of its final price, and tobacco as much as 50 percent. A partner in one importing firm argued that the freight charges from just one successful round trip of a newly built "runner" "would pay its entire cost of construction."[35] Thereafter, only the variable costs of operation had to be deducted before calculating profits.

Six years of warfare had taught the British a great deal about the tactics and strategies employed by the Americans in their attempts to elude hostile cruisers. Thus, in late 1781 and in 1782, the British blockade threatened not only the Delaware, but the entire Atlantic coast under the closest blockade of the war. On the one hand, "the year 1782 was after all the first year that the navy was not required to support major army operations on the continent." On the other hand, both the navy and private adventurers were angry and pushing for revenge after their earlier failures. In the fall of 1781, the British squadron stationed off the Delaware Capes captured several vessels heading for "Philadelphia as well as five ships from a convoy of twenty clearing the Delaware Capes for overseas." American vessels attempting to sail from other ports on the central coast found the task equally difficult. By late spring of 1782, the British squadron operating off the Capes had increased in size and efficiency to the point where "it was seizing almost every vessel attempting to get out." "The coast north of the Delaware experienced similar pressures" and "even Massachusetts Bay felt the force of the blockade spearheaded by two Royal Navy vessels, one a fifty-gun ship." The blockade also began to effect the rest of the domestic economy. For example, "the intensity of the blockade between Cape Cod and Cape Hatteras made land carriage from New England far safer than sea carriage." Moreover, as "the capture rate rose," "the cost of underwriting skyrocketed to the point that most if not all the value of a ship's cargo went to the insurer against the risk of seizure by the enemy." Despite these successes, from the long-run point of view, "the blockade of 1782 failed on two counts. It never completely closed down Philadelphia's navigation nor cut off the region's access to foreign markets."[36]

However, peace was in sight. Taken together, Yorktown and Britain's ongoing relations with its European neighbors – relations that because of "the trend of European politics in the East, in Germany and in the Netherlands told heavily against England, and increased the natural reluctance of any Power to seek the friendship of a beaten nation. In any case, in the existing

35 Buel, *In Irons*, 105–106.   36 Buel, *In Irons*, 217–225.

circumstances peace was a necessity."[37] Thus, on November 30, 1782, nego-
tiators from both belligerents agreed to "The Treaty of Paris" – a treaty
of peace between Britain and the United States, the formal "Treaty of Peace
with Great Britain" of September 3, 1783. In addition to independence,
it gave Americans the right to fish on the Grand Banks, with the right of
citizens of both countries to navigate on the Mississippi River.[38] Although
the British blockades had not led to an American defeat, their impact was
felt throughout the American economy. Because of the difficulty of carrying
on any waterborne commerce during the last years of the war, the series
of blockades did alert American leaders to the "need to consider seriously
the commercial problems with which they would be obliged to deal in a
settlement with Great Britain." In particular, those leaders were faced by
problems raised, first, by the importance of the West Indian trade to the
new nation's commercial system and, then, by the need to secure that trade
in any treaty of peace.[39] Of particular significance "was the British decision
embodied in the Order of Council of July 2, 1783 – to deny the United
States any of the former commercial privileges in the trade of the empire,
particularly the West Indian trade."[40] Thus, Britain continued to maintain
the, then current, version of the Navigation Acts. At the same time, in
the case of ocean commerce, the United States was pushed toward a general
reliance on retaliatory regulations designed and imposed by the government.
The American plans displayed two main features: (1) "unfavorable foreign
regulations were to be countervailed by similar regulations in this country";
and (2) "a new policy of commercial treaties was to be formulated and a
new commission sent abroad to negotiate with the European States."[41] The
treaty provided for peace, but it also laid the foundation for the war and
near-war policies that were to dominate U.S.-British relations for the next
thirty-two years. "Neither Yorktown nor the Peace of Paris made American
independence secure. During the 1780's the young nation suffered humil-
iation at British hands while royalist France, midwife at America's birth,
treated her as an upstart ingrate and sought to maneuver her as a satel-
lite. Even after the Constitution, many Americans considered the nation an
experiment of doubtful permanence."[42]

37 Egerton, *British Foreign Policy*, 75–76.
38 Commager, *Documents*, 117–119.   39 Setser, *Commercial Reciprocity*, 37–38.
40 J. C. A. Stagg, *Mr. Madison's War: Politics, Diplomacy, and Warfare in the Early American Republic, 1783–1830* (Princeton: Princeton University Press, 1983), 7.
41 Setser, *Commercial Reciprocity*, 55.
42 Bradford Perkins, *Prologue to War: England and the United States, 1805–1812* (Berkeley: University of California Press, 1961), 67.

3. FROM REVOLUTION TO WAR

3a. From September 4, 1783, to the Embargo of 1808

3a(1). The Qualitative Story. The postrevolutionary years were marked by continued attempts to negotiate with the European powers for what the Americans considered a "fair" legal environment for international commerce. The British, for example, claiming that there were questions about the relative powers of the state and federal authorities, although expressing a willingness to talk, dragged their feet about any federal government policy. Moreover, even the Americans, themselves, proved unsure of the answer to the question raised by the British.[43] However, the failure of Congress's attempts to impose a national commercial system did not mean that no action was taken against the discriminatory policies of foreign governments. The states moved with vigor; "and not long after the imposition of the restrictions upon the British West India trade all the states except Connecticut had some sort of discriminatory legislation upon their statute books." Even here, however, the results were, at best, negligible; uncoordinated state regulations were, and are, inherently weak; and they are particularly weak when the states are engaged in active competition for a finite level of ocean commerce.[44]

Ultimately, with the adoption of the Constitution, at least in America it was widely assumed that state/federal issues had been resolved.[45] As a result, the foundation of the commercial system that was to govern the thirteen former colonies, now states, was based on four laws that were passed in July and August 1789: the tariff act, the tonnage act, the act to regulate the collection of duties, and the act for the registration and clearing of vessels.[46] The laws did not discriminate among the vessels of different nations, but it obviously reflected a policy designed to protect American industry. The laws also established an American monopoly in the coasting trade. They did not prohibit foreign vessels; but they made such competition noncompetitive "not by prohibiting the participation of foreigners, but by excusing American vessels of fifty tons or less from the necessity of entering and clearing, and other coasting vessels from paying tonnage duties oftener than once a year." Foreign vessels were allowed to enter only the larger

43 Setser, *Commercial Reciprocity*, 58–65, 97.   44 Setser, *Commercial Reciprocity*, 62–64.
45 Article I, section 8 gave Congress the power "to regulate the Commerce with foreign Nations, and among the several States, and with the Indian Tribes."
46 See Setser, *Commercial Reciprocity*, 107, citing *Statutes at Large of the U.S.*, I: 24–27, 27–28, 29, 49, 55–65.

ports, and they were required to pay the tonnage duty on every entry.[47] These rules paralleled but were probably somewhat less stringent than the British Navigation Acts. Some historians have argued that this legislation underlay the observed substitution of American for British vessels in the trade between the United States and Britain; but, in fact, tonnage duties under the new laws were lower than those that had been charged by the individual states; and neither the British merchants nor their government appear to have shown any great concern about the impact of the new laws.[48] The negative reaction of the French was, however, stronger. Not only did the laws place French vessels under the same restrictions as those of the English; but, it was argued, the tonnage duty was a violation of Article V of the 1778 Treaty of Alliance – a clause that had excused the United States from paying a similar duty to that otherwise charged in France; and a clause that had been included, the French alleged, only because the United States laws embodied no such tax.[49]

Although the years 1793 to 1808 included one declared and one unde-clared war with France, historians have labeled that decade and a half the "years of armed neutrality." Initially, the American policies encompassed by the term "armed neutrality" were directed against England; however, the French were not totally absolved. By a Decree of the French National Convention of May 9, 1793, the officers of French warships and privateers were "authorized to seize and carry into ports of the Republic merchant vessels which are wholly or in part laden with provisions, being neutral prop-erty, bound to an enemy's port, or having on board merchandise belonging to an enemy." "Merchandise belonging to an enemy was declared to be 'lawful prize, seizeable for the profit of the captor.' " Initially, American ves-sels were exempted, but only because it was expected 'that the Americans would not abuse this privilege by carrying to her enemies those products by which they ought to assist in the defense of a cause as much their own as hers.' If, however, the Americans did not take measures to lead to the recall of the British declaration of their intent to carry into British ports all the American vessels that were loaded with provisions and vessels that the Royal Navy found bound for French port; and if the American response should prove to be 'insufficient or fruitless,' and the neutrality of the United States "serviceable only to the enemies of France, France would exercise a very natural right in taking measures to prevent a consequence so injurious to her."[50]

47 Setser, *Commercial Reciprocity*, 107–108.   48 Setser, *Commercial Reciprocity*, 108–109.
49 Setser, *Commercial Reciprocity*, 119–120.   50 Egerton, *British Foreign Policy*, 372–373.

Tension with the United Kingdom continued; and, in the spring of 1790, the American government became convinced that the British were unwilling to enter a commercial agreement that was satisfactory to the United States. Both the president and Congress began to consider the passage of a retaliatory navigation bill that would require that only American vessels or those of the country that had produced the goods be allowed to bring imports into the country. As the political discussion warmed, the British government became alarmed about the impact of the proposed American response and dispatched a minister to the American capital. That a bill regulating navigation was not passed in 1791 was due almost solely to that British response; however, the British proposals did not contain the concessions that the Americans demanded. The two governments continued to negotiate for more than a year, but with little success; and, over those months, the international situation changed.[51]

On the one hand, war had again broken out in Europe; and the British interpreted the American discrimination in favor of the treaty states as favoritism to Britain's enemies. On June 8, 1793, the British government issued orders that were "designed to cut off American grain from enemy countries." The British justified the order on the basis of international law. They argued "that by the law of nations all provisions were to be considered as contraband, and as such liable to confiscation in the case when 'the depriving of an enemy of their supplies is one of the means intended to be employed in reducing him to reasonable terms of peace.' " Jefferson argued that provisions were not contraband and that, if the United States were to submit to the rule, it would not be the act of a neutral, but instead, would be close to an act of war against France.[52] There was, however, some progress. For example, in 1793 the British amended the interpretation of the clause in the Orders in Council of 1756 that had forbidden "all trade to neutrals in time of war that was not open to them in times of peace" by limiting it "so as to permit the importation of the produce of the French West India islands into the United States" and its subsequent reexportation to European ports.[53]

On the other hand, relations between the two countries were becoming increasingly strained by issues that were not connected with international

---

51 Egerton, *British Foreign Policy*, 373–375. Louis Martin Sears, *Jefferson and the Embargo* (Durham, NC: Duke University Press, 1927), 45. See also Setser, *Commercial Reciprocity*. 110, 113–114.

52 See the sources cited in Footnote 51.

53 Egerton, *British Foreign Policy*, 374–375. "The Rule of 1756 held that trade closed to a neutral in time of peace could not be opened in time of war and was initially interpreted by the British to prevent American merchants from freighting goods between France and her West Indian colonies." Donald R. Hickey, *The War of 1812: A Forgotten Conflict* (Urbana: University of Illinois Press, 1989), 10. See Chapter 1.

commerce. Still, at first, the American response to the British polices was muted. The initial congressional resolution that was aimed at these policies "was merely a declaration that the commerce of the United States ought to be set on a better footing with regard to foreign nations." However, over time, the response became much more censorious; and, as a result, the crisis in relations was becoming "so serious that mere commercial regulations, even severe ones, would not meet the need."[54]

Such was the political environment when John Jay was dispatched to Britain; and, in the intermediate term, the aim of Jay's mission was to obtain a "treaty of peace and commerce" – a treaty between the two powers that was ratified by the American Senate on June 24, 1795. The Treaty solved some of the most important matters of dispute, and it averted war at the time. However, "it contained certain features profoundly unsatisfactory to the majority of Americans"; and, in the longer term, averted did not mean prevented.[55] Nor did the situation improve. In July 1797, the British prime minister denied that his government had given permission for American vessels to import goods from any place in the world. And, even though "a British court had held that American vessels might legally trade from Europe to India," the American minister to Britain concluded that no further favorable alterations in that country's commercial policy could be anticipated. The British parliamentary acts designed to implement the Jay Treaty and to regulate trade with India were passed on July 4, 1797. This legislation produced substantial dissatisfaction in the United States, and "Jefferson and his friends adopted the attitude that the acts of Parliament constituted convincing evidence of the wickedness of the policy which had produced the Jay Treaty." Nor was that reaction limited to the friends of Jefferson.[56]

Until 1812, as long as the British were heavily involved with the war with Napoleon, they certainly felt that they were in the right. And "right" meant that supplies to the French had to be cut off, that the list of contraband should include anything that might even vaguely contribute to the war effort, and that the navy must have the right to capture neutral vessels on the high seas. The Americans, however, drawing on what were later to become the central tenets of international law – that "free ships make free goods," that the definition of contraband be "limited to those articles that would directly help the French war effort," and "that the only legal blockades were those that named specific ports or areas and stationed ships off the coast to seize ships

54 Setser, *Commercial Reciprocity*, 118.   55 Commager, *Documents*, 165–168.
56 Setser, *Commercial Reciprocity*, 143–144.

as they attempted to enter or leave" – enunciated a quite different vision of international law.[57] The results of these differences between American and British interpretations of a "correct" commercial policy are clear. There were large losses in American exports to the Dutch West Indies, which fell from $5,150,000 in 1799 to $625,000 in 1801, leading to increased complaints against British commercial actions in the West Indies. It has been estimated that, by 1805, American losses due to British seizures in the French West Indies alone totaled $12 million; and the American Secretary of State reported that, between 1803 and 1807, 528 American vessels were lost to British seizures, and 389 to French.[58]

At the same time, as the eighteenth century drew to a close, relations with the French also worsened. As early as 1793, the new revolutionary government began to seize neutral vessels carrying certain specified commodities; and Britain was quick to follow suit.[59] On March 2, 1797, the French government renounced the principle that "free ships make free goods"; and more important, a decree required that American vessels carry a crew list (*rôle d'équipage*) giving names and nationality. American vessels had never carried such a list, and the Americans were given no time to reply. The decree was, in effect, "a declaration of commerce war"; and "'it produced the most extensive and universal devastation of the American commerce.'"[60] In May 1798, the American Secretary of State wrote, "However much reason the Neutral Nations have to complain of her (Great Britain's) measures, the little finger of France in Maritime depredations is thicker than the loins of Britain, and the safety of the portion of the civilized world, not yet subjected by France, greatly depends on the barrier opposed to her boundless ambition and rapacity by the navy of England."[61]

In fact, by 1798 there existed an actual, although limited, naval war between France and the United States.[62] The French demanded both an American loan and that bribes be paid to certain officials. The Americans rejected the demands; Congress abrogated the existing treaties with France; and the government began to organize an army and commission war vessels in preparation for war. There were, in fact, a number of naval actions in

57 Harry L. Coles, *The War of 1812* (Chicago: University of Chicago Press, 1965), 2–4. See also Hickey, *War of 1812*, 11–13.
58 Donald R. Adams Jr., "American Neutrality and Prosperity: 1793–1808: A Reconsideration," *Journal of Economic History*, 40 (December 1980), 732–733; Michael A. Palmer, *Stoddert's War: Naval Operations during the Quasi-War with France, 1798–1801* (Columbia: University of South Carolina Press, 1987), 201, 215.
59 Adams, "American Neutrality," 732.   60 Palmer, *Stoddert's War*, 4–5.
61 Egerton, *British Foreign Policy*, 376, quoting the American Secretary of State.
62 Buel, *In Irons*, 255.

the Caribbean. Estimates indicate that, between June 1786 and June 1798, the French navy and cooperating privateers captured some 316 American vessels, and that, by 1800, the value of the U.S. vessels lost to the French amounted to $20 million. However, the "war" was largely but not entirely one-sided. In 1799, the Americans captured twenty-six French vessels, and the next year that number more than doubled to fifty-eight.[63] The French coup of November 9, 1799, brought Napoleon Bonaparte to power, and he soon agreed that France should come to a settlement with the Americans as a means to further isolate Britain. In December, the offending decrees were repealed and replaced by the law of July 26, 1798.[64] "Although the French government refused to pay an indemnity for past naval spoilations," in the convention of 1800, the French agreed both to stop future attacks and to the U.S. abrogation of the treaties.[65]

Earlier, in 1794, members of Congress realizing that complete naval impotence left them open to attacks on shipping by the North African pirate states had authorized the construction of six large frigates. Unfortunately, four years later, when that body declared a limited naval war against France, only three of the vessels were operational. Over the course of the war, a combination of new construction and the modification of existing commercial vessels increased the number of operational vessels to fifty-four.[66] As the navy expanded, it became obvious that some administrative structure had to be put in place; and, on April 30, 1798, Congress enacted legislation that created the Navy Department and charged the new department with overseeing ongoing strategic and operational naval decisions.[67] As economists tend to say, "supply creates its own demand"; and, as the navy grew, voters pressured their congressmen to expand the navy's duties. Merchants, for example, demanded more naval escorts for their European convoys. Stoddert, then Secretary of the Navy, however, felt that the "first care certainly ought to be the security of our own coast – the next to avail ourselves of the commercial and perhaps political advantages which the present state of the West Indies and Spanish America, is calculated to afford us"; and these goals became his first priority. However, needing the support

---

63 Palmer, *Stoddert's War*, 6, 235. During the two full years of "war," 1799 and 1800, during which the United States Navy operated in the Caribbean, on average, each American vessel captured 5.37 French corsairs; "each British vessel accounting for 0.36 corsairs." Although ties between the United States and Britain were close, the two countries never agreed to share intelligence information nor was there any formal alliance. Britain allowed the American government to purchase badly needed naval and warlike stores, especially cannons and copper, but naval cooperation between the two countries never developed fully. Palmer, pp. 74–77, 235.

64 Palmer, *Stoddert's War*, 192.   65 Setser, *Commercial Reciprocity*, 138–139.

66 Buel, *In Irons*, 255–256.   67 Palmer, *Stoddert's War*, 14.

of the merchant community, he also attempted to deploy American vessels to provide a show of force in European waters; but that attempt ended with little accomplished except "another minor fiasco."[68]

The French attempted to prove to the Americans that an armed confrontation with them could be at least as costly as a similar face-off with the British. Because the Royal Navy had established a fairly effective blockade of France, there was not even a negligible probability that the entire French fleet might be deployed to the Caribbean without first facing a major confrontation with the British. "But fast vessels, individually or in groups, could escape from France's Biscay ports – ports on the Bay of Biscay – that were only distantly blockaded and sail to the Caribbean bringing reinforcements and supplies" to the French fleet operating in that region.[69] These vessels were a serious threat to American commerce. However, when, in July 1798, news of the American decision to confront hostility with hostility, while still maintaining neutrality, reached Paris, the Directorate recognized that their policy had almost certainly failed. But the long lag in European-American communications, coupled with near political anarchy at home, meant that it was late 1799 before the adoption of the Convention of Mortefontaine gave structure to the new French policy toward neutral powers. When Napoleon became First Consul, he was concerned both about international law and about relations with the United States. As a result, in an attempt to align France and America in case of a future war, among his first official acts was to draft a treaty dealing with maritime relations; and the terms of the treaty were so generous that they could have been written by the Americans themselves. However, although terms were never consummated, the treaty was signed.[70] From the U.S. viewpoint, "by establishing a navy and deploying it operationally, the Americans had achieved their aims by displaying national resolve."[71]

As the war with the French neared its end, the United States was faced with the question of the appropriate size of the navy. Although the secretary of the navy pushed for the maintenance of the existing strength, Congress pushed for major reductions. The result was a compromise that, while calling for cutbacks, insured "that a naval force would be maintained and employed." On March 3, 1801, the president signed the Peace Establishment

---

68 Palmer, *Stoddert's War*, 122–123.   69 Palmer, *Stoddert's War*, 69, 75, 233.

70 "The treaty affirmed the principle that free ships make free goods. It recognized the possibility of contraband of war but limited the items to a specified list and exempted foodstuffs. One provision asserted the right of the neutrals to enter all ports not subject to a real blockade. Neutral merchantmen must recognize the right of search, save when in the convoy of warships." Sears, *Jefferson*, 303–304.

71 Palmer, *Stoddert's War*, 233–235.

Act.[72] Although final ratification of the treaty of peace between France and the United States did not occur until December 19, 1801, the U.S. government's policies reflected the belief that peace was at hand. The navy was ordered to continue to provide escorts for convoys, but to "halt hostilities unless the French unexpectedly continued their depredations."[73]

France was, however, not the only threat to American commerce; there also were the British. But threats do not always lead to war; and, as the new century opened, the American leaders were nearly unanimous in their desire for peace with the British – the Northern mercantile community was concerned about the costs, and its membership was dominated by those with an anglophilic bias, whereas, in the South, the majority of the electorate "perceived no motive of self-interest urging them to espouse the cause of France for the sake of Yankee shippers." But France needed allies; and, in an attempt to overcome these biases, from 1800 until 1807, a major thrust of Napoleon's foreign policy was aimed at drawing the United States into the war against the British.[74]

Under the régime of the Jay Treaty, the British government had eased its enforcement of "its despotic maritime regulations"; and it "was often courteous and prompt in redressing grievances."[75] A British Order in 1798 "extended to European neutrals the concession that had been made to the Americans in 1795" – a concession that had allowed American vessels to carry "West Indian produce direct from the islands to their own country, or to Great Britain." It did not, however, permit such produce to be carried to a hostile port or to any other neutral country. The Order was renewed when, in May 1803, war broke out between Britain and France. Although the order did not directly impact American trade, it did give rise to the hope that the British government would adopt a set of policies more in line "to American standards of neutral rights." For example, in reply to American complaints, the British countermanded a navy admiral's proclamation of a blockade of the entire coast of Martinique and Guadeloupe. Instead, the blockade "could apply only to particular ports actually invested by sufficient force, and that neutrals attempting to enter should not be captured unless they had been warned previously."[76]

But, faced by a new war with France, beginning in 1804 the British government began to develop policies that were designed to increase

---

72 Palmer, *Stoddert's War*, 231.
73 Palmer, *Stoddert's War*, 225.
74 Sears, *Jefferson*, 304–305.
75 Setser, *Commercial Reciprocity*, 161.
76 Captain A. T. Mahan, *Sea Power in its Relations to the War of 1812*, 2 vols. (Boston: Little, Brown, 1905), vol. 1, 98–99.

revenues by drawing increasing amounts of commerce into British channels. American produce, even produce carried on enemy and neutral ships, was, first, taken into British colonial ports and from there it was then carried to England in British vessels; British subjects were licensed to use neutral ships to trade with the enemy; and, in May 1805, the Lords Commissioners of Appeal in Prize Causes held that a brief stop at an American port did not neutralize an enemy cargo when the intended final destination was another enemy port."[77] As a result, scores of American vessels were seized and condemned. In the years after 1803, when the European war was renewed, American merchant vessels were never immune from seizure by the British. James Monroe, the Secretary of State, reported later "that from 1805 to 1808 the British captured one American ship every two days." British warships operating off New York searched and seized so many American vessels that "the port was, in effect, blockaded for long periods."[78] In addition, there were seizures, particularly in the West Indies; and, even more troublesome from the point of view of U.S-U.K. relations, Americans, both in and out of government, became alarmed by the rapid increase in the number of American seamen impressed by the Royal Navy. James Madison, then Secretary of State, concluded that "the growing severity of British policies toward neutrals" – policies that were first put into effect in 1805 and policies that reached their peak with the Orders of Council of November 1807 – had little to do with the French war, but were instead, designed to serve the ends of those British elites, particularly the West Indian interests, who were concerned about American competition and had an economic interest in shipping and selling West Indian sugar and coffee in Europe.[79] After 1808, however, the number of "prize captures" declined. In no year between 1809 and 1812 did the number of British captures reach one-half of the 1807 total, "and less than one of every dozen vessels departing from port fell into British hands." The decline, however, reflected not the British effort but the increasing awareness of American shippers and the fact that U.S. law now prohibited trade with the British.[80]

---

77 Perkins, *Prologue to War*, 73–85; Setser, *Commercial Reciprocity*, 162.
78 Setser, *Commercial Reciprocity*, 161–162. The earlier *Polly* decision had "granted the reëxport trade almost complete immunity from seizure." The decision stated that landing of goods in America and payment of even the smallest duties neutralized cargo being borne circuitously from the Caribbean to Europe." In effect, the decision had made the Rule of War of 1756 unenforceable. In the spring of 1805, the *Essex* decision, by condemning a cargo of wine shipped from Barcelona to Havana, but that had been landed briefly in the United States, although technically not repealing the *Polly* decision had, for all intents and purposes, just that effect. Perkins, *Prologue to War*, 79–81.
79 Stagg, *Mr. Madison's War*, 18–19.   80 Perkins, *Prologue to War*, 74.

Congress passed the Non-Importation Law in April 1806; however, the House of Representatives agreed to suspend the act until November 15, awaiting news of the British response. As a piece of economic legislation, it had little effect; and in terms of improving U.S.-British relations, it was worse than useless. "The most important imports from Britain – cottons, cheap woolens, iron and steel – did not appear on the list" of excluded commodities; and, in addition, the law was not seriously enforced. Moreover, it raised English hackles. As an independent congressman wrote, "it has not sufficient energy to operate on the fears, but may wound the pride of Great Britain."[81] In an attempt to "cool off" the situation, the American delegates to Britain signed the Monroe-Pinkney Treaty of 1806. The new treaty was more favorable to the United States than the Jay Treaty that it would replace. From the British point of view, it was clearly a conciliatory gesture. For example, the British agreed to retreat from the current *Essex* restrictions to those of the previous *Polly* decision.[82] The treaty did not, however, call for the halt of the impressment of American seamen; nor did it call for "immediate and prompt redress" to any Americans who were mistakenly impressed – two issues that the Americans felt were very important.[83] President Jefferson, reflecting that position, concluded that "we better have no treaty than a bad one, it will not restore friendship but keep us in a state of constant irritation"; and he refused to submit the treaty to the Senate.[84] Although counterfactuals are, as always, difficult to prove, some historians of the period have argued that the United States "missed an opportunity . . . to substitute peace and prosperity for commercial restrictions and war."[85] What is certainly clear, however, is that tensions between the countries continued to mount.

In June 1807, the British warship *Leopard* attacked the American frigate *Chesapeake*; twenty-three men were killed and eighteen wounded. The *Chesapeake* surrendered; and the British boarded her and took off four suspected British deserters.[86] Although four years of negotiations were to

---

81 Perkins, *Prologue to War*, 112–113. Two years later, in Spring 1808, when the act was "at last seriously enforced," "nonimportation became an important ancillary to the Embargo."

82 Perkins, *Prologue to War*, 132–134.

83 Hickey, *War of 1812*, 14; Setser, *Commercial Reciprocity*, 166, 201–202. "The British agreed not to interfere with the re-export trade as long as American ships paid a small transit duty on their stopover in the United States," and they agreed not to interfere with American shipping within five miles of the American coast; the definition of contraband was narrowed; they agreed "to reduce the duties paid by American ships in British ports"; to allow American merchants continued (although somewhat restricted) access to the British East Indies; and "to indemnify any merchant whose vessel was detained in violation of the treaty."

84 Perkins, *Prologue to War*, 134–135.   85 Hickey, *War of 1812*, 16.

86 Mahan, *Sea Power*, vol. 1, 134, 155–156; Reginald Horsman, *The Causes of the War of 1812* (Philadelphia: University of Pennsylvania Press, 1962), 102.

follow, the American public was outraged. Then in November 1807, the British adopted stringent new commercial regulations that, while aimed primarily at the French, were "regulations that might require temporary sacrifices but [that] would strike down the baneful American re-export trade." These regulations impacted the Americans adversely.[87] These general facts were known to the president (Thomas Jefferson) and to Congress, and they certainly were both on the politician's minds when, on December 18, the president, angered by the *Chesapeake* affair, sent a message to Congress recommending "an inhibition of the departure of our vessels from the ports of the United States."[88] "On the same day that Jefferson's message was received, the Senate passed an Embargo Bill." The bill was sent to the House, returned with amendments; and the amended bill was passed and approved on December 22. Then Secretary of State James Madison had achieved his wish for a radical cure of Anglo-American difficulties.[89]

Nor was it only British policies that inflamed American opinion. In November 1806, Napoleon's Berlin Decree proclaimed a blockade of Britain, excluded from French controlled harbors in Europe any neutral vessel that had stopped in a British port, and declared that all British-made goods, even those owned by neutrals, constituted lawful prizes. Just over a year later, in December 1807, his Milan Decree announced that all neutral vessels submitting to the British trade regulations, or even permitting a British search party to board, were liable to seizure. Thus, Napoleon's policies toward U.S. commerce were nothing short of extensive. Although a sensible policy should have called for maintaining good relations with the Americans, "the Emperor showed as little respect for America's rights and even less for her political importance than did British leaders."[90] The British responded with several Orders in Council that "proclaimed a blockade of all ports from which British goods were excluded and required neutrals who wished to trade with those ports to stop in Britain and pay transit duties first." Although at times circumvented by special licenses and, more frequently, by wholesale evasion, in theory the combined French–British policies closed the door to American shipping. "If American ships complied with French decrees they were subject to seizure by the British, and if they submitted to the British decrees, they could be seized by the French."[91] According to Secretary of State Madison, from 1803 to the Orders of 1807, the British

87 Perkins, *Prologue to War*, 201–202.
88 Perkins, *Prologue to War*, 153–157; Sears, *Jefferson*, 59–60; Stagg, *Mr. Madison's War*, 21–22.
89 Mahan, *Sea Power*, vol. 1, 182–183; Stagg, *Mr. Madison's War*, 21–22.
90 Perkins, *Prologue to War*, 69–72.
91 Horsman, *War of 1812*, 8; Hickey, *War of 1812*, 18.

seized 528 American vessels, and, from November 1807 through 1812, an additional 389 – a total of 917. Between 1803 and the Berlin decree, the French seized 206 American vessels, under the Berlin and Milan decrees another 307, and, after repeal, 45 additional ships, for a total of 558.[92]

Initially, scholars had concluded that, because of the war in Europe, over the years of "armed neutrality," the American economy had prospered. For example, in 1944, Harold Somers summarized a traditional view: "Early in the period [1790–1811], the country gained from the European wars. Production and trade were stimulated. . . . The Non-Importation Act of 1806 and the Embargo of 1808 put this profitable period to an end."[93] More recently, that conclusion has been seriously disputed. In terms of exports and imports – the statistical basis for the earlier conclusion about domestic prosperity – it appears that the years between 1793 and 1807 differed little from the years 1808–1812, a period that had been characterized as years of declining prosperity. Moreover, although American shippers benefited from increased freight rates, it was the American consumers who paid for those increases in terms of higher prices for imported goods; and the economy certainly did not benefit from the initial (1793 to 1799) decline in domestic exports. Thus, Donald Adams concludes, "that scholars of the early national era have overemphasized the benefits of American neutrality while neglecting some of the costs, have discussed the ensuing prosperity without a complete assessment of the distribution of benefits, and have failed to differentiate carefully between changes that occurred because of neutrality and those that most likely would have occurred in the absence of the Continental Wars."[94]

Although the American response had proved somewhat effective, it had also proved costly. Until 1793, American expenditures on the navy were negligible; however, such expenditures reached $411,000 in 1794, exceeded $1 million in 1798, and, in 1800, achieved a pre-1807 peak of $3.4 million (equal to 32 percent of government expenditures). "Average expenditures between 1800 and 1807 were $1.7 million per annum."[95] There were,

---

92 Perkins, *Prologue to War*, 72.
93 Harold M. Somers, "The Performance of the American Economy Before 1865," in Harold F. Williamson, ed., *The Growth of the American Economy: An Introduction to the Economic History of the United States* (New York: Prentice Hall, 1944), 324–327.
94 Adams, "American Neutrality," 714, 720–722. The average figure for real domestic exports for the years 1793–1807 was $24.8 million whereas that for the years 1808–1812 was $25.4 million. For real domestic imports, the comparative figures are $41.8 and $41.1 million.
95 Adams, "American Neutrality," 734. See also Joseph H. Davis and Douglas A. Irwin, "Trade Disruption and America's Early Industrialization" (unpublished 2003), and Claudia D. Goldin and Frank D. Lewis, "The Role of Exports in American Economic Growth during the Napoleonic Era, 1793 to 1807," *Explorations in Economic History* 17 (January 1980), 6–25.

Table 3.4. *Total United States Tonnage and Tonnage in Foreign Trade, 1789–1807*

(1)	(2)	(3)	(4)
Year	Total U.S. Tonnage (000)	Total Tonnage In Foreign Trade (000)	Column 3/Column 2 (percent)
1789	202	124	61.4
1790	478	346	72.4
1791	502	363	72.3
1792	564	411	72.9
1793	521	368	70.6
1794	629	439	69.8
1795	748	529	70.7
1796	832	577	69.3
1797	877	598	68.2
1798	898	603	67.1
1799	939	657	70.0
1800	972	667	68.6
1801	948	631	66.6
1802	892	558	62.6
1803	949	586	61.7
1804	1,042	661	63.4
1805	1,140	744	65.3
1806	1,209	799	66.1
1807	1,269	840	66.2

Source: Donald R. Adams Jr., "American Neutrality and Prosperity, 1793–1808: A Reconsideration," *Journal of Economic History*, 40 (December 1980), 724.

however, not only costs but also benefits. In the *Polly* decision (1800), the British government considered that American vessels shipping goods from France to the United States and then reexporting them to the West Indies did not violate British law. As a result, American reexports increased more than fifty times between 1792 and 1805 (from $1 million to $53 million).[96]

3a(2). The Quantitative Story. In the United States, shipping was important. During the years 1790 to 1807, the shipping industry's economic contribution to the American economy was both substantial and growing. The tonnage of the American merchant fleet rose from 478,000 to 1,269,000 tons; and, of that total, two-thirds was deployed in foreign trade (see Tables 3.4 and 3.5). Robert Gallman has placed per capita income in 1805 at about $70. Between 1790 and 1807, the value of real exports rose from

[96] Douglass C. North, *The Economic Growth of the United States, 1790–1860* (Englewood Cliffs, NJ: Prentice-Hall, 1961), 221. See also Hickey, *War of 1812*, 10.

Table 3.5. *Tonnage of Documented United States Merchant Vessels, 1789–1825*

| | Trade in Which Engaged | | | | Percentage of Total Trade in Which Engaged | | | |
Year	Total Documented Gross Tons (000)	Foreign Trade (000)	Coastal Trade (000)	Whaling & Fishing (000)	Total Documented Gross Tons	Foreign Trade	Coastal Trade	Whaling & Fishing
1789	202	124	69	9	100.0	61.4	34.2	4.5
1790	478	346	104	28	100.0	72.4	21.8	5.9
1791	502	363	106	33	100.0	72.3	21.1	6.6
1792	564	411	121	32	100.0	72.9	21.5	5.7
1793	521	368	122	31	100.0	70.6	23.4	6.0
1794	629	439	163	27	100.0	69.8	25.9	4.3
1795	748	529	184	34	100.0	70.9	24.6	4.5
1796	832	577	218	37	100.0	69.4	26.2	4.4
1797	877	598	237	42	100.0	68.2	27.0	4.8
1798	898	603	251	· 44	100.0	67.1	28.0	4.9
1799	939	657	247	36	100.0	69.9	26.3	3.8
1800	972	667	272	32	100.0	68.7	28.0	3.3
1801	948	631	275	42	100.0	66.6	29.0	4.4
1802	892	558	290	45	100.0	62.4	32.5	5.0
1803	949	586	299	64	100.0	61.7	31.5	6.7
1804	1,042	661	318	64	100.0	63.3	30.5	6.1
1805	1,140	744	333	63	100.0	65.3	29.2	5.5
1806	1,209	799	341	70	100.0	66.0	28.2	5.8
1807	1,269	840	349	79	100.0	66.2	27.5	6.2
1808	1,243	765	421	57	100.0	61.5	33.9	4.6
1809	1,350	907	405	38	100.0	67.2	30.0	2.8
1810	1,425	981	405	39	100.0	68.8	28.4	2.7
1811	1,233	764	420	48	100.0	62.0	34.1	3.9
1812	1,270	759	478	33	100.0	59.8	37.6	2.6
1813	1,167	673	471	23	100.0	57.7	40.4	2.0
1814	1,159	675	466	19	100.0	58.2	40.2	1.6
1815	1,368	854	476	38	100.0	62.4	34.8	2.8
1816	1,372	801	522	49	100.0	58.4	38.0	3.6
1817	1,400	805	525	70	100.0	57.5	37.5	5.0
1818	1,225	590	549	86	100.0	48.2	44.8	7.0
1819	1,261	581	571	108	100.0	46.2	45.3	8.6
1820	1,280	584	588	108	100.0	45.6	45.9	8.4
1821	1,299	594	615	90	100.0	45.7	47.3	6.9
1822	1,325	583	624	118	100.0	44.0	47.1	8.9
1823	1,337	600	618	119	100.0	44.9	46.2	8.9
1824	1,389	637	642	110	100.0	45.9	46.2	7.9
1825	1,423	665	641	116	100.0	46.8	45.0	8.2

Source: U.S. Bureau of the Census, *Historical Statistics of the United States, Colonial Times to 1970*, 2 vols. (Washington, DC, Government Printing Office: 1975), vol. 2, Series Q425–432, 750.

Table 3.6. *American Exports, 1785–1815*

(1)	(2)	(3)	(4)	(5)	(6)	(7)
Year	Total Exports (Millions of Dollars)	Export Price Index	Real Exports (Millions of Dollars)	Real Domestic Exports (Millions of Dollars)	Real Exports Per Capita (Dollars)	Real Domestic Exports Per Capita (Dollars)
1785	14.2	106.0	13.4			
1786	14.4	97.0	14.8			
1787	14.4	92.0	15.7			
1788	15.5	87.0	17.8			
1789	17.5	87.0	20.1			
1790	20.2	100.0	20.2	19.9	5.14	5.07
1791	19.0	85.8	22.2	21.6	5.46	5.32
1792	20.8	81.7	25.4	24.2	6.06	5.76
1793	26.1	97.8	26.7	24.9	6.16	5.75
1794	33.0	103.6	31.9	25.6	7.13	5.73
1795	48.0	153.6	31.2	25.9	6.78	5.61
1796	67.1	172.6	38.9	23.6	8.19	4.98
1797	56.9	174.8	35.5	17.1	6.66	3.49
1798	61.5	207.4	29.7	13.8	5.91	2.74
1799	78.7	220.3	35.7	15.0	6.92	2.90
1800	71.0	145.9	48.6	15.0	9.18	2.83
1801	94.1	154.1	61.1	30.8	11.13	5.62
1802	72.5	131.6	55.1	27.9	9.70	4.91
1803	55.8	132.8	42.1	31.8	7.16	5.41
1804	77.7	147.7	52.6	28.1	8.67	4.63
1805	95.6	156.4	61.1	27.1	9.76	4.33
1806	101.5	142.0	71.5	29.1	11.08	4.50
1807	108.3	136.2	79.5	35.8	11.97	5.38
1808	22.4	115.3	19.5	8.2	2.84	1.20
1809	52.2	116.2	44.9	27.0	6.39	3.84
1810	66.8	128.6	51.9	32.9	7.19	4.56
1811	61.3	128.6	47.7	35.2	6.39	4.72
1812	38.5	127.1	30.3	23.6	3.94	3.07
1813	27.9	126.5	22.0	19.8	2.77	2.49
1814	6.9	127.3	5.4	5.3	0.67	0.65
1815	52.6	182.9	28.7	25.2	3.41	2.98

Source: Adams, "American Neutrality and Prosperity," 736.

$20.2 million to $79.5 million and averaged $40.6 million. On a per capita basis, the increase was from $5.14 to $11.97. Moreover, it is clear that the increase did not reflect a similar expansion of domestic production. The value of real domestic exports did increase, but the increase was only from

Table 3.7. *American Imports, 1785–1815*

(1)	(2)	(3)	(4)	(5)	(6)	(7)
Year	Total Imports (Millions of Dollars)	Import Price Index	Real Imports (Millions of Dollars)	Real Domestic Imports (Millions of Dollars)	Real Imports Per Capita (Dollars)	Real Domestic Imports Per Capita (Dollars)
1785						
1786						
1787						
1788						
1789						
1790	23.8	100.0	23.8	23.5	6.06	5.98
1791	30.5	109.8	27.8	28.0	7.01	6.89
1792	32.5	118.8	27.4	28.5	7.02	6.80
1793	32.6	108.4	30.1	26.9	6.56	6.20
1794	36.0	129.2	27.9	22.0	6.00	4.92
1795	71.3	124.3	57.4	40.1	9.85	8.70
1796	82.9	132.8	62.4	35.7	11.02	7.53
1797	77.4	139.9	55.3	33.4	10.49	6.83
1798	70.6	127.6	55.3	25.6	9.58	5.10
1799	81.1	135.5	59.9	22.5	9.93	4.35
1800	93.3	124.6	74.9	28.8	11.47	5.43
1801	113.4	119.9	94.6	43.7	13.52	7.96
1802	78.3	111.8	70.0	29.6	9.57	5.20
1803	65.7	118.0	55.7	37.5	8.05	6.38
1804	87.0	134.7	64.6	34.4	9.72	5.68
1805	125.5	139.5	90.0	49.7	13.78	7.95
1806	136.6	129.8	105.2	53.2	14.77	8.25
1807	144.7	124.7	116.0	61.8	15.83	9.31
1808	58.1	124.3	46.7	30.4	5.72	4.44
1809	69.0	129.1	47.3	23.9	5.17	3.40
1810	89.4	129.8	68.9	39.7	7.55	5.49
1811	57.9	121.1	47.8	27.0	5.00	3.62
1812	78.8	131.7	59.8	39.8	5.80	5.18
1813	22.2	179.7	12.4	9.3	1.34	1.17
1814	13.0	232.3	5.6	5.2	0.64	0.63
1815	85.4	191.3	44.6	37.0	4.89	4.51

Source: Adams, "American Neutrality and Prosperity," 737, with corrected figures for real imports (column 4).

$19.9 million to $35.8 million; and, in per capita terms, there was only a small increase (from $5.07 to $5.38). The series on the real value of imports show a similar story, although real domestic imports per capita increased more rapidly than did domestic exports (see Tables 3.6 and 3.7). It is, however, interesting to note that during the first war with France (1797–1798) real exports, both total and domestic, did fall; but there is no similar movement during the second war (1801–1803).[97]

Finally, the importance of Great Britain in the market for America exports is underscored by the data reported in Table 3.8. In 1790–1792, Great Britain and Ireland accounted for 31 percent of all U.S. exports, the British West Indies for 10 percent, and Canada for an additional 2 percent. Altogether, the British Empire accounted for 43 percent of American foreign exports.

3b. The Embargo: December 22, 1807, to March 4, 1809

3b(1). The Qualitative Story. Although this book is focused on blockades, the embargo – a policy that could be viewed as an antiblockade – played a major role in the commercial warfare between the United States and Britain, a form of commercial warfare that, in the slightly longer term, ended in actual warfare and in one of the more effective blockades in modern history.

The months leading up to the embargo were marked by an increasing number of seizures of American vessels by the warring European powers. In the words of Senator Smith of Maryland, in private life a shipping merchant, "It has been truly said by an eminent merchant of Salem, that not more than one vessel in eight that sailed for Europe within a short time before the embargo reached its destination. My own experience has taught me the truth of this; and as further proof I have in my hand a list of fifteen vessels, which sailed for Europe between September 1 and December 23, 1807. Three arrived; two were captured by French and Spaniards; one was seized in Hamburg; and nine carried into England. But for the embargo, ships that would have sailed would have fared as ill, or worse. Not one in twenty would have arrived."[98] An embargo, however, was not the only possible response. It is certainly true that the Americans could have continued to export their produce on European, mostly British, ships. Shipowners would have been the losers; but, of course, they were already the losers; however, the costs to the rest of the American economy would not have been large – certainly they would have been smaller than the costs that were imposed by the embargo. The Americans, however, concluded that the British "blockade" was a weapon that, although aimed at the French, was striking at them, and

---

97 The 1797–1798 real exports were about 20 percent less than the average of the two subsequent years. Adams, "American Neutrality," 724, 736, 737. See also Goldin and Lewis, "The Role of Exports," 9.
98 Quoted in Mahan, *Sea Power*, vol. 1, 184–185.

Table 3.8. *Average Annual Exports to Overseas Areas: The 13 Colonies, 1768–1772, and the United States, 1790–1792ᵃ (Thousands of Pounds Sterling: 1768–1772 prices)ᵇ*

Destination	1768–1772	Percentage of Total	1790–1792	Percentage of Total
Great Britain and Ireland	1616	58	1234	31
Northern Europe			643	16
Southern Europe	406	14	557	14
British and Foreign West Indies (1768–1772)	759	27		
British West Indies (1790–1792)			402	10
Foreign West Indies (1790–1792)			956	24
Africa	21	1	42	1
Canadian Colonies	ᶜ		60	2
Other			59	1
TOTAL	2802	100	3953	100

ᵃ The annual average exports for 1790–1792 are taken from export values in the source for the following periods: (1) various days in August 1789 through September 30, 1790; (2) October 1, 1790, through September 30, 1791; and (3) October 1, 1791, through September 30, 1792.

ᵇ Values for 1790–1792 were converted to pounds sterling and 1768–1772 prices on the basis of a Pasche price index implicit in the calculations of the real values of the more important commodity exports. This implicit Pasche index is 4.924, which includes the exchange rate between sterling and dollars, and the change in the average level of prices of those exports between 1768–1772 and 1790–1792 (see footnote 17 for a discussion on the exchange rate and changes in the general level of export prices). This index stems from revaluing the quantities of those annual average commodity exports in 1790–1792 with average prices of the same commodities exported in 1768–1772. Northern Europe includes continental European countries north of Cape Finisterre. Southern Europe includes Spain, the Canary Islands, Portugal, Madeira, the Azores, the Cape Verde Islands, Gibraltar, and other Mediterranean ports in Europe (except French ports). The Foreign West Indies includes the Swedish, Danish, French, and Spanish Caribbean possessions, and Florida and Louisiana. Africa includes North Africa, the west coast of Africa, and the Cape of Good Hope. The Canadian colonies include the British North American colonies, including Newfoundland, and the British Fisheries; and St. Pierre, Miquelon, and the French fisheries. Other destinations include the East Indies, the northwest coast of America, and unknown destinations.

ᶜ Not available.

Source: James F. Shepherd and Gary M. Walton, "Economic Change After the American Revolution: Pre- and Post-War Comparisons of Maritime Shipping and Trade," *Explorations in Economic History*, 13 (October 1976), 406. See original estimates for average annual exports for 1768–1772 in James F. Shepherd and Gary M. Walton, *Shipping, Maritime Trade, and the Economic Development of Colonial North America* (Cambridge: Cambridge University Press, 1972) 94–95; and exports for 1790–1792 in U. S., A. S. P. (1832). See also table 4 of the original article for sources of data on the real value of exports.

that they were the victims of a commercial war in which they were not directly engaged. As victims, they needed to make a positive response that would force their attackers to retreat. Perhaps because it was never seriously enforced, the 1806 Non-Importation Act had not worked to deter the

British. Madison, in public at least, argued that the embargo was not a hostile act, but merely an attempt "to compel the withdrawal of her various maritime measures objectionable to the United States."[99] In fact, however, both politicians and citizens at large viewed the embargo as another, and stronger, response – an openly hostile policy that was, however, still a step away from the ultimate alternative, a military war.[100]

As tensions grew, the Secretary of State, James Madison and the President, Thomas Jefferson, came out strongly in support of an embargo. As Jefferson explained to Congress, the policies adopted by Britain in numerous Decrees and Orders in Council, practically amounted 'to a declaration that every vessel found on the high seas, whatsoever be her cargo, and whatsoever foreign port be that of her departure or destination, shall be deemed lawful prize.'[101] Both men concluded that a strong response was necessary; and both firmly believed in the coercive power of an embargo. They assumed that, with European imports being unavailable, by cutting off Britain and her colonies from the products of American farms, the residents of the empire would soon face starvation.[102] Although there were those in Congress who opposed such action, the Senate pushed the bill ordering the embargo through in one afternoon. "The House of Representatives proved slightly more recalcitrant," but it also went along.[103]

In hindsight, at least, it is clear that, if the embargo was to successfully coerce the British, two conditions had to be met. First, as the embargo would impose substantial costs on the American economy, "successful coercion required the almost unanimous support of the American people."[104] Second, it was necessary that the policy be closely coordinated with European governments operating within the then existing European Continental System. In fact, neither requirement was met. Because the pressure of the embargo induced a level of economic distress – wherever employment depended on commerce, distress was immediate, and it soon spread to other sectors – and because of a broadly based general willingness in the population to believe that national honor was "no less sullied by one-sided trade than by head-in-the-sand withdrawal," opposition proved far deeper than Jefferson had anticipated.[105] Moreover, Americans have always been more than willing to turn a profit; and violations of the restrictions imposed by the embargo

---

99 Mahan, *Sea Power*, vol. 1, 183. See also the more recent works of Hickey and Stagg cited earlier. The interpretations of these scholars are consistent with those of Mahan for most issues of interest.
100 Mahan, *Sea Power*, vol. 1, 185–186.   101 Egerton, *British Foreign Policy*, 382.
102 Perkins, *Prologue to War*, 151.   103 Perkins, *Prologue to War*, 153–154.
104 Perkins, *Prologue to War*, 158
105 Mahan, *Sea Power*, vol. 1, 192; Perkins, *Prologue to War*, 158.

proved very profitable. When the law was passed, there were many American vessels scattered about the world's oceans and ports. Many, perhaps most, remained abroad, thus escaping the embargo's effects.[106] Nor did the owners of many of the vessels that were in port obey the law. Instead, they moved quickly to order their ships to sea. In New Orleans, for example, with the cooperation of the U.S. customs collector, forty-two vessels escaped. "The most notorious violations took place among vessels nominally engaged in the coasting trade" – owners who found that "imaginary bad weather or constructed circumstances" required that their ships make for foreign ports, ports that were sometimes all the way across the Atlantic.[107] In addition, as Gallatin informed Jefferson, at times vessels were secretly loaded and sailed without legally clearing port.[108]

Nor were American entrepreneurs the only source of the weakness of the impact of the embargos. Loopholes in the embargo legislation itself also contributed heavily. On the one hand, the law did not affect foreign ships or goods. Throughout the fifteen months of the Embargo, "large numbers of British ships arrived to sell cargoes of English wares." Foreign ships were supposed to leave in ballast, but many captains broke the law. If they did follow the law, such journeys should have proved unprofitable; however, the withdrawal of American competition turned potential losses into profits. On the other hand, the law never prohibited the export of specie, so cash sales were legal.[109] Congress also passed supplementary legislation that, in addition to somewhat tightening restrictions, was allegedly designed to permit American citizens to bring home property that was stranded abroad; it also authorized the president to license vessels to sail abroad in ballast. Large numbers of vessels were licensed, dispersed in various directions; and many remained away.[110]

Nor was the ocean the only means to undercut the embargo. Across both land and lakes, commodities flowed out of the northern United States; and, as a result of the illegal trade, trade that moved in both directions, and trade that was directed by smugglers, the economies of both Quebec and Halifax boomed.[111] So leaky was the system that Jefferson was forced to conclude "that the embargo law is certainly the most embarrassing we ever had to

---

106 Egerton, *British Foreign Policy*, 383. As an aside, it might be noted that, by an edict issued on April 17, 1808, Napoleon, arguing that no American vessel could be at sea without violating American law, ordered the seizure of all American vessels entering the ports of France, Italy, or the Hanse Towns.

107 Perkins, *Prologue to War*, 160–161.   108 Mahan, *Sea Power*, vol. 1, 196.

109 Perkins, *Prologue to War*, 162.   110 Mahan, *Sea Power*, vol. 1, 197.

111 Mahan, *Sea Power*, vol. 1, 198; Hickey, *War of 1812*, 225–226, points to the "mushrooming trade with Canada," which "American officials found it difficult to halt."

execute. I did not expect a crop of so sudden and rank growth of fraud, and open opposition by force, could have grown up within the United States."[112]

But what about Britain? Underlying the American belief in the effectiveness of the Embargo was the belief that the new policy would effect the British in two ways: (1) it would act directly by reducing the food supplies and push the average British resident toward near starvation; and, thus, it would produce an effective political outcry against the government's commercial policies; and (2) it would operate indirectly by reducing British exports, thus, placing pressure on British manufacturing, in industries owned by members of the upper middle class who had substantial political clout. In terms of the first, the effects on income were much as the Americans expected; but the political response was not. Imports of corn, grain, and meal fell by 84 percent from £920,435 in 1807 to £146,119 in 1808.[113] And the statistics on the poor rate give convincing evidence of the intense suffering in cities throughout the winter of 1807–1808. In Manchester, for example, poor rate expenditures rose from an average of £4,000 to more than £249,000.[114] The state of the economy did produce opposition to the Orders in Council, but the opposition did not produce action. "The members of the opposition were Englishmen and patriots" and, because of the threat of Napoleon "with the empire at stake, minor issues counted little."[115]

Moreover, the statistics on exports are less supportive of the American prediction. Admittedly, some sectors of the economy were badly affected. "Ireland's linen industry, almost entirely dependent upon American flaxseed, suffered as the price bounded up." More important, as the supply of raw cotton dried up, the cotton industry was impacted. At its worst, in Manchester, for example, a city with more than eighty cotton mills, during the year of the embargo only nine operated full time, thirty-one at half-time, and forty-four were closed. However, although the United States had accounted for almost all of British cotton imports and those imports had fallen from forty-four million pounds in 1807 to twelve million pounds in 1808, the size of the decline is, in part, a statistical artifact. On average, imports had been much less than the 1807 figure; and that year's surge had left Britain awash in cotton. Moreover, in 1808 imports from non-American sources totaled thirty million pounds. Much of the remainder of the manufacturing sector

112 Mahan, *Sea Power*, vol. 1, 194.
114 Sears, *Jefferson*, 280.

113 Sears, *Jefferson*, 276–293.
115 Sears, *Jefferson*, 274–275.

Table 3.9. *United Kingdom, Exports, Declared Value, 1806–1808 (£000)*

Year	To Europe	To Africa	To Asia	To U.S.A.	To Americas, non-U.S.A	Total Exports
1806	11,364	1,164	2,938	12,389	10,878	38,733
1807	9,002	765	3,359	11,847	10,439	35,412
1808	9,016	633	3,525	5,242	16,592	35,008
			Percent			
1806	29.3	3.0	7.6	32.0	28.1	100.0
1807	25.4	2.2	9.5	33.5	29.5	100.0
1808	25.8	1.8	10.1	15.0	47.4	100.0

Source: B. R. Mitchell and Phyllis Deane, *Abstract of British Historical Statistics* (Cambridge: Cambridge University Press, 1962), 313.

was hardly effected, and the textile losses were partly offset by the increasing profitability in the shipping industry, as freight rates rose, the effect of the absence of American competition.[116] Overall, in terms of exports, between 1807 and 1808, although shipments to the United States had declined by some 56 percent, exports to other areas, particularly those to Canada and to Central and to South America – markets opened by the Spanish rebellion against Napoleon – had risen; and the overall decline in U.K. exports was a miniscule 1 percent[117] (see Table 3.9).

Given the legal and economic problems, the administration acted with as much vigor as was probably possible. Congress passed supplementary legislation that prohibited all intercourse with foreign countries, including Canada, by land, as well as by sea; authority was given to detain coastal shipping, if evasion was suspected; the small navy cruised off the coast looking for evaders; additional revenue cutters were authorized; and, finally, in January 1809 an Act for the Enforcement of the Embargo was signed into law. "No vessel, coasting or registered, should load, without first having obtained permission from the custom-house, and given bond, in six times the value of the cargo, that she would not depart without a clearance, nor after clearing go to any foreign port, or transfer her lading to any other vessel."[118]

116 Setser, *Commercial Reciprocity*, 161–169; Mahan, *Sea Power*, vol. 1, 199–200; Perkins, *Prologue to War* 167–168. In Bristol, with the withdrawal of the Americans, freight costs for a 330-ton ship to St. Petersburg and return reached £3,300; and for a 199-ton ship to Lisbon and back, £2,000.
117 Perkins, *Prologue to War*, 168–169.
118 Mahan, *Sea Power*, vol. 1, 206–209; Perkins, *Prologue to War*, 163; Hickey, *War of 1812*, 20.

In Europe, the rules had drastically changed. By July, the British government had halted all hostilities in Spain and had lifted the blockade on all Spanish ports except those occupied by the French. The next month, the French evacuated Portugal. Thus, only shortly more than four months after Congress had imposed the embargo, both countries on the Spanish peninsula "were in alliance with Great Britain; their ports and those of their colonies open to British trade."[119]

In America, the costs imposed by the embargo continued to rise; and, voices demanding repeal became ever louder. By the fall of 1808, it was obvious that the embargo had failed. Jefferson had greatly "overestimated British dependence on American supplies and had failed to take into account the possibility that there were alternative suppliers and those trade routes can be adjusted in the face of changing prices. He had accepted congressional restrictions – restrictions that undercut the embargo – and he had expected that the British would have responded rationally to the American policy."[120] On March 1, 1809, Congress acted to repeal the legislation that had underwritten the embargo – legislation that they had enacted little more than fourteen months earlier.[121]

Although the issue can never be fully resolved, some scholars have argued that the embargo was not left in place long enough to avert war; and, had it not been repealed, it might have forestalled a formal war with Britain. Certainly, by early 1809 the British government had begun to display an interest in the restoration of commerce with the United States.[122] If this argument is true, the embargo's failure can, instead, be traced to "a lack of the political will and perseverance to use it, rather than through a lack of economic power."[123] At minimum, then, the embargo was not allowed to avert war.

3b(2). The Quantitative Story. The effect of the embargo is reflected in the data; but even those data still do not provide sufficient evidence to prove if, as earlier scholars believed, the embargo was a failure or if, as some now argue, it was a lack of national will that caused the embargo to fail. However, the reader should bear in mind that the data depended, to a large extent, on official records; and, given the apparent rise in illegal commerce, the American figures may well overstate the embargo's impact. The British data are probably more reliable.

---

119 Mahan, *Sea Power*, vol. 1, 191; Hickey, *War of 1812*, 117, 124, 182.
120 Perkins, *Prologue to War*, 170–171.
121 Egerton, *British Foreign Policy*, 383; Perkins, *Prologue to War*, 181–182.
122 Sears, *Jefferson* 131–142, 319–320; Perkins, *Prologue to War*, 170.
123 Jeffrey A. Frankel, "The 1807–1809 Embargo Against Great Britain," *Journal of Economic History*, 42 (June 1982), 291–292.

Table 3.10. *The Effect of the Embargo on Prices in the United States*

Item	Before Embargo	During Embargo	After Embargo	Embargo/ Non-Embargo
Agricultural Products				
1. Sea Island Cotton	41.600	22.250	26.750	0.661
2. Upland Cotton, Charleston	19.000	11.875	13.031	0.751
3. Upland Cotton, Boston	21.555	16.877	16.333	0.867
4. Flax	15.000	14.887	15.417	0.977
5. Flour	6.903	6.098	7.299	0.861
6. Corn	91.556	79.568	85.240	0.896
7. Farm Products	93.500	71.000	86.500	0.789
8. Foods	146.000	113.000	134.000	0.807
9. Rothenberg Index	113.500	98.600	110.950	0.879
Manufactured Products				
10. 2d Nails	26.000	26.128	27.500	0.982
11. Gun Powder	40.833	59.049	62.667	1.191
12. White Lead	18.500	18.346	20.417	0.952
13. Bristol Glass	15.375	16.387	18.833	0.949
14. Textiles	277.000	279.000	300.500	0.966
15. Chemicals and Drugs	479.500	455.000	510.500	0.919
Terms of Trade (Agr./Mfg.)				
16. Sea Island Cotton/Nails				0.673
17. Sea Island Cotton/Textiles				0.684
18. North Index	109.300	92.800	94.550	0.910
19. Domestic/Imports (Bezanson, et al.)	105.750	90.700	91.650	0.919
20. Agriculture/Industrial (Bezanson, et al.)	91.800	75.300	79.050	0.881
21. Boston Index	100.450	54.900	90.400	0.575

Source: Jeffrey A. Frankel, "The 1807–1809 Embargo Against Great Britain", *Journal of Economic History*, 42 (June 1982), 306. The numbers used in this table are drawn from Frankel's table, despite some apparent minor errors.

In the case of the United States, not surprisingly, the real value of both exports and imports fell sharply – by 60 percent for imports and 75 percent for exports – during 1808 (see Tables 3.6 and 3.7). However, the embargo seems to also have had a longer-term effect. The real values rose in 1809; but, between that year and the beginning of 1814, exports averaged only slightly more than 50 percent and imports slightly more than 40 percent of the 1806–1807 average. Prices, particularly, prices of agricultural products, declined. In the case of farm products, the decline, as compared to the years both before and after the embargo, was about 20 percent; for manufactured goods, however, the fall was only about a quarter of that amount (see Table 3.10). Finally, the terms of trade turned slightly against the United States, and that

Table 3.11. *Terms of Trade Series for the United States, 1790–1815*

(1)	(2)	(3)	(4)	(5)
	North Index	Bezanson Index: Domestic/Imported	Bezanson Index: Agriculture/Industrial	Boston (Adjusted)
Year	(1790 = 100)	(1790 = 100)	(1790 = 100)	(1790 = 100)
1790	100.0	100.0	100.0	100.0
1791	78.1	94.7	92.7	n.d.
1792	68.8	92.8	89.9	90.0
1793	90.2	95.5	96.2	90.1
1794	80.2	90.7	89.7	94.9
1795	123.6	95.5	90.8	126.3
1796	130.0	106.4	97.1	115.3
1797	124.9	106.8	95.5	113.2
1798	162.5	100.9	91.3	92.5
1799	162.6	87.6	84.4	102.8
1800	117.1	94.6	90.7	108.5
1801	128.5	101.6	99.8	103.3
1802	117.7	98.3	88.8	97.0
1803	112.5	100.0	85.1	91.7
1804	109.7	100.0	89.5	101.9
1805	112.1	108.5	98.4	101.8
1806	109.4	105.3	94.0	100.9
1807	109.2	106.2	89.6	100.0
1808	92.8	90.7	75.3	54.9
1809	90.0	87.0	74.7	80.8
1810	99.1	96.3	83.4	100.0
1811	106.2	103.7	83.4	77.4
1812	96.5	85.4	75.1	73.2
1813	70.4	77.8	69.3	79.2
1814	54.8	83.8	67.3	71.3
1815	95.6	93.0	84.0	111.2

Source: Adams, "American Neutrality and Prosperity," 717.

fall caused national income to decline slightly, adding to the direct effects of the embargo on national output (see Tables 3.11 and 3.12).

In the case of England, the embargo adversely affected cotton prices, but had little impact on either prices or exports. Whereas exports to the United States declined from about £12 million to less than half that amount, exports to the rest of the Americas surged from just less than £11 million to £16.6 million. In 1807, the United States had accounted for a third of the United Kingdom's exports, the next year the fraction was only 15 percent.

Table 3.12. *Terms of Trade Impact on Real Gross Domestic Product in the United States, 1791–1815*

(1)	(2)	(3)	(4)
		Domestic/	Agricultural/
	North Index	Imported Index	Industrial Index
Date	(Percent Change)	(Percent Change)	(Percent Change)
1791	−3.09	−0.75	−1.03
1792	−4.04	−1.02	−1.42
1793	−1.38	−0.63	−0.54
1794	−2.79	−1.31	−1.45
1795	3.32	−0.63	−1.30
1796	4.23	0.90	−0.41
1797	3.51	0.96	−0.63
1798	8.81	0.13	−1.23
1799	8.83	−1.75	−2.20
1800	2.41	−0.76	−1.31
1801	4.02	0.23	−0.03
1802	2.50	−0.24	−1.58
1803	1.76	0.01	−2.10
1804	1.37	0.01	−1.48
1805	1.71	1.20	−0.23
1806	1.33	0.75	−0.85
1807	1.30	0.87	−1.47
1808	−1.02	−1.31	−3.48
1809	−1.41	−1.83	−3.57
1810	−0.18	−0.74	−3.34
1811	1.25	0.74	−3.34
1812	−0.70	−2.93	−5.00
1813	−5.95	−4.46	−6.17
1814	−9.09	−3.26	−6.57
1815	−8.84	−1.41	−3.22

Source: Adams, "American Neutrality and Prosperity," 718.

The rest of the Americas had been the recipient of less than 30 percent of U.K. exports in 1807; the next year the figure was over 47 percent. As a result, total exports declined by about £400,000 (about 1 percent) between 1807 and 1808 (see Table 3.9). Although Sea Island cotton prices rose by over 60 percent, other agricultural prices remained relatively steady and the prices of manufactured goods actually fell – by something less than 10 percent (see Table 3.13). Certainly the British economy suffered from unemployment, unemployment that was initially centered in the manufacturing sector, and that gradually spread to other sectors. It remains, however,

Table 3.13. *The Effect of the Embargo on Prices in Great Britain*

Item	Before Embargo	During Embargo	After Embargo	Embargo/ Non-Embargo
Agricultural Products				
1. Sea Island Cotton	53.021	87.500	49.843	1.719
2. Bowed Cotton	32.188	50.438	29.907	1.644
3. Wheat	1,850.000	1,952.000	2,445.000	0.900
4. Barley	936.000	1,042.000	1,154.000	0.997
5. Oats	671.000	800.000	720.000	1.150
6. Cotton	32.750	44.000	35.250	1.294
Manufactured Products				
7. Cotton Twist	36.700	38.000	39.460	0.998
8. Iron Bars	18.500	16.000	n.d.	0.865
9. Copper	16.600	14.700	n.d.	0.886
10. Pig Iron	3,381.000	3,000.000	3,012.000	0.939
11. Bar Iron	8,040.000	7,200.000	7,200.000	0.945
Terms of Trade (Man. /Agr.)				
12. Iron Bars/Sea Island Cotton				0.503
13. Cotton Twist/Sea Island Cotton				0.581

Source: Frankel, "1807–1809 Embargo," 305.

unclear whether the economic damage caused by the embargo, if that policy had been continued, would have brought the government to its knees.

3c. From the Embargo to War

3c(1). The Qualitative Story. The repeal of the embargo was enacted as a part of a new piece of commercial regulation – the Non-Intercourse Act.[124] That Act prohibited immediately the entry of government owned ships of Great Britain and France into any port in the United States. In addition, the law prohibited, after the the following May 20: (1) merchant vessels from those two countries from entering American ports on penalty of forfeiture; and (2) the importation of merchandise from British and French ports. The act also empowered the president "to suspend these prohibitions in respect of either nation" should that nation "revoke or modify its Orders or Decrees so that they should cease to violate the neutral commerce of the United States." "This Act was to remain in force only until the end of the next session of Congress, It was continued in force by the Act of June 28, 1809.[125]

124 Perkins, *Prologue to War*, 181–182.   125 Egerton, *British Foreign Policy*, 383–384.

Perhaps the embargo might have succeeded had the mood of the country been different; what is certain, however, is that the Non-Intercourse regime was too weak to prevent its failure.[126] In New England, the center of antiembargo sentiments and votes, the citizens were "to learn that war suited her even less than the embargo" and that, for a period of years, they were "to forfeit even the political gains" they "had won by the embargo's defeat."[127]

The political regime produced by the embargo, its repeal, and the passage of the Non-Intercourse Act had two other unfortunate aspects. On the one hand, the policies "provided an excuse for ineffective military preparations when force was the only language that the world understood," so that the United States was unprepared for the war that would be declared on June 18, 1812. On the other hand, the "ineffectiveness" of the embargo induced the governments of Europe, particularly Britain, to "believe that commercial coercion could be scorned because it would harm the United States more than those against whom it was wielded." As a result, in the months leading up to the war, the British proved far less willing to compromise in the face of renewed American economic threats.[128]

3c(2). The Quantitative Story. The years between March 1809 and June 18, 1812 – years fraught with the political battles that were to underwrite the declaration of war – show some evidence of changes in the nation's overseas commerce and in its merchant fleet. Total documented tonnage was 1,350,000 in 1809; it rose to 1,425,000 the next year, before declining to 1,270,000 in 1812, a decline of about 6 percent. Perhaps of more interest, the relative importance of the tonnage deployed in the overseas trade declined from about 67 to 60 percent of the total; a decline from 1809 that, at least in part, reflected the increasing tensions between the United States and Europe (see Table 3.5).[129] Somewhat different patterns can be observed for the series on the real value of the nation's exports and imports. The real value of exports averaged $48 million over the years 1809 through 1811, before declining to $30 million in 1812. A different pattern is reflected in the level and composition of the real value of domestic imports. During the year 1812, although the real value of total imports showed a small increase from the 1809–1811 average, the level of domestic imports actually rose by

126 Sears, *Jefferson*, 194–196.   127 Sears, *Jefferson*, 196.
128 Perkins, *Prologue to War*, 174.
129 U.S. Bureau of the Census, *Historical Statistics of the United States, Colonial Times to 1970*, 2 vols. (Washington, DC: Government Printing Office, 1975), vol. 2, Series Q, 418, 750, and Table 3.5.

almost one-third. The outbreak of war had already changed the pattern of the country's waterborne commerce (see Tables 3.6 and 3.7).

4. THE WAR OF 1812

4a. The Qualitative Story

Looking ahead, the history of the war can be divided into three chapters. The first covers the period from the declaration of war until the winter of 1812–1813. During that period, the British government remained reluctant to believe that the declaration was not reversible, and they did not begin to deploy all the nation's military power or in other ways exercise the repressive measures that were available. The second period began on November 27, 1813, when the fleet operating off the American coast was ordered to establish a rigorous commercial blockade of the Delaware and Chesapeake Bays, and it ended with the defeat of Napoleon in April 1814. During the third phase the British, freed from the French threat, and in order "to terminate a conflict at once weakening and exasperating," let loose her military might by rigorously and effectively blockading the entire American coast – "not merely specified places, but 'all the ports, harbors, bays, creeks, rivers, inlets, outlets, islands, and sea-coasts of the United States, from the border of New Brunswick to that of Florida.'"[130]

To summarize, the years leading up to the war, with the renewal of the European War in 1803 and the resulting host of British maritime practices had presented an almost continuous worsening of the relations between Britain and America. Although there were other issues – Canada, for example – the basic difficulties related to ocean commerce and, in particular, to the various manifestations of the British navigation system. The Americans complained about the British definition of contraband, their practice of stopping and searching vessels that might contain illegal goods, and their definition of a legal blockade – Britain had often declared an entire coastline under blockade; and then, to make matters even worse, their navy had seized vessels that were far away from that coast, arguing that the ships were sailing toward the blockaded area – and, particularly, to impressment. The deterioration led, in June 1812, to the American declaration of war against Britain.[131] Jefferson had hoped that the U.S. could avoid war; but Britain,

---

130 Mahan, *Sea Power*, vol. 2, 9–11. The quotation is from the *Naval Chronicle*, vol. xxxi: 475.
131 Horsman, *War of 1812* (New York: Alfred A. Knopf, 1969), 6–7. See also Horsman, *Causes of the War of 1812*, 259–262; Stagg, *Mr. Madison's War*, 5.

fully involved with its war with France, declined to compromise until it was too late.

Writing "in January 1812, Secretary of State Monroe claimed that 6257 Americans had been impressed since 1803." Although his figure was disputed by both the American Federalists and the British, his estimate was widely circulated; and it contributed to the steadily increasing level of public complaints about British commercial policy.[132] On January 9, 1813, Congress, having stalled for almost two years, passed an "act authorizing the construction of the Federal navy's first four line of battleships."[133] And, finally, and very indirectly, one other cause of the war might be traced to the fact that the U.S. government did not realize that earlier the French, although apparently agreeing to revoke the Berlin and Milan decrees, had, in August 1810 issued a secret decree – a decree that Gallatin, on finally learning of its existence, said "it is not a condemnation either in form or in substance; but it certainly announces the intention to condemn." In the United States, the president had based his campaign against the Orders in Council on the strength of the supposed French repeal of the Berlin and Milan decrees. The new information that could be inferred from the publication of the French Decree of St. Cloud certainly called "into question both the legitimacy and necessity of the war against Great Britain"; and, although the information did not become known in the United States until after the declaration of war, Madison's congressional opponents made full use of it as they attacked his policies.[134] Moreover, had the Americans known that they faced problems with the French, as well as the British, they might well not have taken some of the measures that exacerbated their differences with the latter country.[135]

It was clear that the embargo and Non-Intercourse Acts had failed. As the *Niles' Weekly Register* reported in April, "The embargo system, at once the safest and best, has been disgraced by the time-serving conduct of its friends – war or submission present themselves; and all that sophistry can devise, the fear of [un]popularity invent, or personal pusillanimity dictate, cannot offer another alternative." Across the ocean, the British government reaffirmed the existing declaration arguing that, with the "French

---

132 Perkins, *Prologue to War*, 91. After examining the basis of the various estimates, Perkins concludes, "We may settle upon 3,800 as the rock-bottom figure, unchallengeable even on the basis of British calculations and British definitions of citizenship. Beyond that it is impossible to go with any certainty, although it may well be that the widely advertised 6,257 actually reflects something near the truth. The number of seamen impressed might well have been larger," p. 92.

133 Palmer, *Stoddert's War*, 127.

134 Stagg, *Mr. Madison's War*, 305–307. Egerton, *British Foreign Policy*, 384. See Chapter 2.

135 Egerton, *British Foreign Policy*, 384.

repeal being fraudulent, Britain would continue the Orders in Council."[136] Despite the Non-Importation Act, trade with Canada, both by land and sea, continued; and most of the seaborne trade was carried in American vessels – a clear violation of the Non-Intercourse Act. The Americans proved equally adept at smuggling by land and lake. Tariff collectors on the northern frontier complained of the difficulties they encountered in their attempts to enforce the law. For example, "Zebulon M. Pike sought to prosecute smugglers near Plattsburgh, but no court would take cognizance because even the judges had a hand in the trade." Nor was the government able to keep the British fleet from reprovisioning itself in the Americans market. The editors of the Lexington *Reporter* wrote, 'The fact is notorious that the very squadrons of the enemy now annoying our coast . . . derive their supplies from the very country which is the theatre of their atrocities.'[137] A few months later, the Americans were to learn that even a declaration of war was insufficient to halt the practice.

The nations moved closer to war when, on April 1, the president, noting the absence of British concessions, recommended, and three days later Congress passed, first, a ninety-day embargo and, then, new nonexportation measures. "Together these laws prohibited American ships from clearing for foreign ports and barred the export of all goods and specie by land or by sea."[138] However, support for these measures, could hardly be termed overwhelming. In the case of the embargo, it passed the House by a vote of seventy to forty-one with ten abstentions; in the Senate, it passed by a vote of twenty to thirteen.[139]

On June 1, Madison's message to Congress called for a declaration of war. In that message he cited four major grievances that underlay his decision: impressment, illegal blockades, the Orders in Council, "and an allegation that British agents had been responsible for the renewal of Indian warfare on the northwest frontier over the winter of 1811–1812." Both Houses ultimately supported his decision; but, again, the support was not overwhelming. On June 3, "after beating back three attempts at delay, the House passed the war bill by a vote of seventy-nine to forty-nine." Two weeks later, after much debate – a debate marked by the rejection of motions to: (1) "issue letters of marque and reprisal, the same to take effect against France as

136 Perkins, *Prologue to War*, 378, quoting *Niles' Weekly Register*, April 4, 1812.
137 Hickey, *War of 1812*, 167–171.
138 Hickey, *War of 1812*, 39. The president had initially proposed a sixty-day embargo, but Congress extended the period to ninety days.
139 Perkins, *Prologue to War*, 384–385. See also Horsman, *Causes*, 244.

well as England, if positive proof of repeal of the Berlin and Milan decrees was not forthcoming"; and (2) "to limit the war to the high seas" – by a vote of 19 to 13, the Senate concurred. In both Houses, "the vote on the war bill was the closest vote on any declaration of war in American history."[140]

On June 16, just two days before the American Congress declared war, the British Secretary of State for Foreign Affairs, Robert Stewart, the Viscount Castlereagh, "announced in Parliament that the Orders in Council would be suspended." Then, on June 23, before they had received news of the American decision, "Castlereagh made it known that the government had revoked the Orders in Council," scrapping the whole system of blockades and licenses. "The government insisted that the repeal was voluntary, . . . [but] that new measures against American trade would follow if nonimportation continued."[141]

For some months, the British continued to believe that, when the news filtered across the ocean, their action would cause the Americans to reconsider their decisions. As a result, although many American ships were seized, the British did not deploy an extensive blockade of the American coast. Moreover, in part because they needed supplies for their troops on the Iberian Peninsula, they were prepared to, and did, issue licenses for the export of goods from the United States in both American and neutral vessels. In fact, despite the federal government's efforts to enforce the law, a large number of merchants, particularly in New England, did not hesitate to export provisions, "not only to the Peninsula, but also through neutral ports to the British West Indies, and to Newfoundland, New Brunswick, Nova Scotia, and the rest of Canada."[142] However, the American government, if not the New England merchants, proved intransigent. But their intransigence was not based on the public's reaction to the start of open warfare. Even war had not made the commercial hostilities any more popular on the home front. In November, for example, "resolutions to prohibit the export of flour and breadstuffs" were offered in the House; but they were "voted down by a large majority of the Congressmen." Most Representatives had concluded that, less than six months into the conflict, "the war had become

---

140 Stagg, *Mr. Madison's War*, 110–114; Perkins, *Prologue to War*, 407, 414; Hickey, *War of 1812*, 46. See also Horsman, *War of 1812*, 24.
141 Perkins, *Prologue to War*, 337–338; Hickey, *War of 1812*, 42.
142 Horsman, *War of 1812*, 57–58. It was not only the Americans who closed their eyes to the enemy. During the first summer of the war, the British exported some £5,000,000 worth of manufactures to the United States.

so unpopular" that they were unwilling to further anger their constituents by supporting policies that would further reduce "profits from agriculture, even if it meant feeding the enemy." Congress had, in fact, served notice to Madison's administration "that the conquest of Canada would indeed have to be the principal means of bringing Britain to terms."[143]

Throughout 1812, the British blockade was neither extensive, tight, nor particularly effective. As was to be proved again during the American Civil War, a weaker belligerent's best naval strategy, when faced by a blockade, is to deploy the vessels that are directly, or indirectly, under its control to attack enemy shipping on the high seas. So, given the small number of naval vessels in its fleet during 1812 and the two years following, the United States "flooded the seas with privateers." Although the privateers were never able to "win" the battle of the Atlantic, for two years they proved very effective.[144] A year after the declaration of war, on July 29, 1813, faced with the failure to pass an embargo and with the resurgence of American smuggling, the Secretary of the Navy, trying to achieve at least some of the results that he had hoped the embargo would have produced, instructed American warships to attempt to intercept all American trade with the enemy – at most, a second-best result. Moreover, there was even more bad news. Reports from Europe indicated that the power of the nation's "semi-ally," France, was clearly declining; and the threat of peace in Europe – peace that would release British naval forces for duty off the Atlantic coast – further undercut the American position.[145]

In December, however, Madison, in an attempt both to stop trade with the enemy and to increase the economic pressure on Britain, again appealed to Congress to "pass a total embargo on American exports and a ban on all imports known to be of British origin."[146] Despite both the past unpopularity of such a policy and a general skepticism about its potential effectiveness, times had changed; and, despite Federalist opposition, Congress quickly passed a measure that was substantially more stringent than the one they had rejected only four months previously.[147] In its form, the new embargo

---

143 Stagg, *Mr. Madison's War*, 274–275.   144 Mahan, *Sea Power*, vol. 1, 286–289.
145 Stagg, *Mr. Madison's War*, 319–320.
146 The president's message called for four new restrictions: "(1) an embargo prohibiting all American ships and goods from leaving port; (2) a complete ban on the importation of certain commodities customarily produced in the British Empire, such as woolen and cotton goods and rum; (3) a ban against foreign ships trading in American ports unless the master, supercargo, and at least three-quarters of the crew were citizens or subjects of the flag flown by the ship; and (4) a ban on ransoming ships." Hickey, *War of 1812*, 171–172; Stagg, *Mr. Madison's War*, 363.
147 Stagg, *Mr. Madison's War*, 363–364.

reflected its 1809 predecessor; but it was far broader and more sweeping than any previous legislation. All vessels except privateers were restricted to port; "the export of all goods and produce prohibited"; the ocean coasting trade was forbidden; fishing vessels were required to post heavy bonds; "government officials were given broad powers to enforce the law," they could act on suspicion alone, and "penalties for violation were heavy." In fact, the law proved too strong; and, within a week, the government began to relax some of the restrictions imposed by it. Officials were ordered to impound goods only if they had clear evidence that a vessel's operators had intended to violate the law, and Congress enacted new legislation to ease the most severe effects of the law. For example, Nantucket, under threat of starvation, was granted the right to import food and fuel; and "coasting vessels trapped away from home were allowed to return."[148]

The American action was taken in the face of an increasingly effective British blockade. Not even the British navy could completely seal the bays, harbors, and inlets of the whole Atlantic coast; and, initially, because of a European war-induced shortage of vessels, the British efforts were even more limited.[149] In the fall of 1812, the British blockaded the coast from Charleston, South Carolina to Spanish Florida. "By November 1813, the entire coast south of New England was under blockade."[150] Because of concern about the weather, as early as September 1813, a large part of the blockading force was withdrawn from the Chesapeake Bay; and, during the winter, heavy weather and driving snowstorms forced the blockading vessels farther away from other ports as well. Even in the spring, a few American warships managed to escape.[151] However, from the late spring of 1813, the blockade became increasingly effective. In February, a blockade of the Chesapeake and Delaware Bays was officially proclaimed; and, later in the spring, the blockade had been extended to New York, Charleston, Port Royal, Savannah, and the Mississippi. In addition, there were *de facto* blockades – neutral vessels arriving before they were informed of the blockade were warned off or returned to port rather than seized – obstructing other ports that served as bases for the American privateers and naval vessels that

---

148 Hickey, *War of 1812*, 172–173.   149 Horsman, *War of 1812*, 142–143.
150 Hickey, *War of 1812*, 152.
151 Mahan, *Sea Power*, vol. 2: 177–178. In April, both the *President* and the *Congress* escaped from Boston; and the former vessel, on a long cruise that involved taking a dozen prizes, proved an effective American weapon. Both the *United States* and the *Macedonian* escaped from New York, but they were forced by the blockading force to return to New London, Connecticut. Horsman, *War of 1812*, 71–72.

had been harassing British commerce.[152] Finally, in November, the blockade was extended to cover all of Long Island Sound; and, at that point, it stretched all the way along the Atlantic and Caribbean coasts from southern New England to the Mississippi River.[153]

As the year 1813 wore on, the Americans felt the effects of the blockade in a number of ways. On the one hand, in the domestic economy, supplies of imports fell, touching off a speculative surge; and, because of shortages and speculation, prices rose: In August sugar sold for $9.00 a hundredweight in New Orleans and for $26.50 in Baltimore; rice sold for $3.00 a hundredweight in Charleston or Savannah and $12.00 in Philadelphia; and flour that went for $4.50 a barrel in Richmond sold for almost $12.00 in Boston. The New York *Columbian* reported that 'the *mania for commercial speculations* and monopolies is extensive and increasing.'[154]

Not surprisingly, exports also fell. Aggregate real exports in 1813 declined to about one-half the level of 1811, and they amounted to hardly more than a fourth of the average that had obtained over the years before Jefferson's embargo. Although all sections of the country saw their exports decline; in relative terms, the proportion of both the south and the middle states increased, whereas those of New England declined from one quarter of the national total to 40 percent of that fraction.[155] That sector's decline is underscored by a fall 1813 enumeration of 250 idle ships, many rotting, sitting in Boston harbor. Nor was Boston alone; "other seaports in New England experienced a similar fate."[156]

On the other hand, the nature of the American military response also changed. Because most U.S. warships were bottled up in port, there were fewer naval engagements. As a result, although the catch was smaller, privateers were forced to pick up the slack. Most British vessels now sailed in convoy; and, because they were the only places that merchant ships traveled alone and not in convoy, both American privateers and warships were forced to operate either in the British West Indies or off the coast of the British Isles.[157]

And so, the year 1813 came to a close. As 1814 opened, "neither side was satisfied with the naval situation. The British public lamented that the Americans had not been swept from the seas, but the Americans complained that the lack of naval preparations by their government had left the American

---

152 Horsman, *War of 1812*, 68–69.   153 Horsman, *War of 1812*, 143.
154 Hickey, *War of 1812*, 152–153.
155 Mahan, *Sea Power*, vol. 2, 179–181. If both exports and reexports are included in the total, the relative decline of New England is even more marked.
156 Hickey, *War of 1812*, 230–231.   157 Hickey, *War of 1812*, 157.

coastline vulnerable to all manner of British attacks, and the blockade was ruining their trade."[158] In 1814, however, the situation began to change – and, from the American viewpoint, not for the better. The war at sea continued to favor the British. On April 25, the British blockade was extended to New England. The peace treaty between Britain and France was signed on May 30; and, the next day, by British order, the entire American coast, all "ports, harbors . . . and seacoasts were declared to be" under strict blockade.[159] The British naval commander denied a request by the merchants of Halifax to carry on licensed trade with the blockaded ports; and, a few months later, he ordered a series of attacks on the American coast.[160] Moreover, with peace in Europe, the blockade became, not only broader but also more effective; and "the economic bottlenecks that had appeared in 1813 worsened in 1814 as the gluts and shortages in every market increased. Merchants and fishermen could not send their ships to sea, and farmers could not ship their produce" to either foreign or domestic markets.[161] The contemporary view was neatly summarized in a letter published in *Niles' Weekly Register*: 'No sooner had the enemy blockaded our harbors, and extended his line of cruisers from Maine to Georgia, than both foreign and domestic commerce came at once to be reduced to a deplorable state of stagnation; producing in its consequences the utter ruin of many respectable merchants, as well as a great multitude besides.'[162]

The American coastal areas suffered particularly heavily. The number of predatory naval raids, particularly along the hitherto largely untouched New England coast, increased dramatically in both numbers and cost. For example, "in one such raid, a British squadron sailed up the Connecticut River and destroyed twenty-seven vessels valued at $140,000."[163] "The Royal Navy also cut off the nation's coastal islands from the mainland." Although Nantucket was located only thirty miles off the coast, the British navy controlled the intervening water. As a result, in August, "the threat of starvation was so acute that the island had to declare its neutrality. In exchange for surrendering its public stores, supplying British warships, and discontinuing the payment of federal taxes, Nantucket won the right to import provisions and fuel from the mainland and to fish in nearby waters." Other coastal

158 Horsman, *War of 1812*, 153.   159 Coles, *War of 1812*, 89.
160 Horsman, *War of 1812*, 144–145.
161 Hickey, *War of 1812*, 214–215. American exports that had been valued at $61,300,000 in 1811 declined by almost 90 percent to $6,900,000 in 1814, and imports fell from $57,900,000 to $13,000,000, a decline of more than 75 percent.
162 Mahan, *Sea Power*, vol. 2, 207–208. This was the issue of June 17, 1815.
163 Hickey, *War of 1812*, 215.

towns also came to terms. Residents of Cape Cod "paid tribute to avoid bombardment and plundering." On Block Island, a part of Rhode Island, the residents were 'in the daily habit of carrying intelligence and succor to the enemy's squadron'; in response, the Americans cut off all trade between the island and the rest of the world.[164]

By March, Britain was effectively in control of both the Atlantic and Pacific coasts of the United States. Because the blockade was almost complete, with a heavy concentration of vessels off the middle states, any vessel attempting to run the blockade was required to, first, break the blockade as it left port, then sail far out into the ocean to avoid the concentration of British warships, and, then, break the blockade again before it could make port.[165] Data on coastal trade are limited, but the figures for international trade bear out the conclusion that the blockade was very effective. Real exports for the year 1811 had been $47.7 million; by 1813 they had declined to $22 million; and, in 1814, the figure had fallen to $5.4 million. Overall, there was a decline of 89 percent, of which about 40 percent occurred in the last year. In addition, given the reliance on customs duties as a revenue source the government's budget constraint became more binding.

In addition to preventing the passage of further commercial regulations, the news of peace in Europe greatly increased both the number and the vociferousness and clamor of the voices demanding repeal of the Embargo and Non-Importation Acts. Napoleon's defeat also convinced Madison that, if he was to garner any European support for the American position on the rights of neutral commerce, it was necessary that the United States quickly restore trade relations with the European neutrals. Thus, on March 31, less than four months after he had recommended the new restrictions, Madison asked Congress to repeal both acts. In addition, he asked that the "export of specie should also be banned to prevent an unfavorable balance of trade from draining the nation's banks." In his request, he argued that enemy goods could still be barred from the country.[166] In principle, the president and Congress agreed that it was "necessary to remove all restrictions upon commerce, both foreign and domestic."[167] A bill repealing the two acts passed both Houses by large majorities; however, antiwar sentiment was so

164 Hickey, *War of 1812*, 215–216; Horsman, *War of 1812*, 160–161.
165 Coles, *War of 1812*, 88–90, 166; Mahan, *Sea Power*, vol. 1, 201; Stagg, *Mr. Madison's War*, 383. Brian Arthur, at the University of Greenwich, has been writing on naval aspects of the War of 1812. His MA thesis concluded that the British blockade had a major effect on the United States, particularly due to the reductions in tax revenues caused by the decline of imports as the outcome of the effectiveness of the blockade. See Brian Arthur, "The Role of Blockade in the Anglo-American Naval War of 1812" (MA thesis, University of Greenwich, 2002)
166 Hickey, *War of 1812*, 174–175.   167 Mahan, *Sea Power*, vol. 2, 208.

strong that a "bill to outlaw the export of specie failed to win a majority in either house." With the passage of the repeal, Americans were "barred only from trading directly with the enemy, importing enemy-owned goods, or using enemy licenses."[168]

At sea, the war also was not going well for the Americans. Not only had the blockade crushed domestic and international trade and imposed the costs and pain of war directly on the population, but it also gradually spelled the end of effective naval operations. With most of its warships bottled up in port, the navy actually suffered its greatest losses on land rather than at sea. Of the navy's four frigates, the *Constitution*, the *United States*, and the *President* were effectively bottled up in Atlantic ports; and only the *Constitution* was operational. Meanwhile, although they were tied-up in port, the *Columbia*, the *Argus*, and the *Adams* were all lost to British ground attacks.[169] Moreover, the three seventy-four-gun vessels that Congress had authorized – vessels that would have been a match for the British three-deckers – were still under construction.[170]

With most of the navy confined to port, the war at sea was largely left in the hands of the American privateers and British warships. Given the blockade and the British rules governing commercial navigation – rules that did not require their vessels to sail in convoy, if they were operating close to home, the waters off the British Isles, particularly the Irish Sea, became the focus of American activity. Despite the British navy, given the absence of U.S. naval "competition," the Atlantic swarmed with privateers – privateers whose success is reflected in the increase in insurance rates between Liverpool and Halifax – rates that, in 1814, jumped three times, to 13 percent.[171]

With the American coastline under attack, with the navy unable to deliver a telling blow at sea, and with the French surrender, the voices of the anti-war opposition became even louder.[172] "That opposition had always been strong, but the degree of outright Federalist obstruction had fluctuated" with the state of the war.[173] And the events of 1814 did little to quiet the opposition. As far as New England was concerned, it was widely believed, by members of both the administration and the opposition, that it was but a short step from resisting the war, to neutrality, to a separate peace,

168 Hickey, *War of 1812*, 174–175.
169 Hickey, *War of 1812*, 216; Coles, *War of 1812*, 94.
170 Horsman, *War of 1812*, 152. The British admiralty had actually ordered their three-deckers not to engage the 74s should they encounter them.
171 Hickey, *War of 1812*, 217–218.
172 Stagg, *Mr. Madison's War*, 469.   173 Stagg, *Mr. Madison's War*, 469.

and, finally, to secession. For contemporaries, all that was required as evidence of such a scenario was a recognition of the fact that the Federalist opposition had called the Hartford Convention – a meeting that, it was generally believed, was organized by politicians eager to underwrite such a program.[174] Moreover, from the administration's point of view, any solution to the question of continuing the war effectively was further muddled by the continued trade between the United States and the British Empire, particularly Canada. As they had demonstrated earlier, many citizens proved willing to engage in such activity, but not all such trade even violated American law. In September, the British seized eastern Maine; and they made Castine, on the Penobscot River, a port of entry. Even more disturbing was the flow of commerce moving across the border from Canada – trade that not only brought British goods into the United States, but, because of the balance of payments deficit, drained specie from the country, and provided foodstuffs for the British army in Maine. As at Castine, a share of the Canadian trade was waterborne; and the American government did little to prevent it. In the words of a Treasury official, 'neutral vessel and cargo coming from any part of the British dominions, may be admitted to an entry in any part of the United States.' Maine was not the only point of entry. Neutral ships flying Swedish and Spanish colors operated on Lake Champlain. Waterborne imports, however, constituted only a part of the total; the overland trade between British-occupied Maine and Canada represented an even greater proportion; and much of that trade was conducted illegally by American citizens.[175] Profits rather than patriotism had triumphed again.

It was in this environment that the British and American envoys met to discuss a treaty of peace. The war had raised the specter of a replay of the revolution; the United States had fought a naval war with an enemy whose naval supremacy it could not begin the challenge. Moreover, because of monetary and political problems, the government had had a difficult time mobilizing the nation's resources.

In April 1814, the news of the armistice talks spread across the country; and it raised American hopes that a negotiated peace would soon end the fighting. Britain, however, had little reason to concede anything; and the talks stalled over questions of territorial secessions and of future naval policy along the Atlantic coast.[176] By November, however, the British were willing to concede that given "the state of the war, they had no right to demand

---

174 Stagg, *Mr., Madison's War*, 472.   175 Hickey, *War of 1812*, 225–226.
176 Stagg, *Mr. Madison's War*, 385–386.

any concession of territory."[177] After a month of negotiations, a treaty that came to be known as the Treaty of Ghent, was completed on December 24, 1814. "The treaty mentioned none of the maritime issues that had caused the war. It simply restored the *status quo* ante-bellum." It did, however, call for returning all prisoners of war; in addition, both sides agreed not to carry off any enemy property, and, after a certain time, to restore to their owners, any vessels that had been taken as prizes. Hostilities were to end when both sides ratified the agreement, although the treaty "would not be binding until ratifications had been exchanged."[178]

A further treaty was concluded on July 3, 1815. That second treaty included provisions regarding commerce with India, and the "reservation of the rights of each country with regard to the regulation of colonial trade." Most important was the article dealing with the "regulation of direct trade between the United States and the British possessions in Europe." The rules on American–British trade were the most generous that had ever been offered to the United States. All discriminating duties were abolished; "each nation guaranteed that the other" would essentially be granted the equiv-alent of a most favored nation clause, as "all import and export duties on merchandise and [to] all prohibitions on imports should be placed on an equality with all other nations"; the vessels of each country would be placed on an equal footing with the ships of its own "as far as duties and charges were concerned, except that equalization of duties on the cargo should apply only to articles of growth, produce, or manufacture of the country of the vessel's flag."

The 1815 treaty remained the legal basis of commercial relations between the United States and British dominions in Europe for the next fifteen years; and it was never seriously undercut either by the bitter fight over the West India trade or by any of the other controversies that arose between the two countries. Two years later, the bias toward American commerce that was embodied in the treaty was further reinforced by the Navigation Act of March 1, 1817.[179]

After 1815, the cause of the most serious friction between the two coun-tries was still over the old question of American access to the colonial trades – particularly trade with the West Indies. Although treaties failed to solve the problem, economic changes – changes in both countries – greatly reduced the issue's importance. For the Americans, it was the explo-sion of the transoceanic cotton trade – a product of the British industrial

---

177 Mahan, *Sea Power*, vol. 2, 431.   178 Hickey, *War of 1812*, 296.
179 Setser, *Commercial Reciprocity*, 186–187.

revolution — that came to dominate American overseas commerce. "On the British side, the West Indies lost their pre-eminent position as the nation's most valued colonies as the planters there struggled with rising costs and falling returns and with competition from newer areas in the East Indies and Latin America, and then finally had to endure the abolition of slavery."[180]

To close the story, although a military disaster for the United States, the war did have some intermediate and longer-term benefits to the nation. Increased wartime demand provided a stimulus for the growth of the man-ufacturing sector. In addition, throughout the war, capital flowed into New England; and a large fraction of that flow ended up in the hands of "knowledgeable entrepreneurs." Together, the flow and its recipients placed capital in the hands of talented entrepreneurs. Initially, the combination of capital and talented entrepreneurs underwrote the growth of the cotton textile industry; and, in the longer term, they provided the basic struc-ture that, over the following decades, allowed the nation to, first, develop and, then, exploit its comparative advantage in manufacturing.[181] Moreover, despite its outcome, the war proved that the United States was a nation in its own right — a nation with a relatively strong political structure and an emerging national economy. The nascent manufacturing sector made it pos-sible for the country to arm, feed, and clothe its military forces; the nation withstood the British attacks without the major assistance of European allies; and "it survived a three-year war without complete financial collapse. Never again would the republic have to depend on foreign powers for its survival."[182]

4b. The Quantitative Story

As one might expect, given the effectiveness of the British blockade after 1813, the terms of trade moved heavily against the United States. Having reached a favorable 106.2 (1790 = 100) in 1811, the index prepared by Douglass North began to decline as the war broke out; and, by 1814, it had reached 54.8 (see Table 3.11). With peace, however, recovery was swift; and in 1815, the measure stood at 95.6. The series on the tonnage of the merchant fleet, however, displays a much smaller decline during the

---

180 Stagg, *Mr. Madison's War*, 509–513.   181 Coles, *War of 1812*, 268–269.
182 Buel, *In Irons*, 256. Buel claims that the emerging manufacturing sector was, at least in part, a product of the embargo and the era of non-intercourse. See Davis and Irwin, "Trade Disruptions," for a more reserved evaluation.

Table 3.14. *Imports, Exports, Home Consumption, and Stocks of Cotton in Great Britain, 1811–1820*
(Bales)

	Imports into Great Britain						Exports from Great Britain	Consumption in Great Britain	Stocks in Great Britain 12/31
Year	United States	Brazil	Mediterranean	West Indies &c	East Indies &c	Total			
1811	128,192	118,514	974	63,905	14,646	326,231	5,500	285,830	378,900
1812	95,331	98,704	2,012	62,551	2,607	261,205	7,500	309,700	322,900
1813	37,720	137,168	1,899	71,320	1,429	249,536	37,000	344,130	191,300
1814	48,853	150,930	2,740	72,060	13,048	287,631	26,300	347,530	105,100
1815	203,051	91,055	1,291	51,549	22,357	369,303	36,200	325,100	113,100
1816	166,077	128,450	1,272	47,963	30,670	374,432	29,300	337,400	115,800
1817	199,669	114,518	120	44,752	120,202	479,261	26,700	407,000	161,300
1818	207,580	162,499	2,717	48,274	247,659	668,729	55,500	422,700	351,800
1819	205,161	125,415	1,329	29,971	184,259	546,135	66,800	434,300	396,800
1820	302,395	180,086	2,515	28,732	57,923	571,651	28,400	466,900	473,100

Source: Thomas Ellison, *The Cotton Trade of Great Britain* (London: Frank Cass: 1968, first published in 1886), appendix table 1.

war (see Table 3.5). Total documented gross tons had stood at 1,270,000 in 1812 (it had been 1,233,000 the year before), but tonnage declined to 1,167,000 in 1813, and to 1,159,000 in 1814 (a fall of about 9 percent from 1812), before rebounding to 1,368,000 in 1815 and to a pre-1820 peak of 1,400,000 two years later.[183] Of that 1812 to 1814 decline, more than 75 percent is accounted for by foreign tonnage, as opposed to tonnage deployed in coastwise trade or commercial fishing vessels. Moreover, as a fraction of the total, the figure for foreign shipping continued to decline over the remainder of the decade. Foreign shipping had accounted for 60 percent of the total in 1812 and for 58 percent in 1814. By 1820, however, the figure was only about 46 percent. The American economy was changing. Because tonnage of ships resting in port may still be registered, the effectiveness of the British blockade is almost certainly better measured by the data on the real value of exports and imports, and those figures provide a description of an even more efficient British naval effort. In 1811, the value of real exports stood at $47.7 million, by 1814 the value had fallen to $5.4 million,

---

183 Of some interest, although not relevant to this study, the figure for documented tonnage fell to 1,225,000 in 1818. It did not reach the 1817 level again until 1825. That movement, however, may reflect nothing but changes in the way the data are calculated. See Census, *Historical Statistics*, vol. 2, 75.

a decline of more than 88 percent. Moreover, whereas domestic exports had accounted for 74 percent of the total in 1811, they accounted for 98 percent in 1814. The data for the real value of imports also underscores the effectiveness of the blockade. The real value of those imports declined by 91 percent – from $59.8 million in 1812 to $5.6 million in 1814 (see Tables 3.6 and 3.7).[184]

In England, the economic impact of the decline in the imports of American cotton was far less than it had been during the embargo – the British had proved very effective in increasing the range of their suppliers. By 1811, imports of American cotton represented less than 40 percent of the British supply. Thus, between 1812 and 1814, although imports from the United States declined about 50 percent, total British imports of cotton remained above their 1812 level (see Table 3.14).

---

184 For a recent argument that the British blockade was not as successful as argued by Mahan, see Wade G. Dudley, *Splitting the Wooden Wall: The British Blockade of the United States, 1812–1815* (Annapolis: Naval Institute Press, 2003). His major criticism is that the British did not provide sufficient vessels to achieve an effective blockade.

4

The North Blockades the Confederacy, 1861–1865

1. INTRODUCTION

In Chapter 2, the British blockade of the French coast during most of the nearly one hundred years of continuous warfare was shown to be a "defensive blockade." That is, the English defended their country by deploying their fleets off the French ports to prevent that country's naval vessels from putting to sea and attacking the British coast and its colonies. During the American Civil War, the United States "stationed her fleets off the southern ports, not because she feared for her own, but to break down the Confederacy by isolation from the rest of the world, and ultimately by attacking the ports." Although the method was the same as that earlier employed by the British, the purpose of the Northern blockade was "offensive" rather than "defensive."[1]

Much has been written about the Civil War blockade; few historical events have been the subject of more academic controversy. For example, the historian Allan Nevins concludes that "To the east and south on the Atlantic and Gulf coasts the blockade had stiffened until near the end it was perhaps the major element in garroting the South." He reports the words of the Civil War soldier-journalist, T. C. DeLeon, that by 1863 "the blockade had become so thoroughly effective that blankets and shoes had almost given out, and a large portion of the army was barefoot."[2] In a similar vein, Francis B. C. Bradlee writes, "As a military measure, the blockade was of vital

---

1 A. T. Mahan, *The Influence of Sea Power Upon History, 1660–1783* (New York: Dover, 1987; first published 1890), 87. The most recent study of the blockade is by David G. Surdam, *Northern Naval Superiority and the Economics of the American Civil War* (Columbia: University of South Carolina Press, 2001), which brings together seven of his published essays on the topic. Surdam's detailed examination of the blockade and the cotton market represent the necessary starting point for future analysis.

2 Allan Nevins, *The War for the Union: Vol. 4, The Organized War to Victory, 1864–1865* (New York: Charles Scribner's Sons, 1971), 221–222, 272.

importance in the operations of the war; and there is no doubt that without it the South would have won its independence." In the absence of the blockade "the South could have kept on fighting indefinitely; the 'Peace Party' at the North, always powerful in influence and numbers, would have been immensely strengthened. France and England would probably have been led to recognize the government of Jefferson Davis, which of course would have meant its success."[3] At the other extreme, Robert Doughty and Harold E. Raugh Jr., quoting the work of Stephen Wise, note that "[t]he Confederate soldiers had the equipment and food needed to meet their adversaries. Defeat did not come from the lack of material; instead the Confederacy simply no longer had the manpower to resist, and the nation collapsed." The study of embargos by Doughty and Raugh concludes that, while the blockade did have some "devastating effect on the South's economy," it did not weaken the South's war effort as much as sometimes believed. "The Union naval blockade of the Confederate States was, therefore, of limited success."[4]

In the most recent study of the blockade, David Surdam states that "although the blockade failed to 'starve' the Confederacy of all necessary war materiel, it may have constricted the supply and therefore impeded the Confederacy's war-making efforts." More important, however, were two "important achievements: disrupting intraregional trade and denying the Confederacy badly needed revenue from exporting raw cotton and other staple products."[5] The former resulted from the failures of the southern railroad system, but the cause of the decline in the exports of cotton remains debated.

Because the South possessed almost no merchant marine, its navy was not faced with the task of providing for the oceanwide protection of a merchant fleet. Instead, its major assignments involved coastal and river defense and attempts to break the Northern blockade. For the Northern navy, not surprisingly, its assignments reflect the other side of the coin – there was no need to patrol the open seas; instead the navy attempted "to seal the Confederacy off completely from the outside world" and "to cooperate with the army in operations on the coasts and rivers of the Confederacy."[6] The blockade had two equally important objectives: first, to cut off the imports

3 Francis B. C. Bradlee, *Blockade Running During the Civil War; And the Effect of Land and Water Transportation on the Confederacy* (Salem: Essex Institute, 1925), 6, 163.
4 See Stephen R. Wise, *Lifeline of the Confederacy: Blockade Running during the Civil War* (Columbia: University of South Carolina Press, 1988), 7, 226. Robert A. Doughty and Harold E. Raugh Jr., "Embargoes in Historical Perspective," *Parameters*, 21 (Spring 1991), 22.
5 Surdam, *Northern Naval Superiority*, 6. See also pages 1–8, 206–209.
6 Peter J. Parish, *The American Civil War* (New York: Holmes & Meier, 1975), 420.

of manufactured goods, especially munitions of war; and, second, to prevent the export of cotton – the main source of Southern income.[7]

In the remainder of this chapter, we will, first, briefly summarize the blockade strategy of the North and the antiblockade strategy of the South and discuss the effectiveness of their policies and, second, attempt to provide some measures of the effectiveness of the blockade.

2. THE MARITIME STRATEGIES AND POLICIES OF THE NORTH AND SOUTH: 1861–1865

2(1). A Brief History of the Blockade

In a proclamation issued on April 19, 1861, President Lincoln declared a naval blockade of the coast south of South Carolina; "and, eight days later extended the blockade to the North Carolina and Virginia coasts." The proclamation specified that any "vessels attempting to enter or leave blockaded ports would be warned first," and if they attempted to evade the blockade, they would be captured and confiscated. "It was a fantastic gesture, to attempt to patrol better than 3,500 miles of coast with a few dozen ships, and Navy Secretary Welles was among those who hooted at the idea." Moreover, Welles and other well-informed Americans were not alone in their beliefs. Across the Atlantic "nearly every one, including the highest naval authorities abroad, considered that the blockade could not possibly be rigorously enforced, and that it would result in what is known as a 'paper blockade,' which that doubtful science known as 'International Law' does not consider binding." However, Lincoln's "proclamation remained in force, and at the end of April," when sufficient vessels had been assembled to enforce the blockade at Hampton Roads, Virginia, a "more formal announcement of the blockade, with notice to foreign ships," was made at that port.[8] On April 13, two events occurred that were to become major milestones in the "war between the states." First, Fort Sumter fell to what were to become the Confederate forces. Second, the union vessel *Sabine* officially began to blockade the harbor at Pensacola. Although there were other ships in the blockading fleet, it was the *Sabine* that had been assigned the responsibility for closing the port to commerce.[9] Although there were

---

7 Bradlee, *Blockade Running*, 163–165.
8 Bradlee, *Blockade Running*, 9–10; Virgil Carrington Jones, *The Civil War at Sea: Vol. 1, January 1861–March 1862* (New York: Holt, Rinehart, Winston, 1960), 91.
9 Jones, *Civil War at Sea*, vol. 1, 82.

many questions still to be answered – some of which remain unanswered today – Lincoln's much-maligned blockade had been put into effect.

As time passed, in April and May, the blockade of Pensacola tightened. Six ships and a schooner made up the blockading fleet, and the captains were given orders to search all vessels coming into the harbor for munitions. By the end of May, a thin and leaky "blockade extended along the entire Southern coast, from Fort Monroe to the Gulf of Mexico." The blockade at Pensacola was far from airtight, and at other ports on the Atlantic coast it was even less effective. The summer of 1861 still found the blockade a 'token threat,' although the Union attempted to "bluff both Confederate and foreign ships into staying away." Under international law, every Southern port was notified of its effective date; however, the Atlantic squadron had only twenty-two vessels to blockade a coast that included ports such as Norfolk, Beaufort, Wilmington, Charleston, Port Royal, Savannah, and Key West; and there were less than half that many attached to the Gulf squadron to cut off access to Pensacola, Mobile, New Orleans, Galveston, and the intervening coast line. Proclamations do not equal enforcement, and the available vessels could not cover anywhere near the 3,549 miles of coastline (the longest blockade ever deployed by any nation). Moreover, the success of the blockade runner *Adeline* – a vessel that arrived in Savannah amid cheering crowds in early July 1861 – proved that it was possible to use Nassau (a seaport in the Bahamas, a British colony protected by that country's military) as an intermediate point for transshipping neutral commerce from Europe; and, over the next few weeks, Bermuda, Havana, and Matamoras were added to the list of way stations. Moreover, at the same time, intelligence from overseas alerted the Union that, in Europe, vessels were being converted into blockade runners to help supply the Confederacy.[10] Although in a five-month period in late 1861 and early 1862 only fifteen thousand stand of arms reached the South, the number rose to nearly fifty thousand in the following four months.[11] It began to appear that a successful blockade was beyond the reach of the Union.

Over the months leading up to November 1863, "blockade-running developed into a science, carried on by vessels built abroad especially for the purpose of slipping through the cordon of Union ships lying in watch off the Southern coast." The new runners were long (often nine times their width), low (to avoid detection), side-wheel steamers of five to six hundred

---

10 Jones, *Civil War at Sea*, vol. 1, 104–105, 119, 165–166, 168–169.
11 Virgil Carrington Jones, *Civil War at Sea, Vol. 2, March 1862–July 1863* (New York: Holt, Rinehart, Winston, 1962), 247.

tons. "They burned a smokeless coal" and, when running the blockade, they traveled without lights, "the binnacle and fireroom hatches carefully covered, and steam released under water. In daylight they could scarcely be seen a matter of yards away."[12]

Despite the evidence of the quantitative success of the new blockade-runners, as early as February 1862 the blockade of the Southern coast, though still as leaky as a colander, was beginning to have some effect.[13] Moreover, as winter moved into spring, the U.S. navy had begun to join and operate with small bodies of army troops that were occupying parts of the Southern territories. As a result, blockading vessels were able to use these occupied sectors as bases of operation; and there was no longer the need to withdraw blockading vessels to Northern ports for repairs and coal. By the spring of 1862, all the squadrons were well provided with bases.[14]

As a result, by 1863, the blockade was rapidly becoming almost as effective as the Union strategists had hoped for. Although runners still did get through, the fraction of successful runs was growing fewer in number almost every month. "The best available figures, which may be open to question, show that one out of ten blockade runners were taken in 1861, one out of eight in 1862 and one out of four, in 1863." The ratio for 1864 was not more than one out of three, and in 1865, one in two.[15] The blockade had become effective, but, perhaps, in a way that the strategists had not really anticipated. Imports from Europe continued to reach some Southern ports until almost the end of the war. For example, during the six months from June through November 1864, Charleston and Wilmington, together, received from Europe "over 500,000 pairs of shoes, 300,000 blankets, 3.5 million pounds of meat, 1.5 million pounds of lead, 2 million pounds of saltpeter, 50,000 rifles, and 43 cannons," plus large amounts of other essential items. Thus, the blockade probably did not weaken the war effort as much as had been thought. However, the blockade did sharply curtail the import of other manufactured goods; and, thus, it helped touch off a severe, and a morale-devastating, inflation. Of even greater importance, however, was the impact of the blockade and the Southern reduction of cotton production on the export of Southern cotton – the South's international "coin

12 Virgil Carrington Jones, *Civil War at Sea: Vol. 3, July 1863–November 1865* (New York: Holt, Rinehart, Winston, 1962), 74–75.
13 Parish, *American Civil War*, 167.   14 Bradlee, *Blockade Running*, 164–165.
15 Allan Nevins, *The War for the Union: Vol. 3, The Organized War, 1863–1864* (New York: Charles Scribner's Sons, 1971), 28, 333. Nevins is citing the work of Frank Lawrence Owsley, *King Cotton Diplomacy: Foreign Relations of the Confederate States of America* (Chicago: University of Chicago Press, 1931), 285.

Table 4.1. *British Cotton Imports, 1860–1865 (000 bales)*

Year	U.S.	Imports From Other Countries	Total
1860	2,581	786	3,367
1861	1,842	1,194	3,036
1862	72	1,373	1,445
1863	132	1,800	1,932
1864	198	2,389	2,587
1865	462	2,293	2,755
1861–1865	5,287	9,835	15,122
	(Percent of Total)		
1860	76.7	23.3	100.0
1861	60.7	39.3	100.0
1862	5.0	95.0	100.0
1863	6.8	93.2	100.0
1864	7.7	92.3	100.0
1865	16.8	83.2	100.0
1861–1865	35.0	65.0	100.0

Source: Thomas Ellison, *The Cotton Trade of Great Britain* (London: Frank Cass, 1968; first published in 1886), appendix table 1.

of the realm." Exports to Britain fell from about 2.8 million bales during the eleven months from September 1860 to July 1861, a monthly average of about 255,000 bales, to a total of about 400,000 bales during the last three full years of the War, a monthly average of slightly more than 11,000 bales. The new blockade-runners were not well designed to carry bulk commodities (see Table 4.1).[16]

There was yet one more economic effect of the blockade that, until recent work by David Surdam, has received relatively little attention. Although, in 1860, with more than nine thousand miles of track, the Confederacy could boast more total miles than most European countries, once the blockade was in place the system suffered both from weakness in the system's design and from the original choice of the physical capital deployed. Both weaknesses were, in large part, the product of the South's prewar dependence on the much less expensive coastal and river transportation systems. In the years before 1861, the rail system had been largely designed and deployed to supplement and "fill in the gaps" in the waterborne network. By the blockade, the Union Navy reduced Southern railroad capacity, by greatly increasing

16 Doughty and Raugh, "Embargoes," 22; Wise, *Lifeline*, 7.

the demand for shipments by rail via "the blockade-induced loss of water-borne transport" between Confederate ports. In addition, the blockade, combined with Union military victories at Memphis, New Orleans, and Vicksburg, badly disrupted internal river transportation.[17]

Moreover, given the system's design, the increase in shipments diverted to the railroads by the blockade, meant that the railroad's carrying capacity diminished rapidly. In April 1863, the officer charged with monitoring the railroads "detailed the estimated freight capacity for thirty-four of the key Southern railroads. Fourteen of them were only able to run one or fewer trains in each direction per day. None of the lines were able to run more than three trains in each direction per day. The daily tonnage capacity was equally distressing." Thus, the failure of the Southern railroads contributed significantly to the Confederate defeat; and the railroads failure can be traced, in large part, to the blockade. "The Southern railroad system probably was incapable of efficiently supplying the troops and civilians, but the Union naval blockade helped stymie attempts to improve the existing railroads and compounded the inherent inadequacies of these railroads."[18]

The blockade also impacted the South's railways in a less direct fashion. Even with aid from the British and French, it is unlikely that the Confederacy could have been victorious in a prolonged naval race with the North. Given that the new ironclads were quickly making the North's wooden fleet obsolete in the first years of the war, it might have gained an initial superiority. The blockade of the mouth of the Mississippi forced the Southern shipbuilders in New Orleans, "to transport iron and machinery from Virginia and the eastern Confederacy by rail." Moreover, those eastern regions were not endowed with large supplies of iron ore, and the rolling mills that would be capable of turning ore into the two-inch plate that ironclads required. Thus, the blockade, by reducing imports from Europe also diminished the chances of the South deploying a number of the new naval vessels.[19]

The blockade was, however, financially costly; and, because of those costs, the Federal Navy began its gradual reduction of the forces needed on the

17 Surdam, *Northern Naval Superiority*, 39, 53, 72–84, 89, 185–186.

18 Surdam, *Northern Naval Superiority*, 83–84. For a recent argument that the failure of the southern railroads in the Civil War was primarily due to defects of management, see John E. Clark Jr., *Railroads in the Civil War: The Impact of Management in Victory and Defeat* (Baton Rouge: Louisiana State University Press, 2001).

19 Surdam, *Northern Naval Superiority*, 88–90. For example, the New Orleans shipbuilders began to construct an ironclad, the *Mississippi*; however, the vessel was not completed in time to contest Admiral Farragut's attack on that city; and the still-unfinished vessel was destroyed to prevent its capture.

blockade even before the army started demobiliziation.[20] "After the fall of Fort Fisher in North Carolina in January and Wilmington in late February, 1865," naval forces were cut back. In the case of vessels assigned to the blockade, by May 1, "squadrons in home waters were reduced by half," and "the Potomac Flotilla and the Mississippi Squadron were discontinued." Thus, of the 471 vessels assigned to blockade duty in January 1865, only thirty steamers and receiving ships of the blockaders were still on duty in mid-July.[21] "On June 23, 1865, President Andrew Johnson officially ended the blockade. From the first run of the *Bermuda* to the *Lark's* final escape from Galveston, just under 300 steamers tested the blockade. Out of approximately 1,300 attempts, over 1,000 were successful."[22] During the war, 1,149 blockade-runners were captured; of that total, 210 were steamships. In addition, 355 vessels, including 85 steamships, were burned, sunk, driven ashore, or otherwise destroyed, making a total of 1,504 vessels of all classes that were lost. "According to a low estimate, the value of these vessels and their cargoes was thirty-one millions of dollars."[23] "The average lifetime of a blockade runner was just over four runs, or two round trips."[24]

2(2). The Blockade and International Law

It should be remembered that originally seven nations (England, France, Austria, Russia, Sardinia, Turkey, and Prussia) and then, over the next four decades, most other developed countries (a group that did not, however, include the United States) were signators to the Declaration of Paris of 1856 – the first formal attempt to convert what, until then, had been international common law into something akin to a body of international statute law. That Declaration had "abolished privateering, announced that a neutral flag covered all enemy goods save contraband and that neutral goods are not subject to capture, and accepted the usual legal requirement of effectiveness

---

20 Over the course of the war, the Union commissioned almost seven hundred vessels, and many were, at one time or another, assigned to blockade duty. "Many of them were converted merchantmen armed with a few guns" and were deployed as pickets – vessels whose assignments were limited to sounding the alarm when a blockade-runner was spotted. The pursuit would then be carried out by more conventional warships or captured blockade-runners. During the same period, the total Union government expenditures on naval activities amounted to some $567 million; a figure that represented something over eight percent of the Union's total wartime expenditures of $6.8 billion. Surdam, *Northern Naval Superiority*, 206. Nevins, *War for the Union*, vol. 4, 368.
21 Nevins, *War for the Union*, vol. 4: 368.
22 Stephen R. Wise, *Lifeline*, 221. See also Table 4.15.
23 Bradlee, *Blockade Running*, 162–163. See also Table 4.15.
24 Wise, *Lifeline*, 221.

as is the basis for recognition of a blockade."[25] It should not, therefore, be surprising that there were still important questions to be "ironed out" when the War between the American North and the South erupted. The Civil War blockade raised four major questions concerning the interpretation of international law. First, there was the question of defining an ineffective blockade and the related issue of when, because it is or has become ineffective, a blockade could be regarded as legally broken. Second, because a blockade was considered a weapon of international war between sovereign powers, it was necessary to define a sovereign power. Third, there was the question of the nature of a "continuous voyage"; a concept that had been accepted by most European nations but not by the United States. And, fourth, was the question of the legal right of neutral powers to build vessels for belligerents.

Even before the Declaration of Paris, "the law of nations held that blockades must be effective to be recognized," and statistics collected almost daily at every Rebel port proved that the North maintained nothing more than a paper blockade. "From April 29 through August 20, 1861, four hundred ships had entered and cleared Southern ports and sheer numbers proved of that there was no legal interdiction of commerce." Although the North continued to insist that the blockade was legal, the leaders in the South were certain that the European nations would accept the obvious fact that the blockade was not legal.[26] Thus, in early 1862, the Confederate commissioners to England and to France – James M. Mason and John Slidell – were instructed to ask both for diplomatic recognition of the Confederacy and for the termination of what the North declared was a "legal" blockade – a blockade that the Commissioners insisted was ineffective, "and, according to the Declaration of Paris and international law, not binding on neutrals."[27] Again, after a night attack on the northern fleet off Charleston, "the Confederates sent out a vessel with some foreign consuls on board" as invited guests. The consuls found no evidence of any blockading vessels in the area, and issued a statement to that effect. "On the strength of this declaration some Southern authorities claimed that the blockade was technically broken, and could not be technically re-established without a new notification."[28] In these and other instances, France was inclined to accept the Southern position; but that country was unwilling to act unilaterally.

25 Frank E. Vandiver, *Their Tattered Flag* (New York: Harper and Row, 1970), 102.
26 Vandiver, *Tattered Flag*, 102–103.   27 Owsley, *King Cotton*, 226.
28 Mahan, *Influence of Sea Power*, 85.

The British government – a government with, perhaps, a longer time horizon, or at least a government that considered both short- and long-term interests – concluded that, "if a somewhat loose and fallible blockade such as the Union practiced in 1861 received international approval, it would set an invaluable precedent"; and, in the future, this northern precedent could possibly give Britain an immense advantage in the future.[29] In addition, the British government had other concerns. First, the members of the Cabinet concluded that if they did not honor the blockade, their merchant marine might well become a victim of marauding Northern naval vessels. In addition, although they were probably less concerned than they were about the loss of cotton, they were apprehensive about the loss of Northern wheat; there also were worries about the possibility of war with the North, about the potential loss of the profits that they were earning from the sales of arms and ammunitions to both sides, the possibility of a Northern invasion of Canada, and the possibility that involvement might result in political destabilization on the continent. Finally, they realized that, within Britain, there was believed to be a widespread dislike of slavery. "Probably no one factor by itself deterred intervention," but, when all arguments were counted and weighed against the potential benefits of intervention, the government quickly decided to remain neutral.[30] As early as the end of 1861, Lord John Russell, the British Foreign Secretary, "gave answer that he considered the blockade as legal and binding."[31] Thus, "for reasons of potential self-interest, Europe accepted the blockade."[32] The European reaction was an early proof that, scarcely half a decade after the Declaration of Paris, national self-interest proved stronger than statute-based international law. That result was to be repeated time and time again from the 1860s (and before) to the twenty-first century. It should, however, be kept in mind that worries about the potential repercussions of a cutoff of southern cotton continued to haunt both members of the Union government and a substantial number of influential northerners until at least the end of 1863.[33] Those concerns, in turn, did influence the structure and direction of northern policy in regards to cotton exports throughout most of the war.

In the case of Britain, these political and moral arguments must have been very powerful for, initially, that country's view of the North was very

---

29 Parish, *American Civil War*, 408.
30 Surdam, *Northern Naval Superiority*, 199–200. On the mixed British reaction at the start of the Civil War, see R. J. M. Blackett, *Divided Hearts: Britain and the American Civil War* (Baton Rouge: Louisiana State University Press, 2001), Blackett describes the British as mainly antislavery and antiwar.
31 Owsley, *King Cotton*, 253.   32 Vandiver, *Tattered Flag*, 102–103.
33 Surdam, *Northern Naval Superiority*, 195–197.

negative. In 1862, the popular agitation against the United States was so great that it spread to "all the British possessions." The U.S. consul in Nassau, the Bahamas, "became so intimidated that he was afraid to leave the consulate, and at night [N]egro roustabouts serenaded him by standing under his window and singing ribald parodies on the American flag, calling out to him, 'Say, you's got too many stars in dat flag.'"[34] Over time, their views did change – changes that reflected, first, the September 1862 Preliminary Emancipation Proclamation; and, then, in January 1863 the second proclamation – a proclamation that fulfilled the promise of the first legal announcement. At that time the Duke of Argyll said:

It is very easy to point out the logical inconsistency of the Proclamation with an abstract principle on the question of Slavery. But the North has never professed to fight for the abolition of Slavery. I have always looked to the irresistible tendency of events, rather than to the intentions of the North, for the Anti-Slavery effects of the War. Of that tendency – and of its irresistible character – the President's Proclamation is a signal proof – crowning many other proofs, which have been accumulating rapidly as the war went on. Halting, imperfect, and inconsistent as the Proclamation is – interpreted strictly – it has nevertheless been hailed by the Ablititionist Party as a great – irrevocable step – towards their 'Platform.'[35]

In terms of the questions raised by the "sovereign power" issue, the legal arguments were equally muddied. The North could have merely declared the Southern ports closed, but Seward, the Secretary of State, preferred to deploy a blockade because, despite the legal ambiguities about the nature of sovereignty, "Britain and France were much less likely to accept the idea of closing the ports, and that a blockade laid down recognized procedures which all neutrals could accept and follow." Lincoln accepted his opinion. Lincoln and Seward's refusal to recognize a sovereign South, initially undermined their legal position on the issue of sovereignty; however, in 1863, their position was granted legal support (at least in American courts) when the Supreme Court held "that the conflict had a two-fold character as rebellion and war, and that the United States Government could exercise both sovereign and belligerent rights in dealing with the South."[36]

Again, the debates over the issue of the doctrine of a "continuous voyage" threw little light on the role of international law. One of the central reasons for the American government's refusal to become a signator to the Declaration of Paris was that declaration's approval of the concept of a continuous

34 Owsley, *King Cotton*, 325. 35 Vandiver, *Tattered Flag*, 151–152.
36 Parish, *American Civil War*, 406–407.

voyage (i.e., that a vessel could be classified as violating a blockade, if there was proof that the ultimate destination of the cargo was the blockaded port, even if the vessel itself was only on its way to an intermediate destination). However, within a year of the time the Civil War began, the United States extended its blockade to include continuous voyages. In April 1862, the British vessel *Bermuda* was seized; "and the resulting court ruling caused an immediate change in the methods of shipping goods to Nassau or any other neutral port near the Confederacy. No longer did the British flag provide immunity. By the court's decision, a ship could be stopped anywhere on the high seas and seized if her papers gave any hint that the ultimate destination of her cargo was the Confederacy."[37]

Today, after the experience of two world wars, "it seems odd that this doctrine was even questioned." A century and a half ago, however, the school of international lawyers condemned "the proposition that a belligerent might seize a neutral ship for attempted breach of a blockade thousands of miles away from the blockaded coast." The problem was that the international law had been written in the days of sail; and the blockading fleet was not faced by runners operating fast, difficult to detect and to capture, steamships operating between the intermediate neutral ports and Southern harbors.[38] Its new role as a blockading power had replaced the United States' earlier role as the home of potential blockade-runners; and the Americans were quick to grasp this point. The British problems were, of course, the reverse. They had agreed to the doctrine; but when, on February 25, 1863, the U.S.S. *Vanderbilt* seized the British ship *Peterhoff* anchored near St. Thomas, Britain was quick to denounce the capture. Their government claimed that both the *Peterhoff* and the entire trade through Matamoras (a neutral Mexican port bordering Texas) "did not fall within the limits of the 'continuous voyage' doctrine," as it had been approved by Britain. The British argued that "this doctrine held that contraband going to a belligerent via neutral ports could be seized," but it did not cover goods that were moved from the neutral port to the blockaded country, not by sea, but overland. The British argued that it was not possible, before the fact, for the blockading power to determine which goods would be consumed in Mexico and which would be transshipped to the South. The United States held that the doctrine covered the case, because, before the war, the trade through

---

37 Wise, *Lifeline*, 66. "Because of this ruling, some shippers backed off from carrying Southern-bound cargoes, but the majority merely repacked their goods and altered manifests to show Nassau as the freight's final destination."

38 Bradlee, *Blockade Runners*, 34–35.

Matamoras was miniscule. "The war was the only reason for its present size." In the *Peterhoff* case (as well as in several others) the "courts later ruled that the trade such as carried on by the *Peterhoff* was legal, and no blockade was violated, because the United States could not lawfully blockade the Mexican half of the Rio Grande."[39] The British were pleased; the doctrine of the continuous voyage was amended; but, as we shall see, World War I was to drastically alter the British position.

Finally, the question of the right of a neutral to build vessels, including warships, for a belligerent came increasingly under scrutiny. The scrutiny was increased when Union agents discovered that the British firm of Laird was in the process of building a pair of rams that, if completed, were quite capable of sinking blockading vessels.

In 1816, the *Independence*, a vessel dispatched from Baltimore, had been armed and dispatched to Buenos Aires. The case of the *Independence* (renamed the *Santissima Trinidad*) was brought before Justice Story in 1822. He ruled: "The question as to the original illegal armament and outfit of the Independence may be dismissed in a few words. It is apparent that, though equipped as a vessel of war, she was sent to Buenos Ayres as a commercial venture, contraband indeed, but in no shape violating our laws or our national neutrality. If captured . . . during the voyage, she would have been justly condemned as a good prize. . . . But there is nothing in our laws or the laws of nations that forbids our citizens from sending armed vessels as well as munitions of war to foreign ports. It is a commercial adventure which no nation is bound to prohibit, and which only exposes the persons engaged in it to the penalty of confiscation . . ."[40]

Based on this and similar well-established American as well as British precedents, the British government, as reflected in the views of the Solicitor-General and that country's press, contended that Britain, as a neutral nation, had a right to arm and sell vessels of war to belligerents; that guns and powder were not different from warships.[41] This right, it was argued, "was applicable to the building of war vessels in England by the Confederacy," and the United States had no legal grounds of a complaint as long as these

---

39 Nevins, *War for the Union*, vol. 3, 367–368. "Several other ships, such as the *Agnes* and the *Magicienne*, were seized by the Navy while engaged in Mexican trade, but it was impossible" for the North to win in the courts.

40 Owsley, *King Cotton*, 429–433.

41 On October 10, 1863, the *Economist*, commenting on the decision in the case of the *Santissima Trinidad* wrote: "so far then, as mere international law and the obligations of neutrality are concerned, any British merchant might sell an 'Alabama' or an 'Alessandra' to any agent of the Confederate Government, just as he might sell an Armstrong or a Blakely rifled cannon to a Federal agent." *Economist*, October 10, 1863, quoted in Owsley, *King Cotton*, 431.

vessels did not use English ports as a point of departure against American commerce or the American Navy. "The main point was that no vessel was to leave England *armed* and *equipped* unless it was delivered first as an article of commerce at some Confederate port. Before the building or equipping of such a ship could be stopped . . . it would be necessary to find out the intent of the owners, that is, whether they intended to commence operations from the British port or whether they intended to carry the ship to the Confederate ports first and begin operations from there."[42]

The Solicitor-General went on to note that "the 'fitting-out' of a warship for the Confederacy or any belligerent, by England . . . was a violation of the British Foreign Enlistment Act, but not a violation of international law, and the violation of a municipal law such as the Foreign Enlistment Act was a matter for the British government alone − it was not America's business. Not that England would neglect the enforcement of the law, but she would insist on sufficient evidence as in any other municipal law before taking action which would entail losses to British subjects."[43] Unfortunately, it took a long time for the Northerners and the American minister to realize that "the British Government would risk severe legal and political penalties if it halted the building of great and costly ships on a mere suspicion that they might be used improperly."[44]

Despite the American indignation about the *Alabama*, it does appear that "the British Government in general tried honestly to enforce its long-standing neutrality legislation, which among other provisions forbade the construction and equipment in British harbors of ships for belligerents in any war in which Britain remained neutral." Although in this case its efforts were marked by "gross and culpable carelessness," in the end the British government did carry out reasonable enforcement.[45]

Even with no basis in international law, the Union government continued to pressure the British; and, as the tide of war shifted, the British began to listen. In early 1863, they held up delivery of the *Alexandra;* and, although that vessel was finally released, the handwriting was on the wall. Although the *Alabama* escaped to sea by a trick, in July, the British government either stopped the construction or refused to permit the delivery of the *Alexandra*

---

42 Owsley, *King Cotton*, 429. For the entire debate, see *Parliamentary Debates, Commons, Ser. 3*, vol. 170, 33–72.
43 Owsley, *King Cotton*, 429–430, 432.
44 Nevins, *War for the Union*, vol. 3, 499. For example, the elder Lair, owner of the firm that was constructing the rams, was a member of Parliament.
45 Allan Nevins, *The War for the Union, Vol. 2, War Becomes Revolution* (New York: Charles Scribner's Sons, 1960), 266.

(the gunboat being built by Fraser, Trenholm, and Company); of the ironclad that [Lt. James H.] North was having Thompson of Glasgow build, of the armed vessels built for [G. T.] Sinclair; and of the Laird rams, two powerful ironclads, that were obviously built for war. Ultimately, because the government could not legally interfere with private commercial ventures, the British solved the problem by buying the ships that were still in the shipyards and adding them to the Royal Navy. Thus, the Laird rams and the *Alexandra* were exchequered.[46]

It should be noted that, in the summer of 1861, in a somewhat similar and parallel vein, and, again, with British cooperation, the Confederates adopted a strategy that, if international law had been enforced, might well have helped them break the blockade. That ruse involved changing the registration of some of their vessels from U.S. to British ownership, thus technically classifying them – under the law – as neutrals. The vessels involved included the *Gondar*, the *Eliza Bonsall*, the *Alliance*, the *Emily*, the *St. Pierre*, and the *John Fraser* – a significant merchant fleet. The North's response was both rapid and devastating. Gideon Welles, the Secretary of the Navy, ruled that the transfers were fraudulent and "gave orders for the ships to be captured at sight, an action that would cause the question of ownership to be settled in court," but only after the war.[47]

2(3). Cotton Exports: From Weapons to Cash: Southern Strategies

Throughout most of the war, the Confederate government considered cotton the most effective weapon in their armory. A shortage of cotton, it was argued, might actually bring England and France into the war against the North; and, at minimum, it would cause the European countries to support the Southern effort to breach the Union blockade.

During the War, the South pursued three quite different strategies in regard to the export of cotton. In response to the deployment of the Union blockade, in April 1862, President Jefferson Davis, as part of a campaign "to charm England and Europe through public pronouncements" to believe that the South sought only peace and freedom and direct negotiations supported "a straightforward deal to France and to Europe: Confederate cotton for recognition of the Confederacy." He believed that European recognition of independence represented the most certain way to end the blockade. "Once the Confederacy was acknowledged, Lincoln's paper barrier would vanish

46 Vandiver, *Tattered Flag*, 230. Owsley, *King Cotton*, 420–424, 434.
47 Jones, *Civil War at Sea*, vol. 1, 169–170.

in a crush of international commerce. The assumption that cotton was king, a sure fulcrum of power, formed the initial basis for Southern diplomacy."[48] However, President Davis quickly came to realize that countries often have more than a single issue on their international policy agendas.

A second strategy involved the use of cotton exports as an economic weapon to force European recognition and support: in this case, it was the state governments and private citizens, not the Confederacy, that embargoed the export of cotton. "The effectiveness of the embargo, during the year 1861 and far into the winter of 1862, was complete." "It was, as the English had supposed, just as near air-tight as human effort could make it. No embargo in history has been any more strict." From September 1860 to January 1861, 1,488,004 bales of cotton had arrived at the ports of Memphis, New Orleans, Savannah, Mobile, and Charleston; from September 1861 to January 1862, although 4,490,586 bales had been grown during the first year of the war, the figure for arrivals at the enumerated ports was only 9,863 bales.[49] Although some states had passed laws embargoing cotton, many had not. In Charleston, for example, "the Committee of Public Safety, in conjunction with the local authorities, had prevented the exportation of cotton." Public discussion focused on the proposal to legally forbid the export of cotton until the blockade had been halted and independence granted. "The governors of most of the states had been actively opposed to the exportation of cotton, favoring an embargo as a means of coercing Europe, and especially had public safety committees in all seaports, backed by public opinion, been actively engaged in seeing that no vessel loaded with cotton should start through the blockade." Despite these views, although the Confederate Congress passed several laws dealing with cotton, none called for a total embargo. Thus, the embargo was "partly legal, but for the most part extra-legal or actually illegal." However, most European newspapers, including the *Economist*, reported, 'the exportation of cotton was forbidden in the Confederacy.'[50]

It has been argued, both by contemporaries and by subsequent scholars, that the decision to embargo the export of cotton was a disaster. These critics argue that President Davis could have exported enough cotton to Europe in 1861 to provide a solid financial infrastructure for the Confederate economy. This argument, is however, almost certainly fallacious. In the months before

---

48 Vandiver, *Tattered Flag*, 89. Thus, the belief in the political power of "King Cotton" preceded by one century OPEC's use of "King Oil." The relative success, at least in the short run, of "King Oil," suggests that whereas the South may have been less successful, the use of key raw materials as a political and economic weapon may have some potential.
49 Owsley, *King Cotton*, 43.   50 Owsley, *King Cotton*, 40–42.

the blockade became effective, in order to carry that much cotton out of the South would have required some four thousand vessels. Nor could the time period be extended. Once the blockade became effective, it would have required blockade-runners to move the cotton overseas; and, because the Confederacy had no warships to break the blockade, much of the cotton would probably have ended up in Northern prize-courts.[51]

Finally, as the financial noose began to tighten, the Confederate government began to issue "cotton bonds" (bonds that were supported by the stock of cotton in the Confederacy) and bonds that required the purchasers to collect their cotton in the South. Thus, the government was forced to change its export policy yet again.[52] Cotton began to flow overseas. It moved, at first, in a mix of private enterprise and state-owned blockade-runners, and later, as Confederate finances came increasingly under strain, in government-owned or government-regulated vessels. Many states owned blockade-runners that ran regular schedules to intermediate ports, exported state cotton, and imported state supplies. Because the supplies purchased by state-owned vessels added to the demand for supplies generated by the private runners, they drove up prices; and, thus, they contributed to the economic pressure placed on the Southern economy. Needless to say, their activities greatly annoyed many Confederate officials, including the Quartermaster General, the Chief of Ordnance, the Commissary General, and even the Secretary of War.[53]

By the end of 1863, many citizens, as well as the editors of some Southern newspapers, argued that, "had the Confederacy exported all the cotton which reached Europe through the blockade, it could have supplied its armies with all their needs and its citizens with necessities" with only a moderate increase in prices.[54] However, "President Davis had opposed open trading in cotton as long as it had any leverage as diplomatic blackmail." In the summer of 1863, "he relented, and approved the purchases of government blockade runners, government cotton, and the management of foreign and domestic transportation to expand importations. The best

---

51 Nevins, *War for the Union*, vol. 3, 336–337. If there had been no war, a portion of the Southern crop would have been exported to the North – a voyage that did not require vessels capable of crossing the Atlantic. If there had been no blockade, the crop could have been exported gradually over twelve months. Nevins raises the question, "Where would those vessels have been procured in the face of notification of the blockade?"
52 At first, the market for cotton bonds responded well. The bonds "attracted much attention, held around par for a time, and seemed a fine adjunct to the Southern quest for recognition." News of Gettysburg and Vicksburg, however, caused prices to plummet. The initial loan was for $15 million, but with falling prices, interest, and commissions it is likely that the Confederacy received only about $6 million in cash. Vandiver, *Tattered Flag*, 231–233.
53 Vandiver, *Tattered Flag*, 194.   54 Owsley, *King Cotton*, 416.

evidence of his approval was permission to use naval officers as blockade-running captains."[55]

The process of the Southern government's involvement in breaking the blockade continued to inch forward. In early February 1864, the Confederate Congress passed a bill that allowed the President "to regulate all foreign commerce." It gave the president control over the export of a wide range of commodities; and, in order to allow more room for needed imports, it "prohibited the importation of many luxury items." The bill took effect on the first of March. Four days later, a second bill was passed, that reinforced the first. The second bill "required all operators and shippers to make a declaration – giving the names of the vessel's owners, officers, crew, passengers, port of destination, and the quantity and value of the cargo before leaving a southern port." It also required that all vessels except those carrying cotton that supported the cotton bonds or that were under contract to the Confederacy, "were liable to have one-half of their inward and outward stowage taken by the government."[56]

Although the new system was helpful, in March 1865 the Confederate Congress, heavily influenced by a generalized demoralization – the product of fear of an imminent Union victory – and possessed by a willingness to put the blame directly on the president's shoulders, "abandoned the attempt to regulate blockade-running in the interest of the Confederate government and the war effort."[57]

2(4). The Failure of the King Cotton Strategy in Europe

The South's belief in the potential efficacy of cotton as an effective weapon in the war with the Union rested on an economic argument that was widely held, not only in the South, but in Europe and the North as well. Not only was the British textile industry the largest in the nation, but a very large percentage of the English population had come, directly and indirectly, to depend on that industry for its livelihood. The industry, in turn, drew its cotton almost entirely from the United States (see Tables 4.1 and 4.2). It has been estimated that the cotton mills directly employed about five hundred thousand workers, that "the subsidiary cotton industry (including

---

55 Vandiver, *Tattered Flag*, 231.
56 Wise, *Lifeline*, 145–146. The listed exports included cotton, tobacco, military and naval stores, rice, sugar, and molasses. The enumerated imports included brandy and spirits, carpets and rugs, carriages and carriage parts, furniture, marble, wallpaper, bricks, coconuts, gems, antiques, and coin collections. See also Owsley, *King Cotton*, 411–412.
57 Parish, *American Civil War*, 560.

Table 4.2. *British Cotton Imports, 1840–1858 (Pounds)*

Year	Total Imports into Great Britain	Imports from Southern U.S.	Imports from South as Percent of Total
1840	592,488,010	487,856,504	97.1
1841	487,992,355	358,240,964	73.4
1842	531,750,776	414,030,779	77.9
1843	637,193,116	574,738,520	90.2
1844	646,111,304	517,218,662	80.1
1845	721,979,955	626,650,412	86.8
1846	467,856,274	401,949,393	85.9
1847	474,707,615	364,599,291	76.8
1848	713,020,161	600,247,488	84.2
1849	755,469,012	634,504,050	84.0
1850	633,576,861	493,153,112	77.8
1851	757,379,749	596,638,962	78.8
1852	929,782,448	765,630,544	82.3
1853	895,279,749	658,451,796	73.5
1854	887,333,149	722,151,346	81.4
1855	891,751,952	681,629,424	76.4
1856	1,023,886,304	780,040,016	76.2
1857	969,318,896	654,758,048	67.5
1858	931,847,056	732,403,840	78.6

Source: Frank Lawrence Owsley, *King Cotton Diplomacy: Foreign Relations of the Confederate States of America* (Chicago: University of Chicago Press, 1931), 3.

the hosiery, cotton-lace and sewed muslin establishments) around 400,000 more," and that indirect employees ("warehousemen, stevedores, mechanics, bakers, and small trades people in the cotton districts") contributed about 150,000, a total of over 1,000,000 workers. If, as has been estimated, there were three dependents for each employee, the industry accounted for almost 20 percent of the British population.[58]

58 Owsley, *King Cotton*, 8–9. James A. B. Scherer, *Cotton as a World Power: A Study in the Economic Interpretation of History* (New York: Frederick A. Stokes, 1916), 263–264. On January 19, 1861, the editors of the *Economist* reported, "the cotton manufacture, from the first manipulation of the raw material to the last finish bestowed upon it, constitutes the employment and furnishes the sustenance of the largest portion of the population of Lancashire, North Cheshire, and Lanarkshire, of a considerable number in Derbyshire, Leicestershire, Nottinghamshire, and Yorkshire, and of scattered individuals in several other parts of England, Scotland and Ireland and if we take into account the subsidiary trades and occupations and add the dependent members of their families we may safely assume that nearer four than three million are dependent for their daily bread on this branch of our industry." In terms of the labor force, the textile workers represented about 12 percent of the nation's 10,520,000 person labor force. B. R. Mitchell and Phyllis Deane, *Abstract of British Historical Statistics* (Cambridge: Cambridge University Press, 1962), 60. For a rather thorough discussion of "King Cotton," see Surdam, *Naval Superiority*, 111–162.

The Confederate belief in the power of cotton was, however, not realized; and the explanation of that failure has at least two dimensions: one political and one economic. In terms of the first, as we have seen, British government policy was less affected by the short-run than it was by the longer-run implications of a decision to directly support the South; and, in addition, the government feared the loss of vessels in their merchant marine to Union raiders. Still, if the economy had been hit as hard as the employment figures suggest, it would have been difficult for the government to have continued to support its policy of non-interference. Thus, the economic issues become crucially important. In several ways, the overall economic impact was much much less than the "true believers" in the doctrine of King Cotton had assumed.

First, from the point of view of the South, the Civil War commenced at a very inopportune time. Even before Fort Sumter, the threat of a potential failure of the American cotton crop had led Lancashire mill owners to attempt to diversify their sources of supply. In 1858, they had organized the "Cotton Supply Association" – an organization designed to help stimulate cotton production in India, Egypt, and Brazil (see Table 4.3). Then, in 1860, the United States produced a record cotton crop; and the United Kingdom had imported 1,650,000 bales before the war broke out. Instead of a shortage, there was actually a glut of cotton; prices of cloth fell, and many of the mills were forced to shut down in 1861. "Mill owners even longed for an effective blockade to relieve the glut of the market."[59]

The U.S. government also moved to help relieve the expected shortage of cotton in the United Kingdom. In 1862, they fitted out a series of military expeditions whose primary mission was to seize cotton in captured Southern ports; that cotton was "afterwards doled out to England." The first ports to be declared to be open for trade were Beaufort, North Carolina; Port Royal, South Carolina; and New Orleans, Louisiana. "Licenses were granted to foreign vessels by United States consuls and to coasting vessels by the Treasury Department, and the blockade was relaxed so far as related

---

59 Scherer, *Cotton*, 264–265. India alone supplied imports of 563,200 bales in 1860. In 1862, Indian exports accounted for 1,072,439 bales of a total British importation of 1,445,065 bales (74 percent), in 1863 the figures were 1,390,700 and 1,932,200 (72 percent), and, in 1864, 1,798,600 and 2,587,100 (70 percent). Thomas Ellison, *The Cotton Trade of Great Britain* (London 1886), 80–105; Owsley, *King Cotton*, 571. See also Surdam, *Northern Naval Superiority*, 118–153, who argues against there being "a significant temporary or permanent downturn in the demand for American-grown raw cotton," suggesting difficulties in the cotton famine thesis. Also important was the trade diversion created by New York City's no longer being able to help with financing and distributing southern imports and exports. See Robert Greenhealgh Albion, *The Rise of New York Port, 1815–1860* (New York: Charles Scribner's Sons, 1939), 14, 95–121.

Table 4.3. *Cotton Imports to Great Britain, 1856–1860 to 1876–1880 (000 bales)*

Years	U.S.A.	Brazil	West Indies	India	Egypt	Total
1856 to 1860	3,678	153	35	540	162	4,568
1861 to 1865	1,281	201	73	1,380	418	3,353
Change 1856–60 to 1861–65	−2,397	48	38	840	256	−1,215
1866 to 1870	2,528	614	175	1,601	438	5,356
Change 1856–60 to 1866–70	−1,150	461	140	1,061	276	788
1871 to 1875	3,827	690	202	1,484	472	6,675
Change 1856–60 to 1871–75	149	537	167	944	310	2,107
1876 to 1880	5,015	256	92	1,090	469	6,922
Change 1856–60 to 1876–80	1,337	103	57	550	307	2,354

Source: Ellison, *Cotton Trade*, 99.

to those ports, except as 'to persons, property, and information contraband of war.'"[60]

Finally, Lancashire was not Great Britain; and although citizens in the midlands suffered, in other regions of Britain, war-based prosperity reigned. First, although the cotton industry suffered, profits in that industry's competitors soared. Sales and profits in both the linen and woolen industries – industries that had suffered and largely languished in the face of competition from cotton – reawakened, recaptured much of their lost ground, "reaped a unexpected harvest of gold." British farmers also shared in the prosperity.[61] Second, the munitions industry also "waxed fat and greasy" from the war. It has been estimated that the North and South together purchased some $100,000,000 worth of war supplies from Great Britain. That figure does not include the purchases of clothing, tents, shoes, and leather goods, industries that also were major beneficiaries of the war. Third, the blockade running business, despite substantial costs, also proved very profitable. It is estimated that the profits on the one million to the million-and-a-half bales of cotton exported through the blockade seldom netted profits of less than 300 percent, and goods (excluding munitions) that were exported through the blockade frequently netted profits of 500 percent; however,

60 Scherer, *Cotton*, 292–293.
61 In the case of linen, it is estimated that in the three years 1862, 1863, and 1864 realized profits were some £14,500,000 above the normal profits earned in the three years before the war, and profits for 1865 pushed the total to over £20,000,000. The estimates of excess profits for the woolen industry for the years 1862 through 1864 are £17,000,000, with 1865 yielding another £5,000,000. In addition, sheep farmers are estimated to have earned excess profits from raw wool that totaled £8,932,286 over the war years. Owsley, *King Cotton*, 573–576.

recent evidence suggests that, on average those profits were likely much
lower. Finally, and, perhaps most important to the British economy in the
long run, was the almost complete destruction of the American merchant
marine. That destruction was the product, either directly or indirectly, of
Confederate privateers and cruisers. At the beginning of the war, the U.S.
merchant marine, deploying almost six million tons, was practically as large
as the British fleet; it had doubled in size every decade since 1816; and,
in the transatlantic trade with Britain, American vessels represented almost
2.4 times as many tons as its competitor. In direct terms, during the war,
Confederate cruisers and privateers sank or captured some two hundred
ships, in the process destroying about $30 million dollars in property. In indi-
rect terms, however, the costs to the Americans and the profits to Britain
were even greater. Marine insurance rates rose to levels that were higher
than those that had prevailed during the War of 1812, when the British
had effectively blockaded the American coast. Thus, in the minds of both
American and European merchants and shippers, the hazard posed by the
Confederacy appeared so great that they could not be induced to ship their
merchandise on American vessels at any price. As a result, during the war,
the Northern vessels that had not been sunk or captured largely remained in
port; and, at war's end, some 65 percent of the tonnage that was sold went
to English firms. By the end of the war, as is still true today, the American
merchant marine was, for all intents and purposes, extinct; and, from the
1860s until the start of World War II, "Britain ruled the waves."[62] From
one point of view, British economic distress has been exaggerated. "In the
kingdom as a whole the number of persons on relief did not rise materially
during the war, for as heavy as was the unemployment in textile areas, other
industries enjoyed a compensating boom."[63]

2(5). Blockade Runners: Firms and Profits

Once the embargo was lifted, the Confederate government encouraged
blockade running. However, because that government had initially chosen
not to become *directly* involved in blockade running, it was private sector
entrepreneurs who quickly recognized the potential profits in this new, and
what was widely viewed as an inherently lucrative, industry. Hardly had the
blockade been deployed before both individual entrepreneurs and, perhaps
somewhat surprisingly, firms that were organized specifically for the purpose
of blockade-running, entered the industry. "These concerns ranged in size

62 Owsley, *King Cotton*, 573–576.   63 Nevins, *War for the Union*, vol. 2, 263.

from single-ship ventures to large stockholding companies."[64] The importance of companies, as opposed to individual enterprises, is underscored by
the evidence of the blockade-runners that ran in or out of Charleston over
the course of the war (see Table 4.4). Of the total of eighty-seven vessels,
forty-five (52 percent) were owned by such firms; and in terms of the number of steamers running the blockade; the figure was forty-one of sixty-seven
(61 percent).[65] Nor were the blockade-runners solely Confederate enterprises. Although the South contributed a substantial number of vessels and
firms, the Southerners were forced to share the trade with entrants from
England, Canada, Cuba, and the North.

Most English ventures were organized as formal firms; and those firms
first entered the new industry in early 1862. Although the firms were well
financed and employed steam vessels, their managers and captains underestimated the effectiveness of the blockade; and, as a result, the firms often
failed.[66] "Among the first, and least successful, of the British-based ventures was the Navigation Company of Liverpool." Its owners sent six fully
loaded steamers to run the blockade, and all were lost.[67] Another of the
early entrants was Pearson and Company – a firm owned and operated by
Zachariah C. Pearson, a merchant, shipowner, and mayor of Hull. Between
early May and early August 1862, the firm dispatched seven vessels to the
Confederacy. Six were captured by the blockading fleet, and the seventh ran
aground. By the end of the year, the firm was forced to declare bankruptcy.[68]

As the war progressed, however, the foreign firms obtained better vessels;
and their captains came to better recognize the problems raised by the
blockading forces. Thus, despite captures, "losses failed to deter investors";
and the number of blockade-runners rapidly increased.[69] "Freight rates were
enormous, ranging from $300 to $1,000 a ton. But they had to be high in
order to meet expenses. Wages were also high, varying according to the reputation of the ship captain. The more successful might receive $5,000 for a
run, half of it paid in advance. His chief officer would get $1,250; the second
and third officers $750 each; the chief engineer, $2,500; the crew and fire-
men, $250 each, and the pilot $3,500." Despite the costs, and the possibility
of capture, the potential profitability of the enterprises was widely recognized. In 1863, the U.S. consul at Nassau cited a particular vessel that had
expenses of $115,000 on her outward journey. On the return, she brought

64 Wise, *Lifeline*, 107.
65 Bradlee, *Blockade Running*, 96–98; Wise, *Lifeline*, 107.
66 Wise, *Lifeline*, 71.   67 Wise, *Lifeline*, 111, 297, 302, 305, 315, 324.
68 Wise, *Lifeline*, 71.   69 Jones. *Civil War at Sea*, vol. 2, 247–248.

Table 4.4. *Confederacy Blockade Runners Out of Charleston, 1861–1865*

Type of Vessel	Name of Vessel	Owners	Captain
Steamer	Gordon	J. Fraser and Co.	T. J. Lockwood
Steamer	Antonica	J. Fraser and Co.	L. M. Coxetter
Steamer	Margaret and Jessie	J. Fraser and Co.	R. W. Lockwood
Steamer	Pet	A. R. Chisholm and Co.	Foley
Steamer	Calypso	Consolidated Co.	Black
Steamer	Ella and Annie	Bee Co.	Carlin
Steamer	Genera/Moutne	Ravenel and Co.	H. Tilton
Steamer	Hattie	Collie and Co.	H. S. Lebby
Steamer	Fox	J. Fraser and Co.	Brown
Steamer	Badger	J. Fraser and Co.	D. Martin
Steamer	Leopard	J. Fraser and Co.	Peck
Steamer	Lynx	J. Fraser and Co.	E. C. Reid
Steamer	Presto	J. Fraser and Co.	J. Horsey
Steamer	Sumter	J. Fraser and Co.	E. C. Reid
Steamer	Rattlesnake	W. G. Crenshaw	Vzini
Steamer	Colonel Lamb	J. Fraser and Co.	T. J. Lockwood
Steamer	Hope	J. Fraser and Co.	Wm. Hammer
Steamer	Ruby	Collie and Co.	A. Swasey
Steamer	Let Her Be	Chicora Co.	H. Holgate
Steamer	Let Her Rip	Chicora Co.	A. D. Stone
Steamer	Republic	J. Fraser and Co.	F. M. Harris
Steamer	Nina	Ravenel and Co.	Relyea
Steamer	Emily	Bee Co.	Egan
Steamer	Isabel	J. Fraser and Co.	A. Swasey
Steamer	Elizabeth	J. Fraser and Co.	T. J. Lockwood
Steamer	Juno	Confederate States Govt.	Porcher
Steamer	General Whiting	Consolidated Co.	S. Adkins
Steamer	Syren	Cobia and Co.	J. Johnson
Steamer	Nashville	J. Fraser and Co.	Pegram
Steamer	Theodora	J. Fraser and Co.	J. N. Maffitt
Steamer	Beauregard	J. Fraser and Co.	H. Holgate
Steamer	Kate	J. Fraser and Co.	T. J. Lockwood
Steamer	Fanny	Bee Co.	D. Dunning
Steamer	Alice	Bee Co.	Kennedy
Steamer	Caroline	Bee Co.	C. Barkley
Steamer	Dream	Collie and Co.	Lockwood
Steamer	Secret	Collie and Co.	I. Davis
Steamer	Druid	Palmetto Co.	H. Tilton
Steamer	Emma		Hutchlin
Steamer	Raccoon	J. Fraser and Co.	F. M. Harris
Steamer	Banshee	Collie and Co.	Speed
Steamer	Herald	Collie and Co.	Randall
Steamer	Maryland		Combs
Steamer	Fannie		T. Moore

Type of Vessel	Name of Vessel	Owners	Captain
Steamer	Britannic		Zachison
Steamer	Stonewall Jackson		Peck
Steamer	Thistle		M. Murray
Steamer	Julia	Cobia Co.	Swan
Steamer	Gem	Cobia Co.	J. Johnson
Steamer	Prince Albert		
Steamer	Lillian		D. Martin
Steamer	Columbia		Hutchinson
Steamer	Coquette		Coombs
Steamer	Big Scotia		Swan
Steamer	Little Scotia		Swan
Steamer	Little Hattie		
Steamer	General Clinch		Murphy
Steamer	Cecile		Carlin
Steamer	Stag		
Steamer	Pearl		
Steamer	Florine		
Steamer	Stono		
Steamer	Nimoo		
Steamer	Owl	Confederate States Govt.	J. N. Maffitt
Steamer	Little Ada		
Steamer	Jupiter		
Steamer	Falcon		
Ship	Emily St. Pierre	J. Fraser and Co.	Wilson
Brig	Jeff Davis	Hall and Co.	Coxetter
Barque	Etiwan	J. Fraser and Co.	J. Stephens
Brig	West Indian		Amot
Schooner	Beauregard		Hayes
Schooner	Sallie		Lebby
Schooner	E. Waterman		Hawes
Schooner	Savannah		Baker
Schooner	Dixie		T. Moore
Schooner	Major E. Willis	W. M. Hale	W. M. Hale
Schooner	Kent	W. M. Hale	W. M. Hale
Schooner	Ben		
Schooner	Palmetto		A. Swasey
Schooner	J. W. Ladson	Mordecai and Co.	Stone
Sloop	Swallow	Adams and Willis	C. Gould
Pilot Boat	Petrel	Perry	Perry
Pilot Boat	Charleston	William Hone	William Hone
Pilot Boat	Chicora		
Pilot Boat	Leitch		
Pilot Boat	Pride	Street and West	T. Bennett

Source: Frances B. C. Bradlee. *Blockade Running During the Civil War: And the Effect of Land and Water Transportation on the Confederacy* (Salem: Essex Institute, 1925), 96–98.

Table 4.5. *Blockade Running Profits: Schooner "Rob Roy"*

	Item	Value
1	Investment in Vessel	$5,000
2	Net Return on Vessel, Brownsville-Havana	5,804
3	Rate of Return on Successful Outward Voyage	116%

Note: Rate of Return is row 2 divided by row 1.
Source: Stanley Lebergott, 'Through the Blockade' The Profitability and Extent of Cotton Smuggling, 1861–1865," *Journal of Economic History*, 41 (December 1981), 870.

in cotton valued at $234,000, giving her a profit of $119,000."[70] "A few large fortunes were probably made by a few lucky entrepreneurs; however, smaller fortunes were made by a great many."[71]

Unfortunately, however, we still have relatively little aggregate knowledge of the average profitability of a typical blockade-runner. There are partial records from a number of vessels, but, if the secondary literature is to be believed, well-documented records of the revenues, costs, and profits earned by successful blockade-runners exist for only two runners: the schooner *Rob Roy* and the steamer *Banshee*.[72] Lebergott's analysis of the record for a successful roundtrip of the *Rob Roy* estimates a profit rate of 116 percent, whereas that for the *Banshee* indicate profits of 132 percent (see Tables 4.5 and 4.6). It is on these two sets of records that much of the recent historical analysis has been based. Stanley Lebergott, combining those records with the expected loss rate that runners experienced during the years in question, calculates net profit rates at 45 percent for the *Rob Roy* and 101 percent for the *Banshee* – figures substantially below those reflected in earlier analysis.[73] He then turns to the records of three blockade companies that were organized in South Carolina. He finds that, at most, the Chicora Company paid dividends of 42 percent, the Charleston Importing and Exporting Company 38 percent, and the Importing and Exporting Company of South Carolina 41 percent. Using those figures, he then estimates that the returns on successful runs (those in which the "runner" was neither captured or destroyed) were about 67 percent.[74] He

70 Jones, *Civil War at Sea*, vol. 3, 82. See also Wise, *Lifeline*, 111.
71 Nevins, *War of the Union*, vol. 3, 340.
72 William Watson, *Adventures of a Blockade Runner or Trade in Time of War* (London: Macmillan, 1892) and Thomas Taylor, *Running the Blockade* (London: J. Murray, 1897), also Stanley Lebergott, "Through the Blockade. The Profitability and Extent of Cotton Smuggling, 1861–1865," *Journal of Economic History*, 41 (December 1981), 874.
73 Lebergott, "Through the Blockade," 874.
74 The average return of about 40 percent reflects the average loss rate of about 16 percent. Lebergott, "Through the Blockade," 873–879.

Table 4.6. *Blockade Runner Profits: Steamer "Banshee"*

	Item		Values	
1	Investment in Vessel		$168,000	
2	Gross Earnings: Inward	$130,000		
3	Gross Earnings: Outward	120,000		
	Gross Earnings: Total		250,000	
4	Expenses: Pilot and Crew	23,000		
5	Expenses: Refitting	2,000		
6	Expenses: Coal	3,600		
	Expenses: Total		28,600	
7	Net Return		221,400	
8	Rate of Return on Successful Round Trip (row 7 divided by row 1)			132%

Source: Lebergott, "Through the Blockade," 871.

concludes, therefore, that "such rates of return were, of course, high for companies engaged in low risk enterprises. But they proved remarkably low for a wartime industry contesting the U.S. naval blockade and confronted by changing demands of pilots and seamen for wages appropriate to the risk." And, furthermore, that "the infrequency with which any of the hundreds upon hundreds of ships engaged in a second trip running cotton through the blockade suggests that a profit rate of around 40 percent a year was insufficient to cover the risks."[75]

In the months through August 1862, there was mounting evidence that the Confederates and their friends abroad were in the blockade-running business to stay.[76] For example, in the spring of 1862, "Thomas Sterling Begbie, a London shipping merchant, and Peter Denny, senior partner of Denny and Company, a prominent shipbuilding firm," joined to underwrite the blockade running attempts of "Denny's recently completed steamer *Memphis*."[77] In late 1862, "two more British firms, Alexander Collie and Company of Manchester and Edward Lawrence and Company of Liverpool, joined the trade." Collie was backed by numerous wealthy Englishmen; and by February 1863, "the first of his steamers were running the blockade"; and the other soon followed. The voyages were so highly profitable that, before the year was out, he had added two more vessels to his fleet. Again, after an abortive venture in the summer of 1862, in 1863 the Anglo-Confederate Trading Company, a firm organized by the members of the large Liverpool-based shipping firm of Edward Lawrence and Company, became active; and

75 Lebergott, "Through the Blockade," 876–877.
76 Jones, *Civil War at Sea*, vol. 2, 255.   77 Wise, *Lifeline*, 71.

it proved to be quite successful.[78] Even the Canadians joined the parade. For the sole purpose of running the blockade, two Canadian businessmen underwrote the cost of the steamship *Acadia*; and, by December 1863, the vessel was on her way to Nassau to load a cargo of contraband.[79] And so it went. The owners of these firms and their competitors were certainly sympathetic to the Confederate cause, but the primary motivation for their entry into the blockade running business was their desire to make money. In the words of the owner of the *Harriet Pinckney*, "If captured why should he worry? He could lose two steamers out of three and make a profit."[80]

Confederate firms were not, however, shut out of the market. Even though some of the European firms were very successful, "no blockade-running company could compare to John Fraser and Company. By 1863, the Charleston partners had exported over 18,000 bales of cotton, which sold for at least £900,000 ($2,160,000 in gold). With their profits, the partners purchased additional vessels, cotton, merchandise, and some six million dollars worth of Confederate bonds. They also bought, chartered, and built cargo ships to carry supplies across the Atlantic."[81] The Chicora Importing and Exporting Company of South Carolina was also a successful Charleston-based blockade-running firm. Another southern firm was the Importing and Exporting Company of South Carolina. The firm was incorporated, and more than $200,000 of its stock was sold on the open market. The firm exported cotton on its outbound trips, and its managers took orders from local merchants for its inbound cargoes. One of its vessels, the *Alice and Fannie*, a vessel that on average carried 925 bales of cotton on every outbound trip from the Confederacy, earned a profit of over $100,000 per round trip. During the time that it operated, the firm paid dividends of $9,000 Confederate (£120 per share).[82]

Unlike the European firms, "Southern firms also viewed blockade running as a money-making venture, but they realized that their survival as businesses depended on a Confederate victory. For this reason, a strong streak of patriotism ran through their operation, one that, to some extent, would temper their hunger for profits."[83] Thus, unlike the European firms, the Southern vessels were willing to carry dangerous explosive materials; and also "such items as iron plates, small arms, acids, gunpowder, and submarine

---

78 Wise, *Lifeline*, 112, 202–203.   79 Wise, *Lifeline*, 215–216.
80 Jones, *Civil War at Sea*, vol. 2, 247–248.
81 Wise, *Lifeline*, 115–116. The firm accounted for at least twenty-one of the eighty-seven blockade-runners, which ran in or out of Charleston. Bradlee, *Blockade Running*, 96–98.
82 Wise, *Lifeline*, 114–115.   83 Wise, *Lifeline*, 114.

cable for use with underwater mines." These were items that, because of their weight, the European runners shied away from, preferring instead to concentrate on light cargoes, especially luxury consumer goods, that brought them the highest profits. "However, it should be noted that the [private southern] companies did not lose money on these shipments."[84]

2(6). The Blockaded Ports

Although blockade runners operated from more than a dozen ports, to say nothing of the rivers and inlets that marked the several thousand miles of Southern coastline, the general picture of the blockade is captured in the histories of four major ports – ports that were centers of the Confederate and foreign attempts to run the blockade: Charleston; Wilmington, NC; Mobile; and Matamoras. In the case of Charleston, in late 1861, the Union attempted to seal off the port by sinking a "stone fleet" at the entrance to the harbor.[85] With the New Bedford whaling fleet confined to port because of the threat posed by Confederate raiders, the U.S. government purchased ten whaling vessels and added them to the first and second "stone fleets" – vessels that were each loaded with some seventy-five hundred tons of stone, deployed to the southern coast, and ordered to be sunk to block the harbors at Savannah and Charleston. The first fleet sailed from New Bedford bound for Savannah in November 1861 and the second, bound for Charleston, sailed in December 1861. In the words of the editors of the *Whalemen's Shipping List and Merchants' Transcript*, of December 10, 1861, "By this time the first fleet of stone ships is quietly deposited in the Savannah river, and the history of the city of Savannah as a commercial emporium is terminated. Charleston harbor, by a similarly process will have terminated its career as a Southern port before two weeks elapse."[86] Although the effort did reduce the size of the Northern whaling fleet, it had little impact on the Southern port or the activities of the blockade-runners operating to and from that harbor. In an attempt to reduce competition for cargo space, and the use of railroads, warehouses, pilots, and coal, the Ordnance Bureau had concentrated government blockade-running operations in Wilmington, "leaving Charleston almost exclusively in the hands of private shippers."[87] Thus, from the beginning of the War until February 20, 1865, when the

84 Wise, *Lifeline*, 115.   85 Vandiver, *Tattered Flag*, 100.
86 Lance E. Davis, Robert E. Gallman, and Karin Gleiter, *In Pursuit of Leviathan: Technology, Institutions, Productivity, and Profits in American Whaling, 1816–1906* (Chicago: University of Chicago Press, 1997), 97–98, Table 6.8, 238, 442.
87 Wise, *Lifeline*, 120, 163–165.

Table 4.7. *Quarterly Totals of the Number of Steam Blockade Runners Arriving at:*

Year and Quarter	Charleston, S.C.	Wilmington, N.C.
1861-4	1	1
1861 TOTAL	1	1
1862-1	6	1
1862-2	6	1
1862-3	5	1
1862-4	10	3
1862 TOTAL	27	6
1863-1	18	12
1863-2	22	26
1863-3	6	45
1863-4	0	45
1863 TOTAL	46	128
1864-1	1	39
1864-2	6	46
1864-3	11	42
1864-4	15	41
1864 TOTAL	33	168
1865-1	8	0
1865-2	0	0
1865 TOTAL	8	0
TOTAL 1861–4 through 1865–2	115	303

Source: Stephen R. Wise, *Lifeline of the Confederacy: Blockade Running during the Civil War* (Columbia: University of South Carolina Press, 1988), 233–241, 251–254.

Confederates evacuated the city and it fell to Union forces, no fewer than eighty-seven blockade-runners, including sixty-seven steamships, had started from Charleston (see Table 4.4).[88] Although the data on steamships does not represent a complete enumeration of all blockade-runners (see Tables 4.7 and 4.8), it does capture a very substantial majority – over three-quarters of the eighty-seven Charleston blockade-runners (see Table 4.4). Thus, Tables 4.7 and 4.8 probably accurately reflect the trend in blockade-running. From October 1861 until the middle of 1863, Charleston was more important than Wilmington – it was the "host" to sixty-eight runners as opposed to Wilmington's forty-five. Although it never regained its earlier position, either absolutely of relatively, it still remained an important port until early 1865. After the closure of Wilmington, however, more Union

88 Bradlee, *Blockade Running*, 96–98; Wise, *Lifeline*, 210–211.

Table 4.8. *Estimates of the Carrying Capacity of Confederate Blockade Runners, 1861–1865*

Month	Year	Number of Vessels	Steam Vessels Only				Number of Vessels	Estimates of Entire Fleet	
			Monthly Total		Average Vessel Size			Monthly Total	
			Gross Tons	Registered Tons	Gross Tons	Registered Tons		Gross Tons	Registered Tons
October	1861	1	897	716	897	716	1	1,165	930
November	1861	2	848	528	424	264	3	1,101	686
December	1861	2	712	430	356	215	3	925	558
January	1862	2	1,538	1,030	769	515	3	1,997	1,337
February	1862	4	2,486	1,689	622	422	5	3,228	2,193
March	1862	7	3,853	2,527	550	361	9	5,003	3,281
April	1862	4	2,354	1,581	589	395	5	3,057	2,053
May	1862	6	2,140	1,307	357	218	8	2,779	1,697
June	1862	2	1,408	929	704	465	3	1,828	1,206
July	1862	7	5,808	3,845	830	549	9	7,542	4,993
August	1862	6	2,794	1,771	466	295	8	3,628	2,300
September	1862	4	1,882	1,169	471	292	5	2,444	1,518
October	1862	1	398	246	398	246	1	517	319
November	1862	3	1,587	1,008	529	336	4	2,061	1,309
December	1862	5	2,644	1,702	529	340	6	3,433	2,210
January	1863	10	4,468	2,797	447	280	13	5,802	3,632
February	1863	10	4,091	2,426	409	243	13	5,312	3,150
March	1863	12	5,359	2,768	447	231	16	6,959	3,594
April	1863	17	8,853	5,808	521	342	22	11,496	7,542
May	1863	27	12,430	8,034	460	298	35	16,140	10,432
June	1863	19	10,017	6,618	527	348	25	13,007	8,593
July	1863	22	10,175	6,569	463	299	29	13,212	8,530
August	1863	18	7,513	4,724	417	262	23	9,756	6,134
September	1863	17	6,854	4,108	403	242	22	8,900	5,334
October	1863	19	7,214	4,519	380	238	25	9,367	5,868
November	1863	17	6,605	4,099	389	241	22	8,577	5,323
December	1863	20	6,731	4,207	337	210	26	8,740	5,463
January	1864	17	7,528	4,710	443	277	22	9,775	6,116
February	1864	15	8,784	7,702	586	513	19	11,406	10,001
March	1864	16	6,908	4,538	432	284	21	8,970	5,893
April	1864	17	9,371	6,259	551	368	22	12,168	8,127
May	1864	26	13,152	8,480	506	326	34	17,078	11,011
June	1864	27	11,633	7,608	431	282	35	15,105	9,879
July	1864	23	9,226	5,865	401	255	30	11,980	7,616
August	1864	21	10,700	7,120	510	339	27	13,894	9,245
September	1864	20	8,502	5,237	425	262	26	11,040	6,800
October	1864	16	7,024	5,262	439	329	21	9,121	6,833

(continued)

Table 4.8 *(continued)*

Month	Year	Steam Vessels Only					Estimates of Entire Fleet		
			Monthly Total		Average Vessel Size			Monthly Total	
		Number of Vessels	Gross Tons	Registered Tons	Gross Tons	Registered Tons	Number of Vessels	Gross Tons	Registered Tons
November	1864	21	9,566	6,253	456	298	27	12,421	8,120
December	1864	25	11,581	7,566	463	303	32	15,038	9,824
January	1865	10	4,013	2,571	401	257	13	5,211	3,338
February	1865	8	751	459	94	57	10	975	596
March	1865	5	2,453	1,655	491	331	6	3,185	2,149
April	1865	5	2,001	1,332	400	266	6	2,598	1,730
May	1865	2	777	553	389	277	3	1,009	718

Notes: (1): Fleet estimates are based on the ratio of steamers to total blockade runners out of Charleston. Steamer totals are multiplied by 1.2985.

(2): Vessels without gross or registered tons are assumed to be the average of the other blockade runners in the same month and year.

Source: Bradlee, *Blockade Running*, 96–98; Wise, *Lifeline*, 233–328.

vessels joined the blockading fleet, and it became much more difficult for blockade-runners to use the port. Some captains, however, for reasons of "profit or patriotism," continued to run the risk. In early 1865, however, Sherman's army moved into South Carolina and cut the railroads – an action that effectively severed Charleston's trading links with its "customers."[89]

In the case of Wilmington, the time pattern reflected in the steam vessel data are quite different. Although only seven vessels arrived between the outbreak of hostilities and the end of 1862, because of the protection offered by Fort Fisher, no fewer than 296 runners arrived in 1863 and 1864. On January 15, 1865, however, after a very costly three-day ground attack, Fort Fisher was captured. The fall of the fort allowed blockading vessels to enter the Cape Fear River and cut off the port's defenses. Although the city was not officially abandoned until February 25, no runners entered or left the port after the fall of the fort.[90] Thus, the last major eastern port for blockade-runners was closed and occupied; and, although the war continued for another few months, with the loss of the two seaports, the fate of the Confederacy had effectively been sealed.[91]

---

89 Wise, *Lifeline*, 210.
90 Nevins, *War for the Union*, vol. 4, 191–192; Wise, *Lifeline*, 205–207. In the battle for Fort Fisher, the Union army lost 995 men killed, and about another 1,700 wounded or missing.
91 Wise, *Lifeline*, 211–213.

After Charleston and Wilmington had been occupied, the focus of the blockade shifted to the Gulf States. As long as blockade-running was dominated by private enterprise, despite the pressure placed on the Confederate railway network by the need to ship imported supplies to the West, "English shippers preferred to use Nassau and Bermuda" as intermediate ports, because use of those ports "allowed them to operate larger and more profitable vessels than could be employed in the Gulf." Thus, although Mobile, with good railroad and steamship connections, "could have become the major supply center for the Western armies," because of the failure of government policy to provide either incentives or to impose formal regulation on the blockade-runners, it never was. In late 1864, however, with the imposition of regulations designed to ease the burden on Wilmington, and, then, the demise of the eastern ports, some blockade-runners turned their attention to Mobile. The flow, however, was never large; and, on April 12, 1865, Union attacks forced the city's evacuation. Thus, the Confederacy was never able to realize the port's full potential.[92]

With the fall of Mobile, blockade-runners based in Havana turned to the Texas coast for new ports of entry. After the fall of New Orleans, rail connections to the Eastern states ran from Monroe, Louisiana, to Vicksburg, Mississippi. However, "links between Monroe and Texas depended on slow wagon trains, which took weeks to complete the journey."[93]

Although the overland transportation problems were at least as great, it was not one of the harbors on the Texas coast that became the last important Confederate port of entry. Instead, because of the law, it was the Mexican city of Matamoras that, as early as 1862, had become a sore point in the Union blockade – an infection that was only made worse by the collapse of trade through Charleston, Wilmington, New Orleans, and Mobile. A provision of the 1848 treaty of Guadalupe Hidalgo defined the Rio Grande as a neutral river the mouth of which could not be directly blockaded by either the United States or Mexico. In 1862, in the case of the British steamer *Labuan*, the court upheld that interpretation, ruling that, even though the vessel's cargo of cotton had come from Texas, Union warships could not interfere, if the cotton was initially exported to Mexico and then reexported to Europe.[94] The same was true for supplies exported to Mexico and then reexported overland to the Confederacy by land.

---

92 Wise, *Lifeline*, 180–181.

93 Wise, *Lifeline*, 181. "Of the 31,000 miles of railroad in the United States in 1860, only 9,000 were in those states that became part of the Confederacy." Parish, *American Civil War*, 110.

94 Wise, *Lifeline*, 88.

As early as the spring of 1862, Governor Vidaurri had taken over the political structure of Tamaulipas, the state that included the seaport, Matamoras. "He immediately threw the port open to the Confederates." Later, when Juarez replaced Vidaurri, the new governor reaffirmed the policy – he was just as dependent on the income from the duties collected at the border as was his predecessor. In October 1862, the Confederate agent to the border states of Mexico, Juan A. Quintero, reported that he "would be able to put four or five hundred wagons to hauling cotton out of Texas in exchange for supplies and specie." The quantitative estimates of data on the extent of the size of the loophole in the blockade are still in doubt, but the trans-Mississippi department of the Confederacy had been supplied through Matamoras from the beginning of the war. The best estimates suggest that the revenues from the duties collected at Piedras Negras, a major border crossing point, were over $50,000 a month ($1,200,000 was collected there between 1862 and 1864), and there were also several other points of entry to the Confederacy, where the Mexican government collected duty on imports and exports. In total, over the three years, the revenues on such goods could not have been less than $125,000 a month; and, as "trade with the exception of an occasional interruption, was kept open during the entire war," they almost certainly would have risen after the major ports on the east and gulf coasts had been closed.[95] The duties, of course, represented but a fraction of the value of the goods imported and exported (see Table 4.9).

The extent of breach in the blockade is reflected in the changes in the town of Matamoras itself. The population of the once tiny town was increased by the arrival of some twenty thousand speculators, a group drawn from all parts of the globe, and that included a substantial number of Union citizens. Nor were the profits limited to those who migrated. "The trade with New York merchants was heavy and profitable." The town saw rents rise sharply, an English-language newspaper was launched, and a packet line commenced regular service between the town and Havana. "To the very end of the war, after Wilmington had been captured and Memphis brought under effective trade controls, Matamoras remained an open gate in the walls raised about the Confederacy."[96]

---

95 Owsley, *King Cotton*, 126–128, 143–145. Lebergott calculates that, in 1864, the market price for cotton in Houston and Galveston was about 6 cents a pound (Confederate), whereas the price in New York and London was about 55.4 cents a pound (the average of 55 cents in the U.K. and 55.8 cents in New York). Of that total, the Mexican import duty averaged 3.4 cents and that country's export duty, 3.8 cents. Together, they accounted for about 13 percent of the delivered price. Lebergott, "Through the Blockade," 869.

96 Nevins, *War for the Union*, vol. 3, 368–369.

Table 4.9. *Cotton: Blockade Margin (1864, Texas)*

Item	Cost (Cents)	Market Price (Cents)
1 Market Price in C.S.A. (Houston, Galveston)		6.000
2 Value of Export Permit	5.000	
3 Transport: interior to the Rio Grande	3.000	
4 C.S.A Export Duty	0.125	
5 Mexican Import Duty	3.400	
6 Smuggling Cost	12.800	
7 Market Price in Tampico, Mexico		30.300
8 Mexican Export Duty	3.800	
9 Market Price in Havana		34.300
10 Reshipping Cotton in Havana	1.000	
11 Transport to Liverpool	20.000	
12 Market Price in United Kingdom		55.000
13 Market Price in New York City (Gold)		55.800

Source: Lebergott, "Through the Blockade," 869.

2(7). The Data: Exports and Imports

In terms of exports, cotton clearly dominated Southern exports; and, in our attempts to measure the efficiency of the blockade, we will focus on that commodity. Table 4.10 attempts to place the Civil War in the context of the growth of cotton production in the South and the role of cotton exports in the southern economy. There were, not surprisingly, some year-to-year fluctuations in the Southern crop; but, in general, production grew fairly steadily from 1845 through 1861; and, reflecting the Confederate decision to embargo exports at the outbreak of the war, exports had grown fairly steadily from 1845 to 1860. In 1861, production was almost 2.5 times the 1845 base line. Despite the growth of the domestic cotton textile industry (see Table 4.10, and also Table 4.11), exports grew even faster; and the 1860 figure was 3.3 times that baseline.[97]

The figures give some rough measure of the effectiveness of the blockade. Several historians, including Francis B. C. Bradlee, have pointed to the Southern exports that moved through the blockade as evidence of its ineffectiveness. His figures show that between 1861 and 1863 some 130 blockade-runners from Charleston carried 32,050 bales through the blockade; and, again, that runners based in Wilmington moved an additional 27,299 bales

[97] See Table 4.11. Between 1840 and 1860 domestic cotton consumption increased from 236,525 bales to 845,410 bales – an increase of almost 260 percent.

Table 4.10. *United States Production and Exports of Raw Cotton, 1845–1880*

	Equivalent 500-Pound Bales, Gross Weight (Bales)			As a Percentage of 1845 Baseline		
Year	Production	Exports	Percent Exported	Production	Exports	Percent Exported
1845	1,806,110	1,095,116	60.6	100.0	100.0	100.0
1846	1,603,763	1,054,440	65.7	88.8	96.3	108.4
1847	2,128,433	1,628,549	76.5	117.8	148.7	126.2
1848	2,615,031	2,053,204	78.5	144.8	187.5	129.5
1849	1,975,274	1,270,763	64.3	109.4	116.0	106.1
1850	2,136,083	1,854,474	86.8	118.3	169.3	143.2
1851	2,799,290	2,186,461	78.1	155.0	199.7	128.8
1852	3,130,338	2,223,141	71.0	173.3	203.0	117.1
1853	2,766,194	1,975,666	71.4	153.2	180.4	117.8
1854	2,708,082	2,016,849	74.5	149.9	184.2	122.8
1855	3,220,782	2,702,863	83.9	178.3	246.8	138.4
1856	2,873,680	2,096,565	73.0	159.1	191.4	120.3
1857	3,012,016	2,237,248	74.3	166.8	204.3	122.5
1858	3,758,273	2,772,937	73.8	208.1	253.2	121.7
1859	4,309,642	3,535,373	82.0	238.6	322.8	135.3
1860	3,841,416	3,615,032	94.1	212.7	330.1	155.2
1861	4,490,586	10,129	0.2	248.6	0.9	0.4
1862	1,596,653	22,770	1.4	88.4	2.1	2.4
1863	449,059	23,998	5.3	24.9	2.2	8.8
1864	299,372	17,789	5.9	16.6	1.6	9.8
1865	2,093,658	1,301,146	62.1	115.9	118.8	102.5
1866	1,948,077	1,401,697	72.0	107.9	128.0	118.7
1867	2,345,610	1,502,756	64.1	129.9	137.2	105.7
1868	2,198,141	1,300,449	59.2	121.7	118.7	97.6
1869	2,409,597	1,987,708	82.5	133.4	181.5	136.0
1870	4,024,527	2,922,757	72.6	222.8	266.9	119.8
1871	2,756,564	1,824,937	66.2	152.6	166.6	109.2
1872	3,650,932	2,470,590	67.7	202.1	225.6	111.6
1873	3,873,750	2,682,631	69.3	214.5	245.0	114.2
1874	3,528,276	2,504,118	71.0	195.4	228.7	117.1
1875	4,302,818	3,037,650	70.6	238.2	277.4	116.4
1876	4,118,390	2,839,418	68.9	228.0	259.3	113.7
1877	4,494,224	3,197,439	71.1	248.8	292.0	117.3
1878	4,745,078	3,290,167	69.3	262.7	300.4	114.4
1879	5,466,387	3,742,752	68.5	302.7	341.8	112.9
1880	6,356,998	4,453,495	70.1	352.0	406.7	115.5

Source: James A. B. Scherer, *Cotton as a World Power: A Study in the Economic Interpretation of History* (New York: Frederick A. Stokes Company Publishers, 1916), Appendix F, 420, with 1860 export figure corrected.

Table 4.11. *The Growth of Cotton Manufactures by Sections in the United States, 1840–1880*

	Cotton Produced (Bales)	Cotton Consumed (Bales)				Active Cotton Spindles			
		United States	Cotton Growing States	New England States	All Other States	United States	Cotton Growing States	New England States	All Other States
1840	2,063,915	236,525	71,000	158,708	6,817	2,284,631	180,927	1,597,394	506,310
1850	2,469,093	575,506	78,140	430,603	66,763	3,998,022	264,571	2,958,536	774,915
1860	5,387,052	845,410	93,553	567,403	184,454	5,235,727	324,052	3,858,962	1,052,713
1870	3,011,996	796,616	68,702	551,250	176,664	7,132,415	327,871	5,498,308	1,306,236
1880	5,755,359	1,570,344	188,748	1,129,498	252,098	10,653,435	561,360	8,632,087	1,459,988

Year	Percent Consumed United States	Percent of United States Consumption			Active Cotton Spindles Percent of United States Total		
		Cotton Growing States	New England States	All Other States	Cotton Growing States	New England States	All Other States
1840	11.5	30.0	67.1	2.9	7.9	69.9	22.2
1850	23.3	13.6	74.8	11.6	6.6	74.0	19.4
1860	15.7	11.1	67.1	21.8	6.2	73.7	20.1
1870	26.4	8.6	69.2	22.2	4.6	77.1	18.3
1880	27.3	12.0	71.9	16.1	5.3	81.0	13.7

Note: The quantities are given in running bales, except those for production in 1850, 1860, and 1870, which are in equivalent four-hundred pound bales, and those for consumption from 1840 to 1870, which are in equivalent five-hundred pound bales.

Source: Scherer, *Cotton*, Appendix F, 422.

Table 4.12. *Cotton Exports from Charleston, 1861–1863*

Period	Number of Vessels Cleared	Number of Bales Exported	Value of the Cotton Exported
July 1 to September 30, 1861	5	140	$6,657
October 1 to December 31, 1861	11	4,675	534,902
January 1 to March 30, 1862	28	2,195	97,021
April 1 to June 30, 1862	41	1,345	59,007
July 1 to September 30, 1862	7	4,101	223,511
October 1 to December 31, 1862	13	10,220	954,009
January 1 to March 30, 1863	25	9,374	1,179,369
TOTAL	130	32,050	3,054,476

Note: Cotton exported by way of Matamoras (the nearest Mexican port across the Texas boundary line) are included in these figures; however, it may be assumed that the latter did not amount to 5 percent of the total.
Source: Official Records of the Civil War, Series IV, vol. 2, p. 562; cited in Bradlee, *Blockade Running*, 59–60.

overseas during the course of the war (see Tables 4.12 and 4.13). Stanley Lebergott (see Table 4.20) has suggested that the total may have been even higher. For the years 1861 through 1865, he put the total at 446,000 bales.[98]

The aggregate data, however, suggest quite a different conclusion.[99] They indicate a rapid decline in production – from 3.8 million bales in 1860 to less than 300 thousand bales in 1864 (see Table 4.10). Moreover, they show an even more dramatic decline in exports – from a total of 3,615,032 bales in 1860 to 17,789 bales in 1864, a fall of more than 99 percent, to a figure that represents only 1.6 percent of the 1845 export baseline. Moreover, the 1864 total of 17,789 bales almost certainly includes some shipments that were exported from the North – products of the Union strategy that, by legally permitting them to export part of their limited crops to the Union, was designed to relieve the impact of the war on Union sympathizers who lived in the South. Finally, the data from Britain, the South's major prewar customer, tell a similar story. Between the beginning of 1860 and the end of 1864, total cotton imports fell by only 23 percent, whereas imports from the United States declined by 92 percent. In 1860, the United States supplied 77 percent of cotton for Britain's mills; in 1864, the figure was 8 percent (see Table 4.1).

98 Bradlee, *Blockade Running*, 59, 316. Lebergott, "Through the Blockade," 880–881.
99 Lebergott has come to somewhat different conclusions about the production and export of cotton through the blockade during the Civil War, although most of the Southern cotton grown that he points to was produced at the start of the war, with much planted before Fort Sumter. See Lebergott, "Through the Blockade." More recent work is somewhat at odds with his conclusions, indicating the impact of Southern war strategy on cotton production.

Table 4.13. *Confederate Commercial Statistics Shipments of Cotton (from Wilmington, N.C.) since March 1, 1861*

Account	Bales
Niter and Mining Bureau	873
Medical Department	328
Engineer Department	57
Commissary Department	1,248
Quartermaster's Department	1,829
Ordnance Department	1,776
Navy Department	4,861
Treasury Department (12,840)	16,327
and one-half of contract steamers (6,974)	
TOTAL	27,299

Note: 27,299 bales at £40 average = £1,091,960, at \$4.85 = \$5,296,006. Equal in (Confederate) currency @ 25 to 1 = \$132,400,150.
Source: Bradlee, *Blockade Running*, 316.

Thus, on the export side, this preliminary examination of data suggests that, critics of the blockade to the contrary, the naval deployment had some effect. It appears to have impacted exports both directly by cutting the overseas flow, and indirectly, by reducing the Southern cotton crop. These conclusions will be more systematically examined in the following section.

The import story is considerably less clear. There is, for example, no good prewar series on imports to the South; and, under any conditions, what would be required would be a series on imports from both the North and from overseas. Moreover, the data that are reported in the secondary literature on the imports carried through the blockade are neither complete nor systematic. Furthermore, those authors have focused on military supplies, despite the general recognition that, until fairly late in the war, blockade runners focused much more on high-profit luxury goods than on goods that directly supported military operations. On the basis of the secondary literature, we are, therefore, left with a few numbers and some general impressions – impressions that generally suggest that, overall, in terms of Southern imports, the blockade was relatively ineffective.

For example, during the months of July and August 1861, Virgil Jones writes, "the South, an agricultural area, needed supplies and was willing to pay for them with cotton, something that England and other nations wanted to buy." He provides evidence from a single order from the Confederate Ordnance Officer at Richmond – an order for "50,000 to 150,000 pounds of rifle powder, 250,000 to 350,000 pounds of musket powder, 50,000 to 150,000 pounds of cannon powder, 10,000 to 100,000 Minié muskets, 100,000 Enfield rifles, 2,000 artillery sabers, 5,000 breach-loading carbines, 2 thousand Colt's Navy and Army pistols, 200 carboys of nitric acid, 20,000 pounds of block tin and 1,000 boxes of common tin."[100] He does not, however, indicate either whether the order was filled or whether this type of order was common.

Writing about the later years of the war, at a time when the blockade should have been at the peak of its effectiveness, Bradlee writes, "that between October, 1864, and January, 1865, there had been imported through the blockade 500,000 pairs of shoes, 8,000,000 pounds of bacon, 2,000,000 pounds of saltpeter, 50 cannon, etc."[101]

In a similar, although perhaps somewhat less negative, vein, Stephen Wise reports that "By the latter part of 1864, the Confederate armies were almost totally dependent on goods received through the blockade." "From April to November 1864, Lawton's bureau brought in enough supplies to outfit the Confederate soldiers through the last year of the war. Blockade runners carried into Wilmington and Charleston at least 400,000 pairs of shoes and 300,000 blankets along with vast amounts of uniform material." During 1864, the [Ordnance] bureau "reported importing nearly 50,000 rifles, 1,700 pistols, and 4,700 carbines." "From October 1864 to January 1865, the Ordnance Bureau imported nearly 50,000 rifles and carbines, over 400,000 pounds of lead, great quantities of copper, tin, and a vast supply of saltpeter." However, he then goes on to note, first, that during this period reserves of weapons were low and, second, that much greater quantities of arms had been ordered, but not delivered, and that ten to twelve thousand more weapons remained stored in intermediate ports.[102] Thus, he fails to note that, because of the blockade, coastal shipping, an important need for the Southern transport system, was sharply curtailed, a situation made worse by the poor railroad system of the South.[103]

The best systematic quantitative data were collected by Bradlee and those data, when carefully examined, suggest a considerably less negative view of the effectiveness of the blockade (see Table 4.14). Bradlee compares the quantities of fifteen commodities imported into Wilmington and Charleston between the period November 1, 1863, to October 26, 1864, and those brought in between October 26, 1864, and December 8, 1864. For the fifteen, average daily imports declined for nine of the commodities by an

100 Jones, *War at Sea*, vol. 1, 168–169.   101 Bradlee, *Blockade Running*, 81–82.
102 Wise, *Lifeline*, 196, 211–212.   103 Surdam, *Naval Superiority*, 53, 99–100.

Table 4.14. *Imports of Leading Articles at Wilmington and Charleston Since November 1, 1863*

Leading Articles	From 11/1/63 to 10/26/64	From 10/26/64 to 12/8/64	Daily Average		Daily Average Percent Decline
			From 11/1/63 to 10/26/64	From 10/26/64 to 12/8/64	
Leather, packages	666	3	1.84	0.07	96.3
Lead, pigs	12,396	150	34.34	3.41	90.1
Lead, casks	54	0	0.15	0.00	100.0
Saltpeter, packages	9,226	473	25.56	10.75	58.1
Revolvers, packages	97	0	0.27	0.00	100.0
Boots and shoes, packages	2,915	857	8.07	19.48	−140.5
Blankets, bales	2,921	322	8.09	7.32	95.2
Meat, packages	15,194	6,085	42.09	138.30	−227.7
Rifles, cases	2,818	328	7.81	7.45	4.8
Coffee, packages	2,453	540	6.80	12.27	−80.1
Cannon	43	0	0.12	0.00	100.0
Copper, packages	1,452	24	3.95	0.55	86.5
Swords, cases	134	0	0.37	0.00	100.0
Rope, coils	816	104	2.26	2.36	−4.3
Medicine, packages	2,222	417	6.16	9.48	−53.5

Source: Bradlee, *Blockade Running*, 316. No allowance made in calculations for 1864 leap year.

average of 82 percent (with four dropping to zero).[104] As the war progressed, the Confederate government exercised an increasing level of control over the type of imports "run in," substituting military supplies for luxury goods. Over time, then, military supplies became a larger fraction of total imports run through the blockade. Thus, military supplies alone do not provide a good index of total imports; and as a result, an enumeration of all imports would almost certainly have shown a substantially larger decrease.

3. THE QUANTITATIVE STORY

At first glance, it appears that the Northern blockade was not very successful. Over the course of the war, there were no fewer than 6,316 attempts to run the blockade; and, of that number, no fewer than 85 percent (5,389) were successful. Moreover, although the percentage of successful attempts declined from the first year's high of 96.8 percent, it still averaged over

104 Bradlee, *Blockade Running*, 316.

Table 4.15. *Number and Percentage of Successful Runs Through the Blockade,*
1861–1865

		Steam Vessels		
Year	Attempts	Successful Attempts	Unsuccessful Attempts	Percent Successful
1861	1,411	1,407	4	99.7
1862	205	155	50	75.6
1863	545	472	73	86.6
1864	474	401	73	84.6
1865	108	90	18	83.3
TOTAL	2,743	2,525	218	92.1
1862–1865	1,332	1,118	214	83.9
		Sailing Vessels		
Year	Attempts	Successful Attempts	Unsuccessful Attempts	Percent Successful
1861	2,168	2,058	108	94.9
1862	653	413	240	63.2
1863	458	259	199	56.6
1864	249	121	128	48.6
1865	45	13	32	28.9
TOTAL	3,573	2,864	707	80.2
1862–1865	1,405	806	599	57.4
		All Vessels		
Year	Attempts	Successful Attempts	Unsuccessful Attempts	Percent Successful
1861	3,579	3,465	112	96.8
1862	858	568	290	66.2
1863	1,003	731	272	72.9
1864	723	522	201	72.2
1865	153	103	50	67.3
TOTAL	6,316	5,389	925	85.3
1862–1865	2,737	1,924	813	70.3

Note: Price counted as a "successful attempt" any run through the blockade, including packet stops along the coast. Many of the 1861 "attempts" were by coastal packets making stops at several small ports.
Source: Surdam, *Northern Naval Superiority*, Table 1.1, 4.

70 percent during the years from January 1862 until the war ended in 1865 (see Tables 4.15, 4.16, and 4.17). The evidence indicates that steam-driven runners were, on average, more successful than sailing vessels (92 percent compared to 80 percent); and, over the course of the war, the proportion

Table 4.16. *Number of Successful Runs Through the Blockade, 1861–1865*

Year	Atlantic Ports		Gulf Ports		Total Steam	Total Sail	All Vessels
	Steam	Sail	Steam	Sail			
1861	1,036	765	371	1,293	1,407	2,058	3,465
1862	79	184	45	229	124	413	537
1863	347	66	78	193	425	259	684
1864	414	30	84	91	498	121	619
1865	22	2	50	11	72	13	85
TOTAL	1,898	1,047	628	1,817	2,526	2,864	5,390

Notes: (1) 1865 is January through the end of the war.

(2) These numbers for successful steamers, based on Wise, differ slightly from those of Marcus Price underlying Table 4.15. See "Ships that Tested the Blockade of the Carolina Ports, 1861–65," "Blockade Running as a Business in South Carolina during the War between the States, 1861–65," "Ships that Tested the Blockade of the Gulf Ports, 1861–65," and "Ships that Tested the Blockade of the Georgia and East Florida Ports, 1861–65," a series of articles published in American Neptune, 1948, 1949, 1951, 1952, and 1955.

Source: Surdam, *Northern Naval Superiority*, Table 1.2, 5.

of steam runners in the total steadily increased from 24 percent in 1862 to 71 percent in 1865.

The suggested failure of the blockade to reduce the fraction of successful runs after 1861 was, therefore, at least in part, underwritten by improvements in "running" technology, with the substitution of steam for sail, after 1861 (see Table 4.18). In 1861, no fewer than 80 percent of blockade-runners were wooden-hulled; 20 percent had iron hulls; and there were no runners with steel hulls. Over time, the proportion of wooden-hulled vessels declined to 54 percent in 1862, to 15 percent in 1863, to 1 percent in 1864; and, in 1865 there were no wooden-hulled vessels. Meanwhile, the number of iron hulled runners increased to a peak of 82 percent of the total in 1864 before declining to 68 percent in the last five months of the war; and the number of runners with steel hulls, although still totaling less than 4 percent in 1863, accounted for 32 percent in 1865. Oddly enough, however, the proportion of side-wheelers in the total remained high from 1862 onward; and it actually rose to 86 percent in 1864 and to 90 percent the next year. However, more in line with the usual expectations regarding technical change, the fraction of runners propelled by single screws declined from 22 percent of the total in 1862 to zero over the last five months, whereas the figure for double screw-driven blockade-runners rose from 2 percent in 1862 to more than 10 percent in 1864 and 1865.

Other evidence suggests that the blockade was much more effective than these data suggest. Although it is impossible to estimate Southern imports

Table 4.17. Attempts to Run the Blockade, 1861–1865

Year	Steamers in Business	Sailing Vessels in Business	Total Vessels in Business	Attempts by Steamers			Attempts by Sailing Vessels			Total Attempts		
				Successful	Unsuccessful	Total	Successful	Unsuccessful	Total	Successful	Unsuccessful	Total
Carolina Coast												
1861	21	253	274	131	0	131	562	40	602	693	40	733
1862	45	145	190	96	28	124	161	91	252	257	119	376
1863	73	55	128	390	43	433	46	36	82	436	79	515
1864	98	14	112	311	56	367	11	9	20	322	65	387
1865	24	5	29	25	13	38	2	3	5	27	16	43
1861–1865	261	472	733	953	140	1,093	782	179	961	1,735	319	2,054
Gulf Ports												
1861	34	397	431	371	4	375	1,293	53	1,346	1,664	57	1,721
1862	34	222	256	50	18	68	229	131	360	279	149	428
1863	38	216	254	73	26	99	193	136	329	266	162	428
1864	25	119	144	87	13	100	91	82	173	178	95	273
1865	25	33	58	65	4	69	11	28	39	76	32	108
1861–1865	156	987	1,143	646	65	711	1,817	430	2,247	2,463	495	2,958
Georgia and Eastern Florida												
1861	16	78	94	905	0	905	203	15	218	1,108	15	1,123
1862	7	24	31	9	4	13	23	18	41	32	22	54
1863	7	39	46	9	4	13	20	27	47	29	31	60
1864	4	48	52	3	4	7	19	37	56	22	41	63
1865	1	1	2	0	1	1	0	1	1	0	2	2
1861–1865	35	190	225	926	13	939	265	98	363	1,191	111	1,302

Source: Marcus W. Price, American Neptune, Volumes 8, 9, 11, 12, and 15.

Table 4.18. *Technology Adopted by Identified Blockade Runners, Percentages, 1861–1865*

Year	Month	Hull Type					Driving Mechanism			
		Wood	Iron	Iron & Steel	Steel	Total	Side Wheel	Single Screw	Double Screw	Total
1861	October	100.0	0.0	0.0	0.0	100.0	0.0	100.0	0.0	100.0
	November	50.0	50.0	0.0	0.0	100.0	0.0	100.0	0.0	100.0
	December	100.0	0.0	0.0	0.0	100.0	50.0	50.0	0.0	100.0
1861	TOTAL	80.0	20.0	0.0	0.0	100.0	20.0	80.0	0.0	100.0
1862	January	100.0	0.0	0.0	0.0	100.0	100.0	0.0	0.0	100.0
	February	100.0	0.0	0.0	0.0	100.0	66.7	33.3	0.0	100.0
	March	50.0	50.0	0.0	0.0	100.0	83.3	16.7	0.0	100.0
	April	75.0	25.0	0.0	0.0	100.0	100.0	0.0	0.0	100.0
	May	75.0	25.0	0.0	0.0	100.0	50.0	50.0	0.0	100.0
	June	50.0	50.0	0.0	0.0	100.0	50.0	50.0	0.0	100.0
	July	0.0	100.0	0.0	0.0	100.0	57.1	28.6	14.3	100.0
	August	60.0	40.0	0.0	0.0	100.0	83.3	16.7	0.0	100.0
	September	75.0	25.0	0.0	0.0	100.0	75.0	25.0	0.0	100.0
	October	100.0	0.0	0.0	0.0	100.0	100.0	0.0	0.0	100.0
	November	33.3	66.7	0.0	0.0	100.0	66.7	33.3	0.0	100.0
	December	40.0	60.0	0.0	0.0	100.0	100.0	0.0	0.0	100.0
1862	TOTAL	54.2	45.8	0.0	0.0	100.0	75.5	22.4	2.0	100.0
1863	January	44.4	55.6	0.0	0.0	100.0	50.0	40.0	10.0	100.0
	February	10.0	90.0	0.0	0.0	100.0	60.0	40.0	0.0	100.0
	March	8.3	91.7	0.0	0.0	100.0	66.7	25.0	8.3	100.0
	April	13.3	80.0	0.0	6.7	100.0	81.3	18.8	0.0	100.0
	May	8.7	82.6	8.7	0.0	100.0	68.0	24.0	8.0	100.0
	June	18.8	75.0	6.3	0.0	100.0	88.9	5.6	5.6	100.0
	July	22.2	66.7	5.6	5.6	100.0	71.4	14.3	14.3	100.0
	August	25.0	62.5	6.3	6.3	100.0	84.2	5.3	10.5	100.0
	September	6.7	86.7	0.0	6.7	100.0	81.3	12.5	6.3	100.0
	October	11.8	82.4	5.9	0.0	100.0	73.7	15.8	10.5	100.0
	November	0.0	92.3	0.0	7.7	100.0	73.3	20.0	6.7	100.0
	December	13.3	80.0	0.0	6.7	100.0	89.5	5.3	5.3	100.0
1863	TOTAL	14.5	78.8	3.4	3.4	100.0	75.5	17.0	7.5	100.0
1864	January	0.0	93.3	6.7	0.0	100.0	88.2	5.9	5.9	100.0
	February	0.0	91.7	0.0	8.3	100.0	92.9	7.1	0.0	100.0
	March	8.3	83.3	8.3	0.0	100.0	57.1	21.4	21.4	100.0
	April	0.0	93.3	0.0	6.7	100.0	87.5	6.3	6.3	100.0
	May	0.0	82.6	4.3	13.0	100.0	79.2	0.0	20.8	100.0
	June	0.0	79.2	0.0	20.8	100.0	81.5	0.0	18.5	100.0
	July	0.0	90.9	0.0	9.1	100.0	87.0	0.0	13.0	100.0
	August	5.0	70.0	0.0	25.0	100.0	90.0	0.0	10.0	100.0

(continued)

Table 4.18 *(continued)*

		Hull Type					Driving Mechanism			
Year	Month	Wood	Iron	Iron & Steel	Steel	Total	Side Wheel	Single Screw	Double Screw	Total
	September	0.0	66.7	0.0	33.3	100.0	94.4	0.0	5.6	100.0
	October	0.0	78.6	0.0	21.4	100.0	81.3	6.3	12.5	100.0
	November	0.0	78.9	0.0	21.1	100.0	90.5	0.0	9.5	100.0
	December	0.0	78.6	0.0	21.4	100.0	95.8	0.0	4.2	100.0
1864	TOTAL	1.0	82.0	1.5	15.6	100.0	85.9	3.0	11.1	100.0
1865	January	0.0	88.9	0.0	11.1	100.0	70.0	0.0	30.0	100.0
	February	0.0	75.0	0.0	25.0	100.0	100.0	0.0	0.0	100.0
	March	0.0	60.0	0.0	40.0	100.0	100.0	0.0	0.0	100.0
	April	0.0	60.0	0.0	40.0	100.0	100.0	0.0	0.0	100.0
	May	0.0	0.0	0.0	100.0	100.0	100.0	0.0	0.0	100.0
1865	TOTAL	0.0	68.0	0.0	32.0	100.0	90.0	0.0	10.0	100.0

Source: Wise, *Lifeline*, Appendices 5, 7, 9, 11, 13, 15, 17, and 22.

from Europe and the North for the years running up to the War, it is possible to estimate Southern cotton exports. Over the years 1856 through 1860, cotton exports to those regions averaged over 3,500,000 bales a year, or about 292,000 bales a month.[105] Generously assuming that, on average, a blockade-running vessel could carry one thousand bales of cotton, over the months from January 1861 through the end of the war, the successful blockade-runners, although apparently numerous, had the capacity to export only 2,694,500 bales, or about 55,000 bales a month. Taken together, these figures indicate that the successful blockade-runners would have been able to carry about 20 percent of what would probably have been exported if the South had permitted cotton production at the previous level had there been no blockade. If, instead of the one-thousand-bale capacity, the estimate of capacity is reduced to reflect the declining size of the average blockade-runner, the figure is slightly lower, about 14 percent (see Tables 4.19, 4.20, and 4.21).

Finally, the figures on cotton prices appear to confirm the argument that the blockade, in conjunction with the cotton embargo, had a significant impact on the Confederate economy. Although real cotton prices in the United Kingdom increased more than four times between 1860 and 1864 (they fell slightly in 1865 as more and more cotton was received from

105 Ellison, *Cotton Trade*, Table No. 3.

Table 4.19. *Estimated Carrying Capacity of Successful Blockade Runners (Bales of Cotton), 1861–1865*

Year	Number of Successful Attempts	Estimated Number of Successful Outbound Attempts	Number of Bales Carried, if 1000 Bales Capacity	Number of Bales Carried, if Decline in Tonnage is Taken into Account	Average Number of Bales Exported & Sold to the North (1856–1860)	Estimated Excess (+) or Shortage (–) of Capacity 1000 Bales	Estimated Excess (+) or Shortage (–) of Capacity "True Capacity"
1861	3,465	1,732.5	1,732,500	1,732,500	3,501,431	–1,768,931	–1,768,931
1862	568	284.0	284,000	264,120	3,501,431	–3,217,431	–3,237,311
1863	731	365.5	365,500	247,078	3,501,431	–3,135,931	–3,254,353
1864	522	261.0	261,000	209,844	3,501,431	–3,240,431	–3,291,587
1865	103	51.5	51,500	30,797	1,458,930	–1,407,430	–1,428,133
1861–1865	5,389	2,694.5	2,694,500	2,484,339	15,464,654	–12,770,154	–12,980,315

Note: Exports to North estimated at 650,000 bales a year.
Source: Surdam, *Northern Naval Superiority*, 4.

155

Table 4.20. *Bales Run Through the Blockade,*
1861–1865 (thousands)

Type of Ship	Bales
Steamers:	
Carolina Ports	272
Other Ports	94
Sailing Vessels:	
Carolina Ports	14
Other Ports	66
Total, All Ships	446

Source: Lebergott, "Through the Blockade," 880.

non-American sources), the real prices received in the Confederacy declined between 1860 and 1865. Thus, the blockade had a direct impact on the Confederate economy; the result of the declining prices received by Southern cotton farmers. However, it also had a substantial indirect effect. Implied transport costs from the South to the United Kingdom increased sharply. It is small wonder that farmers in Brazil, the West Indies, India, and Egypt found that cotton was a profitable crop; and, once they had entered the market, they did not leave when the blockade was lifted. Although after the war the South did manage to recover her leading role in Britain's cotton imports, it was a smaller role than she had held in the immediate prewar years. Although Surdam argues that "the South fell just short of regaining her former share of the market for raw cotton after the war, she was still able to easily recapture her leading role," in the interim, supporting players had reduced the importance of that role.[106] In the years 1856 to 1860, the South's share of British imports had averaged 81 percent; between 1866 and 1870, it was 47 percent; and even as late as the years 1876 to 1880, it was still only 72 percent. Moreover, given the ability of the new competitors to expand production should prices rise, the South was no longer able to act as an unrestricted "price setter." Because of the increased competition, the economic costs of the blockade were still felt in the South years after Appomattox.[107]

---

106 Surdam, *Naval Superiority*, 128, 129, 153.
107 The non-U.S. sources had accounted for 19 percent of U.K. cotton imports between 1856 and 1860; that figure rose to 62 percent during the war; and, although in the postwar decades their share in the market declined, it still stood at 28 percent in the years 1876 to 1880. See Table 4.3.

Table 4.21. Estimated Number of 400 Pound Bales of Cotton Smuggled Through the Blockade, 1862–1865

Calendar Year	Smuggled by Steamers							Smuggled by Sailing Vessels				Grand Total
	Wilmington	Charleston	Georgia & East Florida	West Florida	Mobile	Texas	Steamer Total	Carolina Ports	Georgia & East Florida Ports	Gulf Ports	Sailing Vessel Total	
1862	4,155	21,388	2,771	693	11,080	3,463	43,550	13,163	1,950	33,800	48,913	92,463
1863	74,790	31,713	2,078	8,311	13,850	1,385	132,127	3,738	1,625	21,125	26,488	158,615
1864	112,878	22,864	0	693	11,773	11,080	159,288	975	1,625	10,075	12,675	171,963
1865	1,385	8,113	0	0	693	18,006	28,197	163	0	1,138	1,301	29,498
TOTAL	193,208	84,078	4,849	9,697	37,396	33,934	363,162	18,039	5,200	66,138	89,377	452,539
Percentage of Steamer Totals and Percentage of Sailing Vessel Totals												
1862	9.5	49.1	6.4	1.6	25.4	8.0	100.0	26.9	4.0	69.1	100.0	
1863	56.6	24.0	1.6	6.3	10.5	1.0	100.0	14.1	6.1	79.8	100.0	
1864	70.9	14.4	0.0	0.4	7.4	7.0	100.0	7.7	12.8	79.5	100.0	
1865	4.9	28.8	0.0	0.0	2.5	63.9	100.0	12.5	0.0	87.5	100.0	
TOTAL	53.2	23.2	1.3	2.7	10.3	9.3	100.0	20.2	5.8	74.0	100.0	
Percentage of Grand Total												
1862	4.5	23.1	3.0	0.7	12.0	3.7	47.1	14.2	2.1	36.6	52.9	100.0
1863	47.2	20.0	1.3	5.2	8.7	0.9	83.3	2.4	1.0	13.3	16.7	100.0
1864	65.6	13.3	0.0	0.4	6.8	6.4	92.6	0.6	0.9	5.9	7.4	100.0
1865	4.7	27.5	0.0	0.0	2.3	61.0	95.6	0.6	0.0	3.9	4.4	100.0
TOTAL	42.7	18.6	1.1	2.1	8.3	7.5	80.2	4.0	1.1	14.6	19.8	100.0

Notes: (1) Mobile contains nine thousand bales from Louisiana during early 1862. Texas does not include raw cotton shipped from the Rio Grande.
(2) 1865 includes first quarter for all ports except Texas (through May).
Source: Surdam, *Northern Naval Superiority*, 171.

As an aside, it might be noted that, although after 1861 the blockade became increasingly effective, at no time was it as successful in cutting off the flow of cotton as was the initial Southern embargo in late 1860 and 1861. Between 1862 and 1864, the blockade had reduced Southern cotton exports from an annual average for 1856 to 1860 of 2,851,431 bales to, assuming the successful blockade-runner carried nothing but cotton and that they were always loaded to capacity, an average of no more than 303,000 bales (a decline of 89 percent). By contrast, the Southern embargo produced in 1861 a decline from the 2,851,431 average to a miniscule total of 10,129 bales (a decline of 99.6 percent).[108]

Overall then, it appears that, although the blockade may not have "garroted" the Confederacy, it did play a significant role in the Union victory. In 1861, the Northern economy was much richer than that of the South; and it was, therefore, better able to absorb the economic costs of the blockade than the South was able to absorb the costs of the lost export revenue. In addition, by cutting off coastal and interdicting river transport, "the blockade forced Southerners to rely more upon their frail railroad network," while, at the same time it "deprived those railroads of necessary supplies of railroad iron, machinery, and supplies."[109] However, it might be noted that its role, although overall probably more significant than any Southern action, might seem, to a casual observer, probably less impressive than the South's initial attempt at suicide – a failed threat that had been designed to force England and France to recognize the Confederate succession.

---

108 If Scherer's estimate of exports from 1862 to 1864 is correct (an average of 21,519 bales) the blockade-induced decline is still only 99.2 percent as compared with the embargo's 99.6 percent. Scherer, *Cotton*, 420.
109 Surdam, *Naval Superiority*, 207.

5

International Law and Naval Blockades during World War I

Britain, Germany, and the United States: Traditional Strategies versus the Submarine

1. INTRODUCTION

World War I saw blockades assume a major role in the strategy adopted by both coalitions of belligerent powers. In some ways, this role merely reflected a continuation of the strategies adopted by the naval forces in earlier European conflicts; but by this time there was one crucial change in technology – the German military's expanded use of the submarine as a weapon of war. Because the submarine had not been a subject included in the earlier formulations of international law, and, as it posed a new set of military and moral problems, over the course of the war, new rules for international behavior were brought to the table, but, even in 1919, there was no satisfactory resolution. The submarine was crucial to the German war effort; but, ultimately, it did not accomplish as much as did the Allies' more traditional blockade. The submarine, nevertheless, did lead to a number of important strategic changes in the organization of, and the responses to, blockades; and it was instrumental in shaping policies that would become critical during World War II.[1]

Because Germany and, even more so, Britain, depended on imports for a significant portion of their food supply, the threat of blockades was an important consideration in the design of domestic policies. Problems with maintaining or increasing domestic production, as well as those arising from attempts to keep imports flowing, confronted both powers, as did issues involving the restriction of unnecessary consumption, if that latter goal was possible to achieve at all. In addition to direct attempts to offset reductions in agricultural manpower, rationing of foodstuffs was introduced by both nations – a dramatic expansion of government powers from earlier wars.

---

1 See the discussion of the submarine in Chapter 1.

A second important political and military development was reflected in
the changes introduced into the British treatment of continental European
neutral countries – countries that had had extensive trading relations with
Germany prior to the onset of World War I. In addition to the standard
provisions regarding neutral trade and continuous voyages, geography gave
rise to the need to limit imports into those neutrals with overland connections to Germany because reexports to the Central Powers could not
be controlled without further military intervention. The resolution of this
problem was achieved by political bargaining; it involved the setting, and
the imposition, of so-called normal (that is prewar) levels of imports of various consumption goods, and, thus, established limits for the quantity of
imported supplies available to the neutrals. Such action defined a new set
of explicit international standards.

There was yet a third twentieth-century change that influenced both the
actual conflict and the analysis of that conflict: the increased power of the
central governments. The central governments' concern with obtaining
the information needed to design effective policies, information often of
a statistical nature, meant that considerably more quantitative data exist for
World War I than for any previous war. In short, the growth of the governments – and of the international agencies concerned with economic and
political problems – has meant that a better statistical (and nonstatistical)
portrait of events is possible.

2. THE WAR

2(1). The Initial Plans

In 1914, submarines were still untested, and they were not an important part of the German naval plans. Instead, the German naval command "believed that the Royal Navy would maintain a close blockade
of the German coast." Based on that assumption, Grand Admiral Alfred
von Tirpitz assumed that after the new coastal defenses (submarines and
mines) and the weather had inflicted major losses on the British, the German
High Seas Fleet would sortie, and, "in a decisive battle, would crush British
naval power for all time." As argued by "one historian of the German
Imperial Navy, 'given that Britain was Germany's primary potential opponent, a brief glance at the...map will confirm the obvious: the British
could bottle up the German fleet...in the North Sea'" by deploying a
distant blockade, "'to close the straits of Dover and the waters between

Scotland and Norway. Despite this Tirpitz failed to develop an alternative strategy.'"[2]

As the British refused to take the German bait, the war at sea, like the war on land, quickly turned into a stalemate. During the first year of the war, the German naval command was divided. "One faction clung to the hope of a great surface battle," despite the evidence that their fleet was badly outnumbered and that the British refused to leave their distant blockade. "Another group concluded that Germany was now involved in a different kind of war, in which naval action had become subsidiary to commercial warfare – that the principal targets of German naval operations would not be enemy warships but the merchant vessels that maintained enemy armies in the field." Ultimately, given the successes scored by submarines against merchant shipping and older British warships, they came to the conclusion that the U-boat, a vessel that could be built quickly and cheaply, "seemed to offer an effective means to retaliate against the British blockade."[3] In 1915, and again in 1917, the "other" group were to get their way.

Although Tirpitz had erred in his reading of the British mind, he was not far wrong. In the early years of the twentieth century, British naval plans had called for an "immediate imposition of a close blockade on the German coast"; and First Sea Lord Admiral John ("Jackie") Fisher "even suggested landing a portion of the British army on Germany's Pomeranian coast" in support of that effort. In 1912, however, after Fisher's initial retirement, it became apparent, even to the senior navy officers, that such thoughts were unrealistic; and "the Admiralty took the momentous decision to abandon the close blockade. By early 1914, the British had determined that in war their 'Grand Fleet' would move to the anchorage of Scapa Flow in the Orkney Islands," whereas "a smaller fleet unit would guard the English Channel."[4]

Even during the years when the navy was committed to a close blockade, officers assigned to the Naval Intelligence Department also had considered the possibility of engaging in economic warfare in the event of an armed conflict with Germany. As early as 1905, they had recognized that Germany

2 Williamson Murray, "Naval Power in World War I," in Colin S. Gray and Roger W. Barnett, eds., *Seapower and Strategy* (Annapolis: Naval Institute Press, 1980), 190–191, including a quote from Holger Herwig, "The Dynamics of Necessity." For a recent, very detailed analysis of this blockade, based on extensive archival research in British sources, see Eric W. Osborne, *Britain's Economic Blockade of Germany, 1914–1919* (London: Frank Cass, 2004).
3 Roger Chickering, *Imperial Germany and the Great War, 1914–1918* (Cambridge: Cambridge University Press, 1998), 89.
4 Murray, "Naval Power," 191.

had become progressively more dependent on its merchant marine to supply food and raw materials to its increasingly industrialized economy. German imports had risen from an average of 5,607 million marks over the years 1900–1902, to an average of 10,369 million marks over the three years 1911–1913, an increase of 85 percent (about 60 percent in real terms).[5] Those officers noted that some imports might be diverted through neutral ports; but they reasoned that the resulting increase in transport costs "would raise prices in Germany at the very time when the financial strain of war was pressing for a reduction"; and they concluded that a "blockade, particularly if indirect shipments to Germany could also be seized, 'would doubtless inflict in the end considerable losses on Germany. . . . But the effect would take time to produce.'"[6] It was recognized that Germany was not an island nation; that less than 20 percent of its national income was derived from exports; and less than a fifth of those were from extra-European countries. The officers also recognized that the Central Powers could quickly take over or easily secure required supplies from neutral neighbors. If, however, certain essential supplies (such as nitrate for fertilizer) could be cut off, the blockade could prove an effective weapon.[7] However, given the time required for a blockade to become effective, the British military command – strongly supported by the army representatives – still concluded that a European land effort was required.

Most Germans were, hardly surprisingly, not unaware of the possibility of a British blockade. Although Tirpitz, lobbying for his grand battle strategy, had denied that it was possible to carry the supplies into Germany that were necessary to replace those that could no longer be carried through the blockaded ports, the General Staff, in hindsight and admittedly somewhat optimistically, "calculated the capacity required to ship the import deficit through Switzerland and Austria at fifty trains a day, each of one hundred railway cars (that makes almost three and a half cars every minute, day and night). With careful management, the staff officers said, this could be done. But they failed to ask whether supplies could actually be purchased anywhere." Given the goals of the military in Germany and in England,

---

5 Current values from B. R. Mitchell, *European Historical Statistics, 1750–1970* (London: Macmillan, 1975), 494.

6 Avner Offer, *The First World War: An Agrarian Interpretation* (Oxford: Clarendon Press, 1989), 227.

7 Paul Kennedy, *The Rise and Fall of British Naval Mastery* (New York: Charles Scribner's Sons, 1976), 253–254; Paul Kennedy, *The Realities Behind Diplomacy: Background Influences on British External Policy, 1865–1980* (London: George Allen and Unwin, 1981), 182–183.

both General Staffs were anxious to prove that "a continental war could not be stopped short by blockade."[8]

2(2). The Narrative Story

The German strategy – a strategy designed to produce a short and relatively costless war – was quickly proved to have been wrong; and, as the war extended into 1915, it became increasingly clear that the conflict was going to be anything but short and costless. On the economic front, both Germany and the Allies saw "imports mounted, exports declined, trade balances became more and more unfavorable." (For Germany, see Table 5.1). "Rates of exchange, as against neutral currencies, steadily fell; prices rose." Also, consumer purchasing power declined, and labor became increasingly scarce.[9]

For the Germans, there was stalemate on the Western Front and, in a parallel fashion, the British decision to mount a distant blockade, instead of deploying their fleet close to shore, meant that the German fleet remained bottled up in the North Sea. The initial British blockade was "aimed at preventing the flow of what international law termed 'absolute contraband' onto the Continent." It was soon extended to include "conditional contraband," such as oil and nitrates; and, by 1915, it had been extended to include foodstuffs.[10] At the same time, although they still refused to use the word blockade, the British put increasing pressure on Germany's border neutrals. Those polices were designed to prevent the neutrals from reexporting their imports to Germany, to guarantee that import licensing facilities were not granted to firms on Allied trade blacklists, and that imports would not be allowed to fall into the hands of such firms, as far as possible. The imports of strategic commodities by bordering neutral countries were to be rationed so that they did not "exceed their normal domestic needs." In addition, they attempted to make certain that the Allies were the principle beneficiaries of both neutral exports and of the services of those countries' merchant fleets, and that the exports of the Central powers were reduced and their exchange rates rendered "as unfavorable as possible."[11] (For an assessment

---

8 Offer, *First World War*, 342.
9 Frank P. Chambers, *The War Behind the War, 1914–1918: A History of the Political and Civilian Fronts* (New York: Harcourt, Brace, 1939), 222–223.
10 Murray, "Naval Power," 202.
11 Maurice Parmelee, *Blockade and Sea Power: The Blockade, 1914–1919, and Its Significance for a World State* (New York: Thomas Y. Crowell, 1924), 72–73.

Table 5.1. *German Foreign Trade, 1913–1918 (Billions of Marks)*

	Foreign Trade at Current Prices			Foreign Trade in Gold Marks			Gold Mark Index (1913 = 100)	
	Imports	Exports	Balance (Imports – Exports)	Imports	Exports	Balance (Imports – Exports)	Imports	Exports
1913	10.8	10.1	0.7	10.8	10.1	0.7	100	100
1914:								
Jan. to July	6.4	6.0	0.4	6.4	6.0	0.4	79	74
August to Dec.	2.1	1.4	0.7	2.1	1.5	0.6		
1915	7.1	3.1	4.1	5.9	2.5	3.4	55	25
1916	8.4	3.8	4.5	6.4	2.9	3.5	59	29
1917	7.1	3.5	3.6	4.2	2.0	2.2	39	20
1918	7.1	4.7	2.4	4.2	2.8	1.4	39	28
August 1914 to Dec. 1918	31.8	16.5	15.3	22.8	11.7	11.1		

Source: G. Hardach, *The First World War* (Berkeley: University of California Press, 1977), 33.

of the efficiency of the British decision to "ration" the imports received by Holland and the Scandinavian countries, see Table 5.2.)[12]

As the "non-blockade" proved increasingly effective, the German navy's helplessness became ever more apparent. There was increasing political pressure within Germany to "do something"; and Tirpitz, supported by the Naval High Command and conservative politicians, urged his government to use the submarine fleet to attack British commerce without warning. In November 1914, without political authorization, he went so far in a newspaper interview as to speak of a German submarine blockade of Britain. The Grand Admiral and the navy high command aside, German conversion to a policy designed to blockade the British Isles by launching an unrestricted submarine assault on merchant shipping was "slow and very hesitant." The navy with some indirect support from the Foreign Office pushed hard, but the Kaiser and the Chancellor resisted.[13] Ultimately, however, despite political opposition and the Kaiser's initial doubts, Tirpitz's views triumphed; and, on February 4, 1915, "the Kaiser signed Germany's first declaration of submarine warfare."[14]

At this time, the Germans launched an unrestricted submarine offensive against the commercial shipping that supported the United Kingdom.[15] The British remote blockade effectively contained surface ships, but it was unable to prevent submarines passing through the wide Northern Sea gap between the Orkneys and Norway.[16] The waters around the British Isles were declared a war zone, and German submarines were empowered to attack without warning every merchant vessel that they encountered regardless of whether they were Allied or neutral. The results were significant but not spectacular. British Empire losses rose from a monthly average of

---

12 See Parmelee, *Blockade*, 430–436; Eli F. Heckscher, Kurt Bergendal, William Keilhau, Einar Cohn, and Thorsteinn Thorsteinsson, *Sweden, Norway, Denmark and Iceland in the World War* (New Haven: Yale University Press, 1930); and on the Netherlands, E. P. DeMonchy, "Commerce and Navigation," in *The Netherlands and the World War: Studies in the War History of a Neutral*, 4 vols. (New Haven: Yale University Press, 1928), vol. 2, 115–162.

13 H. P. Willmott, *Sea Warfare, Weapons, Tactics and Strategy* (Chichester: Anthony Bird, 1981), 53–54. Chambers, *War Behind the War*, 192, 200–201. In February 1915, the Admiralty Chief of Staff, after consulting with Tirpitz and his own officers, gave an assurance that Britain would come round within six weeks of opening the campaign, if all restrictions were removed. W. Hubatsch, *Die Ära Tirpitz: Studien zur deutschen Marinepolitik, 1890–1918* (Berlin, 1955), 129–130, cited in Offer, *First World War*, 363.

14 Chambers, *War Behind the War*, 201.   15 Murray, "Naval Power," 202.

16 Michael Lewis, *The History of the British Navy* (Harmondsworth: Penguin Books, 1957), 245–246. Toward the end of the war the British and Americans "were attempting to lay a 'northern barrage' of mines across to Norway, but the difficulties and the expenses were enormous," and they were never completely successful.

Table 5.2. *Statistics on Imports into Scandinavia and Holland: The Years 1916 and 1917 Compared with Average Prewar Imports*

Commodities	Imports During Year 1916 (Tons)	Imports During Year 1917 (Tons)	Average Yearly Imports During Years 1911–1913 Total Imports Less All Exports (Tons)	Average Yearly Imports During Years 1911–1913 Total Imports (Tons)	Imports During Year 1916 As % of Prewar Total Imports Less All Exports	Imports During Year 1916 As % of Prewar Total Imports	Imports During Year 1917 As % of Prewar Total Imports Less All Exports	Imports During Year 1917 As % of Prewar Total Imports
A. Corn and Grain								
Corn and Flour, Corn Fodder & Oil Cake (including Cake Content of Imported Oil Seeds)	4,104,709	1,734,020	4,582,136	8,706,624	89.58	47.14	37.84	19.92
Malt	18,792	7,259	52,392	64,272	35.87	29.24	13.86	11.29
Rice, Sago, Tapioca, and Macaroni	121,965	22,538	171,840	436,560	70.98	27.94	13.12	5.16
Peas, Beans, & Lentils	6,927	4,297	84,192	140,760	8.23	4.92	5.10	3.05
B. Other Foodstuffs								
Butter	1,107	78		18,096		6.12		0.43
Casings	774	378	528	7,812	146.59	9.91	71.59	4.84
Cocoa Bean and Preparations	23,307	10,841	13,320	48,816	174.98	47.74	81.39	22.21
Coffee	178,031	46,886	101,748	192,096	174.97	92.68	46.08	24.41
Fruit (fresh)	56,030	14,569	27,300	67,392	205.24	83.14	53.37	21.62
Fruit (dried)	31,258	7,617	39,480	40,272	79.17	77.62	19.29	18.91
Honey	2,894	430	2,916	3,024	99.25	95.70	14.75	14.22
Meat	10,471	14,833	6,384	24,084	164.02	43.48	232.35	61.59
Salt	279,769	140,263	463,236	482,220	60.39	58.02	30.28	29.09
Spices	7,691	712	2,868	3,876	268.17	198.43	24.83	18.37
Sugar & Syrup	97,471	55,373	74,484	185,748	130.86	52.47	74.34	29.81
Tea	19,161	1,112	6,156	6,252	311.26	306.48	18.06	17.79
Wines & Spirits	83,598	16,639	25,068	42,060	333.48	198.76	66.38	39.56

C. Oils, Fats, & Gums

Oils & Fats; Animal & Vegetable (including the Oil Content of Imported Oil Seeds, etc.)	321,427	166,283	275,972	585,248	116.47	54.92	60.25	28.41
Margarine	1,029	237	1,980	3,432	51.97	29.98	11.97	6.91
Petrol	48,945	19,431	42,460	43,548	115.27	112.39	45.76	44.62
Petroleum	442,724	158,560	403,080	405,984	109.84	109.05	39.34	39.06
Lubricating Oils	60,277	16,324	58,644	60,480	102.78	99.66	27.84	26.99
Mineral Oils (other kinds)	87,638	28,876	75,384	75,384	116.26	116.26	38.31	38.31
Rosins, Gums and Lacs	20,770	2,391	21,936	49,768	94.68	41.73	10.90	4.80
Rubber, Raw	1,834	256	2,388	9,828	76.80	18.66	10.72	2.60
Rubber, Manufactured	4,047	1,570	4,236	5,676	95.54	71.30	37.06	27.66
Varnishes & Polishes	1,814	1,178	2,052	2,628	88.40	69.03	57.41	44.82
Waxes	6,323	2,014	6,492	7,476	97.40	84.58	31.02	26.94
D. Textiles								
Cordage	8,116	3,777	8,548	15,576	94.95	52.11	44.19	24.25
Cotton (raw and waste)	80,325	23,754	66,192	99,660	121.35	80.60	35.89	23.84
Cotton (yarn & thread)	43,915	20,654	37,704	43,800	116.47	100.26	54.78	47.16
Cotton Manufactures	25,158	15,006	11,196	23,568	224.71	106.75	134.03	63.67
Total Raw & Manufactured Cotton	149,398	59,414	115,092	167,028	129.81	89.44	51.62	35.57
Flax & Linen	3,784	4,152	5,728	5,948	66.06	63.62	72.49	69.80
Hemp & Jute (raw)	23,570	12,810	41,620	58,375	56.63	40.38	30.78	21.94
Jute manufactures	11,062	5,548	10,500	11,824	105.35	93.56	52.84	46.92
Linoleum	6,105	3,770	5,616	5,676	108.71	107.56	67.13	66.42
Wool (raw, tops, waste, & shoddy)	20,033	7,742	17,364	34,932	115.37	57.35	44.59	22.16
Woolen Yarns	3,573	1,629	6,480	7,200	55.14	49.63	25.14	22.63
Woolen Manufactures	9,629	6,822	5,688	8,028	169.29	119.94	119.94	84.98
Total Raw & Manufactured Wool	33,235	16,193	29,532	50,160	112.54	66.26	54.83	32.28
E. Metals & Manufactures Thereof								
Aluminum	172	174	864	2,820	19.91	6.10	20.14	6.17
Antimony	158	40.5	112	124	141.07	127.42	36.16	32.66
Copper & Alloys	27,742	13,232	32,124	133,080	86.36	20.85	41.19	9.94

(continued)

167

Table 5.2 *(continued)*

Commodities	Imports During Year 1916 (Tons)	Imports During Year 1917 (Tons)	Average Yearly Imports During Years 1911–1913: Total Imports Less All Exports (Tons)	Average Yearly Imports During Years 1911–1913: Total Imports (Tons)	Imports During Year 1916: As % of Prewar Total Imports Less All Exports	Imports During Year 1916: As % of Prewar Total Imports	Imports During Year 1917: As % of Prewar Total Imports Less All Exports	Imports During Year 1917: As % of Prewar Total Imports
Iron & Steel	254,394	181,538	1,061,724	2,653,392	23.96	9.59	17.10	6.84
Lead	12,561	4,832	18,948	35,136	66.29	35.75	25.50	13.75
Nickel	188	44	132	144	142.42	130.56	33.33	30.56
Tin	3,406	696	3,888	26,148	87.60	13.03	17.90	2.66
Zinc Crude (spelter)	361	857	1,668	68,196	21.64	0.53	51.38	1.26
F. Other Aticles								
Asphalt	5,039	1,443	11,844	12,000	42.54	41.99	12.18	12.03
Borax & Boric Acid	2,046	1,119	4,428	7,176	46.21	28.51	25.27	15.59
Corkwood	8,875	3,627	8,208	11,088	108.13	80.04	44.19	32.71
Fertilzers:								
(a) Ammonia Sulphate	8,226	2,758	13,872	38,412	59.30	21.42	19.88	7.18
(b) Phosphates	295,412	91,930	465,240	1,001,604	63.50	29.49	19.76	9.18
(c) Soda-Nitrate	146,396	110,373	143,784	263,508	101.82	55.56	76.76	41.89
Graphite	878	496	1,212	1,260	72.44	69.68	40.92	39.37
Hides & Skins	16,464	5,819	5,968	66,432	275.87	24.78	97.50	8.76
Leather	4,503	1,090	2,832	7,260	159.00	62.02	38.49	15.01
Leather Manufactures	1,026	466	1,192	1,768	86.07	58.03	39.09	26.36
Seeds (Grass & Clover)	7,914	3,764	7,176	16,164	110.28	48.96	52.45	23.29
Soda, Ash, Caustic & Sulphate	83,630	32,118	119,196	129,936	70.16	64.36	26.95	24.72
Sulphur	32,833	18,359	52,284	64,596	62.80	50.83	35.11	28.42
Tanning Materials	34,533	7,694	35,612	37,980	96.97	90.92	21.61	20.26
Tobacco	212,233	25,696	31,164	39,216	681.02	541.19	82.45	65.52

Source: Maurice Parmelee, *Blockade and Sea Power: The Blockade, 1914–1919, and its Significance for a World State* (New York: Thomas Y. Crowell, 1924), appendix V, Statistics of Imports into Scandanavia and Holland, 430–436.

Table 5.3. *War Losses of British Empire Merchant Vessels: August 1914 to November 1918*
(Losses of All Classes of Vessels in Gross Tonnage Each Month)

Months	1914	1915	1916	1917	1918	Total 1914–1918
January		32,403	72,234	153,899	173,387	431,923
February		36,636	69,159	310,868	213,045	629,708
March		79,230	98,409	352,344	199,426	729,409
April		29,376	138,689	526,447	214,426	908,938
May		92,924	64,690	345,293	179,395	682,302
June		90,605	32,273	398,773	143,639	665,290
July		56,418	80,925	359,539	163,801	660,683
August	46,603	149,084	43,554	331,370	143,944	714,555
September	79,798	99,731	107,360	186,647	129,483	603,019
October	83,651	54,287	170,120	261,873	56,330	626,261
November	15,730	89,929	180,078	175,194	15,352	476,283
December	26,596	74,848	174,376	257,807		533,627
ANNUAL TOTAL	252,378	885,471	1,231,867	3,660,054	1,632,228	7,661,998

Source: James Arthur Salter, *Allied Shipping Control: An Experiment in International Administration* (Oxford: Clarendon Press, 1921), 355–359. For similar estimates, see C. Ernest Fayle, *War and the Shipping Industry* (London: Oxford University Press, 1927), 417.

46,000 tons in the seven months, August 1914 through February 1915, to an average of over 85,000 tons over the next seven months. Total Allied losses rose from a monthly average of 61,000 to 121,000 over the same period (see Tables 5.3, 5.4, 5.5, and 5.6).

The new strategy was not without its problems. Although there are differences in the precise estimates, there is a general agreement about the order of magnitudes. On the one hand, on the date of the declaration, the German navy had only thirty-seven submarines (only twenty-nine available for frontline duty); and, on average only six were at sea at the same time during the spring of 1915.[17] Over the course of 1915, the Germans lost

---

17 Michelsen puts the number in the fleet on August 10, 1914, at twenty, with sixteen available for duty. Primarily on the basis of the data prepared by Michelsen, both Terraine's and Kemp's data imply that there were probably fewer than twenty-eight completed or commissioned in the fleet at the outbreak of the war, about the same as Michelsen in November 1994. Andreas Michelsen, *Der U-bootskrieg, 1914–1918* (Leipzig: K. F. Koehler, 1925), 182–185; Paul Kemp, *U-boats Destroyed: German Submarine Losses in the World Wars* (Annapolis: Naval Institute Press, 1997), 9–59; John Terraine, *Business in Great Waters: The U-Boat Wars, 1916–1945* (Ware: Wordsworth Editions, 1999), 762–764. See also R. H. Gibson and Maurice Prendergast, *The German Submarine War, 1914–1918* (Annapolis: Naval Institute Press, 2002; first published 1930) and Chickering, *Imperial Germany*, 8–9. See Appendix Tables 5.A.1, 5.A.2, and 5.A.3 on the German submarine fleet.

Table 5.4. *War Losses of British Empire Merchant Vessels: August 1914 to November 1918*
(Losses of All Classes of Vessels in Percentage of Gross Tonnage Each Month)
(Monthly Percentages of Annual Totals)

Months	1914	1915	1916	1917	1918	Total 1914–1918
January		3.66	5.86	4.20	10.62	5.64
February		4.14	5.61	8.49	13.05	8.22
March		8.95	7.99	9.63	12.22	9.52
April		3.32	11.26	14.38	13.14	11.86
May		10.49	5.25	9.43	10.99	8.91
June		10.23	2.62	10.90	8.80	8.68
July		6.37	6.57	9.82	10.04	8.62
August	18.47	16.84	3.54	9.05	8.82	9.33
September	31.62	11.26	8.72	5.10	7.93	7.87
October	33.15	6.13	13.81	7.15	3.45	8.17
November	6.23	10.16	14.62	4.79	0.94	6.22
December	10.54	8.45	14.16	7.04	0.00	6.96
ANNUAL TOTAL	100.00	100.00	100.00	100.00	100.00	100.00

Source: See Table 5.3.

Table 5.5. *War Losses of British Empire Merchant Vessels: August 1914 to November 1918*
(Losses of All Classes of Vessels in Monthly Percentage of Gross Wartime
Monthly Total Tonnage)

Months	1914	1915	1916	1917	1918	Total 1914–1918
January		7.50	16.72	35.63	40.14	100.00
February		5.82	10.98	49.37	33.83	100.00
March		10.86	13.49	48.31	27.34	100.00
April		3.23	15.26	57.92	23.59	100.00
May		13.62	9.48	50.61	26.29	100.00
June		13.62	4.85	59.94	21.59	100.00
July		8.54	12.25	54.42	24.79	100.00
August	6.52	20.86	6.10	46.37	20.14	100.00
September	13.23	16.54	17.80	30.95	21.47	100.00
October	13.36	8.67	27.16	41.82	8.99	100.00
November	3.30	18.88	37.81	36.78	3.22	100.00
December	4.98	14.03	32.68	48.31	0.00	100.00
ANNUAL TOTAL	3.29	11.56	16.08	47.77	21.30	100.00

Source: See Table 5.3.

Table 5.6. *War Losses of Allied and Neutral Merchant Vessels: August 1914 to November 1918*
(Losses of All Classes of Vessels in Gross Tonnage Each Month)

Months	1914	1915	1916	1917	1918	Total 1914–1918
January		48,181	94,817	364,767	303,608	811,373
February		60,190	114,523	536,582	305,509	1,016,804
March		88,369	165,560	590,545	320,708	1,165,182
April		58,500	183,032	866,610	275,016	1,383,158
May		124,983	122,955	574,317	263,420	1,085,675
June		135,638	110,772	665,405	241,380	1,153,195
July		107,044	115,251	549,359	237,941	1,009,595
August	64,752	183,596	165,077	488,675	276,522	1,178,622
September	89,586	147,525	222,438	342,097	166,608	968,254
October	95,282	88,666	344,035	429,459	113,054	1,070,496
November	25,802	144,901	318,704	284,550	24,316	798,273
December	43,978	124,623	348,405	385,759		902,765
ANNUAL TOTAL	319,400	1,312,216	2,305,569	6,078,125	2,528,082	12,543,392

Source: See Table 5.3.

twenty vessels, and they had only forty-four operational U-boats.[18] More-over, even as late as 1917, they were able to keep hardly more than one-third of their subs at sea – maintenance was time and financially consuming.[19]

On the other hand, and ultimately much more important, there were potentially very serious diplomatic problems. Although not always obeyed, international law had established a set of rules to govern the relationship between blockading belligerents and merchant vessels and their passengers and crew, regardless of whether they were belligerents or neutrals – only specific categories of goods were subject to interdiction, vessels could not be sunk without warning, and the safety of passengers and crew were assured. Germany had, in fact, subscribed to these rules; and, for interdiction by surface warships, the rules were not unreasonable. Submarines, however, were a different matter. If the merchant vessels was armed, and as the war progressed more and more were, a submarine commander who ordered

18 Kemp (*U-boats Destroyed*, 11–17) puts the number destroyed in 1915 at twenty-one. Michelsen's (*Der U-bootskrieg*, 185) numbers indicate that on December 10, there were thirty-two operational U-boats of a total of forty-four in the fleet. See also Holger Herwig, *"Luxury" Fleet; The Imperial German Navy, 1888–1918* (London: George Allen and Unwin, 1980), 163–164, as quoted in Murray, "Naval Power," 202, for slightly different numbers.
19 Murray, "Naval Power," 202. Chickering, *Imperial Germany*, 89. The monthly averages for the percentage of submarines at sea are 12.6 for 1914, 20.8 for 1915, 25.9 for 1916, 34.1 for 1917, and 35.6 for 1918; see Appendix Table 5.A.2.

his U-boat to surface in order to warn the merchant vessel and inspect its cargo put his submarine at risk. Although the British having twisted (some might say having made a shambles of) the rules by widening the definition of contraband and applying direct and indirect pressure to neutrals, those policies were directed against property and profits. A successful submarine blockade, however, required that vessels be sunk without warning and, at times, without even having been adequately identified. Such policies were directed against not only profits and property but against civilian lives as well.[20]

It is certainly surprising that the Germans undertook the campaign as if the economic strength and military potential of the United States was of no importance.[21] Moreover, even the first American reaction should have raised some storm flags. In response to the German note declaring the blockade, the American president responded: "If the commanders of German vessels should . . . destroy on the high seas an American vessel or the lives of American citizens, it would be difficult for the Government of the United States to view the act in any other light than as an indefensible violation of neutral rights. . . . The Government of the United States would be constrained to hold the Imperial German Government to a strict accountability for such acts of their naval authorities and to take any steps that it might be necessary to take to safeguard American lives and property and to secure to American citizens the full enjoyment of their acknowledged rights on the high seas."[22]

That note was, however, only the first chapter. In May 1915, "after announcing in a front-page advertisement in the *New York Times* that the liner *Lusitania* would be subject to attack due to a blockade, the Germans actually torpedoed and sank her, killing 1,198 passengers (including 100 Americans)."[23] Neutral reaction – particularly American reaction – was vocal, strident, and swift. The Americans accused the Germans of barbarism;

20 Chickering, *Imperial Germany*, 90.
21 Murray, "Naval Power," 202–203. The explanation for the German failure to recognize the potential economic and military strength of the United States is in doubt. However, it may reflect a common military failing – a belief that winning a battle is more important than winning the war. Given the friction between the military, naval, and civilian leadership, it is possible that the naval high command thought that the chance to make the navy a major part of the German war effort led them to deliberately downplay the potential negative long-term consequences of the decision to launch unrestricted submarine warfare. In this action they may have been tacitly supported by the army who, given the stalemate on the Western Front, may well have feared a civilian-led peace offensive.
22 Chambers, *War Behind the War*, 202. The note was signed by the Secretary of State William Jennings Bryan, but the real authors were President Woodrow Wilson and Robert Lansing, Counseller of the State Department.
23 Murray, "Naval Power," 203. Chickering, *Imperial Germany*, 90.

and politicians reacted. Senator Lodge declared, "My heart is more moved by the thought of a drowned baby than by an unsold bale of cotton." The historian Frank Chambers concluded, "Germany's malpractices on the high seas were more criminal and spectacular than England's."[24] At the same time, initial German success was not spectacular – in March and April 1915, U-boats sank less than 116,000 tons of Allied shipping.[25] Although the navy strongly disagreed, at this stage of the war the civilians in the government, particularly Chancellor Theobald von Bethmann-Hollweg, the civilian head of the German federal government, and the diplomats in the Foreign Office, fearing that the blockade would draw the United States and the Netherlands into the war on the Allied side, concluded that the price of a continued submarine blockade was too high. The war was still less than a year old; and so, in 1915, political priorities won out. At first, the German government merely limited the blockade to the waters around the British Isles; but then, in September, for all intents and purposes, they called it off completely.[26]

The Admiralty's staff, however, continued to promote the view that economic warfare, including an unrestricted submarine blockade of the United Kingdom, was a strategy that was capable of leading to a German victory.[27] Throughout 1916, the navy waged an unremitting campaign to renew the blockade. That campaign was summarized in the chief of staff's memorandum of December 22. That memorandum identified two targets – "the British wheat supply and the merchant tonnage that carried it" – that, if destroyed, could bring Britain to her knees before the United States could fully deploy its resources on the side of the Allies.[28] Those words were only a precursor of deeds; and, by early 1916, Germany had entered into a new "intensive" phase of the submarine campaign.

The claim of the German admiralty that Britain could be brought to surrender as a result of increased submarine warfare and some fortuitous events has generated debates, both among contemporaries and in subsequent historical writings. That starvation would have occurred within six weeks or, possibly at most about six months, as argued by the admiralty in a series of rhetorical documents designed to influence policy, has sometimes been translated into a statement of actual fact about the British conditions. It is of interest that the British themselves did not seem to have a similar expectation, not unreasonably, given that, throughout World War I, home

---

24 Chambers, *War Behind the War*, 199.   25 Murray, "Naval Power," 203.
26 Chickering, *Imperial Germany*, 90–91.   27 Offer, *First World War*, 357.
28 Murray, "Naval Power," 203–204, Offer, *First World War*, 357.

production and imports were not markedly, if at all, lower than the prewar levels.

The German forecasts were based on some moderately careful, if ultimately proved to be erroneous, calculations made by an economist, Hermann Levy. These estimates, as described later, included arguments based on British and allied shipping losses; an expected shortfall in wheat exports from the United States and Canada – a shortfall that meant an increased demand for ships to obtain the required imports from more distant countries; and the "terror" imposed on neutral traffic that would dramatically reduce this possible source of alternative shipping.[29] Although estimated Allied losses to submarines were initially accurate, and U.K. food imports did decline slightly over the course of the war, the forecast of neutral behavior was completely inaccurate, at least in the case of the United States. The mystery to be explained is not about the nature of the German forecast but, rather, the reliance on it in later historical writings.

As mentioned earlier, the critical December memorandum was largely based on the work of Professor Doctor Hermann Levy, a student of British agriculture. He noted that Britain did not hold large stocks of grain (at minimum six and a half weeks and at maximum seventeen weeks' supply), but instead depended on a continuous flow of imports of grain from all over the world. Levy's assumptions regarding British stocks appear to have been somewhat understated. Postwar research by Beveridge has, for example, shown that the stocks of wheat (including flour as wheat) held on September 1 represented 36.3 percent of the total of imports and domestic produced consumption in the year 1914, 39.6 percent in 1915, 36.2 percent in 1916, 45.9 percent in 1917, and 47.9 percent in 1918. For barley, the ratios were 76.8 percent, 77.5 percent, 74.5 percent, 82.7 percent, and 88.7 percent; and for oats, they were 77.4 percent, 79.6 percent, 85.2 percent, 81.6 percent, and 84.7 percent.[30] Although the import and home production series are for the calendar, not the seasonal, year, they are closely correlated with the ratio of September stocks to imports and home production in the September to August seasonal years. Citing official British sources, Levy concluded, based on a Royal Commission Report, that "if wheat imports were cut off when domestic stocks were already exhausted, there would be a rise in prices, a dangerous panic, and a shortage so serious that the war could not

29 Offer, *First World War*, 354–367.
30 Sir William H. Beveridge, *British Food Control* (New Haven: Yale University Press, 1928), 346–347, 354–358, 359.

be carried on." By the next summer, "Professor Levy reported that overseas harvests were poor"; North America would not have an export surplus; the British would have to turn to South America, India, and Australia; and, because of the increased distance, those imports would require more merchant tonnage.[31]

Later studies have shown that Levy's analysis was badly flawed, as were the supporting arguments provided, (some say "cooked"), by the naval bureaucracy. His assumptions about the size of stocks aside, his conclusions about public reactions were based on anecdotes drawn from newspapers and parliamentary speeches. The calculations of necessary tonnage were suspect, and proved to be wrong. The arguments ignored the possibility of relative price-induced substitution both in terms of the decision to allocate tonnage and in terms of the profitability, and therefore the choices of home versus foreign production of foodstuffs. The arguments were so weak that even some German politicians – politicians with no military expertise – were able to point out that there were major gaps in the analysis. Those gaps included, but were not limited to, the omission from the calculations of "the 1.7 million tons of Austrian-German shipping interned in the United States and the one million plus tons yearly capacity of the Allied dockyards," to say nothing of the American shipbuilding capacity that might come on line should that country enter the war.[32]

But analytical correctness does not always carry the day in a political debate. In the summer of 1916, the inconclusive result of the Battle of Jutland, the subsequent retreat of the German fleet to its North Sea ports, the reimposition of the British distant blockade, and the deadlock on the Western Front appeared to imply a long-run strategic stalemate. The apparent lengthening of the war far into the foreseeable future, the German army's recognition that there would be no victory in 1915 or 1916, and the impact of the British blockade on the domestic economy weakened the effectiveness of the moral argument against indiscriminate sinkings and again tipped the balance back to the advocates of unrestricted submarine warfare.[33] This time, however, the proponents encompassed a much broader base. Not

31 Cited in Offer, *First World War*, 357, 359. For a further discussion of British wheat supplies, their origin, and distribution, see *Supply of Food and Raw Material in Time of War: Royal Commission: Minutes of Evidence*, PP 1905 Cd. 2644 XXXIX, and Andrew Millar, *Wheat and Its Products: A Brief Account of the Principal Cereal: Where It Is Grown and the Modern Method of Producing Wheaten Flour* (London: Pitman, 1916), both cited by Offer.
32 Offer, *First World War*, 362–364, Murray, "Naval Power," 203.
33 Willmott, *Sea Warfare*, 53–54; Chickering, *Imperial Germany*, 90–92.

only had the Social Democrats in the Reichstag joined the coalition, but the German public also had begun to clamor for unrestricted submarine warfare. "The chancellor remained more skeptical"; he was no softer than his military protagonists; but he had a better assessment of the costs and benefits of the blockade; and he could not bring himself to support such a gamble.[34] However, in October, the Centrum party in the Reichstag's Committee of Supplies passed a resolution to the effect that, if the German Supreme Command (O.H.L.) "should come to a decision in favor of the unrestricted submarine warfare, the Chancellor could rely on the confidence of the Reichstag only by his unqualified support of that decision."[35]

In March 1916, the French Channel packet, the *Sussex*, was torpedoed without warning, and some eighty civilians (including several Americans) were killed or injured. Initially, the Germans claimed that the vessel had not been sunk by a submarine; but "fragments of a German torpedo were found embedded in the hull." The American response was a near ultimatum to the German government: "unless the Imperial German Government 'should now immediately declare and effect an abandonment of its present method of submarine warfare against passenger and freight carrying vessels, the Government of the United States can have no other choice but to sever diplomatic relations with the German Empire altogether.'" In May, the Germans bowed to American pressure. Their note to Washington contained "a disavowal and a general abandonment of its previous attitude. In future the German submarine would abide by the rules of cruiser warfare." For the moment, the 'intensified' phase of the German campaign had ended; and the threat of American entry into the war was removed.[36]

On January 9, 1917, however, under increasing pressure, both military and civilian, the Kaiser made the decision to renew unrestricted submarine warfare on February 1. Bethmann-Hollweg remained in office for another six months; but, under continuous conservative attack, he was forced to resign in July. One unanticipated cost of the strategic decision was the pressure put on the German/Austrian alliance. The German decision had been made unilaterally; their allies were not informed until after the submarines had put to sea. Although ultimately forced to accept the German decision, King Charles made it clear that he fully agreed with his civilian advisers and was opposed to the "declaration of unrestricted submarine war by Austria-Hungary." Unfortunately, because of the alliance, his country was forced to share the risks, stigma, and ultimate costs of Germany's decision to resume

34 Chickering, *Imperial Germany*, 92; Chambers, *War Behind the War*, 342.
35 Chambers, *War Behind the War*, 342.   36 Chambers, *War Behind the War*, 277–279.

all-out submarine attacks.[37] "In January 1917, Germany notified the United States and the Allies of the resumption of unrestricted submarine attacks and, after several attacks on American ships, the United States declared war on Germany on 6 April 1917." The cost of the German decision was to be very high.[38]

Based on Levy's analysis and their own studies (to say nothing of common sense), the German bureaucracy recognized that "wheat was almost the sole ingredient of bread in Britain, and some 80 per cent was imported. Furthermore, the quantities imported (about six million tons a year) corresponded quite closely with the U-boats' sinking capacity." Moreover, once released, the U-boat captains did not disappoint their superiors. "Sinkings matched the forecast in the first six months, and continued to be a serious drain on the British war economy until the very end of the war."[39] The losses of Allied and neutral shipping rose from 537,000 tons in February, to 591,000 tons in March, to 867,000 tons in April.[40] Of that total, losses of British Empire shipping amounted to 311,000 tons in February, 352,000 tons in March, and 526,000 tons in April, nearly 60 percent of the total. The new blockade also had a significant impact on the American merchant marine. Over the thirty months of war from August 1914 through January 1917, U.S. losses had totaled 31,000 tons, and no vessels had been sunk in twenty-one of those thirty months. In February, March, and April 1917, American losses totaled 48,000 tons – about 2.4 percent of all Allied losses (see Tables 5.7, 5.8, 5.9, 5.10, 5.11, and 5.12).

"From February 1917, up to the end [of the war], almost 4,000 ships were lost, of nearly eight and a half million tons." And over some 15,000 British merchant seamen lost their lives. Over the same period, the Germans lost 191 submarines.[41] A measure of the efficiency of the German U-boat fleet, based the allied and neutral tonnage lost per U-boat (or per U-boat at sea), indicates relatively unchanged efficiency from the start of the war until the beginning of 1917 (see Table 5.12). Thereafter, efficiency increased for several months, but then it began a continued decline that lasted from June or July 1917 until the end of the war. This decline accompanied the expanded use of convoys by Allied shippers.

---

37 Chambers, *War Behind the War*, 344, 354–357, 375–376.
38 Robert A. Doughty and Harold E. Raugh, Jr., "Embargoes in Historical Perspective," *Parameters*, 21 (Spring 1991), 27.
39 Offer, *First World War*, 359, 366–367.
40 B. H. Liddell Hart, *Strategy*, 2nd rev. ed. (New York: Praeger, 1967), 202–204; Chambers, *War Behind the War*, 413. See also James Arthur Salter, *Allied Shipping Control: An Experiment in International Administration* (Oxford: Clarendon Press, 1921), 357–359. These three sets of estimates differ slightly, and we have presented the Salter numbers.
41 Lewis, *History of the British Navy*, 243.

Table 5.7. *War Losses of Allied and Neutral Merchant Vessels: August 1914 to November 1918*
(Losses of All Classes of Vessels in Gross Tonnage)

Country	1914	1915	1916	1917	1918	Total 1914–1918
United States	0	16,154	14,720	165,965	142,230	339,069
Belgium	34	21,523	16,045	35,609	30,590	103,801
Brazil	0	0	2,258	10,022	0	12,280
British Empire	252,378	885,471	1,231,867	3,660,054	1,632,228	7,661,998
Cuba	0	0	0	0	1,510	1,510
France	14,414	93,987	169,829	459,454	178,107	915,791
Greece	2,462	15,751	86,106	236,070	57,699	398,088
Italy	48	39,379	233,318	336,522	150,453	759,720
Japan	0	23,457	16,075	57,267	22,557	119,356
Peru	0	0	0	1,374	0	1,374
Portugal	0	871	1,041	16,933	9,281	28,126
Romania	285	0	4,434	0	0	4,719
Russia	4,094	34,821	33,552	97,567	13,049	183,083
Uruguay	0	0	0	1,957	1,638	3,595
Argentina	0	0	0	2,522	1,753	4,276
Denmark	11,176	20,621	59,321	123,600	28,989	243,707
Netherlands	11,974	29,350	71,002	88,617	11,026	211,969
Norway	11,902	94,206	276,861	659,949	137,398	1,180,316
Persia	758	0	0	0	0	758
Spain	0	3,762	46,296	58,667	59,766	168,491
Sweden	9,875	32,863	42,844	65,976	49,808	201,366
TOTAL	319,400	1,312,216	2,305,569	6,078,125	2,528,082	12,543,393

Source: Salter, *Allied Shipping Control*, 355–359.

The Germans had failed to anticipate both the Allied responses and the naval, economic, financial, and military, power of the Americans.[42] Hindsight has shown that it was the knowledge that the Americans would soon arrive "that alone held the Anglo-French armies in the field during the disastrous spring of 1918."[43] Moreover, it was American financial resources that kept the Allied economies from bankruptcy during the same period.

American involvement aside, the British response to the renewed blockade had three major components. First, almost certainly of most importance, was the British innovation of a very broad set of domestic food policies. At the outbreak of the war, the British government had not prepared a plan for dealing with food shortages. In August 1914, although there was no

42 By the end of the war there were more American than British troops deployed on the Western Front.
43 Willmott, *Sea Warfare*, 55.

Table 5.8. *War Losses of Allied and Neutral Merchant Vessels: August 1914 to November 1918 (Losses of All Classes of Vessels in Gross Tonnage; Each Country as a Percentage of Annual and Wartime Totals)*

Country	1914	1915	1916	1917	1918	Total 1914–1918
United States	0.00	1.23	0.64	2.73	5.63	2.70
Belgium	0.01	1.64	0.70	0.59	1.21	0.83
Brazil	0.00	0.00	0.10	0.16	0.00	0.10
British Empire	79.02	67.48	53.43	60.22	64.56	61.08
Cuba	0.00	0.00	0.00	0.00	0.06	0.01
France	4.51	7.16	7.37	7.56	7.05	7.30
Greece	0.77	1.20	3.73	3.88	2.28	3.17
Italy	0.02	3.00	10.12	5.54	5.95	6.06
Japan	0.00	1.79	0.70	0.94	0.89	0.95
Peru	0.00	0.00	0.00	0.02	0.00	0.01
Portugal	0.00	0.07	0.05	0.28	0.37	0.22
Romania	0.09	0.00	0.19	0.00	0.00	0.04
Russia	1.28	2.65	1.46	1.61	0.52	1.46
Uruguay	0.00	0.00	0.00	0.03	0.06	0.03
Argentina	0.00	0.00	0.00	0.04	0.07	0.03
Denmark	3.50	1.57	2.57	2.03	1.15	1.94
Netherlands	3.75	2.24	3.08	1.46	0.44	1.69
Norway	3.73	7.18	12.01	10.86	5.43	9.41
Persia	0.24	0.00	0.00	0.00	0.00	0.01
Spain	0.00	0.29	2.01	0.97	2.36	1.34
Sweden	3.09	2.50	1.86	1.09	1.97	1.61
TOTAL	100.00	100.00	100.00	100.00	100.00	100.00

Source: See Table 5.7.

shortage of most foodstuffs, sugar was in short supply; and the government organized a Royal Commission on Sugar Supplies and "The Home Secretary assumed a monopoly of all sugar imports." Moreover, in the winters of 1914–1915 and 1915–1916 the government did make secret purchases of wheat from Argentina and began to accumulate some emergency stocks. Still, the issue of food imports was not considered serious.

By 1916, however, some leaders, including Lloyd George had become concerned about the potential problems of the supply of food. In July 1916, Parliament passed the Output of Beer Restriction Bill – an act that was estimated to save 150,000 tons of imports annually (a comment on the British diet) – and the Board of Trade created a Departmental Committee on Prices. Three months later, a Royal Commission on Wheat Supplies was established, but the government was still committed to a policy of

Table 5.9. *War Losses of Allied and Neutral Merchant Vessels: August 1914 to November 1918*
(Losses of All Classes of Vessels in Gross Tonnage; Each Year's Losses as a Percentage
of Total Wartime Losses for that Country)

Country	1914	1915	1916	1917	1918	Total 1914–1918
United States	0.00	4.76	4.34	48.95	41.95	100.0
Belgium	0.03	20.73	15.46	34.31	29.47	100.0
Brazil	0.00	0.00	18.39	81.61	0.00	100.0
British Empire	3.29	11.56	16.08	47.77	21.30	100.0
Cuba	0.00	0.00	0.00	0.00	100.00	100.0
France	1.57	10.26	18.54	50.17	19.45	100.0
Greece	0.62	3.96	21.63	59.30	14.49	100.0
Italy	0.01	5.18	30.71	44.30	19.80	100.0
Japan	0.00	19.65	13.47	47.98	18.90	100.0
Peru	0.00	0.00	0.00	100.00	0.00	100.0
Portugal	0.00	3.10	3.70	60.20	33.00	100.0
Romania	6.04	0.00	93.96	0.00	0.00	100.0
Russia	2.24	19.02	18.33	53.29	7.13	100.0
Uruguay	0.00	0.00	0.00	54.44	45.56	100.0
Argentina	0.00	0.00	0.00	58.99	41.01	100.0
Denmark	4.59	8.46	24.34	50.72	11.90	100.0
Netherlands	5.65	13.85	33.50	41.81	5.20	100.0
Norway	1.01	7.98	23.46	55.91	11.64	100.0
Persia	100.00	0.00	0.00	0.00	0.00	100.0
Spain	0.00	2.23	27.48	34.82	35.47	100.0
Sweden	4.90	16.32	21.28	32.76	24.74	100.0
TOTAL	2.55	10.46	18.38	48.46	20.15	100.0

Source: See Table 5.7.

noninterference.[44] Such a policy was not, however, able to withstand the effects of the tightening submarine blockade.

On November 20, 1916, on the eve of Germany's declaration of unrestricted submarine warfare, by Orders in Council, the British Government "compulsorily lengthened the extraction of flour from wheat to 76 percent"; and British consumers began to eat "war bread."[45] On the

---

44 The President of the Board of Trade, Walter Runciman, in a speech to the House of Commons said: "But the thing we want to avoid in this country is ... to put ourselves in the position of a blockaded people. Bread tickets, meat coupons, all those artificial arrangements are harmful, and they are harmful to those who have least with which to buy. . . . We want to avoid any rationing of our people in food." Quoted in Chambers, *War Behind the War*, 418, 419.

45 For a discussion of extraction rates, usually 70 percent, and the legal changes that permitted wartime stretching of the wheat supply, see M. K. Bennett, "Wheat and War, 1914–18 and Now," *Wheat Studies of the Food Research Institute*, 16 (November 1939), 69–72, for the discussion of extraction rates. See also Chambers, *War Behind the War*, 420.

Table 5.10. *War Losses of American Merchant Vessels: August 1914 to November 1918*
(Losses of All Classes of Vessels in Gross Tonnage Each Month)

Months	1914	1915	1916	1917	1918	Total 1914–1918
January		3,374	0	0	2,981	6,355
February		4,050	0	4,443	9,771	18,264
March		0	0	20,886	4,922	25,808
April		3,331	0	22,846	2,660	28,837
May		0	0	18,065	13,505	31,570
June		0	2,294	20,104	28,699	51,097
July		1,924	0	27,106	5,909	34,939
August	0	1,571	0	6,487	46,937	54,995
September	0	1,904	0	13,095	14,574	29,573
October	0	0	692	16,855	9,202	26,749
November	0	0	11,734	16,075	3,070	30,879
December	0	0	0	0		0
ANNUAL TOTAL	0	16,154	14,720	165,962	142,230	339,066

Source: Salter, *Allied Shipping Control*, 355–359.

Table 5.11. *War Losses of American Merchant Vessels: August 1914 to November 1918*
(Losses of All Classes of Vessels in Percentage of Gross Tonnage Each Month)
(Monthly Percentages of Annual and Wartime Totals)

Months	1914	1915	1916	1917	1918	Total 1914–1918
January		20.89	0.00	0.00	2.10	1.87
February		25.07	0.00	2.68	6.87	5.39
March		0.00	0.00	12.58	3.46	7.61
April		20.62	0.00	13.77	1.87	8.50
May		0.00	0.00	10.89	9.50	9.31
June		0.00	15.58	12.11	20.18	15.07
July		11.91	0.00	16.33	4.15	10.30
August	0.00	9.73	0.00	3.91	33.00	16.22
September	0.00	11.79	0.00	7.89	10.25	8.72
October	0.00	0.00	4.70	10.16	6.47	7.89
November	0.00	0.00	79.71	9.69	2.16	9.11
December	0.00	0.00	0.00	0.00	0.00	0.00
ANNUAL TOTAL	0.00	100.00	100.00	100.00	100.00	100.00

Source: See Table 5.10.

Table 5.12. *Measures of Benefits and Costs and the Efficiency of the German Submarine Campaigns*

Year & Month	Wartime Shipping Losses (Gross Tonnage)							Submarines (Numbers of Vessels)			Allied & Neutral Tonnage Lost Per U-Boat in Fleet	Allied & Neutral Tonnage Lost Per U-Boat at Sea	Allied & Neutral Tonnage Lost Per U-Boat Sunk
	British Empire	France	Italy	Russia	United States	Other Allied & Neutral Nations	Total Allied & Neutral Nations	Total Fleet	At Sea	Sunk			
1914													
August	46,603	0	0	717	0	17,432	64,752	20	2	2	3,238	32,376	32,376
September	79,798	0	48	0	0	9,740	89,586	24	2	0	3,733	44,793	–
October	83,651	2,221	0	3,377	0	6,033	95,282	27	8	0	3,529	11,910	–
November	15,730	5,183	0	0	0	4,889	25,802	28	3	1	922	8,601	25,802
December	26,596	7,010	0	0	0	10,372	43,978	28	4	2	1,571	10,995	21,989
1914 TOTAL	252,378	14,414	48	4,094	0	48,466	319,400	25.40	3.80	1.00	2,515	18,788	63,880
1915													
January	32,403	4,390	0	1,315	3,374	6,699	48,181	27	4	2	1,784	12,045	24,091
February	36,636	14,487	0	0	4,050	5,017	60,190	27	1	0	2,229	60,190	–
March	79,230	4,909	0	0	3,331	4,230	88,369	27	6	3	3,273	14,728	29,456
April	29,376	399	8	9,061		16,333	58,500	26	6	1	2,250	9,750	58,500
May	92,924	3,857	1,373	251	0	27,943	124,983	35	8	0	3,571	15,623	124,983
June	90,605	1,419	1,987	5,155	1,924	37,086	135,638	40	10	3	3,391	13,564	45,213
July	56,418	6,962	0	16,403	1,571	23,350	107,044	44	10	3	2,433	10,704	35,681
August	149,084	2,212	0	1,265	1,904	29,464	183,596	45	13	3	4,080	14,123	61,199
September	99,731	16,409	3,420	1,145		24,916	147,525	46	14	2	3,207	10,538	73,763
October	54,287	20,430	1,220	0		12,729	88,666	44	7	1	2,015	12,667	88,666
November	89,929	12,124	20,939	226	0	21,683	144,901	42	9	1	3,450	16,100	144,901
December	74,848	6,389	10,432	0	0	32,954	124,623	44	8	0	2,832	15,578	–
1915 TOTAL	885,471	93,987	39,379	34,821	16,154	242,404	1,312,216	37.25	8.0	1.58	2,936	13,669	69,064
1916													
January	72,234	1,298	4,277	0	0	17,008	94,817	41	4	0	2,313	23,704	–
February	69,159	13,221	3,301	6,966	0	21,876	114,523	41	10	0	2,793	11,452	–
March	98,409	20,871	2,790	327	0	43,163	165,560	47	11	2	3,523	15,051	82,780
April	138,689	5,795	336	844	0	37,368	183,032	52	20	3	3,520	9,152	61,011
May	64,690	12,583	25,400	593	0	19,689	122,955	58	7	2	2,120	17,565	61,478
June	32,273	9,868	36,635	762	2,294	28,940	110,772	65	15	1	1,704	7,385	110,772

July	80,925	5,574	18,302	1,107	0	9,343	115,251	72	28	3	1,601	4,116	38,417
August	43,554	8,876	60,750	2,774	0	49,123	165,077	74	21	1	2,231	7,861	165,077
September	107,360	13,142	22,439	1,153	692	78,344	222,438	80	21	1	2,780	10,592	222,438
October	170,120	27,379	22,240	13,685	11,734	109,919	344,035	87	17	1	3,954	20,237	344,035
November	180,078	21,850	6,658	114	0	98,270	318,704	93	29	5	3,427	10,990	63,741
December	174,376	29,372	30,190	5,227	0	109,240	348,405	97	34	3	4,005	14,570	116,135
1916 TOTAL	1,231,867	169,829	233,318	33,552	14,720	622,283	2,305,569	67.25	18.08	1.83	2,893	11,138	104,799
1917													
January	153,899	48,131	22,207	5,213	0	135,317	364,767	103	20	2	3,541	18,238	182,384
February	310,868	38,321	37,748	10,213	4,443	135,989	537,582	111	38	4	4,843	14,147	134,396
March	352,344	40,836	15,607	2,822	20,886	158,050	590,545	128	36	3	4,614	16,404	196,848
April	526,447	38,811	51,350	15,878	22,846	201,275	856,607	127	42	2	6,745	20,395	428,304
May	345,293	27,348	22,975	12,918	18,065	147,718	574,317	130	42	7	4,418	13,674	82,045
June	398,773	53,534	38,233	6,475	20,104	148,286	665,405	132	61	2	5,041	10,908	332,703
July	359,539	33,135	30,542	6,851	27,106	102,266	559,439	130	42	6	4,303	1,320	93,240
August	331,370	42,452	29,491	9,742	6,487	69,133	488,675	128	45	3	3,818	10,859	162,892
September	186,647	67,243	2,724	10,973	13,095	61,415	342,097	139	59	13	2,461	5,798	26,315
October	261,873	18,388	52,762	6,946	16,855	72,635	429,459	140	55	5	3,068	7,808	85,892
November	175,194	32,435	5,826	2,604	16,075	52,416	284,550	137	30	7	2,077	9,485	40,650
December	257,807	18,800	27,057	7,032	0	75,063	385,759	134	60	9	2,879	6,429	42,862
1917 TOTAL	3,660,054	459,434	336,522	97,667	165,962	1,359,563	6,079,202	128.25	44.17	5.25	3,950	11,470	96,495
1918													
January	173,387	31,420	28,285	9,642	2,981	57,893	303,608	132	33	9	2,300	9,200	33,734
February	213,045	11,484	28,623	0	9,771	42,586	305,509	129	50	3	2,368	6,110	101,836
March	199,426	15,795	37,964	0	4,922	62,601	320,708	127	37	5	2,525	8,668	64,142
April	214,426	23,143	5,254	1,189	2,660	28,344	275,016	125	44	7	2,200	6,250	39,288
May	179,395	21,207	18,168	1,309	13,505	29,836	263,420	125	55	14	2,107	4,789	18,816
June	143,639	15,799	9,520	0	28,699	43,723	241,380	112	36	3	2,155	6,705	80,460
July	163,801	18,761	14,065	0	5,909	35,405	237,941	121	45	6	1,966	5,288	39,657
August	143,944	26,782	570	909	46,937	57,380	276,522	124	45	7	2,230	6,145	39,503
September	129,483	4,854	380	0	14,574	17,317	166,608	128	43	7	1,302	3,875	23,801
October	56,330	8,862	7,624	0	9,202	31,036	113,054	121	54	7	934	2,094	16,151
November	15,352	0	0	0	3,070	5,894	24,316	–	–	–	–	–	–
1918 TOTAL	1,632,228	178,107	150,453	13,049	142,230	412,015	2,528,082	124.40	44.20	6.8	1,847	5,200	33,798

183

Source: Salter, *Allied Shipping Control*, 355–359; Table 5A-2; Michelsen, *Der U-bootskrieg*, 186.

22nd, the Shipping Control Committee reported that the stocks of wheat were running down; that the country was living from "hand to mouth"; and that "while the Wheat Commission have purchased 700,000 quarters in North America," "there were no steamers to bring the wheat to England."

In response, the prime minister created a new ministerial position, the Food Controller. The new Ministry controlled all imported foodstuffs; "it formed purchasing organizations in Canada and the United States"; and "it requisitioned home-produced meat, butter, cheese and potatoes." Over the last years of the war, its annual purchases averaged £900,000,000. It bought domestic commodities at prices that encouraged the British farmer to maximize production; and it had absolute power to fix consumer prices. Moreover, in order to hold prices down, at times it subsidized the difference between its dictated purchase prices and the prices consumers were required to pay. By the end of 1917, prices of all principal foodstuffs had been fixed at every step of the production and distribution process, from the farm or ship to the retail store.

In parallel, a Food Production Department was established within the Board of Agriculture; and the Board's president "began his two-years' drive to restore British agricultural" prosperity. Prices had been fixed at what were thought to be profitable levels, but the labor shortage still constrained production. The Department oversaw policies that guaranteed that farmers were protected from the draft and released from military service and that "schoolboys on holiday and German prisoners" were assigned to jobs on farms; and it underwrote the organization of the Woman's Land Army and directed its members to productive jobs in the countryside. By 1918, these efforts had resulted in increases in domestic production of 60 percent in wheat, 50 percent in oats, and 40 percent in potatoes over the figures for the same products in 1914, and the homegrown percentage of the wheat and flour, barley, oats, and peas and beans consumed in Britain had increased from 46 to 60 percent. In the case of wheat and flour, for example, between 1914 and 1918 domestic production had risen from 1,685 to 2,496 thousand tons – an increase of 48 percent. Despite the loss of grassland to crops, "milk production remained level"; and the production of "livestock showed only a slight decrease."[46]

---

46 Chambers, *War Behind the War*, 418–424. For a full discussion of the means by which the British attempted to maintain the agricultural labor force and agricultural production during World War I, see the essays on "Great Britain and Ireland: The Maintenance of the Supply of Agricultural Labour in England and Wales During the War," *International Review of Agricultural Economics*, 13 (January–February, March–April, May, November, 1922), 85–105, 234–262, 312–337, 777–793. See Beveridge, *British Food Control*, 359.

Second, and from a military point of view, was the tactical reorganization of the merchant fleet from individual voyages into convoys. Naval convoys were hardly a new innovation. As discussed earlier, in the ninth, tenth, and eleventh centuries, the Venetians employed convoys for the protection of their river trade with the inland cities of what had been the Holy Roman Empire. By the middle of the thirteenth century, they were conducting convoys up the Po as far as the junction with the Mincio and "up the Adige as far as Legnago."[47] Later convoys had been used by the Spain to protect her American treasure fleets and by the French during the nearly century-long series of wars with England.

The lessons of history, however, meant little to the British Admiralty in the early years of the war. Convoys are not without their problems: they are slow and difficult to organize; the delays incurred by ships waiting for the convoy to form are costly; the speed of the convoy is governed by the speed of the slowest vessel; and the arrival of a convoy can cause port congestion. For centuries, those economic issues had raised serious questions to shipowners, whose primary concern was profits. In the eyes of the Admiralty, however, there were other problems as well. Admiral Sir John Jellicoe, the First Sea Lord, opposed the convoy system on the grounds that there were insufficient escorting craft; and, given his views of the nature of naval warfare, he would not hear of denuding the Grand Fleet of its destroyers. Others in the British High Command argued that the captains of merchant ships, having had no experience in sailing or maneuvering in company, could not be trusted to keep "close station," that the convoy might be dispersed by fog or storm, that the convoy would offer a very large and inviting target to German submarines, and that the convoy might be raided by units of the German surface fleet.[48]

The facts, however, were largely otherwise. The opponents' estimates of the required number of escorts were inflated; there were sufficient numbers of escort vessels to cover the twenty or so merchant ships that would, on average, arrive each day. The Ministry of Shipping was in a position to quickly organize the assembly of vessels at convenient points. Individual ships, forced to zig-zag, were often slower than the slowest tramp in a convoy. The merchant captains proved that they were more than capable of keeping station. Furthermore, the impact on the morale of the seamen

---

47 Frederic C. Lane, *Venice: A Maritime Republic* (Baltimore: Johns Hopkins University Press, 1973), 61, 62; see Chapter 1.
48 For a later discussion of the convoy issue, explaining (defending) his earlier position, see Earl Jellicoe, *The Submarine Peril: The Admiralty Policy in 1917* (London: Cassell and Company, 1934), particularly 96–120.

was profound. "If a ship was hit, rescue was assured"; and, as a result, the crew could devote their entire energy "to their proper work of navigation." The secrecy of the convoy's routes and destinations could be more easily preserved than if individual ships needed to use wireless means to obtain instructions and thus revealed their location.[49]

The battle between the convoy's proponents and its detractors was fought out during the tenure of Sir Edward Carson as First Lord of the Admiralty. He was continually torn between his loyalty to Jellicoe and the senior naval bureaucracy and the pressure applied by the prime minister. Pressed by the cadre of younger naval officers, and supported by the Shipping Controller and the Secretary of the War Cabinet, Sir Maurice Hankey, Lloyd George had begun to attribute the mounting losses at sea to the stubborn unimaginativeness of the Admiralty chiefs. He pointed to the experimental convoys that employed trawlers to transport colliers from England to France – convoys that, in the months of March, April, and May 1917, had involved the movement of 4,013 vessels across the Channel with a loss of only nine ships. The American naval representative, Admiral Sims, was impressed and reported favorably to his government; that government, in turn, raised the possibility of contributing American destroyers to the effort, if the British moved to innovate a strategy that involved convoys.[50] In England, the prime minister resolved to 'take peremptory action on the question of convoys'; and, in May, the Admiralty, under pressure from the War Cabinet, "officially consented to a trial convoy from Gibraltar." "In mid-May the Admiralty appointed a Committee on Convoys" and established a Convoy Department. By early summer, "the convoy system was operating regularly on routes from America, Gibraltar, Dakar and in the North Sea." The convoys' success convinced the prime minister to remove the team at the Admiralty, which he considered had originally blocked innovation of the new strategy. Under its new commander, Sir Eric Geddes, "the convoy system was extended in every direction," and to outgoing as well

49 The counteranalysis was made by Commander Reginald Henderson, a leading advocate of the convoy system. In calculating the number of escorts that would be required, the Admiralty had put the total number of sailings and arrivals at about 2,500 per week. Henderson discovered that, of the 2,500 movements, only 120 to 145 per week involved oceangoing ships forced to transit the U-boat danger zones. Those were the only ships that would be affected by the innovation of convoys; the rest were mostly engaged in coastal traffic. Andrew Gibson and Arthur Donovan, *The Abandoned Ocean: A History of United States Maritime Policy* (Columbia: University of South Carolina Press, 2000), 111–112. See also Chambers, *War Behind the War*, 415.

50 Jellicoe, *Submarine* Peril, 112–113, 123. In May, soon after the entry of the United States into the war, six "destroyers arrived in Queenstown harbor to begin convoy duty. Many more destroyers were to follow." Gibson and Donovan, *Abandoned Ocean*, 112. Chambers, *War Behind the War*, 417.

Table 5.13. *Convoy Losses and Sailings (All Convoys Through November 23, 1918)*

	Number of Ships	Total Gross Tonnage	Percent Ships	Percent Gross Tonnage
Homeward Bound				
1. Escorted Safely	9,250	49,541,313	98.89	98.97
2. Torpedoed in Convoy	61	305,643	0.65	0.61
3. Lost by Marine Perils	12	64,540	0.13	0.13
4. Lost While Not in Convoy	31	145,633	0.33	0.29
TOTAL SAILINGS	9,354	50,057,129	100.00	100.00
Outward Bound				
1. Escorted Safely	7,289	36,832,412	99.32	99.13
2. Torpedoed in Convoy	41	279,640	0.56	0.75
3. Lost by Marine Perils	4	17,819	0.06	0.05
4. Lost While Not in Convoy	5	26,419	0.06	0.07
TOTAL SAILINGS	7,339	37,156,290	100.00	100.00

Source: C. Ernest Fayle, *Seaborne Trade, Volume III, The Period of Unrestricted Submarine Warfare: History of the Great War* (New York: Longmans, Green, 1924), Appendix C, 472–473. Percentages as computed by Fayle.

as incoming voyages. "Between mid–summer 1917 and November 1918, 16,657 ships were convoyed to or from British shores with a loss of only 0.71 percent."[51]

The results of the innovation bordered on the spectacular. Taking together all convoys, both outward- and inward-bound, that sailed through November 23, 1918 – a total of 16,693 vessels aggregating 87,213,419 tons – only 102 ships of 585,283 tons were torpedoed while in convoy (0.61 percent of the vessels and 0.67 percent of the tonnage), whereas 16,539 vessels of 86,373,725 tons (99.1 percent of the vessels and 99.04 percent of the tonnage) arrived safely in port (see Table 5.13).[52] The German blockade had finally been broken, although it is not clear if the blockade could have been before this, if the Admiralty had adopted this ten–century–old strategy earlier in the war.

Third, for the first time since the war began, the Allies began to effectively coordinate their shipping efforts. During the first years of the war, the British government had found no need and, therefore, made no effort to control

51 Chambers, *War Behind the War*, 417, Offer, *First World War*, 220–221.
52 A total of fifty-two vessels (254,411 tons) were lost from non-war–related accidents or while traveling outside the convoy.

even British merchant shipping. The laws of supply and demand continued
to allocate space, and freight charges reflected "the varying stringencies of
the war." As long as the war was thought to be of short duration, the government was not inclined to introduce a bureaucratic machine to replace
these market functions. By the end of 1915, however, it had become clear
that it would not be a short war; and submarine attacks had become more
deadly. In November, "the Board of Trade appointed two committees to
provide a tentative control." "The Ship Licensing Committee supervised all
British tonnage not under government requisition." "The Requisitioning
(Carriage of Foodstuffs) Committee was empowered to requisition British
ships for the importation of food, especially of wheat." The next month,
the Admiralty appointed a Port and Transit Executive Committee, whose
duties included overseeing the improvement of conditions in British ports,
the task of preventing submarine induced "irregular congestion" in ports
and their approaches, and the job of "defending port labour against excessive
recruitment into the army." The problems, however, continued to mount;
and, in, January the Cabinet established the Shipping Control Committee –
a committee charged with exercising "general supervision over the whole
field of shipping problems." Although helping alleviate some requisitioning
and cross-Channel problems, the Committee, unfortunately, had no executive powers; and its major impact was to underscore the seriousness of the
problem and "confer the Cabinet's blessing on the work" of the other two
committees.

Finally, in December 1916, the Ministry of Shipping was established.
The new Ministry launched a major shipbuilding and purchase program –
a program designed to build over one million tons of merchant shipping
annually, as well as to make substantial purchases of new and existing vessels abroad. Total additions to Britain's merchant fleet – additions that had
averaged 884,000 tons in the years 1911 through 1913 – totaled 1,265,000
tons in 1917 and 1,269,000 tons in 1918. Although the tonnage of new
vessels built in the United Kingdom or ordered from abroad declined from
the prewar average of 806,000 to a low of 321,000 in 1916, it rebounded
to 753,000 in 1917 and to 946,000 in 1918. Purchases from foreigners had
increased from the 1911–1913 average of 30,000 tons to 218,000 in 1917
and to 249,000 in 1918; and other additions (including transfers from the
colonies) increased substantially, although irregularly, from the prewar average of 48,000 tons to a total of 407,000 in 1915, 110,000 in 1916, and
294,000 in 1917. Although declining, thereafter such "other" additions still
totaled 74,000 tons in the last year of the war (see Tables 5.14, 5.15, 5.16,
5.17, 5.18, and 5.19).

Table 5.14. *British and World Shipbuilding Tonnage of Merchant Vessels of 100 Tons Gross or Larger Launched Each Year (1,000 Gross Tons)*

Year	United Kingdom	United States	Japan	Other	World Total
1911–1913 Average	1,825	173	56	908	2,962
1914	1,683	163	86	920	2,852
1915	651	157	49	344	1,201
1916	608	385	146	549	1,688
1917	1,163	821	350	604	2,938
1918	1,348	2,602	490	1,007	5,447
1919	1,620	3,580	612	1,332	7,144
1920	2,056	2,349	457	1,001	5,863
1921	1,538	995	227	1,581	4,341
1922	1,031	79	83	1,255	2,448
1923	646	96	72	829	1,643
COUNTRY TOTAL: 1914–1918	5,453	4,128	1,121	3,424	14,126
COUNTRY TOTAL: 1914–1923	12,344	11,227	2,572	9,422	35,565

Source: Fayle, *War and the Shipping Industry*, 416.

Table 5.15. *British and World Shipbuilding Tonnage of Merchant Vessels of 100 Tons Gross or Larger Launched Each Year (Percentage of World Total)*

Year	United Kingdom	United States	Japan	Other	World Total
1911–1913 Average	61.61	5.84	1.89	30.65	100.00
1914	59.01	5.72	3.02	32.26	100.00
1915	54.20	13.07	4.08	28.64	100.00
1916	36.02	22.81	8.65	32.52	100.00
1917	39.58	27.94	11.91	20.56	100.00
1918	24.75	47.77	9.00	18.49	100.00
1919	22.68	50.11	8.57	18.65	100.00
1920	35.07	40.06	7.79	17.07	100.00
1921	35.43	22.92	5.23	36.42	100.00
1922	42.12	3.23	3.39	51.27	100.00
1923	39.32	5.84	4.38	50.46	100.00
COUNTRY TOTAL: 1914–1918	38.60	29.22	7.94	24.24	100.00
COUNTRY TOTAL: 1914–1923	34.71	31.57	7.23	26.49	100.00

Source: See Table 5.14.

Table 5.16. *British and World Shipbuilding Tonnage of Merchant Vessels of 100 Tons Gross or Larger Launched Each Year (Ratio to National Total 1914–1918)*

Year	United Kingdom	United States	Japan	Other	World Total
1911–1913 Average	33.47	4.19	5.00	26.52	20.97
1914	30.86	3.95	7.67	26.87	20.19
1915	11.94	3.80	4.37	10.05	8.50
1916	11.15	9.33	13.02	16.03	11.95
1917	21.33	19.89	31.22	17.64	20.80
1918	24.72	63.03	43.71	29.41	38.56
COUNTRY TOTAL: 1914–1918	100.00	100.00	100.00	100.00	100.00

Source: See Table 5.14.

The Ministry of Shipping worked closely with the American Shipping Committee; in cooperation with other agencies, "it exerted absolute control over the allocation of freight space"; it drastically reduced the level of nonessential imports; "it placed the entire British mercantile fleet, tramps and liners alike, under requisition at 'Blue Book' rates; and" insofar as was possible, "it concentrated purchases in the nearest markets" so that the length and duration of ocean voyages was minimized. The Committee went a long way toward solving the problems of British maritime

Table 5.17. *British and World Shipbuilding Tonnage of Merchant Vessels of 100 Tons Gross or Larger Launched Each Year (Ratio to National Total 1914–1923)*

Year	United Kingdom	United States	Japan	Other	World Total
1911–1913 Average	14.78	1.54	2.18	9.64	8.32
1914	13.63	1.45	3.34	9.76	8.02
1915	5.27	1.40	1.91	3.65	3.38
1916	4.93	3.43	5.68	5.83	4.75
1917	9.42	7.31	13.61	6.41	8.26
1918	10.92	23.18	19.05	10.69	15.32
1919	13.12	31.89	23.79	14.14	20.09
1920	16.66	20.92	17.77	10.62	16.49
1921	12.46	8.86	8.83	16.78	12.21
1922	8.35	0.70	3.23	13.32	6.88
1923	5.23	0.86	2.80	8.80	4.62
COUNTRY TOTAL: 1914–1923	100.00	100.00	100.00	100.00	100.00

Source: See Table 5.14.

Table 5.18. *Merchant Vessels Launched During the War Period (100 Tons Gross or Larger)*

Where Launched	1914 Vessels	1914 Tons	1915 Vessels	1915 Tons	1916 Vessels	1916 Tons	1917 Vessels	1917 Tons	1918 Vessels	1918 Tons	1914–1918 Vessels	1914–1918 Tons
Panel A: Vessels & Tonnage												
United Kingdom & Dominions	714	1,706,000	354	664,000	342	630,000	366	1,229,000	485	1,579,000	2,261	5,808,000
United States (Coast & Lakes)	94	201,000	84	177,000	211	504,000	326	998,000	929	3,033,000	1,644	4,913,000
Rest of the World (Excluding Germany & Austria)	389	499,000	301	351,000	407	544,000	395	683,000	430	786,000	1,922	2,863,000
TOTAL	1197	2,406,000	739	1,192,000	960	1,678,000	1,087	2,910,000	1,844	5,398,000	5,827	13,584,000
Panel B: Percentage of Annual Total												
United Kingdom & Dominions	59.6	70.9	47.9	55.7	35.6	37.5	33.7	42.2	26.3	29.3	38.8	42.8
United States (Coast & Lakes)	7.9	8.4	11.4	14.8	22.0	30.0	30.0	34.3	50.4	56.2	28.2	36.2
Rest of the World (Excluding Germany & Austria)	32.5	20.7	40.7	29.4	42.4	32.4	36.3	23.5	23.3	14.6	33.0	21.1
TOTAL	100.0	100.0	100.0	100.0	100.0	100.0	100.0	100.0	100.0	100.0	100.0	100.0
Panel C: Percentage of 1914–1918 Total												
United Kingdom & Dominions	31.6	29.4	15.7	11.4	15.1	10.8	16.2	21.2	21.5	27.2	100.0	100.0
United States (Coast & Lakes)	5.7	4.1	5.1	3.6	12.8	10.3	19.8	20.3	56.5	61.7	100.0	100.0
Rest of the World (Excluding Germany & Austria)	20.2	17.4	15.7	12.3	21.2	19.0	20.6	23.9	22.4	27.5	100.0	100.0
TOTAL	20.5	17.7	12.7	8.8	16.5	12.4	18.7	21.4	31.6	39.7	100.0	100.0

Source: Salter, *Allied Shipping Control*, 361.

Table 5.19. Additions and Deductions from Tonnage on the Register of the United Kingdom, 1911–1922, Steamships Only
(In 1,000 tons net)

	Average 1911–13	1914	1915	1916	1917	1918	1919	1920	1921	1922
					Panel A: Additions					
New Vessels[1]	806	788	453	321	753	946	884	675	570	682
Purchased from Foreigners[2]	30	64	68	23	218	249	8	50	91	100
Transferred from Colonies	10	61	30	23	38	26	18	17	34	29
Other Additions[3]	38	30	377	87	256	48	789	488	956	268
TOTAL ADDITIONS	884	943	928	454	1,265	1,269	1,699	1,230	1,651	1,079
					Panel B: Deductions					
Wrecked	121	83	176	162	297	191	87	168	46	71
Broken Up	30	10	8	3	3	2	2	10	8	11
Sold Foreign[4]	398	354	121	14	21	18	640	429	504	509
Transferred to Colonies	32	39	32	174	48	4	27	31	141	48
Other Deductions[5]	28	196	560	714	2,324	1,162	106	161	797	149
TOTAL DEDUCTIONS	609	682	897	1,067	2,693	1,377	862	799	1,496	788
Net Increase or Decrease	275	261	31	-613	-1,428	-108	837	431	155	291

Notes:
[1] Includes new vessels built abroad to orders of Shipping Controller.
[2] Includes foreign vessels taken over by Shipping Controller.
[3] Includes tonnage added in consequence of remeasurement, prizes of war, and ex-enemy vessels transferred after the war.
[4] Includes in 1919 and 1920 foreign vessels handed back by Shipping Controller.
[5] Includes losses by war risks, and in 1921 the closing of provisional register in respect to ex-enemy ships now reregistered.

Source: Fayle, War and the Shipping Industry, 422:

Table 5.20. *The Balance of Demand For, and Supply of, Food in the United Kingdom,*
1914–1918 (Billions of Calories)

	Average 1909–13	1914	1915	1916	1917	1918
A. Potential Demand	51.0	52.5	53.7	54.4	55.1	55.3
B. Total Supply						
Imports	29.6	34.2	31.8	31.1	29.2	27.9
Home Production	21.1	21.4	21.9	19.4	20.6	21.2
Food Controls					3.7	7.5
TOTAL SUPPLY	50.7	55.6	53.7	50.5	53.5	56.6
C. Surplus (+) or Shortage (−). [B−A]	−0.3	3.1	0.0	−3.9	−1.6	1.3
D. C as a Percentage of A	−0.6	5.9	0.0	−7.2	−2.9	2.4

Source: P. E. Dewey, "Food Production in the United Kingdom, 1914–1918," in *Transactions of the Royal Historical Society,* 5th Series, 30 (1980), 88.

coordination; but questions of British-French synchronization remained unresolved.[53]

In December 1917, the Allied Maritime Transport Council (AMTC) was organized; and, with the responsible Ministers from each country appointed as members, it became an effective international allocative agency. Thus, from December onward, the AMTC allocated all the tonnage, both domestic and foreign, that was employed by the Allies. "Not a bushel of wheat, not a shell, not a man was carried over the sea except by its sanction. England, France and Italy were secured their most necessary imports. Expeditionary forces in Salonika, Mesopotamia and Palestine were maintained at strength. Two million American troops were safely landed in France."[54]

Overall, given the German goals, the British efforts appear to have been fairly successful. In terms of total supply, although shortages of available calories existed in 1916 (7 percent) and 1917 (3 percent), there were surpluses in both 1914 (6 percent) and 1918 (2 percent), and an equal balance of supply and demand in 1915. Given that, in the prewar years, the average deficit was 0.6 percent, the wartime performance appears to be reasonably good (see Table 5.20).[55] The wartime increases in the percentage of domestic production of certain foodstuffs, such as all cereals and pulses, and butter and margarine, have already been noted. Although, by 1918,

53 Chambers, *War Behind the War,* 411–414, 434–435.
54 Chambers, *War Behind the War,* 435–436.
55 A part of the potential shortage was, of course, offset by imports both in the prewar and war time periods. Beveridge, *British Food Control,* 311. P. E. Dewey, "Food Production and Policy in the United Kingdom, 1914–1918," *Transactions of the Royal Historical Society,* 5th series, 30 (1980), 71–89.

Table 5.21. *Weekly Consumption of Principal Foods in the United Kingdom in 1914–1918 as a Percentage of Average Consumption 1909 to 1913*

Commodity	Average 1909–1913	1914	1915	1916	1917	1918
	Panel A: Pounds Per Head of the Population					
Flour	100.0	98.8	97.0	101.2	109.6	112.1
Butchers' Meat	100.0	96.6	93.6	88.7	82.4	62.3
Bacon and Ham	100.0	100.0	123.5	129.4	105.9	135.3
Butter	100.0	96.8	87.1	74.2	64.5	54.8
Margarine	100.0	127.3	181.8	218.2	218.2	200.0
Lard	100.0	100.0	118.2	100.0	72.7	136.4
Potatoes	100.0	116.9	121.0	110.9	104.6	143.3
Sugar	100.0	102.1	108.2	82.9	68.5	63.7
	Panel B: Pounds Per "Man"					
Flour	100.0	98.8	97.7	101.8	110.5	113.1
Butchers' Meat	100.0	96.7	94.7	89.8	82.4	62.7
Bacon and Ham	100.0	100.0	122.0	129.3	107.3	136.6
Butter	100.0	97.3	89.2	75.7	64.9	54.1
Margarine	100.0	123.1	184.6	230.8	223.1	207.7
Lard	100.0	100.0	115.4	100.0	76.9	138.5
Potatoes	100.0	116.4	121.8	111.8	105.7	144.1
Sugar	100.0	102.3	109.2	83.9	69.0	63.8

Source: Sir William H. Beveridge, *British Food Control* (New Haven: Yale University Press, 1928), 311.

the weekly consumption per capita of butcher's beef, butter, and sugar were below the prewar averages, the consumption of flour (12 percent), bacon and ham (35 percent), lard (36 percent), potatoes (43 percent), and margarine (100 percent) were all above that baseline (see Table 5.21 for consumption and Table 5.22 for imports).

France was never faced with the level of food problems that confronted the British. Domestic agriculture was still sufficient to provide the bulk of the population's foodstuffs. Mobilization had reduced labor reserves; but, under strict government controls, women, children, prisoners of war, and refugees had been recruited as replacements. By 1916, however, some problems had emerged. The cost of living had risen by 40 percent, with no corresponding increase in wages. That year the harvest of wheat, rye, legumes, and potatoes was only 65 percent of normal. Flour was sometimes scarce; sugar was a luxury; and imports of coal from Britain declined steadily. As in Britain,

Table 5.22. *United Kingdom, Net Food Imports, 1914–1918*

Commodity	Average 1910–13	1914	1915	1916	1917	1918
	Panel A. Billions of Calories					
Cereals[1]	14.0	16.3	15.0	16.5	16.6	15.2
Meat	3.5	4.0	4.0	3.8	3.4	4.6
Dairy Products	3.5	3.5	3.5	2.5	1.9	1.2
Sugar[2]	6.6	8.5	7.4	6.5	5.9	5.4
Poultry & Eggs	0.2	0.2	0.2	0.1	0.1	0.1
Fish	0.1	0.2	0.2	0.2	0.1	0.2
Fruit	0.9	0.9	0.9	0.9	0.4	0.3
Potatoes & Vegetables	0.8	0.6	0.6	0.6	0.8	0.9
TOTAL	29.6	34.2	31.8	31.1	29.2	27.9
	Panel B: Imports as Percentage of 1910–1913 Average					
Cereals[1]	100.0	116.4	107.1	117.9	118.6	108.6
Meat	100.0	114.3	114.3	108.6	97.1	131.4
Dairy Products	100.0	100.0	100.0	71.4	54.3	34.3
Sugar[2]	100.0	128.8	112.1	98.5	89.4	81.8
Poultry & Eggs	100.0	100.0	100.0	50.0	50.0	50.0
Fish	100.0	200.0	200.0	200.0	100.0	200.0
Fruit	100.0	100.0	100.0	100.0	44.4	33.3
Potatoes & Vegetables	100.0	75.0	75.0	75.0	100.0	112.5
TOTAL	100.0	115.5	107.4	105.1	98.6	94.3

Notes:
[1] As flour at prewar extraction rates.
[2] Including cocoa and chocolate.
Source: Dewey, "Food Production," 81.

the German submarine blockade made it difficult to make up the shortages through increases in imports; and, as in both Britain and Germany, the French government took action – action supported in this instance by private initiative. "Sugar was rationed, and saccharin authorized in all commercial preparations. A series of *arrêtés* prescribed two pastry-less days, two confectionary-less days and then two meatless days per week. Bread was twelve hours old when sold. Restaurants and hotels simplified their menus and served only two courses per meal. Decrees rationing bread and then prohibiting pastries altogether followed in the course of the year."[56] The

56 Chambers, *War Behind the War*, 395–396.

nature of those actions, however, suggest something of the relative seriousness of the problems vis-à-vis the problems that faced the British and the
German economies.

The American Declaration of April 1917 changed the entire nature of the
naval war. Between then and November 1918, the United States "supplied
Britain with more than half of its bread and flour, and some 80 percent of
its meat and fats." Moreover, the United States loaned Britain the money
to pay for the food.[57] At the same time, although the Allies had succeeded
in reducing imports into Germany from the United States, imports that
were passed through neutral hands, they had not been able to cut them off
completely. However, "the moment the United States itself became a belligerent Germany's principal reservoir was completely dried up." With the
addition of the United States to the Alliance, the rules of the Allied blockade
were extensively revised.[58] In particular, the Allies set out to accomplish two
goals: "(1) To forbid any exportation whatever to neutral countries adjacent to Germany" and "(2) To proceed to exchange products with these
same neutrals if the latter were able to supply the Allies with goods that
would be useful to them." Thus, in the future, trade between the Allies and
the neutrals would be conducted by truck and barter. The Committee of
Restriction then asked the United States: (1) "To forbid the export of any
goods not consigned to organizations having authority to supervise their
consumption in neutral countries or destined to firms entered upon the
black lists" and (2) "To adhere to the agreements which were already in
force with neutral countries adjacent to the enemy."[59]

The United States, however, with its far more extensive view of the nature
of an effective economic encirclement, declined to unilaterally accept the
agreements that its allies had concluded with the neutrals. Instead, it set out

---

57 Offer, *First World War*, 376.
58 Guichard, *The Naval Blockade, 1914–1918* (New York: D. Appleton, 1930), 96–99. Over the years
from 1913, to 1916 Britain's exports to North Sea neutrals had increased from "£42 million in
1913, to £66 million in 1915, and £76 million in 1916"; Britain's economy, to say nothing of its
businessmen, "would have been inconvenienced by total prohibition of trade with neutrals." In Rear
Admiral Consett's postwar memoirs (*The Triumph of Unarmed Forces*), "he described the behaviour
of British traders up to 1916 as disgraceful. The author, who was formerly British naval attaché
at Copenhagen during the war, adduced figures to prove the extent of the assistance as regards
provision and raw material that had been afforded to Germany by the Scandinavian countries, and
added that this assistance had only been rendered possible by means of British imports into Scandinavia
which took place in considerable quantities during the first two years of the war and were, to say
the least of it, authorized by the British Government." Quoted in Guichard, *Naval Blockade*, 99,
64–65.
59 Guichard, *Naval Blockade*, 98–99.

to design a policy that would "retain for the United States as many of its products as it needed, then to supply the most urgent needs of the Allies, and finally to send the balance to neutrals on condition that the amount so sent did not exceed the quotas already fixed by the Allies." In conformity with these principles, President Wilson signed a proclamation of General Embargo – a proclamation that forbid the export of corn, fodder, petrol, cast iron, fertilizers, arms, ammunition, and explosives from any port in the United States without a special license. Furthermore, in order to allow time to examine the situation existing in each neutral country, the government prohibited the export of any foodstuffs to any neutral country "adjacent to Germany" before December 1917. To the extent that their existing arrangements permitted, the French and British governments agreed to assist in implementing the embargo "by every means in their power."[60]

Finally, the United States, in addition to seizing German ships interned in American ports and adding them to the Allied merchant fleet, launched a major shipbuilding program, a program that was designed to substantially increase the number of vessels that were available to the Allies, and, in the long run, to swamp the German submarine blockade. The initial government grant was $750 million; but, within a few months, the total had been increased to $2.9 billion – a figure that represented "twice the value of the entire world fleet engaged in international trade prior to 1914." To assure that the money spent would quickly produce vessels, the prices offered to the shipbuilders were much above existing world levels – contracts were awarded that paid $145 a ton, at a time when ships of the same type were being built in England for $75 per ton. When, in 1921, the program was ultimately completed, the average price paid for all vessels constructed was $200 a ton. Although not a single vessel financed by the program was added to the merchant fleet in 1917, by that year the American shipyards had already begun to have some influence on the war. American production of large (over 100-ton) merchant vessels had averaged only 173,000 tons during the years 1911 through 1913. By 1917 that figure had increased to 821,000 tons; and the next year, as the government program "kicked in," it accounted for an additional 2,602,000 tons, almost one-half (48 percent) of the world total (see Table 5.14). However, despite that figure, the major impact of the American government's program was, almost certainly, symbolic. Although many of the vessels were not finished until long after the

---

60 Guichard, *Naval Blockade*, 98–101.

Armistice was signed, knowledge of the program could not have failed to significantly influence German policies and morale.[61]

No matter how close the German blockade of Britain came to succeeding – and the facts suggest it was not close – in the longer term, the British (and then the British and American) blockade of Germany was to have a much greater impact on the outcome of the war. Almost as soon as the war began, the Eitzbacher Commission "of academic experts and officials" in Germany began an urgent study of Germany's food situation. Before the war, imported food had generated about 19 percent of the calories consumed in Germany; for protein the fraction was 27 percent and for fats 42 percent. Under wartime conditions – with an army in the field reducing civilian production and the soldiers consuming more than their prewar quantities of food, the fractions would be expected to be higher – perhaps "a quarter of the calories and a third of the protein." The outlook was serious, but the commission was optimistic. The food available, it reported, although not sufficient to support peacetime consumption, still stood above the standard of physiological necessity. By reducing waste and making reasonable substitutions, the economy should be able to meet about 90 percent of the caloric and 87 percent of the protein requirements.[62]

The outbreak of the war brought both an increasingly effective British blockade, a blockade that, by cutting off the supply of nitrates, soon led to a drop of about 25 percent in German domestic agricultural production, and an increased drain on the nation's food supplies as Allied success on the Western Front meant that the urban population of Belgium could no longer depend on imports from overseas. Although German production of a number of food crops in 1917 was lower than in 1918, in general, output declined throughout the war. In 1918, production of rye was 66 percent of the 1913 total, wheat, 56 percent, summer barley, 58 percent, potatoes, 56 percent, oats, 49 percent, and meadow hay, 76 percent. The importance of the lack of nitrates and the impact of the scarcity of labor was underscored

---

61 Gibson and Donovan, *Abandoned Ocean*, 113–114. C. Ernest Fayle, *War and the Shipping Industry* (New Haven: Yale University Press, 1927), 416.

62 Offer, *First World War*, 25. For a description of the falling German imports of foodstuffs and fertilizers over the course of the war, see Parmelee, *Blockade*, 202–232. The decline in imports was almost 100 percent. The magnitude of the domestic decline was attributed to the drain of agricultural labor to the military. There was apparently also poor weather during the war. For an analysis of the attempts by Germany to maintain its agricultural labor supply, see August Skalweit, "Germany: The Maintenance of the Agricultural Labour during the War," *International Review of Agricultural Economics*, 13 (December, 1922), 836–890. During the war, the Germans attempted to retain, via various legal measures, the migrant foreign laborers (mainly from Poland and Russia and Poles from Eastern Europe) who were caught in Germany at the start of the war, as well to utilize prisoners of war, mainly from Russia. See also Bennett, "Wheat and War," 72–88.

Table 5.23. *Crops In Germany, 1913–1918 (Alsace-Lorraine has been excluded)*

Year	Rye	Wheat	Summer Barley	Potatoes	Oats	Meadow Hay
			Panel A: Metric Tons			
1913	12,129,505	4,417,908	3,564,576	52,854,683	9,504,002	28,047,208
1914	10,349,481	3,789,662	3,049,616	44,696,408	8,846,987	28,000,119
1915	9,094,339	3,705,936	2,415,672	52,885,181	5,890,129	23,174,120
1916	8,902,843	2,999,385	2,745,088	24,691,170	6,928,293	27,707,899
1917	6,977,191	2,226,005	1,821,238	34,410,982	3,628,253	21,646,289
1918	8,009,090	2,458,418	2,064,590	29,469,718	4,680,755	21,414,969
			Panel B: Tonnage as a Percentage of 1913			
1913	100.00	100.00	100.00	100.00	100.00	100.00
1914	85.32	85.78	85.55	84.56	93.09	99.83
1915	74.98	83.88	67.77	100.06	61.98	82.63
1916	73.40	67.89	77.01	46.72	72.90	98.79
1917	57.52	50.39	51.09	65.10	38.18	77.18
1918	66.03	55.65	57.92	55.76	49.25	76.35
			Panel C: Harvest Per Hectare in Metric Tons			
1913	1.91	2.40	2.22	15.91	2.20	4.90
1914	1.66	2.00	1.99	13.57	2.07	5.01
1915	1.43	1.97	1.54	15.18	1.31	4.03
1916	1.49	1.88	1.84	9.00	1.95	5.06
1917	1.26	1.54	1.28	13.74	1.04	3.92
1918	1.39	1.71	1.51	10.80	1.43	3.45
			Panel D: Harvest Per Hectare as a Percentage of 1913			
1913	100.00	100.00	100.00	100.00	100.00	100.00
1914	86.91	83.33	89.64	85.29	94.09	102.24
1915	74.87	82.08	69.37	95.41	59.55	82.24
1916	78.01	78.33	82.88	56.57	88.64	103.27
1917	65.97	64.17	57.66	86.36	47.27	80.00
1918	72.77	71.25	68.02	67.88	65.00	70.41

Note: Summer barley figures for 1916 include winter as well as summer barley.
Source: Parmelee, *Blockade*, 212.

by the reduction in harvest per hectare of each of those crops – in the prewar years German agriculture had been characterized by its intensive application of fertilizer and labor (see Table 5.23).[63]

63 Suggestive of a decline in labor and fertilizer in German agriculture during World War I, is the relatively sharp fall in the output per hectare over the course of the war. British crops, by contrast had basically an unchanged yield per acre at this time. Sir Thomas Hudson Middleton, *Food Production in War* (Oxford: Clarendon Press, 1923) 313–314. See also Parmelee, *Blockade*, 212.

Runs on stores in the first months of the war resulted in substantial price increases for various staples, including bread, meat, and milk.[64] The government's initial response was hastily improvised, and often led to unanticipated results. "Capping the price of milk, for example, resulted quickly in a milk shortage, as farmers either switched to producing butter and cheese, or they slaughtered their livestock for sale."

By late 1914 it was clear that price controls alone would not work; and the government moved to completely suspend the market mechanism and replace it with rationing. Again the policy had not been worked out in advance; and, while its innovation generated a maze of bureaucratic regulations, it did little to solve the food problem.[65] The food situation still had certainly not reached crisis, or perhaps even serious, proportions. The occupation of Russian Poland had helped the situation. By 1915, Polish farmers were being compelled to sell their output to Germany "at low, administered prices." Thus, Polish potatoes, clover, oats, sugar beets, and livestock (to say nothing of wood, cotton, wool, and flax) helped relieve shortages in Germany.[66] Still, in retrospect, it appears that "the authorities had responded much too slowly"; and it was 1916 before the geographically fractured allocation system was replaced by a single national infrastructure.[67]

Thereafter, however, despite improvements in the government regulatory structure, the situation gradually became much worse. The food shortage "was due in part to the withdrawal of many millions of workers from agriculture and industry;" but such a reallocation would not have been critical, if it had not been for the increasing "rigor of the Allied blockade."[68]

In terms of the labor shortage, the government's Auxiliary Service Law provided for the compulsory employment, for the duration of the war, of every male citizen between seventeen and sixty years of age who was not already in the military service. Women were not included, but an intensive propaganda campaign drew them into the labor force as well. However, prewar German agriculture had achieved some of the world's highest yields by applying large amounts of labor and fertilizer to the land. The blockade had cut off a large fraction of the fertilizer, and the military had called up about two-thirds of the male agricultural labor force – some 3.3 million men.

---

64 In the city of Karlsruhe, for example, between June and December the price of bread increased by 26 percent, pork by 15 percent, butter by 25 percent, milk by 9 percent, and potatoes by 10 percent. Between December 1914 and June 1915, those prices had again increased by 24, 68, 7, 8, and 64 percent. Chickering, *Imperial Germany*, 41–43.
65 Chickering, *Imperial Germany*, 42–44.   66 Chickering, *Imperial Germany*, 85.
67 Offer, *First World War*, 61.   68 Parmelee, *Blockade*, 236–237.

Given the demands of the military, the draftees were among "the strongest and most efficient workers" in Germany, and they also possessed much of human capital that had been invested in the knowledge and skills required to produce those high agricultural yields. They were never adequately replaced by the civilians drafted by the Auxiliary Service Law or the women and children who were drawn into the labor force by some combination of wages, patriotism, and the propaganda campaign.[69]

The blockade, in turn, had only gradually begun to tighten as the British rewrote the rules of international law, and it "was only perfected after the United States joined the war." By 1918, however, although the data are somewhat suspect, it appears that, in terms of gold marks, imports into Germany had declined to about 39 percent of their 1913 level; and, since gold had depreciated, "the level of merchandise imports was probably about one–fifth of the pre–war level by 1918" (see Table 5.1).[70] What is certain is that the war had cut off direct imports from five enemy nations that, together in 1913, had accounted for 46 percent of Germany's total imports (see Table 5.24).[71]

By 1917, the decline that had marked "Central European harvests since 1913 had been halted and some crops had even made a recovery"; and, by year's end, the economic situation was sufficiently better as to convince the High Command that the civilian population "could be relied upon to hold out for the duration of another year's campaign." "However, even with some recovery, over the last year of the War, the blockade and the labor shortage combined to keep the German civilian population in a state of chronic want." The evidence is clear. "The Inter-Allied Scientific Food Commission at Paris in March 1918 [had] estimated that the nutrition required by men weighing 154 pounds and working eight hours a day was 3,300 calories, but that the quantity could be decreased temporarily by 10% without bodily injury." Thus, minimal nutrition requirements were about 3,000 calories a day. For an entire population of men, women, and children, the daily requirement was estimated at about 2,500 calories; and the minimal requirement was about 2,280 calories. At the beginning of the war, the average German consumed about 3,280 calories per day, or about 31 percent more than the long-run requirement and some 44 percent more than the minimum.

69 Offer, *First World War*, 62; Chickering, *Imperial Germany*, 80–81.
70 Hardach, *First World War*, Table 6, 33; Offer, *First World War*, 61–62.
71 The five are: France, 5.4 percent, Italy, 3.0 percent, Russia, 13.3 percent, the United Kingdom, 8.1 percent, and the United States, 15.9 percent. Mitchell, *European Historical Statistics*, Table F2, 526, Table F1, 494. There is evidence that, in the early years, because of imports through neutral countries, there was still some indirect trade.

Table 5.24. *Germany Foreign Trade by Country (millions of marks)*

						Exports					
Year	Total	Austria–Hungary	Belgium	France	Italy	Netherlands	Russia	Sweden	U.K.	U.S.A.	Total Enumerated
1900	4,611	486	253	277	123	364	325	137	862	440	3,267
1901	4,431	464	236	249	123	372	318	110	907	385	3,164
1902	4,678	480	261	253	125	392	344	118	958	449	3,380
1903	5,015	500	268	272	131	417	379	131	982	469	3,549
1904	5,223	555	277	274	141	410	315	147	985	495	3,599
1905	5,732	580	312	293	164	433	368	156	1,042	542	3,890
1906	6,359	649	356	383	231	443	406	177	1,067	637	4,349
1907	6,847	717	343	449	303	452	438	187	1,060	653	4,602
1908	6,399	737	323	438	311	454	450	174	997	508	4,292
1909	6,597	767	349	455	289	454	445	156	1,015	606	4,536
1910	7,475	822	391	543	324	499	547	191	1,102	633	5,052
1911	8,106	918	413	599	348	532	625	192	1,140	640	5,407
1912	8,967	1,035	493	689	401	609	680	197	1,161	698	5,963
1913	10,097	1,105	551	790	394	694	880	230	1,438	713	6,795
1914											
1915											
1916											
1917											
1918											
1919		Austria									
1920	3,709										
1921	2,976										
1922	6,188										
1923	5,338	305	112	67	245	685	73	271	557	475	2,790
1924	6,674	313	106	114	240	648	89	286	612	491	2,899
1925	9,284	320	344	489	425	996	250	342	937	604	4,707
1926	10,415	311	418	670	486	1,127	266	401	1,163	744	5,586
1927	10,801	366	441	562	462	1,119	330	409	1,178	776	5,643
1928	12,055	425	489	693	547	1,175	403	431	1,180	796	6,139
1929	13,486	441	609	935	602	1,355	354	476	1,306	991	7,069
1930	12,036	360	601	1,149	484	1,206	431	494	1,219	685	6,629

						Imports					
Year	Total	Austria–Hungary	Belgium	France	Italy	Netherlands	Russia	Sweden	U.K.	U.S.A.	Total Enumerated
1900	5,769	704	215	303	181	209	717	104	719	1,004	4,156
1901	5,421	684	183	272	178	192	716	84	553	986	3,848
1902	5,631	696	194	304	189	195	760	80	557	893	3,868
1903	6,003	724	206	330	196	187	826	90	594	935	4,088
1904	6,354	703	231	365	187	212	819	99	615	943	4,174
1905	7,129	752	273	402	211	246	1,091	119	718	992	4,804
1906	8,021	811	291	434	241	242	1,070	150	825	1,237	5,301

		Imports									
Year	Total	Austria-Hungary	Belgium	France	Italy	Netherlands	Russia	Sweden	U.K.	U.S.A.	Total Enumerated
1907	8,745	813	297	454	285	228	1,108	172	977	1,320	5,654
1908	7,663	752	262	420	236	231	946	145	697	1,283	4,972
1909	8,519	755	290	485	288	253	1,364	142	723	1,263	5,563
1910	8,927	759	326	509	275	259	1,387	164	767	1,188	5,634
1911	9,683	739	340	524	285	298	1,634	183	809	1,343	6,155
1912	10,674	830	387	552	305	345	1,528	214	843	1,586	6,590
1913	10,751	827	345	584	318	333	1,425	224	876	1,711	6,643
1914											
1915											
1916											
1917											
1918											
1919		Austria									
1920	3,929										
1921	5,732										
1922	6,301										
1923	6,150	131	85	186	150	201	92	95	1,015	1,172	3,127
1924	9,132	134	204	694	372	426	126	121	827	1,709	4,613
1925	12,429	176	415	558	496	743	205	269	944	2,196	6,002
1926	9,984	116	343	378	388	543	323	234	576	1,603	4,504
1927	14,114	211	548	806	528	698	433	370	963	2,073	6,630
1928	13,931	232	474	741	467	710	379	253	894	2,026	6,176
1929	13,359	202	447	642	443	701	426	350	865	1,790	5,866
1930	10,349	181	325	519	365	561	436	304	639	1,307	4,637

Source: B. R. Mitchell, *European Historical Statistics: 1750–1970* (New York: Macmillan, 1975), 494, 526–527.

As the war progressed, however, civilian consumption of a broad range of foodstuffs was continually reduced. Before the war, the average German consumed some 342 grams of bread a week; with rationing, consumption was initially set at 225 grams, a figure that was first reduced to 200 grams and, that, by the end of the agricultural year 1917–1918, to 160 grams – less than half of prewar consumption. Prewar weekly consumption of meat has been estimated at 950 grams; in 1918, the average weekly ration in urban areas was 135 grams. Similar reductions occurred in the rations of fats (from more than 25 grams to 7) and milk. Nor were these the only foodstuffs where rations fell well below peacetime consumption. By 1918, although rations for sugar and potatoes were more than 80 percent of the prewar levels, the legal rations of fish, eggs, lard, butter, cheese, pulses, and vegetable fats ranged from 5 to 28 percent of that standard (see Table 5.25).

Table 5.25. *Germany: Wartime Rations versus Peacetime Consumption*
(Peacetime Consumption = 100)

Commodity	July 1916 to July 1917	July 1917 to July 1918	July 1918 to December 1918
Meat	31	20	12
Fish	51	–	5
Eggs	18	13	13
Lard	14	11	7
Butter	22	21	28
Cheese	3	4	15
Rice	4	–	–
Pulses	14	1	7
Sugar	49	56 to 67	80
Vegetable Fats	39	41	17
Potatoes	71	94	94
Flour	53	47	48

Source: Hardach, *First World War*, Table 13, 119.

Moreover, in many cases, particularly, in towns and cities, there was seldom sufficient supply to permit citizens to acquire even the legal ration.

Overall, rations per head had fallen to 1,344 calories by the autumn of 1916 and to 1,100 calories by the summer of 1917. Furthermore, it appears that, because of waste in cooking and the low levels of digestibility of much of the available food, the actual nutritive value was probably no more than 1,000 calories. "If these estimates are correct, the nutrition of the civilian population had fallen in 1917 to less than 30% of its pre-war average, and to less than 50% of the normal minimum of 2,280 calories."[72]

The full impact of continued shortfall was, however, only really felt in the longer term. Over the course of the war, German deaths on the battlefield and from wounds totaled 1,486,952, and military deaths from sickness added another 134,082 to that figure. Over the four years 1914–1915 to 1917–1918, the excess of deaths in the civilian population over the number of deaths in 1913 was 762,796. Furthermore, over those years, the figure increased from 88,235, to 121,174, to 259,627, to 293,760. The rise in civilian deaths is, of course, merely a reflection of the increases in mortality rates. For example, between 1913 and 1918 female mortality rates rose

---

72 Parmelee, *Blockade*, 213–220; Chickering, *Imperial Germany*, 141–144; Chambers, *War Behind the War*, 483–484.

Table 5.26. *Female Mortality and Female Infant Mortality in Germany and in England and Wales*

Year	Deaths per 1000 Females			Deaths per 1000 Females aged 0 to 1		
	Germany	England	Germany as a Percent of England	Germany	England	Germany as a Percent of England
1913	14.3	12.2	117.2	137	96	142.7
1914	15.2	12.4	122.6	148	93	159.1
1915	15.3	13.2	115.9	135	96	140.6
1916	15.2	11.7	129.9	128	80	160.0
1917	17.6	11.4	154.4	136	85	160.0
1918	21.6	14.6	147.9	143	86	166.3
1919	16.7	11.9	140.3	131	78	167.9
1920	15.3	10.9	140.4	118	69	171.0
1921	13.6	10.2	133.3	120	72	166.7
1922	13.9	10.5	132.4	116	66	175.8
1923	13.6	9.3	146.2	119	60	198.3

Source: Avner Offer, *The First World War: An Agrarian Interpretation* (Oxford: Clarendon Press, 1989), 35–36.

from 14.3 to 21.6 deaths per thousand, and the mortality rate for female infants age 0 to 1 rose from 137 to 143 (see Table 5.26).[73] Although the blockade was certainly not directly responsible for all of the excess of deaths nor for the entire rise in female mortality, it obviously played a major role. At the same time, the birth rate in Germany was declining – the decrease in the number of births during the years 1914–1919, as compared to the years 1910–1913, was about four million. Although most of the decline can be attributed to the separation of soldiers and sailors from their families, "German writers on this subject have usually assumed that one-fourth of this total estimated decrease of births, namely, one million births, can be attributed to the blockade."[74]

The blockade also had an indirect impact on the German war effort. German military morale began to suffer as the war dragged on; and the German High Command noted that declines in morale were significantly higher in units that had been reinforced by new recruits, troops transferred from the homeland, and soldiers returning from leave. The generals blamed this infection on news of the food shortages at home, and they concluded

[73] Of the total of 1,621,034, it is estimated 73,319 succumbed to earlier wounds or sickness after the end of the war. Parmelee, *Blockade*, 222; Offer, *First World War*, 35–36.

[74] Parmelee, *Blockade*, 223. Offer, *First World War*, 33, estimates these lost births at three million.

that it was the reports of suffering in the civilian population that was at the root cause of the decline in morale.[75] Moreover, although the failure of the final German offensive of 1918 – an offensive that came very close to splitting the British and French armies apart – can, in part, be attributed to Ludendorff's failure to define the objectives and his failure to reinforce the major breakthrough, in even larger part it can be attributed to the substantial number of German troops, troops that had been on minimal rations for the past two years, who stopped to loot British supply dumps.[76] The looted foodstuffs were partially consumed by the looters themselves, but a not insignificant fraction was shipped back to Germany to relieve the suffering of families, relatives, and friends.

3. THE EFFICIENCY OF THE NAVAL BLOCKADES DEPLOYED DURING THE WAR

3(1). *The Allied Blockade of Germany*

3(1a). Quantitative Measures. Jutland aside, there were few direct naval confrontations between the Allied blockading fleets and German forces. Instead, the presence of the British and, later, the American, navy was sufficient to keep the German merchant marine "bottled up" at home, whereas economic and political pressure, as well as the threat of military action, partly closed Germany to imports passing through neutrals like Holland and the Scandinavian countries. It is, however, difficult to measure directly the impact of a blockade on trade that does not occur.

The United States, however, was a country that had accounted for about 15 percent of total German imports. U.S. exports to Germany had averaged $309 million in the years 1911–1913, and still amounted to $345 million in 1914. By 1915, however, the figure had declined to $29 million and, by 1916, the last year before America entered the war, to a mere $2 million. The 1915 and 1916 declines provide some measure of the effectiveness of the British blockade on trade across the Atlantic. The U.S. experience may provide a reasonable index of all German "overseas" trade; and, to the extent it does, it provides high marks for the British-deployed distant

---

75 Offer, *First World War*, 61.
76 "Critics of the military pointed out that one of the main reasons for discontent within the army was inequality in the distribution of rations, with the officers enjoying superior food in their messes, while troops in the rear, with access to the black market, to their own gardens, and to animals, lived better than troops in the line." Offer, *First World War*, 60–61, 72–74.

blockade. However, the data on trade with Germany's close neighbors suggest a somewhat less sanguine conclusion.

In the case of Denmark, in the years 1911–1913, exports to Germany averaged 174 million kroner, and accounted for less than 30 percent of the Danish export total. During the war, that country's exports to Germany rose to a peak of 691 million kroner in 1916, at which time they represented almost 60 percent of all Danish exports. Thereafter, they declined slightly, but even in 1918 they still totaled 308 million, 43 percent of the Danish total. Over the entire war, Germany accounted for an average of 455 million kroner, 49 percent of Denmark's 923 million total (see Table 5.27).

In the case of Sweden, in the prewar years, Germany had accounted for an average of 161 million kroner and for just more than a fifth of that country's exports. By 1915, exports to Germany had climbed to 486 million, or some 37 percent of the total. They declined thereafter; but, even in 1918, they still amounted to 293 million kroner; representing over 21 percent of all Swedish exports. Over the entire four years of the war, exports to Germany averaged 349 million kroner and accounted for more than one-quarter of that Scandinavian country's exports. Moreover, it was only in 1918 that the fraction fell below the 1913 level.

The Norwegian experience also reflects what might be termed the Scandinavian pattern. Prewar exports to Germany averaged 58 million kroner, about 17 percent of Norway's export total. During the first three years of the war, exports to Germany rose rapidly; they peaked in 1916 at 292 million kroner, about 30 percent of the country's total. Over the entire fifty-two months of the war, those exports averaged 159 million kroner, 2.75 times the prewar average, and more than a fifth of total Norwegian exports. It was only in 1918 that the percentage fell below the 1911–1913 average; and, even then, the 85 million kroner total was 147 percent of the prewar average.

Finally, exports from the Netherlands appear to have been more effected by the blockade than those from the Scandinavian countries. In the prewar years, shipments to Germany averaged 1,463 million gulden, just less than half of the country's total exports. Over the course of the war, total exports fell steadily, from 2,505 to 386 million gulden; and the 566 million annual average of exports to Germany represented only about two-fifths of Dutch total exports (see Table 5.27).

Overall, then, for Germany's Scandinavian neighbors, it appears that the blockade tightened, but only gradually. In all three countries, the 1918 exports to Germany exceeded the prewar average. In the case of the Netherlands, the blockade appears to have been somewhat more effective;

Table 5.27. *Total Exports and Exports to Germany*

Denmark (million kroner)			
Year	Total	Germany	% German
1911	537	160	29.8
1912	597	182	30.5
1913	637	179	28.1
Avg. 1911–13	590	174	29.5
1914	780	301	38.6
1915	979	487	49.7
1916	1,177	691	58.7
1917	970	490	50.5
1918	710	308	43.4
Avg. 1914–18	923	455	49.3

Sweden (million kroner)			
	Total	Germany	% German
1911	664	134	20.2
1912	760	171	22.5
1913	817	179	21.9
Avg. 1911–13	747	161	21.5
1914	772	175	22.7
1915	1,316	486	36.9
1916	1,556	438	28.1
1917	1,350	352	26.1
1918	1,350	293	21.7
Avg. 1914–18	1,269	349	27.5

Norway (million kroner)			
	Total	Germany	% German
1911	298	51	17.1
1912	336	55	16.4
1913	393	67	17.0
Avg. 1911–13	342	58	17.0
1914	410	76	18.5
1915	677	193	28.5
1916	988	292	29.6
1917	791	150	19.0
1918	755	85	11.3
Avg. 1914–18	724	159	22.0

The Netherlands (millions of gulden)			
	Total	Germany	% German
1911	2,732	1,357	49.7
1912	3,113	1,555	50.0
1913	3,083	1,478	47.9
Avg. 1911–13	2,976	1,463	49.2
1914	2,505	1,125	44.9
1915	1,749	714	40.8
1916	1,347	520	38.6
1917	821	317	38.6
1918	386	154	39.9
Avg. 1914–18	1,361.6	566	41.6

Source: Mitchell, *European Historical Statistics*, 494–497, 516, 541–542, 545, 566.

but a part of the reduction can almost certainly be attributed to the general breakdown of international trade.[77]

However, because, to a large extent, the "profits" from the blockade were realized only in the long run; and, because most of the literature has focused on the impact of the blockade on the German home front, the best available measures probably involve comparisons of British/German food consumption and health – measures that are, of course, affected by weather and the shortage of labor as well as by the relative effectiveness of the Allied blockade of Germany and the German submarine blockade of Britain. Note that the weather and the labor shortage should have affected both Britain and Germany, whereas Holland was impacted by the weather alone. The 1913 to 1918 increase in the relative German/British female death rates – an increase of 26 percent for all females and of 16.5 percent for those aged 0 to 1 – is indicative (see Table 5.26). A comparison of the relative daily rations proposed in Britain and those adopted in Germany show even greater differences – the German "normal" ration was about 70 percent of the suggested British figure – and that difference is understated because the British proposed rations could have been met, whereas the German legal rations represented maximum legal consumption, and were frequently unmet (see Table 5.28). Finally, a comparison of weekly per capita consumption of principal foods in Britain, Germany, and the Netherlands in 1918 indicates that, for bread and flour, British consumption was 107 percent of the prewar level, for meats it was 62 percent, and for fats 88 percent. The German averages for the same commodities were 63, 22, and 27 percent. In the case of Holland, a country not directly affected by the blockade, the levels were 42, 29, and 53 percent of the prewar standard (see Table 5.29).[78]

3(1b). The Historiography. Of the two blockades, the British *cum* American blockade of Germany has, at least in the English language literature, the far greater historiography. Although, because of their inability to control the Baltic, the British had never officially declared a blockade, their Orders in Council of March 11, 1915 and the January 1916 "Statement of the Measures adopted to Intercept the Seaborne Commerce of Germany," can, for all intents and purposes, be viewed as announcements of a blockade; and they were largely so viewed by most neutral nations. However, from the British point of view, as it was legally not a blockade, it was not subject to

---

77 U.S. Bureau of the Census, *Historical Statistics of the United States, Colonial Times to 1970*, 2 vols. (Washington, DC: Government Printing Office, 1975), vol. 2, 903. Mitchell, *European Historical Statistics*, 494–566.
78 Offer, *First World War*, 35–36, 52. Beveridge, *British Food Control*, 316, 390–391.

Table 5.28. *Scale of Daily Rations Proposed in Britain and Comparison with Germany*

| Commodity | Heavy Workers | | Ordinary Manual Workers | | Normal Ration | | |
	Germany	United Kingdom	Germany	United Kingdom	Germany	United Kingdom Adolescents included	Normal
Bread	7.375 lbs.	9.000 lbs	6.125 lbs.	8.000 tbs.	4.375 lbs.	7.000 lbs.	6.000 lbs.
Meat	0.750 lbs.	3.000 lbs.	9.000 ozs.	3.000 lbs.	9.000 ozs.	3.000 lbs.	2.000 lbs.
Fats	4.500 ozs.	0.750 lbs.	3.167 ozs.	0.750 lbs.	3.167 ozs.	0.500 lbs.	0.500 lbs.
Sugar	0.333 lbs.	0.500 lbs.	0.333 lbs.	0.500 lbs.	0.333 lbs.	0.500 lbs.	0.500 lbs.
Potatoes	9.375 lbs.	7.000 lbs.	7.125 lbs.	6.000 lbs.	7.125 lbs.	5.000 lbs.	4.000 lbs.
Total Calories Per Day	2,184	3,070	1,760	2,841	1,460	2,081	
Ratio to U.K. Total Calories (%)	71.14	100.00	61.95	100.00	70.16	100.00	

Note: Calories for "Normal Ration" for United Kingdom is weighted average of adolescents and normal.
Source: Beveridge, *British Food Control,* 390–391.

Table 5.29. *Weekly Per Capita Consumption of Principal Foods in the United Kingdom, Germany, and Holland, Pre-War and in 1918*

| Commodity | United Kingdom | | | Germany | | | Holland | | |
	Pre-War (lbs.)	1918 (lbs.)	1918 Percent of Pre-War (%)	Pre-War (lbs.)	1918 (lbs.)	1918 Percent of Pre-War (%)	Pre-War (lbs.)	1918 (tbs.)	1918 Percent of Pre-War (%)
Bread and Flour	6.12	6.57	107.4	6.44	4.06	63.0	7.25	3.06	42.2
Meats	2.50	1.54	61.6	2.25	0.49	21.8	1.50	0.44	29.3
Sugar	n.d.	0.50	n.d.	n.d.	0.33	n.d.	n.d.	0.52	n.d.
Fats	0.51	0.45	88.2	0.56	0.15	26.8	0.70	0.37	52.9

Source: Beveridge, *British Food Control,* 316.

international law. Thus, not only was the definition of contraband expanded to include almost everything but also the doctrine of continuous voyage was extended until even its original innovator, the Americans, might not have recognized it.[79] In 1915 and 1916, the British introduced a series of programs designed, in addition to blockading the ports of Germany, (1) "to stop the arrival in neutral countries of an undue quantity of imports by sea"; (2) "to ensure the imports which the Allies had allowed to go through being retained in the neutral country where they were landed"; and (3) "to divert from the Central Empires the home production of the neutrals."[80]

Given the publicity attached to the blockade, it is not surprising that the war was hardly over before politicians and historians began to assess the blockade's productivity. Originally, their conclusions were decidedly mixed. Only a month after the Armistice, British Prime Minister Herbert Asquith proclaimed, "with all deference to our soldiers this war had been won with sea power." The economic blockade of Germany enforced by the Navy allegedly was *the* critical lever for Allied victory.[81] At almost the same time, the journalist G. A. Schreiner, perhaps partly blinded by the customs that constrained behavior during the heyday of the gold standard, argued that the blockade, if it was imposed at all, was imposed far too soon, because "it is certain that the Central states governments would have been bankrupt long ago had they been able to buy in the foreign market *ad libitum*."[82] Despite Asquith, views that undervalued the contribution of the navy and the blockade, initially held sway in the academic community.

A few historians did choose a middle position. For example, Maurice Parmelee noted, on the one hand, that there were large holes in the blockade (holes, initially, in Italy and, throughout the war, in Switzerland, Holland, and the Scandinavian countries) and that, even before the outbreak of hostilities, the Germans had at least partially prepared themselves to hold out against a British blockade. On the other hand, he also recognized that the "blockade controlled not only the importation and exportation of commodities, but also the transmission of financial credit and the communication of information." He concluded that, taking all aspects together, "the

79 Parmelee, *Blockade*, 38–40, 43–44. For a discussion of the concept of a continuous voyage, see Chapter 1.
80 Guichard, *Naval Blockade*, 75–77.
81 Quoted in Colin S. Gray, *The Leverage of Sea Power: The Strategic Advantage of Navies in War* (New York: Free Press, 1992), 211.
82 G. A. Schreiner, *The Iron Ration: The Economic and Social Effects of the Allied Blockade of Germany and the German People* (London: Harper and Brothers, 1918), 336–337, as quoted in Parmelee, *Blockade*, 239.

blockade, nevertheless, did much injury to the Central Powers."[83] The "middle grounders" were, however, in the distinct minority.

Gradually, however, in the postwar decades, both the British public and the country's historians, influenced, perhaps, by the deaths on the battle-fields of France, began to reevaluate the role of the blockade. Thus, by the 1930s, it was the navy and the blockade strategy that had become almost solely responsible for the Allied victory. For example, Sir Basil Liddell Hart, Britain's most distinguished military historian, wrote, "The Navy was to win no Trafalgar, but it was to do more than any other factor towards winning the war for the Allies. For the Navy was the instrument of the blockade, and as the fog of war disperses in the clearer light of these postwar years that blockade is seen to assume larger and larger proportions, to be more and more clearly *the decisive agency* in the struggle."[84] And, he argued, "among the causes of Germany's surrender the blockade is seen to be the most funda-mental. Its existence is the surest answer to the question whether but for the revolution the German armies could have stood firm on their own frontiers. For even if the German people, roused to a supreme effort in defense of their own soil, could have held the Allied armies at bay, the end could only have been postponed – because of the grip of sea-power, Britain's historic weapon."[85] As late as 1957, Michael Lewis wrote, "The economic blockade was beyond question the primary cause of her [the German] collapse. The interlocked armies, loudly slaughtering each other over the shell-pocked battlefields, held men's gaze to the last. But the war was not really decided there. It was lost and won on the misty sea-approaches to Britain and Western Europe."[86] "In part, this British attitude was the product of interwar folk-lore. The Germans after 1918 had fostered the legend that the so-called 'hunger blockade' of the First World War had in the end starved out the country and destroyed its will to resist."[87] But the widespread acceptance of that myth in England was fueled "by the desire to make a case for a return to what allegedly had been the traditional British way in warfare; subsidizing continental clients, establishing supremacy at sea by the defeat in battle or blockade of the enemy's navy and merchant marine, exploiting maritime command for control of seaborne trade, conducting occasional land campaigns in, as well as raids upon, coastal regions . . . and providing a continental commitment for direct support of European allies."[88] Given

83 Parmelee, *Blockade*, 234–237.
84 Cited in Gray, *Leverage of Sea Power*, 178.
85 Liddell Hart, *Strategy*, 218.
86 Lewis, *History of the British Navy*, 253.
87 Gordon Wright, *The Ordeal of Total War, 1939–1945* (New York: Harper and Row, 1968), 53.
88 Gray, *Leverage of Sea Power*, 179.

the number of World War I battlefield deaths, it is hardly surprising that the argument for a reversion to "traditional" strategy seemed to become ever more cogent as the storm clouds of World War II gathered on the horizon.

More recent historical work has tended toward more Parmelee-like conclusions, particularly when the example of World War I was used as an argument for the imposition of a blockade in the late twentieth century. Some historians, H. P. Willmott, for example, still argued in 1981 that the "Britain's geographical position, across German lines of communication with the outside world, enabled her gradually but remorselessly to strangle the life out of Germany and her allies." But, even Willmott acknowledged that "the British blockade, however, was not just a naval affair: the emergence of total war ensured that the naval aspects of the blockade had to be supplemented by the use of other nonmilitary aspects of power."[89] Others historians, although acknowledging the importance of the blockade, have tended to make it, although, perhaps the most important, still only one of a number of reasons for the Allied triumph. In 1966, for example, F. S. Northedge wrote, "with no considerable assistance from her allies," Germany "had held the rest of the world at bay, had beaten Russia, had driven France, the military colossus of Europe for more than two centuries, to the end of her tether, and in 1917, had come within an ace of starving Britain into surrender."[90] Although one may question whether France, in 1914, was the military colossus of Europe, or that the German blockade "came within an ace of starving Britain into surrender," to Northedge, the blockade was an effective device in a "world" allied against the Germans. A similar argument had been made as early as 1928 by Sir Herbert Richmond. Richmond wrote, "It was only owing to the fact that the land frontiers of the enemies were sealed by the armies, and that every nation of importance was either actively assisting with her navies at sea, or passively by withholding trade, that the eventual degree of isolation was procured which contributed to their victory."[91] By the late 1980s, Williamson Murray had concluded that "seapower alone could not have had a decisive impact on the First World War. However, the exercise of sea control and the economic and strategic implications that accrued to the Allies by that exercise played a crucial role in the defeat of the German Empire and its allies."[92]

89 Willmott, *Sea Warfare*, 34–35.
90 F. S. Northedge, *The Troubled Giant: Britain Among the Great Powers* (London: 1988, first published 1966), 623, as cited in Chickering, *Imperial Germany*, 200.
91 H. W. Richmond, *National Policy and Naval Strength and Other Essays* (London: Longmans, Green, 1928). 142.
92 Murray, "Naval Power," 207.

Finally, Avner Offer, in his careful examination of the German economy also comes to a very similar conclusion. He argues that "to sum up the evidence of public health: the siege economy did not give rise to famine. People did not, as a rule, drop dead on the streets." He notes that "Germany was able to continue purchasing with its own currency overseas," that the "German economy held up much better than British blockade planners supposed," and that "at the end of the war Germany still had about £112 million in gold at the pre-war rate of exchange (say, US $ 535 million), which supported the currency and facilitated foreign borrowing and imports." He concludes that "Whether starved of foreign goods by an actual blockade, or by the inability to buy them, the German economy was simply too weak to take on the combined power of the *entente* and the United States."[93]

As the quantitative evidence indicates, and after some four decades in the academic wilderness, the historians now appear to have reached a general consensus: that Britain's distant blockade was an effective weapon in the Allied arsenal, but, unlike the American blockade of the Japanese mainland in World War II or the atomic bomb, it was not a weapon that by itself could have brought the war to an end.

3(2). The German Submarine Blockade of Britain

3(2a). Quantitative Measures. In the case of the German U-boat blockade, because there were continuous clashes between German warships and Allied merchantmen, there are at least three reasonably direct quantitative measures of the efficiency of the blockade: changes in the volume and structure of British imports, the net gains and losses of the Allied merchant fleets, and comparisons of the number of German submarines deployed, first, with allied vessels lost and, second, with the number of submarines sunk.

Table 5.30 compares the value of British imports for domestic consumption in the prewar years 1911–1913 with the years of the war. In the baseline years, such imports averaged £16.4 per capita. That figure declined steadily over the course of the war, from £15.0 in 1914 to £12.8 in 1918, averaging £14.4. Because the war caused major misallocations in international transport, it is unlikely that the entire decline in British trade can be attributed to the submarine campaign; however, it should be noted that the sharpest declines in imports occurred during the years (1916 to 1918) of unrestricted German submarine warfare, as did the sharpest decline in exports.[94] An

---

93 Offer, *First World War*, 38, 65, 76.
94 Werner Schlote, *British Overseas Trade from 1700 to the 1930's* (Oxford: Basil Blackwell, 1952), 130.

Table 5.30. *British Imports, 1911–1918*

Year	Population (In millions)	Imports (millions of constant pounds)	Imports per capita
1911	45.3	704.2	15.5
1912	45.4	756.6	16.7
1913	45.6	768.7	16.9
Avg. 1911–1913	45.4	743.2	16.4
1914	46.0	691.7	15.0
1915	44.3	749.8	16.9
1916	43.7	639.4	14.6
1917	43.3	534.7	12.3
1918	43.1	551.2	12.8
Avg. 1914–1918	44.1	633.4	14.4

Source: Mitchell and Deane, *Abstract*, 10; Werner Schlote, *British Overseas Trade From 1700 to the 1930s* (Oxford: Basil Blackwell, 1952), 131–133.

examination of the spatial distribution of imports, although providing only indirect light on the efficiency of the U-boat blockade, clearly underscores one of the costs imposed on Germany by the High Command's decision to deploy the blockade. Annual imports into Britain from America had averaged only £133 million over the years 1911 to 1913 – 20 percent of Britain's total imports – and, even in 1914, they totaled only £139 million (22 percent). Thereafter, however, they rose steadily; and, by 1918, they totaled £515 million – 43 percent of all British imports. Over the years of direct American involvement, those imports amounted to £892 million and represented 42 percent of the British total; and the Americans financed those imports (see Tables 5.31, 5.32, and 5.33). Moreover, given the German goal of "starving out" the British, the American contribution becomes, perhaps, even more important. By 1918, the United States accounted for 52 percent of all wheat and flour imported into Britain, 31 percent of fresh meats, 84 percent of bacon and hams, 94 percent of lard, 38 percent of dairy products, and 64 percent of sugar (see Table 5.34; see also Tables 5.35, 5.36, 5.37, and 5.38).

In terms of the British merchant marine, the U–boat campaign appears to have been somewhat more successful.[95] Although there are some differences

---

95 The data do not separate war losses by cause (submarine, surface vessel, aircraft, or mines). The evidence, however, suggests that, particularly after January 1915, submarines were by far the most important cause, and, that, therefore, total sinkings, provides a good index of submarine sinkings. We, therefore, assign all losses to U-boats. Moreover, to the extent that the index is biased, it is in favor of the cost-effectiveness of the submarines.

Table 5.31. *United Kingdom: Declared Values of Imports by Region, 1905–1928 (millions of pounds)*

Year	North & North-East Europe	Western Europe	Central & South-East Europe	Southern Europe & North Africa	Turkey & the Middle East	The Remainder of Africa	Asia	U.S.A.	British North America	The West Indies	Central & South America	Total Enumerated Imports
1905	66.0	86.0	61.7	26.6	20.9	11.8	57.2	114.7	26.2	3.4	49.0	523.5
1906	65.7	89.2	66.0	30.2	23.4	13.0	62.4	131.1	28.7	3.8	47.4	560.9
1907	69.0	88.3	68.7	32.1	28.9	16.7	71.7	134.3	25.8	3.6	52.7	591.8
1908	66.2	82.7	65.7	27.1	23.1	14.2	53.8	123.9	24.8	3.8	60.7	546.0
1909	73.2	87.2	69.0	27.4	25.4	16.9	63.8	118.4	25.5	3.8	61.5	572.1
1910	81.8	91.8	72.8	28.5	26.3	19.7	79.5	117.6	26.2	6.3	65.9	616.4
1911	82.1	91.2	79.1	29.3	27.9	19.1	83.8	122.7	25.3	3.8	56.6	620.9
1912	83.0	101.2	80.8	31.0	33.5	20.9	97.2	134.6	27.7	5.3	70.3	685.5
1913	86.0	104.4	90.2	30.6	27.6	22.9	92.6	141.7	31.5	6.1	73.7	707.3
1914	75.4	88.3	54.9	31.0	22.4	23.9	93.5	138.6	32.4	7.1	66.2	633.7
1915	77.8	71.7	0.3	40.5	24.4	33.4	130.7	237.8	42.2	12.6	100.1	771.5
1916	78.4	65.5	0.1	50.7	28.5	38.6	151.8	291.8	60.5	18.4	91.8	876.1
1917	69.6	54.4	0.0	42.6	34.3	39.6	148.3	376.3	85.1	24.4	91.6	966.2
1918	58.2	55.9	0.0	68.0	55.2	47.1	157.8	515.4	125.3	31.0	121.2	1,235.1
1919	78.8	94.3	1.5	76.9	72.2	74.4	230.4	541.6	117.8	29.4	138.7	1,456.0
1920	145.5	197.0	36.3	78.2	86.1	80.6	238.6	563.3	97.4	41.0	201.9	1,765.9
1921	86.7	145.3	33.1	43.9	39.4	48.5	101.5	274.8	63.8	13.1	112.2	962.3
1922	94.1	128.4	39.0	42.2	45.5	42.7	100.6	221.8	56.8	15.7	98.2	885.0
1923	110.0	143.0	54.5	47.0	46.4	46.4	130.0	210.7	55.5	16.1	107.0	966.6
1924	126.5	166.6	64.5	51.2	50.8	52.2	142.4	241.2	67.8	21.3	128.2	1,112.7
1925	129.9	166.6	70.1	51.1	45.3	60.2	160.5	245.3	72.6	22.3	120.9	1,144.8
1926	127.7	169.1	97.9	42.8	38.7	53.7	137.9	228.9	65.6	13.3	111.5	1,087.1
1927	134.1	169.5	83.1	47.9	40.1	56.2	142.7	200.2	57.4	16.8	122.7	1,070.7
1928	130.9	161.8	81.0	45.5	41.6	60.0	127.0	188.4	59.2	22.9	122.6	1,040.9

Source: Mitchell and Deane, *Abstract*, 316–323.

216

Table 5.32. *United Kingdom: Percent of Declared Values of Imports by Region, 1905–1928*

Year	North & North-East Europe	Western Europe	Central & South-East Europe	Southern Europe & North Africa	Turkey & the Middle East	The Remainder of Africa	Asia	U.S.A.	British North America	The West Indies	Central & South America	Total Enumerated Imports
1905	12.6	16.4	11.8	5.1	4.0	2.3	10.9	21.9	5.0	0.6	9.4	100.0
1906	11.7	15.9	11.8	5.4	4.2	2.3	11.1	23.4	5.1	0.7	8.5	100.0
1907	11.7	14.9	11.6	5.4	4.9	2.8	12.1	22.7	4.4	0.6	8.9	100.0
1908	12.1	15.1	12.0	5.0	4.2	2.6	9.9	22.7	4.5	0.7	11.1	100.0
1909	12.8	15.2	12.1	4.8	4.4	3.0	11.2	20.7	4.5	0.7	10.7	100.0
1910	13.3	14.9	11.8	4.6	4.3	3.2	12.9	19.1	4.3	1.0	10.7	100.0
1911	13.2	14.7	12.7	4.7	4.5	3.1	13.5	19.8	4.1	0.6	9.1	100.0
1912	12.1	14.8	11.8	4.5	4.9	3.0	14.2	19.6	4.0	0.8	10.3	100.0
1913	12.2	14.8	12.8	4.3	3.9	3.2	13.1	20.0	4.5	0.9	10.4	100.0
1914	11.9	13.9	8.7	4.9	3.5	3.8	14.8	21.9	5.1	1.1	10.4	100.0
1915	10.1	9.3	0.0	5.2	3.2	4.3	16.9	30.8	5.5	1.6	13.0	100.0
1916	8.9	7.5	0.0	5.8	3.3	4.4	17.3	33.3	6.9	2.1	10.5	100.0
1917	7.2	5.6	0.0	4.4	3.5	4.1	15.3	38.9	8.8	2.5	9.5	100.0
1918	4.7	4.5	0.0	5.5	4.5	3.8	12.8	41.7	10.1	2.5	9.8	100.0
1919	5.4	6.5	0.1	5.3	5.0	5.1	15.8	37.2	8.1	2.0	9.5	100.0
1920	8.2	11.2	2.1	4.4	4.9	4.6	13.5	31.9	5.5	2.3	11.4	100.0
1921	9.0	15.1	3.4	4.6	4.1	5.0	10.5	28.6	6.6	1.4	11.7	100.0
1922	10.6	14.5	4.4	4.8	5.1	4.8	11.4	25.1	6.4	1.8	11.1	100.0
1923	11.4	14.8	5.6	4.9	4.8	4.8	13.4	21.8	5.7	1.7	11.1	100.0
1924	11.4	15.0	5.8	4.6	4.6	4.7	12.8	21.7	6.1	1.9	11.5	100.0
1925	11.3	14.6	6.1	4.5	4.0	5.3	14.0	21.4	6.3	1.9	10.6	100.0
1926	11.7	15.6	9.0	3.9	3.6	4.9	12.7	21.1	6.0	1.2	10.3	100.0
1927	12.5	15.8	7.8	4.5	3.7	5.2	13.3	18.7	5.4	1.6	11.5	100.0
1928	12.6	15.5	7.8	4.4	4.0	5.8	12.2	18.1	5.7	2.2	11.8	100.0

Source: See Table 5.31.

Table 5.33. *United Kingdom: Declared Values and Percentages of Imports by Region, 1905–1928: War and Peace – Annual Averages (millions of pounds)*

Year	North & North-East Europe	Western Europe	Central & South-East Europe	Southern Europe & North Africa	Turkey & the Middle East	The Remainder of Africa	Asia	U.S.A.	British North America	The West Indies	Central & South America	Total Enumerated Imports
				Panel A: Values (Annual Averages)								
1905–1913	74.8	91.3	72.7	29.2	26.3	17.2	73.6	126.6	26.9	4.4	59.8	602.7
1914–1918	71.9	67.2	11.1	46.6	33.0	36.5	136.4	312.0	69.1	18.7	94.2	896.5
1919–1928	116.4	154.2	56.1	52.7	50.6	57.5	151.2	291.6	71.4	21.2	126.4	1,149.2
				Panel B: Percent of Accumulated Total								
1905–1913	12.4	15.2	12.1	4.8	4.4	2.9	12.2	21.0	4.5	0.7	9.9	100.0
1914–1918	8.0	7.5	1.2	5.2	3.7	4.1	15.2	34.8	7.7	2.1	10.5	100.0
1919–1928	10.1	13.4	4.9	4.6	4.4	5.0	13.2	25.4	6.2	1.8	11.0	100.0

Source: See Table 5.31.

Table 5.34. *United Kingdom: Percentages of Food Imports (Gross) from Various Sources in 1913 and 1918*

Country	Wheat & Flour 1913	Wheat & Flour 1918	Meat 1913	Meat 1918	Bacon & Hams 1913	Bacon & Hams 1918	Lard 1913	Lard 1918	Dairy Produce 1913	Dairy Produce 1918	Sugar 1913	Sugar 1918
U.S.A (including Cuban sugar)	34.7	52.3	1.6	31.2	44.9	83.7	92.1	93.7	0.2	37.8	11.6	63.5
Canada	22.5	25.1	0.1	5.0	5.8	15.2	3.7	3.3	10.4	20.6	0.0	0.0
Argentina	12.3	15.5	49.5	32.1	0.0	0.0	0.0	0.0	0.6	4.5	0.0	0.0
India	15.3	0.8	0.0	0.0	0.0	0.0	0.0	0.0	0.0	0.0	0.2	0.0
Australia & New Zealand	8.7	4.6	36.5	22.5	0.0	0.0	0.0	0.0	11.3	22.2	0.0	0.0
Russia	4.1	0.0	0.0	0.0	0.0	0.0	0.0	0.0	19.8	0.0	0.0	0.0
Netherlands	0.0	0.0	4.6	0.0	0.0	0.0	0.0	0.0	22.7	8.9	9.6	1.1
Uruguay	0.0	0.0	4.4	5.5	0.0	0.0	0.0	0.0	0.0	0.0	0.0	0.0
Denmark	0.0	0.0	0.0	0.0	0.0	0.0	0.0	0.0	19.3	3.1	0.0	0.0
Germany	0.0	0.0	0.0	0.0	40.9	0.0	0.0	0.0	0.0	0.0	47.6	0.0
Austria-Hungary	0.0	0.0	0.0	0.0	0.0	0.0	0.0	0.0	0.0	0.0	18.2	0.0
Java	0.0	0.0	0.0	0.0	0.0	0.0	0.0	0.0	0.0	0.0	0.0	14.3
Other Countries	2.4	1.7	3.3	3.7	8.4	0.9	4.2	3.0	15.7	2.9	12.8	21.1
TOTAL	100.0	100.0	100.0	100.0	100.0	100.0	100.0	100.0	100.0	100.0	100.0	100.0
Actual Quantity (thousand tons)	6,135.0	4,632.0	878.0	660.0	286.0	601.0	111.0	139.0	621.0	360.0	1,969.0	1,306.0

Source: Beveridge, *British Food Control*, 135.

Table 5.35. *United Kingdom: Percentages of Total Supplies of Principal Foodstuffs that were Imported and Home-Grown Respectively in 1909–1913 and in Each Year 1914 to 1918*

| | United Kingdom | | | | | | | | | | | |
| | Percentage Home Grown | | | | | | Percentage Imported | | | | | |
Commodity	1909–13	1914	1915	1916	1917	1918	1909–13	1914	1915	1916	1917	1918
Wheat & Flour (as equivalent grain)	21.3	22.8	28.4	21.9	23.8	35.1	78.7	77.2	71.6	78.1	76.2	64.9
Barley	56.7	65.8	64.4	59.9	73.7	84.7	43.3	34.2	35.6	40.1	26.3	15.3
Oats	76.6	80.6	80.1	82.6	85.2	88.8	23.4	19.4	19.9	17.4	14.8	11.2
Peas & Beans	64.5	69.3	64.7	62.1	43.3	56.1	35.5	30.7	35.3	37.9	56.7	43.9
Total (above cereals & pulses)	43.8	46.4	49.5	45.3	49.9	60.1	56.2	53.6	50.5	54.7	50.1	39.9
Beef & Veal	66.4	64.0	64.6	68.5	73.0	59.1	33.6	36.0	35.4	31.5	27.0	40.9
Mutton	55.5	52.1	54.6	62.6	71.3	67.7	44.5	47.9	45.4	37.4	28.7	32.3
Other Meat	71.0	62.0	63.4	66.0	58.1	40.5	29.0	38.0	36.6	34.0	41.9	59.5
Total Meat	64.3	60.7	62.0	66.5	70.0	57.8	35.7	39.3	38.0	33.5	30.0	42.2
Bacon & Hams	31.3	28.8	24.5	23.2	21.8	10.6	68.7	71.2	75.5	76.8	78.2	89.4
Lard	21.5	19.6	16.4	16.5	15.2	5.4	78.5	80.4	83.6	83.5	84.8	94.6
Fish	88.3	83.5	71.0	68.5	69.7	72.9	11.7	16.5	29.0	31.5	30.3	27.1
Milk (fresh)	100.0	100.0	100.0	100.0	100.0	100.0	0.0	0.0	0.0	0.0	0.0	0.0
Milk (condensed)	45.6	44.0	39.2	39.7	43.4	29.5	54.4	56.0	60.8	60.3	56.6	70.5
Butter	37.7	38.8	39.5	53.4	55.9	56.6	62.3	61.2	60.5	46.6	44.1	43.4
Cheese	25.3	24.7	22.7	23.1	21.0	25.8	74.7	75.3	77.3	76.9	79.0	74.2
Margarine	50.8	50.6	52.8	48.3	66.9	94.1	49.2	49.4	47.2	51.7	33.1	5.9
Potatoes	96.3	97.8	98.6	98.4	99.1	99.4	3.7	2.2	1.4	1.6	0.9	0.6

Source: Beveridge, *British Food Control*, 359.

Table 5.36. *United Kingdom, Potential Food Supply, 1914–1918 (Billions of Calories)*

	Average 1909–13	1914	1915	1916	1917	1918
Potential Food Demand	51.0	52.5	53.7	54.4	55.1	55.3
Less Imports	29.6	34.2	31.8	31.1	29.2	27.9
Net	21.4	18.3	21.9	23.3	25.9	27.4
Potential Shortage (−) or Surplus (+)	n.a.	3.1	−0.5	−1.9	−4.5	−6.0
Surplus or Shortage as a Percentage of Demand	n.a.	5.9	−0.9	−3.5	−8.2	−10.8

Source: Dewey, "Food Production," 82.

Table 5.37. *United Kingdom: Stocks of Principal Foods on September 1 of Each Year, 1914 to 1919*

Commodity	Stocks as a percentage of Stocks at September 1st 1914					
	1914	1915	1916	1917	1918	1919
Wheat (including flour as wheat)	100.0	103.4	96.9	122.6	127.0	95.4
Barley	100.0	74.4	84.0	82.1	83.3	75.4
Oats	100.0	111.8	107.2	125.5	149.7	120.8
Bacon & Ham	100.0	315.0	313.3	245.0	782.5	513.3
Other Meat	100.0	113.4	56.0	92.4	117.1	176.5
All Meat	100.0	140.9	91.0	113.2	207.7	222.4
Butter	100.0	76.9	59.8	81.1	94.1	104.7
Margarine	100.0	153.6	128.6	242.9	67.9	142.9
Lard	100.0	284.1	206.1	330.5	293.9	203.7
All Fats	100.0	145.5	109.7	170.6	150.2	137.6
Cheese	100.0	151.9	113.2	121.7	197.7	93.8
Condensed Milk	100.0					
Sugar	100.0	113.0	104.6	138.2	323.7	186.3
Tea	100.0	111.3	119.6	57.7	123.5	180.7
Cocoa	100.0	142.4	329.9	410.4	97.9	520.1
Oil-seeds	100.0	84.5	128.3	106.7	68.7	65.0
Oilcakes & Meal	100.0	75.9	94.7	97.7	55.6	89.3

Source: Beveridge, *British Food Control*, 319.

Table 5.38. *United Kingdom: Daily Food Consumption, 1914–1918*

	Average 1909–13	1914	1915	1916	1917	1918
Calories Per "Average Man"	3,442	3,454	3,551	3,418	3,320	3,358
As a Percentage of 1909–1913	100.0	100.3	103.2	99.3	96.5	97.6

Source: Dewey, "Food Production," 72.

due to the definition of the British Empire, Tables 5.39 and 5.40 tell a similar story. If the United States had not been involved, formally or informally, construction in Britain and the Dominions would not have been able to make up the wartime losses in any year after 1914. Moreover, in 1917 the British deficit was 2,431 thousand tons. American participation, although insufficient to overcome all losses in 1915, 1916, and 1917, did, however, greatly reduce those deficits. Moreover, in 1918, American construction turned a 53,000-ton British deficit into a 2,838-thousand-ton Allied surplus; and, for the entire war, it turned an 1,854,000-ton deficit into a 2,720,000-ton surplus. Thus, at war's end, the Allied merchant fleet was larger than it had been before the Germans launched their two U-boat offensives. Moreover, it is difficult to underestimate the impact on German morale, when civilians and troops became aware that the Americans were able to launch an additional 3.6 *million* tons in 1919.[96]

Finally, a comparison between the German submarine fleet and allied and neutral losses provides a third measure of the costs and benefits of the German U-boat campaign. First, in terms of submarines at sea, tonnage losses per submarine rose from 84,000 tons in 1914, to 164,000 in 1915. Because of the submarine fleet's weak performance in June, July, and August, the total declined to 127,000 in 1916. Although the annual total in 1917 rose to over 137,000 tons, the widespread innovation of convoys reduced monthly sinkings. Sinkings had averaged 15,000 tons a month for the first eight months, fell to less than half that amount in September, October, November, and December. Never again, after September 1917, were monthly sinkings per submarine at sea to total as much as 10,000 tons. In fact, the monthly average from that September until the end of the war was less than 6,000 tons (see Table 5.12).

Furthermore, over the years 1914 to 1918, in order to keep averages of 4, 8, 18, 44, and 44 submarines at sea per year, it was necessary to maintain a total fleet of 25, 37, 67, 128, and 124 U-boats, an average wartime ratio of just more than 1 in 3. As a result, sinkings per submarine in the fleet totaled only 13,000 tons in 1914, 35,000 in 1915, 34,000 in 1916, 47,000 in 1917, and 20,000 in the last year of the war.

Second, the figures on allied and neutral losses per submarine sunk indicated something about improvements in antisubmarine warfare. The widespread innovation of the convoy – the convoy provided what appeared

---

96 Fayle, *War and the Shipping Industry*, 416.

Table 5.39. *British Empire Merchant Marine: Construction Gains and War-Related Losses (August 1914 to October 1918)*

Month & Quarter	Gains	Losses	Net Change
1914			
July			
August	82,000	47,000	35,000
September	72,000	80,000	−8,000
3rd Quarter	154,000	127,000	27,000
October	140,000	84,000	56,000
November	94,000	15,000	79,000
December	96,000	27,000	69,000
4th Quarter	330,000	126,000	204,000
1914 TOTAL	484,000	253,000	231,000
1915			
January	101,000	32,000	69,000
February	74,000	36,000	38,000
March	71,000	79,000	−8,000
1st Quarter	246,000	147,000	99,000
April	110,000	29,000	81,000
May	63,000	93,000	−30,000
June	71,000	92,000	−21,000
2nd Quarter	244,000	214,000	30,000
July	59,000	56,000	3,000
August	41,000	149,000	−108,000
September	56,000	100,000	−44,000
3rd Quarter	156,000	305,000	−149,000
October	54,000	54,000	0
November	51,000	90,000	−39,000
December	71,000	75,000	−4,000
4th Quarter	176,000	219,000	−43,000
1915 TOTAL	822,000	885,000	−63,000
1916			
January	40,000	72,000	−32,000
February	27,000	69,000	−42,000
March	26,000	98,000	−72,000
1st Quarter	93,000	239,000	−146,000
April	21,000	139,000	−118,000
May	58,000	65,000	−7,000
June	34,000	32,000	2,000
2nd Quarter	113,000	236,000	−123,000
July	48,000	81,000	−33,000
August	46,000	44,000	2,000
September	24,000	107,000	−83,000
3rd Quarter	118,000	232,000	−114,000

(continued)

Table 5.39 *(continued)*

Month & Quarter	Gains	Losses	Net Change
October	69,000	170,000	−101,000
November	68,000	180,000	−112,000
December	83,000	174,000	−91,000
4th Quarter	220,000	524,000	−304,000
1916 TOTAL	544,000	1,231,000	−687,000
1917			
January	76,000	154,000	−78,000
February	92,000	311,000	−219,000
March	158,000	352,000	−194,000
1st Quarter	326,000	817,000	−491,000
April	77,000	526,000	−449,000
May	81,000	345,000	−264,000
June	147,000	399,000	−252,000
2nd Quarter	305,000	1,270,000	−965,000
July	72,000	360,000	−288,000
August	109,000	331,000	−222,000
September	106,000	187,000	−81,000
3rd Quarter	287,000	878,000	−591,000
October	126,000	262,000	−136,000
November	112,000	175,000	−63,000
December	151,000	258,000	−107,000
4th Quarter	389,000	695,000	−306,000
1917 TOTAL	1,307,000	3,660,000	−2,353,000
1918			
January	95,000	173,000	−78,000
February	88,000	213,000	−125,000
March	146,000	199,000	−53,000
1st Quarter	329,000	585,000	−256,000
April	99,000	214,000	−115,000
May	164,000	179,000	−15,000
June	160,000	144,000	16,000
2nd Quarter	423,000	537,000	−114,000
July	160,000	164,000	−4,000
August	120,000	144,000	−24,000
September	197,000	129,000	68,000
3rd Quarter	477,000	437,000	40,000
October	144,000	56,000	88,000
November	–	–	–
December	–	–	–
4th Quarter	144,000	56,000	88,000
1918 TOTAL	1,373,000	1,615,000	−242,000

Source: Salter, *Allied Shipping Control*, 362–363.

Table 5.40. *British Empire and American Merchant Shipping Losses and New Vessel Construction*
(thousands of gross tons)

	Panel A: Wartime Losses					
	1914	1915	1916	1917	1918	1914–1918
United Kingdom & Dominions	253	885	1,232	3,660	1,632	7,662
United States	0	16	15	166	142	339
TOTAL	253	901	1,247	3,826	1,774	8,001
	Panel B: New Vessel Construction					
United Kingdom & Dominions	1,706	664	630	1,229	1,579	5,808
United States	201	177	504	998	3,033	4,913
TOTAL	1,907	841	1,134	2,227	4,612	10,721
	Panel C: Net Additions or Subtractions					
United Kingdom & Dominions	1,453	−221	−602	−2,431	−53	−1,854
United States	201	161	489	832	2,891	4,574
TOTAL	1,654	−60	−113	−1,599	2,838	2,720

Source: Salter, *Allied Shipping Control*, 355–358, 361.

to be a profitable target and attracted submarines to the very parts of the ocean where the Allied antisubmarine force were concentrated – began to make that form of deployment an offensive, as well as a defensive, weapon. There also were some improvements in antisubmarine technology. Tonnage lost per submarine sunk averaged almost 68,000 tons per month in 1914 and 1915; it increased to 105,000 tons per month in 1916, before declining to 96,000 tons per month in 1917, and to 34,000 tons per month in 1918. Again, although averaging about 160,000 tons through the first eight months of 1917, the figure for September through December was less than 43,000 tons a month; and, over the last fourteen months of the war, it never again totaled as much as 90,000 tons. There can be no doubt, convoys were a crucial innovation.

3(2b). The Historiography. General Erich Ludendorff, in retirement, "remarked that the requirements of totalitarian warfare will ever ignore the cheap theoretical desire to abolish unrestricted U-boat warfare," whereas aircraft would in future combine with submarines at sinking every ship that tried to reach the enemy's ports – 'even vessels sailing under neutral flags.'" In this and other comments, he appeared to realize that military power rests in part, at least, on an economic foundation. However, his vision of the way the next war would be fought centered on military clashes similar to his 1918 offenses. "For him the offensive was still a battle-process in which the infantry would be helped forward by artillery, machine guns, and tanks until it 'overwhelms the enemy in a man-to-man fight.'"[97] Ludendorf still believed that the war had been lost on the Western Front, not in the seas around the British Isles.

The historian H. P. Willmott voices an intermediate assessment; although accepting the fact that the major cause of the German defeat was the gradual build-up of the forces that opposed her, "The simple truth of the situation was that the Germans managed to get themselves into a disastrous strategic position as a result of their own myopia and their failure to defeat France in 1914." Overall, he provides a mixed assessment of the submarine blockade: "By a very narrow margin the German unrestricted submarine campaign failed, but the failure was decisive in that it provoked the American intervention."[98] Michael Lewis, however, views the German strategy as one designed to guarantee an Allied victory. Although noting the blockade was "nearly strangling us," he writes, "Germany, however, played into our hands. Like Napoleon, she declared a blockade on us, but, unlike Napoleon who could not make it effective, Germany thought that she could – with her submarines. But this involved methods of unheard of barbarity."[99] Of the three, Lewis probably comes the closest to the truth; but the quantitative evidence seems to suggest that the blockade never brought Britain within a few weeks or months of starvation. It certainly did, however, trigger the American entry into the war. That entry opened wide a source of supplies and finance that guaranteed that the British would never starve to death, to say nothing of injecting some two million fresh troops into the Allied armies fighting on the Western Front.

4. INTERNATIONAL LAW REVISITED

It is clear that, by the end of the war, the policies adopted by Britain, Germany, and the United States had made a shambles of that part of international law that dealt with naval blockades. Given the British refusal to ratify the Declaration of London, despite the fact that the major belligerents gave lip service to those amended rules, the Declaration was a dead letter at the outbreak of the war. On the question of contraband, there was no agreed definition; and, "on October the 30th, by Order of Council, the British Government asserted the right to intercept conditional contraband, if consigned 'to order', that is in blank." Thereafter, the shipper was forced

97 Liddell Hart, *Strategy*, 226.   98 Willmott, *Sea Warfare*, 54–55.
99 Lewis, *History of the British Navy*, 251–252.

to prove his 'innocence of intent by showing the name of a genuine consignee.' Four days later, the British declared the entire North Sea a 'military area'; and, despite the fact that they had not formally declared a blockade, their naval vessels began diverting neutral merchant vessels to Allied ports, so that they could be searched.[100]

In February 1915, the Germans, arguing that noncontraband articles bound for Germany had been seized on neutral vessels, declared an all-out submarine war. "Allied merchantmen in a 'war area' comprising the coasts of the British Isles and northern France were liable to be destroyed without warning and without consideration for the lives of crews or passengers. Neutral ships in the same waters would be exposed to danger, for the *ruse-de-guerre*, which allowed the ships of a belligerent to fly a neutral flag, made it impossible to distinguish the nationality. The German government officially maintained that its action had been forced on it by the Allies' disregard of the law of contraband and in particular of the Declaration of Paris."[101]

The next month, the British and French governments retaliated with the Reprisals Orders of March 1915. They announced that they would, in the future, seize any goods at sea whose "'destination, ownership, or origin' were presumed to be hostile." The order, for all intents and purposes, "gave the Allies complete freedom to apply the doctrine of continuous voyage to whatever articles they wished, whether absolute or conditional contraband, or whether consigned to a known or unknown importer."[102]

Nor was the United States exempt from the popular game of adding new additions to the list of "infractions" of international law. With the exception of its innovation of the concept of continuous voyage during the Civil War, it can be argued that, up to the time of its entrance into World War I in 1917, "the United States had invariably advocated the freedom from seizure upon the sea of all private property belligerent as well as neutral with the exception of contraband of war." During the years 1914 to 1917, the American government protested against both sides' alleged violations of international law. It protested against the belligerents floating mines in the North Sea; it protested against the German "war zone" policy of unrestricted submarine warfare; it protested British merchant vessels flying the American flag; it protested against the Central Powers sinking American ships and

---

100 Chambers, *War Behind the War*, 134–135.
101 Chambers, *War Behind the War*, 135. It should be noted that the German deportation of Belgium citizens to Germany to augment that country's labor force also "contravened any normal interpretation of international law; and those deportations were carried out with extreme brutality." Chambers, *War Behind the War*, 215.
102 Chambers, *War Behind the War*, 135–136.

killing American citizens; and, in 1915, it denounced the British blockade as illegal. No sooner, however, had the United States entered the war, than the government deployed naval units to help enforce the "illegal" British blockade; and, in addition, it innovated a number of policies of its own – many of them policies that it, alone, had the financial power to implement. The history of the American attitude toward blockades, both in the Civil War and again during World War I, "furnishes a good illustration of the manner in which nations are prone to act in accordance with their interests of the moment, even though such actions are inconsistent with their previous policy," to say nothing of violating international law.[103]

By the end of the war, historians spoke of the "inchoate" state of international law. The British (and American) economic "blockade" was certainly a major attempt to control world industry and commerce. It affected not only imports and exports but also involved attempts to stimulate production of certain commodities by subsidies and the fixing of minimum prices, to limit the production of other commodities by fiat, to monopolize the sources of many raw materials, and to alter trade routes by the control of shipping. Given the "state" of international law, historians were hesitant to charge the Allies with imposing "illegal" embargoes on particular neutral countries; but they did acknowledge that "the blockade demonstrated the feasibility of such regulation and control on a large scale"; and they recognized that, in the future, if there were another major war, that there would likely be attempts to implement such measures again. Some of these, however, also went on to suggest that the basic solution for "imperialism of all kinds and the wars which arise therefrom is the World State."[104] The first conclusion provides a legitimate insight into what were to be the policies adopted by the belligerents in World War II. However, given the demonstrated unwillingness of the World War I belligerents to abdicate their military decisions to a court of international law, it is hard to understand how those same scholars could conclude that, in the future, major powers would be willing to surrender their decision-making power to a "World State" – particularly a World State with no ability to enforce its decisions. It would take at least another quarter century before that lesson was learned, if, in fact it has yet been learned.

5. CONCLUSIONS

We wish to make a few brief concluding remarks – remarks designed to place the World War I experience with blockades in a broader perspective

---

103 Parmelee, *Blockade*, 63–68.   104 Parmelee, *Blockade*, 45–48, 331, 383–384.

and to indicate the role played by the opinions of historians, politicians, and the men on the street as to what really happened in helping to shape the interwar period and the planning for World War II.

First, as expected, despite the international conferences and other agreements about the accepted wartime rules to be followed by belligerents, those belligerents operated as they wished, guided almost solely by their own self-interests. The belligerents, Allied and Central Powers alike, violated the rights of neutral traders as provided in the still unratified Declaration of the London Conference of 1909 as regards both to interference with neutral voyages and to the tactics that could be employed to sink the vessels engaged in such a voyage. Moreover, when countries shifted from neutral to belligerent status, as the United States did in 1917, there were dramatic changes in their attitude toward the remaining neutral powers – changes that again reflected self-interest.

World War I saw the first major deployment of a revolutionary new technology, the submarine. Rules governing the "legal" tactics that submarines could adopt had not been covered in the existing international protocols; thus, there was much room for debate about just how the existing rules could be modified to deal with the innovation of the new warships without emasculating them. Those issues, however, were not even theoretically resolved until two decades after the war had ended. Even then, however, once World War II began, and the Germans launched major submarine attacks on Allied shipping, the prior new agreements were once again ignored by all of the belligerent powers. Clearly, any international agreement had, at most, a limited impact, once military operations began.

Second, World War I saw blockades imposed by both the Germans and the British (the latter with subsequent American cooperation). The German blockade was primarily a submarine blockade, whereas the British deployed a more traditional surface fleet–based effort. The early years of the war saw effective German submarine attacks on both Allied and neutral ships, with sinkings exceeding the Allies capacity to build new vessels. Later, however, the belated adoption of the centuries–old convoy technology reduced the submarine kill-ratios, and therefore the effectiveness of the German blockade, to acceptable levels. The delay in the adoption of the convoy does raise an important question; what would have been the impact of the blockade, if the Admiralty had been blessed with the same vision as the Venetian admirals centuries earlier?

An at least equally important contribution to the Allied victory was made by the Germans themselves; their U-boat attacks brought the United States into the war on the Allied side. The American financial and military contributions, including the deployment of the American navy, the world's second or third largest, in support of the British convoys, cannot be minimized; however, perhaps equally important, was the was the addition of American shipbuilding capacity to the Allied shipyards. By 1918, those shipyards had launched more than three million tons of merchant shipping; and, as a result, after four years of war *and* the German submarine blockade, the Allied merchant marine was some 2.7 million tons larger than it had been in August 1914.

In large part due to the shortfall in domestic production, but also in part due, to the effectiveness of the Allied blockade, by 1918, the Germans faced a food crisis. It appears that the blockade directly accounted for about a quarter of the decline in German food consumption; the other three-quarters of the fall can be traced to the decline in domestic production. Although the blockades, by cutting off the supply of nitrates, made an indirect contribution, most of the reduction in domestic production can be traced to the military's demands for manpower and to bad weather. However, despite its relative small direct contribution, and, because the Allies continued the blockade from the November armistice until the signing of peace at Versailles, some eight months later, the Allied tactics were blamed for the German civilian suffering; and the blockade itself was held up as an example of British savagery. Those conclusions continued to dominate German thinking during the interwar period and World War II.

The German blockade of Britain, despite the numbers of ships sunk, had much less of an impact on British food consumption. British imports declined only slightly, and domestic production was maintained (and in some cases increased) (see Tables 5.33, 5.34, 5.35, and 5.36. For the general increase in stocks of key foods during the war, see Table 5.41). As a result, in spite of the U-boats, there was little change in the domestic consumption of food by the citizens of the United Kingdom.

Despite the evidence, several scholars have tended to reach a very strange conclusion about the effectiveness of the German submarine blockade – namely, that the blockade had come within six weeks (or six months) of starving the British into submission. The widespread belief in that conclusion led, during the interwar period, to a growing concern for the future among politicians and normal citizens alike. The conclusion was, however, reached without a careful examination of the food supplies that were available; instead, they were based on German propaganda – propaganda that was used by the German military to support their call for an increase in the magnitude and extent of the German U-boat campaign against Allied and neutral shipping. Nevertheless, taken together, the actual, and the alleged, efficiency of the submarine as a weapon of war greatly influenced the policies of both the British and American navies before and during World War II.

In a set of policies that were to be widely copied by both sides during World War II, both Britain and Germany introduced rationing of food and other consumer goods in an effort to "fairly" allocate limited supplies. The Germans introduced rationing earlier, and their program encompassed more commodities than did the British counterpart; but both countries witnessed a massive increase in central government bureaucracies, as new administrative structures were introduced to handle problems raised by the blockades and other wartime measures. In both cases, these bureaucracies were to play a key role in the interwar period, as well as during World War II.

Table 5.A.1. *Estimates of Construction and Destruction of the German Submarine Fleet, 1914–1918 (end of each month)*

Year	Month	Constructed	Destroyed
1914	August	1	2
	September	2	0
	October	2	0
	November	2	1
	December	2	2
1915	January	5	2
	February	5	0
	March	3	3
	April	8	1
	May	8	0
	June	4	3
	July	6	3
	August	2	3
	September	2	2
	October	2	1
	November	5	1
	December	5	0
1916	January	5	0
	February	5	0
	March	7	2
	April	7	3
	May	7	2
	June	10	1
	July	9	3
	August	10	1
	September	15	1
	October	10	1
	November	10	5
	December	5	3
1917	January	3	2
	February	5	4
	March	6	3
	April	6	2
	May	7	7
	June	11	2
	July	9	6
	August	9	3
	September	12	13
	October	6	5
	November	6	7
	December	11	9

Year	Month	Constructed	Destroyed
1918	January	7	9
	February	7	3
	March	8	5
	April	8	7
	May	12	14
	June	12	3
	July	23	6
	August	17	7
	September	15	7
	October	15	7
	November	0	1

Notes: Vessels constructed are evenly assigned over the months that saw the class completed.
Sources: Andreas Michelsen, *Der U-bootskreig, 1914–1918* (Leipzig, K. F. Koehler, 1925), 182–185, 186; and John Terraine, *Business in Great Waters, The U-Boat Wars, 1916–1945* (Ware: Wordsworth Editions, 1999), 762–764.

Table 5.A.2. *The German Submarine Fleet (On the tenth day of every month) August 1914 through October 1918*

Year & Month	At Sea	At Base	In Dockyard	Total
1914				
August	0	16	4	20
September	2	20	2	24
October	8	14	5	27
November	3	15	10	28
December	4	15	9	28
1915				
January	4	12	11	27
February	1	15	11	27
March	6	6	15	27
April	6	5	15	26
May	8	8	19	35
June	10	15	15	40
July	10	22	12	44
August	13	23	9	45
September	14	18	14	46
October	7	19	18	44
November	9	22	11	42
December	8	24	12	44
1916				
January	4	23	14	41
February	10	11	20	41
March	11	20	16	47
April	20	23	9	52
May	7	25	26	58
June	15	18	32	65
July	28	21	23	72
August	21	27	26	74
September	21	36	23	80
October	17	41	29	87
November	29	25	39	93
December	34	20	43	97
1917				
January	20	32	51	103
February	38	31	42	111
March	36	43	49	128
April	42	40	45	127
May	42	25	63	130
June	61	24	47	132
July	42	28	60	130
August	45	30	53	128
September	59	27	53	139

Year & Month	At Sea	At Base	In Dockyard	Total
October	55	39	46	140
November	30	26	81	137
December	60	17	57	134
1918				
January	33	29	70	132
February	50	29	50	129
March	37	18	72	127
April	44	18	63	125
May	55	17	53	125
June	36	15	61	112
July	45	17	59	121
August	45	10	69	124
September	43	5	80	128
October	54	0	67	121

Source: Michelsen, *Der U-bootskrieg*, 182–185.

Table 5.A.3. *The German Submarine Fleet-Percentage Distribution: Sea, Base,*
or Dockyard (On the tenth day of every month)

Year & Month	At Sea	At Base	In Dockyard	Total
1914				
August	0.00	80.00	20.00	100.00
September	8.33	83.33	8.33	100.00
October	29.63	51.85	18.52	100.00
November	10.71	53.57	35.71	100.00
December	14.29	53.57	32.14	100.00
1915				
January	14.81	44.44	40.74	100.00
February	3.70	55.56	40.74	100.00
March	22.22	22.22	55.56	100.00
April	23.08	19.23	57.69	100.00
May	22.86	22.86	54.29	100.00
June	25.00	37.50	37.50	100.00
July	22.73	50.00	27.27	100.00
August	28.89	51.11	20.00	100.00
September	30.43	39.13	30.43	100.00
October	15.91	43.18	40.91	100.00
November	21.43	52.38	26.19	100.00
December	18.18	54.55	27.27	100.00
1916				
January	9.76	56.10	34.15	100.00
February	24.39	26.83	48.78	100.00
March	23.40	42.55	34.04	100.00
April	38.46	44.23	17.31	100.00
May	12.07	43.10	44.83	100.00
June	23.08	27.69	49.23	100.00
July	38.89	29.17	31.94	100.00
August	28.38	36.49	35.14	100.00
September	26.25	45.00	28.75	100.00
October	19.54	47.13	33.33	100.00
November	31.18	26.88	41.94	100.00
December	35.05	20.62	44.33	100.00
1917				
January	19.42	31.07	49.51	100.00
February	34.23	27.93	37.84	100.00
March	28.13	33.59	38.28	100.00
April	33.07	31.50	35.43	100.00
May	32.31	19.23	48.46	100.00
June	46.21	18.18	35.61	100.00
July	32.31	21.54	46.15	100.00
August	35.16	23.44	41.41	100.00
September	42.45	19.42	38.13	100.00

Year & Month	At Sea	At Base	In Dockyard	Total
October	39.29	27.86	32.86	100.00
November	21.90	18.98	59.12	100.00
December	44.78	12.69	42.54	100.00
1918				
January	25.00	21.97	53.03	100.00
February	38.76	22.48	38.76	100.00
March	29.13	14.17	56.69	100.00
April	35.20	14.40	50.40	100.00
May	44.00	13.60	42.40	100.00
June	32.14	13.39	54.46	100.00
July	37.19	14.05	48.76	100.00
August	36.29	8.06	55.65	100.00
September	33.59	3.91	62.50	100.00
October	44.63	0.00	55.37	100.00

Source: See Table 5.A.2.

6

Legal and Economic Aspects of Naval Blockades

The United States, Great Britain, and Germany in World War II

INTRODUCTION

By World War I, improvements in technology, particularly the innovation of long-range coastal defense guns, mines, and submarines, had all but ruled out "close blockades" of the type that characterized warfare from the English-French continental wars of the eighteenth century through at least the American Civil War. Earlier, most blockades were "close blockades," that "must be confined to ports and coasts belonging to or occupied by the enemy." By 1914, however, "*close*" blockades had been replaced by "*distant*" ones. The blockading vessels were now almost always positioned further out to sea, with a corresponding potential for more contact with nonbelligerent shipping; however, as long as the blockade can adequately restrict movements into and out of enemy ports, this form of interdiction is considered legally valid.[1]

Another important change is that although in the twentieth century most blockades have been enforced by government-owned-and-operated vessels, in the past the blockading vessels have included private ships operating under letters of marque as government approved privateers. Historically, the distinction between private and government blockades raised a number of issues including legal questions of controls over appropriate behavior and domestic questions involving the relative size of peacetime and wartime navies.[2]

---

1 Wolff Heintschel von Heinegg, "Naval Blockade," in Michael M. Schmitt (ed.), *International Law across the Spectrum of Conflict; Essays in Honour of Professor L. C. Green on the Occasion of His Eightieth Birthday* (Newport: Naval War College, 2000), 209, 211.
2 Maurice Parmelee, *Blockade and Sea Power: The Blockade, 1914–1919, and Its Significance for a World State* (New York: Thomas Y. Crowell, 1924), 61–63.

Given its precursors and the size of the conflagration, it is not surprising that policies adopted during World War I almost entirely rewrote the rules of naval blockades; and the history of the war itself appeared to confirm that, in the future, the convoy was to become the ultimate weapon against a "distant" blockade. Between 1914 and 1918, there were two major blockades: a British "distant" blockade of Germany – a blockade aimed at severing that country's external sources of supply of food and military material – and a German submarine-based blockade of the British Isles – a blockade designed to cut Great Britain off from food produced in the empire and the United States.[3] The lessons or the presumed lessons of both blockades were to have a major impact on the blockades of World War II.

In the case of the British blockade, it was the restrictions imposed on neutral nations that were to have the most important long-term impact. British strategy called for a "distant" blockade of Germany, designed to prevent merchant ships from reaching Germany and also to tempt the German surface fleet into a major battle in the North Sea. The first of these goals was achieved, and the second partially so. However, in the early stages of the war, Germany was able to draw on imports from Denmark, Norway, and Sweden – imports of commodities that before the war had often been imported into the Scandinavian countries from Britain, France, the Americas, and Asia. The British responded with an expanded version of the American doctrine of "continuous voyage" – an extension designed to pressure the neutral nations bordering the Central Powers. The rules were rewritten to guarantee: (1) that imports into those countries were not reexported to the Central Powers and that those imports could not be used as substitutes for the neutral's exports to those powers; (2) that "import licensing facilities should be refused to individuals and firms on Allied trade black lists," and that imports should not fall into the hands of such individuals and firms; (3) that the rations of supplies permitted into the neutral countries were "not to exceed their normal domestic needs"; (4) that, insofar as was possible, the neutral's export surpluses should be directed toward the Allies and that the neutral's merchant fleet should be used to support Allied trade; and (5) that the Central Powers exports were reduced as far

---

3 It should be remembered that Great Britain "never formally declared a blockade" during World War I. Because British naval forces were never able to enter the Baltic, they could not prevent ocean trade between Germany and the Scandanavian countries; and, therefore, within the terms of both the Declaration of Paris and the Declaration of London, the blockade could not have been "effective." Parmelee, *Blockade*, 38.

as possible, and that their exchange rates were made "as unfavorable as possible."[4]

To effect these ends, a system of import quotas was introduced in 1915; and, despite vigorous protests by the neutrals, by 1916 it had been extended to include Holland, Switzerland, Denmark, Norway, and Sweden.[5] The blockade, coupled with the drain on German civilian manpower that resulted from the military demands of the eastern and western fronts, proved effective. Economic conditions in Germany deteriorated and civilian discontent rose. In response to the resulting domestic threat, the German high command launched the 1918 offensive in the West – an offensive that, although nearly achieving victory, ended in disaster. Although, in part, the offensive failed because of ineffective coordination, in even larger part it failed because substantial numbers of German troops – troops who had been on minimal rations for the past two years – stopped to loot Allied supply dumps for food.

In the case of the German blockade, the set of wartime "rules" was rewritten, and the importance of convoys was underscored. Both those new rules and the reemergence of the convoy were to play crucial roles in naval engagements a quarter century later when World War II broke out. Unlike the British blockade with the use of their surface fleet, the German blockade was mounted by submarines. Although a battleship, a cruiser, or even a destroyer could stop a merchantman at sea with little threat to itself, a submarine that surfaced to identify a potential target and take it into port was at serious risk from even a lightly armed vessel. In February 1915, as the British blockade tightened, the German military turned to a policy of "unrestricted submarine warfare against the commercial shipping that supported the British Isles." The initial assault managed to sink almost 116,000 tons of shipping in March and April, but even that relatively small success, when coupled with the following month's sinking of the *Luisitania*, with its 1,198 passengers, nearly brought the United States into the war. The fear of U.S. involvement persuaded the Germans to temporarily halt unrestricted submarine warfare.[6] Two years later, however, the British blockade, coupled with the domestic manpower demands of what, by then, had become a total war, pushed the German economy to the brink of collapse and led the German leaders to resume unrestricted submarine warfare, despite their

---

4 Parmelee, *Blockade*, 72–73.
5 Louis Guichard, *The Naval Blockade, 1914–1918* (New York: D. Appleton, 1930), 76–77.
6 Williamson Murray, "Naval Power in World War I," in Colin S. Gray and Roger W. Barnett, eds., *Seapower and Strategy* (Annapolis: Naval Institute Press, 1980), 202, 203, 205–206, 207.

full realization and acceptance as almost certain, of the risk that such action would bring the United States into war against them.[7] They believed that Britain's dependence on seaborne supplies to feed and clothe its civilian and military populations was a weak point in that country's defenses, and they concluded that the "inherently quicker effect of the submarine form of blockade lent force to the argument that this grand-strategical form of indirect approach would inflict a mortal blow" before the United States could respond. Their conclusions proved incorrect; but, in fact, in terms of contemporary perception they appear to have been not far off the mark. Shipping losses rose from 536,582 tons in February to 866,650 tons in April 1917; and by the time Allied countermeasures and Germany's insufficient submarine resources combined to produce a progressive decline in the blockade's effectiveness, it was perceived, although almost certainly erroneously, that Britain's food supply was sufficient for only another six weeks.[8]

Two factors ultimately combined to reduce the effectiveness of that blockade. First, the German High Command had not prepared for a massive submarine blockade; the number of German submarines proved insufficient to mount a full-scale and extended blockade; and they were able to add only a very few additional vessels through new construction. At the same time, the entry of the United States into the war meant that the Allies could deploy an increasingly large combined naval force to attack the blockading forces. Second, the Allies were able to deploy that force in a manner that proved very effective. In the words of B. H. Liddell Hart, first written in 1930 "the convoy system was the main agent of salvation." At first the senior officers in the British Admiralty, despite the "close-looming disaster," strongly opposed the introduction of the convoy system. However, in April 1917, the increasingly vocal advocacy of the junior officers – an advocacy strongly

---

7 Murray, "Naval Power," 202–205.

8 Robert A. Doughty and Harold E. Raugh Jr., "Embargoes in Historical Perspective," *Parameters* 21 (Spring 1991), 27; B. H. Liddell Hart, *Strategy* (2d rev. ed., New York: Praeger, 1967), 202; B. H. Liddell Hart, *A History of the World War, 1914–1918* (2nd rev. ed.) (London: Faber & Faber, 1934), 400–401. The view that Britain had been pushed to the edge was widely held in Britain both during the war and in the interwar period. Recently, however, Avner Offer has produced evidence that the crisis was far less grave, and that the German submarine fleet was never able to seriously threaten Britain's food supply, Avner Offer, *The First World War: An Agrarian Interpretation* (Oxford: Clarendon Press, 1989), 357–367. Moreover, P. E. Dewey has shown that claims of a British food shortage were much overdrawn. P. E. Dewey, "Food Production and Policy in the United Kingdom, 1914–1918" *Transactions of the Royal Historical Society*, 5th series, 30 (1980), 71–89. The six-week figure was the claim made by the German navy, but there also seems to have been some British belief in that conclusion. See also J. A. Salter, *Allied Shipping Control: An Experiment in International Administration* (Oxford: Clarendon Press, 1921), 121,122, 358. See Chapter 5 for a more complete discussion of these issues.

reinforced by the intervention of Lloyd George – led the Admiralty to sanction an experiment on inbound shipping on the Gibralter and North Sea routes. The convoy system proved immediately successful; and, when the arrival of the American flotillas increased the number of destroyers available for escort duty, convoys were extended to the transatlantic routes. "The loss of shipping in such convoys was reduced to a bare one per cent and when, in August, the convoys were extended to outward bound shipping the British loss fell next month below the 200,000 ton level." By the end of 1917, the submarine menace, if not broken, had been at least subdued.[9]

2. THE START OF WORLD WAR II

The years between the two world wars saw changes in both the institutional environment and in the thinking of the military planners in all three of the soon-to-be Atlantic belligerents. First, in terms of the institutional environment, "when the Germans signed the London Submarine Agreement in 1935, they undertook to observe the terms of the Geneva Convention in regard to submarine warfare." Under the agreement, "the U-boat commander was obliged to stop a target merchant vessel before he attacked it, to order the crew to their lifeboats, and, when he had sunk the vessel, by whatever means, to ensure that the lifeboats would hold all the survivors." Hardly surprisingly, given the experience of World War I, such scrupulous conduct, although initially followed by some of the early commanders, did not last long.[10] On the day the war began, the German submarine U-30 torpedoed and sank the British passenger ship *Athenia* with the loss of 112 (or 118) lives. Second, as part of the Chamberlain government's appeasement process, Britain surrendered the right to utilize "the west coast ports of the Irish Republic in case of war." Those ports had played a crucial role in breaking the German blockade during World War I. Although, in hindsight, historians have severely criticized the action, given the Admiralty's then view of convoys, it was perhaps hardly surprisingly that the Naval Command failed to appeal the proposal to surrender the right to use the bases.[11]

---

9 Liddell Hart, *World War*, 403.
10 Philip Kaplan and Jack Currie, *Convoy: Merchant Sailors at War, 1939–1945* (Annapolis: Naval Institute Press, 1998), 35.
11 Holger H. Herwig, "Innovation Ignored: The Submarine Problem – Germany, Britain, and the United States, 1919–1939," in Williamson Murray and Allan R. Millett, eds., *Military Innovation in*

At the most basic level, the British navy appeared to have largely forgotten that convoys, almost alone, "had played the crucial role in blunting the U-boat offensive in 1917." "Convoys fell by the wayside because naval professionals despised the dull and monotonous work of escorting convoys. They viewed convoys as a temporary expedient rather than a tool of war."[12] "Both convoy protection and antisubmarine work were tedious and dull, unlikely to attract either funds or recruits. For naval officers, appointment 'plums' led to the main battle fleet – at worst, to its protective destroyer screen."[13] "The naval staff encouraged the complacency. In autumn 1935, it endorsed evasive routing of merchant ships and argued that it would employ convoys only if rerouting 'should prove ineffective.'"[14] In that year, Lord E. M. C. Stanley, the Admiralty's Parliamentary and Financial Secretary, told the House of Commons that "the convoy system will be introduced" only "when sinkings are so great that the country no longer feels justified in allowing ships to sail by themselves" and that "antisubmarine systems were 'so very much better than they were during the [Great] War that we should want fewer protective vessels in the convoy.'"[15]

The outbreak of war, however, caused some revision of those attitudes at the Admiralty, if not among the officers assigned to the fleet. The *Athenia* was sunk on September 3, and "the first British convoy sailed three days later. But years of neglect had taken their toll on British preparedness: insufficient escorts, unsuitable escort types, cruisers without effective antisubmarine devices, inadequately trained antisubmarine groups, lack of air power on convoy routes, and diversion of escort craft from the 'defensive' convoy patrols to 'offensive' hunting groups characterized British antisubmarine operations."[16] It would, however, be 1943 before the underlying attitudes of the officer corps were to change. By then, "the Battle of the Atlantic took on a certain glamour"; the Atlantic had become a fashionable combat

---

the Interwar Period (Cambridge: Cambridge University Press, 1996), 246,251. See also Clay Blair, *Hitler's U-boat War: The Hunters, 1939–1942* (New York: Modern Library, 2000), 67; S. W. Roskill, *The War at Sea, 1939–1945*, Vol. 1, *The Defensive* (London: Her Majesty's Stationery Office, 1954), 103. Blair provides an estimate of 118 deaths, and Terraine (see footnote 29) a figure of 112. Part of this difference reflects losses in the recovery process.

12 Herwig, "Innovation Ignored," 243–244.   13 Herwig, "Innovation Ignored," 263.

14 Herwig, "Innovation Ignored," 248.

15 Herwig, "Innovation Ignored," 248: quoting Hansard, *Parliamentary Debates (House of Commons)*, 5th Series, ccic, columns 674–677. For a thorough discussion of *The Defeat of the Enemy Attack on Shipping, 1939–1945*, described as "the most powerful justification of the convoy system of warfare ever written," see the volume edited by Eric J. Grove, from the Naval Staff History, *Second World War* (Aldershot: Ashgate, 1998). The basic conclusion was that, in World War II as in World War I and earlier: "convoy was the surest measure of bringing to action and defeating enemy raiders, surface and submarine, sent out to attack our merchant ships," ix.

16 Herwig, "Innovation Ignored," 251.

arena; and, as a result, "commands in the Western Approaches were eagerly sought."[17]

If the British navy had forgotten the lessons of World War I, the most generous conclusion one can reach is that their American counterparts had never learned them. The years from 1918 to 1939 may have been long enough to cloud the best memories, but the Americans had had an additional two years and three months to examine the effectiveness of the new German submarine blockade and to watch "the British flounder in their efforts to master the threat. Nevertheless, American leaders responsible for the defense of merchant shipping along the East Coast of the United States and in the Caribbean resolutely set themselves against learning anything from the British" experience.[18] And among those "leaders" it was the naval bureaucracy that was largely to blame for this state of affairs. In addition to failing to make any tactical preparation for antisubmarine warfare, the U.S. Navy displayed not only a rooted aversion to learning anything from the recent experience of the Royal Navy, but also they seemed equally unwilling to accept the conclusions that had been voiced by American Admiral W. S. Sims in 1917. "The senior American commanders, acknowledging the lack of small craft, instead of striving with might and main to remedy the evil of 1941, used it as an argument against convoy just as alarmists in the Admiralty had done twenty-five years earlier. So the fatal doctrine was propounded that 'a convoy without adequate protection is worse than none'; and such vessels as were available, including destroyers from the Atlantic Fleet, were wasted in the vain hunts and 'tram-line' patrols that had exerted their fatal lure in the Royal Navy for too long."[19]

Jumping somewhat ahead of the story, the result of that attitude was, as Rear Admiral Samuel E. Morison later wrote, a "merry massacre" that cost the Allies over 1.5 million tons of shipping in early 1942.[20] A British intelligence officer summed up the situation neatly in a comment directed to the chief of American Admiral Ernest King's staff: "The trouble is, Admiral, it is not only your bloody ships you are losing. A lot of them are ours."[21]

---

17 Kaplan and Currie, *Convoy*, 80–81.   18 Herwig, "Innovation Ignored," 252.

19 John Terraine, *Business in Great Waters: The U-Boat Wars, 1916–1945* (Ware: Wordsworth Editions, 1989), 413. The phrasing of the "fatal doctrine" has been attributed to Vice-Admiral Adolphus Andrews, Commander of the Eastern Sea Frontier.

20 Samuel Eliot Morison, *The Battle of the Atlantic, September 1939–May 1943* (Boston: Little, Brown, 1947), 128, 142.

21 Quoted in Eliot A. Cohen and John Gooch, *Military Misfortunes, The Anatomy of Failure in War* (New York: Free Press, 1990), 60. The staff member was Rear Admiral Richard S. Edwards.

3. A MODERN CASE STUDY: THE GERMAN WORLD WAR II
BLOCKADE OF THE BRITISH ISLES

3(1). Introduction

Despite earlier rumbles – the German reoccupation of the Saar, Franco's battles in Spain, the Japanese push into China, and Italy's incursion into Abyssinia – World War II officially began on September 3, 1939, when, two days after the German invasion of Poland, both Britain and France, honoring their treaties, declared war against Nazi Germany. It was, however, another twenty-seven months before the United States and Japan were to join the war; and, with their entry, World War II became a truly worldwide conflagration. Between September 1939 and August 1945, there were to be three major naval blockades: (1) the British-French supply blockade that was initially directed against Germany, but was later expanded to include Italy; (2) the German submarine blockade designed to cut off supplies to Great Britain (a blockade that was later expanded to include the east coast of the United States); and (3) the American blockade of the Japanese home islands.

For an economic blockade to be effective, three conditions must be met. First, "the economy of the blockaded power must be vulnerable"; if it has taken the precaution to stockpile scarce resources, then even if the blockade is effective, it may be a long while before the blockade is pro-ductive. Second, "the blockading power must have the means . . . to cut off the supply of goods to its enemy from outside his border." Third, "the blockading power must be able to secure the acquiescence or co-operation, of neutral powers, whether adjacent to the enemy or supplying him from overseas."[22]

Once Germany had overrun France and Eastern Europe, the now solely British blockade, although in place throughout the war, had almost no impact on the final outcome. In 1944 and 1945, the American blockade of the Japanese home islands effectively cut Japan off from the rest of Asia; and, almost certainly proved to be the most effective economic blockade of the three-hundred-year history of naval roadblocks. In fact, if the Allies had been able to accurately assess the actual impact of the blockade, Hiroshima and Nagasaki might well have proved unnecessary since the "lack of available shipping had destroyed the country's wartime economy long before the

---

22 W. N. Medlicott, *The Economic Blockade*, 2 vols. (London: His Majesty's Stationery Office, 1952), vol. 1, 2–3.

air raids began."[23] Any complete history of World War II must include a study of all three blockades. In this chapter, however, we focus only on the second of the three, the German attempt to sever the economic connections between the British Isles and North and South America. Of the three, that blockade consumed the largest fraction of Allied and Axis resources; and it also provides an excellent example of a short-run success coupled with long-run failure. Although "the strategic effectiveness of maritime blockade of the supply of goods, and indeed of economic warfare broadly pursued, must depend on the political, social, economic, military, and geostrategic particulars of a specific case," an analysis of the German submarine blockade and the allied efforts to breach it yields a number of important insights into the factors that effect the success of blockades more generally considered.[24]

3(2). The Strategic Background

The original German strategy set very modest goals: first, "constant disturbance of British operations in building up their blockade"; second, "to afford 'assistance to the conduct of the war in the Atlantic by keeping as many enemy forces as possible tied up'"; and third, to achieve an "occasional brief" opening of the British blockade sufficient to allow for passage of combat forces into the Atlantic. Because the leadership of the *Kreigsmarine* did not expect to be able to find a submarine base with easy access to the Atlantic, they were not prepared to mount an all-out submarine blockade of the British Isles. As late as April 1939, Admiral Karl Doenitz had insisted that Germany required at least three hundred submarines, if submarine warfare was to "achieve decisive success against Britain." The High Command's long-run "Z" plan, however, promised only 162 U-boats capable of operating in the Atlantic by 1948, with fewer by 1940. With the fall of France, however, the German "Army and Air Force, with naval assistance in Norway, changed the geostrategic terms of engagement for the German counterblockade of Britain."[25] The Germans moved quickly to capitalize on the new opportunity, but the effort was to suffer from the earlier decision on the level of submarine production.

In Britain, throughout the 1930s, the threat of submarines to seaborne commerce had been heavily discounted. The reasons for this high rate of

23 Akira Hara, "Japan: Guns Before Rice," in Mark Harrison, *The Economics of World War II* (Cambridge: Cambridge University Press, 1998), 256; See Chapter 7.

24 Colin S. Gray, *The Leverage of Sea Power: The Strategic Advantage of Navies in War* (New York: Free Press, 1992), 38–39.

25 Gray, *Leverage of Sea Power*, 37.

discount are not certain; but they probably included the British experience in the latter days of World War I when they were able to blunt the German submarine menace, the navy's faith in the new ASDIC/sonar technology, a faith that led them into a false sense of security concerning their ability to detect and destroy enemy submarines, and the belief, like that held by the German naval command, that Germany would not be able to acquire bases on the open Atlantic. Thus, the British were possibly even less prepared to counter a submarine blockade than the Germans were to initiate such action.[26]

In the case of the United States, in 1939 the country was not only a neutral, but a neutral forced to operate under the constraints imposed by the U.S. Neutrality Act of 1937. However, between 1939 and December 7, 1941, in part because American vessels were being sunk in transatlantic routes, the American definition of neutrality changed markedly. To a degree these changes were rooted in the newly enacted U.S. Neutrality Act of 1939 (an act that "relaxed" some of the strictures of the earlier legislation), but in even larger measure, changes depended, on the Executive's modification of the legal rules.[27] Those informal modifications included, but were not limited to, the transfer of fifty old destroyers to the British, lend-lease, a shift in anti-submarine warships from the Pacific to the Atlantic, and "the assignment of our own naval vessels to escort our merchant shipping on threatened transatlantic routes."[28] In fact, by the time war was officially declared, a state of open economic warfare between Germany and the United States had existed for months.

The battle for control of the Atlantic sea lanes opened on September 3, 1939, when the submarine U-30, in defiance of treaties that Germany had signed as recently as 1936, "torpedoed without warning the unarmed, unescorted British passenger steamer *Athenia*," "with the loss of 112 (or 118) lives, including women and children." "Before long, 'no holds were barred,' except what humanity and fear of reprisal dictated." Until June 1940, Britain seemed to be in a position to win the Battle of the Atlantic without allied support – although convoys were still not universally employed, they were employed on major intercontinental routes; and although submarines did sink some forty-seven vessels in the North

26 Roskill, *Defensive*, 54–55.
27 For the texts of the two Neutrality Acts, see Henry Steele Commager, ed., *Documents of American History* 6th ed. (New York: Appleton-Century-Croft, 1958), 558–562, 600–604.
28 Samuel Eliot Morrison, *The Two-Ocean War* (Boston: Little, Brown, 1963), 28. Morison, *Battle of the Atlantic*, 27; Ernest J. King, *U.S. Navy at War, 1941–1945, Official Reports to the Secretary of the Navy* (Washington, DC: United States Navy Department, 1946), 79.

Atlantic in 1939, Halifax-U.K. convoys suffered no losses from submarines in 1939.[29]

The first ship in a Halifax-U.K. convoy to be torpedoed, a straggler, was sunk in February 1940; but the fall of France put an entirely new face on the situation. By then the German U-boat fleet had been enlarged; and, more important, Admiral Doenitz was now able to base his vessels in Normandy and Brittany. Within hours of the signing of the Franco–German armistice, Doenitz flew to the western coast of France to search out potential bases for German U-boats. He chose five: Brest, Lorient, St. Nazaire, La Pallice, and Bordeaux. "Meanwhile, his staff loaded a special train with torpedoes, spare parts, and other gear and sent it to Paris. From there the train was routed to Lorient, where an advanced party of staff and technicians established the first U-boat base."[30] Taken together, these changes nearly doubled the number of submarines that could be continuously maintained in the western Atlantic.[31] On August 17, 1940, Hitler declared a "counter blockade" of the British Isles, and he warned that neutral shipping would be sunk on sight. Submarines from Brest, Lorient, St. Nazaire, La Pallice, and Bordeaux could cruise as far as 20° West longitude, well beyond the range of British air and some surface escorts. The Germans shifted their entire submarine fleet to the Atlantic, and the blockade became increasingly effective.

3(3). The Production Function (1): Technology, Capital, and Labor

The primary mission of the German submarine fleet was to cut the sea routes to the British Isles; the goal of the British, Canadians, and Americans was to keep those lanes open. Over the course of the war, the Germans improved their tactics, innovated and improved their command structure, produced larger, faster, and better armed U-boats; and, by the spring of 1944, had submarines equipped with schnorkels that made them much more difficult to locate. Similarly, over the same years, Allied antisubmarine strategy and tactics evolved – an evolution that, like the German, encompassed both technical and organizational innovations. In the words of the naval historian Samuel Eliot Morison, "The United States and Allied Navies and merchant

---

29 Samuel Eliot Morison, *The Atlantic Battle Won, May 1943-May 1945* (Boston: Little, Brown, 1960), 3; Morison, *Battle of the Atlantic*, 9, 22. Terraine, *Business*, 767. The number of ships sunk between the start of the war and the end of June 1940 was 141. See also footnote 11.
30 Clay Blair, *Hitler's U-boat War: The Hunters, 1939–1942* (New York: Modern Library, 2000), 172. Morison, *Battle of the Atlantic*, 22–26.
31 Morison, *Battle of the Atlantic*, 22. Blair, *Hunters*, 179.

services thwarted the submarine by efforts all along the line, and in four dimensions: Doctrine; Research; Training; Production."[32]

3(3a). The German Experience. In the case of tactics, for example, U-boats initially operated individually, submerged before approaching a convoy, and, by preference, chose to attack in morning or evening twilight when ships were silhouetted against the sky. By late 1940, however, those submarines were organized into wolf-packs – eight to twenty submarines controlled by daily radio messages from a command post in Lorient and charged with shadowing convoys by day and attacking at night.[33] Moreover, the wolf-packs were soon supplied by "milch cows" (U-tankers of Types IX and X) that replaced the supply ships; and replenished the raider's fuel, provisions, and torpedoes.[34] As a result, the attack submarines were able to remain at sea for much longer periods. By the end of 1943, the "cows refueled and replenished nearly 400 U-boats in the waters south and north of the Azores."[35] As an indication of their initial success, on the night of 3–4 April 1941, a wolf-pack attacking first in the "black pit" – latitude 58° 20'N and longitude 28° 10'W – sank ten out of twenty-two ships in a transatlantic convoy.[36]

However, not all the changes in tactics introduced by Doenitz proved to be productive. First, Doenitz's desire to retain tactical control of his submarines was so intense that, even after he became aware that the submarines' radio messages were being monitored by Allied "Huff-Duff" and that the information was being used to locate his U-boats, he continued his daily radio exchanges with each U-boat engaged in operations.[37] It was only when the too-little and too-late success of the schnorkel-equipped submarines – as the new U-boats didn't surface, they could not use their radios – had shackled the Allied HF/DF, was it clear how much Doenitz's desire to retain tight control had cost the German effort. In 1943 he lost faith in the German antiradar countermeasures, and made what may have been his second greatest single mistake. Until then, German submarines had been ordered to surface at night to recharge their batteries. Radar had made it possible to locate the surfaced U-boats, and a number had been sunk by

---

32 Morison, *Atlantic Battle Won*, 244–247.
33 Morison, *Two-Ocean War*, 35; Morison, *Battle of the Atlantic*, 25.
34 Kaplan and Currie, *Convoy*, 101.
35 Morison, *Atlantic Battle Won*, 128; S. W. Roskill, *The War at Sea, 1939–1945 Vol. 2, The Period of Balance* (London: Her Majesty's Stationery Office, 1956), 207–208.
36 Morison, *Two-Ocean War*, 35, 382–383; Morison, *Battle of the Atlantic*, 56.
37 Morison, *Atlantic Battle Won*, 58

allied aircraft. Because the submarines had achieved some success with their new antiaircraft guns, Doenitz reversed his previous policy and ordered the submarines to dive by night and to surface to charge their batteries during the day. Moreover, once surfaced, he ordered his crews 'to stay on the surface and fight it out with the aircraft.'[38] The new policy did manage to destroy a number of planes; but, in the end, this tactic "played into the hands of the Allied air forces by furnishing them with more surface targets." The ultimate cost to the Germans was a substantial number of submarines.[39] A third example of command error can be found in Doenitz's "integral tonnage" concept. Until the end of the war, Doenitz believed that "the main task of U-boats was to sink enemy tonnage without regard to route, place, or cargo, in the hope of keeping ahead of replacement by new construction." Thus, "a Liberty ship returning empty from Africa was as good a target as a heavy-laden Liberty ship proceeding to Great Britain." As a result, when Allied forces began to sink submarines on the North Atlantic routes, he redirected his forces to the South Atlantic and Indian Oceans – regions that were peripheral to the invasion of Europe – instead of sustaining the attacks on the "transatlantic troop and merchant convoys."[40]

Some German command mistakes, however, cannot be blamed on the Grand Admiral. In particular, he shares no responsibility for the failure to coordinate submarine and airborne resources or the failure, until far too late, to mobilize German scientific resources. In the probably inflated view of one historian, "one boon Doenitz lacked which his enemies enjoyed was a close cooperation with air forces and scientists. It was the unbeatable combination of surface and air power and scientific research that enabled the British and American antisubmarine forces to win."[41]

In the case of submarine–air force cooperation, the Allies had some major problems, but they appear miniscule when compared with those of the Germans. Doenitz and Goering disliked each other, and there was very little cooperation between the Luftwaffe and the U-boats. "In 1941 Doenitz had managed to get one air squadron placed under his operational control," but, "although Hitler ordered that it continue to support the submarines," Goering soon managed to regain operational control. Moreover, the squadron, based on French airfields, never had more than thirty bombers; a number that was totally insufficient to provide both necessary convoy

---

38 Roskill, *Period of Balance*, 371; Morison, *Atlantic Battle Won*, 58–59.
39 Morison, *Atlantic Battle Won*, 245.
40 Morison, *Two-Ocean War*, 563; Morison, *Atlantic Battle Won*, 58.
41 Morison, *Two-Ocean War*, 564.

reconnaissance and to cover U-boats entering and leaving port. Although two airforce squadrons, "based in northern Norway and Finland were supposed to cooperate with the U-boats" in their attacks on Russian convoys, the continued complaints of the submarine skippers suggests that they were far less effective than their Allied counterparts.[42]

In innovations ranging from centimeter radar, to cryptography, to penicillin, the Allies had made highly productive use of their scientific resources. It was only at the very end of the war that the Germans made any serious attempt to mobilize the scientific community to produce military technology. Although in 1942 the Germans were initially able to break the British codes, from May 1943 until the war's end, they were unable to repeat that accomplishment.[43] Again, because of failure to assign a first-rate scientist to analyze Allied radar until the end of 1943, it was 1944 before the Germans realized that Allied radar was operating on the "ten" (actually 9.8) centimeter band; "and by the time they had drawn the correct conclusions regarding Allied radar developments it was too late to reverse the trend of the Atlantic battle."[44] "Owing to Hitler's disregard of operational scientists, the Germans never produced a jamming device suitable for U-boats until very late in the war." Doenitz finally "managed to invoke Hitler's authority to stop the drafting of submarine builders into the Army," but the battle over the proper role of scientists continued almost until the end of the war.[45] As early as the end of 1943, in Doenitz's assessment, "the Allies by their skill in 'radio location' had wrested the advantage of surprise from the U-boats. Science, not superior strategy or tactics, he insisted, had done this; and, he added bitterly, he might have worsted the enemy in that realm if German scientists had not stupidly been absorbed into the armed forces instead of being kept at work in their laboratories. These men were now being released from military service in order 'to catch up in the field of high-frequency research to equal the achievements of the enemy.'" It was, however, 1945 before they did manage to make up at least some of the slack.[46]

---

42 Morison, *Atlantic Battle Won*, 75.   43 Roskill, *Period of Balance*, 208.

44 S. W. Roskill, *The War at Sea, 1939–1945, Vol. 3, The Offensive, Part I, 1st June 1943–31st May 1944* (London: Her Majesty's Stationery Office, 1960), 33.

45 Morison, *Battle of the Atlantic*, 316.

46 Morison, *Atlantic Battle Won*, 246. For a collection of documents on Allied intelligence based on the interception of German radio communications, in which the editor's conclusion is that "Communications intelligence did not win the Battle of the Atlantic by itself, but it greatly increased the effectiveness of Allied naval and air forces, shortening the conflict by months, if not years." See David Syrett, ed., the *Battle of the Atlantic and Signals Intelligence: U-Boat Situations and Trends, 1941–1945* (Aldershot: Ashgate, 1998), xxxiv. Syrett's bibliographic note (p. xi) is useful not only in describing the historiography related to breaking the German U-Boat codes, but also in distinguished books on submarine warfare written prior in the detailed knowledge of Allied code-breaking and those written subsequently.

Doenitz's focus on the crucial role played by Allied radar was partially correct; however, both then and later, he refused to believe that the Allies might have broken the German *Enigma* code. In his own words, "We repeatedly checked our security instructions to ensure as far as possible that our intentions were not being betrayed. That a widespread spy network was at work in our bases in occupied France was something we obviously had to assume. . . . Our ciphers were checked and rechecked, to make sure they were unbreakable; and on each occasion the head of the Naval Intelligence Service at Naval High Command adhered to his opinion that it would be impossible for the enemy to decipher them. And to this day [1958], as far as I know, we are not certain whether or not the enemy did succeed in breaking our ciphers during the war."[47] In fact, although the British were not able to continuously read the German *Enigma* code, they had initially broken it as early as March 1941.

Doenitz did, however, recognize the contributions of the "German 'B-Service', our Cryptographic Section, which time and again succeeded in breaking enemy ciphers. As a result U–boat Command received not only the British signals and routing instructions sent to convoys, but also, in January and February 1943, the British 'U–boat Situation Report', which was transmitted to commanders of convoys at sea and which gave the known and presumed distributions of U–boats in the different areas. These 'Situation Reports' were of greatest value to us in our efforts to determine how the enemy was able to find out about our U–boat dispositions and with what degree of accuracy he did so." In fact, the Germans were able to read, more or less accurately, the British codes during thirty of the thirty-four months between September 1939 and June 1943. In the latter month, however, a secure ciphering system was introduced by both the Royal Navy and the Royal Canadian Navy; and, later, the adoption of the Combined Cipher Machine for all allied Atlantic communication – a system that was never penetrated by the *xB-Dienst* – meant that the Germans were never again able to again break the Allied codes.[48]

In terms of the command structure of the blockading submarine force, at the outbreak of war the German navy had been under the command of Grand Admiral Erich Raeder, whereas the U–boats were under the command of Admiral Karl Doenitz, who reported to Raeder. In January 1943, Hitler promoted Doenitz to the rank of Grand Admiral and made him Commander in Chief, Navy. Only then was new naval construction

---

47 Karl Doenitz, *Memoirs: Ten Years and Twenty Days* (Annapolis: Naval Institute Press, 1990; first published 1958), 324–325.
48 Doenitz, *Memoirs*, 325.

limited to submarines. Doenitz was finally able to convince Hitler "to stop the drafting of submarine builders into the Army," but he was never able to convince Goering to give him the air reconnaissance support that he felt was required.[49]

In terms of size, speed, and armament, the new submarines were faster as well as larger than the earlier models; and by 1943 they were equipped with antiaircraft guns, acoustic torpedoes, and "Aphrodite" radar decoy.[50] Moreover, the new submarines could operate at depths up to 600 feet, nearly twice the 309-foot limits of the earlier models.[51]

Finally, facing the heavy U-boat losses in April and May 1943, the Germans, in an attempt "to improve the survival prospects of their submarines," took a second look at two Dutch submarines that had been captured in 1940 – submarines that were fitted with a 'schnorkel' air intake and diesel exhaust mast.[52] Initially, the Germans had attached no great importance to the 'new' innovation. "Successful trials took place in July 1943, and, by the middle of the following year thirty operational boats had been fitted. The "schnorkel" enabled the U-boats to charge their electric batteries while remaining at periscope depth, it reduced the likelihood of being sighted or detected by radar while charging batteries, and it permitted operations to be restarted in waters which had recently been made prohibitively dangerous by our air patrols" – planes that were fitted with ten-centimeter radar.[53]

Although "hailed by some historians and engineers as another great technical achievement, the snort was not that by a long shot. Rather it was a miserable, temporary device that German U-boat crews hated absolutely." "Mounted on the port side just forward of the bridge, the exhaust or wake of the snorts clouded the raised periscopes, reducing submerged visibility." When the schnorkel was used, the suction inside the boat was so great that, if pressure dropped too far, the diesel engines had to be shut down and the boat shifted to battery power. Moreover, despite all efforts to overcome the problem, diesel fumes seeped into the boat, causing headaches, blurred

49 Morison, *Battle of the Atlantic*, 316; Roskill, *The Offensive, Part I*, 15.
50 The XXI, for example, was a streamlined 1500-ton U-boat that could travel at up to 17.5 knots submerged and had a surface range of 19,000 miles at six knots. See Morison, *Atlantic Battle Won*, 60–61, 138; Roskill, *Defensive*, Appendix G, 591 and *Period of Balance*, Appendix K, 475.
51 Roskill, *Period of Balance*, 207.
52 The "schnorkel" had been invented by a Dutch naval officer in 1927; and it had been installed on four submarines that escaped to England in 1940. The British, however, saw no use for the equipment, and it was removed before the four began to operate under British control. Roskill, *Offensive, Part I*, fn. 1, 18.
53 Roskill, *Offensive, Part I*, 18.

vision, and more serious problems. The crews "resisted its installation on their boats and used it not continuously as often depicted, but only very sparingly (ordinarily about four hours a day) to charge batteries, owing to the high fuel oil consumption experienced when running submerged on diesels." Because of crew complaints and technical faults, the Germans actually innovated "schnorkel" boats much more slowly than many have thought.[54] Despite their drawbacks, the boats proved quite successful; but, happily, from the point of view of the Allies, it was a case of too little and too late.

Over the course of the war, the Germans U-boat flotilla was the beneficiary of a series of technological advances in both offensive and defensive weaponry. Those advances included a new radar detector called *Wanze*, the T-5 Zaunkönig (Wren) antiescort acoustic or homing torpedo, the G7a FAT I (looping) and the G7e FAT II (looping and circling) torpedoes, an improved version of the Pi2 pistol for the G7e (electric) torpedoes, a pistol that could be set for either impact or magnetic demolition, improved search radar, a convoy contact buoy to mark the path of a convoy, and radar deceivers known as *Aphrodite* and *Thetis*. In addition, the boats began to carry more and better antiaircraft guns. The *Wanze*, however, could still not detect the Allies' radar.[55]

3(3b). The Allied Experience. Over the years between 1939 and 1945, Allied (first British and Canadian and then British, American, and Canadian) anti-submarine strategy and tactics evolved.[56] In terms of technology, there is no obvious one weapon that led to victory in the Atlantic, although escort carriers, plane-mounted microwave radar, and the old "Huff-Duff" – "the high-frequency direction-finder, a pointer for the Fleet" – are all possible candidates.[57] There also were a number of other technical innovations that played a significant role in breaking the blockade.

The organizational innovation of the Atlantic convoy was clearly crucially important to victory over the German blockade; but the convoys would not have been as effective, if it had not been for the integration of air and sea forces. Thus, airplane design and production played a role, as did the ability of the Allies to operate from airbases in the United States, Canada, Greenland, Great Britain, and, ultimately, Iceland. However, even with better aircraft and additional bases there still remained a "black pit" in the middle of the ocean that could not be covered by even the newly designed PB4Y

54 Blair, *Hunted*, 314–315.
55 Blair, *Hunted*, 315–316.
56 Morison, *Atlantic Battle Won*, 247–248.
57 Morison, *Atlantic Battle Won*, 363–364.

(or B-24) Liberators, no matter where they were based.[58] The escort carriers changed that situation; they "broadened the protection of a convoy," so that even in the middle of the ocean, it was as well covered as if it were "passing through coastal waters within reach of land-based planes."[59] "The first escort carrier, the *Audacity*, closed the air gap on the Gibraltar route in September 1941," but it was the Americans who produced most of, and operated many of, the escort carriers. The first American escort carrier, the U.S.S. *Bogue*, went into action in March 1943; and a steady stream followed thereafter.[60]

One of the most famous of the hunter-killer groups was "Johnny Walker's Support Group 2, five sloops plus the jeep carriers *Nairana* and *Activity*." In February 1944, operating in the middle Atlantic west of the British Isles over a two-week period, the group, using depth charges and Hedgehogs, "sank five more U-boats making a total of six kills in a single twenty-eight day cruise."[61]

Radar permitted aircraft, as well as surface ships, to locate submarines that were surfaced to replenish their batteries long before the crew of the submarine was aware that it had been detected. Although Germany, Britain, and the United States were all experimenting with radar, Britain was first to deploy an operational model. Airborne radar sets had been installed on both British and American aircraft in 1942. Thus, it is not surprising that, within a year of the Allied airborne radar deployment, the Germans had developed a search receiver for radar operating on meter-wave length; and, by October 1942, they had begun installing it in their submarines. The design was somewhat crude; but the receivers sufficed to give U-boats warning of the approach of Allied aircraft; and the initial Allied advantage was temporarily lost.[62] That advantage was, however, regained with the development in Britain of the cavity magnetron and its innovation as the source of power for a ten-centimeter microwave aircraft radar.[63] Despite delays

---

58 The problem became less acute after late 1943 when Portugal gave the Allies permission to base planes in the Azores. Morison, *Atlantic Battle Won*, 42–46.
59 Morison, *Battle of the Atlantic*, 401.
60 Morison, *Atlantic Battle Won*, 38–39, 76–80, 244; Roskill, *Period of Balance*, 366–367.
61 The five were U-762, U-238, U-734, U-424, and U-264. In addition, the group also sank U-592 on January 31. With the exception of fifty-one submariners rescued from the U-264, there were no other survivors. Blair, *Hunted*, 498.
62 Morison, *Battle of the Atlantic*, 226.
63 The cavity magnetron was invented by John Randall and graduate student Henry Boot. It was first tested in February 1940. It made radar miniaturization possible; and, it has been argued, "lifted radar from an electronic stone age to the present day." An early prototype "picked up the *periscope* of a submerged submarine at a range of more than seven miles." Blair, *Hunters*, 128–129. The quotation is from Brian Johnson, *The Secret War* (New York: Methuen, 1978).

created by bureaucratic arguments between the British Coastal and Bomber commands, American imports were soon mounted on Allied planes. The new 'S-band' radar "did the trick and, as the German search receiver failed to detect them, the enemy was completely in the dark as to what was guiding our planes to the U-boats." German efforts to develop "radar warning devices were hamstrung by the German assumption that centimetric radar was not technically possible. When they did finally realize that it was possible, it was the belief of the tactical commanders of the submarine fleet "that the British were not employing it operationally."[64]

So successful was the new equipment that, in January 1944, Hitler stated that, "The obvious decline in U-boat successes has been due to only one invention of the enemy." Even after the Germans realized that the Allies had a centimeter-band radar, they never managed to develop a way to detect or to jam it.[65] Despite the innovation of the even more effective three-centimeter radar toward the end of the war, the German innovation of 'schnorkel' submarines reduced the effectiveness of Allied radar. The "Germans had now fitted search receiver aerials on the schnorkel funnels and, although they were only designed to cover the metric radar band, they would respond to a centimetric set, if the transmitting source was strong and fairly close. This was enough to alert the U-boat crews."[66]

The third major innovation was the high frequency direction-finders developed by the British. The principle was relatively simple, an extension of the single loop-finder that vessels use to get bearings on radio beams from known stations on the shore. Instead of a single loop, the British located direction-finders all along the coast; and, thus, were able to obtain cross-bearings on submarines making their daily reports to Admiral Doenitz. The bearings were reported to the Admiralty, where specially trained teams integrated the findings and "were able to plot the course of a submarine across the Atlantic."[67] The weapon played a major role in the initial victory over the submarines; but it became largely ineffective, once Doenitz accepted that he could not conduct daily conversations with the "schnorkels".

---

64 Morison, *Battle of the Atlantic*, 226. Alan Beyerchen, "From Radio to Radar: Interwar Military adaptation to Technological Change in Germany, the United Kingdom, and the United States," in Murray and Millet, eds., *Military Innovation*, 295.
65 Morison, *Atlantic Battle Won*, 247; Roskill, *Period of Balance*, 205; Morison, *Battle of the Atlantic*, 225–226.
66 S. W. Roskill, *The War at Sea, 1939–1945, Vol. 3, The Offensive, part II, 1st June 1944–14th August 1945* (London: Her Majesty's Stationery Office, 1961), 288.
67 Morison, *Battle of the Atlantic*, 226–227.

There also were a number of other innovations that, although individually less important, together played an important role in the ultimate weakening of the blockade. New weapons included more effective depth charges and new methods of deploying them, the Leigh Light, the "Foxer," "Sono" buoys, and the new class of destroyer escorts. In terms of aircraft weapons, a "more powerful depth charge fitted with the new shallow-firing pistol, which entered service in mid-1942"; and the 600-pound antisubmarine bomb was available as an alternative to the depth charge. On shipboard and aircraft, the 300-pound depth charge remained the primary weapon; "but most ships were fitted also with the ahead-throwing weapons known as 'Hedgehog' or 'Squid,'" weapons that could throw the depth charge ahead of a submarine – a valuable addition to the arsenal, since ships frequently lost sonar contact as they made their final approach to a submarine.[68] In response to the German innovation of the acoustic torpedo the Allies deployed the "Foxer" – a noise-making machine towed astern of a ship that attracted the acoustic torpedo to itself. Although the first models had problems, by February 1944 a much-improved version had been introduced; and the Admiralty was able to announce "that an 'escort vessel, with Foxer operating should be immune from acoustic torpedoes.'"[69] Aircraft also were increasingly equipped with electronic buoys that, when dropped from an airplane, "kept an automatic hydrophone watch, transmitting the propeller noises from a submerged U-boat to a patrolling aircraft by wireless."[70] Finally, the Leigh searchlight made it possible for attacking aircraft to illuminate surfaced submarines; and, when used with radar, it proved particularly effective.[71]

The history of the Leigh light, however, suggests something of the problems that faced both sets of belligerents. Aircrews attacking submarines needed some way of "seeing" the submarine during the last mile of their aircraft's approach. In late 1940, Humphry de Verde Leigh, an officer in the Coastal Command, suggested a possible solution – "a very powerful, steerable searchlight, mounted on a retractable bed in the underside of the fuselage." His commander strongly endorsed the proposal and set Leigh to work designing and building a prototype. There were some technical difficulties; but also because of "bureaucratic inertia, and indifference, it

68 Roskill, *Offensive, Part II*, 288–289; Roskill, *Period of Balance*, 205. Morison, *Atlantic Battle Won*, 159.
69 Roskill, *Offensive, Part I*, 40–41; Morison, *Atlantic Battle Won*, 159.
70 Roskill, *Offensive, Part II*, 288–289.
71 Morison, *Atlantic Battle Won*, 83; Roskill, *Period of Balance*, 205.

was to take Leigh a full eighteen months to work out the bugs, to gain full approval from the Air Ministry, and to get the searchlight into combat, yet another serious British lapse."[72]

In a somewhat different dimension, although delayed by other demands on the nation's shipyards, by December 1942, the U.S. Navy had commissioned some 260 new destroyer escorts (DEs) – smaller and cheaper than their big brothers, they were nearly as effective in antisubmarine work.[73]

As with technology, there also were important innovations in organization. If productivity were the sole criteria, the innovations in the organization of convoys were almost certainly the most important; however, because of the interdependence of the innovations, it seems appropriate to discuss them in the following order: the scientists, fleet organization, convoys, and the U-boat killer groups, the integration of air and sea units, and, finally, training.

From the point of view of Admiral Doenitz, it was the ability of the Allies to organize the efforts of the scientific community that wrested control of the Atlantic and that broke the German blockade.[74] Whether his assessment is correct or not is still unclear; but, it is certainly true that British and American scientists had provided many technical developments of inestimable value and placed them in the hands of the naval forces.[75] The crucial importance of centimeter band radar has already been noted; but the scientists' contributions were not limited to technological innovations. For example, they "worked out an entire complex of search patterns" for regaining underwater contacts with submarines; they determined the most "effective search speed, altitude and airborne time for patrol planes"; "they proved that three destroyers searching abreast were more than three times as effective as a single destroyer"; they "proved that an air 'umbrella' over a convoy was far less potent a protection than a wide-ranging search on front and flanks." They also "carried out an extensive and important survey of

---

72 Blair, *Hunters*, 216.   73 Morison, *Two-Ocean War*, 245.
74 Morison, *Atlantic Battle Won*, 246; Morison, *Battle of the Atlantic*, 202–265.
75 Roskill, *Period of Balance*, 208. "A member of the Anti-Submarine Warfare Division of the British Naval Staff produced the following piece of doggeral at this time:

> "Gaily the backroom boys,
> Peddling their gruesome toys,
> Come in and make a noise,
> Oozing with science!
> Humbly their aid we've sought;
> Without them we're as nought;,
> For modern wars are fought,
> By such alliance."

convoy routing and control"; and they organized "counter-measures which stymied the German acoustic torpedo as soon as it appeared."[76]

At the organizational level, "the Atlantic antisubmarine campaign has been a closely integrated international operation." There was constant interchange of information between the Admiralty and the U.S. Navy. Initially, there was a considerable mixture of forces – both British and Canadian vessels operated as part of the U.S. coastal escorts, and some U.S. destroyers were seconded to British groups in the Atlantic and even occasionally in north Russian waters. As Allied strength increased, however, more clearly defined areas of national responsibility were designated.[77] Moreover, administrative control of antisubmarine operations continued to improve over the course of the war. On the American side, Admiral King became convinced that a fleet organization for antisubmarine warfare was a military necessity; and on May 1, 1943, the U.S. Tenth Fleet was organized to combine "all existing antisubmarine activities."[78] Thereafter, the Tenth Fleet, the Operational Training Command Atlantic Fleet, and the Antisubmarine Development Detachment Atlantic Fleet together "made for efficiency in administration and uniformity in training; as soon as a new device was approved, it could be adopted with confidence that escorts and antisubmarine aircraft would be properly instructed in its use."[79] The table of organization of the Tenth Fleet was expanded to include the handling of all naval *Enigma* intelligence – intelligence that had to be closely guarded to prevent leaks.

The Tenth Fleet's Washington-based senior personnel could deal directly with London by secure teletype; and they could then digest the flow of information from the *Enigma* decrypts, recommend convoy diversions, and direct "other highly secret ASW operations without the need to divulge the reasons for them to subordinate commanders." Again, however, this organizational innovation was not completely free of problems. Although the Tenth Fleet was ostensibly organized to combine all antisubmarine activities, in fact it was initially organized to combine *almost* all antisubmarine activities. The Army Air Force ASW command – twenty-seven squadrons on line with more to be added soon – was initially not placed under the control of the Tenth Fleet. It would be several months before the "awkward – and hugely wasteful – internal struggle between the Army and Navy over control of land-based ASW aircraft" – would be resolved, and those aircraft

76 Morison, *Battle of the Atlantic*, 224.   77 King, *U.S. Navy at War, 1941–1945*, 81.
78 Morison, *Atlantic Battle Won*, 21; Morison, *Two-Ocean War*, 245.
79 Morison, *Atlantic Battle Won*, 245.

brought under naval control.[80] The Americans were, however, certainly not alone in their need to solve problems raised by interservice rivalry. Both the British and the Germans faced similar, and, in both cases, less easily resolved, interservice struggles for control.

In Britain, "the notorious neglect of Coastal Command had led to a proposal that it be transferred from the Air Ministry to the Admiralty." Churchill initially opposed the transfer, but he ordered an investigation. That investigation "brought to light in shocking detail the shortcomings of the command." As a result, although the Coastal Command was left in the Air Ministry for administrative purposes, on April 15, 1941, operational control of the organization was transferred to the Admiralty. "Thereafter naval requirements – U-boat hunting in particular – were to take precedence over all other missions."[81]

The experience of World War I strongly indicated that convoy and escort were by far the most effective means of countering a U-boat blockade. It was not that the British had ignored that lesson from World War I. It was, perhaps, that they had also drawn conclusions about the value of submarines from that same wartime experience. Because Germany had no submarine force until 1935, the Admiralty had not vigorously pursued antisubmarine warfare.[82] It was not until the end of 1938, when the Germans announced that they would expand their submarine fleet until they had reached parity with the British that the Admiralty began to plan seriously for the possibility of a U-boat war. Even then, however, their plans were strongly influenced by the widely held belief that sonar, developed near the end of World War I and greatly improved in the 1920s and 1930s had rendered submarines virtually obsolete. By the outset of the War, that belief had seriously distorted the shape of the British navy; and, as a result, there was an acute shortage of escort vessels.

Although there was no debate about the necessity of convoying – the Admiralty's plans required that, with the outbreak of war, all British merchant vessels were to be placed under the operational control of the government, and all Commonwealth vessels, except those slower than nine or faster than fifteen knots, were to travel in convoy.[83] In addition, "the government had created on paper a convoy control organization and had indoctrinated thousands of merchant marine officers in convoy tactics and procedures,

---

80 Blair, *Hunted*, 309.   81 Blair, *Hunters*, 247.
82 Blair, *Hunters*, 71.
83 On convoys, see Chapters 1 and 5; see Gove, ed., *Defeat of the Enemy Attack*, 29–37; Blair, *Hunters*, 71–72.

such as station keeping, zigzagging, communications." Every new escort vessel had to spend a month in training. In addition, they had put together "a list of retired Royal Navy officers who were to be recalled to serve for the convoy control organization and at sea."[84] The question, however, still remained, convoyed by whom?

By October 1939, the Allies had organized most merchant shipping into convoys. Worldwide, however, the British navy had only 175 fleet destroyers; and more than 40 percent of them were of World War I vintage. Moreover, most of the modern destroyers were required for fleet support duties – screens, scouting, port protection, and other tasks. In addition, in 1939 and 1940, much of the remaining escort strength was dissipated on hunting and patrolling. All told, there were only about seventy-five old destroyers, most not equipped with sonar, and some thirty smaller sloops available for escort duty. That fleet was augmented "for inshore, or coastal, escort in the British Isles," by a few coal-burning trawlers – trawlers fitted with guns and depth charges, but trawlers were too slow to catch a submarine. Thus, the early convoys were very lightly protected; and, in the North Atlantic, with the exception of the important Halifax Fast convoys, they were only escorted for a few hundred miles at the beginning and end of their journeys to-and-from Britain. Those convoys proved vulnerable to submarine attack; but the evidence shows that merchant vessels traveling in convoy, even vessels in a lightly or partly escorted convoy, were sunk significantly less often than vessels traveling by themselves – that is unescorted.

By the end of 1940, however, the British and Canadians had added 121 corvettes to their fleet of escorts.[85] With the growth of the escort fleet, it became possible to begin to expand training from a ship and its crew to an entire "Escort Group." These "groups were composed of a number of vessels," more or less permanently teamed up, and assigned as a single entity to convoys. "The performance of the groups, manned almost solely by wartime conscripts or volunteers, was ragged at first and never perfect, but gradually became quite proficient."[86] Nor were the British alone. The Americans were slow "to institute convoys off their eastern seaboard in the early days of 1942, when comparatively few U-boats inflicted such heavy losses on independently-routed shipping."[87] Gradually, however, the British were able to deploy fully protected convoys and the Americans came to understand the value of such convoys.

84 Blair, *Hunters*, 72.
85 Blair, *Hunters*, 71–72, 109–110, 215. "At the outbreak of the war, a total of only 185 British ships had sonar: 100 modern destroyers, forty-five sloops and old destroyers, and forty trawlers."
86 Blair, *Hunters*, 247.   87 Roskill, *Offensive, Part I*, 265.

In the British, and perhaps also the American, case, the delay not only reflected the professional naval officers view of convoy duty but also the fact that "the Royal Navy did not fully appreciate the deadly threat of the wolfpacks." Moreover, there was a general belief among those same planners that, in general, U-boats operated under water and launched their attacks while submerged. As a result, the navy placed too much faith "in the combination of their Asdic underwater sensor (later known as sonar) and depth-charges as the main defense against" submarine attacks. In fact, early in the war, the German submarines most frequently launched their assault on the surface after dark. Although the submarines could be "attacked by gunfire, neither Asdic nor depth-charges were of any use."[88] "It was not until strong air support became available, and the American Hudsons, Liberators, and Catalinas joined the British Sunderlands and Ansons on ocean patrol, that the hunting U-boats were obliged to 'go down into the cellar' more and more often, and to stay below the surface longer." Only then did the escort vessels' Asdic and depth charges begin to prove themselves. By 1945, depth charges thrown from escorts had sunk 158 U-boats and, together with those dropped from aircraft, had accounted for about 43 percent of all U-boat sinkings.[89] By then, the productivity of "the new convoys" was well known to all the belligerents.

Even before the entry of the Americans into the war, in January 1941, British-American staff conversations had focused on the need for shared responsibility for Atlantic convoys; and, in February 1942, they began to define their joint strategic responsibilities. On July 1, a "Change of Operational Control" line designating areas of British and American responsibility for escort was established in the Atlantic. Initially, it generally followed the 26° West meridian; and, although the line was altered from time to time, the principle of passing control back and forth at some point in the Atlantic remained unchanged until the end of the war.[90]

By August 1942, another important organizational change had been innovated, "the ingenious and efficient Interlocking System, by which ships were run" on schedules that were almost as tightly controlled as airline schedules are today. Although the "System involved thousands of ships and scores of routes," it was, in fact, relatively simple. First, "Northbound coastal convoys were timed to arrive in New York just before a transatlantic convoy sailed for Great Britain. Second, the two main [North-South] convoys, to which all others were tied in were the Key West–New York and return and

88 Kaplan and Currie, *Convoy*, 36. 89 Kaplan and Currie, *Convoy*, 37, 41.
90 Roskill, *Period of Balance*, 111.

the Guantanamo–New York and return." Local convoys fed into the two southern termini on schedules designed to minimize lost shipping days.[91] By 1943, the Year of the Convoy, the Interlocking System had been extended south to Rio; and, with "better escorts, improved convoy discipline and increased air coverage," it had become very effective.[92] In order to free U.S. destroyers for troop convoys, the British and Canadian navies took over the major responsibility for convoy escort in the northern Atlantic, with the United States assuming responsibility for the tanker convoys running between Britain and the Dutch West Indies. Thereafter, "'Fast' 9-knot HX convoys sailed from Halifax for Londonderry every seven days, followed three or four days later by a $6\frac{1}{2}$ knot SC convoy, which sailed from Sydney, except from December through April, when that harbor was apt to be frozen." "Both convoys were fed at the American end by Boston-Halifax convoys designated BX and XB, which received ships from various coastal routes and formed up at Cape Cod Bay or Boston Harbor."[93] By 1944, authorities had come to realize that fewer escorts would be needed if convoys were reclassified into three, rather than two classes; and, after April, "the convoys in both directions were divided into Fast, Medium and Slow categories." Many of the east-west convoys consisted of more than one hundred vessels, whereas outward-bound convoys frequently had as many as eighty ships. The risk of port congestion "was reduced by detaching groups of the faster ships towards the end of the journeys." "The convoy system, the linchpin of Allied maritime strategy, was now virtually world-wide, and in April 1944 Britain and America between them were operating no less than 236 separate series of trade and military convoys."[94]

The answer to the question of the optimal size of a convoy also was finally accepted. Despite the navy's experience during World War I and Rollo Appleyard's by then quarter century old mathematical analysis, until 1943 the Admiralty clung to "the shibboleth that 'the larger the convoy the greater the risk.'" In fact, the reverse was true. Appleyard's 1918 study for the Royal Navy on "the law of convoy size" had proved that "whereas escorts protect the convoy's perimeter and not the individual ships within, and whereas large convoy's perimeter is only slightly larger than that of a small convoy, 'the area occupied by the ships increases as the square, while the perimeter is directly proportional to the length of the radius.' In short,

91 Morison, *Battle of the Atlantic*, 260.   92 Morison, *Atlantic Battle Won*, 245–246.

93 Morison, *Battle of the Atlantic*, 318. "The reverse of the HX and SC were still designated ON and ONS respectively"; Roskill, *Period of Balance*, 358.

94 Roskill, *Offensive, Part I*, 259.

what counts is not the ratio of merchant ships to escorts, but the ratio of the attack area around the convoy to the number of close escorts. The larger the convoys, the further the Admiralty could spread the small numbers of escort vessels then available."[95]

Finally, although it took a while for the navy to implement local superiority of force, it came to be recognized that "concentration of effort" was as important at sea as on the land and in the air. "Captain Frederick 'Johnny' Walker, the champion escort group leader in the North Atlantic," employed his escort group as a semi-independent submarine hunting unit with great success; and even Winston Churchill "was persuaded that offensive patrols by such groups as 'Walker's chicks', as they were known in Liverpool, paid better dividends than simply shepherding the convoys."[96]

That step was taken when, within the convoys, there was a major innovation in the positioning of the aircraft supporting units and their surface escorts. Initially, the baby flattops "had taken station between the two center columns of merchant ships"; and their escorts had been integrated into the general convoy screen. The configuration, however, "involved constant danger of collision" between the carrier and the merchantmen "whenever planes were launched and recovered." The continual maneuvering in and out of the convoy exhausted the carrier's deck officers; and, in terms of the time and effort involved, the system proved unproductive. In May 1943, the commodore in command of a support group that consisted of the carrier U.S.S. *Bogue* and her screen, having employed the traditional disposition in his earlier and unfruitful crossings, "took station astern of the convoy commander's column, then pulled his own escorts out of the screen, and operated as one group within visual signaling distance of the convoy."[97] From this semi-independent aviation group, it was only a minor step to the innovation of the "roving U-boat killer outfit – a group composed of an escort carrier" and its screen. The group used the convoys as bait "to hunt down submarines wherever HF/DF fixes indicated their presence."[98] With this innovation, the convoy had become an offensive, as well as a defensive, weapon in the battle with the U-boat enforced blockade.

An examination of the convoy battles in the North Atlantic reveals two consistent features; which together underscore the importance of an integrated air and sea convoy. First, "with only rare exceptions, U-boats broke off their attacks as soon as air escorts joined a convoy;" and second, "as soon as the air escorts left they pressed in once again." These observations

95 Herwig, "Innovation Ignored," 250–251.   96 Kaplan and Currie, *Convoy*, 83.
97 Morison, *Atlantic Battle Won*, 80.   98 Morison, *Two-Ocean War*, 366.

make "plain the extent to which the complete integration of our sea and air escorts wrested the initiative from the enemy."[99] Thus, by May 1943, "the Allies had demonstrated that both fast and slow convoys, if provided with air as well as surface escort and support, could cross the North Atlantic in either direction with slight if any loss, no matter how many U-boats were deployed against them; and that, during the passage, submarines could be killed by surface and air escorts before they ever came within sight of merchant-ship targets."[100]

Interallied and interservice organizational innovations, however, were not always so easily achieved. It is clear that a unified air command for all antisubmarine work would have proved very productive; but, although frequently proposed, every such proposal "foundered on the unwillingness of Britain or the United States to surrender any measure of sovereignty within their own strategic zones, and on the very real difficulty of integrating the functions of the British Admiralty and Ministry of War Transport with the corresponding American departments." The war ended without an integrated air command; "and it was left for the post-war Governments of the North Atlantic Treaty Organization to accept and introduce measures similar to those" discussed during the war.[101]

Finally, there was the matter of training, an issue that had received scant attention in either the United States or the United Kingdom in the years leading up to the war. Soon after the outbreak of hostilities, however, both navies came to recognize "that normal naval training was not enough to qualify sailors to hunt and kill submarines; special training was required not only in tactics," but in the use of the rapidly expanding armory of antisubmarine weapons. Both the Admiralty and the Navy Department introduced special training schools – schools freely opened to members of other allied navies; the U.S. schools even accepted "students" from Latin American and other neutral navies.[102]

3(4). The Production Function (2a): Output, The Qualitative Story

The swings in the effectiveness of the German submarine blockade of the Allies are captured in Figure (see also Tables 6.1 and 6.2). During the fall of 1939, on average about twenty-nine vessels with a carrying capacity of about 105,000 tons were sunk each month; and the numbers were only slightly higher (thirty-one and 119,000) during the first six months of 1940.

---

99   Roskill, *The Offensive, Part I*, 264–265.   100 Morison, *Atlantic Battle Won*, 84.
101 Roskill, *Period of Balance*, 361–362.   102 Morison, *Atlantic Battle Won*, 7–9.

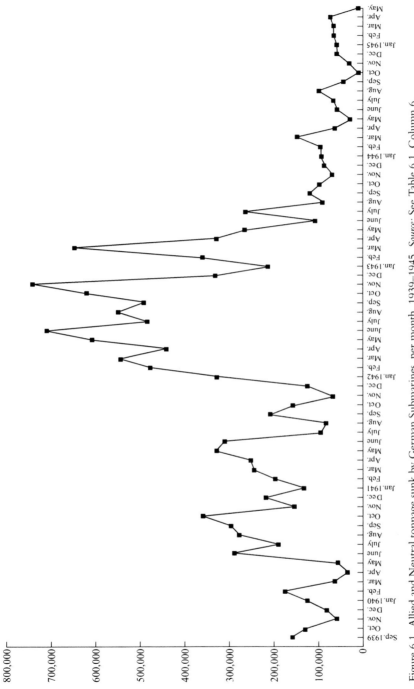

Figure 6.1. Allied and Neutral tonnage sunk by German Submarines, per month, 1939–1945. *Source:* See Table 6.1, Column 6.

Table 6.1. *Allied and Neutral Shipping Lost, Monthly Totals, September 1939 to August 1945*

Month	Year	Tonnage of Allied and Neutral Shipping Lost By Theater					Allied and Neutral Tonnage Lost to Submarine Attack		Lost by Area			Percent Lost in Atlantic – Arctic
		North Atlantic	United Kingdom	South Atlantic	Other	Total	Tonnage Lost to Submarines	Percent of Total Lost to Submarines	Atlantic-Arctic	Other	Total	
		(1)	(2)	(3)	(4)	(5)	(6)	(7)	(8)	(9)	(10)	(11)
September	1939	104,829	84,965	5,051	0	194,845	153,879	79.0				
October		110,619	63,368	22,368	0	196,355	134,807	68.7				
November		17,895	155,668	0	706	174,269	51,589	29.6				
December		15,852	152,107	21,964	0	189,923	80,881	42.6				
January	1940	35,970	178,536	0	0	214,506	111,263	51.9				
February		74,759	152,161	0	0	226,920	169,566	74.7				
March		11,215	95,794	0	0	107,009	62,781	58.7				
April		24,570	133,648	0	0	158,218	32,467	20.5				
May		49,087	230,607	6,199	2,568	288,461	55,580	19.3				
June		296,529	208,924	0	80,043	585,496	284,113	48.5				
July		141,474	192,331	31,269	21,839	386,913	195,825	50.6				
August		190,048	162,956	0	44,225	397,229	267,618	67.4				
September		254,553	131,150	17,801	45,117	448,621	295,335	65.8				
October		286,644	131,620	0	24,721	442,985	352,407	79.6				
November		201,341	92,713	0	91,661	385,715	146,613	38.0				
December		239,304	83,308	0	26,956	349,568	212,590	60.8				
January	1941	214,382	36,975	58,585	10,298	320,240	126,782	39.6				
February		317,378	51,381	0	34,634	403,393	196,783	48.8				
March		364,689	152,862	0	12,155	529,706	243,020	45.9				
April		260,451	99,031	21,807	306,612	687,901	249,375	36.3				
May		324,550	100,655	11,339	74,498	511,042	325,492	63.7				
June		318,740	86,381	10,134	16,770	432,025	310,143	71.8				

Month	Year											
July		97,813	15,265	0	7,897	120,975	94,209	77.9				
August		83,661	19,791	0	27,247	130,699	80,310	61.4				
September		184,546	54,779	15,526	31,091	285,942	202,820	70.9				
October		154,593	35,996	5,297	22,403	218,289	156,554	71.7				
November		50,215	30,332	4,953	19,140	104,640	62,196	59.4				
December		50,682	56,845	6,275	469,904	583,706	124,070	21.3				
January	1942	276,795	19,341	0	123,771	419,907	327,357	78.0	270,348	57,009	327,357	82.6
February		429,891	11,098	0	238,643	679,632	476,451	70.1	427,733	42,403	470,136	91.0
March		534,064	15,147	13,125	271,828	834,164	537,980	64.5	511,552	20,446	531,998	96.2
April		391,044	54,589	48,177	180,647	674,457	431,664	64.0	388,182	49,474	437,656	88.7
May		576,350	59,396	9,081	60,223	705,050	607,247	86.1	586,149	21,098	607,247	96.5
June		623,545	2,655	26,287	181,709	834,196	700,235	83.9	603,402	96,692	700,094	86.2
July		486,965	22,557	23,972	84,619	618,113	476,065	77.0	425,864	50,185	476,049	89.5
August		508,426	0	35,494	117,213	661,133	544,410	82.3	526,329	18,081	544,410	96.7
September		473,585	1,892	57,797	34,053	567,327	485,413	85.6	454,548	30,826	485,374	93.6
October		399,715	12,733	148,142	77,243	637,833	619,417	97.1	585,510	28,794	614,304	95.3
November		508,707	6,363	58,662	234,022	807,754	729,160	90.3	636,907	74,973	711,880	89.5
December		262,135	9,114	43,496	34,157	348,902	330,816	94.8	287,730	56,142	343,872	83.7
January	1943	172,691	15,819	16,116	56,733	261,359	203,128	77.7	181,767	21,276	203,043	89.5
February		288,625	4,925	21,656	87,856	403,062	359,328	89.1	312,004	47,324	359,328	86.8
March		476,349	884	61,462	154,694	693,389	627,377	90.5	567,401	59,976	627,377	90.4
April		235,478	9,926	7,129	92,147	344,680	327,943	95.1	276,790	51,153	327,943	84.4
May		163,507	1,568	40,523	93,830	299,428	264,852	88.5	211,929	52,923	264,852	80.0
June		18,379	149	11,587	93,710	123,825	95,753	77.3	37,825	57,928	95,753	39.5
July		123,327	72	64,478	177,521	365,398	252,145	69.0	136,106	108,381	244,487	55.7
August		10,186	19	15,368	94,228	119,801	86,579	72.3	27,941	58,617	86,558	32.3
September		43,775	0	10,770	101,874	156,419	118,841	76.0	46,892	71,949	118,841	39.5
October		56,422	0	4,663	78,776	139,861	97,407	69.6	53,886	43,521	97,407	55.3
November		23,077	13,036	4,573	103,705	144,391	66,585	46.1	29,917	36,629	66,546	45.0
December		47,785	6,086	0	114,653	168,524	86,967	51.6	47,785	39,182	86,967	54.9

(continued)

269

Table 6.1 (continued)

Month	Year	Tonnage of Allied and Neutral Shipping Lost By Theater					Allied and Neutral Tonnage Lost to Submarine Attack		Lost by Area			
		North Atlantic	United Kingdom	South Atlantic	Other	Total	Tonnage Lost to Submarines	Percent of Total Lost to Submarines	Atlantic–Arctic	Other	Total	Percent Lost in Atlantic – Arctic
		(1)	(2)	(3)	(4)	(5)	(6)	(7)	(8)	(9)	(10)	(11)
January	1944	36,065	6,944	0	87,626	130,635	92,278	70.6	36,065	56,213	92,278	39.1
February		12,577	4,051	0	100,227	116,855	92,923	79.5	7,048	85,875	92,923	7.6
March		36,867	0	4,695	116,398	157,960	142,944	90.5	41,562	101,382	142,944	29.1
April		34,224	468	13,539	34,141	82,372	62,149	75.4	47,763	14,386	62,149	76.9
May		0	0	17,277	10,020	27,297	24,424	89.5	17,277	7,147	24,424	70.7
June		4,294	75,166	3,268	21,356	104,084	57,875	55.6	38,556	19,319	57,875	66.6
July		15,480	19,038	14,062	30,176	78,756	63,351	80.4	33,175	30,176	63,351	52.4
August		5,685	54,834	0	57,785	118,304	98,729	83.5	40,944	57,785	98,729	41.5
September		16,535	21,163	0	7,107	44,805	43,368	96.8	37,698	5,670	43,368	86.9
October		0	1,722	0	9,946	11,668	7,176	61.5	0	7,176	7,176	0.0
November		7,828	8,880	0	21,272	37,980	29,592	77.9	15,567	14,025	29,592	52.6
December		5,458	85,639	0	43,816	134,913	58,518	43.4	51,338	7,180	58,518	87.7
January	1945	29,168	46,553	0	7,176	82,897	56,988	68.7	56,988	0	56,988	100.0
February		32,453	48,551	7,136	7,176	95,316	65,233	68.4	58,057	7,176	65,233	89.0
March		23,684	83,664	3,656	0	111,004	65,077	58.6	65,077	0	65,077	100.0
April		32,071	49,619	0	22,822	104,512	72,957	69.8	72,957	0	72,957	100.0
May		5,353	4,669	0	7,176	17,198	10,022	58.3	10,022	0	10,022	100.0

Sources: Columns (1) thru (5) S. W. Roskill, *The War at Sea* (London: His Majesty's Stationery Office, 1954–1961); *Defensive*, 617–618; *Period of Balance*, 486; *Offensive*, *Part I*, 389; *Offensive*, *Part II*, 478.

Column (6) Roskill, *The War at Sea*, *Defensive*, 615–616; *Period of Balance*, 485; *Offensive*, *Part I*, 388; *Offensive*, *Part II*, 477.

Column (8) thru (11) Samuel Eliot Morison. *The Battle of the Atlantic* (Boston: Little, Brown, 1947). 412: Morison, *The Atlantic Battle Won* (Boston: Little, Brown, 1960), 367.

Table 6.2 *Allied and Neutral Shipping Lost, Quarterly and Annual Totals, September 1939 to August 1945*

		Tonnage of Allied and Neutral Shipping Lost By Theater					Allied and Neutral Tonnage Lost to Submarine Attack		Lost by Area			
Year	Quarter	North Atlantic	United Kingdom	South Atlantic	Other	Total	Tonnage Lost to Submarines	Percent of Total Lost to Submarines	Atlantic-Arctic	Other	Total	Percent Lost in Atlantic – Arctic
		(1)	(2)	(3)	(4)	(5)	(6)	(7)	(8)	(9)	(10)	(11)
1939	4*	249,195	456,108	49,383	706	755,392	421,156	55.8				
1940	1	121,944	426,491	0	0	548,435	343,610	62.7				
1940	2	370,186	573,179	6,199	82,611	1,032,175	372,160	36.1				
1940	3	586,075	486,437	49,070	111,181	1,232,763	758,778	61.6				
1940	4	727,289	307,641	0	143,338	1,178,268	711,610	60.4				
1941	1	896,449	241,218	58,585	57,087	1,253,339	566,585	45.2				
1941	2	903,741	286,067	43,280	397,880	1,630,968	885,010	54.3				
1941	3	366,020	89,835	15,526	66,235	537,616	377,339	70.2				
1941	4	255,490	123,173	16,525	511,447	906,635	342,820	37.8				
1942	1	1,240,750	45,586	13,125	634,242	1,933,703	1,341,788	69.4	1,209,633	119,858	1,329,491	91.0
1942	2	1,590,939	116,640	83,545	422,579	2,213,703	1,739,146	78.6	1,577,733	167,264	1,744,997	90.4
1942	3	1,468,976	24,449	117,263	235,885	1,846,573	1,505,888	81.6	1,406,741	99,092	1,505,833	93.4
1942	4	1,170,557	28,210	250,300	345,422	1,794,489	1,679,393	93.6	1,510,147	159,909	1,670,056	90.4
1943	1	937,665	21,628	99,234	299,283	1,357,810	1,189,833	87.6	1,061,172	128,576	1,189,748	89.2
1943	2	417,364	11,643	59,239	279,687	767,933	688,548	89.7	526,544	162,004	688,548	76.5

(continued)

271

Table 6.2 (*continued*)

Year	Quarter	Tonnage of Allied and Neutral Shipping Lost By Theater					Allied and Neutral Tonnage Lost to Submarine Attack		Lost by Area			Percent Lost in Atlantic – Arctic
		North Atlantic	United Kingdom	South Atlantic	Other	Total	Tonnage Lost to Submarines	Percent of Total Lost to Submarines	Atlantic-Arctic	Other	Total	
		(1)	(2)	(3)	(4)	(5)	(6)	(7)	(8)	(9)	(10)	(11)
1943	3	177,288	91	90,616	373,623	641,618	457,565	71.3	210,939	238,947	449,886	46.9
1943	4	127,284	19,122	9,236	297,134	452,776	250,959	55.4	131,588	119,332	250,920	52.4
1944	1	85,509	10,995	4,695	304,251	405,450	328,145	80.9	84,675	243,470	328,145	25.8
1944	2	38,518	75,634	34,084	65,517	213,753	144,448	67.6	103,596	40,852	144,448	71.7
1944	3	37,700	95,035	14,062	95,068	241,865	205,448	84.9	111,817	93,631	205,448	54.4
1944	4	13,286	96,241	0	75,034	184,561	95,286	51.6	66,905	28,381	95,286	70.2
1945	1	85,305	178,968	10,792	14,352	289,217	187,298	64.8	180,122	7,176	187,298	96.2
1945	2**	37,424	54,288	0	29,998	121,710	82,979	68.2	82,979	0	82,979	100.0
1939	*	249,195	456,108	49,383	706	755,392	421,156	55.8				
1940		1,805,494	1,793,748	55,269	337,130	3,991,641	2,186,158	54.8				
1941		2,421,700	740,293	133,916	1,032,649	4,328,558	2,171,754	50.2				
1942		5,471,222	214,885	464,233	1,638,128	7,788,468	6,266,215	80.5	5,704,254	546,123	6,250,377	91.3
1943		1,659,601	52,484	258,325	1,249,727	3,220,137	2,586,905	80.3	1,930,243	648,859	2,579,102	74.8
1944		175,013	277,905	52,841	539,870	1,045,629	773,327	74.0	366,993	406,334	773,327	47.5
1945	***	122,729	233,056	10,792	44,350	410,927	270,277	65.8	263,101	7176	270,277	97.3

* September through December.
** April through May 10 only.
*** January through May 10 only.
Source: See Table 6.1.

By the middle of 1940, however, with the French Atlantic coast in German hands, and despite counterattacks by British and Canadian escorts, U-boat attacks on convoys became more intense; and the blockade became substantially more effective. For example, convoy HX-112, consisting of forty-one merchant vessels and seven escorts lost five ships in March; and, the next month, a wolf-pack broke up convoy SC-26 and sank ten of twenty-two vessels. Overall, between July 1940 and June 1941, a total of 548 ships totaling 2,921,983 tons (a monthly average of forty-six vessels and more than 243,000 tons) were lost to German submarine attacks.[103]

Thereafter the situation eased. On the one hand, new routings made the convoys more difficult to locate. "Between 22 July and 10 August, nine convoys, totaling five hundred thirty-three ships" sailed from Halifax and Sydney to the United Kingdom; and although some twenty-five turned back because of collisions or engine trouble, none were lost to enemy action. On the other hand, although the United States had still not officially entered the war, U.S. Admiral Stark came to the conclusion that 'the situation is obviously critical in the Atlantic. In my opinion, it is hopeless except as we take strong measures to save it. The effect on the British of sinkings with regard both to the food supply and essential material to carry on the war is getting progressively worse.' In response to his concerns, in April and May 1941, the American navy transferred one carrier, three battleships, four light cruisers, and two squadrons of destroyers from the Pacific to the Atlantic, where they soon joined in limited partnerships with the British and Canadians. Because the Germans were still reluctant to meet the Americans head on, the results were immediate; over the last six months of the year, losses fell to a monthly average of twenty-eight ships totaling some 120,000 tons – a figure comparable to the losses suffered during the first nine months of the war and less than one-half the monthly tonnage lost between July 1940 and June 1941.[104]

However, when the United States officially did enter the war, the German Navy took its gloves off. Although the United States was granted a few weeks grace during the period from December 7 to mid-January 1942, the attacks on Allied, particularly U.S., shipping, started in earnest soon thereafter.[105] In January alone, sixty-two ships totaling more than 327,000 tons were sunk; for the entire year the figures were 1,160 vessels of almost 6.3 million tons (a monthly average of ninety-seven vessels and 525,000 tons).[106] As if to make up for their reticence during the months of

103 Morison, *Battle of the Atlantic*, 56; Roskill, *Defensive*, 615–616.
104 Morison, *Battle of the Atlantic*, 56–57, 71; Roskill, *Defensive*, 615–616.
105 Roskill, *Period of Balance*, 95.
106 Morison, *Battle of the Atlantic*, 132; Roskill, *Period of Balance*, 485–486.

"phony" war, the Germans hit the Americans particularly hard; during the first six months, U.S. merchant marine losses "from enemy action already surpassed those suffered during the entire course of World War I."[107] On the day following the declaration of war, Hitler decided to attack American coastal shipping; and it was there, rather than on the transatlantic convoy routes, that the sinkings were concentrated.[108] Although probably no more than a dozen submarines were operating continuously in the Eastern Sea Frontier, in the first four months of 1942 they sank no fewer than 137 ships totaling 828,000 tons. Then, gradually moving south into the Gulf of Mexico, the Yucatan Channel, the waters off western Cuba, and the Panama Canal, in March, April, May, and June they sank another 160 to 170 ships totaling 870,000 tons.[109] In total, the massacre carried out along the Atlantic coast "was as much a national disaster as if saboteurs had destroyed a half dozen of our biggest war plants." "The U-boats were undoubtedly helped by enemy agents and clandestine radio transmissions from the United States," and the Germans also had managed to break the American codes; however, they also received a significant level of help from American citizens and politicians. One of the ugliest features of the war was the refusal "of local communities to dim their waterfront lights, or of the military authorities to require them to do so, until more than three months after the German submarine offensive began." "When this obvious defense measure was first proposed, squawks went all the way from Atlantic City to southern Florida that the 'tourist season would be ruined.' Miami and its luxurious suburbs threw up six miles of neon-light glow, against which the southbound shipping that hugged the reefs to avoid the Gulf Stream was silhouetted. Ships were sunk and seamen drowned in order that the citizenry might enjoy business and pleasure as usual."[110] In addition, the merchant marine itself

---

107 Morison, *Battle of the Atlantic*, 200.

108 During the first year of the war, the U.S. Navy took part in escorting 9,481 merchant ships in 250 different transatlantic convoys with a total loss of only 132 ships, 1.4 percent. Morison, *Battle of the Atlantic*, 315; *Atlantic Battle Won*, 7.

109 Morison, *Atlantic Battle Won*, 7–8. "The German Navy ... pulled off one of the greatest merchant-ship massacres in history during the first four months of 1942, by keeping an average of a dozen U-boats constantly in the Eastern Sea Frontier, relieving them every two weeks and refueling them from tanker submarines stationed 300 miles east of Bermuda."

110 Morison, *Battle of the Atlantic*, 128–130; Morison, *Two-Ocean War*, 109. "During the summer of 1942, Doenitz declared: 'our submarines are operating close inshore along the coast of the United States of America, so that bathers and sometimes entire coastal cities are witnesses to that drama of war, whose visual climaxes are constituted by the red glorious of blazing tankers.' No frantic boast this; burning tankers were not infrequently sighted from fashionable Florida resorts, and on June 15 two large American freighters were torpedoed by a U-boat within full view of thousands of pleasure-seekers at Virginia Beach." Morison, *Battle of the Atlantic*, 157. The Doenitz quote is from translation in *Monthly Report, Army Air Forces A/S Command* (mimeographed pamphlet) (Oct. 1942), 16.

contributed to the "merry massacre" by continuing the unrestricted use of ship's radios. Finally, the American navy was slow to innovate coastal convoys – it was not until April 1 that even a partial convoy system was innovated; and this omission added to the total cost.[111]

The failure of the Americans to quickly adopt convoying along the eastern seaboard was the unfortunate product of two very different "readings of history." First, the American naval officers stationed in London were shocked by the sinkings of British vessels in May and June 1940. Although most of the sunken ships were merchant vessels sailing alone – that is, unescorted – the Americans believed that they had been sailing in thinly escorted convoys; and they "concluded that to sail merchant ships in thinly escorted convoys was unwise or even foolish." As the sinkings in the western approaches continued into the fall, the American observers became steadily more convinced that what was their erroneous conclusion – that a poorly escorted convoy was worse than no convoy at all – was correct. Such a convoy, they concluded, presented the German wolf-packs a convenient mass target – "too many eggs in one vulnerable basket"; and, unfortunately, their views were accepted and became the policy of the Navy Department in Washington. A very costly mistake.

Second, as late as 1941, the U.S. navy had no ships other than destroyers suitable for deep ocean convoy escort. That fact was either a result of poor navy planning or of a very bad political decision. Initially, the former conclusion was widely accepted and the blame was placed on Admiral King. More recently, as new evidence has emerged, it appears that the fault lay in the political sector. When the Secretary of the Navy presented President Roosevelt with the plans for an improved version of the British frigate, the president approved the British request to build fifty such vessels; but he denied the navy's request to produce destroyer escorts (DEs) for itself. Moreover, he continued to reject similar requests from the Secretary of the Navy and from Admiral Stark "right up to – and beyond – America's entry into the war."

In part, that decision may be explained by the president's desire to invade Europe as quickly as possible, while at the same time launching an island-hopping campaign in the Pacific. To achieve those goals, it was necessary to build some twelve thousand to twenty-four thousand landing craft. In part, the decision may be explained by a belief that the way to defeat the U-boats was to produce more merchant vessels than the submarines could sink. Certainly "Roosevelt awarded a higher priority to building merchant

111 Roskill, *Period of Balance*, 95–96.

ships than to any convoy escorts other than small SCs and PCs." Finally, and arguably weighing most heavily in the decision, was Roosevelt's personal biases – biases at least partially shaped by his experience as Assistant Secretary of the Navy during World War I. "Roosevelt had a 'predilection for small antisubmarine craft', which could be mass-produced cheaply and quickly when the need arose." Furthermore, Roosevelt 'was a small-boat seaman himself and loved to cruise on little things like the [165-foot presidential yacht] *Potomac* and he liked small ships.' As a result of his urging, "the Navy had contracted for prototypes of two such vessels: a 110-foot, 14-knot, wood-hull submarine chaser (SC) and a 173-foot, 22-knot, steel hulled patrol craft (PC)." Unfortunately, neither craft was capable of combating the submarine on the high seas. In one angry letter to Admiral Stark, Secretary Knox characterized Roosevelt's policy as "Blind Folly."[112]

Overall, in 1942 the Germans should have been somewhat pleased by the results of their Atlantic blockade. Total Allied losses were very high. Although "convoys were increasingly successful in protecting trade routes," escorts were sinking relatively few submarines. Only twenty-one German and seven Italian submarines were sunk by Allied navies during the first half of the year, while, during the same period, the Germans had built 123.[113] Over the first seven months of 1942, only thirty-two, 3.9 percent of the U-boats at sea (about one month's production), had been destroyed, whereas the submarines had, on average, sunk three hundred tons of merchant shipping per submarine per day.[114]

A very large proportion of the total Allied losses had been sunk in American waters; however, as American defenses and methods had begun to improve, it could hardly be expected that those sinkings would continue at the same rate.[115] In fact, after July, as defense measures improved, German submarines moved away from the American coast. In the case of the American coast, there were only three sinkings in July and none during the rest of the year.[116] Thus, the year closed on a hopeful note for the Allies. In December total Allied sinkings had fallen to fifty-four ships of 288,000 tons, less than half of the tonnage lost in the previous month; however, Allied hopes were premature. Although better weapons and tactics were coming on line, the drop in sinkings was not yet a reflection of their impact in coastal and North Atlantic waters; instead, it mirrored Doenitz's decision

---

112 Blair, *Hunters*, 173, 448–449, 450–451, 480.   113 Morison, *Two-Ocean War*, 135.
114 Roskill, *Period of Balance*, 111, 113, 467–468.   115 Roskill, *Period of Balance*, 111–112.
116 Morison, *Battle of the Atlantic*, 312.

to concentrate on troop and supply convoys destined for North Africa – convoys that proved "too fast and cagey for his wolves to catch."[117] From the Allied point of view, victory was still not in sight; at best, the situation was summarized by Winston Churchill's comment that the period, from July 1942 to April 1943, marked "the end of the beginning."[118]

The evidence, however, suggests that Churchill was too optimistic. The first five months of 1943 could hardly be considered a victory – or even a stand-off. Losses totaled 314 ships of almost 1.8 million tons, a monthly average of sixty-three vessels of 357,000 tons. The latter figure, although only about two-thirds of the 1942 total, was well above those of 1939, 1940, and 1941. It has been argued by the historian of the U.S. Navy in World War II that "only once before since the sixteenth century had Anglo-American supremacy in the Atlantic been so seriously threatened as in the twelve months beginning in April 1943. That was exactly twenty-five years earlier," during the first German submarine blockade.[119] The British, however, argued that the situation in the spring of 1943 was even more precarious. The Admiralty, looking at those long months, concluded "the Germans never came so near to disrupting communication between the New World and the Old as in the first twenty days of March 1943." It is certainly true that during that month, submarines sank 108 ships of 627,000 tons, but the threat to transatlantic trade was certainly less than in the contemporary perceptions.[120]

In the first twenty days of March, eighty-five ships were lost in the North Atlantic alone; and the German losses were a mere six U-boats.[121] Since August 1942, in the area between Iceland and the Azores, the Germans had deployed numerous wolf-packs. Packs were strung out across the transatlantic convoy routes but they were concentrated in the "Black Pit" that lay outside the range of land-based aircraft.[122] Although the average monthly sinkings per submarine had declined from its peak in the months before the Americans had innovated coastal convoys, a decline from twelve thousand to two thousand tons, the number of U-boats deployed had increased sufficiently to keep the total sinkings close to their earlier levels.[123] "Every day [in April] on the American half of the North Atlantic convoy route, there

---

117 Morison, *Battle of the Atlantic*, 324–325.   118 Morison, *Battle of the Atlantic*, 403.
119 Morison, *Battle of the Atlantic*, 201; Roskill, *Period of Balance*, 485.
120 Roskill, *The Period of Balance*, 367, 485. Of the ships sunk, nearly two-thirds were "sunk in convoy," a source of great concern to the Naval Staff.
121 Morison, *Atlantic Battle Won*, 65.   122 Morison, *Two-Ocean War*, 240.
123 Morison, *Battle of the Atlantic*, 407.

were five or six convoys at sea, making all together 206 ships and 38 escorts."
There were also, on average, some forty-nine submarines in pursuit of each
convoy.[124] However, the evidence will show that both Morison and the
Admiralty overstated their claims of early German successes.

Wherever the truth may be, it is certainly true that by May 1943, the
situation had changed markedly. Between land-based aircraft, baby flattops,
and centimeter radar, the Germans lost forty-one submarines in that month
alone; and the "rate of exchange" had fallen from about one submarine lost
per 100,000 tons to one submarine for every 5,169 tons.[125] For example, in
April and May, fifty-one submarines were deployed against convoy ONS-5.
Although the escort was never more than nine vessels, and it was usually
smaller, only thirteen merchantmen out of forty-three were sunk; and the
Germans lost six U-boats.[126] Two weeks later, SC-130 of thirty-eight ships
escaped the thirty-two U-boats that were deployed against it and reached
port intact and undamaged. This time, the Germans, lost five submarines
to the escorts and the convoy's air-support.[127] On May 17, slow convoy
ONS-7 lost the S.S. *Aymeric* to a submarine attack – the submarine was
sunk an hour later – but the "*Aymeric* was the last merchantship sunk from
a northern transatlantic convoy until mid-September."[128]

On May 22, having already lost thirty-three submarines during the month
(German losses had risen from 13 to 30 percent of those at sea), the high
command concluded that they must accept defeat and withdrew the surviv-
ing submarines to, in Doenitz's words, "areas less endangered by aircraft."[129]
Withdrawal might have been wise; but the Grand Admiral could well have
chosen a better area for his next operations. In fact, he chose the Central Transatlantic Convoy Route – a route "teeming with valuable targets"
as "the United States Navy was then convoying hundreds of troop trans-
ports, fast tankers, and slow freighters crammed with military supplies, in
preparation for the invasion of Sicily in July and of Italy in September."
"Unfortunately for German hopes, the Navy was uncommonly well prepared to protect troop convoys with fast escorts and escort carriers." No
sooner were the redeployed submarines on station, than they "became the
victim of an antisubmarine offensive unique for the rapidity with which tactical innovations were introduced."[130] In particular, they were the victims of

---

124 Morison, *Battle of the Atlantic*, 404–405.   125 Morison, *Atlantic Battle Won*, 83.
126 Morison, *Atlantic Battle Won*, 76.   127 Morison, *Atlantic Battle Won*, 79.
128 Morison, *Atlantic Battle Won*, 77.
129 Roskill, *Period of Balance*, 377; *Offensive, Part I*, 15; Morison, *Atlantic Battle Won*, 108.
130 Morison, *Atlantic Battle Won*, 108–109.

the innovation of the roving U-boat killer outfit and of land-based aircraft operating from the Azores.[131] Doenitz then ordered his submarines back to the North Atlantic, but the results were no better. Between September 20 and October 19, the Germans managed to sink four escorts and eight merchantmen, but the cost was eighteen submarines.[132]

"In the Atlantic as a whole, August was a banner month for antisubmarine warfare. For the second time since the war began, more submarines than merchant ships were sunk; 26 of the former, as against only four of the latter."[133] "Between 18 May and 18 September 1943, 62 convoys comprising 3546 merchant ships crossed between America and Britain by the northern transatlantic route and not one ship was lost." During the months of November and December, an additional "seventy-two ocean convoys totalling 2,218 ships reached their destinations without suffering any losses."[134]

By the end of the year, there was no part of the Atlantic where submarines were safe from being located by aircraft; in fact, the German high command "seriously considered whether the submarine campaign should be given up altogether, since the U-boats were no longer paying their cost in terms of shipping sunk."[135] During the last seven months of the year, the German Navy had lost 141 submarines. The change was reflected in the attitudes of the submariners themselves. Within the submariners' officer corps, there was a serious debate about whether or not the tonnage war should continue; and two of the most highly decorated captains (Suhren and Topp) came out strongly against continuation. They argued that given the "immense losses" and the lack of even "the slightest prospect of success" the U-boats should be withdrawn. Even Doenitz was torn, but he ultimately decided to continue the fight. Until then, Doenitz "had enjoyed nearly divine status among the men in the U-boat force"; but "his order to fight on with such patently inferior weapons was seen by an embittered few as a cold-blooded decision to send his loyal corps to a certain death."[136] In hindsight, it is clear that, by May, "the Germans had lost the strategic initiative in the Atlantic war," and that, despite some later surges of sinkings, it was already "too late to restore the balance, let alone tip the scales in the German favor." In the British and American high commands, "the almost desperate

---

131 Morison, *Two-Ocean War*, 366; Roskill, *Offensive, Part I*, 55.
132 Morison, *Atlantic Battle Won*, 149.   133 Morison, *Atlantic Battle Won*, 132.
134 Morison, *Two-Ocean War*, 376; Roskill, *Offensive, Part I*, 54–55.
135 Morison, *Battle of the Atlantic*, 401–402.
136 Blair, *Hunted*, 353–354; Roskill, *Offensive, Part I*, 375.

feelings of mid–1942 were now replaced by sober confidence of eventual victory."[137]

The explanation of ebb and flow of the Battle of the North Atlantic had yet another dimension: the countervailing efforts of the "Boys at Bletchley Park" to break the German *Enigma*-based naval codes and those of their counterparts in Germany's *xB-Dienst* to solve the mysteries of the British merchant marine ciphers. The success and failure of brains and technology deployed by both the Germans and the Allies to acquire access to the naval codes employed by the other side closely parallel the flows of the Battle of the Atlantic itself. That is the contribution of science. For the Germans, the story is captured in the efforts of the men of *xB-Dienst* to read Allied naval ciphers 1 through 5; and, for the Allies, it was the efforts of the cryptanalysts at the Government Code and Cipher School (GC&CS) at Bletchley Park teamed, later, with their American counterparts in Washington to read the German naval codes – codes that included Hydra, Triton, and Tetis and that were encrypted by the German *Enigma* machine – a machine the British called *Ultra*.[138]

In terms of the German effort, "*xB-Dienst* had begun its penetration of British naval ciphers as far back as 1935–6, monitoring signals and observing corresponding movements in the Mediterranean during the period of the Abyssinian war crisis." By November 1939, the Germans were able to determine, despite the British belief that is was a closely guarded secret, that Loch Ewe was being used as a base for the Home Fleet. In January 1940, their ability to read the British codes was briefly checked "when a new Merchant Navy Code was introduced." During the Norwegian campaign they were able to "read between 30 and 50% of British naval signals without any undue delay." A month later, a copy of Naval Cypher No.1 was captured in Bergen, thereafter the cryptographers at *xB-Dienst* were able to 'read the bulk of the traffic with very little delay.'" In August, however, the British replaced Cypher No. 1 with the Naval Cypher No. 2; and this change, despite *xB-Deinst's* contributions to the first wolf-pack attacks on British convoys, limited that group's ability to read British codes until September 1941. Soon thereafter, however, the British replaced Cypher No. 2 with Cypher No. 3; and it was early 1942 before the Germans succeeded in reconstructing that codebook. Moreover, in March they captured a Naval Cypher No. 4 codebook from a merchant vessel in northern waters. Thus, from February until December, *xB-Dienst* was able to read as much

137 Morison, *Atlantic Battle Won*, 10; Roskill, *Offensive, Part I*, 53.
138 Terraine, *Business*, 257–258, 425, 712. The British called the German Hydra, Dolphin, and the German Triton, Shark.

as 80 percent of British naval traffic. However, although somewhat successful directing U-boat packs against a series of Atlantic convoys, their success was somewhat qualified – for example, in the weeks leading up to November 1942, *xB-Dienst* delivered no warnings of the 350 vessels that sailed from the United States and Britain in support of the landings in North Africa.[139] It was only after the Allied troops were ashore that Doenitz learned of the landings – and, even then, he was only notified by a telephone call from Africa. But, in the early months of 1943 *"B-Deinst* continued to supply good convoy intelligence to the U-boat Command." Fortunately, for the allies, at the end of May, U-boat control committed three horrendous breaches of communications security. *"B-dienst* had intercepted and decrypted Allied warnings in Naval Cypher Number 3 to all Allied convoys that three [American submarines] ... were to operate at certain positions along the North Atlantic run during their return to the States." U-boat control relayed the Allied information; and its messages were decoded by the Allies, who immediately recognized that Naval Cypher Number 3 had been broken by the Germans. As a result, in June 1943 the British Admiralty were finally persuaded that their convoy ciphers were insecure and "both Cyphers No. 3 and No. 4 were replaced by No. 5;" "and a secure ciphering system was introduced for both the Royal Navy and the RCN." By January 1944, the U.S. Navy "was fully integrated into this system;" and "all three Navies were in process of adopting the Combined Cipher Machine (CCM) for all their Atlantic communications, and this was never penetrated by the *xB-Dienst*."[140]

The pattern of the successes and failures of the "Boys from Bletchley Park" is strikingly similar; although happily, from the Allied point of view, the long-run results were much better. "With the help of captured materials, a great increase in the number of bombes and other mechanical devices, and inspired mathematical and intellectual solutions, Allied codebreakers at Bletchley Park and in Washington and elsewhere slowly but steadily broke deeper into Axis military, diplomatic, and merchant-marine codes." "The quantity of precise information that the allies amassed on the enemy forces and intentions in 1943 and later was without precedent in history, and it became an increasingly larger factor in Allied military decisions."[141]

---

139 In October 1942, for example, on the basis of an intercepted signal, Doenitz was able to place sixteen U-boats in the path of SC 107, then on passage through Canadian waters. The result was an Allied disaster.

140 Details in this paragraph are from Terraine, *Business*, 227, 257, 258, 426, 454, 490, 496, 628, 699 (note 39), 747 (note 94). Blair, *Hunted*, 310–311.

141 Blair, *Hunted*, 159. For detailed information on this, see Syrett, ed., *Battle of the Atlantic*.

In the long run, the British were more successful than the German *B-Deinst*; however, not only were they slower to get into action, but, initially, the GC&CS cryptanalysts also were understaffed, overworked, and grossly underfunded. Because of the need to maintain the utmost secrecy, the work at Bletchley Park was neither understood nor appreciated by the London bureaucrats charged with the allocation of military resources. As a result, until October 1941 the codebreakers were not given the support that their work deserved, let alone the support they desired. On October 21, however, four senior cryptanalysts sent an extraordinary letter directly to Churchill, begging for help. They pointed out that owing to 'shortage of staff' and "'overworking'" that they "had to cease night shifts, with the result that 'the finding of the [Enigma] naval keys is being delayed at least twelve hours every day.'" "In response to the letter, Churchill directed that Bletchley Park be given 'all they want on extreme priority.'" Thereafter, the "boys" were gradually able to build a full head of steam; but it took time.[142]

Although they were much slower "off the mark," in March 1941 the British recovered a spare set of *Enigma* rotors "on the abandoned armed trawler *Krebs*"; and that discovery permitted the GC&CS cryptanalysists "to read the whole of the German radio traffic for February and some days in March." By May 10, they also had broken the whole of April traffic and were reading May messages with delays of only three to seven days. On May 7, the Royal Navy seized the weather ship *Munchen* – a vessel equipped with both *Enigma* and the Hydra settings – and took the machine and settings intact. The GC&CS were, as a result, able to read traffic in June almost as soon as it was received. Two days later, the Navy captured the U-110; and the net included the settings for the very high-grade "officer only" naval signals and the *Kurzsignale* ("Short Signals") code. The Germans used the latter code along with standardized messages that, taken together, were designed to use their speed to defeat D/F fixes. The May Hydra settings were, unfortunately, destroyed. In June, the capture of the weather ship, *Lauenberg*, gave Bletchley Park the ability to read July current traffic from *Heimische Gerwässer* ("Home Waters"). In November, however, the Germans innovated a new *Enigma* signal (Triton). Because they used the new signal only with submarines in the Atlantic for the British, the German innovation although serious, proved only a major setback, rather than the catastrophe that it might have been. In February 1942, however,

142 Blair, *Hunters*, 387–388; Terraine, *Business*, 628.

the Germans added a fourth rotor to the *Enigma* machines on their Atlantic communications network; and they altered Triton. As a result, for nine months British decrypting of German messages was "blacked out." In the middle of December 1942, the four-wheel Triton key was partially broken; and, although significantly slowed by the backlog of undecoded messages and by the failure to completely master the new Triton, some important decrypts were achieved. In March 1943, however, the Germans innovated a new code for Triton causing a nine-day *Enigma* blackout. Fortunately, for the British, the U-boats continued to use the three-wheeled machine for short messages and weather reports. In July, the Germans introduced an alternative fourth wheel; and, "for the first three weeks of July and the first ten days of August," and again in September, decrypts were greatly delayed. However, the arrival in August of the American four-wheel high-speed bombes "made it possible to overcome these obstacles" much more rapidly than previously had been possible; "and *Enigma* remained a first Class Intelligence source for the rest of the war." Finally, in December 1943, the British/American team both mastered Triton and solved the mystery of the signal produced by a new German machine called *Geheimschreiber* – a machine that used a teleprinter code instead of Morse. The machine produced a stream of radio traffic that the Germans thought was as secure as landline teleprinter messages and that they used for their highest level and most important messages. On average, in every month from then until the end of the war, Bletchely Park was successfully decrypting some 250 of these "Fish" messages as well as about 84,000 of the more common *Enigma* messages.[143]

Thus far, the effectiveness of the blockade has been described in terms of thrust and parry of the Allied and German navies; that description ignores one important component of the Allied victory over the Atlantic blockade – the ability of the Allies, particularly the Americans, to produce merchant ships to replace those lost to submarines. As Doenitz realized, as long as his submarines were sinking more ships than the Allies were building, the final victory remained in balance. Although Allied losses of ships in convoy had never fallen below the gains in merchant shipping from new construction and other sources, until July 1943, "total losses had so far always exceeded our gains." In that month, however, "the rising curve of Allied merchant ship construction overtook and crossed the more slowly rising curve of sinkings; and never again did the former fall below the latter."[144] Most of the construction was American, built under the guidance of the Maritime

143 Terraine, *Business*, 325, 424–425, 527, 627, 754 (note 19).
144 Roskill, *Period of Balance*, 378–379.

Commission and the War Shipping Administration Board. The first Liberty ship was launched in September 1941; the first Victory ship (about the same size but 50 percent faster) two years later. "In 1942, 727 ships of 55.5 million tons were constructed. By April 1943 the Maritime Commission was building 140 ships of a million tons per month; and by the end of the year these figures were doubled." For a Liberty ship, within 18 months, the time of construction had been lowered from 105 days to 14 days, with one vessel actually completed in less than five days.[145] Until the autumn of 1943, Doenitz had defended his submarine losses "on the ground that the U-boats were sinking merchant tonnage faster than the Allies could replace it. But the ships constructed monthly were by now equivalent to ten-fold the monthly losses; new construction by the end of October had more than replaced the total losses of all Allied merchant shipping since the beginning of the war."[146]

By 1944, for all intents and purpose, all vessels sailing across the North Atlantic moved in convoys. Between January and March, 105 convoys with 3,360 merchant ships crossed the northern Atlantic; and only three vessels were lost. Never again were Allied convoys seriously threatened. In March, Doenitz "tacitly admitting defeat, he evacuated a large area in the central Atlantic." He "cancelled all further operations against convoys."[147] The few U-boats that did operate successfully during 1944 were more likely than not to have been 'schnorkelers'; but, despite the 'schnorkel' spurt (a loss of 132 vessels of 773,000 tons in 1944) merchant ship losses to U-boats fell to an wartime low of four ships in May. "The most dramatic evidence of Allied mastery of the U-boat came in the Normandy operation of June 1944. Doenitz alerted 58 U-boats to break it up, but not one got near the invasion area."[148]

One would have thought that the successes of 1944 would have led to a relaxation of Allied fears as the year 1945 began, but such was not the case. The First Sea Lord wrote, "We are having...a difficult time with the U-boats. There is no doubt that this 'Schnorkel' has given them a greater advantage than we first reckoned on." Moreover, the total size of

---

145 Morison, *Two-Ocean War*, 132–133; Andrew Gibson and Arthur Donovon, *The Abandoned Ocean: A History of United States Maritime Policy* (Columbia: University of South Carolina Press, 2000), 166. The American effort is neatly captured in the following, almost certainly apocryphal, story: "One lady who had been invited to christen one of the Liberty ships was standing ready for the launching with a champagne bottle in her hand when she noticed that the keel had yet to be laid. She enquired to Henry Kaiser what he thought she should do. 'Just start swinging, Ma'am,' he replied."

146 Morison, *Atlantic Battle Won*, 149.   147 Roskill, *Offensive, Part I*, 258.

148 Morison, *Two-Ocean War*, 382–383; Roskill, *Offensive, Part II*, 479.

the German submarine fleet was still increasing – thirty new boats were added in January 1945; and losses had dropped from eighteen per month in 1944 to two-thirds that figure. Thus, in March, the German submarine fleet reached its wartime peak strength of 463 vessels; and the new additions were the greatly improved Types XXI and XXIII.[149]

During the last month of 1944, the Germans, having discovered that with "schnorkels" their submarines could successfully operate in British coastal waters, dispatched large numbers of U-boats from their Baltic and Norwegian bases and deployed them off the East Coast of Britain, in the Western Approaches, and even in the English Channel. By January 1945, their area of operation had expanded to include the Irish Sea where an escort carrier was sunk. By February, at least twenty-seven submarines were sinking Allied ships in an area that had not been threatened since 1941. The British navy was forced to deploy over four hundred escort vessels and eight hundred Coastal Command planes; but, despite that effort, between January and the beginning of May, the submarines sank fifty-one ships of 253,000 tons in the Atlantic. Early in the New Year, four of the new submarines also moved into the western Atlantic; but all were sunk by the American hunter-killer groups. This assault was not, however, the final German effort directed at the United States.[150] In the last month of the war, the Germans, in great strength, again made a determined effort to reach the eastern coast of the United States. The strike was thwarted by a U.S. fleet task force that, during an engagement lasting several days, sank five U-boats. Only two days before V-E day, a last German U-boat was sunk off Block Island, Rhode Island.[151]

"Although the submarine menace" did not end until Germany surrendered – the last attack on British coastal shipping was in May 1945, the Allied navies and air forces had effectively broken the blockade before the end of 1943. "In March and April [of that year] the submarines had wrought great havoc along the North Atlantic convoy routes, in July they had put on a blitz in the South Atlantic, and in September they had boiled up into the high latitudes with new tactics and weapons." But, by year's end, the "rate of exchange" between merchant ships and submarines – a rate that had equaled ten merchant vessels sunk per submarine at the outset of the war – had become about two submarines per merchant vessel.[152] Even during the days of their most effective attacks, in 1942 and early 1943, the losses they inflicted, despite the Admiralty's views, were never enough to

149 Roskill, *Offensive, Part II*, 285.
151 King, *U.S. Navy at War*, 205.

150 Morison, *Two-Ocean War*, 558–559.
152 Morison, *Atlantic Battle Won*, 244.

disrupt Atlantic communication; and, during the remainder of the war, the German submarine fleet could best be viewed not as operating an effective blockade but as fighting a series of defensive operations comparable to the French commerce-raiding strategy of the Napoleonic wars. In the twelve months from June 1, 1944, 135 convoys with 7,157 vessels, totaling more than 50,000,000 gross tons arrived in U.K. ports from overseas. Given the new tactics, convoys could be larger and the ratio of merchantmen to escorts higher. Convoys were clearly becoming more efficient.[153]

Counterfactuals are always difficult to construct; however, although the Allied success in breaking the blockade can, in large part, be attributed to success in strategy, tactics, and technology, it is not clear that the result would have been very much different had the convoys, the air support, and the Huff Duff and radar been significantly less effective. British and American reserves of shipping and American ship building capacity were so great that the Allies could have accepted even greater losses than those suffered in 1943. From January 1943 through December 1944, American shipyards alone produced an average of a million tons a month of new merchant ships – a total of twenty-four million over two years. Perhaps, if the strategic bombing and the continental invasion had been less successful, the Germans might have ultimately produced a submarine fleet capable of successfully blockading Great Britain; but, as it was, there was never any real likelihood that Britain would starve or even that the Allied land campaigns would be seriously handicapped, let alone halted, through losses at sea.[154]

3(5). *The Production Function (2b): Costs and Output, the Quantitative Story*

The data reported in Tables 6.1 through 6.14 capture the quantitative measures of costs and outputs of the German submarine blockade, including

---

153 Morison, *Atlantic Battle Won*, 63–64; King, *U.S. Navy at War*, 206.
154 Roskill, *Offensive, Part II*, 290–291; King, *U.S. Navy at War*, 206; Morison, *Atlantic Battle Won*, 363. The blockade was, however, costly to both sides. The Allies sank some 781 U-boats, with the loss of some 32,000 officers and men. The German and Italian submarines sank 2,828 Allied and neutral merchant vessels of some 14.7 million tons as well as 187 British Commonwealth and American warships. The British, alone, lost almost 30,000 merchant sailors; and the total Allied losses (including American merchant mariners, passengers, and sailors on the sunken warships) came to at least 40,000 men, women, and children. We have examined the data in *Axis Submarine Successes* by Jurgen Rohwer, as published by the Naval Institute Press in 1983, which may be more thorough than earlier estimates but would not present significant changes for the issues under discussion. The same pattern is true for Axel Niestlé, *German U-Boat Losses During World War II: Details of Destruction* (Annapolis: Naval Institute Press, 1998). Niestlé (1–4) provides a brief summary of the various estimates. His estimates are highly correlated with earlier estimates.

Allied and neutral tonnage lost to submarines. They also capture the pattern of thrust and counterthrust that have marked the belligerents' responses to the imposition of blockades between countries of relatively equal economic and military strength.

From the German point of view, it was the tonnage of vessels sunk by submarines that provides the best measure of the "output"; but, even from the German point of view, sinkings were not necessarily the best measure of the economic effectiveness of the submarine blockade – the costs incurred in those sinkings also must be considered. As Tables 6.1 and 6.2 indicate, total Allied losses from all causes rose from something more than 750,000 tons in the fourth quarter of 1939 to more than 1.6 million tons in the second quarter of 1941; losses fell briefly over the rest of 1941, but surged to 2.2 million in the second quarter of 1942 (reaching a total of almost 7.8 million tons for the year). Thereafter the decline was fairly regular from 3.2 million tons in 1943 to slightly over one million tons in 1944.

Of the total of Allied and neutral vessel losses, submarines accounted for about 55 percent in 1939 and 1940; submarine sinkings may have fallen to 50 percent of the total in 1941; but they accounted for between 74 and 80 percent in 1942, 1943, and 1944, before declining to 64 percent in the last five months of the war.[155] In contrast, aircraft sank about 13 percent, mines 7 percent (but more than one-third in 1939 and one-fifth in 1945, when the war was centered more closely on the waters near Europe), and raiders, e-boats, and others, about 12 percent (see Table 6.3). In terms of location, more than 90 percent of Allied and neutral tonnage lost to submarine attack in the U-boat "heydays" of 1942 and the first quarter of 1943 were operating in the "Atlantic-Arctic" theater. Thereafter, however, sinkings in that very crucial route declined to less than half the total in 1944. The "North Atlantic" itself accounted for less than 17 percent of all losses that year before rising again in the few months of 1945, months that saw very few sinkings anywhere (see Tables 6.4 and 6.5).

Over the course of the war, despite U-boat losses that increased from an average of 29 per year in 1940–1941, to 237 in 1943, and to 242 in 1944, the German submarine force increased in size from less than sixty vessels to a fleet of more than 400 in 1943, 1944, and early 1945 (see Table 6.7). Moreover, of the 839 subs built between January 1942 and May 1945,

155 The percent of losses due to submarines exceeded 90 percent in seven of the 36 months in 1942, 1943, and 1944. The figure for 1941 reflects 421,000 tons of "unknown and other" causes. This includes 213 vessels, totaling 316,000 tons in December alone. If the excess of "unknown and other" in that year is distributed across all "known" categories, submarines would have accounted for about 55 percent of the total in that year as well.

Table 6.3. *Causes of Loss of Allied and Neutral Shipping from Enemy Action, Annual, 1939–1945*

Year	Submarines	Aircraft	Mines	Warship Raider	Merchant Raider	E-Boat	Unknown & Other	Total
				Panel A: Tonnage				
1939	421,156	2,949	262,542	61,337	0	0	7,253	755,237
1940	2,186,158	580,074	509,889	96,986	366,644	47,985	203,905	3,991,641
1941	2,171,754	1,017,422	230,842	201,823	226,527	58,854	421,336	4,328,558
1942	6,266,215	700,020	104,588	130,461	194,625	71,156	323,632	7,790,697
1943	2,586,905	424,411	108,658	0	41,848	15,138	43,177	3,220,137
1944	773,327	120,656	95,855	7,840	0	26,321	21,630	1,045,629
1945	281,716	44,351	93,663	0	0	10,222	8,869	438,821
1939–1945	14,687,231	2,889,883	1,406,037	498,447	829,644	229,676	1,029,802	21,570,720
				Panel B: Percentages of Total Loss				
1939	55.8	0.4	34.8	8.1	0.0	0.0	1.0	100.0
1940	54.8	14.5	12.8	2.4	9.2	1.2	5.1	100.0
1941	50.2	23.5	5.3	4.7	5.2	1.4	9.7	100.0
1942	80.4	9.0	1.3	1.7	2.5	0.9	4.2	100.0
1943	80.3	13.2	3.4	0.0	1.3	0.5	1.3	100.0
1944	74.0	11.5	9.2	0.7	0.0	2.5	2.1	100.0
1945	64.2	10.1	21.3	0.0	0.0	2.3	2.0	100.0
1939–1945	68.1	13.4	6.5	2.3	3.8	1.1	4.8	100.0

Source: Roskill, *Offensive: Part II*, 479.

Table 6.4. *German Submarine Fleet Changes, Monthly, September 1939 to May 1945*

Month	Year	Percent of Total Loss to Submarines	Percent Sunk in Atlantic-Arctic	Tonnage Lost per Submarine		Commissioned minus Sunk (1)	Comparison of Subs Added to Subs Sunk			Percent of Submarine Fleet Operational
				Operational Fleet	Total Fleet		Ratio Commissioned to Sunk (1)	Built minus Sunk (2)	Ratio Built to Sunk (2)	
September	1939	79.0		3,140	2,700	−1	0.50			86.0
October		68.7		2,996	2,365	−4	0.20			78.9
November		29.6		1,258	905	0	1.00			71.9
December		42.6		2,186	1,419	0	1.00			64.9
January	1940	51.9		3,477	1,987	1	1.50			57.1
February		74.7		4,710	3,140	−1	0.75			66.7
March		58.7		1,531	1,185	0	1.00			77.4
April		20.5		706	624	0	1.00			88.5
May		19.3		1,390	1,069	4	5.00			76.9
June		48.5		8,356	5,571	5				66.7
July		50.6		6,994	3,840	5	3.50			54.9
August		67.4		9,558	4,866	4	2.33			50.9
September		65.8		10,938	5,006	8				45.8
October		79.6		13,052	5,506	9	10.00			42.2
November		38.0		5,639	2,008	8	5.00			35.6
December		60.8		8,858	2,625	10				29.6
January	1941	39.6		5,763	1,425	15				24.7
February		48.8		8,199	2,071	16				25.3
March		45.9		8,679	2,337	11	3.20			26.9
April		36.3		7,793	2,207	15	8.50			28.3
May		63.7		7,570	2,543	17	18.00			33.6

(continued)

Table 6.4 (continued)

Month	Year	Percent of Total Loss to Submarines	Percent Sunk in Atlantic-Arctic	Tonnage Lost per Submarine Operational Fleet	Total Fleet	Comparison of Subs Added to Subs Sunk Commissioned minus Sunk (1)	Ratio Commissioned to Sunk (1)	Built minus Sunk (2)	Ratio Built to Sunk (2)	Percent of Submarine Fleet Operational
June		71.8		5,743	2,169	14	4.50			37.8
July		77.9		1,449	596	22	23.00			41.1
August		61.4		1,147	470	20	7.67			40.9
September		70.9		2,704	1,102	21	11.50			40.8
October		71.7		1,957	791	21	11.50			40.4
November		59.4		749	291	18	4.60			38.8
December		21.3		1,426	535	13	2.30			37.5
January	1942	78.0	82.6	3,597	1,315	13	5.33	17	6.67	36.5
February		70.1	91.0	4,717	1,825	14	8.00	16	9.00	38.7
March		64.5	96.2	4,847	1,971	11	2.83	13	3.17	40.7
April		64.0	88.7	3,567	1,515	16	6.33	20	7.67	42.5
May		86.1	96.5	4,781	2,024	16	5.00	16	5.00	42.3
June		83.9	86.2	5,265	2,223	17	6.67	20	7.67	42.2
July		77.0	89.5	3,400	1,438	9	1.82	7	1.64	42.3
August		82.3	96.7	3,446	1,592	10	2.00	11	2.22	46.2
September		85.6	93.6	2,742	1,371	10	1.91	7	1.70	50.0
October		97.1	95.3	3,160	1,697	7	1.44	7	1.44	53.7
November		90.3	89.5	3,628	1,950	10	1.77	4	1.31	53.7
December		94.8	83.7	1,606	864	18	4.60	21	5.20	53.8
January	1943	77.7	89.5	958	517	17	3.83	15	6.00	53.9
February		89.1	86.8	1,626	892	4	1.21	0	1.00	54.8
March		90.5	90.4	2,728	1,519	8	1.53	8	1.53	55.7
April		95.1	84.4	1,366	772	8	1.53	8	1.53	56.5

Month									
May	88.5	80.0	1,157	629	−17	0.59	−15	0.63	54.4
June	77.3	39.5	439	229	7	1.41	8	1.47	52.2
July	69.0	55.7	1,218	608	−17	0.54	−11	0.70	49.9
August	72.3	32.3	439	209	−5	0.80	−4	0.84	47.6
September	76.0	39.5	639	288	12	2.33	11	2.10	45.0
October	69.6	55.3	557	236	0	1.00	0	1.00	42.5
November	46.1	45.0	385	159	7	1.37	5	1.25	41.2
December	51.6	54.9	509	203	18	3.25	20	3.50	40.0
January 1944	70.6	39.1	549	212	5	1.33	6	1.40	38.5
February	79.5	7.6	553	212	1	1.05	−1	0.95	38.3
March	90.5	29.1	856	324	−4	0.84	−2	0.92	37.9
April	75.4	76.9	374	140	−4	0.81	2	1.10	37.4
May	89.5	70.7	141	55	−4	0.82	−2	0.91	39.2
June	55.6	66.6	306	130	−7	0.72	−13	0.48	42.4
July	80.4	52.4	337	146	−7	0.70	−10	0.60	43.3
August	83.5	41.5	571	233	−19	0.47	−20	0.43	40.9
September	96.8	86.9	276	105	−4	0.81	−1	0.95	38.1
October	61.5	0.0	51	18	8	1.42	5	1.42	35.2
November	77.9	52.6	208	72	15	3.14	15	3.14	34.7
December	43.4	87.7	409	140	8	1.57	17	2.31	34.3
January 1945	68.7	100.0	396	134			7	1.58	33.9
February	68.4	89.0	432	153			3	1.14	35.4
March	58.6	100.0	412	152			−11	0.69	37.0
April	69.8	100.0	440	170			−49	0.13	38.7
May	58.3	100.0							

Note: Sunk (1) is based on data in Roskill; Sunk (2) is based on Morison.

Source: See Tables 6.1 and 6.3.

Table 6.5 *German Submarine Fleet Changes, Quarterly and Annual, September 1939 to May 1945*

Year	Quarter	Percent of Allied Shipping Lost to Submarines (1)	Percent Sunk in Atlantic – Arctic (2)	Tonnage Lost Per Submarine — Operational Fleet (3)	Tonnage Lost Per Submarine — Total Fleet (4)	Comparison of Subs Added to Subs Sunk — Commissioned Minus Sunk (5)	Ratio Commissioned to Sunk (1) (6)	Built Minus Sunk (2) (7)	Ratio Built to Sunk (2) (8)	Percent of Submarine Fleet Operational (9)
1939	4*	55.8		9,794	7,389	−5	0.44			75.4
1940	1	62.7		9,457	6,324	0	1.00			66.9
1940	2	36.1		9,304	7,203	6	2.00			77.4
1940	3	61.6		27,426	13,796	17	4.40			50.3
1940	4	60.4		27,725	9,793	27	10.00			35.3
1941	1	45.2		22,970	5,902	42	9.40			25.7
1941	2	54.3		20,582	6,914	46	7.57			33.6
1941	3	70.2		5,391	2,207	63	11.50			40.9
1941	4	37.8		4,114	1,597	13	4.06			38.8
1942	1	69.4	91.0	13,286	5,141	38	4.45	46	5.18	38.7
1942	2	78.6	90.4	13,694	5,797	49	5.90	54	5.50	42.3
1942	3	81.6	93.4	7,492	4,399	29	1.91	25	1.57	46.3
1942	4	93.6	90.4	8,355	4,490	35	2.03	32	1.94	53.7

Year										
1943	1	87.6	89.2	5,384	2,952	29	1.73	23	1.62	54.8
1943	2	89.7	76.5	3,007	1,634	−2	0.97	1	1.01	54.4
1943	3	71.3	46.9	2,327	1,105	−10	0.86	−5	0.93	47.5
1943	4	55.4	52.4	1,451	598	25	1.47	26	1.49	41.2
1944	1	80.9	25.8	1,957	748	2	1.03	3	1.05	38.2
1944	2	67.6	71.7	821	326	−15	0.78	−13	0.81	39.7
1944	3	84.9	54.4	1,190	486	−30	0.63	−30	0.63	40.8
1944	4	51.6	70.2	671	233	31	1.91	37	2.16	34.7
1945	1	64.7	96.2	1,240	440			−2	0.97	35.4
1945	2**	68.2	100.0	1,000	387			−45	0.09	38.7
1939	*	55.8		9,794	7,389	−5	3.76			75.4
1940		54.8		16,860	9,365	50	3.17			55.5
1941		50.2		9,827	3,562	203	6.80			36.2
1942		80.8	90.8	10,669	4,906	151	2.74	157	2.65	46.0
1943		80.3	74.8	3,156	1,560	21	1.18	45	1.19	49.4
1944		74.0	47.5	1,175	451	−12	0.95	−3	0.99	38.4
1945	***	65.7	97.3	1,120	396			−47	0.49	36.3

* September through December.
** April through May 10 only.
*** January through May 10 only.
Source: See Table 6.4.

660 were the 500 ton Type VII-C, 146 were the 740 ton Type 1X-C, and 32 were the 1200 ton Type 1X-D. All were larger, faster, had longer ranges, and carried more torpedoes than the 250-ton boats that had comprised the bulk of the fleet in 1939.[156]

As a measure of the economic efficiency of a blockade, although total sinkings are important, the fraction of the fleet that is operational and the tonnage of vessels sunk per submarine are of at least equal importance in any cost/benefit calculation. In terms of the first, because of the need for "shake-down" cruises and training a rapid build-up increases the fraction of the fleet that is nonoperational. Thus, in 1939, 75 percent of the fleet was operational; but that figure fell to 55 percent in 1940 and to 36 percent in 1941. It rose somewhat, to 46 percent, in 1942, and 49 percent in 1943, before falling to 37 percent in the last seventeen months of the war. In the case of tonnage of vessels sunk per submarines, the figures in Tables 6.6, 6.7, 6.8, and 6.9, capture the increasing efficiency of the Allied antiblockade measures – particularly of the innovation of the aircraft-supported convoy and first, meter, and then, centimeter, band radar. Average sinkings per operational submarine rose in the last half of 1940 and the first two quarters of 1941, before falling between July and December. In response to the American entry into the war and the subsequent broadening of the "battlefield," the average rose over the first two quarters of 1942; but, thereafter the decline was sharp and fairly steady to 1945.[157] Moreover, an increasing fraction of those sinkings were not on the "North Atlantic Highway," the major route from North America to the British Isles. The percentage sunk in the Atlantic-Arctic area fell from more than 90 percent in 1942, to 75 percent in 1943, to less than 50 percent in 1944 (see Table 6.5). In that latter year, more than half of the million plus tons lost were sunk in theaters other than in the North Atlantic, the area around the United Kingdom, and the South Atlantic (see Table 6.10).

Moreover, by 1943 the sinkings were becoming more costly to the Germans in terms of the submarines lost. For example, from 1939 through 1942, the annual ratios of the number of submarines destroyed (sunk) to the average number of operational submarines, were .21, .72, .64, and .59. For 1943, however, they were 1.16, for 1944, 1.47, and for the first five

---

156 The Type VII-C carried 14 torpedoes, had a range of 6,500 miles and was capable of 17.0 knots on the surface, Type IX-C carried 21 to 23 torpedoes, had an 11,000-mile range, and was capable of 18.2 knots on the surface, and Type IX-D carried 27 torpedoes, with a 23,700-mile range, and a surface speed of 19.2 knots. There were also ten 9,300-ton Type XIV, with a torpedo capacity of 9, a surface speed of 14.4 knots, and a 9,300-mile cruising range. Morison, *Atlantic Battle Won*, 60.

157 In terms of tonnage sunk per U-boat in the fleet, the figures and trends are roughly parallel.

Table 6.6. *The German Submarine Fleet, Monthly Totals, September 1939 to May 1945*

Month	Year	Operational	Training and Trials	Total	Commissioned during Previous Quarter	Built	Sunk (1)	Sunk (2)
		(1)	(2)	(3)	(4)	(5)	(6)	(7)
September	1939	49	8	57	1		2	
October		45	12	57	1		5	
November		41	16	57	1		1	
December		37	20	57	1		1	
January	1940	32	24	56	3		2	
February		36	18	54	3		4	
March		41	12	53	3		3	
April		46	6	52	5		5	
May		40	12	52	5		1	
June		34	17	51	5		0	
July		28	23	51	7		2	
August		28	27	55	7		3	
September		27	32	59	8		0	
October		27	37	64	10		1	
November		26	47	73	10		2	
December		24	57	81	10		0	
January	1941	22	67	89	15		0	
February		24	71	95	16		0	
March		28	76	104	16		5	
April		32	81	113	17		2	
May		43	85	128	18		1	
June		54	89	143	18		4	
July		65	93	158	23		1	
August		70	101	171	23		3	
September		75	109	184	23		2	
October		80	118	198	23		2	
November		83	131	214	23		5	
December		87	145	232	23		10	
January	1942	91	158	249	16	20	3	3
February		101	160	261	16	18	2	2
March		111	162	273	17	19	6	6
April		121	164	285	19	23	3	3
May		127	173	300	20	20	4	4
June		133	182	315	20	23	3	3
July		140	191	331	20	18	11	11
August		158	184	342	20	20	10	9
September		177	177	354	21	17	11	10
October		196	169	365	23	23	16	16

(continued)

Table 6.6 *(continued)*

Month	Year	Operational	Training and Trials	Total	Commissioned during Previous Quarter	Built	Sunk (1)	Sunk (2)
		(1)	(2)	(3)	(4)	(5)	(6)	(7)
November		201	173	374	23	17	13	13
December		206	177	383	23	26	5	5
January	1943	212	181	393	23	18	6	6
February		221	182	403	23	19	19	19
March		230	183	413	23	23	15	15
April		240	185	425	23	23	15	15
May		229	192	421	24	26	41	41
June		218	200	418	24	25	17	17
July		207	208	415	20	26	37	37
August		197	217	414	20	21	25	25
September		186	227	413	21	21	9	10
October		175	237	412	26	26	26	26
November		173	247	420	26	25	19	20
December		171	257	428	26	28	8	8
January	1944	168	268	436	20	21	15	15
February		168	271	439	21	19	20	20
March		167	274	441	21	23	25	25
April		166	278	444	17	23	21	21
May		173	268	441	18	20	22	22
June		189	257	446	18	12	25	25
July		188	246	434	16	15	23	25
August		173	250	423	17	15	36	35
September		157	255	412	17	20	21	21
October		141	260	401	21	17	13	12
November		142	267	409	22	22	7	7
December		143	274	417	22	30	14	13
January	1945	144	281	425		19	14	12
February		151	275	426	n.d.	25	22	22
March		158	269	427	n.d.	25	32	36
April		166	263	429	n.d.	7	55	56
May		n.d.	n.d.	n.d.	n.d.	1	28	36

Sources: (1) thru (5) Roskill, *Defensive*, 614; *Period of Balance*, 475, *Offensive, Part I*, 364. Data extrapolated between end of quarter reports.
(6) Roskill, *Defensive*, 599–601; *Period of Balance*, 467–471; *Offensive, Part I*, 365–372; *Offensive, Part II*, 463–469.
(7) Morison, *Battle of the Atlantic*, 415; Morison, *Atlantic Battle Won*, 366.

Table 6.7. *The German Submarine Fleet, Quarterly and Annual Totals, September 1939 to May 1945*

Year	Quarter	Number of German Submarines						
		Operational	Training & Trials	Total	Commissioned	Built	Sunk (1)	Sunk (2)
		(1)	(2)	(3)	(4)	(5)	(6)	(7)
1939	4*	43	14	57	4		9	
1940	1	36	18	54	9		9	
	2	40	12	52	15		6	
	3	28	27	55	22		5	
	4	26	47	73	30		3	
1941	1	25	71	96	47		5	
	2	43	85	128	53		7	
	3	70	101	171	69		6	
	4	83	131	215	69		17	
1942	1	101	160	261	49	57	11	11
	2	127	173	300	59	66	10	10
	3	158	184	342	61	55	32	30
	4	201	173	374	69	66	34	34
1943	1	221	182	403	69	60	40	40
	2	229	192	421	71	74	73	73
	3	197	217	414	61	68	71	72
	4	173	247	420	78	79	53	54
1944	1	168	271	439	62	63	60	60
	2	176	268	444	53	55	68	68
	3	173	250	423	50	50	80	80
	4	142	267	409	65	69	34	32
1945	1	151	275	426	0	69	68	70
	2**	83	132	215	0	8	83	92
1939	*	43	14	57	4		9	
1940		32	26	59	73	0	23	–
1941		55	97	152	238	0	35	–
1942		147	173	319	238	244	87	85
1943		205	210	415	279	281	237	239
1944		165	264	429	230	237	242	240
1945	***	124	218	341	0	77	151	162

* September through December.
** April through May 10 only (two months).
*** January through May 10 only.
Source: See Table 6.6; also German Naval History, *The U-boat War in the Atlantic, 1939–1945* (London: HMSO, 1989), 72, 112, diagram 30.

Table 6.8. German Submarine Data, Monthly, September 1939 to May 1945

Month	Year	Tonnage of Allied & Neutral Shipping Lost to Submarines	Number of Submarines								Allied Tonnage Lost Per Operational German Submarine	Allied Tonnage Lost Per Total German Submarines	Allied Tonnage Lost Per German Submarine Sunk (1)	Allied Tonnage Lost Per German Submarine Sunk (2)
			Operational	Training & Trials	Total	Built or Commissioned	Sunk (1)	Sunk (2)	Built or Commissioned Minus Sunk (1)	Built or Commissioned Minus Sunk (2)				
September	1939	153,879	49	8	57	1	2		−1		3,140	2,700	76,940	
October		134,807	45	12	57	1	5		−4		2,996	2,365	26,961	
November		51,589	41	16	57	1	1		0		1,258	905	51,589	
December		80,881	37	20	57	1	1		0		2,186	1,419	80,881	
January	1940	111,263	32	24	56	3	2		1		3,477	1,987	55,632	
February		169,566	36	18	54	3	4		−1		4,710	3,140	42,392	
March		62,781	41	12	53	3	3		0		1,531	1,185	20,927	
April		32,467	46	6	52	5	5		0		706	624	6,493	
May		55,580	40	12	52	5	1		0		1,390	1,069	55,580	
June		284,113	34	17	51	5	0		4		8,356	5,571		
July		195,825	28	23	51	7	2		5		6,994	3,840	97,913	
August		267,618	28	27	55	7	3		5		9,558	4,866	89,206	
September		295,335	27	32	59	8	0		4		10,938	5,006		
October		352,407	27	37	64	10	1		8		13,052	5,506	352,407	
November		146,613	26	47	73	10	2		9		5,839	2,008	73,307	
December		212,590	24	57	81	10	0		8		8,858	2,625		
January	1941	126,782	22	67	89	15	0		10		5,763	1,425		
February		196,783	24	71	95	16	0		15		8,199	2,071		
March		243,020	28	76	104	16	5		16		8,679	2,337	48,604	
April		249,375	32	81	113	17	2		15		7,793	2,207	124,688	
May		325,492	43	85	128	18	1		17		7,570	2,543	325,492	
June		310,143	54	89	143	18	4		14		5,743	2,169	77,536	
July		94,209	65	93	158	23	1		22		1,449	596	94,209	
August		80,310	70	101	171	23	3		20		1,147	470	26,770	
September		202,820	75	109	184	23	2		21		2,704	1,102	101,410	

Month	Year													
October		156,554	80	118	198	23	2		21		1,957	791	78,277	
November		62,196	83	131	214	23	5		18		749	291	12,439	
December		124,070	87	145	232	23	10		13		1,426	535	12,407	
January	1942	327,357	91	158	249	16	3	3	13	13	3,597	1,315	109,119	109,119
February		476,451	101	160	261	16	2	2	14	14	4,717	1,825	238,226	238,226
March		537,980	111	162	273	17	6	6	11	11	4,847	1,971	89,663	89,663
April		431,664	121	164	285	19	3	3	16	16	3,567	1,515	143,888	143,888
May		607,247	127	173	300	20	4	4	16	16	4,781	2,024	151,812	151,812
June		700,235	133	182	315	20	3	3	17	17	5,265	2,223	233,412	233,412
July		476,065	140	191	331	20	11	11	9	9	3,400	1,438	43,279	43,279
August		544,410	158	184	342	20	10	9	10	11	3,446	1,592	54,441	60,490
September		485,413	177	177	354	21	11	10	10	11	2,742	1,371	44,128	48,541
October		619,417	196	169	385	23	16	16	7	7	3,160	1,697	38,714	38,714
November		729,160	201	173	374	23	13	13	10	10	3,628	1,950	56,089	56,089
December		330,816	206	177	383	23	5	5	18	18	1,606	864	66,163	66,163
January	1943	203,128	212	181	393	23	8	6	17	20	958	517	33,855	67,709
February		359,328	221	182	403	23	19	19	4	4	1,626	892	18,912	18,912
March		627,377	230	183	413	23	15	15	8	8	2,728	1,519	41,825	41,825
April		327,943	240	185	425	23	15	15	8	8	1,366	772	21,863	21,863
May		264,852	229	192	421	24	41	41	-17	-17	1,157	629	6,460	6,480
June		95,753	218	200	418	24	17	17	7	7	439	229	5,633	5,633
July		252,145	207	208	415	20	37	37	-17	-17	1,218	608	6,815	6,815
August		86,579	197	217	414	20	25	25	-5	-5	439	209	3,463	3,463
September		118,841	186	227	413	21	9	10	12	11	639	288	13,205	11,884
October		97,407	175	237	412	26	26	26	0	0	557	236	3,746	3,746
November		66,585	173	247	420	26	19	19	7	6	385	159	3,504	3,329
December		86,967	171	257	428	26	8	8	18	18	509	203	10,871	10,871

(continued)

Table 6.8 (continued)

Month	Year	Tonnage of Allied & Neutral Shipping Lost to Submarines	Number of Submarines								Allied Tonnage Lost Per Operational German Submarine	Allied Tonnage Lost Per Total German Submarines	Allied Tonnage Lost Per German Submarine Sunk (1)	Allied Tonnage Lost Per German Submarine Sunk (2)
			Operational	Training & Trials	Total	Built or Commissioned	Sunk (1)	Sunk (2)	Built or Commissioned Minus Sunk (1)	Built or Commissioned Minus Sunk (2)				
January	1944	92,278	168	268	436	20	15	15	5	5	549	212	6,152	6,152
February		92,923	168	271	439	21	20	20	1	1	553	212	4,646	4,646
March		142,944	167	274	441	21	25	25	-4	-4	856	324	5,718	5,718
April		62,149	166	278	444	17	21	21	-4	-4	374	140	2,959	2,959
May		24,424	173	268	441	18	22	22	-4	-4	141	55	1,110	1,110
June		57,875	189	257	446	18	25	25	-7	-7	306	130	2,315	2,315
July		63,351	188	246	434	16	23	25	-7	-9	337	146	2,754	2,534
August		98,729	173	250	423	17	36	32	-19	-15	571	233	2,742	2,821
September		43,368	157	255	412	17	21	18	-4	-1	276	105	2,065	2,065
October		7,176	141	260	401	21	13	12	8	9	51	18	552	598
November		29,592	142	267	409	22	7	7	15	15	208	72	4,227	4,227
December		58,518	143	274	417	22	14	13	8	9	409	140	4,180	4,501
January	1945	56,988	144	281	425	19	14	12	5	7	396	134	4,071	4,749
February		65,233	151	275	426	25	22	22	3	3	432	153	2,965	2,965
March		65,077	158	269	427	25	32	36	-7	-11	412	152	2,034	1,808
April		72,957	166	263	429	7	55	56	-48	-49	440	170	1,326	1,303
May		10,022	n.d.	n.d.	n.d.	1	20	36	-27	-35			358	278

Source: See Tables 6.1 and 6.6.

Table 6.9. German Submarine Data: Quarterly and Annual Totals, September 1939 to May 1945

(Quarterly Totals)   *(Monthly Totals)*

Year	Quarter	Total Tonnage of Allied & Neutral Shipping Lost To Submarines	Monthly Average of Allied & Neutral Shipping Lost To Submarines	Monthly Average Operational	Monthly Average Training & Trials	Total	Built or Commissioned	Sunk (1)	Sunk (2)	Built or Commissioned Minus Sunk (1)	Built or Commissioned Minus Sunk (2)	Allied Tonnage Lost Per Operational German submarine	Allied Tonnage Lost Per Total German Submarines	Allied Tonnage Lost Per German Submarine Sunk (1)	Allied Tonnage Lost Per German Submarine Sunk (2)
1939	4*	421,156	105,289	43.00	14.00	57.00	4	9		-5		2,449	1,847	46,795	
1940	1	343,610	114,537	36.33	18.00	54.33	9	9		0		3,152	2,108	38,179	
	2	372,160	124,053	40.00	11.67	51.67	15	6		9		3,101	2,401	62,027	
	3	758,778	252,926	27.67	27.33	55.00	22	5		17		9,142	4,599	151,756	
	4	711,610	237,203	25.67	47.00	72.67	30	3		27		9,242	3,264	237,203	
1941	1	566,585	188,862	24.67	71.33	96.00	47	5		42		7,657	1,967	113,317	
	2	885,010	295,003	43.00	85.00	128.00	53	7		46		6,861	2,305	126,430	
	3	377,339	125,780	70.00	101.00	171.00	69	6		63		1,797	736	62,890	
	4	342,820	114,273	83.33	131.33	214.67	69	17		52		1,371	532	20,166	
1942	1	1,341,788	447,263	101.00	160.00	261.00	49	11	11	38	38	4,428	1,714	121,981	121,981
	2	1,739,146	579,715	127.00	173.00	300.00	59	10	10	49	49	4,565	1,932	173,915	179,915
	3	1,505,888	501,963	158.33	184.00	342.33	61	32	30	29	31	3,170	1,466	47,059	50,196
	4	1,679,393	559,798	201.00	173.00	374.00	69	34	34	35	35	2,785	1,497	49,394	49,394
1943	1	1,189,833	396,611	221.00	182.00	403.00	69	40	40	29	29	1,795	984	29,746	32,158
	2	688,548	229,516	229.00	192.33	421.33	71	73	73	-2	-2	1,002	545	9,432	9,432
	3	457,565	152,522	196.67	217.33	414.00	61	71	72	-10	-11	776	368	6,445	6,355
	4	250,959	83,653	173.00	247.00	420.00	78	53	53	25	25	484	199	4,735	4,647
1944	1	328,145	109,382	167.67	271.00	438.67	62	60	60	2	2	652	249	5,469	5,469
	2	144,448	48,149	176.00	267.67	443.67	53	68	68	-15	-15	274	109	2,124	2,124
	3	205,448	68,483	172.67	250.33	423.00	50	80	81	-30	-31	397	162	2,568	2,739
	4	95,286	31,762	142.00	267.00	409.00	65	34	32	31	33	224	78	2,803	2,978
1945	1	187,298	62,433	151.00	275.00	426.00	69	68	70	1	-1	413	147	2,754	2,676
	2**	82,979	41,490	166.00	263.00	429.00	8	83	92	-75	-84	250	97	1,000	902
1939	*	421,156	105,289	43.00	14.00	57.00	4	9		-5	4	2,449	1,847	35,996	
1940		2,186,158	182,180	32.42	26.00	58.42	76	23		53	76	5,620	3,119	23,763	
1941		2,171,754	180,980	55.25	97.17	152.42	238	35		203	238	3,276	1,188	15,513	
1942		6,266,215	522,192	146.83	172.50	319.33	238	87	85	151	153	3,556	1,635	18,007	18,430
1943		2,586,905	215,576	204.92	209.67	414.58	279	237	238	42	41	1,052	520	2,729	2,717
1944		773,327	64,427	164.58	264.00	428.58	230	242	241	-12	-5	392	150	799	802
1945	***	270,277	22,726	123.80	217.60	341.40	77	151	162	-74	-85	437	158	1,074	1,001

Number of Submarines columns: Monthly Average Operational, Monthly Average Training & Trials, Total, Built or Commissioned, Sunk (1), Sunk (2), Built or Commissioned Minus Sunk (1), Built or Commissioned Minus Sunk (2).

* September through December.   ** April through May 10 only.   *** January through May 10 only.   Source: Tables 6.3 and 6.6.

301

Table 6.10. *Allied and Neutral Shipping Lost, Monthly Totals, September 1939 to May 1945*

		Tonnage Lost by Theater					Percentage Lost by Theater				
Month	Year	North Atlantic	United Kingdom	South Atlantic	Other	Total	North Atlantic	United Kingdom	South Atlantic	Other	Total
		(1)	(2)	(3)	(4)	(5)	(1)	(2)	(3)	(4)	(5)
September	1939	104,829	84,965	5,051	0	194,845	53.8	43.6	2.6	0.0	100.0
October		110,619	63,368	22,368	0	196,355	56.3	32.3	11.4	0.0	100.0
November		17,895	155,668	0	706	174,269	10.3	89.3	0.0	0.4	100.0
December		15,852	152,107	21,964	0	189,923	8.3	80.1	11.6	0.0	100.0
January	1940	35,970	178,536	0	0	214,506	16.8	83.2	0.0	0.0	100.0
February		74,759	152,161	0	0	226,920	32.9	67.1	0.0	0.0	100.0
March		11,215	95,794	0	0	107,009	10.5	89.5	0.0	0.0	100.0
April		24,570	133,648	0	0	158,218	15.5	84.5	0.0	0.0	100.0
May		49,087	230,607	6,199	2,568	288,461	17.0	79.9	2.1	0.9	100.0
June		296,529	208,924	0	80,043	585,496	50.6	35.7	0.0	13.7	100.0
July		141,474	192,331	31,269	21,839	386,913	36.6	49.7	8.1	5.6	100.0
August		190,048	162,956	0	44,225	397,229	47.8	41.0	0.0	11.1	100.0
September		254,553	131,150	17,801	45,117	448,621	56.7	29.2	4.0	10.1	100.0
October		286,644	131,620	0	24,721	442,985	64.7	29.7	0.0	5.6	100.0
November		201,341	92,713	0	91,661	385,715	52.2	24.0	0.0	23.8	100.0
December		239,304	83,308	0	26,956	349,568	68.5	23.8	0.0	7.7	100.0
January	1941	214,382	36,975	58,585	10,298	320,240	66.9	11.5	18.3	3.2	100.0
February		317,378	51,381	0	34,634	403,393	78.7	12.7	0.0	8.6	100.0
March		364,689	152,862	0	12,155	529,706	68.8	28.9	0.0	2.3	100.0
April		260,451	99,031	21,807	306,612	687,901	37.9	14.4	3.2	44.6	100.0
May		324,550	100,655	11,339	74,498	511,042	63.5	19.7	2.2	14.6	100.0
June		318,740	86,381	10,134	16,770	432,025	73.8	20.0	2.3	3.9	100.0
July		97,813	15,265	0	7,897	120,975	80.9	12.6	0.0	6.5	100.0

Month	Year									
August		83,661	19,791	0	27,247	130,699	64.0	15.1	0.0	20.8	100.0
September		184,546	54,779	15,526	31,091	285,942	64.5	19.2	5.4	10.9	100.0
October		154,593	35,996	5,297	22,403	218,289	70.8	16.5	2.4	10.3	100.0
November		50,215	30,332	4,953	19,140	104,640	48.0	29.0	4.7	18.3	100.0
December		50,682	56,845	6,275	469,904	583,706	8.7	9.7	1.1	80.5	100.0
January	1942	276,795	19,341	0	123,771	419,907	65.9	4.6	0.0	29.5	100.0
February		429,891	11,098	0	238,643	679,632	63.3	1.6	0.0	35.1	100.0
March		534,064	15,147	13,125	271,828	834,164	64.0	1.8	1.6	32.6	100.0
April		391,044	54,589	48,177	180,647	674,457	58.0	8.1	7.1	26.8	100.0
May		576,350	59,396	9,081	60,223	705,050	81.7	8.4	1.3	8.5	100.0
June		623,545	2,655	26,287	181,709	834,196	74.7	0.3	3.2	21.8	100.0
July		486,965	22,557	23,972	84,619	618,113	78.8	3.6	3.9	13.7	100.0
August		508,426	0	35,494	117,213	661,133	76.9	0.0	5.4	17.7	100.0
September		473,585	1,892	57,797	34,053	567,327	83.5	0.3	10.2	6.0	100.0
October		399,715	12,733	148,142	77,243	637,833	62.7	2.0	23.2	12.1	100.0
November		508,707	6,363	58,662	234,022	807,754	63.0	0.8	7.3	29.0	100.0
December		262,135	9,114	43,496	34,157	348,902	75.1	2.6	12.5	9.8	100.0
January	1943	172,691	15,819	16,116	56,733	261,359	66.1	6.1	6.2	21.7	100.0
February		288,625	4,925	21,656	87,856	403,062	71.6	1.2	5.4	21.8	100.0
March		476,349	884	61,462	154,694	693,389	68.7	0.1	8.9	22.3	100.0
April		235,478	9,926	7,129	92,147	344,680	68.3	2.9	2.1	26.7	100.0
May		163,507	1,568	40,523	93,830	299,428	54.6	0.5	13.5	31.3	100.0
June		18,379	149	11,587	93,710	123,825	14.8	0.1	9.4	75.7	100.0
July		123,327	72	64,478	177,521	365,398	33.8	0.0	17.6	48.6	100.0
August		10,186	19	15,368	94,228	119,801	8.5	0.0	12.8	78.7	100.0
September		43,775	0	10,770	101,874	156,419	28.0	0.0	6.9	65.1	100.0
October		56,422	0	4,663	78,776	139,861	40.3	0.0	3.3	56.3	100.0
November		23,077	13,036	4,573	103,705	144,391	16.0	9.0	3.2	71.8	100.0
December		47,785	6,086	0	114,653	168,524	28.4	3.6	0.0	68.0	100.0

(continued)

Table 6.10 (continued)

Month	Year	Tonnage Lost by Theater					Percentage Lost by Theater				
		North Atlantic	United Kingdom	South Atlantic	Other	Total	North Atlantic	United Kingdom	South Atlantic	Other	Total
		(1)	(2)	(3)	(4)	(5)	(1)	(2)	(3)	(4)	(5)
January	1944	36,065	6,944	0	87,626	130,635	27.6	5.3	0.0	67.1	100.0
February		12,577	4,051	0	100,227	116,855	10.8	3.5	0.0	85.8	100.0
March		36,867	0	4,695	116,398	157,960	23.3	0.0	3.0	73.7	100.0
April		34,224	468	13,539	34,141	82,372	41.5	0.6	16.4	41.4	100.0
May		0	0	17,277	10,020	27,297	0.0	0.0	63.3	36.7	100.0
June		4,294	75,166	3,268	21,356	104,084	4.1	72.2	3.1	20.5	100.0
July		15,480	19,038	14,062	30,176	78,756	19.7	24.1	17.9	38.3	100.0
August		5,685	54,834	0	57,785	118,304	4.8	46.4	0.0	48.8	100.0
September		16,535	21,163	0	7,107	44,805	36.9	47.2	0.0	15.9	100.0
October		0	1,722	0	9,946	11,668	0.0	14.8	0.0	85.2	100.0
November		7,828	8,880	0	21,272	37,980	20.6	23.4	0.0	56.0	100.0
December		5,458	85,639	0	43,816	134,913	4.0	63.5	0.0	32.5	100.0
January	1945	29,168	46,553	0	7,176	82,897	35.2	56.2	0.0	8.7	100.0
February		32,453	48,551	7,136	7,176	95,316	34.0	50.9	7.5	7.5	100.0
March		23,684	83,664	3,656	0	111,004	21.3	75.4	3.3	0.0	100.0
April		32,071	49,619	0	22,822	104,512	30.7	47.5	0.0	21.8	100.0
May		5,353	4,669	0	7,176	17,198	31.1	27.1	0.0	41.7	100.0

Sources: Columns (1) through (5): Roskill, *Defensive*, 617–618; *Period of Balance*, 486; *Offensive, Part I*, 389; *Offensive, Part II*, 478.

Table 6.11. *Allied and Neutral Shipping Lost, Quarterly and Annual Totals, September 1939 to May 1945*

Year	Quarter	Tonnage of Allied and Neutral Shipping Lost By Theater					Percentage of Allied and Neutral Shipping Lost By Theatre				
		North Atlantic	United Kingdom	South Atlantic	Other	Total	North Atlantic	United Kingdom	South Atlantic	Other	Total
		(1)	(2)	(3)	(4)	(5)	(1)	(2)	(3)	(4)	(5)
1939	4*	249,195	456,108	49,383	706	755,392	33.0	60.4	6.5	0.1	100.0
1940	1	121,944	426,491	0	0	548,435	22.2	77.8	0.0	0.0	100.0
	2	370,186	573,179	6,199	82,611	1,032,175	35.9	55.5	0.6	8.0	100.0
	3	586,075	486,437	49,070	111,181	1,232,763	47.5	39.5	4.0	9.0	100.0
	4	727,289	307,641	0	143,338	1,178,268	61.7	26.1	0.0	12.2	100.0
1941	1	896,449	241,218	58,585	57,087	1,253,339	71.5	19.2	4.7	4.6	100.0
	2	903,741	286,067	43,280	397,880	1,630,968	55.4	17.5	2.7	24.4	100.0
	3	366,020	89,835	15,526	66,235	537,616	68.1	16.7	2.9	12.3	100.0
	4	255,490	123,173	16,525	511,447	906,635	28.2	13.6	1.8	56.4	100.0
1942	1	1,240,750	45,586	13,125	634,242	1,933,703	64.2	2.4	0.7	32.8	100.0
	2	1,590,939	116,640	83,545	422,579	2,213,703	71.9	5.3	3.8	19.1	100.0
	3	1,468,976	24,449	117,263	235,885	1,846,573	79.6	1.3	6.4	12.8	100.0
	4	1,170,557	28,210	250,300	345,422	1,794,489	65.2	1.6	13.9	19.2	100.0
1943	1	937,665	21,628	99,234	299,283	1,357,810	69.1	1.6	7.3	22.0	100.0
	2	417,364	11,643	59,239	279,687	767,933	54.3	1.5	7.7	36.4	100.0
	3	177,288	91	90,616	373,623	641,618	27.6	0.0	14.1	58.2	100.0
	4	127,284	19,122	9,236	297,134	452,776	28.1	4.2	2.0	65.6	100.0

(continued)

Table 6.11. (continued)

Year	Quarter	Tonnage of Allied and Neutral Shipping Lost By Theater					Percentage of Allied and Neutral Shipping Lost By Theatre				
		North Atlantic	United Kingdom	South Atlantic	Other	Total	North Atlantic	United Kingdom	South Atlantic	Other	Total
		(1)	(2)	(3)	(4)	(5)	(1)	(2)	(3)	(4)	(5)
1944	1	85,509	10,995	4,695	304,251	405,450	21.1	2.7	1.2	75.0	100.0
	2	38,518	75,634	34,084	65,517	213,753	18.0	35.4	15.9	30.7	100.0
	3	37,700	95,035	14,062	95,068	241,865	15.6	39.3	5.8	39.3	100.0
	4	13,286	96,241	0	75,034	184,561	7.2	52.1	0.0	40.7	100.0
1945	1	85,305	178,968	10,792	14,352	289,217	29.5	61.8	3.7	5.0	100.0
	2**	37,424	54,288	0	29,998	121,710	30.7	44.6	0.0	24.6	100.0
1939	*	249,195	456,108	49,383	706	755,392	33.0	60.4	6.5	0.1	100.0
1940		1,805,494	1,793,748	55,269	337,130	3,991,641	45.2	44.9	1.4	8.4	100.0
1941		2,421,700	740,293	133,916	1,032,649	4,328,558	55.9	17.1	3.1	23.9	100.0
1942		5,471,222	214,885	464,233	1,638,128	7,788,468	70.2	2.8	6.0	21.0	100.0
1943		1,659,601	52,484	258,325	1,249,727	3,220,137	51.5	1.6	8.0	38.8	100.0
1944		175,013	277,905	52,841	539,870	1,045,629	16.7	26.6	5.1	51.6	100.0
1945	***	122,729	233,056	10,792	44,350	410,927	29.9	56.7	2.6	10.8	100.0

* September through December.
** April through May 10 only.
*** January through May 10 only.
Source: See Table 6.10.

306

months of 1945, 1.22. Similarly, the ratio of submarines commissioned to submarines sunk was .44, 3.2, and 6.8 for the years 1939 through 1941. However, for the three years 1942, 1943, and 1944 it was 2.7, 1.2, and 1.0. And in 1945, although the Germans managed to build 77 submarines, the Allies sank either 151 or 162 (see Tables 6.6 and 6.7).[158]

But submarine sinkings and submarine losses were, at most, only half of the picture. They might well have been the whole story, if the Allies had not been able to add to the stock of merchant shipping after the outbreak of hostilities; but, unfortunately from the German point of view, such was not to be the case. In fact, the ability of the Allies, particularly the Americans, to build merchant ships makes the German submarine construction effort appear almost preindustrial. In 1939 the Allies built and delivered about 380,000 tons of new shipping. In that year, German submarines alone sank some 421,000 tons. If other causes of loss are added, the Allied merchant fleet was 376,000 tons smaller at the end of the year than it was on September 3. In 1940, the Allied shipyards added 1,418,000 tons, and in 1941 another 1,975,000 tons; but losses to submarines and other causes swamped the effort. During 1940 and 1941 the Allied fleet had shrunk by an additional 4,938,000 tons. At that point, however, the efforts of Henry Kaiser and his peers began to be felt. In 1939, 1940, and 1941, the Americans had produced 39, 45, and 59 percent of the total of Allied merchantmen built and delivered. Over the ensuing three years and the first five months of 1945, American shipyards were responsible for 79, 89, 89, and 94 percent of the total; and it was a much larger total. Allied production added 8,757,000 tons in 1942, 20,126,000 in 1943, 15,578,000 in 1944, and 5,497,000 in 1945. So successful was the effort that by 1944 the U.S. government had begun to reduce its orders for merchant vessels. As a result, despite total losses from 1942 to 1945 of 12,465,000 tons (9,897,000 to submarines), in May 1945 the Allied merchant fleet was 37,493,000 tons larger than it had been at the end of December 1941 (see Table 6.13).[159]

If a hypothetical German submarine fleet had been able to sustain the actual level of tonnage sunk per submarine needed to offset Allied production, they would have had to build and commission twenty-two submarines in 1939, twelve in 1940, and twenty-five in 1941. In fact, although

---

158 The ratio of sunk to total fleet were .16, .39, .23, .27, .57, .56, .44.

159 It might be noted, that, on the other war front, although the Japanese built or captured more than 900,000 tons of civilian shipping in 1942, thereafter construction and capture lagged and the stock of merchant shipping declined (due largely to the U.S. naval attacks) to 1.5 million tons by August 1945. Over the same period the tonnage "available" had declined by almost 4.6 million tons. Roskill, *Offensive, Part II*, 367.

Table 6.12. Allied Merchant Vessel Construction, Monthly Totals, September 1939 to May 1945

Month	Year	Tonnage of Allied and Neutral Shipping Lost to All Causes	Tonnage of Allied and Neutral Shipping Lost to Submarines	Tonnage of Merchant Vessels Built and Delivered by U.S. Shipyards	Est. Tonnage Built and Delivered by U.K. Shipyards	Est. Tonnage of Merchant Vessels Built and Delivered by U.S. & U.K. Shipyards	Net Change in the Stock of Allied Merchant Shipping Due to Allied Production	Net Change in the Stock of Allied Merchant Shipping Due to U.S. Production	US Percent of Merchant Vessels Built and Delivered by U.S. & U.K. Shipyards	Actual Number of Operational German Submarines	Allied Tonnage Lost Per Operational German Submarine	Number of Additional Operational Submarines Needed to Offset Allied Production	Number of Additional Operational Submarines Needed to Offset U.S. Production	Actual Number of German Submarines Commissioned or Built	Percent of Submarines Commissioned or Built to Needed
		(1)	(2)	(3)	(4)	(5)	(6)	(7)	(8)	(9)	(10)	(11)	(12)	(13)	(14)
September	1939	194,845	153,879	56,965	57,750	114,715	−80,130	−137,880	49.7	49	3,140	37	18	1	2.74
October		196,355	134,807	17,840	57,750	75,590	−120,765	−178,515	23.6	45	2,996	25	6	1	3.96
November		174,269	51,589	27,776	57,750	85,526	−88,743	−146,493	32.5	41	1,258	68	22	1	1.47
December		189,923	80,881	45,966	57,750	103,716	−86,207	−143,957	44.3	37	2,186	47	21	1	2.11
January	1940	214,506	111,263	39,734	65,000	104,734	−109,772	−174,772	37.9	32	3,477	30	11	3	9.96
February		226,920	169,566	18,827	65,000	83,827	−143,093	−208,093	22.5	36	4,710	18	4	3	16.86
March		107,009	62,781	48,072	65,000	113,072	6,063	−58,937	42.5	41	1,531	74	31	3	4.06
April		158,218	32,467	64,219	65,000	129,219	−28,999	−93,999	49.7	46	706	183	91	5	2.73
May		288,461	55,580	44,457	65,000	109,457	−179,004	−244,004	40.6	40	1,390	79	32	5	6.35
June		585,496	284,113	32,399	65,000	97,399	−488,097	−553,097	33.3	34	8,356	12	4	5	42.90
July		386,913	195,825	105,121	65,000	170,121	−216,792	−281,792	61.8	28	6,994	24	15	7	28.78
August		397,229	267,618	31,514	65,000	96,514	−300,715	−365,715	32.7	28	9,558	10	3	7	69.32
September		448,621	295,335	40,709	65,000	105,709	−342,912	−407,912	38.5	27	10,938	10	4	8	82.78
October		442,985	352,407	59,658	65,000	124,658	−318,327	−383,327	47.9	27	13,052	10	5	10	104.70
November		385,715	146,613	90,403	65,000	155,403	−230,312	−295,312	58.2	26	5,639	28	16	10	36.29
December		349,568	212,590	62,924	65,000	127,924	−221,644	−286,644	49.2	24	8,858	14	7	10	69.24
January	1941	320,240	126,782	48,605	67,917	116,522	−203,718	−271,635	41.7	22	5,763	20	8	15	74.19
February		403,393	196,783	40,519	67,917	108,436	−294,957	−362,874	37.4	24	8,199	13	5	16	120.98
March		529,706	243,020	114,605	67,917	182,522	−347,184	−415,101	62.8	28	8,679	21	13	16	76.08
April		687,901	249,375	119,431	67,917	187,348	−500,553	−568,470	63.7	32	7,793	24	15	17	70.71
May		511,042	325,492	117,421	67,917	185,338	−325,704	−393,621	63.4	43	7,570	24	16	18	73.52
June		432,025	310,143	103,266	67,917	171,183	−260,842	−328,759	60.3	54	5,743	30	18	18	60.39
July		120,975	94,269	94,341	67,917	162,258	41,283	−26,634	58.1	65	1,449	112	65	23	20.54

Month	Year													
August		130,699	80,310	129,342	67,917	197,259	66,560	−1,357	65.6	70	1,147	172	113	23	13.38
September		285,942	202,820	86,335	67,917	154,252	−131,690	−199,607	56.0	75	2,704	57	32	23	40.32
October		218,289	156,554	75,296	67,917	143,213	−75,076	−142,993	52.6	80	1,957	73	38	23	31.43
November		104,640	62,196	138,254	67,917	206,171	101,531	33,614	67.1	83	749	275	184	23	8.36
December		583,706	124,070	92,350	67,917	160,267	−423,439	−491,356	57.6	87	1,426	112	65	23	20.47
January	1942	419,907	327,357	198,122	153,583	351,705	−68,202	−221,785	56.3	91	3,597	98	55	16	16.37
February		679,632	476,451	290,054	153,583	443,637	−235,995	−389,578	65.4	101	4,717	94	61	16	17.01
March		834,164	537,980	291,473	153,583	445,056	−389,108	−542,691	65.5	111	4,847	92	60	17	18.51
April		674,457	431,664	402,182	153,583	555,765	−118,692	−272,275	72.4	121	3,567	156	113	19	12.20
May		705,050	607,247	610,338	153,583	763,921	58,871	−94,712	79.9	127	4,781	160	128	20	12.52
June		834,196	700,235	711,936	153,583	865,519	31,323	−122,260	82.3	133	5,265	164	135	20	12.17
July		618,113	476,065	773,167	153,583	926,750	308,637	155,054	83.4	140	3,400	273	227	20	7.34
August		661,133	544,410	725,805	153,583	879,388	218,255	64,672	82.5	158	3,446	255	211	20	7.84
September		567,327	485,413	95,267	153,583	248,850	−318,477	−472,060	38.3	177	2,742	91	35	21	23.14
October		637,833	619,417	851,922	153,583	1,005,505	367,672	214,089	84.7	196	3,160	318	270	23	7.23
November		807,754	729,160	855,071	153,583	1,008,654	200,900	47,317	84.8	201	3,628	278	236	23	8.27
December		348,902	330,816	1,108,653	153,583	1,262,236	913,334	759,751	87.8	206	1,606	786	690	20	2.93
January	1943	261,359	203,128	942,876	183,417	1,126,293	864,934	681,517	83.7	212	958	1,175	984	23	1.96
February		403,062	359,328	1,136,108	183,417	1,319,525	916,463	733,046	86.1	221	1,626	812	699	23	2.83
March		693,389	627,377	1,440,828	183,417	1,624,245	930,856	747,439	88.7	230	2,728	595	528	23	3.86
April		344,680	327,943	1,533,239	183,417	1,716,656	1,371,976	1,188,559	89.3	240	1,366	1,256	1,122	23	1.83
May		299,428	264,852	1,660,970	183,417	1,844,387	1,544,959	1,361,542	90.1	229	1,157	1,595	1,436	24	1.50
June		123,825	95,753	1,554,845	183,417	1,738,262	1,614,437	1,431,020	89.4	218	439	3,957	3,540	24	0.61
July		365,398	252,145	1,549,751	183,417	1,733,168	1,367,770	1,184,353	89.4	207	1,218	1,423	1,272	20	1.41
August		119,801	86,579	1,571,534	183,417	1,754,951	1,635,150	1,451,733	89.5	197	439	3,993	3,576	20	0.50
September		156,419	118,841	1,526,824	183,417	1,710,241	1,553,822	1,370,405	89.3	186	639	2,677	2,390	21	0.78
October		139,861	97,407	1,566,102	183,417	1,749,519	1,609,658	1,426,241	89.5	175	557	3,143	2,814	26	0.83
November		144,391	66,585	1,539,037	183,417	1,722,454	1,578,063	1,394,646	89.4	173	385	4,475	3,999	26	0.58
December		168,524	86,967	1,902,952	183,417	2,086,369	1,917,845	1,734,428	91.2	171	509	4,102	3,742	26	0.63
January	1944	130,635	92,278	1,095,369	142,500	1,237,869	1,107,234	964,734	88.5	168	549	2,254	1,994	20	0.89
February		116,855	92,923	1,304,334	142,500	1,446,834	1,329,979	1,187,479	90.2	168	553	2,616	2,358	21	0.80
March		157,960	142,944	1,413,530	142,500	1,556,030	1,398,070	1,255,570	90.8	167	856	1,818	1,651	21	1.16
April		82,372	62,149	1,439,901	142,500	1,582,401	1,500,029	1,357,529	91.0	166	374	4,227	3,846	17	0.40
May		27,297	24,424	1,386,579	142,500	1,529,079	1,501,782	1,359,282	90.7	173	141	10,831	9,821	18	0.17

(continued)

Table 6.12 (continued)

Month	Year	Tonnage of Allied and Neutral Shipping Lost to All Causes (1)	Tonnage of Allied and Neutral Shipping Lost to Submarines (2)	Tonnage of Merchant Vessels Built and Delivered by U.S. Shipyards (3)	Est. Tonnage Built and Delivered by U.K. Shipyards (4)	Est. Tonnage of Merchant Vessels Built and Delivered by U.S. & U.K. Shipyards (5)	Net Change in the Stock of Allied Merchant Shipping Due to Allied Production (6)	Net Change in the Stock of Allied Merchant Shipping Due to U.S. Production (7)	US Percent of Merchant Vessels Built and Delivered by U.S. & U.K. Shipyards (8)	Actual Number of Operational German Submarines (9)	Allied Tonnage Lost Per Operational German Submarine (10)	Number of Additional Operational Submarines Needed to Offset Allied Production (11)	Number of Additional Operational Submarines Needed to Offset U.S. Production (12)	Actual Number of German Submarines Commissioned or Built (13)	Percent of Submarines Commissioned or Built to Needed (14)
June		104,084	57,875	1,218,314	142,500	1,360,814	1,256,730	1,114,230	89.5	189	306	4,444	3,979	18	0.41
July		78,756	63,351	1,114,910	142,500	1,257,410	1,178,654	1,036,154	88.7	188	337	3,731	3,309	16	0.43
August		118,304	98,729	975,749	142,500	1,118,249	999,945	857,445	87.3	173	571	1,959	1,710	17	0.87
September		44,805	43,368	912,685	142,500	1,055,185	1,010,380	867,880	86.5	157	276	3,820	3,304	17	0.45
October		11,668	7,176	975,503	142,500	1,118,003	1,106,335	963,835	87.3	141	51	21,967	19,167	21	0.10
November		37,980	29,592	1,028,941	142,500	1,171,441	1,133,461	990,961	87.8	142	208	5,621	4,937	22	0.39
December		134,913	58,518	1,001,746	142,500	1,144,246	1,009,333	866,833	87.5	143	409	2,796	2,448	22	0.79
January	1945	82,897	56,988	1,074,226	70,750	1,144,976	1,062,079	991,329	93.8	144	396	2,893	2,714	19	0.66
February		95,316	65,233	1,145,828	70,750	1,216,578	1,121,262	1,050,242	94.2	151	432	2,816	2,652	25	0.89
March		111,004	65,077	1,133,868	70,750	1,204,618	1,093,614	1,022,864	94.1	158	412	2,925	2,753	25	0.85
April		104,512	72,957	839,503	70,750	910,253	805,741	734,991	92.2	166	440	2,071	1,910	7	0.34
May		17,198	10,022	950,010	70,750	1,020,760	1,003,562	932,812	93.1	–	–	–	–	–	–

Notes: Col. (5): Col. (3) plus Col. (4).
Col. (6): Col. (1) minus Col. (5).
Col. (7): Col. (5) minus Col. (3).
Col. (8): Col. (3) divided by Col. (5).
Col. (10): Col. (2) divided by Col. (9).
Col. (11): Calculated.
Col. (12): Calculated.
Col. (14): Calculated.

Source: Cols. (1)(2), Table 6.1; Panel A Col. (3), U.S. Maritime Commission, *Official Construction Record Number 108,* 3–17; Col. (4), King, *U.S. Navy at War, 1911–1945,* 206; Col. (9), Table 6.6; Panel A Col. (10), Table 6.3, Panel A: Col. (13), Table 6.6 (Panel A).

Table 6.13. *Allied Merchant Vessel Construction, Quarterly and Annual Totals, September 1939 to May 1945*

Year	Quarter	Tonnage of Allied & Neutral Shipping Lost To All Causes (1)	Tonnage of Allied & Neutral Shipping Lost To Submarines (2)	Tonnage of Merchant Vessels Built Delivered by U.S. Shipyards (3)	Est. Tonnage of Merchant Vessels Built and Delivered by U.K. Shipyards (4)	Est. Tonnage of Merchant Vessels Built and Delivered by U.S. & U.K. Shipyards (5)	Net Change in the Stock of Allied Merchant Shipping Due to Allied Production (6)	Net Change in the Stock of Allied Merchant Shipping Due to U.S. Production (7)	U.S. Percent of Merchant Vessels Built and Delivered by U.S. & U.K. Shipyards (8)	Average Number of Operational German Submarines (9)	Allied Tonnage Lost Per Operational German Submarine (10)	Number of Additional Operational Submarines Needed to Offset Allied Production (11)	Number of Additional Operational Submarines Needed to Offset U.S. Production (12)	Actual Number of German Submarines Commissioned or Built (13)	Percent of Submarines Commissioned or Built to Needed (14)
1939	4*	755,392	421,156	148,547	231,000	379,547	−375,845	−606,845	39.1	43	17,567	22	8	4	18.5
1940	1	548,435	343,610	106,633	195,000	301,633	−246,802	−441,802	35.4	36	15,095	20	7	9	45.0
1940	2	1,032,175	372,160	141,075	195,000	336,075	−696,100	−891,100	42.0	40	25,804	13	5	12	92.1
1940	3	1,232,763	758,778	177,344	195,000	372,344	−860,419	−1,055,419	47.6	28	44,558	8	4	22	263.3
1940	4	1,178,268	711,610	212,985	195,000	407,985	−770,283	−965,283	52.2	26	45,907	9	5	30	337.6
1941	1	1,253,339	566,585	203,729	203,750	407,479	−845,860	−1,049,610	50.0	25	50,811	8	4	47	586.1
1941	2	1,630,968	885,010	340,118	203,750	543,868	−1,087,100	−1,290,850	62.5	43	37,929	14	9	53	369.6
1941	3	537,616	377,339	310,018	203,750	513,768	−23,848	−227,598	60.3	70	7,680	67	40	69	103.1
1941	4	906,635	342,820	305,900	203,750	499,650	−396,985	−600,735	60.0	83	10,880	47	28	69	147.3
1942	1	1,933,703	1,341,788	779,649	460,750	1,240,399	−693,304	−1,154,054	62.9	101	19,146	65	41	49	75.6
1942	2	2,213,703	1,739,146	1,724,456	460,750	2,185,206	−28,497	−489,247	78.9	127	17,431	125	99	59	47.1
1942	3	1,846,573	1,505,888	1,594,239	460,750	2,054,989	208,416	−252,334	77.6	158	11,663	176	137	61	34.6
1942	4	1,794,489	1,679,393	2,815,646	460,750	3,276,396	1,481,907	1,021,157	85.9	201	8,928	367	315	69	18.8
1943	1	1,357,810	1,189,833	3,519,812	550,250	4,070,062	2,712,252	2,162,002	86.5	221	6,144	662	573	69	10.4
1943	2	767,933	688,548	4,749,054	550,250	5,299,304	4,531,371	3,981,121	89.6	229	3,353	1,580	1,416	71	4.5
1943	3	641,618	457,565	4,648,109	550,250	5,198,359	4,556,741	4,006,491	89.4	197	3,262	1,593	1,425	61	3.8
1943	4	452,776	250,959	5,008,091	550,250	5,558,341	5,105,565	4,555,315	90.1	173	2,617	2,124	1,914	78	3.7
1944	1	405,450	328,145	3,813,233	427,500	4,240,733	3,835,283	3,407,783	89.9	168	2,418	1,754	1,577	62	3.5
1944	2	213,753	144,448	4,044,794	427,500	4,472,294	4,258,541	3,831,041	90.4	176	1,215	3,682	3,330	53	1.4
1944	3	241,865	205,448	3,003,344	427,500	3,430,844	3,188,979	2,761,479	87.5	173	1,401	2,449	2,144	50	2.0
1944	4	184,561	95,286	3,006,190	427,500	3,433,690	3,249,129	2,821,629	87.5	142	1,300	2,642	2,313	65	2.5
1945	1	289,217	187,298	3,353,922	212,250	3,566,172	3,276,955	3,064,705	94.0	151	1,917	1,862	1,751	69	3.7
1945	2**	121,710	82,979	1,789,513	141,500	1,931,013	1,809,303	1,667,803	92.7	166	733	2,634	2,441	7	0.3
1939	*	755,392	421,156	148,547	231,000	379,547	−375,845	−606,845	39.1	43	17,567	22	8	4	18.5
1940		3,991,641	2,186,158	638,037	780,000	1,418,037	−2,573,604	−3,353,604	45.0	32	123,135	12	5	73	633.9
1941		4,328,558	2,171,754	1,159,765	815,000	1,974,765	−2,353,793	−3,168,793	58.7	55	78,345	25	15	238	944.2
1942		7,788,468	6,266,215	6,913,990	1,843,000	8,756,990	968,522	−874,478	79.0	147	53,043	165	130	238	144.2
1943		3,220,137	2,586,905	17,925,066	2,201,000	20,126,066	16,905,929	14,704,929	89.1	205	15,714	1,281	1,141	279	21.8
1944		1,045,629	773,327	13,867,561	1,710,000	15,577,561	14,531,932	12,821,932	89.0	165	6,353	2,452	2,183	230	9.4
1945	***	410,927	270,277	5,143,435	353,750	5,497,185	5,086,258	4,732,508	93.6	155	2,655	2,070	1,937	76	3.7

* September through December.   ** April through May 10 only.   *** January through May 10 only.

* April through May 10 only.   *** January through May 10 only.

Source: Table 6.12.

they only commissioned 4 in 1939, they produced 73 in 1940, and 238 in 1941. In 1942, although they needed 165 additional submarines to offset the Allied efforts; they commissioned an additional 238, or 144 percent of their requirement. The last twenty-nine months of the war were, however, something else again. In 1943, they would have needed to commission 1,281 additional U-boats, they managed 279. In 1944, they would have needed 2,452, they managed 230; and in 1945 the requirement was 2,070, and German production was 76. Thus, from January 1943 through May 1945, of the numbers that would have been required to offset Allied production, the German navy managed to commission or build just 22, 9, and 4 percent. Of the 5,802 submarines that would have been needed to offset Allied construction, the Germans can blame American shipyards for 5,260 or 91 percent (see Table 6.13).

Finally, in order to get a feeling for the relative contribution of convoys, science, and tactics as opposed to vessel production in breaking the German submarine blockade, one might want to pose the counterfactual: "if convoys, science, and tactics had not reduced the number of sinkings per submarine, would the German effort have destroyed the Allied merchant fleet?" Assume that the German submarine fleet could have continued to sink Allied vessels at the same level as they had in the "heydays" of 1942, would then German submarine production been sufficient to offset the efforts of the Allied shipbuilders? Tables 6.14 and 6.15 provide a tentative answer. In terms of operational submarines, the Germans would have needed an additional 226 U-boats in 1942, 726 in 1943, 451 in 1944, and 359 in 1945. To support that number of operational submarines (assuming the actual operational to total ratios), the Nazis would have need an additional 492 submarines in 1942, 1,469 in 1943, 1,175 in 1944, and 991 in 1945. In fact, as noted above, they managed to commission or build 238 in 1942, 279 in 1943, 230 in 1944, and 76 in 1945. Those figures represent 105 percent of the operational requirement in 1942, 38 percent in 1943, 51 percent in 1944, and 21 percent in 1945. The percentage figures for the "total" requirement are even more telling: 48, 19, 20, and 8 percent. Clearly, convoys, technology, and tactics made a major contribution to breaking the blockade; but the contribution of American shipyards was at least equally important. Moreover, there is one other conclusion that can be drawn from this exercise in counterfactual history: it probably doesn't pay to attempt to blockade a country that has both nearly infinite resources (i.e., costs are no consideration) and entrepreneurs of the likes of Henry Kaiser, who, by introducing mass production technology and integrated sources of supply managed over

Table 6.14. The Counterfactual: What if There had been no Change in Antisubmarine Tactics? (Monthly)

Month	Year	Tonnage of Allied & Neutral Shipping Lost to Submarines	Number of Submarines Operational	Number of Submarines Total	Allied Tonnage Lost Per Operational German Submarine	Allied tonnage Lost Per Total German Submarines	Counterfactual Allied & Neutral Shipping Lost to German Submarines	Counterfactual Tonnage Lost Per Operational German Submarine	Counterfactual Tonnage Lost Per Total German Submarines	Est. Tonnage of Merchant Vessels Built and Delivered by U.S. & U.K. Shipyards	Number of Additional Operational Submarines Needed to Offset Allied Production	Number of Additional Total Submarines Needed to Offset Allied Production	Actual Number of German Submarines Commissioned or Built	Percent of Operational Submarines Commissioned or Built to Needed	Percent of Total Submarines Commissioned or Built to Needed
		(1)	(2)	(3)	(4)	(5)	(6)	(7)	(8)	(9)	(10)	(11)	(12)	(13)	(14)
January	1942	327,357	91	249	3,597	1,315	473,467	5,203	1,901	351,705	68	185	16	23.7	8.7
February		476,541	101	261	4,717	1,825	473,467	4,688	1,814	443,637	95	245	16	16.9	6.5
March		537,980	111	273	4,847	1,971	473,467	4,265	1,734	445,056	104	257	17	16.3	6.6
April		431,664	121	285	3,567	1,515	473,467	3,913	1,661	555,765	142	335	19	13.4	5.7
May		607,247	127	300	4,781	2,024	473,467	3,728	1,578	763,921	205	484	20	9.8	4.1
June		700,235	133	315	5,265	2,223	473,467	3,560	1,503	865,519	243	576	20	8.2	3.5
July		476,065	140	331	3,400	1,438	473,487	3,382	1,430	926,750	274	648	20	7.3	3.1
August		544,410	158	342	3,446	1,592	473,467	2,997	1,384	879,388	293	635	20	6.8	3.1
September		485,413	177	354	2,742	1,371	473,467	2,675	1,337	248,850	93	186	21	22.6	11.3
October		619,417	196	365	3,160	1,697	473,467	2,416	1,297	1,005,505	416	775	23	5.5	3.0
November		729,160	201	374	3,628	1,950	473,467	2,356	1,266	1,008,654	428	797	23	5.4	2.9
December		330,816	206	383	1,606	864	473,467	2,298	1,236	1,262,236	549	1,021	23	4.2	2.3
January	1943	203,128	212	393	958	517	473,467	2,233	1,205	1,126,293	504	935	23	4.6	2.5
February		359,328	221	403	1,626	892	473,467	2,142	1,175	1,319,525	616	1,123	23	3.7	2.0
March		627,377	230	413	2,728	1,519	473,467	2,059	1,146	1,624,245	789	1,417	23	2.9	1.6
April		327,943	240	425	1,366	772	473,467	1,973	1,114	1,716,656	870	1,541	23	2.6	1.5
May		264,852	229	421	1,157	629	473,467	2,068	1,125	1,844,387	892	1,640	24	2.7	1.5
June		95,753	218	418	439	229	473,467	2,172	1,133	1,738,262	800	1,535	24	3.0	1.6
July		252,145	207	415	1,218	608	473,467	2,287	1,141	1,733,168	758	1,519	20	2.6	1.3
August		86,579	197	414	439	209	473,467	2,403	1,144	1,754,951	730	1,535	20	2.7	1.3
September		118,841	186	413	639	288	473,467	2,546	1,146	1,710,241	672	1,492	21	3.1	1.4
October		97,407	175	412	557	236	473,467	2,706	1,149	1,749,519	647	1,522	26	4.0	1.7
November		66,585	173	420	385	159	473,467	2,737	1,127	1,722,454	629	1,528	26	4.1	1.7
December		86,967	171	428	509	203	473,467	2,769	1,106	2,086,369	754	1,886	26	3.5	1.4

(continued)

Table 6.14. *(continued)*

Month	Year	Tonnage of Allied & Neutral Shipping Lost to Submarines	Number of Submarines Operational	Number of Submarines Total	Allied Tonnage Lost Per Operational German Submarine	Allied tonnage Lost Per Total German Submarines	Counterfactual Allied & Neutral Shipping Lost to German Submarines	Counterfactual Tonnage Lost Per Operational German Submarine	Counterfactual Tonnage Lost Per Total German Submarines	Est. Tonnage of Merchant Vessels Built and Delivered by U.S. & U.K. Shipyards	Number of Additional Operational Submarines Needed to Offset Allied Production	Number of Additional Total Submarines Needed to Offset Allied Production	Actual Number of German Submarines Commissioned or Built	Percent of Operational Submarines Commissioned or Built to Needed	Percent of Total Submarines Commissioned or Built to Needed
January	1944	92,278	168	436	549	212	473,467	2,818	1,086	1,237,869	439	1,140	20	4.6	1.8
February		92,923	168	439	553	212	473,467	2,818	1,079	1,446,834	513	1,342	21	4.1	1.6
March		142,944	167	441	856	324	473,467	2,835	1,074	1,556,030	549	1,449	21	3.8	1.4
April		62,149	166	444	374	140	473,467	2,852	1,066	1,582,401	555	1,484	17	3.1	1.1
May		24,424	173	441	141	55	473,467	2,737	1,074	1,529,079	559	1,424	18	3.2	1.3
June		57,875	189	446	306	130	473,467	2,505	1,062	1,360,814	543	1,282	18	3.3	1.4
July		63,351	188	434	337	146	473,467	2,518	1,091	1,257,410	499	1,153	16	3.2	1.4
August		98,729	173	423	571	233	473,467	2,737	1,119	1,118,249	409	999	17	4.2	1.7
September		43,368	157	412	276	105	473,467	3,016	1,149	1,055,185	350	918	17	4.9	1.9
October		7,176	141	401	51	18	473,467	3,358	1,181	1,118,003	333	947	21	6.3	2.2
November		29,592	142	409	208	72	473,467	3,334	1,158	1,171,441	351	1,012	22	6.3	2.2
December		58,518	143	417	409	140	473,467	3,311	1,135	1,144,246	346	1,008	22	6.4	2.2
January	1945	56,988	144	425	396	134	473,467	3,288	1,114	1,144,976	348	1,028	19	5.5	1.8
February		65,233	151	426	432	153	473,467	3,136	1,111	1,216,578	388	1,095	25	6.4	2.3
March		65,077	158	427	412	152	473,467	2,997	1,109	1,204,618	402	1,086	25	6.2	2.3
April		72,957	166	429	440	170	473,467	2,852	1,104	910,253	319	825	7	2.2	0.8
May		10,022	n.d.	n.d.											

Source: Column (6): Average monthly sinkings January 1942 through May 1943. See text.

Table 6.15. *The Counterfactual: What if There had been no Change in Antisubmarine Tactics? (Quarterly and Annually)*

Year	Quarter	Tonnage of Allied & Neutral Shipping Lost To Submarines (1)	Number of Submarines (Monthly Average) Operational (2)	Total (3)	Allied Tonnage Lost Per Operational German Submarines (4)	Allied Tonnage Lost Per Total German Submarines (5)	Counterfactual Allied & Neutral Shipping Lost to Submarines (6)	Counterfactual Tonnage Lost Per Operational German Submarines (7)	Counterfactual Tonnage Lost Per Total German Submarines (8)	Tonnage of Merchant Vessels Built and Delivered by U.S. & U.K. Shipyards (9)	Additional Operational Submarines Needed to Offset Allied Production (10)	Additional Total Submarines Needed to Offset Allied Production (11)	Number of German Submarines Commissioned or Built (12)	Percent Operational Submarines Commissioned or Built to Needed (13)	Percent Total Submarines Commissioned or Built to Needed (14)
1942	1	1,341,788	101	261	13,285	5,141	1,420,401	14,063	5,442	1,240,399	88	228	49	55.6	21.5
	2	1,739,146	127	300	13,694	5,797	1,420,401	11,184	4,735	2,185,206	195	462	59	30.2	12.8
	3	1,505,888	158	342	9,511	4,399	1,420,401	8,971	4,149	2,054,989	229	495	61	26.6	12.3
	4	1,679,393	201	374	8,355	4,490	1,420,401	7,067	3,798	3,276,396	464	863	69	14.9	8.0
1943	1	1,189,833	221	403	5,384	2,952	1,420,401	6,427	3,525	4,070,062	633	1,155	69	10.9	6.0
	2	688,548	229	421	3,007	1,634	1,420,401	6,203	3,371	5,299,304	854	1,572	71	8.3	4.5
	3	457,565	197	414	2,327	1,105	1,420,401	7,222	3,431	5,198,359	720	1,515	61	8.5	4.0
	4	250,959	173	420	1,451	598	1,420,401	8,210	3,382	5,558,341	677	1,644	78	11.5	4.7
1944	1	328,145	168	439	1,957	748	1,420,401	8,472	3,238	4,240,733	501	1,310	62	12.4	4.7
	2	144,448	176	444	821	326	1,420,401	8,070	3,202	4,472,294	554	1,397	53	9.6	3.8
	3	205,448	173	423	1,190	486	1,420,401	8,226	3,358	3,430,844	417	1,022	50	12.0	4.9
	4	95,286	142	409	671	233	1,420,401	10,003	3,473	3,433,690	343	989	65	18.9	6.6
1945	1	187,298	151	426	1,240	440	1,420,401	9,407	3,334	3,566,172	379	1,070	69	18.2	6.5
	2*	82,979	166	429	500	193	946,934	11,409	4,415	1,931,104	169	437	7	4.1	1.6
1942		6,256,215	147	319	42,676	19,623	5,681,604	38,694	17,792	8,756,990	226	492	238	105.2	48.4
1943		2,586,905	205	415	12,624	6,240	5,681,604	27,726	13,704	20,126,066	726	1,469	279	38.4	19.0
1944		773,327	165	429	4,699	1,804	5,681,604	34,521	13,257	15,577,561	451	1,175	230	51.0	19.6
1945	**	270,277	124	341	1,747	633	2,367,335	15,298	5,547	5,497,185	359	991	76	21.1	7.7

* April through May 10 only.   ** January through May 10 only.

Source: See Table 6.14. See text.

the course of the war to reduce the time needed to build a Liberty ship from 105 to 14 days.[160]

4. SOME STILL UNANSWERED QUESTIONS

The history of the Battle of the Atlantic raises a number of questions whose answers have more general implications for military and economic policy, but many of those questions still remain largely unanswered. For example, it has often been argued that the problem with the military in every country is that the "high command" is always prepared to fight the last war. In this case, however, a strategy based on the lessons of the last war would have proved highly profitable in terms of both lives and vessels saved. The question remains, "Why was one of the most important lessons of 1916–1917 lost?"

Given the experience of World War I, how is it possible to explain the lag in the introduction of truly effective convoys by both the American and the British naval authorities? In the latter case, given what was then perceived as a near-tragic experience in World War I, when only the belated introduction of the convoy was thought to have saved the country from imminent disaster, it is still unclear why, on the eve of World War II, there should have been so prolonged a discussion and so much hesitation before adopting the tactics that had apparently proved so profitable more than twenty years earlier. The British did not hesitate to innovate convoys, but decisions during the interwar period had led to a Navy that was hard pressed to produce effective convoys. The shortage of escort vessels, coupled with initial attempts to make the convoy an offensive as well as a defensive weapon – attempts made at a time when there was insufficient air support – meant that the convoys suffered much greater losses than they would have had more resources been devoted to providing the escorts needed to make convoys truly effective. Still, even the weakly escorted convoys proved more effective than merchant vessels traveling alone.

Moreover, even given the resources the British devoted to the education of merchant marine officers in convoy tactics and, thanks largely to the Americans and the arrival of an adequate number of escort vessels, there was still a delay in recognizing and then formalizing the structure of an "effective" convoy and in educating the personnel who were "on the line" in how to effectively employ that structure. It was, for example, 1944 before

---

160 Gibson and Donovan, *Abandoned Ocean*, 166; also Stephen B. Adams, *Mr. Kaiser Goes to Washington: The Rise of a Government Entrepreneur* (Chapel Hill: University of North Carolina Press, 1997), 114–115, for a less impressive estimate of the decline.

the Admiralty finally issued the formally authorized "Admiralty Convoy Instructions to Escorts"; until then the choice of tactics had been largely left up to the officers "on the spot."[161] Those officers ultimately learned the needed lessons, but their education was both time consuming and not cheap.

In the case of the United States, the lag is far more difficult to explain. Despite the Americans' ability to closely observe both twenty-six months of "secondhand" war and the toll of ships lost off the east coast in the first fifteen months of the "shooting war," it was March 1943 before Admiral Ernest King, Commander in Chief of the U.S. Fleet, announced his considered opinion that convoys were not only the best means to protect shipping but also provided the best bait for U-boats. In fact, the American response once again demonstrates two important truths. First, it is certainly correct that history can provide important lessons for current policy, but it will not provide such useful lessons unless history is correctly interpreted. It may well have been the case that the American response would have been quicker and more effective, if the officers in the naval bureaucracy had not observed the British convoy losses over the first twenty-seven months of the war. That those convoys suffered substantial losses is certainly correct; but those observations, when coupled with the data on total sinkings, led the American naval command to conclude that weakly escorted convoys are worse than no convoys at all. What the admirals failed to note, however, was that the losses of vessels not traveling in convoys were significantly larger than the losses in lightly escorted convoys. Second, politics do matter. The British decision to produce few escort vessels in the prewar years, although in hindsight certainly a flawed decision, was at least a decision made on the basis of reasoned assumptions about the potential effectiveness of submarines and sonar and about German intentions and their ability to wage a submarine campaign. The American policy about the construction of escort vessels, on the other hand, was heavily influenced by President Roosevelt's personal beliefs about the relative effectiveness of small SC and PC vessels as compared with larger and better equipped DE's as convoy escorts. That belief, although partly based on his memories of World War I, also was partly rooted in his love for small craft. Moreover, he did not allow his belief to be shaken by the opinions of the naval professionals. In the words of Samuel Eliot Morison, the historian of U.S. naval operations: "The entire experience of the war demonstrated that the heavily escorted

161 Roskill, *Offensive, Part II*, 402–404.

merchant convoy, supplemented by an escort carrier group on its flank, was by far the best way to get U-boats, because the merchantmen acted as bait."[162] World War II proved that the convoy with air support was an effective offensive weapon as well as a superb defensive one; however, the experience of World War I had proved its defensive potency almost a quarter century before the Battle of the Atlantic was joined.

Second, it also appears to be true that, at times, the military was better prepared to fight the last war than the present one. How else can one explain the behavior of both the British and Germans in the case of "schnorkel" submarines? The "schnorkel" had been invented in Holland in 1927, and, between then and 1940, a number of Dutch "schnorkelers" had been added to that nation's fleet. With the fall of the Netherlands, some of those submarines had been taken over by the British and some had been captured by the Germans. In Britain, the "schnorkels" were removed before the submarines were added to the Royal Navy, and they were never reinstalled. In Germany, it took three years for the naval authorities to recognize the benefits of the Dutch invention; and, by then, despite some limited success, it was far too late for the few "schnorkel" submarines that were actually built to make any significant contribution to the effectiveness of either the blockade or the total war effort. Moreover, it is also clear that the lesson once learned may have been learned too well. "Schnorkels" were more effective in the face of radar, but they were not the end all of submarine design.

Third, given the importance of the blockade from both the Axis and Allied points of view, it is difficult to understand the role played by the preferences of one or a small group of decision makers or by the role of domestic politics in major military decisions. The impact of Doenitz's desire to micromanage the blockade – for example, his decision to require that his submarines report in daily by radio, despite the fact that those messages allowed the British to track individual submarines, his order that submarines remain surfaced when attacked by enemy aircraft, despite the losses inflicted, and his belief in integral tonnage, that is that a ton is a ton is a ton, despite the fact that ships supplying England were more important to the war effort than ships supplying Brazil and that loaded vessels were a more valuable prize than empty ones – particularly stand out. However, those are not the only examples of personal interference. The animosity between Doenitz and Goering that led to insufficient aircraft support for the submarine blockade, and, despite the protests of the military professionals, Hitler's refusal to employ

162 Morison, *Two-Ocean War*, 28.

German scientists and engineers in developing submarine technology and tactics, until it was too late, are also examples of the petty preferences that proved very costly to the German effort.

Nor were the Germans alone. Interservice and international rivalry, for example, the Royal Airforce's reluctance to divert bombers to the antisubmarine campaign, and both British and Americas unwillingness to integrate their armed forces, imposed heavy costs on both countries. In the case of bombers, it is clear that the British failed to see the potential of the B-24 as a highly effective ASW weapon. If, as early as June 1941, "the War Cabinet assigned more of Bomber Command's four-engine, long-range, radar-equipped, land-based aircraft to Coastal Command," "the 'U-boat peril' could have been reduced dramatically." "A number of studies would show that a Coastal Command ASW force of merely a hundred B-24s could well have decisively crushed the U-boat peril in the summer of 1941, sparing the Allies the terrible shipping losses in the years ahead." "Given the loss of Allied shipping to U-boats in 1942, the failure to take that step (as Admiral King repeatedly urged) was yet another painful lapse by Prime Minister Churchill and others in London who were bedazzled and blinded by the enticing doctrine" of the RAF, a doctrine that "promised a cheap, easy victory over Germany through airpower alone."[163] A similar decision was made in the case of the submarine bunkers or "pens" built by the Germans at Brest, Lorient, St. Nazaire, and La Pallice. These steel-reinforced concrete bunkers continued to shelter German submarines even after the Allies had recaptured Paris. "RAF reconnaissance aircraft took photographs of the foundations of the first bunkers at Lorient and La Pallice." Thus, the British were well warned; but bomber command continued to assign priority to targets in Germany; and construction of the pens continued with only sporadic and ineffective interference from the RAF. This decision was yet another example of a serious lapse of strategic planning; one "the British were to regret and one the Americans could never fathom."[164] In a somewhat different dimension, the same arguments can be made for the response to the political complaints of the business communities of American East Coast cities – complaints that, despite continued pressure from the military, effectively prevented urban dim-outs and contributed heavily to American losses in the early months of the war.

There are also clearly some general lessons provided by the German blockade and the Allied attempts to break it. First, in the modern world there

163 Blair, *Hunted*, 152, *Hunters*, 319.   164 Blair, *Hunters*, 205.

should be no barriers between the military and the scientific communities, nor between the entrepreneurs in a free enterprise competitive society and the production of military supplies. In both cases, the absence of barriers may produce some failures, but there may well be major breakthroughs that the military professionals alone simply cannot envision. It was well into the war before the German military believed that such a thing as radar could exist, let alone be effectively innovated as an antisubmarine weapon. German scientists had long been aware of that possibility. Ford's attempt to build aircraft at Willow Run may have been a failure, but the German blockade was as much overcome by Henry Kaiser's shipbuilding innovations as it was by innovations in military tactics and technology.[165]

Second, even in the days of international organizations, in this case the League of Nations, international law will seldom, perhaps never, constrain a major belligerent's behavior, if that law interferes with a country's effective prosecution of a major war. Weak nations and underdeveloped countries may be constrained, but the policies adopted by both the United States and Germany demonstrated time and again the ineffectiveness of heretofore well-recognized principles of international law when those principles came in conflict with military goals. In the American case, tourism may have been sacred, but international (and, in 1940 and 1941, even domestic) law was not.

165 The ill-fated ice-aircraft carrier of Operation Habakkuk provides yet another example of failed military-civilian efforts.

7

The American Submarine and Aerial Mine Blockade of the Japanese Home Islands, 1941–1945

1. INTRODUCTION

As the history of blockades over the years has shown, the success of any economic blockade depends, to a large extent, upon several key factors – factors that vary with the domestic resources and the geographic location of the nation that the blockade is directed against and the military resources at the disposal of the blockading power. First, "the economy of the blockaded power must be vulnerable" – given the resource and industrial base, a naval blockade directed against the United States, for example, would be almost certain to fail. Second, the blockading nation must have sufficient military power to have control of sea and land routes that connect the enemy with other nations; and, thus, enable it "to cut off the supply of goods to its enemy from outside his border." Third, "the blockading power must be able," either through military force or diplomatic pressure, "to secure the acquiescence or cooperation of neutral powers" that might be able to supply the blockaded country from overseas.[1] In summary, then, economic warfare, to be successful, depends "on the ability to restrict an enemy's economy to a small and known stock of basic resources." The blockade of Japan was successful because that country had been "driven back from her imperial outposts to the limited economic base of the Home Islands and Korea." By the end of 1943, the United States and its allies had sufficient naval and air power to effectively enforce such a blockade.[2]

The principal weapons deployed "to enforce the blockade were submarines, direct attacks by aircraft, and mine-laying and of those three; the

---

1 W. N. Medlicott, *The Economic Blockade*, 2 vols. (London: Her Majesty's Stationery Office, 1952), vol. 1, 2–3. See Chapter 1.
2 Alan S. Milward, *War, Economy and Society, 1939–1945* (Berkeley: University of California Press, 1977), 320–321.

submarines achieved by far the greatest successes." For the submarines, it was 1943 and 1944 that saw their greatest successes; "and it was they who then struck lethal blows at the foundation stones of the entire Japanese war economy."[3] In the end, next to the atomic bomb, the American submarine fleet was, arguably, destined to be remembered as the most devastating weapon deployed in the Pacific campaign. Although it played a role in the battles of Midway and the Philippine Sea, its major contribution was its steady, and unremitting, focus on the annihilation of the Japanese merchant marine. American "submarines waged *and won* the war against Japanese commerce, in effect sundering Japan's sea lines of communications."[4] Submarines were responsible for only one-third of the Japanese combat ships sunk. Over 55 percent of the merchant tonnage sent to the bottom was due to U.S. submarines. Despite the addition of over 800,000 tons of merchant shipping by conquest and 3.3 million tons by new construction, Japanese mercantile tonnage declined from about 6 million tons at the beginning of the war to 1.5 million tons at the end. Moreover, by 1945, almost the entire remaining fleet consisted of small wooden vessels operating in the Inland Sea. After the war, General Tojo stated that "the destruction of her merchant marine was one of the three factors that defeated Japan." Recent research has indicated that he had, almost certainly, underestimated its role.[5]

2. SUBMARINE AND BLOCKADE STRATEGIES: OFFENSIVE AND DEFENSIVE

In the run up to World War II, both the American and Japanese Naval bureaucracies almost completely failed to comprehend the potential contribution of the submarine as an effective commerce raider. In the U.S. case, since 1911, the navy's General Board had defined only two roles for submarines: to be deployed, first, as defensive coastal protection, and, second, as minor supporting players in offensive fleet operations. "The failure of Imperial Germany's unrestricted U-boat offensive in 1917–1918 confirmed established U.S. beliefs that commerce raiding was *not* the proper employment for submarines. Moreover, after 1919 the navy's civilian leadership

---

3 S. W. Roskill, *The War at Sea 1939–1945, Vol. 3 The Offensive, Part II, 1st June 1944–14th August 1945* (London: Her Majesty's Stationery Office, 1981), 367–369.

4 Holger H. Herwig, "Innovation Ignored: The Submarine Problem – Germany, Britain, and the United States, 1919–1939," in Williamson Murray and Allen R. Millett, eds., *Military Innovation in the Interwar Period* (Cambridge: Cambridge University Press, 1996), 252.

5 Samuel Eliot Morison, *The Two-Ocean War: A Short History of the United States Navy in the Second World War* (Boston: Little, Brown, 1963), 493–494, 511.

argued that submersibles were violations of international law. Finally, the naval planning group for the [1936] London Conference advised the chief of naval operations that 'the national conscience' would never permit use of submarines in 'the destruction of enemy merchant shipping'. In short, the national strategic culture militated against the conduct of unrestricted submarine warfare." As early as 1920, "a minority within the navy, however, was hesitant to forego submarine warfare." That opposition was in part, at least, rooted in the belief that no scrap of paper was, by itself, sufficient to effectively outlaw any weapons system. For example, Captain H. H. Bemis "argued that it would be 'criminal' for the United States to 'abolish submarines,' especially with the potential threat posed by the Japanese in the Pacific." His position was supported by Theodore Roosevelt Jr., then Assistant Secretary of the Navy, who argued that, " 'against the two island empires − Great Britain and Japan,' − it was imperative that Washington 'not permit our hands to be tied as regards submarines.' "[6] History has proved that, in at least one regard, they were correct.

The critics of the submarine were unable to rid the navy of the undersea craft; but their arguments did mean that, as late as 1941, the U.S. Navy had not managed to articulate, let alone adopt, a coherent commerce-raiding submarine strategy. "On 7 December 1941," Franklin D. Roosevelt endorsed Admiral Harold R. Stark's proposal that, "in response to Pearl Harbor," the navy begin "unrestricted submarine warfare against Japan"; and he informed congressional leaders "that American policy in the Pacific was simply 'strangulation of Japan − strangulation altogether.' " Given the government's "strident opposition" to Germany's decision to launch unrestricted submarine warfare during World War I, one might wonder about the decision; but, once again, it underscores the adaptability of "morality" in the face of national self-interest.

Ultimately the policy proved a tremendous success − over the course of the war, some 300 U.S. submarines were to conduct more than 1,500 sorties against Japanese shipping in the process, sinking 4,779,902 tons of merchant shipping as well as warships "weighing in" at 540,192 tons, a total of 50.3 percent of all Japanese tonnage sunk.[7] But, ultimately was not immediately − in the shorter term, although weak links in the Japanese economy were discovered, "they were never attacked for long enough or

6 Herwig, "Innovation Ignored," 253. See also, Ernest Andrade Jr., "Submarine Policy in the United States Navy, 1919–1941," *Military Affairs*, 35 (April 1971), 50–56.
7 Herwig, "Innovation Ignored," 252–253. See also Charles A. Lockwood, *Sink Em All: Submarine Warfare in the Pacific* (New York: Dutton, 1951), 27. The 4,779,902 figure is from Herwig. For other estimates, see Table 7.5.

frequently enough, because forces were diverted to other tempting but less useful targets or other forms of warfare altogether."[8]

In the case of both offensive and defensive strategies – that is of employing submarines against enemy commerce and of defending against submarines and submarine supported blockades – the Japanese certainly had the worst record of any of the major belligerents. Offensively, they made "the most astonishing misuse of submarines." Despite their possession of the "long lance" torpedo, probably the finest undersea weapon deployed by any of the warring powers, and, in the face of the historical lessons of World War I and of the then (that is, in 1940 and 1941) currently observable evidence about the Battle of the Atlantic, they "still failed to attack Allied commerce in the Pacific." As a result, most of the merchant ships that sailed from the west coast of the United States in support of, first, the material buildup and, then, the military campaigns in the Pacific were able to sail singly and without escort – the Allies found it unnecessary to divert naval resources to convoying activity.[9]

Even stranger – perhaps, given the dependence of the island nation on its overseas trade, unexpected would be a better description – was the Japanese failure to adopt any antisubmarine strategy until it was far too late. "Throughout the war, they devoted virtually no resources to protecting their own sea lines of communication."[10] If there is a "rational" explanation for this failure, perhaps it lies in the mindset of the Japanese military leaders who, until V-J day, refused to face the possibility that they might ever be forced to wage a defensive war.[11] Or, perhaps, it reflects the Navy's belief that, if the war was to be won, it had to be won quickly before the resources of the United States could be effectively deployed. For example, in a statement made by Admiral Yamamoto to Prince Konoye shortly after the Tripartite Pact of September 1940 brought Japan into the Axis, the Admiral is quoted as saying:

If I am told to fight regardless of consequences, I shall run wild considerably for the first six months or a year, but I have utterly no confidence for the second or third years.[12]

---

8 Milward, *War*, 299.
9 Williamson Murray, "Innovation: Past and Present," in Murray and Millett, eds., *Military Innovation*, 321–322.
10 Morison, *Two-Ocean War*, 279, 496–497; Murray, "Innovation," 321–323.
11 Morison, *Two-Ocean War*, 496–497.
12 Quoted in Samuel Eliot Morison, *The Rising Sun in the Pacific, 1931–April 1942* (Boston: Little, Brown, 1963), 46.

Others in the naval hierarchy appear to have held similar views. They saw that the Japanese navy "could hardly go over to the defensive." "Yamamoto had foreseen if not all the details then certainly the basic framework of the Japanese difficulties, and he had warned that the only way the Japanese could secure their objectives in a war with the United States was to dictate terms of peace inside the White House. In saying this, Yamamoto recognized that it was impossible to achieve victory. The problem that he and his colleagues faced in the opening months of 1942 was how to achieve the impossible."[13]

Although either explanation is consistent with the Japanese decisions in 1942 and 1943 to construct twenty new aircraft carries and "to convert a *Yamato* class battleship hull to the super-carrier *Shinano*"– vessels that would be of no use in any defensive campaign – the second possible explanation seems the more probable. Certainly those resources could have been employed to construct several hundred destroyers and small escort vessels. Given, however, the recognized competency of the Japanese naval hierarchy, their allocation of resources suggests that these decisions seemed reasonable.[14]

Moreover, when they finally did recognize the submarine threat, it was clearly a case of "way too little and way too late." Although Japanese merchant losses had risen over the years from 1941 through 1944, it was not until November 1943, that those losses skyrocketed (see Tables 7.1, 7.2, and 7.3).

It was not until late 1943 that the Japanese, in an attempt to reverse the trend, introduced a general convoy system. "But the late hour at which they adopted such measures, combined with the inadequate strength allocated to the naval command concerned, the failure to exploit the possibilities of shore-based air escort, and the lack of any control over the requisitioning of ships for military purposes destroyed the effectiveness of the new policy." As late as 1945, the Japanese General Escort Command controlled only fifty-five long-range vessels; and their convoys had very little air cover.[15] "The Japanese ended the war with the same antisubmarine equipment that they had at the beginning – not very accurate depth charges and aircraft bombs; and they never solved the mathematical problem of where to drop a depth charge to do damage. They had no method of assessing [the efficiency of

13 H. P. Willmott, *Empires in the Balance: Japanese and Allied Pacific Strategies to April 1942* (Annapolis: Naval Institute Press, 1982), 453.
14 Morison, *Two-Ocean War*, 496–497; Willmott, *Empire*, 453–454.
15 Roskill, *Offensive, Part II*, 367–368.

Table 7.1. Japanese Vessels Claimed Sunk and Actually Sunk by U.S. Submarines, By Base, By Month, December 1941 to July 1945

Date of Submarine's Departure		Submarine Base	Vessels		Tonnage (thousands)		Actual Sinkings as a % of Claimed	
Month	Year		Wartime Credit	JANAC Credit	Wartime Credit	JANAC Credit	Vessels	Tonnage
December	1941	Pearl Harbor	8.00	4.00	50.200	14.100	50.0	28.1
		Manila	21.00	6.00	120.400	29.500	28.6	24.5
		TOTAL	29.00	10.00	170.600	43.600	34.5	25.6
January	1942	Pearl Harbor	4.00	4.00	23.200	12.701	100.0	54.7
		Australia	6.00	1.00	23.000	4.124	16.7	17.9
		TOTAL	10.00	5.00	46.200	16.825	50.0	36.4
February	1942	Pearl Harbor	10.00	7.00	74.200	24.145	70.0	32.5
		Australia	7.00	3.00	34.000	14.840	42.9	43.6
		Alaska	–	–	–	–	–	–
		TOTAL	17.00	10.00	108.200	39.985	58.8	36.0
March	1942	Pearl Harbor	8.00	4.00	49.000	16.415	50.0	33.5
		Fremantle	5.00	4.00	19.500	12.587	80.0	64.5
		Alaska	–	–	–	–	–	–
		TOTAL	13.00	8.00	68.500	29.002	61.5	42.3
April	1942	Pearl Harbor	26.00	18.00	151.500	74.843	69.2	49.4
		Fremantle	4.00	3.00	28.300	12.800	75.0	45.2
		Brisbane	2.00	2.00	11.700	10.044	100.0	85.8
		Alaska	–	–	–	–	–	–
		TOTAL	32.00	23.00	191.500	97.687	71.9	51.0
May	1942	Pearl Harbor	2.00	–	30.900	–	–	–
		Fremantle	6.00	7.00	33.700	26.800	116.7	79.5
		Brisbane	–	–	–	–	–	–
		Alaska	–	–	–	–	–	–
		TOTAL	8.00	7.00	64.600	26.800	87.5	41.5

June	1942	Pearl Harbor	6.00	4.00	38.200	12.700	66.7	33.2
		Fremantle	6.00	4.00	47.100	23.200	66.7	49.3
		Brisbane	1.00	1.00	1.100	2.626	100.0	238.7
		Alaska	7.00	4.00	11.000	3.700	57.1	33.6
		TOTAL	20.00	13.00	97.400	42.226	65.0	–
July	1942	Pearl Harbor	25.00	14.00	188.400	60.550	56.0	32.1
		Fremantle	4.00	4.0	25.100	18.962	100.0	75.5
		Brisbane	3.00	2.00	22.200	14.428	66.7	65.0
		Alaska	1.00	–	9.300	–	–	–
		TOTAL	33.00	20.00	245.000	93.940	60.6	–
August	1942	Pearl Harbor	15.00	12.00	103.100	43.709	80.0	42.4
		Fremantle	3.00	2.00	19.500	7.000	66.7	35.9
		Brisbane	1.00	–	1.500	–	–	–
		Alaska	–	–	–	–	–	–
		TOTAL	19.00	14.00	124.100	55.709	73.7	40.9
September	1942	Pearl Harbor	19.00	20.00	136.700	94.600	105.3	69.2
		Fremantle	5.00	2.00	34.900	9.800	40.0	28.1
		Brisbane	6.00	3.00	42.600	14.685	50.0	34.5
		Alaska	–	–	–	–	–	–
		TOTAL	30.00	25.00	214.200	119.085	83.3	55.6
October	1942	Pearl Harbor	9.00	3.00	52.500	12.500	33.3	23.8
		Fremantle	7.00	7.00	43.500	30.900	100.0	71.0
		Brisbane	7.00	–	43.000	–	–	–
		Alaska	1.00	1.00	3.000	2.864	100.0	95.5
		TOTAL	24.00	11.00	142.000	46.264	45.8	32.6

(continued)

Table 7.1 (continued)

Date of Submarine's Departure		Submarine Base	Vessels		Tonnage (thousands)		Actual Sinkings as a % of Claimed	
Month	Year		Wartime Credit	JANAC Credit	Wartime Credit	JANAC Credit	Vessels	Tonnage
November	1942	Pearl Harbor	12.00	9.00	74.900	40.100	75.0	53.5
		Fremantle	–	1.00	–	0.600	–	–
		Brisbane	3.00	1.00	8.700	2.000	33.3	23.0
		Alaska	–	–	–	–	–	–
		TOTAL	15.00	11.00	83.600	42.700	73.3	51.1
December	1942	Pearl Harbor	18.00	13.00	87.700	37.300	72.2	42.5
		Fremantle	7.00	6.00	40.600	16.200	85.7	39.9
		Brisbane	5.00	5.00	36.000	29.798	100.0	82.8
		Alaska	–	–	–	–	–	–
		TOTAL	30.00	24.00	164.300	83.298	80.0	50.7
January	1943	Pearl Harbor	13.00	7.00	96.200	54.210	53.8	56.4
		Fremantle	7.00	3.00	29.700	11.750	42.9	39.6
		Brisbane	15.00	12.50	85.900	44.550	83.3	51.9
		Alaska	–	–	–	–	–	–
		TOTAL	35.00	22.50	211.800	110.510	64.3	52.2
February	1943	Pearl Harbor	22.50	17.50	138.100	58.411	77.8	42.3
		Fremantle	2.00	2.00	6.800	7.000	100.0	102.9
		Brisbane	4.00	1.00	18.400	3.000	25.0	16.3
		Alaska	–	–	4.300	–	–	–
		TOTAL	31.50	20.50	167.600	68.410	65.1	40.8
March	1943	Pearl Harbor	10.50	9.50	74.500	43.700	90.5	58.7
		Fremantle	7.00	3.00	44.200	19.000	42.9	43.0
		Brisbane	1.00	1.00	8.500	5.000	100.0	58.8
		Alaska	1.00	–	9.000	–	–	–
		TOTAL	19.50	13.50	136.200	67.700	69.2	49.7

Month	Year	Location						
April	1943	Pearl Harbor	23.00	19.00	152.600	78.510	82.6	51.4
		Fremantle	8.00	5.00	36.100	31.000	62.5	85.9
		Brisbane	–	2.00	–	12.300	–	–
		Alaska	1.00	–	3.000	–	–	–
		TOTAL	32.00	26.00	191.700	121.810	81.3	63.5
May	1943	Pearl Harbor	16.00	18.00	103.900	77.800	112.5	74.9
		Fremantle	9.00	5.00	54.100	13.600	55.6	25.1
		Brisbane	3.00	2.00	13.900	6.100	66.7	43.9
		Alaska	2.00	2.00	6.200	6.264	100.0	101.0
		TOTAL	30.00	27.00	178.100	103.764	90.0	58.3
June	1943	Pearl Harbor	26.00	17.00	192.600	74.740	65.4	38.8
		Fremantle	2.00	1.00	20.000	5.000	50.0	25.0
		Brisbane	3.00	2.00	13.000	7.000	66.7	53.8
		Alaska	1.00	1.00	8.200	5.430	100.0	66.2
		TOTAL	32.00	21.00	233.800	92.170	65.6	39.4
July	1943	Pearl Harbor	14.00	12.00	90.600	39.940	85.7	44.1
		Fremantle	5.00	4.00	27.000	16.500	80.0	61.1
		Brisbane	1.00	1.00	6.600	5.871	100.0	89.0
		Alaska	–	–	–	–	–	–
		TOTAL	20.00	17.00	124.200	62.311	85.0	50.2
August	1943	Pearl Harbor	22.00	18.00	144.100	71.272	81.8	49.5
		Fremantle	8.00	5.00	48.200	21.662	62.5	44.9
		Brisbane	6.00	3.00	30.100	9.394	50.0	31.1
		Alaska	–	–	–	–	–	–
		TOTAL	36.00	26.00	222.400	102.298	72.2	46.0

(continued)

Table 7.1 (continued)

Date of Submarine's Departure		Submarine Base	Vessels		Tonnage (thousands)		Actual Sinkings as a % of Claimed	
Month	Year		Wartime Credit	JANAC Credit	Wartime Credit	JANAC Credit	Vessels	Tonnage
September	1943	Pearl Harbor	24.00	18.00	199.600	100.619	75.0	50.4
		Fremantle	16.00	10.00	96.800	40.287	62.5	41.6
		Brisbane	4.00	3.00	25.100	18.600	75.0	74.1
		Alaska	1.00	1.00	4.000	1.368	100.0	34.2
		TOTAL	45.00	32.00	325.500	160.874	71.1	49.4
October	1943	Pearl Harbor	44.00	31.00	289.700	128.506	70.5	44.4
		Fremantle	10.00	4.00	67.100	21.173	40.0	31.6
		Brisbane	8.00	6.00	47.100	26.100	75.0	55.4
		Alaska	–	–	–	–	–	–
		TOTAL	62.00	41.00	403.900	175.779	66.1	43.5
November	1943	Pearl Harbor	25.00	18.00	188.000	113.859	72.0	60.6
		Fremantle	14.00	11.00	93.000	47.670	78.6	51.3
		Brisbane	10.00	8.00	74.200	43.072	80.0	58.0
		Alaska	–	–	–	–	–	–
		TOTAL	49.00	37.00	355.200	204.601	75.5	57.6
December	1943	Pearl Harbor	37.00	32.00	223.100	137.190	86.5	61.5
		Fremantle	17.00	13.00	127.400	61.348	76.5	48.2
		Brisbane	6.00	6.00	34.700	28.000	100.0	80.7
		Alaska	–	–	–	–	–	–
		TOTAL	60.00	51.00	385.200	226.538	85.0	58.8
January	1944	Pearl Harbor	62.00	50.00	433.300	223.113	80.6	51.5
		Fremantle	12.00	7.00	63.400	29.831	58.3	47.1
		Brisbane	–	–	–	–	–	–
		TOTAL	74.00	57.00	496.700	252.944	77.0	50.9

330

Month	Year	Location						
February	1944	Pearl Harbor	30.00	25.00	163.000	92.561	83.3	56.8
		Fremantle	10.00	9.00	72.200	60.700	90.0	84.1
		Brisbane	9.00	6.00	48.100	25.740	66.7	53.5
		TOTAL	49.00	40.00	283.300	179.001	81.6	63.2
March	1944	Pearl Harbor	33.00	24.00	190.600	102.882	72.7	54.0
		Fremantle	7.00	4.00	50.600	15.474	57.1	30.6
		Brisbane	1.00	1.00	6.800	2.800	100.0	41.2
		TOTAL	41.00	29.00	248.000	121.156	70.7	48.9
April	1944	Pearl Harbor	31.00	25.50	173.100	106.228	82.3	61.4
		Fremantle	35.00	26.50	232.800	92.881	75.7	39.9
		Brisbane	4.00	5.00	18.800	21.900	125.0	116.5
		TOTAL	70.00	57.00	424.700	221.009	81.4	52.0
May	1944	Pearl Harbor	41.00	32.50	233.500	130.532	70.4	55.9
		Brisbane	1.00	1.00	5.700	6.440	100.0	113.0
		Fremantle	19.00	14.00	67.500	44.695	73.7	66.2
		TOTAL	61.00	47.50	306.700	181.667	77.9	59.2
June	1944	Pearl Harbor	66.00	48.00	426.100	216.584	72.7	50.8
		Fremantle	21.00	14.00	139.500	74.743	66.7	53.6
		Brisbane	12.00	10.00	58.300	33.480	83.3	57.4
		TOTAL	99.00	72.00	623.900	324.807	72.7	52.1
July	1944	Pearl Harbor	51.00	28.00	270.000	137.957	54.9	51.1
		Fremantle	34.00	22.00	240.000	116.700	64.7	48.6
		Brisbane	3.00	3.00	8.600	6.950	100.0	80.8
		TOTAL	88.00	53.00	518.600	261.607	60.2	50.4

(continued)

Table 7.1 *(continued)*

Date of Submarine's Departure		Submarine Base	Vessels		Tonnage (thousands)		Actual Sinkings as a % of Claimed	
Month	Year		Wartime Credit	JANAC Credit	Wartime Credit	JANAC Credit	Vessels	Tonnage
August	1944	Pearl Harbor	66.00	38.50	390.900	164.763	58.3	42.1
		Fremantle	13.00	10.50	40.900	27.507	80.8	67.3
		Brisbane	4.00	2.00	10.700	4.300	50.0	40.2
		TOTAL	83.00	51.00	442.500	196.570	61.4	44.4
September	1944	Pearl Harbor	59.00	42.00	345.724	165.675	71.2	47.9
		Fremantle	42.50	32.33	258.900	144.190	76.1	55.7
		Brisbane	5.00	4.00	43.000	37.141	80.0	86.4
		TOTAL	106.50	78.33	647.624	347.006	73.5	53.6
October	1944	Pearl Harbor	62.50	49.00	438.500	303.023	78.4	69.1
		Fremantle	35.50	22.66	205.400	84.241	63.8	41.0
		Brisbane	1.00	0.50	0.700	2.849	50.0	407.0
		TOTAL	99.00	72.16	644.600	390.113	72.9	60.5
November	1944	Pearl Harbor	25.50	15.50	166.600	56.520	60.8	33.9
		Fremantle	14.00	12.00	76.200	60.094	85.7	78.9
		Brisbane	1.00	–	1.000	–	–	–
		TOTAL	40.50	27.50	243.800	116.614	67.9	47.8
December	1944	Pearl Harbor	32.50	18.00	195.500	73.441	55.4	37.6
		Fremantle	6.00	5.00	30.700	13.354	83.3	43.5
		Brisbane	–	–	–	–	–	–
		TOTAL	38.50	23.00	226.200	86.795	59.7	38.4
January	1945	Pearl Harbor	21.00	17.00	71.400	33.194	81.0	46.5
		Fremantle	11.00	10.00	62.500	40.773	90.9	65.2
		Brisbane	–	–	–	–	–	–
		TOTAL	32.00	27.00	133.900	73.967	84.4	55.2

Month	Year							
February	1945	Pearl Harbor	18.00	11.50	78.200	43.698	63.9	55.9
		Fremantle	18.00	17.00	85.600	36.283	94.4	42.4
		TOTAL	36.00	28.50	163.800	79.980	79.2	48.8
March	1945	Pearl Harbor	30.00	23.00	94.500	49.351	76.7	52.2
		Fremantle	13.00	6.00	36.200	20.520	46.2	56.7
		TOTAL	43.00	29.00	130.700	69.870	67.4	53.5
April	1945	Pearl Harbor	24.00	18.00	78.700	30.801	75.0	39.1
		Fremantle	14.00	5.00	31.900	6.967	35.7	21.8
		TOTAL	38.00	23.00	110.600	37.768	60.5	34.1
May	1945	Pearl Harbor	62.00	46.00	213.900	87.869	74.2	41.1
		Fremantle	7.00	6.00	32.300	16.896	85.7	52.3
		TOTAL	69.00	52.00	246.200	104.765	75.4	42.6
June	1945	Pearl Harbor	20.00	6.00	38.600	6.710	30.0	17.4
		Fremantle	5.00	8.00	6.300	5.579	160.0	88.6
		TOTAL	25.00	14.00	44.900	12.278	56.0	27.4
July	1945	Pearl Harbor	18.00	14.00	62.600	35.049	77.8	56.0
		Fremantle	6.00	2.00	12.200	1.389	33.3	11.4
		TOTAL	24.00	16.00	74.800	36.438	66.7	48.7

Source: Clay Blair Jr., *Silent Victory: The U.S. Submarine War Against Japan* (Philadelphia: J. B. Lippincott Co., 1975), 900–983. JANAC refers to the determinations of sinkings of Japanese ships of over five hundred gross tons by the Joint Army–Navy Assessment Committee as reported in February 1947. The Joint Army–Navy Assessment Committee was established in January 1943 to assess Japanese naval and merchant ship losses. Their estimates adjusted downward the initial wartime estimates of losses (Blair, 900).

Table 7.2. Japanese Merchant Vessels Sunk During World War II by Submarines, Other Agents, and All Causes, By Month, December 1941 to July 1945

Year	Month	Sunk By Submarines		Sunk by Other Agents		Total Sunk		Percentage Sunk by Submarines		Average Vessel Tonnage Sunk	
		Number of Vessels	Gross Tonnage (000)	Number of Vessels	Gross Tonnage (000)	Number of Vessels	Gross Tonnage (000)	Number of Vessels	Gross Tonnage (000)	By Submarines (000) Tons	By Others (000) Tons
1941	December	6	31.694	6	26.064	12	57.758	50.00	54.87	5.282	4.344
1941	TOTAL	6	31.694	6	26.064	12	57.758	50.00	54.87	5.282	4.344
1942	January	7	28.351	10	45.514	17	73.865	41.18	38.38	4.050	4.551
	February	4	15.142	5	22.149	9	37.291	44.44	40.60	3.786	4.430
	March	11	41.927	9	61.168	20	103.095	55.00	40.67	3.812	6.796
	April	7	32.997	2	9.799	9	42.796	77.78	77.10	4.714	4.900
	May	22	94.582	2	10.546	24	105.128	91.67	89.97	4.299	5.273
	June	6	20.021	4	18.498	10	38.519	60.00	51.98	3.337	4.625
	July	9	39.012	3	23.319	12	62.331	75.00	62.59	4.335	7.773
	August	19	83.748	4	30.533	23	114.281	82.61	73.28	4.408	7.633
	September	12	45.939	2	8.539	14	54.478	85.71	84.33	3.828	4.270
	October	28	133.717	8	43.280	36	176.997	77.78	75.55	4.776	5.410
	November	9	39.358	21	128.895	30	168.253	30.00	23.39	4.373	6.138
	December	15	56.310	10	32.054	25	88.364	60.00	63.73	3.754	3.205
1942	TOTAL	149	631.104	80	434.294	229	1,065.398	65.07	59.24	4.236	5.429
1943	January	24	112.759	10	46.126	34	158.885	70.59	70.97	4.698	4.613
	February	10	55.367	11	37.295	21	92.662	47.62	59.75	5.537	3.390
	March	23	94.961	14	52.579	37	147.540	62.16	64.36	4.129	3.756
	April	18	88.699	8	44.025	26	132.724	69.23	66.83	4.928	5.503
	May	30	128.138	4	6.523	34	134.661	88.24	95.16	4.271	1.631
	June	23	98.160	3	6.948	26	105.108	88.46	93.39	4.268	2.316
	July	17	70.320	8	14.041	25	84.361	68.00	83.36	4.136	1.755
	August	19	79.932	5	20.132	24	100.064	79.17	79.88	4.207	4.026

Year	Month										
1943	September	31	135.540	14	43.426	45	178.966	68.89	75.74	4.372	3.102
	October	26	128.088	13	30.005	39	158.093	66.67	81.02	4.926	2.308
	November	46	232.333	24	88.474	70	320.807	65.71	72.42	5.051	3.686
	December	29	121.917	24	85.131	53	207.048	54.72	58.88	4.204	3.547
	TOTAL	296	1,346.214	138	474.705	434	1,820.919	68.20	73.93	4.548	3.440
1944	January	53	249.672	42	105.696	95	355.368	55.79	70.26	4.711	2.517
	February	53	252.526	59	266.171	112	518.697	47.32	48.68	4.765	4.511
	March	30	122.921	37	140.884	67	263.805	44.78	46.60	4.097	3.808
	April	24	92.592	14	35.736	38	128.328	63.16	72.15	3.858	2.553
	May	58.5	246.790	5.5	11.801	64	258.591	91.41	95.44	4.219	2.146
	June	48	197.330	23	81.154	71	278.484	67.61	70.86	4.111	3.528
	July	51	220.643	15	31.278	66	251.921	77.27	87.58	4.326	2.085
	August	46	234.012	20	61.01	66	295.022	69.70	79.32	5.087	3.051
	September	43	170.514	77	248.598	120	419.112	35.83	40.68	3.965	3.229
	October	68.5	328.810	61.5	183.568	130	512.378	52.69	64.17	4.800	2.985
	November	51.5	230.446	45.5	190.58	97	421.026	53.09	54.73	4.475	4.189
	December	19.5	104.736	23.5	83.551	43	188.287	45.35	55.63	5.371	3.555
	TOTAL	546	2,450.992	423	1,440.027	969	3,891.019	56.35	62.99	4.489	3.404
1945	January	21	95.403	80	339.245	101	434.648	20.79	21.95	4.543	4.241
	February	15	55.745	18	45.796	33	101.541	45.45	54.90	3.716	2.544
	March	25.5	65.856	55.5	128.793	81	194.649	31.48	33.83	2.583	2.321
	April	19	68.164	33	57.509	52	125.673	36.54	54.24	3.588	1.743
	May	16	31.194	102	239.509	118	270.703	13.56	11.52	1.950	2.348
	June	46	91.339	77	154.591	123	245.930	37.40	37.14	1.986	2.008
	July	14	29.497	131	280.405	145	309.902	9.66	9.52	2.107	2.140
	August	5	15.433	43	83.661	48	99.094	10.42	15.57	3.087	1.946
	TOTAL	161.5	452.631	539.5	1,329.509	701	1,782.140	23.04	25.40	2.803	2.464

Note: Monthly average for 1945 year is based on 7.5 months (cease-fire ordered August 15, 1945).

Source: Joint Naval Assessment Team, *Japanese Merchant and Shipping Losses During World War II by All Causes* (Washington, DC: Government Printing Office, February 1947), 29–99.

Table 7.3. *Japanese Vessels Claimed Sunk and Actually Sunk by U.S. Submarines, Monthly Totals,*
December 1941 to July 1945

Date of Submarine's Departure		Vessels		Tonnage (000)		Actual Sinkings as a % of Claimed	
Year	Month	Wartime Credit	JANAC Credit	Wartime Credit	JANAC Credit	Vessels	Tonnage
1941	December	29.00	10.00	170.600	43.600	34.5	25.6
1941	TOTAL	29.00	10.00	170.600	43.600	34.5	25.6
1942	January	10.00	5.00	46.200	16.825	50.0	36.4
	February	17.00	10.00	108.200	38.985	58.8	36.0
	March	13.00	8.00	68.500	29.002	61.5	42.3
	April	32.00	23.00	191.500	97.687	71.9	51.0
	May	8.00	7.00	64.600	26.800	87.5	41.5
	June	20.00	13.00	97.400	42.226	65.0	43.4
	July	33.00	20.00	245.000	93.940	60.6	38.3
	August	19.00	14.00	124.100	51.709	73.7	40.9
	September	30.00	25.00	214.200	119.085	83.3	55.6
	October	24.00	11.00	142.000	46.264	45.8	32.6
	November	15.00	11.00	83.600	42.700	73.3	51.1
	December	30.00	24.00	164.300	83.298	80.0	50.7
1942	TOTAL	251.00	171.00	1,549.600	687.521	68.1	44.4
1943	January	35.00	23.50	211.800	110.510	67.1	52.2
	February	31.50	20.50	167.600	68.411	65.1	40.8
	March	19.50	13.50	136.200	67.700	69.2	49.7
	April	32.00	26.00	191.700	121.810	81.3	63.5
	May	30.00	27.00	178.100	103.764	90.0	58.3
	June	32.00	21.00	233.800	92.170	65.6	39.4
	July	20.00	17.00	124.200	62.311	85.0	50.2
	August	36.00	26.00	222.400	102.298	72.2	46.0
	September	45.00	32.00	325.500	160.874	71.1	49.4
	October	62.00	41.00	403.900	175.779	66.1	43.5
	November	49.00	37.00	355.200	204.601	75.5	57.6
	December	60.00	51.00	385.200	226.538	85.0	58.8
1943	TOTAL	452.00	335.50	2,935.600	1,496.766	74.2	51.0
1944	January	74.00	57.00	496.700	252.944	77.0	50.9
	February	49.00	40.00	283.300	179.001	81.6	63.2
	March	41.00	29.00	248.000	121.156	70.7	48.9
	April	70.00	57.00	424.700	221.009	81.4	52.0
	May	61.00	47.50	306.700	181.667	77.9	59.2
	June	99.00	72.00	623.900	324.807	72.7	52.1
	July	88.00	53.00	518.600	261.607	60.2	50.4
	August	83.00	51.00	442.500	196.570	61.4	44.4
	September	106.50	78.33	647.624	347.006	73.5	53.6
	October	99.00	72.16	644.600	390.083	72.9	60.5
	November	40.50	27.50	243.800	116.614	67.9	47.8
	December	38.50	23.00	226.200	86.795	59.7	38.4
1944	TOTAL	849.00	607.49	5,106.624	2,679.259	71.5	52.5

Date of Submarine's Departure		Vessels		Tonnage (000)		Actual Sinkings as a % of Claimed	
Year	Month	Wartime Credit	JANAC Credit	Wartime Credit	JANAC Credit	Vessels	Tonnage
1945	January	32.00	27.00	133.900	73.967	84.4	55.2
	February	36.00	28.50	163.800	79.981	79.2	48.8
	March	43.00	29.00	130.700	69.871	67.4	53.5
	April	38.00	23.00	110.600	37.768	60.5	34.1
	May	69.00	52.00	246.200	104.765	75.4	42.6
	June	25.00	14.00	44.900	12.289	56.0	27.4
	July	24.00	16.00	74.800	36.438	66.7	48.7
	August	0.00	0.00	0.000	0.000		
1945	TOTAL	267.00	189.50	904.900	415.079	71.00	45.9

Source: See Table 7.1.

their] antisubmarine attacks," because, in their view, every attack resulted in a sunken submarine.[16]

3. U.S. TECHNOLOGY: SUBMARINES, TORPEDOS, AND MINES

The American submarine was destined to become one of the most devastating weapons of the Pacific campaign; however, its emergence as the weapon of choice was initially not obvious; and it was certainly not instantaneous. "Karl Lautenschläger has identified five general principles that govern the use of submarines in naval warfare": (1) submarines "possess no inherent immunity against countermeasures"; (2) "navies have trouble integrating submarines into existing force structures and operational concepts"; (3) "competing wartime demands on submarines often preclude their achieving full potential"; (4) "submarine campaigns provide neither quick nor simple routes to victory"; and (5) "submarine and surface fleets are not alternatives; navies almost never possess a clear either–or choice."[17] The problems raised by the second of these five principles already have been noted. The United States also found that the efficiency of the efforts that the Navy directed against the Japanese economy were impacted by the third, fourth, and fifth, as well.

When, after 1918, the American navy began to replace its aging submarines and, later, as it began to build up its undersea fleet, the choice of

---

16 Morison, *Two-Ocean War*, 496–497.
17 Karl Lautenschläger, "The Submarine in Naval Warfare, 1901–2001," *International Security*, 11 (Winter 1986–1987), 94–140. Cited in Herwig, "Innovation Ignored," 227–228.

the type of submarine to be added to the fleet was, at least in part, dictated by the number and location of the country's naval bases – few and far between. Either because of the preferences of the naval bureaucracy, or because of lack of intelligence, the navy had never acquired the equivalent of Germany's "milch cows." As a result, American submarines had to be "capable of self-sustained cruising for long periods over great distances." Given that constraint, when the war began, the majority of the fleet consisted of "large fleet-type submarines of greater endurance, reliability, and comfort than the smaller types favored by European powers."[18] Moreover, in 1940, the fleet contained vessels that had been built as long ago as 1918. Hardly surprisingly, over those interwar years there had been considerable technological improvement. On average, the American submarines displaced about 1,500 tons and were manned by a crew averaging seven officers and seventy men. They had a cruising range of about ten thousand miles; carried supplies for sixty days, and could operate at speeds of twenty knots on the surface and nine knots while submerged.[19] The interwar technological improvements flowed from both design changes and, particularly, from advances in engine performance. By 1940, the design changes and engine improvements had come together to produce the *Tambor* class submarines; probably the best American submarine of the war. Those twelve submarines were each nearly twice the size of the typical German boats, and they were powered by four diesel engines. Most important, the *Tambor* (and subsequent classes) possessed both speed and maneuverability. Moreover, with four engines, they could continue to cruise while charging their batteries; and they were air-conditioned. The latter quality made them livable in the tropics and kept up morale during the long Pacific cruises. Throughout the war, the Pacific submarine fleet was based largely at Pearl Harbor, and Brisbane and Fremantle in Australia. Initially a few submarines also had been based at Manila and in Alaska and later, although their primary bases were still in Pearl Harbor and Australia, tactically many sortied from "advanced" bases near Japan.[20]

At the end of the war, the Americans came to realize that their submarines had been technically inferior to those of the Germans. The German submarines had better speed both on the surface and while submerged; "they

18 Morison, *Two-Ocean War*, 494. The majority of American submarines displaced about 1,500 tons. The exceptions were the older S-boats (800 to 1,100 tons), but they had largely been retired by 1943. The navy also had three larger U.S. submarines (*Argonaut, Narwhal,* and *Nautilus*), vessels built in 1928 and 1930; and they ran up to 2,700 tons displacement. For the listing of the nineteen classes of submarines operational at some time between 1940 and 1945, see Samuel Eliot Morison, *Supplement and General Index* (Boston: Little, Brown, 1962), 54–60.
19 Morison, *Two-Ocean War*, 494.
20 Herwig, "Innovation Ignored," 258; Morison, *Two-Ocean War*, 497.

could dive deeper and faster"; and they had "superior sonar, optics, diesel engines, and batteries." Moreover, both the Germans and the Japanese had built submarines with schnorkels. However, given the constraint imposed by few and distant U.S. bases and the benefits derived from the failure of torpedoes the Japanese countersubmarine strategies, the American submarines proved more than adequate for the tasks assigned to them. Moreover, they might have proved even more effective, had American overall military strategy not been twisted by politics and the personal desires of some military leaders.[21]

The same cannot be said for American torpedoes. The Japanese had entered the war with the world's best torpedo, and they had ended the war with torpedoes that were still better than anything the U.S. Bureau of Ordinance had managed to produce.[22] During their Norwegian campaign, the Germans also had encountered torpedo problems – their torpedoes often failed to hit their target; and, when they did, they often failed to explode. The major problems were in the contact pistol – a mechanism that, because of its faulty action and the ineffectiveness of the initial charge, was liable to fail when the angle of incidence was less than 50° – and in the level of pressure maintained in the balance chambers. Those problems had, however, been almost completely overcome by December 1942.[23]

In the case of the American fleet, the problems were both more serious and not so quickly solved. In fact, unlike much of naval history, the story of the American torpedo has the flavor of a good political scandal. In the words of one student of the war, "the torpedo scandal of the U.S, submarine force in World War II was one of the worst in the history of any kind of warfare."[24] During much of 1942 and 1943 the navy depended on a single source for its torpedoes, "the torpedo factory at Newport [Rhode Island] that was under the direct patronage of the Rhode Island congressional delegation." Moreover, in designing its new torpedoes, the Bureau of Ordinance had developed a badly flawed magnetic exploder – an exploder that depended on the target's magnetic field to provide the "trigger" to set it off. Moreover, the Bureau had never tested any torpedoes with live warheads. Instead, because of the alleged costs involved, even after Pearl Harbor, the Bureau continued to test only torpedoes with light, dummy warheads. When live explosives were used in combat, the torpedoes were heavier and, hardly

21 Clay Blair, Jr., *Silent Victory: The U.S. Submarine War Against Japan* (Philadelphia: J. B. Lippincott, 1975), 881–882. Morison, *Two-Ocean War*, 493–500.
22 Blair, *Silent Victory*, 881.
23 Karl L. Doenitz, *Memoirs: Ten Years and Twenty Days* (Annapolis: Naval Institute Press, 1990, first published 1958), 91–94.
24 Blair, *Silent Victory*, 879.

surprisingly, ran as much as eleven feet deeper than they were designed to, therefore often passing under the target vessel rather than striking it and exploding. Moreover, even when the torpedo physically came in contact with the target, the "contact exploder was so fragile that a direct hit was often sufficient to destroy it without causing the torpedo to explode."

"Nothing in three years of war caused the Bureau of Ordinance to lose faith in its torpedos." Multiple reports of malfunctions from the Pacific fleet were insufficient to convince the Bureau to test their torpedos; instead, they argued that the cause of the failure lay with the submarine crews. The complaints of the officers of the submarine *Sargo* finally forced the Bureau to send an investigating officer to the Pacific fleet to examine those alleged crew mispractices. Although the investigator could "not point out a single fault" in the crew's "preparations and maintenance procedures," his report, reflecting the Bureau's concern with potential political fallout, placed the blame for the torpedo failures on the *Sargo's* crew; and the officers of "the Bureau of Ordinance reaffirmed their position that the Mark XIV torpedoes ran at their set depth." It would be the summer of 1943 before U.S. submarines were finally equipped with torpedoes that, although inferior to those of their Japanese competitors, still worked with a fairly high degree of probability.[25] By then, the torpedo problems were finally largely solved. Both the Mark XIV steam and the Mark XVIII electric torpedo were largely debugged, and "the production bottlenecks had been overcome." Within a few months, boats going on patrol were outfitted with the new torpedoes (on average, about three-quarters electric and one-quarter steam torpedoes); in addition, "the speed of the electric had been increased to, about forty knots, depending on water temperature."[26]

In the case of mines, the story is less grim. Magnetic mines had been deployed by the British against merchant shipping in 1917; and, during World War II, the Germans were quick to seize and, ultimately, to improve on that tactic by adding pressure mines to their armory.[27] During the war,

25 Herwig, "Innovation Ignored," 259–260; Blair, *Silent Victory*, 71,170.
26 Blair, *Silent Victory*, 694.
27 In October 1939, German mines sank 11 Allied vessels totaling 29,490 tons, in November the figures were 27 and 120,985, and in December 32 and 82,557. John Terraine, *Business in Great Waters* (Ware: Wordsworth Editions, 1989), 33, 34, 225, 699 (note 36). "The Germans realised that their best weapon available to them was the new pressure-operated mine," – a mine that was "almost impossible to sweep; – but they refused to risk compromising the invention by using it prematurely and in fact no pressure mines were laid before D-Day." Roskill, *Offensive, Part II*, 15. The British had, in fact, recovered one of the new mines in November 1939. S. W. Roskill, *The War at Sea, 1939–1945. vol. 1, The Defensive* (London: Her Majesty's Printing Office 1954), 100. S. W. Roskill, *The War at Sea, 1939–1945 Vol. 3. The Offensive, Part I: 1st June 1943–31st May 1944* (London: Her Majesty's Printing Office, 1960), 29.

the British and the Germans used both submarines and surface vessels and, near the end of the war, airplanes, to lay their mines. The Americans initially depended on the magnetic mine. Their innovation – an innovation later copied by the Germans – was the use of aircraft to deploy those mines in locations that were difficult for submarines and surface vessels to reach. In "February 1943, Liberators of the U.S. Tenth Air Force, which were based in Calcutta, had laid mines in the Rangoon river delta"; and other parallel missions soon followed.[28] Just over a year later, on March 31, 1944, "specially equipped Avenger squadrons from the [aircraft carriers] *Lexington, Bunker Hill*, and *Hornet*," in a successful effort to prevent Japanese warships from escaping planned American air attacks and mined two passages to the main harbor at Palau.[29] Finally, in the closing months of the war (between March 27 and August 15, 1945), U.S. Army Air Force B-29 long-range bombers operating out of the Marianas dropped more than twelve thousand mines in the waters between Japan and the "Inner Zone" (Manchuria, Korea, and North China). Those mines were all of the "influence" type (that is, mines that did not require direct contact), and they were usually aimed by radar and released from "heights between five and eight thousand feet." Most had variable delay mechanisms; and, during the final weeks of the war, the standard magnetic and acoustic mines were supplemented by the "new" pressure-operated variety. "It was not long before these tactics completely overwhelmed the Japanese minesweeping service." Although the submarine had been the first and, in terms of the entire wartime effort, remained, the most important instrument of the blockade of the Home Islands, "it was the air-laid mines which finally strangled Japan."[30]

4. THE QUANTITATIVE STORY: THE DATA

The quantitative data on the war against Japan are brought together in Tables 7.1 through 7.23. Over the entire war, some three hundred U.S. submarines operating from bases in Alaska, Brisbane, Fremantle, Manila, and Pearl Harbor, conducted over fifteen hundred sorties against Japanese shipping. Although the actual totals fell short of the wartime claims, the submarines were officially credited with sinking 1,314 vessels totaling 5,320,094

---

28 Roskill, *Offensive, Part II*, 352.
29 "The aviators, who did not like this assignment, called themselves the 'Flying Miners,' with an improvised emblem of crossed shovel and pick-axe." Samuel Eliot Morison, *New Guinea and the Marianas, March 1944–August 1944* (Boston: Little, Brown, 1953), 32.
30 Roskill, *Offensive, Part II*, 370–371.

tons.[31] Of that total, and most relevant to this discussion, 1,113 vessels totaling 4,779,902 tons were merchant ships (see also Tables 7.2 and 7.3).[32] All told, Japanese merchant vessel losses due to submarines increased from a monthly average of 6 vessels and 31,694 tons in December 1941, to 12.42 vessels and 52,592 tons in 1942, to 24.67 vessels and 112,185 tons in 1943, and to 45.5 vessels and 204,249 tons in 1944. Finally, the seven and one-half months before the cease fire of August 15, 1945 saw the submarines' monthly vessel total fall to an average of 21.53 vessels; and, with few large ships remaining in the Japanese fleet, the average monthly tonnage figure fell to 60,351. The tonnage of the average vessel sunk by "other agents" fell from 3,404 in 1944 to 2,464 in 1945, whereas the figure for the submarine fleet fell from 4,489 tons to 2,803 tons. In terms of the total losses of merchantmen, the submarine fleet accounted for 50.0 percent of the number of vessels and 54.8 percent of tonnage in December 1941, 65.1 percent of the vessels and 59.2 percent of the tonnage in the twelve months of 1942, 68.2 percent of the vessels and 73.9 percent of the tonnage in 1943, 56.3 percent of the vessels and 63.0 percent of the tonnage in 1944, but only 23.0 percent of the vessels and 25.4 percent of the tonnage in the seven and one-half months of 1945. Overall, submarines accounted for 52.6 percent of the vessels and 60.4 percent of the Japanese merchant tonnage losses due to U.S. forces over the forty-five months of the war.

The cost of that effort, in terms of submarines lost, amounted to a wartime total of 49 − 1 in 1941, 6 in 1942, 15 in 1943, 19 in 1944, and 8 in 1945. And, when set against the merchant ship sinking, those losses work out to an "exchange ratio of 31,694 tons per submarine lost in December 1941, 105,184 for the year 1942, 89,748 in 1943, 129,000 in 1944, and 56,579 in 1945. Those figures work out to an average of 100,258 tons for the entire forty-five and a half months of the war.[33]

Although it was the merchant vessels that were the target of the blockade, as merchant vessels accounted for over 80 percent of the total tonnage sunk,

---

31 Herwig, citing Lockwood, *Sink Em All*, puts the tonnage sunk at 4,779,902 tons of merchant shipping and 540,192 tons of warships, a total of 5,320,094 tons. Herwig, "Innovation Ignored," 252–253.

32 In addition, British and Dutch submarines accounted for some sinkings. See footnote 33.

33 Blair, *Silent Victory*, 900–983, 991–992, and Table 7.1. It should be noted that the figures are for Allied submarine sinkings. Although American submarines were by far the most important, British and Dutch submarines were responsible for three vessels of 16,731 tons in December 1941, five vessels of 29,009 tons in 1942, four vessels of 15,344 tons in 1943, twenty-two vessels of 41,277 tons in 1944, and five vessels of 4,728 tons in 1945 − a total of thirty-nine vessels of 107,089 tons. Overall, these sinkings represented 3.4 percent of the number of merchant vessels and 2.2 percent of the merchant tonnage sunk by submarines. Joint Army-Navy Assessment, *Japanese Naval and Merchant Shipping Losses*, viii.

it does not appear unreasonable to examine the data on the total vessels sunk during the 1,578 sorties from Pearl Harbor, Manila, Brisbane, Alaska, and Fremantle.[34] It should, however, be noted that the figures for vessels and tonnage lost refer to the month that the submarine departed its base, not necessarily the month that the vessels in question were sunk. As a result, these figures in Tables 7.4 and 7.5 are not directly comparable to those reported in Table 7.1.

In December 1941, each sortie resulted in .19 vessels and 807 tons of shipping sunk – figures that work out to an average of .006 vessels and 25 tons per submarine day at sea. Over the twelve months ending in December 1942, each submarine sank .55 vessels totaling 2,228 tons (.013 vessels and 54 tons per day at sea). During 1943 the average per sortie was .93 vessels and 4,181 tons (.022 vessels and 99 tons per day). Over the next year, the averages had again increased – this time to 1.17 vessels of 5,728 tons (.024 vessels and 106 tons per day). However, as the Japanese navy and merchant fleet shrank, so did the measured efficiency of the U.S. submarines – to .55 vessels of 1,207 tons (.012 and 27 tons per day) in the seven and one-half months of 1945 (see Table 7.5).

In an attempt to sort out the effects of changes in efficiency from changes in the number and range of targets, somewhat different efficiency measures were calculated – measures using as a base the number of Japanese merchant vessels "at risk" rather than the number sunk (see Table 7.6). The adjustment compensates for the number of targets; however, it does not compensate for the fact that, with fewer vessels, the concentration of vessels per square mile had declined or for the fact that the remaining vessels were operating close to shore and in other areas that it was difficult for submarines to reach vessels. Not surprisingly, therefore, although the adjustment reduces, it does not eliminate, the decline in the efficiency measures over the last seven and one-half months of the war.

These figures on vessels and tonnages sunk taken together with the data on the number of submarines lost imply "trade-off" ratios of 10 vessels and 43,600 tons in December 1941 (see Table 7.5). For the months January to December 1942, that figure had risen to an average of 14.25 vessels of 57,293 tons. The figures for the sorties departing in 1943 were higher – 27.88 vessels of 124,730 tons per submarine. That year the navy had lost fifteen submarines and more than 1,100 men, but the fleet continued to grow.

---

34 Later in the war, although the vessels continued to be based in Pearl Harbor and Australia, many were actually deployed from for "advanced" naval bases.

Table 7.4. *Japanese Vessels Sunk by U.S. Submarines, By Base, By Month, December 1941 to August 1945 and Measures of Economic Efficiency*

Date of Submarine's Departure		Submarine Base	JANAC Credit		Number of Submarines	Total Days at Sea	Sunk per Submarine		Sunk per Submarine Day at Sea	
Month	Year		Vessels	Tonnage (000)			Vessels	Tonnage (000)	Vessels	Tonnage (000)
December	1941	Pearl Harbor	4.00	14.100	11	483	0.36	1.282	0.008	0.029
		Manila	6.00	29.500	43	1,234	0.14	0.686	0.005	0.024
		TOTAL	10.00	43.600	54	1,717	0.19	0.807	0.006	0.025
January	1942	Pearl Harbor	4.00	12.701	6	337	0.67	2.117	0.012	0.038
		Australia	1.00	4.124	8	248	0.13	0.516	0.004	0.017
		TOTAL	5.00	16.825	14	585	0.36	1.202	0.009	0.029
February	1942	Pearl Harbor	7.00	24.145	7	359	1.00	3.449	0.019	0.067
		Australia	3.00	14.840	18	583	0.17	0.824	0.005	0.025
		Alaska	0.00	0.000	2	30	0.00	0.000	0.000	0.000
		TOTAL	10.00	38.985	27	972	0.37	1.444	0.010	0.040
March	1942	Pearl Harbor	4.00	16.415	4	200	1.00	4.104	0.020	0.082
		Australia	4.00	12.587	8	393	0.50	1.573	0.010	0.032
		Alaska	0.00	0.000	1	12	0.00	0.000	0.000	0.000
		TOTAL	8.00	29.002	13	605	0.62	2.231	0.013	0.048
April	1942	Pearl Harbor	18.00	74.843	12	649	1.50	6.237	0.028	0.115
		Fremantle	3.00	12.800	8	333	0.38	1.600	0.009	0.038
		Brisbane	2.00	10.044	4	108	0.50	2.511	0.019	0.093
		Alaska	0.00	0.000	2	47	0.00	0.000	0.000	0.000
		TOTAL	23.00	97.687	26	1,137	0.88	3.757	0.020	0.086
May	1942	Pearl Harbor	0.00	0.000	19	394	0.00	0.000	0.000	0.000
		Fremantle	7.00	26.800	9	482	0.78	2.978	0.015	0.056
		Brisbane	0.00	0.000	6	185	0.00	0.000	0.000	0.000
		Alaska	0.00	0.000	6	198	0.00	0.000	0.000	0.000
		TOTAL	7.00	26.800	40	1,259	0.18	0.670	0.006	0.021

Month	Year	Location								
June	1942	Pearl Harbor	4.00	12.700	7	356	0.57	1.814	0.011	0.036
		Fremantle	4.00	23.200	6	286	0.67	3.867	0.014	0.078
		Brisbane	1.00	2.626	5	122	0.20	0.525	0.008	0.022
		Alaska	4.00	3.700	5	186	0.80	0.740	0.022	0.020
		TOTAL	13.00	42.226	23	960	0.57	1.836	0.014	0.044
July	1942	Pearl Harbor	14.00	60.550	11	608	1.27	5.505	0.023	0.100
		Fremantle	4.00	18.962	10	522	0.40	1.896	0.008	0.036
		Brisbane	2.00	14.428	8	240	0.25	1.804	0.008	0.060
		Alaska	0.00	0.000	9	311	0.00	0.000	0.000	0.000
		TOTAL	20.00	93.940	38	1,681	0.53	2.472	0.012	0.056
August	1942	Pearl Harbor	12.00	43.703	9	364	1.33	4.857	0.033	0.120
		Fremantle	2.00	7.000	4	246	0.50	1.750	0.008	0.028
		Brisbane	0.00	0.000	5	137	0.00	0.000	0.000	0.000
		Alaska	0.00	0.000	5	162	0.00	0.000	0.000	0.000
		TOTAL	14.00	50.709	23	909	0.61	2.205	0.015	0.056
September	1942	Pearl Harbor	20.00	94.600	8	418	2.50	11.825	0.048	0.226
		Fremantle	2.00	9.800	5	294	0.40	1.960	0.007	0.033
		Brisbane	3.00	14.685	8	320	0.38	1.836	0.009	0.046
		Alaska	0.00	0.000	4	115	0.00	0.000	0.000	0.000
		TOTAL	25.00	119.085	25	1,147	1.00	4.763	0.022	0.104
October	1942	Pearl Harbor	3.00	12.500	10	467	0.30	1.250	0.006	0.027
		Fremantle	7.00	30.900	6	290	1.17	5.150	0.024	0.107
		Brisbane	0.00	0.000	12	487	0.00	0.000	0.000	0.000
		Alaska	1.00	2.864	8	234	0.13	0.358	0.004	0.012
		TOTAL	11.00	46.264	36	1,478	0.31	1.285	0.007	0.031

(continued)

345

Table 7.4 (continued)

Date of Submarine's Departure		Submarine Base	JANAC Credit		Number of Submarines	Total Days at Sea	Sunk per Submarine		Sunk per Submarine Day at Sea	
Month	Year		Vessels	Tonnage (000)			Vessels	Tonnage (000)	Vessels	Tonnage (000)
November	1942	Pearl Harbor	9.00	40.100	10	510	0.90	4.010	0.018	0.079
		Fremantle	1.00	0.600	1	53	1.00	0.600	0.019	0.011
		Brisbane	1.00	2.000	7	359	0.14	0.286	0.003	0.006
		**	0.00	0.000	2	44	0.00	0.000	0.000	0.000
		TOTAL	11.00	42.700	20	966	0.55	2.135	0.011	0.044
December	1942	Pearl Harbor	13.00	37.300	10	446	1.30	3.730	0.029	0.080
		Fremantle	6.00	16.200	5	225	1.20	3.240	0.027	0.072
		Brisbane	5.00	29.798	5	238	1.00	5.960	0.021	0.125
		Alaska	0.00	0.000	4	89	0.00	0.000	0.000	0.000
		TOTAL	24.00	83.298	24	998	1.00	3.471	0.024	0.083
January	1943	Pearl Harbor	7.00	54.210	8	357	0.88	6.776	0.020	0.152
		Fremantle	3.00	11.750	3	145	1.00	3.917	0.021	0.081
		Brisbane	13.50	44.550	9	398	1.15	4.950	0.034	0.112
		Alaska	0.00	0.000	2	51	0.00	0.000	0.000	0.000
		TOTAL	23.50	110.510	22	951	1.07	5.023	0.025	0.116
February	1943	Pearl Harbor	17.50	58.411	10	459	1.75	5.841	0.038	0.127
		Fremantle	2.00	7.000	3	161	0.67	2.333	0.012	0.043
		Brisbane	1.00	3.000	5	111	0.20	0.600	0.009	0.027
		Alaska	0.00	0	2	45	0.00	0.000	0.000	0.000
		TOTAL	20.50	68.411	20	776	1.03	3.421	0.026	0.088

Month	Year	Location								
March	1943	Pearl Harbor	9.50	43.700	11	407	0.86	3.973	0.023	0.107
		Fremantle	3.00	19.000	4	104	0.75	4.750	0.029	0.183
		Brisbane	1.00	5.000	3	171	0.33	1.667	0.006	0.029
		Alaska	0.00	0.000	2	50	0.00	0.000	0.000	0.000
		TOTAL	13.50	67.70	20	732	0.68	3.385	0.018	0.092
April	1943	Pearl Harbor	19.00	78.510	17	745	1.12	4.618	0.026	0.105
		Fremantle	5.00	31.000	3	125	1.67	10.333	0.040	0.248
		Brisbane	2.00	12.300	4	181	0.50	3.075	0.011	0.068
		Alaska	0.00	0.000	5	158	0.00	0.000	0.000	0.000
		TOTAL	26.00	121.810	29	1,209	0.90	4.200	0.022	0.101
May	1943	Pearl Harbor	18.00	77.800	15	641	1.20	5.187	0.028	0.121
		Fremantle	5.00	13.600	4	212	1.25	3.400	0.024	0.064
		Brisbane	2.00	6.100	4	217	0.50	1.525	0.009	0.028
		Alaska	2.00	6.264	3	79	0.67	2.088	0.025	0.079
		TOTAL	27.00	103.764	26	1,149	1.04	3.991	0.023	0.090
June	1943	Pearl Harbor	17.00	74.740	24	1,031	0.71	3.114	0.016	0.072
		Fremantle	1.00	5.000	2	76	0.50	2.500	0.013	0.066
		Brisbane	2.00	7.000	5	240	0.40	1.400	0.008	0.029
		Alaska	1.00	5.430	5	177	0.20	1.086	0.006	0.031
		TOTAL	21.00	92.17	36	1,524	0.58	2.560	0.014	0.060
July	1943	Pearl Harbor	12.00	39.940	17	808	0.71	2.349	0.015	0.049
		Fremantle	4.00	16.500	3	111	1.33	5.500	0.036	0.149
		Brisbane	1.00	5.871	6	272	0.17	0.979	0.004	0.022
		Alaska	0.00	0.000	3	90	0.00	0.000	0.000	0.000
		TOTAL	17.00	62.311	29	1,281	0.59	2.149	0.013	0.049

(continued)

Table 7.4 (continued)

Date of Submarine's Departure		Submarine Base	JANAC Credit		Number of Submarines	Total Days at Sea	Sunk per Submarine		Sunk per Submarine Day at Sea	
Month	Year		Vessels	Tonnage (000)			Vessels	Tonnage (000)	Vessels	Tonnage (000)
August	1943	Pearl Harbor	18.00	71.272	18	724	1.00	3.960	0.025	0.149
		Fremantle	5.00	21.662	6	315	0.83	3.610	0.016	0.022
		Brisbane	3.00	9.394	6	271	0.50	1.561	0.011	0.035
		Alaska	0.00	0.000	4	120	0.00	0.000	0.000	0.000
		TOTAL	26.00	102.298	34	1,430	0.76	3.009	0.018	0.072
September	1943	Pearl Harbor	18.00	100.619	25	1,057	0.72	4.025	0.017	0.095
		Fremantle	10.00	40.287	6	238	1.67	6.715	0.042	0.169
		Brisbane	3.00	18.600	2	81	1.50	9.300	0.037	0.230
		Alaska	1.00	1.368	4	113	0.25	0.342	0.000	0.012
		TOTAL	32.00	160.874	37	1,489	0.86	4.348	0.021	0.108
October	1943	Pearl Harbor	31.00	128.506	21	952	1.48	6.119	0.033	0.135
		Fremantle	4.00	21.173	5	175	0.80	4.235	0.023	0.121
		Brisbane	6.00	26.100	6	250	1.00	4.350	0.024	0.104
		Alaska	0.00	0.000	1	28	0.00	0.000	0.000	0.000
		TOTAL	41.00	175.779	33	1,405	1.24	5.327	0.029	0.125
November	1943	Pearl Harbor	18.00	113.859	19	756	0.95	5.993	0.024	0.151
		Fremantle	11.00	47.670	7	307	1.57	6.810	0.036	0.155
		Brisbane	8.00	43.072	5	190	1.60	8.614	0.042	0.227
		Alaska	0.00	0.000	1	20	0.00	0.000	0.000	0.000
		TOTAL	37.00	204.601	32	1,273	1.16	6.394	0.029	0.161
December	1943	Pearl Harbor	32.00	137.900	24	1,184	1.33	5.716	0.027	0.116
		Fremantle	13.00	61.348	8	341	1.63	7.669	0.038	0.180
		Brisbane	6.00	28.000	5	253	1.20	5.600	0.024	0.111
		Alaska	0.00	0.000	3	87	0.00	0.000	0.000	0.000
		TOTAL	51.00	226.538	40	1,865	1.28	5.663	0.027	0.121

January	1944	Pearl Harbor	50.00	223.113	26	1,235	1.92	8.581	0.040	0.181
		Fremantle	7.00	29.831	7	345	1.00	4.262	0.020	0.086
		Brisbane	0.00	0.000	0	0	0.00	0.00	0.00	0.00
		TOTAL	57.00	252.94	33	1,580	1.73	7.665	0.036	0.160
February	1944	Pearl Harbor	25.00	92.561	20	934	1.25	4.628	0.027	0.099
		Fremantle	9.00	60.700	10	485	0.90	6.070	0.019	0.125
		Brisbane	6.00	25.740	4	183	1.50	6.435	0.033	0.141
		TOTAL	40.00	179.00	34	1,602	1.18	5.265	0.025	0.112
March	1944	Pearl Harbor	24.00	102.882	27	1,389	0.89	3.810	0.017	0.074
		Fremantle	4.00	15.474	2	86	2.00	7.737	0.047	0.180
		Brisbane	1.00	2.800	6	363	0.17	0.467	0.003	0.008
		TOTAL	29.00	121.156	35	1,838	0.83	3.462	0.016	0.066
April	1944	Pearl Harbor	25.50	106.228	29	1,417	0.88	3.663	0.018	0.075
		Fremantle	26.50	92.881	14	721	1.89	6.634	0.037	0.129
		Brisbane	5.00	21.900	3	193	1.67	7.300	0.026	0.113
		TOTAL	57.00	221.009	46	2,331	1.24	4.805	0.024	0.095
May	1944	Pearl Harbor	32.50	130.532	26	1,176	1.25	5.020	0.028	0.111
		Fremantle	1.00	6.440	11	470	0.09	0.585	0.030	0.014
		Brisbane	14.00	44.695	1	50	14.00	44.695	0.280	0.894
		TOTAL	47.50	181.667	38	1,696	1.25	4.781	0.028	0.107
June	1944	Pearl Harbor	48.00	216.584	32	1,596	1.50	6.768	0.030	0.136
		Fremantle	14.00	74.743	12	491	1.17	6.229	0.029	0.152
		Brisbane	10.00	33.480	8	359	1.25	4.185	0.028	0.0295
		TOTAL	72.00	324.807	52	2,441	1.38	6.246	0.029	0.133

(continued)

Table 7.4 (continued)

Date of Submarine's Departure		Submarine Base	JANAC Credit		Number of Submarines	Total Days at Sea	Sunk per Submarine		Sunk per Submarine Day at Sea	
Month	Year		Vessels	Tonnage (000)			Vessels	Tonnage (000)	Vessels	Tonnage (000)
July	1944	Pearl Harbor	28.00	137.957	23	1,217	1.22	5.998	0.023	0.113
		Fremantle	22.00	116.700	13	626	1.69	8.977	0.035	0.186
		Brisbane	3.00	6.950	2	97	1.50	3.475	0.031	0.072
		TOTAL	53.00	261.61	38	1,940	1.39	6.884	0.027	0.135
August	1944	Pearl Harbor	38.50	164.763	34	1,753	1.13	4.846	0.022	0.094
		Fremantle	10.50	27.507	12	427	0.88	2.292	0.025	0.064
		Brisbane	2.00	4.300	5	269	0.40	0.860	0.007	0.016
		TOTAL	51.00	196.57	51	2,449	1.00	3.854	0.021	0.080
September	1944	Pearl Harbor	42.00	165.675	35	1,719	1.20	4.734	0.024	0.096
		Fremantle	32.33	144.190	17	718	1.90	8.482	0.045	0.201
		Brisbane	4.00	37.141	5	172	0.80	7.428	0.023	0.216
		TOTAL	78.33	347.006	57	2,609	1.37	6.088	0.030	0.133
October	1944	Pearl Harbor	49.00	303.023	35	1,683	1.40	8.658	0.029	0.180
		Fremantle	22.66	84.241	20	976	1.13	4.212	0.023	0.086
		Brisbane	0.50	2.819	1	46	0.50	2.819	0.011	0.061
		TOTAL	72.16	390.083	56	2,705	1.29	6.966	0.027	0.144
November	1944	Pearl Harbor	15.50	56.620	24	1,230	0.65	2.355	0.013	0.046
		Fremantle	12.00	60.094	10	529	1.20	6.009	0.023	0.114
		Brisbane	0.00	0.000	1	26	0.00	0.000	0.000	0.000
		TOTAL	27.50	116.614	35	1,785	0.79	3.332	0.015	0.065
December	1944	Pearl Harbor	18.00	73.441	31	1,479	0.58	2.369	0.012	0.050
		Fremantle	5.00	13.354	11	610	0.45	1.214	0.008	0.022
		Brisbane	0.00	0.000	3	99	0.00	0.000	0.000	0.000
		TOTAL	23.00	86.795	45	2,188	0.51	1.929	0.011	0.040

January	1945	Pearl Harbor	17.00	33.194	33	1,788	0.52	1.006	0.010	0.019
		Fremantle	10.00	40.773	11	476	0.91	3.707	0.021	0.086
		Brisbane	0.00	0.000	2	115	0.00	0.000	0.000	0.000
		TOTAL	27.00	73.967	46	2,379	0.59	1.608	0.011	0.031
February	1945	Pearl Harbor	11.50	43.698	22	1,182	0.52	1.986	0.010	0.037
		Fremantle	17.00	36.283	14	658	1.21	2.592	0.026	0.055
		TOTAL	28.50	79.981	36	1,840	0.79	2.222	0.015	0.043
March	1945	Pearl Harbor	23.00	49.351	32	1,376	0.72	1.542	0.017	0.036
		Fremantle	6.00	20.520	19	798	0.32	1.080	0.008	0.026
		TOTAL	29.00	69.871	51	2,174	0.57	1.370	0.013	0.032
April	1945	Pearl Harbor	18.00	30.801	33	1,509	0.55	0.933	0.012	0.020
		Fremantle	5.00	6.967	13	506	0.38	0.536	0.010	0.014
		TOTAL	23.00	37.768	46	2,015	0.50	0.821	0.011	0.019
May	1945	Pearl Harbor	46.00	87.869	44	2,142	1.05	1.997	0.021	0.041
		Fremantle	6.00	16.896	13	558	0.46	1.300	0.011	0.030
		TOTAL	52.00	104.765	57	2,700	0.91	1.838	0.019	0.039
June	1945	Pearl Harbor	6.00	6.710	30	1,506	0.20	0.224	0.004	0.004
		Fremantle	8.00	5.579	10	408	0.80	0.558	0.020	0.014
		TOTAL	14.00	12.289	40	1,914	0.35	0.307	0.007	0.006
July	1945	Pearl Harbor	14.00	35.049	36	1,612	0.39	0.974	0.009	0.022
		Fremantle	2.00	1.389	15	450	0.13	0.093	0.004	0.003
		TOTAL	16.00	36.438	51	2,062	0.31	0.714	0.008	0.018
August	1945	Pearl Harbor	0.00	0.000	13	364	0.00	0.000	0.000	0.000
		Fremantle	0.00	0.000	4	52	0.00	0.000	0.000	0.000
		TOTAL	0.00	0.000	17	416	0.00	0.000	0.000	0.000

Note: Lost submarines without date of loss have been assigned one-half the average patrol length for the month in question.

Source: Blair, *Silent Victory*, 900–983.

Table 7.5. *Japanese Merchant Vessels Sunk by U.S. Submarines, By Month, December 1941 to August 1945 and Measures of Economic Efficiency*

Date of Submarine's Departure		JANAC Credit		Number of Submarines	Total Days at Sea	Sunk per Submarine		Sunk per Submarine Day at Sea	
Year	Month	Vessels	Tonnage (000)			Vessels	Tonnage (000)	Vessels	Tonnage (000)
1941	December	10.00	43.600	54	1,717	0.19	0.807	0.006	0.025
1941	TOTAL	10.00	43.600	54	1,717	0.19	0.807	0.006	0.025
1942	January	5.00	16.825	14	585	0.36	1.202	0.009	0.029
	February	10.00	38.985	27	972	0.37	1.444	0.010	0.040
	March	8.00	29.002	13	605	0.62	2.231	0.013	0.048
	April	23.00	97.687	26	1,137	0.88	3.757	0.020	0.086
	May	7.00	26.800	40	1,259	0.18	0.670	0.006	0.021
	June	13.00	42.226	23	960	0.57	1.836	0.014	0.044
	July	20.00	93.940	38	1,681	0.53	2.472	0.012	0.056
	August	14.00	50.709	23	909	0.61	2.205	0.015	0.056
	September	25.00	119.085	25	1,147	1.00	4.763	0.022	0.104
	October	11.00	46.264	36	1,478	0.31	1.285	0.007	0.031
	November	11.00	42.700	20	966	0.55	2.135	0.011	0.044
	December	24.00	83.298	24	998	1.00	3.471	0.024	0.083
1942	TOTAL	171.00	687.521	309	12,697	0.55	2.228	0.013	0.054
1943	January	22.50	110.510	22	951	1.02	5.023	0.024	0.116
	February	20.50	68.411	20	776	1.03	3.421	0.026	0.088
	March	13.50	67.700	20	732	0.68	3.385	0.018	0.092
	April	26.00	121.810	29	1,209	0.90	4.200	0.022	0.101
	May	27.00	103.764	26	1,149	1.04	3.991	0.023	0.090
	June	21.00	92.170	36	1,524	0.58	2.560	0.014	0.060
	July	17.00	62.311	29	1,281	0.59	2.149	0.013	0.049
	August	26.00	102.298	34	1,430	0.76	3.009	0.018	0.072
	September	32.00	160.874	37	1,489	0.86	4.348	0.021	0.108

Year	Month							
	October	41.00	175.779	33	1,405	1.24	5.327	0.029	0.125
	November	37.00	204.601	32	1,273	1.16	6.394	0.029	0.161
	December	51.00	226.538	40	1,865	1.28	5.663	0.027	0.121
1943	TOTAL	334.50	1,496.766	358	15,084	0.93	4.181	0.022	0.099
1944	January	57.00	252.944	33	1,580	1.73	7.665	0.036	0.160
	February	40.00	179.001	34	1,602	1.18	5.265	0.025	0.112
	March	29.00	121.156	35	1,838	0.83	3.462	0.016	0.066
	April	57.00	221.009	46	2,331	1.24	4.805	0.024	0.095
	May	47.50	181.667	38	1,696	1.25	4.781	0.028	0.107
	June	72.00	324.807	52	2,441	1.38	6.246	0.029	0.133
	July	53.00	261.607	38	1,940	1.39	6.884	0.027	0.135
	August	51.00	196.570	51	2,449	1.00	3.854	0.021	0.080
	September	78.33	347.006	56	2,609	1.40	6.197	0.030	0.133
	October	72.16	390.113	56	2,705	1.29	6.966	0.027	0.144
	November	27.50	116.714	35	1,785	0.79	3.332	0.015	0.065
	December	23.00	86.795	45	2,188	0.51	1.929	0.011	0.040
1944	TOTAL	607.49	2,679.289	519	25,164	1.17	5.728	0.024	0.106
1945	January	27.00	73.967	46	2,379	0.59	1.608	0.011	0.031
	February	28.50	79.981	36	1,840	0.79	2.222	0.015	0.043
	March	29.00	69.871	51	2,174	0.57	1.370	0.013	0.032
	April	23.00	37.768	46	2,015	0.50	0.821	0.011	0.019
	May	52.00	104.765	57	2,700	0.91	1.838	0.019	0.039
	June	14.00	12.289	40	1,914	0.35	0.307	0.007	0.006
	July	16.00	36.438	51	2,062	0.31	0.714	0.008	0.018
	August	0.00	0.000	15	416	0.00	0.000	0.000	0.000
1945	TOTAL	189.50	415.079	342	15,500	0.55	1.207	0.012	0.027

Source: See Table 7.4 which gives breakdown by submarine base.

353

Table 7.6. Tonnage of Japanese Merchant Vessels "At Risk" and Efficiency Measures: By Month, December 1941 to August 1945

Year	Month	Fleet Additions & Subtractions During Previous Month — Captured & Salvaged Gross Tonnage (000)	Built Gross Tonnage (000)	Total Sunk Gross Tonnage (000)	Tonnage — Available at Beginning of Month Gross Tonnage (000)	Total Sunk During Month Gross Tonnage (000)	Percent of Available Tonnage Sunk During Month	Total of Available Tonnage — Sunk by Submarines Gross Tonnage (000)	Percent of Available Tonnage Sunk by Submarines	Number of Submarine Sorties	Number of Submarine Days at Sea	Percent of Available Tonnage — Sunk per Submarine Sortie	Sunk per Submarine Day at Sea
1941	December	.0	.0	57.758	5,993.902	57.758		31.694	0.53	54	1,717	0.01	0.00031
1941	TOTAL	.0	.0	57.758		57.758		31.694		54	1,717		
1942	January	106.907	5.904	57.758	6,051.660	73.865	1.22	28.351	0.47	14	585	0.03	0.00180
	February	47.125	21.672	73.865	6,046.592	37.291	0.62	15.142	0.25	27	972	0.01	0.00026
	March	47.125	21.672	37.291	6,078.098	103.095	1.70	41.927	0.69	13	605	0.025	0.00114
	April	47.125	21.672	103.095	6,043.800	42.796	0.71	32.997	0.55	26	1,137	0.02	0.00048
	May	47.125	21.672	42.796	6,069.801	105.128	1.73	94.582	1.56	40	1,259	0.04	0.00124
	June	47.125	21.672	105.128	6,033.470	38.519	0.64	20.021	0.33	23	960	0.01	0.00035
	July	47.125	21.672	38.519	6,063.748	62.331	1.03	39.012	0.64	38	1,681	0.02	0.00038
	August	47.125	21.672	62.331	6,070.214	114.281	1.88	83.748	1.38	23	909	0.06	0.00152
	September	47.125	21.672	114.281	6,024.730	54.478	0.90	45.939	0.76	25	1,147	0.03	0.00066
	October	47.125	21.672	54.478	6,039.049	176.997	2.93	133.717	2.21	36	1,478	0.06	0.00150
	November	47.125	21.672	176.997	5,930.849	168.253	2.84	39.358	0.66	20	966	0.03	0.00069
	December	47.125	21.672	168.253	5,831.393	88.364	1.52	56.310	0.97	24	998	0.04	0.00097
1942	TOTAL	625.282	244.296	1,034.792		1,065.398		631.104		309	12,697		
1943	January	47.125	21.672	88.364	5,811.825	158.885	2.73	112.759	1.94	22	951	0.09	0.00204
	February	9.086	64.090	158.885	5,726.116	92.662	1.62	55.367	0.97	20	776	0.05	0.00125
	March	9.086	64.090	92.662	5,706.630	147.540	2.59	94.961	1.66	20	732	0.08	0.00227
	April	9.086	64.090	147.540	5,632.266	132.724	2.36	88.699	1.57	29	1,209	0.05	0.00130
	May	9.086	64.090	132.724	5,572.718	134.661	2.42	128.138	2.30	26	1,149	0.09	0.00200
	June	9.086	64.090	134.661	5,511.233	105.108	1.91	98.160	1.78	36	1,524	0.05	0.00117

Year	Month												
1943	July	9.086	64.090	105.108	5,479.301	84.361	1.54	70.320	1.28	29	1,281	0.04	0.00100
	August	9.086	64.090	84.361	5,468.116	100.064	1.83	79.932	1.46	34	1,430	0.04	0.00102
	September	9.086	64.090	100.064	5,441.228	178.966	3.29	135.540	2.49	37	1,489	0.07	0.00167
	October	9.086	64.090	178.966	5,335.438	158.093	2.96	128.088	2.40	33	1,405	0.07	0.00171
	November	9.086	64.090	158.093	5,250.521	320.807	6.11	232.333	4.42	32	1,273	0.14	0.00348
	December	9.086	64.090	320.807	5,002.890	207.048	4.14	121.917	2.44	40	1,865	0.06	0.00131
	TOTAL	147.071	726.662	1,702.235		1,820.919		1,346.214		358	15,084		
1944	January	9.086	64.090	207.048	4,869.019	355.368	7.30	249.672	5.13	33	1,580	0.16	0.00325
	February	2.970	141.600	355.368	4,658.221	518.697	11.14	252.526	5.42	34	1,602	0.16	0.00338
	March	2.970	141.600	518.697	4,284.094	263.805	6.16	122.921	2.87	35	2,331	0.08	0.00123
	April	2.970	141.600	263.805	4,164.859	128.328	3.08	92.592	2.22	46	1,696	0.05	0.00131
	May	2.970	141.600	128.328	4,181.101	258.591	6.18	246.790	5.90	38	2,441	0.16	0.00242
	June	2.970	141.600	258.591	4,067.080	278.484	6.85	197.330	4.85	52	2,441	0.09	0.00199
	July	2.970	141.600	278.484	3,933.166	251.921	6.41	220.643	5.61	38	1,940	0.15	0.00289
	August	2.970	141.600	251.921	3,825.815	295.022	7.71	234.012	6.12	51	2,449	0.12	0.00250
	September	2.970	141.600	295.022	3,675.363	419.112	11.40	170.514	4.64	56	2,609	0.08	0.00178
	October	2.970	141.600	419.112	3,400.821	512.378	15.07	328.810	9.67	56	2,705	0.17	0.00357
	November	2.970	141.600	512.378	3,033.013	421.026	13.88	230.446	7.60	35	1,785	0.22	0.00426
	December	2.970	141.600	421.026	2,756.557	188.287	6.83	104.736	3.80	45	2,188	0.08	0.00174
	TOTAL	41.756	1,621.690	3,909.780		3,891.019		2,450.992		519	25,767		
1945	January	2.970	141.600	188.287	2,711.847	434.648	16.03	95.403	3.52	46	2,379	0.08	0.00148
	February	0.905	86.087	434.648	2,364.191	101.541	4.29	55.745	2.36	36	1,840	0.07	0.00128
	March	0.905	86.087	101.541	2,349.642	194.649	8.28	65.856	2.80	51	2,174	0.05	0.00129
	April	0.905	86.087	194.649	2,241.985	125.673	5.61	68.164	3.04	46	2,015	0.07	0.00151
	May	0.905	86.087	125.673	2,203.304	270.703	12.29	31.194	1.42	57	2,700	0.02	0.00052
	June	0.905	86.087	270.703	2,019.593	245.930	12.18	91.339	4.52	40	1,914	0.11	0.00236
	July	0.905	86.087	245.930	1,860.655	309.902	16.66	29.497	1.59	51	2,062	0.03	0.00077
	August	0.905	86.087	309.902	1,637.745	99.094	6.05	15.433	0.94	15	416	0.06	0.00227
	TOTAL	9.305	744.209	1,871.333		1,782.140		452.631		342	15,500		

Note: Figures for "Captured & Salvaged" and "Built" are assumed to be evenly distributed over the year.
Source: Table 7.2.

There had been fifty-three submarines operating out of the Pacific bases on the January 1, 1943; by the next New Year's Day, 1944, despite the losses, there were seventy-five. Moreover, "these 75 were almost all fleet submarines, as most of the aged S-boats had been retired to training centers."[35] Given the increase in fleet size and quality and, with the victory in the Battle of the Philippine Sea, the release of more submarines to pursue Japanese merchant shipping, it is hardly surprising that the year 1944 saw the "trade-off" figures rebounding to a wartime high of 50.6 vessels and 223,274 tons.[36] Again, however, as the Japanese fleet declined in size and targets became harder to find, the averages fell to 25.3 vessels and only 55,344 tons over the last seven and a half months of the War (see Tables 7.1 and 7.5).

From a slightly different viewpoint, Table 7.7 provides a comparison between the measured efficiency of German submarines in the Atlantic, and U.S. and allied submarine fleets that were deployed in the Pacific. The measure, of course, captures both the efficiency of the submarines and the efficiency of the antisubmarine tactics deployed by the Allies and by the Japanese. In the opening months of the war, as the Germans were enjoying the "happy times" off the American east coast and the American submarines were partially engaged in supporting the offensive actions of what was left of that country's surface fleet, the Germans enjoyed a significant advantage. Over the first eleven months of 1942 they sank, on average, 3,923 tons of merchant shipping for every submarine lost. Over the same period, the figure for the Allied Pacific fleet was 2,115 – a German/Allied ratio of 1.85 to 1. Atlantic convoys and the failure of the Japanese to deploy any effective antisubmarine strategy quickly underwrote a reversal of that efficiency measure. From December 1942 through May 1943 the monthly average for the German Atlantic effort had fallen to 1,574 and that for the United States and its Pacific allies had risen to 3,915 – a German/Allied ratio of 0.40. The deployment of the Hunter-Killer groups in the Atlantic reduced the average German tonnage figure to 555 tons over the twelve months June 1943 to May 1944, while, over the same period, the U.S. and Allied Pacific figures edged up to a monthly average of 4,619 tons – a German/Allied ratio of 0.12. Finally, the defeat of the Japanese fleet in the Battle of the Philippine Sea released a significant number of U.S. submarines from their fleet supporting duties, and although the German monthly average fell to 308 tons, over the seven months from June to December 1944, the U.S. and Allied figure, despite the growing shortage of targets in November and December, rose to 5,058 – a German/Allied ratio of 0.06.

35 Morison *Two-Ocean War*, 497–499.   36 Morison, *Two-Ocean War*, 504.

Table 7.7. *Comparison of Merchant Tonnage Sunk by Submarines: Japanese by U.S. & Allied Submarines and Allied by German Submarines*

Year	Month	Tonnage Sunk per Operational Submarine		Ratio of German to U.S. Efficiency
		German	U.S. & Allies	
1941	December	1,426	807	1.77
1941	Average	1,426	807	1.77
1942	January	3,597	1,202	2.99
	February	4,717	1,444	3.27
	March	4,847	2,231	2.17
	April	3,567	3,757	0.95
	May	4,781	670	7.14
	June	5,265	1,836	2.87
	July	3,400	2,472	1.38
	August	3,446	2,205	1.56
	September	2,742	4,763	0.58
	October	3,160	1,285	2.46
	November	3,628	2,135	1.70
	December	1,606	3,471	0.46
1942	Average	3,730	2,228	1.67
1943	January	958	5,023	0.19
	February	1,626	3,421	0.48
	March	2,728	3,385	0.81
	April	1,366	4,200	0.33
	May	1,157	3,991	0.29
	June	439	2,560	0.17
	July	1,218	2,149	0.57
	August	439	3,009	0.15
	September	639	4,348	0.15
	October	557	5,327	0.10
	November	385	6,394	0.06
	December	509	5,663	0.09
1943	Average	1,002	4,278	0.26
1944	January	549	7,665	0.07
	February	553	5,265	0.11
	March	856	3,462	0.25
	April	374	4,805	0.08
	May	141	4,781	0.03
	June	306	6,246	0.05
	July	337	6,884	0.05
	August	571	3,854	0.15
	September	276	6,197	0.04
	October	51	6,966	0.01
	November	208	3,332	0.06
	December	409	1,929	0.21
1944	Average	386	5,728	0.07
1945	January	396	1,608	0.25
	February	432	2,222	0.19
	March	412	1,370	0.30
	April	440	821	0.54
1945	Average	420	1,207	0.35

Source: See Tables 6.8 and 7.5.

Table 7.8. *Areas of Operation: U.S. Submarines in the Pacific by Month of Departure December 1941 through December 1942*

Area of Operation	Dec. 1941	Jan. 1942	Feb.	Mar.	Apr.	May	June	July	Aug.	Sept.	Oct.	Nov.	Dec.	Total
Alaska	0	0	2	1	2	6	5	9	5	4	8	2	4	48
Banda Sea	0	0	0	1	0	0	0	0	0	0	0	0	0	1
Barrier	0	3	16	0	0	0	0	0	0	0	0	0	0	19
Bismark	0	0	0	0	0	0	0	0	0	0	0	0	0	0
Bonins	0	0	0	0	0	0	0	0	0	0	0	0	0	0
Carolinas	0	2	0	0	0	0	0	0	0	0	0	0	0	2
Celebes	9	3	0	0	0	1	0	3	1	0	0	0	0	17
China Sea, East	0	1	2	0	4	0	3	1	2	2	1	1	0	17
China Sea, South	0	0	0	0	0	2	2	2	1	3	0	0	0	10
Camranh Bay	0	0	0	0	1	0	0	0	0	0	0	0	0	1
Davao	0	0	0	0	1	0	0	0	0	0	0	0	0	1
Empire	3	1	2	2	2	1	3	4	1	5	1	4	5	34
Flores Sea	0	0	0	0	0	0	0	0	0	0	0	0	0	0
Formosa	4	0	1	0	0	0	0	0	0	0	0	0	0	5
Formosa Strait	0	0	0	0	0	0	0	0	0	0	0	0	0	0
Gilberts	0	0	0	0	0	0	0	0	0	0	0	0	0	0
Halmahera	0	0	0	0	0	0	0	0	0	0	0	0	0	0
Hongkong	2	0	0	0	0	0	0	0	0	0	0	0	0	2
Indochina	6	1	0	1	0	2	2	1	2	0	3	0	1	19
Japan Sea	0	0	0	0	0	0	0	0	0	0	0	0	0	0
Java Sea	0	0	0	2	0	0	0	1	0	0	0	0	0	5
Kendari	0	0	0	0	0	0	1	0	0	0	0	0	0	1
Kuriles & Hokkaido	0	0	0	0	0	0	0	0	0	0	0	0	0	0
Lingayen	1	0	0	0	0	0	0	0	0	0	0	0	0	1
Luzon, East	5	0	0	0	0	0	0	0	0	0	0	0	0	5
Luzon, South	5	0	0	0	0	0	0	0	0	0	0	0	0	5
Luzon, West	8	0	0	0	0	0	0	0	0	0	0	0	0	8
Luzon Strait	0	0	0	0	0	0	0	0	0	0	0	0	0	0
Makassar Straits	0	0	0	0	0	1	0	0	0	0	0	0	0	1
Malacca Straits	0	0	0	0	0	0	0	0	0	0	0	0	0	0
Manila	0	0	0	0	0	2	1	2	0	1	0	1	1	8
Marcus Island	0	0	0	0	0	0	0	0	0	0	0	0	0	0
Marianas	0	0	1	0	1	0	0	0	0	0	0	0	0	2
Marshalls	4	1	1	1	1	0	0	0	0	0	0	0	0	8
Midway	0	0	0	0	0	17	0	0	0	0	0	0	0	17
Palau	0	0	0	0	0	0	0	0	0	0	0	0	0	0
Philippine Sea	0	0	0	0	0	0	0	0	0	0	0	0	0	0
Philippines	0	0	0	0	1	0	0	0	0	0	0	0	0	1
Polar Circuit	0	0	0	0	0	0	0	0	0	0	0	0	0	0

Area of Operation	Dec. 1941	Jan. 1942	Feb.	Mar.	Apr.	May	June	July	Aug.	Sept.	Oct.	Nov.	Dec.	Total
Siam Gulf	0	0	0	0	0	0	0	0	0	0	0	0	0	0
Solomons	0	0	0	0	4	6	5	7	5	6	11	1	2	47
Special Mission	3	2	2	4	3	0	0	0	2	0	0	0	0	16
Sulu Sea	0	0	0	0	0	0	0	0	0	0	0	0	0	0
Sunda Strait	0	0	0	0	0	0	0	0	0	0	0	0	1	1
Fremantle–Brisbane	0	0	0	0	3	1	1	0	0	0	0	0	1	6
Pearl Harbor–Australia	0	0	0	1	2	1	0	2	0	3	4	6	3	22
Truk	0	0	0	0	1	0	0	6	4	1	8	5	4	29
Wake	0	0	0	0	0	0	0	0	0	0	0	0	0	0
Yellow Sea	0	0	0	0	0	0	0	0	0	0	0	0	0	0
December 1941 to December 1942	50	14	27	13	26	40	23	38	23	25	36	20	24	359

Source: Blair, *Silent Victory*, 900–983.

Tables 7.8, 7.9, 7.10, and 7.11 provide information about changes in the deployment of the Allied Pacific submarine fleet. Over the years from December 1941 to August 1945, there were forty-nine different designated areas of operation, and the changes in the number of sorties into each provide evidence of the changing nature of submarine assignments as the war pushed Japan back toward the Home Islands and the blockade became more effective (see Table 7.11). From December 1941 through December 1942, the number of areas in which U.S. and Allied submarines operated was thirty-four; the number fell to twenty-seven in 1943, twenty-four in 1944, and fell again to seventeen in 1945. Over the same years, a pronounced trend can be observed in the increase in the proportion of sorties directed to the "top 1" and "top 5" areas of operation – from 13 percent to 30 percent and from 50 percent to 83 percent. In terms of the areas of increased concentration, the percentage directed to the areas nearest the Japanese Home Islands (Empire, East China Sea, South China Sea, and Japan Sea) rose from 17 percent in 1942, to 35 percent in 1943 and 1944, and to 75 percent in 1945. Moreover, if Empire is excluded, the increase is from 7, to 20, to 21, and to 45 percent (see Table 7.12).

Tables 7.1 and 7.2 suggest something of the problems that faced a submarine commander as he attempted to evaluate the success of his mission.

Table 7.9. *Areas of Operation: U.S. Submarines in the Pacific by Month of Departure*
January 1943 through December 1943

Area of Operation	Jan.	Feb.	Mar.	Apr.	May	June	July	Aug.	Sept.	Oct.	Nov.	Dec.	Total
Alaska	2	2	2	3	3	5	3	4	4	1	1	3	33
Bandu Sea	0	0	0	0	0	0	0	0	0	0	0	0	0
Barrier	0	0	0	0	0	0	0	0	0	0	0	0	0
Bismark	0	0	0	0	0	5	5	4	2	4	4	3	27
Bonins	0	0	0	0	0	0	0	0	0	0	1	1	2
Carolines	0	0	0	0	0	0	0	0	0	0	0	0	0
Celebes	0	0	0	0	0	0	0	1	1	0	1	2	5
China Sea, East	1	3	0	4	3	4	4	3	7	6	3	6	44
China Sea, South	0	1	1	0	1	0	0	3	5	2	4	4	21
Camranh Bay	0	0	0	0	0	0	0	0	0	0	0	0	0
Davao	0	1	0	0	0	0	0	0	0	0	0	0	1
Empire	3	1	4	6	4	6	5	6	5	5	3	6	54
Flores Sea	0	1	0	0	0	0	0	0	0	0	0	0	1
Formosa	0	0	0	0	0	0	0	0	0	0	0	0	0
Formosa Strait	0	0	0	0	0	0	0	0	0	0	0	0	0
Gilberts	0	0	0	0	0	0	0	0	1	0	1	0	2
Halmahera	0	0	0	0	0	0	0	0	0	0	0	0	0
Hongkong	0	0	0	0	0	0	0	0	0	0	0	0	0
Indochina	0	0	0	0	2	0	0	0	0	0	0	0	2
Japan Sea	0	0	0	0	0	3	0	2	0	0	0	0	5
Java Sea	1	0	1	1	0	1	0	0	0	0	0	0	4
Kendori	0	0	0	0	0	0	0	0	0	0	0	0	0
Kuriles & Hokkaido	0	0	0	1	1	0	1	1	0	0	0	0	4
Linguyen	0	0	0	0	0	0	0	0	0	0	0	0	0
Luzon, East	0	0	0	0	0	0	0	0	0	0	0	0	0
Luzon, South	0	0	0	0	0	0	0	0	0	0	0	0	0
Luzon, West	0	0	0	0	0	0	0	0	0	0	0	0	0
Luzon Strait	0	0	0	0	0	0	0	0	0	0	0	0	0
Makassar Straits	0	0	0	0	0	0	0	1	0	1	0	0	2
Malacca Straits	0	0	1	0	0	0	0	0	0	0	0	0	1
Manila	1	0	1	1	0	0	0	0	0	1	0	0	4
Marcus Island	0	0	0	0	0	0	0	0	0	0	0	0	0
Marianas	0	1	0	0	1	1	1	0	1	4	0	3	12
Marshalls	1	1	1	2	1	1	1	1	2	1	3	1	16
Midway	0	0	0	0	0	0	0	0	0	0	0	0	0
Palau	1	2	1	2	1	3	1	2	4	2	2	1	22
Philippine Sea	0	0	0	0	0	0	0	0	0	0	0	0	0
Philippines	0	0	0	0	0	0	0	0	0	0	0	0	0
Polar Circuit	0	0	0	0	0	0	0	0	0	0	0	0	0
Siam Gulf	0	0	0	0	0	0	0	0	0	0	0	0	0
Solomons	5	5	2	3	4	0	0	0	0	0	0	0	19
Special Mission	0	0	0	2	0	0	0	0	0	1	1	0	4
Sulu Sea	0	0	0	0	0	0	0	0	0	0	0	0	0
Sunda Strait	1	0	0	0	0	0	0	0	0	0	0	0	1
Fremantle-Brisbane	0	0	2	1	2	2	1	1	2	1	0	4	16
Pearl Harbor-Australia	4	0	1	2	1	1	4	3	0	2	2	4	24
Truk	2	2	3	1	2	4	3	2	2	2	6	2	31
Wake	0	0	0	0	0	0	0	0	1	0	0	0	1
Yellow Sea	0	0	0	0	0	0	0	0	0	0	0	0	0
January 1943 to December 1943	22	20	20	29	26	36	29	34	37	33	32	40	358

Source: Blair, *Silent Victory*, 900–983.

Table 7.10. *Areas of Operation: U.S. Submarines in the Pacific by Month of Departure, January 1944 through December 1944*

Area of Operation	Jan.	Feb.	Mar.	Apr.	May	June	July	Aug.	Sept.	Oct.	Nov.	Dec.	Total
Alaska	0	0	0	0	0	0	0	0	0	0	0	0	0
Bandu Sea	0	0	0	0	0	0	0	0	0	0	0	0	0
Barrier	0	0	0	0	0	0	0	0	0	0	0	0	0
Bismark	0	1	0	0	0	0	0	0	0	0	0	0	1
Bonins	0	0	2	4	5	2	4	1	1	4	1	1	25
Carolinas	0	0	0	0	0	0	0	0	0	0	0	0	0
Celebes	0	2	1	3	6	3	1	3	0	2	0	0	21
China Sea, East	6	4	2	1	0	3	2	3	4	9	4	8	46
China Sea, South	2	4	1	4	2	5	5	5	6	10	9	10	63
Camranh Bay	0	0	0	0	0	0	0	0	0	0	0	0	0
Davo	0	0	3	2	0	5	2	3	0	0	0	0	15
Empire	1	3	2	8	5	6	4	8	12	8	5	12	74
Flores Sea	0	0	0	0	0	0	0	0	0	0	0	0	0
Formosa	0	0	0	0	0	0	1	0	2	1	0	0	4
Formosa Strait	0	0	0	0	0	0	0	0	0	0	0	0	0
Gilberts	0	0	0	0	0	0	0	0	0	0	0	0	0
Halmahera	1	0	1	0	1	0	0	0	0	0	0	0	3
Hongkong	0	0	0	0	0	0	0	0	0	0	0	0	0
Indochina	1	0	0	1	0	0	0	1	0	1	0	0	4
Japan Sea	0	0	0	0	0	0	0	0	0	0	0	0	0
Java Sea	0	0	0	0	0	0	0	0	1	0	0	0	1
Kendori	0	0	0	0	0	0	0	0	0	0	0	0	0
Kuriles & Hokkaido	0	0	0	0	0	0	0	0	0	0	0	0	0
Linguyen	0	0	0	0	0	0	0	0	0	0	0	0	0
Luzon, East	0	0	0	0	0	0	0	0	0	0	0	0	0
Luzon, South	0	0	0	0	0	0	0	0	0	0	0	0	0
Luzon, West	0	0	0	0	0	0	0	0	0	0	0	0	0
Luzon Strait	1	0	4	2	1	8	5	5	10	6	5	2	49
Makassar Straits	1	1	0	0	0	0	0	0	0	0	0	0	2
Malacca Straits	0	0	0	0	0	0	0	0	0	0	0	0	0
Manila	0	0	0	3	0	2	2	0	3	0	0	0	10
Marcus Island	0	0	0	0	0	0	0	0	0	0	0	0	0
Marianas	6	1	5	4	4	0	0	0	0	0	0	0	20
Marshalls	0	0	0	0	0	0	0	0	0	0	0	0	0
Midway	0	0	0	0	0	0	0	0	0	0	0	0	0
Palau	2	1	5	3	0	2	2	1	0	0	0	0	16
Philippine Sea	0	0	0	0	4	4	0	4	0	0	0	0	12
Philippines	0	0	0	0	0	0	0	0	0	0	0	0	0
Polar Circuit	0	2	1	1	3	2	2	2	2	2	4	1	22
Siam Gulf	0	0	0	0	0	0	0	0	0	0	0	0	0
Solomons	0	0	0	0	0	0	0	0	0	0	0	0	0
Special Mission	1	1	0	0	2	3	1	2	4	2	1	1	18
Sulu Sea	0	0	0	0	0	1	0	1	0	0	0	0	2
Sunda Strait	0	1	0	0	1	0	0	0	0	0	0	0	2
Fremantle-Brisbane	5	6	4	4	3	4	2	10	5	4	4	7	58
Pearl Harbor-Australia	1	4	2	4	0	1	4	1	7	7	2	3	36
Truk	4	3	2	2	1	1	1	1	0	0	0	0	15
Wake	0	0	0	0	0	0	0	0	0	0	0	0	0
Yellow Sea	0	0	0	0	0	0	0	0	0	0	0	0	0
January 1944 to December 1944	32	34	35	46	38	52	38	51	57	56	35	45	519

Source: Blair, *Silent Victory*, 900–983.

Table 7.11. *Areas of Operation: U.S. Submarines in the Pacific, by Month of Departure, January 1945 through August 1945*

Area of Operation	Jan.	Feb.	Mar.	Apr.	May	June	July	Aug.	Total
Alaska	0	0	0	0	0	0	0	0	0
Bandu Sea	0	0	0	0	0	0	0	0	0
Barrier	0	0	0	0	0	0	0	0	0
Bismark	0	0	0	0	0	0	0	0	0
Bonins	2	0	1	0	0	0	0	0	3
Carolinas	0	0	0	0	0	0	0	0	0
Celebes	0	0	0	0	0	0	0	0	0
China Sea, East	9	7	10	8	9	6	5	1	55
China Sea, South	11	12	14	8	10	9	15	4	83
Camranh Bay	0	0	0	0	0	0	0	0	0
Davo	0	0	0	0	0	0	0	0	0
Empire	10	7	13	13	17	19	18	6	103
Flores Sea	0	0	0	0	0	0	0	0	0
Formosa	0	0	1	0	0	0	1	0	2
Formosa Strait	0	2	1	0	0	0	0	0	3
Gilberts	0	0	0	0	0	0	0	0	0
Halmahera	0	0	0	0	0	0	0	0	0
Hongkong	0	0	0	0	0	0	0	0	0
Indochina	0	0	0	0	0	0	0	0	0
Japan Sea	0	0	0	0	9	0	6	1	16
Java Sea	0	0	2	4	0	1	1	0	8
Kendori	0	0	0	0	0	0	0	0	0
Kuriles & Hokkaido	0	0	0	0	0	0	0	0	0
Linguyen	0	0	0	0	0	0	0	0	0
Luzon, East	0	0	0	0	0	0	0	0	0
Luzon, South	0	0	0	0	0	0	0	0	0
Luzon, West	0	0	0	0	0	0	0	0	0
Luzon Strait	4	1	2	0	0	0	0	0	7
Makassar Straits	0	0	0	0	0	0	0	0	0
Malacca Straits	0	0	0	0	0	0	0	0	0
Manila	0	0	0	0	0	0	0	0	0
Marcus Island	0	0	0	0	0	0	1	0	1
Marianas	0	0	0	0	0	0	0	0	0
Marshalls	0	0	0	0	0	0	0	0	0
Midway	0	0	0	0	0	0	0	0	0
Palau	0	0	0	0	0	0	0	0	0
Philippine Sea	0	0	0	0	0	0	0	0	0
Philippines	0	0	0	0	0	0	0	0	0
Polar Circuit	0	0	0	5	4	1	2	3	15
Siam Gulf	0	0	1	0	0	0	0	0	1
Solomons	0	0	0	0	0	0	0	0	0
Special Mission	3	0	0	0	0	0	0	0	3
Sulu Sea	0	0	0	0	0	0	0	0	0
Sunda Strait	0	0	0	0	0	0	0	0	0
Fremantle-Brisbane	3	4	3	6	5	3	1	0	25
Pearl Harbor-Australia	3	3	3	1	3	0	0	0	13
Truk	0	0	0	1	0	1	1	0	3
Wake	0	0	0	0	0	0	0	0	0
Yellow Sea	1	0	0	0	0	0	0	0	1
January 1945 to August 1945	46	36	51	46	57	40	51	15	342

Source: Blair, *Silent Victory*, 900–983.

Table 7.12. *Measures of the Concentration/Dispersion of Allied Pacific Submarine Fleet: Sorties to 49 Areas of Operation, December 1941 to August 1945*

Year	Number of Areas Sortied	Number Sortied as % of 49	Total Number of Sorties	Average Number per Area	Number of Sorties to the Most Visited of the 49 Areas			
					Top 1 Percent		Top 5 Percent	
					Number	Percent of Total Sorties	Number	Percent of Total Sorties
December 7, 1941 through December 31, 1942	34	69.4	359	10.6	48	13.4	180	50.1
January 1, 1943 through December 31, 1943	27	55.1	358	13.3	54	15.1	182	50.8
January 1, 1944 through December 31, 1944	24	49.0	519	21.6	74	14.3	290	55.9
January 1, 1945 through August 15, 1945	17	34.7	342	20.1	103	30.1	282	82.5

Source: Tables 7.8 through 7.11; Blair, *Silent Victory*, 900–983.

As postwar evaluations were to prove, in December 1941 actual sinkings were only about a quarter of both the number of vessels and the tonnage claimed. Thereafter, there was a marked improvement, but claims still far exceeded actual sinkings. From 1942 through 1945, the number of vessels sunk averaged about 70 percent of those claimed, but the tonnage claims continued to be about twice the actual figure. After the war, Vice Admiral Charles Andrews Lockwood Jr., who from 1943 until the end of the war, had commanded the submarines based in Pearl Harbor, laid the blame for the large discrepancies on defective torpedoes. He maintained that a total of 14,748 torpedoes had been fired; and, had they all "hit, and detonated as designed, the claims might well have been closer to actuality."[37] Given the data, however, his argument appears less than persuasive. From early in 1942 until the end of the war, the claim/sinking ratios for both vessels and

37 Blair, *Silent Victory*, 879.

Table 7.13. *Japanese Merchant Losses to Mines January 1945–August 1945*

Month	Number of Vessels	Tonnage (Thousands)	Average Vessel Tonnage (Thousands)	Percent of Total Sinkings	
				Vessels	Tonnage
January	8	18.464	2.308	7.92	4.25
February	5	11.252	2.250	15.15	11.08
March	6	20.434	3.406	7.41	10.50
April	17	33.500	1.971	32.69	26.66
May	65	163.683	2.518	55.08	60.47
June	59	122.546	2.077	47.97	49.83
July	65	154.681	2.380	44.83	49.91
August	16	37.129	2.321	33.33	37.47

Source: Joint Naval Assessment Team, *Japanese Merchant and Shipping Losses*, 78–99.

tonnage were fairly constant and do not appear to reflect any significant change at the time that the new torpedoes came on line.

Finally, Table 7.13 captures the shift in the blockade from submarines to aircraft deployed mines. In the first three months of 1945, those mines accounted for 8.88 percent of vessel and 6.86 percent of tonnage losses; however, over the next five months, they accounted for 45.67 percent of vessel and 48.65 percent of tonnage losses. Once airbases within striking distance of the Home Islands had become operational, as far as the blockade was concerned, the submarine had become largely unnecessary.

5. THE JAPANESE ECONOMY IN WORLD WAR II

From a strictly military point of view, these measures of efficiency and "trade-off" are of particular importance. However, in terms of measuring the economic impact of the blockade, questions of the effect of the blockade on the Japanese domestic economy are certainly of importance. However, in the absence of something comparable to the detailed series of Carnegie-funded studies of World War I, the evidence is fragmented and less focused; and any conclusions are less certain than those based on the military evidence. Moreover, because of the economic drains and the changes in Japanese governmental priorities that were imposed by the war, the official data on imports and exports are far less complete than they were both before and after the war. What evidence there is, however, appears to provide substantial support for the conclusion that the blockade was

Table 7.14. *Japanese External Trade, 1940–1946 (Millions of Yen)*

	Historical Statistics				Strategic Bombing Survey				Price Indices, 1940 = 100	
	Calendar Year				Fiscal Year					
	Current Yen		Constant 1940 Yen		Current Yen		Constant 1940 Yen			
					Merchandise				Historical	
Year	Imports	Exports	Imports	Exports	Imports	Exports	Imports	Exports	Statistics	Morita's
1940	4,653	5,418	4,653	5,418	3,087	4,219	3,087	4,219	100	100
1941	4,088	4,384	4,008	4,290	2,198	2,888	2,035	2,674	102	108
1942	2,924	3,506	2,785	3,339	1,477	2,010	1,070	1,457	105	138
1943	2,939	3,055	2,648	2,752	1,607	1,778	1,030	1,140	111	156
1944					1,161	1,321	611	695	124	190
1945									182	
1946	4,069	2,260	364	202					1,118	

Source: B. R. Mitchell, *International Historical Statistics: Africa, Asia, & Oceania, 1750–1988*, 2nd revised edition (New York: Stockton Press, 1995), 525, 530, 936: Over-All Economic Effects Division, The United States Strategic Bombing Survey, *The Effects of Strategic Bombing on Japan's War Economy*, Table B-13, 91, Table B-15, 96.

effectively strangling the Japanese economy. It must be kept in mind that Japan was engaged in a war with many of the country's major prewar trading partners; and that, as a result, even in the absence of a blockade, international trade would have been badly affected. The data presented below provide a substantial amount of evidence bearing on the effectiveness of the naval blockade.

The official data on total imports and exports (see Table 7.14) are fairly complete for the years 1940 through 1943; and they suggest that even as early as 1942, the war had begun to have an impact. It seems reasonable to assume that the decline in constant yen exports and imports from 1941 to 1942 – a decline of about a third – reflects, not the blockade, but the severance of trade with prewar partners – partners that had become active enemies. However, the decline from 1942 to 1943 and, particularly, the decline from 1943 to 1944 captures the impact of the submarine attacks on Japanese merchant shipping. The 1942 to 1943 decline in constant yen imports was below 5 percent. In sharp contrast, the fall from 1943 to 1944 was a more significant 41 percent. For some countries, the import data are more complete; and they underscore the importance of the blockade (see Table 7.15). In the case of China, between 1941 and 1945, real exports to Japan fell in successive years by 12, 19, 23, and 78 percent – an overall decline of

Table 7.15. Japanese Trade with Selected Partners, 1940–1946 (Millions of Yen)

Year	China				Indonesia				Germany			
	Current Yen		Constant 1940 Yen		Current Yen		Constant 1940 Yen		Current Yen		Constant 1940 Yen	
	Imports	Exports	Imports	Exports	Imports	Exports	Imports	Exports	Imports	Exports	Imports	Exports
1940	759	1,896	759	1,896	125	173	125	173	83	75	83	75
1941	859	1,676	846	1,651	154	161	152	159	70	35	69	34
1942	1,223	1,514	1,169	1,447	13	16	12	15	40	39	38	37
1943	1,326	1,302	1,197	1,175	100	56	90	51	121	15	109	14
1944	1,707	1,123	1,378	907	68	48	55	39	10	1	8	1
1945	854	372	468	204	1	6	–	3	3	–	2	–
1946	285	268	25	24	–	–	–	–	50	–	4	–

Source: Mitchell, International Historical Statistics: Africa, Asia, & Oceania, 588, 589, 936.

88 percent. For Indonesia, the wartime decline was from 159 million yen to zero, and, for Germany, from 34 million yen to zero.

Thanks to the Strategic Bombing Survey, the data on subcategories of commodities are somewhat more complete; and they tell a similar story. In the case of bulk commodities, imports totaled 20.0 million tons in 1941, 19.4 million in 1942, 16.4 million in 1943, 10.1 million in 1944, and 2.7 million in 1945. Although only mildly affected by the war between the end of 1941 and the end of 1942, by 1944 those imports were, on average, only 54 percent of the 1940 baseline; and by the next year the figure was less than 13 percent (see Table 7.16). Imports of oil and oil products also reflected the effects of the tightening blockade. Imports from the "Inner Zone" rose between 1941 and 1942 and peaked at 4,597,000 barrels during the first quarter of 1943. Thereafter imports began to decline. They averaged 3,301,000 over the three quarters from July 1943 through March 1944 and 1,244,000 a quarter between April 1944 and March 1945. Overall, the monthly average declined from 1,532,000 barrels in April to June 1943 to 254,000 over the three months January to March 1945, a decline of 83 percent (see Table 7.17).

Perhaps more important from the point of view of the welfare of the average Japanese, the pattern of imports of food tell a similar story. Over the decade 1931–1940, imports of basic foods accounted for just less than one-fifth of Japanese consumption. In 1941 the figure was 20.3 percent. Those imports declined only slightly between 1941 and the end of 1942, but they had fallen to about one-eighth of consumption in 1943 and 1944 and to just 9.4 percent in 1945 (see Table 7.18). Those declines are reflected in the fall in the imports of staple foods. Rising slightly (by 4 percent) between 1941 and 1942, they declined by more than 50 percent between 1942 and 1943, before collapsing further as the blockade tightened. They fell by about one-third between the end of 1943 and the end of 1944 and by 70 percent the next year. For the year 1945, imports of staple foods totaled only 237,000 tons, 9 percent of the 1941 figure (see Table 7.19).

The decline in food imports effected domestic consumption. Although real GNP remained remarkably strong throughout most of the war (it grew from 40.3 billion yen in 1941 to 49.3 billion in 1944), consumer expenditures declined steadily – from 65 percent of the total in 1941 to 38 percent in 1944. Food and tobacco accounted for 37 percent of GNP in 1941, but only 24 percent in 1944 (see Table 7.20). Nor was it only the labor input that was impacted; the decline in imports effected production of a wide range of commodities. Coal imports averaged over 500,000 tons a month through the end of 1943, but had fallen to 16 percent of that level over the first

Table 7.16. *Japanese Imports of Bulk Commodities, 1940–1945 (Metric Tons)*

Product	1940	1941	1942	1943	1944	1945
Coal	7,011,000	6,459,000	6,388,000	5,181,000	2,635,000	548,000
Iron ore	6,073,000	6,309,000	4,700,000	4,298,000	2,153,000	341,000
Bauxite	275,000	150,000	305,000	909,000	376,000	15,500
Iron and steel	621,000	921,000	993,000	997,000	1,097,000	170,000
Scrap Iron	2,104,000	246,000	50,000	43,000	21,000	12,000
Lead	100,100	86,530	10,990	24,880	16,810	4,000
Tin	10,500	5,500	3,800	26,800	23,500	3,600
Zinc	23,500	7,900	8,500	10,100	6,100	2,500
Phosphorite & phosphate	710,400	396,500	342,100	236,700	89,600	23,000
Dolomite & magnesite	409,600	506,300	468,700	437,500	287,100	65,900
Salt	1,728,300	1,438,900	1,499,800	1,425,100	989,700	386,900
Soybean cake	333,900	337,700	449,500	304,500	384,700	163,400
Soybeans	648,500	572,400	698,800	590,600	728,800	606,900
Rice & paddy	1,694,000	2,232,700	2,629,200	1,135,800	783,200	151,200
Other grains & flours	269,300	267,400	823,300	750,100	506,600	231,400
Raw rubber	27,500	67,600	31,400	42,100	31,500	17,900
TOTAL	22,039,600	20,004,430	19,402,090	16,412,180	10,129,610	2,743,200
Ratio to 1940 Imports						
Coal	100.00	92.13	91.11	73.90	37.58	7.82
Iron ore	100.00	103.89	77.39	70.77	35.45	5.62
Bauxite	100.00	54.55	110.91	330.55	136.73	5.64
Iron and steel	100.00	148.31	159.90	160.55	176.65	27.38
Scrap Iron	100.00	11.69	2.38	2.04	1.00	0.57
Lead	100.00	86.44	10.98	24.86	16.79	4.00
Tin	100.00	52.38	36.19	255.24	223.81	34.29
Zinc	100.00	33.62	36.17	42.98	25.96	10.64
Phosphorite & phosphate	100.00	55.81	48.16	33.32	12.61	3.24
Dolomite & magnesite	100.00	123.61	114.43	106.81	70.09	16.09
Salt	100.00	83.26	86.78	82.46	57.26	22.39
Soybean cake	100.00	101.14	134.62	91.19	115.21	48.94
Soybeans	100.00	88.27	107.76	91.07	112.38	93.59
Rice & paddy	100.00	131.80	155.21	67.05	46.23	8.93
Other grains & flours	100.00	99.29	305.72	278.54	188.12	85.93
Raw rubber	100.00	245.82	114.18	153.09	114.55	65.09
TOTAL	100.00	90.77	88.03	74.47	45.96	12.45

Source: Over-All Economic Effects Division, *Effects*, Appendix Table C-106, 187.

six months of 1945. Finished steel production peaked at 467,000 tons a month in 1943, but had declined to 164,000 tons over the first three months of 1945 – a fall of 65 percent. The pattern of production of aluminum ingots is even more striking – from a monthly average of 11,757 tons in 1943 to a

Table 7.17. *Japanese Oil and Oil Products Imported from the Inner Zone (Thousands of Barrels) (Years are April through March)*

Year	Quarter	Crude Oil	Other	Total
1940		22,050	15,110	37,160
1941	April to June	3,004	2,645	5,649
	July to September	0	1,041	1,041
	October to December	0	1,052	1,052
	January to March	126	504	630
	Year Total	3,130	5,242	8,372
1942	April to June	1,133	265	1,398
	July to September	1,861	393	2,254
	October to December	3,093	899	3,992
	January to March	2,059	821	2,880
	Year Total	8,146	2,378	10,524
1943	April to June	3,712	885	4,597
	July to September	2,264	1,164	3,428
	October to December	2,546	1,105	3,651
	January to March	1,326	1,498	2,824
	Year Total	9,848	4,652	14,500
1944	April to June	994	893	1,887
	July to September	224	881	1,105
	October to December	423	799	1,222
	January to March	0	761	761
	Year Total	1,641	3,334	4,975

Notes: "Other" includes aviation gasoline, motor gasoline, diesel, fuel, and lubricating oil. It does not include kerosene, gas oil, and miscellaneous products.
Source: Over-All Economic Effects Division, *Effects*, Table C-51, 135.

mere 554 tons during 1945 – a decline of 95 percent. Again, although the decline was less spectacular, civilian consumption of crude rubber declined by over 40 percent between 1941 and 1945.[38]

6. THE QUALITATIVE STORY

Although U.S. and allied submarines had sunk some 175 Japanese ships totaling over 700,000 tons, 155 (663,000 tons) of them merchant vessels, the first thirteen months of the war could hardly be termed a roaring success. Only three submarines were lost to enemy action, but three others had

38 Over-All Economic Effects Division, The United States Strategic Bombing Survey, *The Effects of Strategic Bombing on Japan's War Economy* (Washington, D.C.: Government Printing Office, 1946), Tables c-44, 129; c-25, 117; c-29, 120; c-65, 152.

Table 7.18. *Percentage of Food Derived from Imports, Japan Proper, 1931–1940 Average, Annually 1941–1945*

Type of Food	Average 1931–1940 Percent Imported	1941 Percent Imported	1942 Percent Imported	1943 Percent Imported	1944 Percent Imported	1945 Percent Imported
Rice	17.0	22.0	19.0	10.0	8.0	3.0
Wheat	11.0	1.0	1.0	1.0	0.0	0.0
Barley	0.0	0.0	0.0	0.0	0.0	0.0
Naked barley	0.0	0.0	0.0	0.0	0.0	0.0
Soybeans	67.0	72.0	68.0	66.0	73.0	71.0
Potatoes	0.0	0.0	0.0	0.0	0.0	0.0
Sweet Potatoes	0.0	0.0	0.0	0.0	0.0	0.0
Vegetables	0.0	0.0	0.0	0.0	0.0	0.0
Fruits	0.0	0.0	0.0	0.0	0.0	0.0
Fish	4.0	3.0	3.0	3.0	2.0	1.0
Sugar	34.0	82.0	83.0	79.0	77.0	56.0
Other grains & beans	37.0	52.0	34.0	24.0	46.0	35.0
Other foods	5.0	4.0	3.0	1.0	0.0	0.0
Weighted Average	19.0	20.3	18.7	12.7	12.1	9.4

Source: Over-All Economic Effects Division, *Effects*, Table C-205, 239.

grounded, and one had been captured in the Philippines. Moreover, even as late as December 1942, within the Navy's strategic plans their mission remained relatively undefined. They had been employed for coastal defense, for blockading, for interception of capital ships, for interdicting merchant

Table 7.19. *Imports of Staple Foods, 1937–1945 (1,000 Metric Tons)*

Year of Consumption (November to October)	Foreign	Korea	Formosa	Total
1937	48	1,123	809	1,980
1938	25	1,692	829	2,546
1939	26	948	660	1,634
1940	1,331	66	464	1,861
1941	1,638	551	328	2,517
1942	1,457	873	284	2,614
1943	880	–	302	1,182
1944	–	583	217	800
1945	–	237	–	237

Note: Korea 1943 by extrapolation.
Source: Over-All Economic Effects Division, *Effects*, Table C-195, 235.

Table 7.20. *Japanese Gross National Product, Fiscal Years (Billions of 1940 Yen)*

	1940	1941	1942	1943	1944
Gross National Product	39.8	40.3	40.6	45.1	49.3
Consumer Expenditures:					
Food & Tobacco	15.5	14.8	18.9	13.3	11.7
Clothing & Furnishings	3.5	3.5	2.9	2.7	1.4
Other	7.7	7.7	7.0	6.4	5.7
Total Consumer Expenditures	26.7	26.0	28.8	22.4	18.8
Panel B: Expenditures as a Share of Gross National Product					
Gross National Product	100.00	100.00	100.00	100.00	100.00
Consumer Expenditures:					
Food & Tobacco	38.94	36.72	46.55	29.49	23.73
Clothing & Furnishings	8.79	8.68	7.14	5.99	2.84
Other	19.35	19.11	17.24	14.19	11.56
Total Consumer Expenditures	67.09	64.52	70.94	49.67	38.13
Panel C: Expenditures as a Ratio to 1940 Level					
Gross National Product	100.00	101.26	102.01	113.32	123.87
Consumer Expenditures:					
Food & Tobacco	100.00	95.48	121.94	85.81	75.48
Clothing & Furnishings	100.00	100.00	82.86	77.14	40.00
Other	100.00	100.00	90.91	83.12	74.03
Total Consumer Expenditures	100.00	97.38	107.87	83.90	70.41

Source: Over-All Economic Effects Division, *Effects*, Table 3, 15.

shipping, for commando raids, for delivering and retrieving guerrillas and spies, for minelaying, for reconnaissance, for delivering supplies and evacuating personnel, for shifting military staff around in the Asiatic theater, and to act as "beacons" and weather forecasters in support of carrier raids.[39]

Although the most successful of these efforts was probably the interdiction of enemy merchant shipping, even those efforts did not seriously interfere with Japanese foreign trade. "Imports of bulk commodities – coal, iron ore, bauxite, rice, lead, tin, zinc and so on – for 1942 remained about the same as for 1941, about 20 million tons" (see Table 7.16). Moreover, Japan had entered the war with about 5,996,607 tons of cargo vessels and tankers; and, by January 1, 1943, with additions from construction and capture, that figure had shrunk by only 185,000 tons – only about 3 percent. Moreover,

39 Blair, *Silent Victory*, 359–360.

Table 7.21. *The Japanese Merchant Navy, Gains and Losses, 1941–1945*

Year	Sunk (tons)	Captured and Salvaged (tons)	Built (tons)	Available on 31st December (tons)	Net Gain or Loss (+ or −) (tons)
1941 (from 7th Dec.)	57,758	106,907	5,904	6,051,660	55,053
1942	1,065,398	565,504	260,059	5,811,825	−239,835
1943	1,820,919	109,028	769,085	4,869,019	−942,806
1944	3,892,019	35,644	1,699,203	2,711,847	−2,157,172
1945 (to 15th Aug.)	1,782,140	5,880	559,563	1,495,150	−1,216,697
TOTALS	8,618,234	822,963	3,293,814	–	−4,501,457

Note: Tonnage sunk includes marine casualties, which accounted for the heavy total of ninety-seven ships (approximately 269,000 tons).
Source: S. W. Roskill, *The War at Sea, 1939–1945. Vol. 3 The Offensive, Part II*, 1st June 1944 to 14th April 1945 (London: Her Majesty's Printers Office, 1981), 367.

of the 1,123,156 tons lost at sea, submarines accounted for only 662,798 or 59 percent.[40]

There were three major causes of the relatively poor submarine performance. First, there were the problems associated with torpedo failure. Second, there were serious issues of poor performance by the officers commanding the submarines. During 1942, "about 40 skippers out of 135 – almost thirty percent" – were relieved "because of poor health, battle fatigue, or nonproductivity, mostly the last." Third, and most important, however, were the strategic and tactical choices made by the highest levels of the naval command. Those men, a group that included Admirals King, Nimitz, and Hart, "failed to set up a broad, unified strategy for Pacific submarines aimed at a single specified goal: interdicting Japanese shipping in the most efficient and telling manner." Like the initial decision not to employ convoys on the east coast of the United States, the other lessons of the Battle of the Atlantic had still not "sunk home."[41]

In most dimensions, the blockade was more successful in 1943 than it had been during the first thirteen months of the war. All told, 434 merchant vessels of 1,820,919 tons were sunk, and submarines accounted for nearly 70 percent of the vessels (296) and 74 percent of the tonnage (1,346,214). Despite new construction – construction that underwrote an increase in tanker tonnage – the tonnage of the Japanese merchant fleet declined by some 943,000 tons (see Tables 7.6 and 7.21).[42] More important, the blockade

---

40 Blair puts the net loss in shipping at only 89,000 tons. Blair, *Silent Victory*, 360.
41 Blair, *Silent Victory*, 361–362.
42 Blair puts the sinkings of tankers by submarines at 150,000 tons and the gains from construction and conversion at 327,000 tons. Blair, *Silent Victory*, 552.

began to impact Japanese foreign trade. For example, imports of bulk commodities fell by some 15 percent – from 19.4 to 16.4 million tons (see Table 7.16).[43] The blockade was clearly not yet strangling the Japanese economy, but the noose was beginning to tighten.

Although there was a decrease in the "exchange" ratio from 28.5 vessels and 114,762 tons to 24.3 vessels and 109,402 tons sunk per submarine lost, by other measures there was an improvement in the performance of the undersea fleet. Given that there were about an equal number of sorties, total Japanese losses rose from 171 vessels and 688,521 tons to 334.5 vessels and 1,496,766 tons, increases of 96 and 117 percent, respectively. Losses per submarine deployed rose from .55 vessels and 2,228 tons to .93 vessels and 4,181 tons, and losses per submarine day at sea rose from .013 vessels and 54 tons to .022 vessels and 99 tons (see Table 7.5).

The improvement rested, in part, on the "solution" to the torpedo problem, and, in part, on the fleet commanders restructuring of their strategic goals. Submarines were deployed more imaginatively; it was as if the commanders had finally, "after much trial and error, learned how to fight a submarine war and got the equipment to do it." The skippers' lack of aggressiveness remained a problem; although because of a shortage of commanders fewer were relieved for lack of productivity. At the organizational level, the first wolf-packs were deployed, but they still contributed little to the attacks on enemy shipping.[44]

"In one sense it could be said that the U.S. submarine war against Japan did not truly begin until the opening days of 1944. What had come before had been a learning period, a time of testing, of weeding out, of fixing defects in weapons, strategy, and tactics, of waiting for sufficient numbers of submarines and workable torpedoes. Now that all was set, the contribution of the submarine force would be more than substantial: it would be decisive."[45]

From January through December of 1944, 969 Japanese merchantmen totaling 3,892,019 tons were sunk by Allied forces; and of that total 546 vessels of 2,450,992 tons (63 percent) fell victim to allied submarine attack. Sinkings per submarine increased over the previous year by .24 vessels and about 1,500 tons, and sinkings per submarine day at sea rose by .002 vessels and 7 tons. Those gains represented improvements in efficiency of 26 and 24 percent per submarine; but, reflecting the longer cruises, only 9 and 7 percent per day at sea.

---

43 Blair, *Silent Victory*, 552.   44 Blair, *Silent Victory*, 551–554.
45 Blair, *Silent Victory*, 554.

The Japanese merchant marine had begun the year with 4,869,019 tons of shipping. Over the course of the year an additional 35,644 tons were captured or salvaged and 1,699,203 tons were built; however, at year's end, the Japanese could deploy only 2,711,847 tons, a net loss of 2,157,172 tons. Over the first thirty-seven months of the war, the merchant fleet had declined by 55 percent; and two-thirds of that total occurred in the last twelve months (see Table 7.21). The impact of the increasingly effective blockade was reflected in a 6.3 million ton (an almost 40 percent) decline in the imports of bulk commodities. Moreover, "the flow of oil from the southern regions to Japan was almost completely stopped after the invasion of Mindoro" in December. Despite the losses, in September 1944 a tanker fleet estimated at about 700,000 tons had been "engaged in transporting oil from the south to the home islands. By the end of the year this figure had been reduced to about 200,000 tons. Reserve stocks were so low that Japanese leaders launched experiments in making oil from potatoes."[46]

With the torpedo problem largely solved, the June victory in the battle of the Philippine Sea made it possible to release a substantial number of well-armed submarines for the pursuit of Japanese merchant shipping. Moreover, as the areas of Allied occupation expanded north and west, it became possible to move the submarine bases closer to the combat areas. Advance bases in Milne Bay, Manus, Mios Woendi, Majuro, Saipan, and Guam were opened. With travel time reduced, the new advance bases meant shorter, more productive, sorties.[47] Although the "skipper" problem was still not solved, the widespread innovation of wolf-pack tactics also added to the increasing productivity of the fleet. The combination of more submarines, better torpedoes, bases closer to the combat area, and the deployment of aggressive wolf-packs meant that, in early summer, "the area which Comsubpac named 'Convoy College,' extending across the East China Sea from Luzon Strait to Formosa and the coast of China – became the scene of great destruction." For example, "the 'Mickey Finns' (*Guardfish, Piranha, Thresher*, and *Apogon*), a wolf-pack under command of Captain W. V. O'Regan, were the first 'freshman' to cross this watery campus; and their five-day semester cost the Japanese some 41,000 more tons of merchant shipping." By September wolf-packs were "vigorously and successfully combing waters around Formosa." Again, Commander G. R. Donaho's wolf-pack (*Picuda, Redfish*, and *Spadefish*), operating "east of Formosa, sank three or four merchant ships out

---

46 Blair, *Silent Victory*, 816–817.
47 Between more submarines and less travel time, 1944 saw a total of 520 war patrols as compared with about 350 in 1941–42 and 1943. Blair, *Silent Victory*, 816–817.

of a single convoy"; and, by the end of the patrol his "pack" had eliminated 64,456 tons of enemy shipping.[48] Altogether, from July through November, the new bases and tactics had resulted in the sinking of 260 vessels of 1,184,425 tons.

"For all practical purposes, the U.S. submarine war against Japanese shipping ended in December 1944." Submarines deployed "in the Yellow and East China Seas and off the coast of Japan were seldom encountering good targets."[49] "The enemy ships that were left were forced to operate in the confined waters of the Sea of Japan or the Yellow Sea, running very close to shore and holing up in harbors at night, making it almost impossible for submarines to get at them."[50] Those facts are reflected in the data. Although the monthly average of the number of merchant vessels sunk increased by 9 percent when compared with 1944, the average tonnage fell by 37 percent. Moreover, both the number of vessels and the tonnage sunk by submarines fell very sharply – by 56 percent for the case of vessels and by 73 percent in the case of total tonnage. Other efficiency measures tell a similar story. The vessels and tonnage sunk per submarine deployed fell by 53 and 78 percent, respectively, whereas the figures for sinkings per day deployed fell to 50 percent for vessels and 74 percent for tonnage. Similarly, in terms of efficiency, the "exchange rate" of submarines sunk per vessel and per ton both rose.

However, the blockade remained an important weapon. By March 1945, communications between the Japanese Home Islands and the "Outer Zone" had been almost completely severed. But, had there been no blockade, Japan could still have drawn on supplies from the "Inner Zone" – Manchuria, Korea, and North China. This time, however, operation "Starvation" was mainly carried out by B-29s, long range bombers operating from the Marianas. During the 142 days between March 27 and the end of hostilities, they laid twelve thousand mines in the waters between the "Inner Zone" and the Home Islands.[51] Between April and August, those mines accounted for 222 merchant vessels of 511,539 tons – 45 percent of vessel and 47 percent of tonnage losses (see Tables 7.2 and 7.13). It was the mines dropped from aircraft that finally strangled Japan.

The submarines did, however, continue to play a role. By January, the main bases had been shifted from Pearl Harbor to Guam and from Australia to Subic Bay in the Philippines.[52] Advancing Allied forces had driven Japanese shipping back to the shallow waters off the coasts of Japan and the Asiatic

48 Morison, *Two-Ocean War*, 504–505.
49 Morison, *Victory in the Pacific*, 285.
50 Blair, *Silent Victory*, 819.
51 Roskill, *Offensive, Part II*, 370–371.
52 Roskill, *Offensive, Part II*, 368; Morison, *Two-Ocean War*, 510.

mainland. Despite the dangers, American submarines quickly followed the Japanese. For example, in April, the "*Tirante* entered a patrolled anchorage in Quelpart Island to blow up a 10,000-ton tanker and two 1,500-ton escort vessels, which were peacefully lying at anchor."[53]

Among the most successful of the submarine operations over the entire course of the war was the sortie of the nine submarines involved in "Operation *Barney*, the invasion of the Sea of Japan, the only remaining body of water where enemy shipping still moved freely." In June, American submarines reentered the Sea of Japan for the first time since July 1943. Under the command of Commander E. T. Hydeman, the nine, designated *Hydeman's Hell Cats: Hydeman's Hep Cats* (*Sea Dog, Crevalle*, and *Spadefish*), *Piece's Pole Cats* (*Tunny, Skate*, and *Bonefish*) and *Risser's Bob Cats* (*Flying Fish, Bowfin*, and *Tinosa*) – sailed from Pearl Harbor and from Guam between May 27 and 29. The nine passed through Tsushima Strait on June 5 and 6, and reached their assigned patrol stations three days later. Over the next eleven days, Hydeman in *Sea Dog* sank six merchantmen, Germershausen in *Spadefish* sank five, Latham in *Tinosa* sank four, Lynch in *Skate* sank three merchantmen and one submarine, Steinmetz in *Crevalle* sank three merchantmen, and Edge in *Bonefish*, Risser in *Flying Fish*, and Tyree in *Bowfin* each sank two. The total was twenty-seven merchant vessels of 54,784 tons and one submarine. Only one submarine, *Bonefish*, was lost during the operation. The success of this mission convinced Admiral Lockwood to deploy seven other submarines into the Sea of Japan. Of that group, "Charles Robert Clark, Jr., in *Sennet* . . . sank the most ships: four for 13,105 tons." Six of the seven continued to operate in the Sea of Japan until V-J Day.[54]

In late June and July, Gene Fluckey took *Barb* on patrol to Hokkaido and the Kuriles. He sank three trawlers with his deck gun; he bombarded shore bases with both rockets and gunfire, in the process "destroying three sampans at dockside." He sank a lugger and a sampan with gunfire and a frigate with his last torpedoes. Finally, while cruising off the east coast of Karafuto, he "noted a railroad running along the coast and sent a commando party ashore to set demolition charges on the tracks." As they were returning to the submarine, a train set off the charges and destroyed an engine, twelve freight cars, two passenger cars, and a mail car.[55]

53 King, *U.S. Navy at War*, 201–202.
54 Morison, *Victory in the Pacific*, 291–293; Morison, *Two-Ocean War*, 510; Blair, *Silent Victory*, 859–865; Roskill, *Offensive, Part II*, 368.
55 Blair, *Silent Victory*, 866–867.

By July 1945, "the Japanese Merchant Navy had suffered so heavily, and its losses were mounting so rapidly, that it was becoming impossible to feed the population and keep the nation's industries in production. But to a great extent, the seriousness of Japan's economic plight was shrouded from Allied eyes. Although we realized that there was no longer any possibility of her disputing control of the seas, we did not know that the blockade had brought her within measurable distance of collapse."[56]

7. CONCLUSION

As noted earlier, successful economic warfare depends "on the ability of the blockading power to restrict an enemy economy to a small and known stock of basic resources." Unlike in World War I, in World War II the geographic extent of the German conquests gave that nation "control of the resources and trade of virtually a whole continent." Thus, the Allied blockade played virtually no role in Germany's defeat. However, in the Pacific War, the results were just the opposite. When Yamamoto's onslaught failed to bring the Allies to their knees in the first six months of the war, given the productive capacity of the American economy, in hindsight at least, it appears that it was almost inevitable that the Japanese would be "driven back from her imperial outposts to the limited economic base of the Home Islands and Korea." Once that situation had occurred, the forces deployed in the economic offensive were truly in the driver's seat – the submarine and air deployed mines effectively strangled the Japanese economy.[57] The Allied blockade of the Home Islands was as efficient as the Allied blockade of Germany some quarter century before – and it may have been the most effective naval blockade in history.

Based on its experience during World War I, by the 1930s, Germany led the world in submarine tactics; the United States, by contrast, had done little to prepare for undersea warfare, neither in terms of equipment nor in training. Moreover, the United States, Britain, Japan, and Germany did not show "any special expertise or interest in antisubmarine warfare." "For the United States, Britain, and Japan the strategic reason for worrying about the safety of their merchant fleets would seem obvious, but their navies did not stress the mission."[58] The American debacle produced Doenitz's "merry

---

56 Roskill, *Offensive, Part II*, 365.   57 Milward, *War*, 321.
58 Allan R. Millet, "Patterns of Military Innovation in the Interwar Period," in Murray and Millet, eds., *Military Innovation*, 338–339.

times" in the spring and summer of 1942, but at least the American naval leaders learned their lesson. The same could not be said for the Japanese naval bureaucracy.

By late 1943, with the Japanese main fleet no longer a significant offensive threat and with the Americans gradually refining their offensive submarine strategies and tactics, the American submarine fleet became a central player in the ultimate defeat of Japan. At war's end, the United States Strategic Bombing Survey reported: "The war against shipping was perhaps the most decisive single factor in the collapse of the Japanese economy and logistic support of Japanese military and naval power. Submarines accounted for the majority of vessel sinkings and the greater part of the reduction in tonnage," altogether some 1,159 merchant vessels of 4,912,635 tons (see Table 7.6).[59] Moreover, those losses were inflicted by a submarine force composed of only about fifty thousand officers and men – a figure that included both back-up personnel and staff – about 1.6 percent of the total naval force. "In other words, a force representing less than 2 percent of the U.S. Navy accounted for 55 percent of Japan's maritime losses."[60] Nor were the losses restricted to vessels; the loss of merchant marine seamen was equally heavy. "Japan began the war with 122,000 merchant marine personnel. About 116,000 of these became casualties: 27,000 killed, 89,000 wounded or 'otherwise incapacitated.' Of this total, the majority of the casualties – 16,200 killed [60 percent] and 53,400 wounded or 'otherwise incapacitated' [again 60 percent] – were inflicted by submarine attack."[61]

The data on the impact of the blockade on the Japanese economy in general, and on the food supply in particular, have already been noted; and it was very substantial. In parallel to the qualitative microhistory of the submarines and airplanes that carried out that blockade, it appears appropriate to include the following piece of Japanese socioeconomic history. Although their experience may not have been typical, over the years 1940 through December 1945, the consumption of staple food by coal miners declined from one thousand to seven hundred grams per day. At the same time, consumption by other adults in the coal miners' households fell from 800 to 290 grams. Over the same period, the output of coal per man per month declined from twenty-one tons in 1940 to four tons in November 1944 (see Table 7.22). What was also significant over the course of the war was

---

59 See also Blair, *Silent Victory*, 879. There is a small discrepancy from the totals given by the Joint Naval Assessment Team for U.S. forces of 1,113 vessels and 4,779,902 tons. Adding in naval vessels sunk and the vessels sunk by other Allied forces, the totals are 3,032 vessels sunk and 10,583,755 tons, over 90 percent by U.S. forces.

60 Blair, *Silent Victory*, 879.   61 Blair, *Silent Victory*, 878.

Table 7.22. *Japan: Food Consumption by Coal Miners and Their Families,*
1938–1945

| Year | Consumption of Staple Good | | Coal Output |
	Per Worker Per Day (grams)	Per Adult Per Day (grams)	Per Man Per Month (tons)
1938	1,200	900	24
1939	1,000	800	23
1940	1,000	800	21
1941	700	325	17
1942	700	325	16
1943	700	325	19
1944	700	325	12
1945	700	290	8
November 1945	705	325	4

Source: Over-All Economic Effects Division, *Effects*, Table C-175, 229.

the inflation and rapid rise in black market prices of goods and other commodities, which gave rise to major political and economic problems (see
Table 7.23).

In summary, although there is general agreement about the role of the
submarine blockade in the defeat of Japan, two further questions have been
raised. Both are still subjects of debate. On the one hand, it has been argued
that, had the Americans been more prepared to fight an offensive submarine campaign in December 1941, Japan could have been defeated much
earlier. There is, however, some danger in transposing their success in the
months between June 1943 to December 1944 back to the first year and a
half of the war. With other commitments and with an insufficient number
of submarines, the Americans might only have alerted the Japanese to the
seriousness of the threat. Although they might have done considerable damage, even if they had had torpedoes that worked, and they did not, attacks
in 1942 would probably have not been sufficient to bring the Empire to the
point of collapse. "With time to react, [and do as the Americans had done in
the Atlantic], the Japanese might have marshaled the resources necessary to
master the submarine." As it was, "when the onslaught hit their unprepared
forces in 1943, the Japanese had no chance against a strong, well-prepared,
and numerous U.S. submarine fleet."[62]

62 Herwig, "Innovation Ignored," 260.

Table 7.23. *Prices of Food on the Japanese Black Market (Yen)*

Commodity	Unit	Official Price	December 1943	June 1944	November 1944	July 1945
Rice	1 sho	0.5	3.0	14.0	22.0	35.0
Wheat Flour	1 kan	1.5	8.0	22.0	30.0	40.0
Soy Bean	1 sho	0.4	3.0	5.5	7.0	12.0
Potatoes	1 kan	0.5	2.5	3.5	8.0	13.0
Soy	1 sho	0.8	3.0	5.0	13.0	38.0
Edible Oil	1 sho	2.9	15.0	40.0	120.0	220.0
Dried Bonito	1 kan	14.6	70.0	150.0	220.0	520.0
Butter	1lb	3.8	6.5	30.0	60.0	60.0
Pork	100 momme	1.0	3.0	14.0	17.0	27.0
Beef	100 momme	1.6	3.5	13.5	20.0	30.0
Sugar	1 kan	2.2	50.0	200.0	300.0	530.0
Salt	1 kan	5.0	30.0	45.0	40.0	40.0
Salted Salmon	1 kan	4.4	15.0	33.0	35.0	25.0

Prices of Food on the Japanese Black Market as a Percentage of Official Prices

Rice	1 sho	100	600	2,800	4,400	7,000
Wheat Flour	1 kan	100	533	1,467	2,000	2,667
Soy Bean	1 sho	100	750	1,375	1,750	3,000
Potatoes	1 kan	100	500	700	1,600	2,600
Soy	1 sho	100	375	625	1,625	4,750
Edible Oil	1 sho	100	517	1,379	4,138	7,586
Dried Bonito	1 kan	100	479	1,027	1,507	3,562
Butter	1 lb	100	171	789	1,579	1,579
Pork	100 momme	100	300	1,400	1,700	2,700
Beef	100 momme	100	219	844	1,250	1,875
Sugar	1 kan	100	2,273	9,091	13,636	24,091
Salt	1 kan	100	600	900	800	800
Salted Salmon	1 kan	100	341	750	795	568
Unweighted Average		100	589	1,781	2,829	4,829

Notes: 1 sho equals 1.80391 liters; 1 kan equals 3.75 kilograms; 1 momme equals 3.75 grams.
Source: Over-All Economic Effects Division, *Effects*, Table C-168, 225.

On the other hand, what would have happened if the United States had adopted a very different overall naval strategy? In early 1944, Admiral King and his staff began to object to the idea of "battering our way through the Philippines." Instead, "he proposed that the Philippines be bypassed altogether and that the Allied forces move directly against Formosa." He argued that "Japan could be strangled by a submarine blockade while U.S. carrier units and B-29s basing from the Marianas pounded her warmaking potential to rubble." It was certainly "a bold and imaginative plan." "While it is doubtful that air strikes on the Japanese homeland would have inflicted sufficiently severe damage (as time would prove), a submarine blockade could well have been decisive."

"When MacArthur heard about this new idea, he was outraged." Not only would he have been unable to "return"; but, "if the new strategy were adopted, General MacArthur would play only a minor role" in the last phases of the Pacific War. The new strategy was debated at the highest levels. Although Roosevelt personally had no direct part in the final decision, "the Joint Chiefs of Staff, vastly overrating Japan's ability to continue the war of production and strongly influenced by General Marshall, who finally backed MacArthur's concept, decided the original plan for liberating the Philippines should be adhered to." Although counterfactuals are always difficult to prove, given the effectiveness of the U.S. blockade in 1943–1945, it could be argued that "Pacific strategy was dictated by political expediency and the considerable ego of General Douglas MacArthur." "In giving way to his arguments, the Joint Chiefs [may have] committed the United States to thousands of unnecessary casualties."[63] Directly, it led to a ground campaign in the Philippines; a campaign that was still in progress when Japan surrendered. Indirectly, it diverted a part of the submarine fleet from its attacks on merchant commerce to support of invasion forces and guerrilla activity, to photographic reconnaissance, to lifeguard duty, and to scouting – "all of which reduced the number of submarines on anticommerce patrol and needlessly prolonged the war."[64]

During World War II, "economic warfare did no real harm to neutral states even if it virtually destroyed existing international law on neutrality." It did, at most, "only limited damage to the German economy"; but, if it had not been for the atom bomb, it might have, and practically did, cripple the Japanese economy. "It might have been more successful against Germany and Japan if better understood and more consistently and accurately pursued." The success of economic warfare against an industrialized nation depends in large part on the blockading power acquiring "a very exact knowledge of the functioning" of an enemy's economy – an economy that is frequently highly

63 Blair, *Silent Victory*, 693–695. This decision may have triggered the then often-heard plaintive note from our forces deployed in the Pacific: "Stick with Mac and you'll never get back."
64 Blair, *Silent Victory*, 693–695.

complex.[65] Although by 1947 the Strategic Bombing Surveys may have
made the American military sufficiently aware of the problems of wartime
Axis economies, by then the war had been over for two years and; during
World War II that knowledge was insufficient. As a result, our strategic
decisions were badly flawed. In the case of Japan, the Allies never realized
how close the Japanese economy was to collapse. If they had, perhaps the
decision to drop the atomic bomb would have gone the other way. However,
it is still not clear that, given the Japanese military's control of the political
process, that economic collapse alone would have meant the end of the war
and have removed the need to invade the Home Islands.

65 Milward, *War*, 328.

8

Blockades without War

From Pacific Blockades to Sanctions

1. BLOCKADES AND SANCTIONS

The laws of international relations deal with three broad categories of actions in response to disagreements among nations, or four, if one option is to do nothing and maintain the current situation. The three categories are: (1) amicable measures short of war; (2) nonamicable measures short of war; and (3) war. The first of these are formal understandings among nations designed to avoid warfare. They are usually based on some mutual agreement – the product of negotiations that could include mediation or arbitration. The second represents an attempt to avoid warfare through the adoptions of policies that impose a sufficiently high cost on the targeted nation that the target submits to certain terms to avoid military action. These policies – often termed "sanctions" – include measures of an economic, political, or diplomatic nature that are imposed unilaterally by one nation or by a coalition of nations. Among economic sanctions are Pacific blockades and various other forms of restrictions on trade, financial flows, and the movement of people. What types of sanctions to impose, and what their appropriate breadth and magnitude should be, are necessary questions that must be answered by any potential targeting nation (or nations); and the answers to those questions indicate the wide range of actions that are possible.

War involves a declared military action among two or more nations, although there remain questions of exactly what actions constitute a war and what the participants choose to call those actions. Wars, unlike the measures short of war, have long been marked by specific legal codes and rules regarding the behavior of both belligerent powers and third parties; these rules have been spelled out in great detail; and they have been modified as the technology of warfare has changed. Although these rules may be, and frequently have been, violated during actual wars, the legal definition of expected behavior is quite detailed. In the case of measures short of war, whether amicable or nonamicable, there is no generally accepted legal definition of what constitutes a sanction.

It is not, however, true that sanctions remain undefined in the literature. It is generally recognized that it is a prerogative of government to take coercive measures to discourage undesirable behavior. That prerogative is sometimes extended beyond the borders of the injured state or states, and such extensions have been widely referred to as international sanctions. Sanctions are defined "to mean the deliberate, government-inspired withdrawal, or threat of withdrawal, of customary trade or financial relations. 'Customary' does not mean 'contractual'; it simply means the levels of trade and financial activity that would probably have occurred in the absence of sanctions." Foreign policy goals are "defined to encompass changes expressly and purportedly sought by the sender state in the political behavior of the target state," excluding here such foreign policy goals that can be "the normal realm of economic objectives sought in banking, commercial, and tax negotiations between sovereign states."[1] In the words of Daoudi and Dajani, sanctions are the "penalty attached to transgression and breach of international law." They are unilateral or "collective actions against a state considered to be violating international law" designed "to compel that state to conform."[2] In the past, they have involved diplomatic, economic, and military actions. As such, sanctions represent a middle road between a "diplomatic slap on the wrist" and "more extreme measures, such as covert action or military measures."[3] Most studies of the efficiency of sanctions have focused on the degree to which the target relies on the sender for its imports and exports and on the economic and political stability of the target. Because "sender countries are more likely to enjoy a dominant market position as suppliers of exports than as purchasers of imports," historically, when weapons against trade have been deployed, the sender is more likely to have used export rather than import controls.[4] The greater the reliance on these exports, and the weaker the target, the more likely it is that the sanction will succeed. Furthermore, it appears probable that, the longer the sanctions remain in

---

1 Jonathan Eaton and Alan Sykes, "International Sanctions," in Peter Newman, ed., *The New Palgrave Dictionary of Economics and Law*, vol. 2 (New York: Macmillan, 1998), 352–359. Gary Clyde Hufbauer, Jeffrey J. Schott, and Kimberley Ann Elliott, *Economic Sanctions Reconsidered: History and Current Policy*, 2nd ed. (Washington, DC: Institute for International Economics, 1990), 11.
2 See M. S. Daoudi and M. S. Dajani, *Economic Sanctions: Ideals and Experience* (London: Routledge and Kegan Paul, 1983), 5, 8.
3 Hufbauer, Schott, and Elliott, *Economic Sanctions Reconsidered*, 11.
4 Hufbauer, Schott, and Elliott, *Economic Sanctions Reconsidered*, 65.

force, the higher will be the costs incurred by the target; and that empirical relationship probably helps explain the apparent positive correlation between the duration of the sanction and the level of success.[5]

Again, it appears that the type of "sanctions which are most likely to precipitate the desired political change in the target country are those which concentrate income losses on groups benefiting from the target country's policy, those which signal political support to opposition interest groups, or those which threaten increased pain in the future and therefore create an incentive for individual supporters of the target government to free ride on the political activities of their group as a whole."[6] In operational terms, because of the sender's political structure, a sanction might be imposed or "renewed only occasionally ... but enforced continuously"; and legislation can be enacted that would require "the executive or judiciary to lift sanctions as soon as the target performed as specified."[7] Finally, to prevent the target from adopting and adjusting, the imposition of a sanction should be swift; and the sender should "be wary of devoting resources to securing multilateral cooperation," as such "cooperation is far from a prerequisite of successful sanctions."[8]

Economists, political scientists, lawyers, as well as interested laymen, have explored the underlying reasons for the imposition of sanctions: and, although there is a general consensus, there is still a lack of precise agreement. For example, Eaton and Engers argue that there are two types of actions that senders might wish to effect. "One is the target's ongoing choice of some action, such as its debt service payments, trade policies, pollution, or degree of protection of intellectual property. Another is the target's once and for all choice of an irreversible action, such as ceding territory, releasing a hostage, extraditing an accused criminal, or relinquishing power to a new government."[9] Hufbauer, Schott, and Elliott identify five major foreign policy goals that sanctions have been used to achieve: (1) "change target country

5 Jaleh Dashi-Gibson, Patricia Davis, Benjamin Radcliff, "On the Determinants of the Success of Economic Sanctions: An Empirical Analysis," *American Journal of Political Science*, 41 (April 1997), 609–610. It has been argued, conversely, that the longer the period of sanctions, the less successful they will be.

6 William H. Kaempfer and Anton D. Lowenberg, "The Theory of International Economic Sanctions: A Public Choice Approach," *American Economic Review*, 78 (September 1988), 792.

7 Because of limits on time and competing responsibilities, a legislature is not in a good position to immediately change legislation in response to the target's reaction. Jonathan Eaton and Maxim Engers, "Sanctions," *Journal of Political Economy*, 100 (October 1992), 901.

8 Richard N. Haas, "Sanctioning Madness," *Foreign Affairs*, 76 (November/December 1997), 6; Daniel W. Drezner, *The Sanctioning Paradox: Statecraft and International Relations* (Cambridge: Cambridge University Press, 1999), 312–313.

9 Eaton and Engers, "Sanctions," 901–902.

policies in a relatively modest way"; (2) "destabilize the target government"; (3) "disrupt a minor military adventure"; (4) "impair the military potential of the target country"; and (5) "change target country policies in a major way."[10]

However, the type of sanction also must be considered. The most common are restrictions imposed on exports and imports; but those that affect the target's finance – for example, by freezing assets, by cutting off the access of the ruling elites to foreign assets and currency have proven even more important and effective.[11]

If the international political situation is relatively stable, the imposition of tough sanctions by a sender country that is relatively equal in size to the potential target is not likely to touch off a war. Thus, the primary constraint on the sender's behavior "is the economic impact of the lost business with the target." Given the potential costs, the options of the sender are "(1) to do nothing and accept the status quo, (2) to impose sanctions that are stringent enough to have an economic impact on the target, but also result in a high cost for the source, or (3) to impose sanctions that are relatively limited in scope because of the unwillingness of the source states to bear the economic costs of forgoing lost business with the target."[12]

Although sanctions most frequently have been a response to an action or a policy of the target, "in some cases domestic political goals" of the sender have been the force behind their imposition, to solve some internal political difficulties. Such measures may, by "inflaming patriotic fever" "or by quenching the public thirst for action," strengthen the political position of the government in power.[13]

The distinction between wartime and peacetime measures can be seen in a comparison of military blockades with so-called Pacific blockades. Military blockades are wartime measures between adversaries that are designed to restrict the inflow of necessary goods or the export of commodities – exports that are necessary to earn the foreign exchange required to purchase those

10 See Hufbauer, Schott, and Elliott, *Economic Sanctions Reconsidered*, 38. In each case, they have provided an illustration. They are (1) "human rights, terrorism, and nuclear nonproliferation cases"; (2) U.S. campaigns against Fidel Castro "and the Soviet campaign against Marshal Tito"; (3) "UK sanctions against Argentina over the Falkland Islands"; (4) "World Wars I and II and the COCOM sanctions against the Soviet Union and its allies"; and (5) "the UN campaign against South Africa." See Stefanie Ann Lenway, "Between War and Commerce: Economic Sanctions as a Tool of Statecraft," *International Organization*, 42 (Spring 1988), 404.
11 Dashi-Gibson et al., "Determinants," 610. See Lenway, "Between War and Commerce" 404.
12 Lenway, "Between War and Commerce," 422.
13 Examples include the U.S. sanctions against Japan in the months leading up to World War II, and those directed by the United States against Moammar Gadhafi's adventures in northern Africa. Huffbauer, Schott, and Elliott, *Economic Sanctions Reconsidered*, 3.

"necessary" imports. Since the mid-nineteenth century, the established rules of blockades have been the products of a series of international conferences; and those rules include specific provisions that regulate the actions permitted to belligerents, as well as belligerent powers' behavior vis-à-vis neutral third parties.[14] Blockades represent a part of an overall military strategy – a strategy aimed at doing damage to and weakening enemies. Such blockades generally last as long as the war itself; peace presumably brings the end of the blockade (although World War I does provide an exceptional case of the length of time that might elapse between the cessation of hostilities and the lifting of the blockade – during that time the belligerent powers awaited the signing of the peace treaty). Although these international rules are not always followed, they do define an expected standard of behavior in wartime; and they provide a legal basis for international lawsuits during and after the war.

Conversely, Pacific blockades are measures used in peacetime to achieve specific ends without the need for military action; they have no legal status; and, consequently, there are no set of rules governing appropriate behavior. They generally have been applied by larger and stronger powers against smaller nations; and they have been introduced and ended when the imposer decides that no declaration of war or an armistice is required. The ending could be due either to the success of the Pacific blockade in achieving the desired ends or to the willingness of the imposer to accept some degree of failure, because he finds it economically or politically undesirable to continue. In the case of such Pacific blockades, there are no formal rules that have been agreed on by an international organization; and indeed, by most standards, such blockades may be classified as an example of an illegal activity – coercion designed to achieve some desired ends.

2. PACIFIC BLOCKADES

Over the past half-century, we have become used to hearing that "sanctions" have been leveled by one country or by a group of countries that feel they have been injured by an "illegal" action of another nation or an assembly of nations. As a result, the word *sanction* has become an integral part of the international vocabulary. Since the establishment of the League of Nations in the aftermath of World War I, such short-of-war actions that targeted a suspected international miscreant have become common. The United States has been primarily responsible for almost 65 percent of the 120 sanctions that were imposed between 1970 and 1998. Western Europe ranks second as

14 See Chapter 1.

a primary sender; but, with only 22 percent, that region pales in comparison to the United States.[15] However, such actions had been a part of the world's armory for nearly a century before the League leveled its first official peace-time "sanction." Today, in a global economy with countries linked by financial and trade networks, such sanctions are, in part, enforced by actions directed at those economic and financial links. Even now, however, it has sometimes proved necessary to supplement those attacks on the economic and financial links with the imposition of naval blockades. For example, in response to Iraq's 1990 invasion of Kuwait, and after the United Nations imposed comprehensive trade sanctions against the invader, U.S. ships in the Gulf were joined by British, French, and Soviet vessels; and the United States announced that ships attempting to break through the international cordon would be stopped by force if necessary.[16] However, even with this wider set of weapons, the level of success has not been high. In the earlier period, such blockades often were the only method of coercing recalcitrant nations to pay their alleged debts to the international community. Not surprisingly, then, as now, the results were, at best, mixed.

Although historically most blockades have been deployed by belligerent powers in wartime, because of attempts at international coercion short of war there have been some blockades that involved neither war nor belligerent powers. The legal status of such "Pacific" blockades (the term originated about 1850) has only gradually evolved; but, they emerged in the nineteenth century as almost the only coercive tool, short of war, designed and deployed to settle international disputes; and, in recent years, such blockades have continued to be mounted as one enforcement mechanism for what have come to be called "economic sanctions." In this century, Pacific blockades have been initiated by both individual countries and by international organizations (the UN and NATO, to cite but two examples).

A Pacific blockade involves the deployment of a naval force charged with "interrupting commercial intercourse with certain ports or coasts of a state,

---

15 Kimberley Ann Elliott and Gary Clyde Hufbauer, "Same Song, Same Refrain? Economic Sanctions in the 1990's," *American Economic Review*, 89 (May 1999), 404–405.

16 Margaret P. Doxey, *International Sanctions in Contemporary Perspective*, 2nd ed. (Basingstoke: Macmillan, 1997), 84. The U.S. action was based on Article 51 of the UN Charter. In this case, the original Pacific blockade was transformed into a belligerent blockade when twenty-eight nations, acting on the basis of UN Security Council Resolution 678 (1990), launched a military attack on the Iraqi forces. See Ludwig Weber, "Blockade, Pacific," in Peter Macalister-Smith, ed., *Encyclopedia of Public International Law*, vol. 1 (Amsterdam: North Holland, 1992), 412, 415. As an aside, it might be noted that while American naval vessels attempted to intercept Iraqi tankers trying to smuggle oil through the Gulf, neither the United States nor the UN have made any attempt to stop the equally illegal trade through Turkey. Turkey is a member of NATO and an American ally, and this loophole is clearly a result of an American attempt to assuage an ally's "misgivings about America's policy on Iraq." *Economist* (April 8, 2000), 25.

with a view of securing redress for an international wrong" either by way of threats or by the weakening of the targeted nation as a result of the restrictions on its trade that are imposed by the blockade. Such blockades were a product of the wave of globalization that marked the latter part of the nineteenth century. The right to deploy "a pacific blockade has never been regarded as a war measure; nor does it resemble, except in name, the belligerent right of blockade which is sanctioned by international law." Over the years from 1827 until the first decade of the twentieth century, such blockades had been "resorted to, to secure redress for an offence at international law, in cases in which reparation has been demanded, but refused or unnecessarily delayed." Moreover, such blockades have typically been initiated by powers that were militarily "very much stronger" than was the targeted nation; and, in the exercise of the right to deploy the Pacific blockades, "the tendency has been to regard the practice as a measure of international police, in which several powers have concurred as to the justice of the proceeding and the necessity for its exercise."[17]

Given the gradual emergence of the first extensive global economy, it is not surprising that the first recorded "Pacific" blockade dates from the nineteenth century. In 1827, during the Greek fight for independence from Turkey, Britain, France, and Russia deployed a fleet off the Greek coast to prevent the supply and reinforcement of the Turkish and Egyptian forces fighting in Greece. Although none of the three major powers were at war with Turkey, and, although their fleets were ordered not to fire a shot unless they were opposed, "the allied admirals determined to force a battle with the Turkish fleet." Someone did open fire; and the blockading force responded. In four hours, in what has since been termed the Battle of Navarino, the entire Turkish and Egyptian fleets (over 150 vessels) had been sunk, with the loss of over four thousand men.[18] The "great powers" lost no vessels and fewer than 150 men. Thus, did the first Pacific blockade end – not quite pacifically?

From that date until the outbreak of World War I, at least nineteen and, perhaps, as many as twenty-one such Pacific blockades were deployed. They were generally mounted by powerful European states against smaller nations in Europe and emerging nations in Latin America and Asia. The list of targeted states included, in addition to Turkey in 1827, Portugal in 1831, The Netherlands in 1832–1833, Panama in 1837, Mexico in 1838, Argentina

---

17 George B. Davis, *The Elements of International Law* (New York: Harper and Brothers, 1900), 267–269. 477–478.
18 Ian Brownlie, *International Law and the Use of Force by States* (Oxford: Clarendon Press, 1963), 30–31. See Albert E. Hogan, *Pacific Blockade* (Oxford: Clarendon Press, 1908), 73–76.

in 1838–1840, Nicaragua in 1842, and again in 1844, Argentina again in 1845–1850, Greece in 1850, Sicily in 1860–1861, Brazil in 1862–1863, Bolivia in 1879, China in 1884–1885, Greece, again, in 1886, Zanzibar in 1888–1889, Siam in 1893, Greece (Crete), yet again, in 1897, and Venezuela in 1902–1903. In addition, there may have been a Pacific blockade that targeted Colombia in 1834 and another aimed at San Salvador in 1842. Almost without exception, the targeted countries were small and underdeveloped. The list of targeting countries included Great Britain (twelve times), France (eleven times), Italy and Germany (three times each), Russia and Austria (twice each), and Chile once. Clearly, the "great powers" had found a weapon that they thought cost-effective. Although today multilateral sanctions have become the order of the day, over the years 1827 to 1903, there were fourteen such Pacific blockades that were deployed by a single nation as compared with only seven that drew support from more than a single country.[19]

3. PEACETIME SANCTIONS

Pacific blockades are one method of enforcing what have come to be called economic "sanctions." In international relations, sanctions have been defined as nonamicable measures short of war. They have been pursued for a rather broad variety of international goals – to forestall war or to achieve some other political and economic ends. For example, the goals have included freedom, democracy, a better environment, human rights, labor rights, nuclear nonproliferation, the freeing of captured citizens, the reversal of the capture of land, or, more generally, any actions of a targeted nation with which the targeting nation or group of nations disagreed. Although in the past there have been numerous examples of such sanctions, it has only been in the twentieth century that, as part of the general effort to seek political ends via diplomatic and economic means, the deployment of sanctions has become both frequent and widespread. Sanctions have become the standard weapon of both individual nations and international organizations in their attempts to maintain world peace. Thus, in the recent past, the nature of sanctions has been expanded to encompass a broad range of goals, and a much wider set of policies designed to adversely impact the targeted nation or nations have been innovated.[20]

---

19 Hogan, *Pacific Blockade*, 73–157. Hogan presents a brief narrative of the background to and outcome of each of these Pacific blockades.
20 Hufbauer, Schott, and Elliott, *Economic Sanctions Reconsidered*, 7.

In the absence of formal declarations of war and of a specific status in international law for coercive measures undertaken short of war, the limits on the imposition and magnitude of sanctions are established either by the levels of coercion that world public opinion finds acceptable or by the basic power relations among and within nations. In terms of world opinion, it is clear that the sending country has almost always attempted to make its sanctions proportional to the extent of the alleged "crime." In the words of one scholar, "to make reprisals either disproportioned to the provocation, or in excess of what is needed to obtain redress, is to commit a wrong."[21] These limits apply both to the extent of the sanctions and to the degree to which they are enforced. As unilateral actions undertaken by the imposing party or parties, they can be introduced, modified, or ended without agreement by the targeted nation.

The most basic form of sanctions entails interference with foreign trade – exports, imports, or both. Reduction of the exports of the targeted nation, by reducing income, is meant to reduce that state's financial ability to purchase needed supplies in the world market. Restrictions on the imports of the targeted nation might involve a total ban of all commodities or only a more selective set of restrictions on specific military equipment or on certain types of technologically sophisticated materials that are needed to support the state's military and productive capacity. Moreover, when trade sanctions are deployed, sending countries are more likely to use export rather than import restrictions. In general, the initiating power is more likely to have a more nearly monopolistic position in its export than in its import market. In addition, in the case of the United States – the chief targeting country – "Congress has given the president much greater flexibility to restrain exports than to slow imports."[22] Given the importance of international financial flows, it is not surprising that restriction on flows of capital and money also have been implemented frequently, as have reductions or cessation of foreign aid subsidies – subsidies that were intended to benefit the smaller, targeted nations. In the modern world – a world characterized by globalization and welfare transfers to underdeveloped and developing nations – such controls on financial flows tend to be more effective than direct restrictions on trade.

21 William Edward Hall, cited in Dr. Omer Yousif Elagab, *The Legality of Non-Forcible Counter-Measures in International Law* (Oxford: Clarendon Press, 1988), 16.
22 Hufbauer, Schott, and Elliott, *Economic Sanctions Reconsidered*, 65–66. "Import quotas are generally a tool of commercial policy, imposed to protect domestic industries by specifying maximum levels of imports. In the past, however, the government has revised quotas for various commodities to achieve foreign policy and national security goals. The same is true for tariffs ..." Congressional Budget Office, *The Domestic Costs of Sanctions on Foreign Commerce* (Washington, DC: Congressional Budget Office, 1999), 15.

"Alternative financing may be harder to find and is likely to carry a higher price (i.e., a higher interest rate); and require greater credit security, because of the uncertainties that sanctions create." In addition, "official development assistance may be irreplaceable"; and, such financial restrictions "may interrupt a wide range of trade flows even without the imposition of explicit trade sanctions."[23]

Other forms of coercive measures have included the withholding of diplomatic recognition, the boycotting of athletic and cultural events, and the sequestering of property of citizens of the targeted country. Closer to military actions, although still without a formal declaration of war, are the deployment of naval demonstrations, direct military retaliation or reprisal, and the temporary occupation of territories. All of these measures have been included under the rubric of sanctions – sanctions intended to intimidate the target country and to force it to adopt a new course of action more in line with the targeters' wishes. It should be noted, however, that, in a vast majority of the cases of sanctions imposed between 1914 and 1940, those "sanctions were usually imposed to disrupt military adventures or to complement a broader war effort." "In the period following World War II, other foreign policy motives have become increasingly common, but sanctions were still deployed on occasion to force a target country to withdraw its troops from border skirmishes, to abandon plans of territorial acquisition, or to desist from other military adventures."[24]

It should be noted, however, that most such sanctions are not costless to implement. Thus, the targeter almost always bears some economic burden from the introduction of sanctions that limit trade or that disrupt other relations among and between nations (both targets and neutrals). It is highly likely that domestic firms will lose sales when trade, aid, or financial flows are disrupted. Moreover, the sender's trading partners may respond by diversifying their sources of supply and their structure of production to the detriment of the sender. In addition, "sanctions increase the long-term uncertainty, and therefore the cost, of doing business abroad" as costs are imposed on domestic firms.[25] "Unilateral sanctions may also have national costs if they undermine the reputation of U.S. businesses as reliable suppliers."[26] Furthermore, in 1992, Congress and the Clinton administration angered U.S. companies by taking some unilateral embargos a step farther. New

---

23 Hufbauer, Schott, and Elliott, *Economic Sanctions Reconsidered*, 70.
24 Hufbauer, Schott, and Elliott, *Economic Sanctions Reconsidered*, 5.
25 Hufbauer, Schott, and Elliott, *Economic Sanctions Reconsidered*, 75.
26 Congressional Budget Office, *The Domestic Costs of Sanctions*, 10.

laws have broadened the sanctions against Cuba, Iran, and Libya, not only by banning U.S. companies from trading with these countries but also by punishing foreign corporations that continued to trade by preventing those foreign corporations, under certain conditions, from doing business in the United States or with American companies.[27] In the long-term, trade and financial relations between the United States and emerging markets are likely to be much greater than they are at present. Thus, even though the current costs appear low, if U.S. imposed sanctions slowed growth in those relatively new markets, the United States could pay a high price in the future.[28]

In some cases, the sanctions are imposed multilaterally, based on a formal agreement among nations; but, in other cases – cases that are legally more uncertain – imposing nations may attempt to involve third countries and persuade them to go along with the sanctions, even though they were not directly involved at their inception. It should be clear that, in a globalized world, sanctions tend to be ineffective unless there is a high degree of international cooperation. "International trade suggests that for a homogenous good with a high substitution elasticity, only a sender coalition responsible for more than half of the supply of that good can significantly influence the terms of trade."[29] Moreover, such "sanctions may alienate allies abroad and business interests at home." As a result, they may impose substantial political costs. Thus, international cooperation is very important; and, in terms of a sanction's efficiency, "the mirror image of international cooperation with the sender country is the support the target country receives from its neighbors and allies." "Target countries are seldom cut off from alternative markets or financial sources when sanctions are imposed; trade and financial channels usually remain open, even though at a higher cost."[30] A list of the sanctions imposed by individual countries and international organizations between 1914 and 1990, as presented by Hufbauer, Schott, and Elliott, with the dates covered are reported in Tables 8.1 and 8.2, and a decadal estimate of successes and costs is reported in Table 8.3.

27 Louis Uchitell, "Who's Punishing Whom? The Trade Ban is a Boomerang, U.S. Companies Say," *New York Times*, Business Day, (September 11, 1996), D1 and D4. In 2000 Congress amended "the embargo on trade with Cuba, agreed to last year by the United States Congress, allowing sales of food and medicine. But this imposed tight conditions, such as requiring cash payment." *Economist* (November 24, 2001), 60.

28 Congressional Budget Office, *The Domestic Costs of Sanctions*, 31–32.

29 Drezner, *Sanctions Paradox*, 15.

30 One example of the response to such economic/political costs is the passage of the British Protection of Trading Interests Act (a legal barrier that has spread to France, Denmark, Australia, and other countries) designed "to counteract the impact of others' sanctions on their own foreign policy and economic interests." Hufbauer, Schott, and Elliott, *Economic Sanctions Reconsidered*, 12–13, 45.

Table 8.1. *Summary of Economic Sanctions for Foreign Policy Goals, 1914–1990*

Case (a)	Sender and Target	Active Years	Success Score (b) (index)	Cost to Target (c) (millions of dollars)	Cost as Percentage of GNP (d)	Cost per Capita (dollars)	Trade Linkage (e) (percents)	GNP Ratio: Sender to Target (f)	Type of Sanction (g)	Cost to Sender (h) (index)
14-1	UK v Germany	1914–18	12	843.0	7.1	12.58	9	1	X, M, F	4
17-1	US v Japan	1917	4	23.0	0.8	0.44	21	13	X	2
18-1	UK v Russia	1918–20	1	446.0	4.1	2.49	19	1	X, M, F	3
21-1	League v Yugoslavia	1921	16	nd	nd	nd	27	37	nd	2
25-1	League v Greece	1925	16	nd	nd	nd	36	56	nd	2
32-1	League v Paraguay & Bolivia	1932–35	6	4.0	3.0	1.03	74	224	X	2
33-1	UK v USSR	1933	12	4.0	negl	negl	13	1	M	2
35-1	UK, League v Italy	1935–36	1	86.0	1.7	1.98	16	6	X, M, F	3
38-1	UK, US v Mexico	1938–47	9	2.0	0.2	0.11	70	75	M, F	2
39-1	Alliance Powers v Germany, Japan	1939–45	12	688.0	1.6	5.00	15	2	X, M, F	4
40-1	US v Japan	1940–41	1	88.0	0.9	1.21	31	11	X, F	3
44-1	US v Argentina	1944–47	4	29.0	0.8	1.82	19	58	X, F	2
46-1	Arab League v Israel	1946–	4	258.0	4.1	123.00	3	2	X, M, F	4
48-1	US v Netherlands	1948–49	16	14.0	0.2	1.43	9	45	F	1
48-2	India v Hyberdad	1948	12	18.0	2.0	1.10	99	22	X, F	2
48-3	USSR v US, UK, France	1948–49	1	258.0	0.1	1.05	1		X, M	3
48-4	USSR v Yugoslavia	1948–55	1	–76.0	–2.5	4.47	13	52	X, M, F	1
48-5	US, COCOM v USSR, COMECON	1948	6	706.0	0.2	2.28	24	3	X	3
49-1	US, CHINCOM v China	1949–70	1	106.0	0.5	0.20	38	13	X, M, F	3
50-1	US, UN v North Korea	1950–	2	8.0	1.2	0.83	20	378	X, M, F	2
51-1	UK, US v Iran	1951–53	12	186.0	14.3	11.14	42	235	X, M, F	1
54-1	USSR v Australia	1954	1	90.0	0.5	5.56	3	18	M	2
54-2	India v Portugal	1954–61	8	negl	negl	negl	negl	13	X, M, F	2
54-3	Spain v UK	1954–84	6	5.0	negl	0.10	1	0.2	X, M	2
54-4	US, S. Vietnam v North Vietnam	1954–	1	129.0	3.1	3.96	1	358	X, M, F	2

56-1	US v Israel (intermittent episodes)	2	1956–83	16.0	0.1	4.13	22	218	X, F	2
56-2	UK,US, France v Egypt	9	1956	138.0	3.4	5.87	23	160	X, F	2
56-3	US v UK, France	12	1956	167.0	0.3	3.25	10	7	F	2
56-4	US v Laos	9	1956–62	5.0	4.2	2.08	2	4,372	F	1
57-1	Indonesia v Netherlands	8	1957–62	69.0	0.7	6.27	3	0.2	X, M, F	2
57-2	France v Tunisia	1	1957–63	7.0	0.9	1.75	66	76	F	
58-1	USSR v Finland	16	1958–59	45.0	1.1	10.23	19	58	X, M, F	2
60-1	US v Dominican Republic	16	1960–62	16.0	1.9	5.52	56	596	X, M, F	2
60-2	USSR v China	4	1960–70	287.0	0.5	0.42	46	4	X, M, F	4
60-3	US v Cuba	1	1960–	114.0	4.4	16.76	47	173	X, M, F	3
61-1	US v Ceylon	16	1961–65	8.7	0.6	0.86	6	375	F	1
61-2	USSR v Albania	1	1961–65	3.0	0.6	1.76	51	494	X, M, F	2
61-3	Western Allies v German D. Republic	1	1961–62	nd	nd	nd	12	40	nd	2
62-1	US v Brazil	12	1962–64	110.0	0.6	1.49	49	30	F	
62-2	UN v South Africa	6	1962–	273.0	2.8	15.08	77	130	X, F	3
62-3	USSR v Romania	1	1962–63	nd	nd	nd	41	24	nd	2
63-1	US v United Arab Republic	16	1963–65	54.0	1.4	1.93	15	153	F	1
63-2	Indonesia v Malaysia	1	1963–66	29.0	1.0	3.14	7	2	X, M	4
63-3	US v Indonesia	8	1963–66	110.0	2.0	1.05	25	145	F	1
63-4	US v South Vietnam	12	1963	9.0	0.3	0.59	20	206	F	1
63-5	UN, Org. for African Unity v Portugal	8	1963–74	11.0	0.3	1.25	15	10	X, M, F	2
64-1	France v Tunisia	9	1964–66	12.0	1.5	2.67	48	106	M, F	2
65-1	Us v Chile	12	1965–66	0.5	negl	0.06	37	98	M, F	2
65-2	US v India	16	1965–67	41.0	negl	0.08	24	13	F	
65-3	UK, UN v Rhodesia	12	1965–79	130.0	13.0	28.89	69	1,388	X, M, F	3
65-4	US v Arab League	6	1965–	8.0	negl	0.06	10	31	X, F	2
67-1	Nigeria v Biafra	12	1967–70	220.0	15.2	14.67	50	3	X, M, F	3
68-1	US v Peru	1	1968	33.0	0.7	2.60	10	186	F	1
68-2	US v Peru	12	1968–74	35.0	0.7	2.72	10	186	F	

(continued)

Table 8.1 *(continued)*

Case (a)	Sender and Target	Active Years	Success Score (b) (index)	Cost to Target (c) (millions of dollars)	Cost as Percentage of GNP (d)	Cost per Capita (dollars)	Trade Linkage (e) (percents)	GNP Ratio: Sender to Target (f)	Type of Sanction (g)	Cost to Sender (h) (index)
71-1	US v India, Pakistan	1971	2	117.0	0.2	0.18	19	16	X, F	1
72-1	UK, US v Uganda	1972–79	12	36.0	2.6	3.44	22	860	X, M, F	2
73-1	Arab League v US, Netherlands	1973–74	9	5,697.0	0.4	25.55	3	0.04	X	1
73-2	US v South Korea	1973–77	4	333.0	1.8	9.60	29	78	F	1
73-3	US v Chile	1973–	6	54.0	0.6	5.29	18	187	F	1
74-1	US v Turkey	1974–78	1	77.0	0.2	1.92	12	42	F	1
74-2	Canada v India	1974–76	4	33.0	negl	0.06	2	2	X, F	2
74-3	Canada v Pakistan	1974–76	4	13.0	0.1	0.18	2	14	X	2
75-1	US, Canada v South Korea	1975–76	16	nd	nd	nd	32	87	nd	2
75-2	US v USSR	1975–	6	102.0	negl	0.40	4	2	M, F	2
75-3	US v Eastern Europe	1975–	8	37.0	negl	0.51	1	5	M, F	1
75-4	US v South Africa	1975–82	4	2.0	negl	0.08	12	43	X	2
75-5	US v Kampuchea	1975–79	1	42.0	6.8	6.27	negl	2,523	X; M, F	1
76-1	US v Uruguay	1976–81	6	10.0	0.3	3.57	10	452	X, F	
76-2	US v Taiwan	1976–77	16	17.0	0.1	1.01	32	100	X	
76-3	US v Ethiopia	1976–	6	–160.0	–5.5	–5.67	22	592	M, F	2
77-1	US v Paraguay	1977–81	6	2.0	0.1	0.71	13	959	F	
77-2	US v Guatemala	1977–86	6	21.0	0.4	3.17	37	355	F	
77-3	US v Argentina	1977–83	6	62.0	0.1	2.38	13	38	X, F	2
77-4	Canada v Japan, EC	1977–78	9	115.0	negl	0.31	2	0.1	X	2
77-5	US v Nicaragua	1977–79	12	22.0	1.0	9.48	27	913	X, F	1
77-6	US v El Salvador	1977–81	6	13.0	0.5	3.02	32	685	F	
77-7	US v Brazil	1977–84	9	94.0	0.1	0.84	19	12	F	1
78-1	China v Albania	1978–83	1	43.0	3.3	16.54	34	249	X, M, F	2
78-2	US v Brazil	1978–81	4	5.0	negl	0.04	22	11	X	2

(continued)

78-3	US v Argentina	4	1978–82	0.2	negl	negl	14	34	X	2
78-4	US v India	4	1978–82	12.0	negl	0.02	13	18	X	2
78-5	US v USSR	1	1978–80	51.0	negl	0.19	3	2	X	2
78-6	Arab League v Egypt	1	1978–83	–77.0	–0.4	–1.88	4	16	X, M, F	3
78-7	China v Vietnam	3	1978–88	254.0	3.5	5.20	12	41	F	1
78-8	US v Libya	4	1978–	246.0	1.3	90.74	20	118	X, M, F	3
79-1	US v Iran	12	1979–81	3,349.0	3.8	90.51	13	28	X, M, F	3
79-2	US v Pakistan	1	1979–	34.0	0.2	0.43	10	114	F	1
79-3	Arab League v Canada	12	1979–	7.0	negl	0.30	2	1	X, M, F	2
79-4	US v Bolivia	6	1979–82	48.0	1.7	8.73	22	562	F	
80-1	US v USSR	1	1980–81	525.0	negl	2.00	4	2	X	3
80-2	US v Iraq	4	1980–	22.0	0.1	1.71	5	69	X	2
81-1	US v Nicaragua	8	1981–90	45.0	3.2	16.67	33	1727	X, M, F	3
81-2	US v Poland	9	1981–87	246.0	0.1	6.83	4	17	X, M, F	2
81-3	US v USSR	1	1981–82	480.0	negl	1.79	2	2	X	3
81-4	EC v Turkey	6	1981–82	300.0	0.5	6.47	34	40	F	
82-1	UK v Argentina	12	1982	979.0	0.6	34.84	5	3	X, M, F	2
82-2	Netherlands, US v Surinam	9	1982–88	80.0	7.8	202.53	37	2,565	F	1
82-3	South Africa v Lesotho	16	1982–86	27.0	5.4	19.29	100	103	X, M	2
83-1	Australia v France	1	1983–86	negl	negl	negl	negl	0.3	X	2
83-2	US v USSR	1	1983	negl	negl	negl	2	2	M	2
83-3	US v Zimbabwe	4	1983–88	27.0	0.4	3.55	7	462	F	1
83-4	US, Org East Carib States v Grenada	8	1983	negl	negl	negl	1	32,900	X, M, F	2
84-1	US v Iran	6	1984–	130.0	negl	2.83	3	25	X, M, F	2
85-1	US v South Africa	6	1985–	550.0	0.8	17.19	12	54	X, M, F	2
86-1	US v Syria	6	1986–	4.0	negl	0.39	3	189	X, F	2
86-2	US v Angola	2	1986–	4.0	negl	0.44	25	437	F	2
87-1	US v Panama	4	1987–90	319.0	6.0	138.70	50	854	M, F	3

Table 8.1 (continued)

Case (a)	Sender and Target	Active Years	Success Score (b) (index)	Cost to Target (c) (millions of dollars)	Cost as Percentage of GNP (d)	Cost per Capita (dollars)	Trade Linkage (e) (percents)	GNP Ratio: Sender to Target (f)	Type of Sanction (g)	Cost to Sender (h) (index)
87-2	US v Haiti	1987–90	6	56.0	2.9	10.37	74	2,383	F	1
87-3	US v El Salvador	1987–88	16	nd	nd	nd	42	1,006	F	
88-1	Japan, West Germany, US v Burma	1988–	6	234.0	2.1	5.85	22	803	F	1
88-2	US, UK v Somalia	1988–	4	49.0	2.0	6.90	10	1,429	F	1
89-1	India v Nepal	1989–90	9	132.0	4.6	7.25	28	94	X, M	2
89-2	US v China	1989–	1	322.0	0.1	0.29	10	13	X, F	2
89-3	US v Sudan	1989–	1	91.0	0.1	3.96	7	408	F	1
90-1	US, UN v Iraq	1990–	nd	21,600.0	48.0	1,255.81	100	242	X, M, F	4

(a) Case numbers are those in Table 1. 1 of the source.

(b) The success score is an index on a scale of 1 to 16, found by multiplying the policy result index by the sanctions contribution index (see Tables 3.1 through 3.5 of the source).

(c) The cost to target is expressed in millions of current U.S. dollars, as estimated in the case abstracts in vol. 2. Parentheses indicate a gain to the target country.

(d) The cost as a percentage of GNP is the cost of sanctions to the target country as a percentage of its GNP. Parentheses indicate a gain.

(e) The trade linkage equals the average of presanction target–country exports to the sender country (as a percentage of the total target–country exports) and imports from the sender country (as a percentage of total target–country imports).

(f) The GNP ratio is the ratio of the sender country's GNP to the target country's GNP.

(g) Types of sanction include the interruption of commercial financial, aid, and other official finance (F), the interruption of exports from the sender country to the target country (X), and the interruption of imports by the sender country from the target country (M).

(h) The cost to sender is an index number scaled from 1 to 4. Key: 1 = net gain to sender; 2 = little effect; 3 = modest welfare loss to sender; 4 = major loss to sender.

Source: Gary Clyde Hufbauer, Jeffrey J. Schott, and Kimberly Ann Elliott, *Economic Sanctions Reconsidered: History and Current Policy*, 2nd ed. (Washinton, DC: Institute for International Economics, 1990), 16–27, 84–90.

Table 8.2. *Dating of Sanctions, 1914–1990*

Case (a)	Sender and Target	Active Years	Targeting Country	Date Begun	Date Ended
14-1	UK v Germany	1914–18	UK	11–3–15	(if prior to 1990)
17-1	US v Japan	1917	US	7–9–17	
18-1	UK v Russia	1918–20	UK	11–11–18	1–16–20
	(first imposed)				
	(extended)			9–29–19	
21-1	League v Yugoslavia	1921			
25-1	League v Greece	1925			
32-1	League v Paraguay & Bolivia	1932–35			
33-1	UK v USSR	1933	UK	3–20–33	7–1–33
35-1	UK, League v Italy	1935–36	League	11–10–35	7–4–36
38-1	UK, US v Mexico	1938–47			
39-1	Alliance Powers v	1939–45	UK	11–?–39 (G)	5–19–45
	Germany, Japan		US	12–?–41 (J)	9–1–45
40-1	US v Japan	1940–45	US	6–15–40	9–1–45
44-1	US v Argentina	1944–47	US	6 to 10–44	6–4–47
46-1	Arab League v Israel	1946–	Arab League	1946	still in effect
48-1	US v Netherlands	1948–49	US	12–2–48	1949
48-2	India v Hyberdad	1948	India	7–?–48	1948
48-3	USSR v US, UK, France	1948–49	USSR	3–30–48	9–30–49
48-4	USSR v Yugoslavia	1948–55	USSR	2-Late-48	7–29–55
48-5	US, COCOM v USSR, COMECON	1948	US,COCOM	6–15–48	still in effect
49-1	US, CHINCOM v China	1949–70	US, CHINCOM	10–??–49	1969–70
50-1	US, UN v North Korea	1950–	US, UN	6–30–50	still in effect
51-1	UK, US v Iran	1951–53	UK, US	1951	1953
54-1	USSR v Australia	1954	USSR	4–24–54	1954?
54-2	India v Portugal	1954–61	India	8–??–54	12–18–61
54-3	Spain v UK	1954–84	Spain	4–19–54	11–??–84
54-4	US, S. Vietnam v North Vietnam	1954–	US, S. Vietnam	Summer 54	still in effect
56-1	US v Israel (intermittent episodes)	1956–83	Us	Early 57	5–25–83
56-2	UK,US, France v Egypt	1956	UK, US, France	7–28–56	8–1–56
56-3	US v UK, France	1956	US	1956	1956
56-4	US v Laos	1956–62	US	Fall 1956	1962
57-1	Indonesia v Netherlands	1957–62	Indonesia	11–??–57	7–4–63
57-2	France v Tunisia	1957–63	France	5–29–57	8–9–63
58-1	USSR v Finland	1958–59	USSR	Late 1958	1–??–59
60-1	US v Dominican Republic	1960–62	US	8–21–60	1–4 to 6–62
60-2	USSR v China	1960–70	USSR	7–??–60	1970
60-3	US v Cuba	1960–	US	10–19–60	still in effect
61-1	US v Ceylon	1961–65	US	8–8–62	1965
61-2	USSR v Albania	1961–65	USSR	1–??–61	??
61-3	Western Allies v German D. Republic	1961–62	Western Allies	(1961–1962?)	

(continued)

Table 8.2 *(continued)*

Case (a)	Sender and Target	Active Years	Targeting Country	Date Begun	Date Ended
62-1	US v Brazil	1962–64	US	2–28–62	4–1–64
62-2	UN v South Africa	1962–	UN	11–6–62	still in effect
62-3	USSR v Romania	1962–63	USSR	1962	1963
63-1	US v United Arab Republic	1963–65	US	1963	1965
63-2	Indonesia v Malaysia	1963–66	Indonesia	9–27–63	3–??–67
63-3	US v Indonesia	1963–66	US	11–??–63	??–??–66
63-4	US v South Vietnam	1963	US	1963	1963
63-5	UN, Org. for African Unity v Portugal	1963–74	O for AU UN	1963 12–21–65	1974
64-1	France v Tunisia	1964–66	France	5–??–64	5–??–66
65-1	US v Chile	1965–66	US	1965	2–14–66
65-2	US v India	1965–67	US	6–30–65	2–??–67
65-3	UK, UN v Rhodesia	1965–79	UK UN	11–??–65 12–16–66	??–??–79 12–??–79
65-4	US v Arab League	1965–	US	6–30–65	still in effect
67-1	Nigeria v Biafra	1967–70	Nigeria	1967	1–1–70
68-1	US v Peru	1968	US	5–15–68	10–??–68
68-2	US v Peru	1968–74	US	1968	2–19–74
70-1	US v Chile	1970–73	US	11–9–70	??–??–73
71-1	US v India, Pakistan	1971 1971	US US	5-Early-71 (P) 12–1–71 (I)	
72-1	UK, US v Uganda	1972–79	UK	1972 (UK)	1979
73-1	Arab League v US, Netherlands	1973–74	US, Arab League	10–19 to 28–73 10–19 to 28–73	3–18–74 (US) 7–??–74 (N)
73-2	US v South Korea	1973–77	US	1973	1977
73-3	US v Chile	1973–	US	12–11–73	still in effect
74-1	US v Turkey	1974–78	US	8–14–74	9–27–78
74-2	Canada v India	1974–76	Canada	5–22–74	1976
74-3	Canada v Pakistan	1974–76	Canada	11–??–74	1976
75-1	US, Canada v South Korea	1975–76	US, Canada	6–??–75	1976
75-2	US v USSR	1975–	US	1–??–75	still in effect
75-3	US v Eastern Europe	1975–	US	6–10 to 13–75	still in effect
75-4	US v South Africa	1975–82	US	1975	4–??–82
75-5	US v Kampuchea	1975–79	US	5–16–75	1979
76-1	US v Uruguay	1976–81	US	10–1–76	7–1–81
76-2	US v Taiwan	1976–77	US	8–29–76	Early 77
76-3	US v Ethiopia	1976–	US	Early 76	still in effect
77-1	US v Paraguay	1977–81	US	1977	7–1–81
77-2	US v Guatamala	1977–86	US	3–??–77	??–??–86
77-3	US v Argentina	1977–83	US	2–??–77	12–??–83
77-4	Canada v Japan, EC	1977–78	Canada	1–1–77	1–16–78

Case (a)	Sender and Target	Active Years	Targeting Country	Date Begun	Date Ended
77-5	US v Nicaragua	1977–79	US	6–15–77	Fall 79
77-6	US v El Salvador	1977–81	US	summer 77	1981
77-7	US v Brazil	1977–84	US	2–24–77	2–6–84
78-1	China v Albania	1978–83	China	7–11–78	10–4–83
78-2	US v Brazil	1978–81	US	3–10–78	10–??–81
78-3	US v Argentina	1978–82	US	3–9–78	7–19–82
78-4	US v India	1978–82	US	3–10–78	7–29–82
78-5	US v USSR	1978–80	US	7–18–78	80 (add to Afghan)
78-6	Arab League v Egypt	1978–83	Arab League	9–24–78	12–22–83
78-7	China v Vietnam	1978–88	China	2 or 3–??–78	2–17–88
78-8	US v Libya	1978–	US	1978	still in effect
79-1	US v Iran	1979–81	US	3–9–79	1981
79-2	US v Pakistan	1979–80	US	4–6–79	1–??–80
79-3	Arab League v Canada	1979–	Arab League	6–18–79	10–29–79
79-4	US v Bolivia	1979–82	US	11–2–79	10–??–82
80-1	US v USSR	1980–81	US	1–4–80	4–24–81
80-2	US v Iraq	1980–	US	2–6–80	3–1–82 (??)
81-1	US v Nicaragua	1981–90	US	1–22–81	3–13–90
81-2	US v Poland	1981–90	US	12–23–81	2–19–87
81-3	US v USSR	1981–82	US	12–23–81	11–13–82
81-4	EC v Turkey	1981–82	EC	12–??–81	12–1–82
82-1	UK v Argentina	1982	UK	4–6–82	8–10–82
82-2	Netherlands, US v Surinam	1982–88	Netherlands, US	12–??–82	1988??
82-3	South Africa v Lesotho	1982–83	South Africa	12–??–82	1983
83-1	Australia v France	1983–86	Australia	6–9–83	1986
83-2	US v USSR	1983	US	9–5–83	9–28–83
83-3	US v Zimbabwe	1983–88	US	12–19–83	4–10–87?
83-4	US, Org East Carib States v Grenada	1983	US, OECS	6–??–83	11–??–83
84-1	US v Iran	1984–	US		
85-1	US v South Africa	1985–	US	9–9–85	
86-1	US v Syria	1986–	US		
86-2	US v Angola	1986–	US		
87-1	Us v Panama	1987–90	US	4–3–87	1–25–90
87-2	US v Haiti	1987–90	US	1990	
87-3	US v El Salvador	1987–88	US	1988	
88-1	W. Germany, Japan, US v Burma	1988–	W. Germany, Japan, US		
88-2	US, UK v Somalia	1988–	US		
89-1	India v Nepal	1989–90	India		1990
89-2	US v China	1989–	US	6–5–89	
89-3	US v Sudan	1989–	US		
90-1	US, UN v Iraq	1990–	US, UN	8–2–90	still in effect

Source: See Table 8.1.

Table 8.3 *Quinquennial Averages, Economic Variables, 1914–1990*

Years	Annual Average Number of Sanctions	Success Score (b) (index)	Cost to Target (c) (millions of dollars)	Cost as Percentage of GNP (d)	Cost per Capita (dollars)	Trade Linkage (e) (percents)	GNP ratio: Sender to Target (f)	Cost to Sender (h) (index)
1914–1918	0.40	5.67	437.33	4.00	5.17	16.33	5.00	3.00
1919–1923	0.20	16.00	nd	nd	nd	27.00	37.00	2.00
1924–1928	0.20	16.00	nd	nd	nd	36.00	56.00	2.00
1929–1933	0.40	9.00	4.00	1.53	0.52	43.50	112.50	2.00
1934–1938	0.40	5.00	44.00	0.95	1.05	43.00	40.50	2.50
1939–1943	0.40	6.50	388.00	1.25	3.11	23.00	6.50	3.50
1944–1948	1.40	6.29	172.43	0.70	19.31	24.00	26.06	2.29
1949–1953	0.60	5.00	100.00	5.33	4.06	33.33	208.67	2.00
1954–1958	2.20	6.64	61.01	1.31	3.93	13.68	480.04	1.82
1959–1963	2.80	7.36	85.39	1.37	4.15	33.36	170.14	2.07
1964–1968	1.60	10.00	59.94	3.91	6.47	32.25	251.38	1.88
1969–1973	1.20	7.50	1,066.67	1.18	10.20	18.00	207.17	1.17
1974–1978	5.20	5.69	41.45	0.49	5.56	15.17	281.27	1.65
1979–1983	3.40	6.53	332.02	1.42	23.28	16.56	2,270.43	1.94
1984–1990	2.17	5.58	1,957.58	5.56	120.83	29.69	610.54	1.85

Source: Table 8.1 and table notes.

4. SANCTIONS OF THE LEAGUE OF NATIONS AND
THE UNITED NATIONS

Although sanctions and pacific blockades have a long history, the more formal legal discussion of their legitimacy dates only from the twentieth century with the formation, first, of the League of Nations and, then, the United Nations. The Charters of both of these organizations included provisions for collective action, whether by collective decisions made after some particular event or else by collective action automatically undertaken under certain previously specified circumstances. These actions were designed to punish aggressors and, hopefully, to avoid wars. In the case of the League of Nations, the power to deploy sanctions was primarily embodied in Article 16 of the League's Covenant, "which authorizes and contemplates collective economic and military sanctions against a state that resorts to war in disregard of its covenants – peacefully to settle its disputes under articles 12, 13, or 15."[31] In the case of the United Nations, the power is rooted in Articles 2(4), 39, 41, 42, 43, and 46 of that organization's Charter and in the Uniting for Peace Resolution of 1950. Article 2(4), as interpreted, "does not impose any constraint on economic coercion."[32] Articles 41 and 42 give the Security Council power to enforce Article 39. That latter article defines the purpose of enforcement action as being "to maintain or to restore international peace and security." Article 43 "provides that member states should conclude special agreements with the Council to make available, when needed, armed forces to maintain peace and security." Finally, the Uniting for Peace Resolution of 1950 authorizes the General Assembly, by a two-thirds vote, "to take action against an aggressor, if the council is unable to act because of a veto."[33]

---

31 Edwin R. Borchard, "Sanctions, International," in *Encyclopedia of the Social Sciences*, Edwin R. A. Seligman, ed. (New York: Macmillan, 1930), vol. 13, 528. The power of the League to impose effective sanctions suffered a mortal blow when the sanctions imposed on Italy for its invasion of Ethiopia were secretly violated by the British and the French (Hoare-Laval Agreement). Lawrence Ziring, Jack C. Plano, and Roy Olton, *International Relations: A Political Dictionary* (Santa Barbara: ABC-CLIO, 1995), 319.
32 Elagab, *Legality of Non-Forcible Counter-Measures*, 200–201. Ziring, et al., *International Relations*, 358.
33 Marjorie M. Whiteman, ed., *Digest of International Law*, vol. 12 (Washington, DC: Government Printing Office, 1971), 361; Ziring, et al., *International Relations*, 358. It might be noted that the power of the United States to impose sanctions is based largely on International Economic Powers Act (IEEPA), the Trading with the Enemy Act (TWEA), the United Nations Participations Act, and the Export Administration Act. In addition, several pieces of legislation are directed at particular states. They include the Iraq Sanctions Act, the International Security and Development Act, the Cuban Democracy Act, the Cuban Liberty and Democratic Solidarity Act, and the Antiterrorism and Effective Death Penalty Act. Finally, some sanctions have been imposed by presidential Executive Orders. Among U.S. statutes focusing on the regulation of trade are the various tariff and trade acts, including the Trade Act of 1974. "Section 301 of the 1974 Act authorizes retaliation against a wide

The League of Nations undertook four cases of collective action: in 1921 (vs. Yugoslavia); 1925 (vs. Greece); 1932–1935 (vs. both Paraguay and Bolivia, to settle the Chaco War); and, most notably, and most unsuccessfully, against Italy in 1935–1936. Because it captures the problems of imposing effective sanctions without widespread international support and because it underscores the weakness of the League, the mid-1930s case of the attempt by the United Kingdom and the League of Nations to impose sanctions on Italy – sanctions aimed at effecting that latter county's withdrawal from Abyssinia – appears particularly enlightening. The exact location of the border between Abyssinia and Italian Somaliland had long been an issue between Italy and Abyssinia; and on December 5, 1934, the dispute triggered a military clash between the armed forces of the two countries. Over the next ten months, drawing on the Anglo-French-Italian treaty of 1906, both France and England sought a negotiated solution; but their attempts to halt the conflict were unsuccessful. On January 3, 1935, Abyssinia appealed to the Council of the League of Nations under Article 11 of its charter. Drawing on the Italian-Abyssinian Treaty of 1928, the League submitted the dispute to arbitration; but that course of action proved unsuccessful. In September, the League, acting under Article 15.3, appointed a committee with representatives from five countries (the United Kingdom, France, Poland, Spain, and Turkey) to investigate the Abyssinian complaint. On October 5, 1935, Italy invaded Abyssinia; the League council immediately appointed a committee with representatives from six nations to investigate the incursion; and, two days later, that committee found Italy guilty of violating Article 12. Between October 11 and 19, the League approved proposals designed to embargo the supply of arms, prohibit imports from and loans and credits to, and further embargo exports of certain materials (a list, however, that did not include coal, oil, or steel) to Italy. However, in private meetings with the British, the French Prime Minister had insisted that the committee take no action that might lead to war. On November 2, the French effectively derailed an attempt to further expand the list of embargoed commodities. The next month, the British Foreign Secretary and the French Prime Minister worked out an agreement designed to underwrite the transfer of a part of Abyssinian territories to Italy. However, the "secret" agreement was leaked, causing a scandal in the United Kingdom that resulted in the resignation of the British Foreign Secretary and made both British and any

---

range of 'unfair' practices. Some break treaty obligations while others are simply 'unreasonable or discriminatory.'" Congressional Budget Office, *The Domestic Costs of Sanctions*, 19–20; Eaton and Sykes, "International Sanctions," 354

possible American participation in enforcing the agreement impossible. On March 2, 1936, the new British Foreign Secretary, Anthony Eden, advocated oil sanctions against Italy; but both his cabinet colleagues and the French government, fearing a major war in Europe, blocked his proposal. On April 15, the "League addresses [a] 'supreme appeal' to Italy to cease hostilities, but [the] Italian delegation insists on *de facto* recognition of military position." Thus, on May 5, Italian forces entered Addis Ababa, the Abyssinian capital; and, on July 4, by a vote of forty-four to one, the League of Nations voted to discontinue its sanctions.[34] In this case, sanctions failed because two major European countries refused to follow the restrictions imposed by the League.

Initially, the United Nations made less frequent use of economic sanctions; such sanctions were imposed only four times between 1946 and 1965. In several cases, however, the sanctions that the UN did mount were long-lived. From 1990 to 1998, there have been more frequent applications of sanctions (nine), and those sanctions have most often been applied within Africa.[35]

In addition to the sanctions collectively imposed by international organizations, there have been sanctions deployed by a diverse set of nations operating individually or in loose confederation. Some have been imposed by an individual country, some by coalitions of several nations. However, most have been mounted by a single country, perhaps with a few of their allies, against one nation. Regional blocs also have imposed sanctions, at times by voluntary decisions made at the time or, at other times, by prior treaty agreement. The size of the coalition has varied; the ultimate size most often reflected the bargaining power displayed by the targeting country in its attempts to get other nations to join in.

One basic fact stands out. As we have noted, in the case of both individual and multiple country sanctions, the imposing country or countries have almost always been both larger and more economically and militarily powerful than the target country. The evidence suggests that sanctions are more successful "when the threatened measure costs the sender little, relative

---

34 Gary Clyde Hufbauer, Jeffrey J. Schott, and Kimberly Ann Elliott, *Economic Sanctions Reconsidered: Supplemental Case Histories*, 2nd ed. (Washington, DC: Institute for International Economics, 1990), 33–34.

35 Between 1990 and 1998, nineteen of the fifty sanctions (38 percent) that were imposed were directed at Africa. Next in order of importance were Latin America with nine (18 percent) and the Soviet Union/Former Soviet Union eight (16 percent). Between 1970 and 1989, only eleven of the sixty-eight (16 percent) were directed at Africa. In that earlier period, nineteen (28 percent) were directed at Latin America and fourteen (21 percent) at Asian countries. Elliott and Hufbauer, "Same Song, Same Refrain?," 405. See also Hufbauer, Schott, and Elliott, *Economic Sanctions Reconsidered*, 16–20.

to the gain from modifying the target's behavior while the damage to the target is large relative to the cost of complying with the sender's will."[36] Taken together, these facts would suggest that the sender is often very much larger and more powerful than the target, an intuition that is borne out by the evidence. "In most cases, the sender's GNP is over ten times greater than the target's GNP; and in over half, the ratio is greater than fifty." In the sanctions studied by Hufbauer, Schott, and Elliott, "in cases involving modest goals the sender's economy is on average more than 200 times larger than the target's economy, and in cases involving destabilization the average ratio exceeds 400. For cases involving the disruption of military adventures, military impairment, and other major policy change, the results indicate less of a size differential between sender and target. However, there is still a significant mismatch in economic clout: in 77 percent of the disruption of military adventure cases, 30 percent of the military impairment cases, and 60 percent of the other major change cases, the sender country's GNP was over 10 times the size of the target country's GNP."[37] Moreover, "the target will be more reluctant to acquiesce if it anticipates multiple disputes, because its concessions represent a transfer of political leverage to the sender country, magnifying the impact of its concessions in the target's eyes."[38] This imbalance in power means that reciprocal sanctions by the targeted state are seldom employed or, if used, they have tended to be ineffective. Moreover, the difference in size and power also has meant that the timing of the imposition and termination of sanctions has been mainly at the option of the imposer.

5. THE EFFECTIVENESS OF SANCTIONS

Before beginning an examination of the effectiveness of sanctions, let us return to a brief history of sanctions and Pacific blockades. As described earlier, in the nineteenth century there were an estimated twenty-one Pacific blockades, most of them imposed by France and Great Britain. In this period, the nature of the colonial empires meant that sanctions were often viewed as matters of internal policy. Thus, more formal measures involving international relations and legal rules were not required. Moreover, although about one-third of the total involved coalitions of several different countries, the coalition almost invariably included Great Britain. In the years before 1900,

---

36 Drezner, *Sanctions Paradox*, 308; Eaton and Engers, "Sanctions," 409.
37 Hufbauer, Schott, and Elliott, *Economic Sanctions Reconsidered*, 63, 98–99.
38 Drezner, *Sanction Paradox*, 308.

only one sanction was imposed by a non-European nation. Of the twenty-one, seven were aimed at European nations, eleven were directed at Latin America, two (both by France) at Asia, and one at Africa – the latter in an attempt to halt the slave trade. In that case, the British had mounted a major blockade of the West African coast to stop the transatlantic slave trade; and this blockade was implemented against all vessels carrying slaves from Africa.

A second notable nineteenth-century example of political interference with international trade was the embargo imposed on European trading by the United States from 1807 to 1809. In an attempt to avoid involvement in the Napoleonic Wars, the aim of the American policy was to reduce that nation's trade with all other powers and to starve Great Britain by denying it the benefits of trade with the United States. In that effort, "1,500 American ships, 20,000 seamen, and $60,000,000 worth of cargo" were confined to port. The embargo severely damaged the American domestic economy. It was reported that, in 12 hours after the news of the Embargo, flour fell from $5\frac{1}{2}$$ to $2\frac{1}{2}$ [*sic*] . . . and Tobacco from $5\frac{1}{2}$ to 3$ and everything in proportion and [*sic*] God [*sic*] only knows the result. In 1808, exports fell from $108 million to $22 million. The revenue of the United States government shrank from $17 million to $7.8 million. American merchants lost their best customers for cotton, tobacco, and flour." Britain was able to find alternative sources of imports – exports from Canada boomed; and, in retrospect, it is clear that the embargo hurt the sender (the United States) far more than the target (Great Britain).[39] This policy was clearly not successful; it did little to reduce British trade; it badly damaged the U.S. economy; and ultimately it led to the War of 1812.

In the twentieth century, before World War II, there were, in addition to the four cases of sanctions levied by the League of Nations, only seven other cases of sanctions. They included one against Russia by Great Britain, and several aimed at Japan; five of the seven were imposed during the decade of the 1930s.

The use of all types of sanctions, if not their success, increased dramatically in the aftermath of World War II. They were frequently the result of the collective action of the United Nations and related regional organizations, but also they were the product of the Cold War conflict, a conflict primarily

39 Solveig Singleton and Daniel T. Griswold, "Introduction," in Solveig Singleton and Daniel T. Griswold, eds., *Economic Casualties: How U.S. Foreign Policy Undermines Trade, Growth, and Liberty* (Washington, DC: Cato Institute, 1999), ix–x; Donald R. Adams Jr., "American Neutrality and Prosperity, 1793–1808: A Reconsideration," *Journal of Economic History*, 40 (December 1980), 713–737; Jeffrey A. Frankel, "The 1807–1809 Embargo against Great Britain," *Journal of Economic History*, 42 (June 1982), 291–308. See also Chapter 3.

between the United States and the U.S.S.R. Including the eleven sanctions imposed by the United Nations, often with a significant U.S. role, there were fifteen in the 1950s, twenty in the 1960s, thirty-seven in the 1970s, twenty-three in the 1980s, and at least fifty in the 1990s. Between 1960 and 1990, the majority of sanctions were imposed unilaterally, most frequently by the United States; but, in the last decade of the twentieth century, a large fraction were imposed by intergovernmental coalitions. Although a more active role was now played by the countries of Western Europe, these coalitions usually included, if they were not originated by, the United States; the second most frequent targeter of sanctions was the United Kingdom; but that nation was responsible for less than one-third of the number of those initiated by the United States.

The most sophisticated and detailed examination of the success of sanctions, by Hufbauer, Schott, and Elliott, suggest that they have not been an overly effective tool of international relations.[40] For example, some scholars point to the 1980 U.S. embargo on grain exports to the Soviet Union as "the classic case of economic sanctions gone awry." The embargo did "raise the costs of grain to the Soviets by an estimated $225 million. But the Soviets were able to obtain grain from new sources." The price increases did not dissuade them from their Afghanistan adventure. "The economic cost to the United States was a loss of $2.3 billion in sales to the Soviet Union." The total costs to the American economy were, however, almost certainly much higher. For example, "U.S. grain producers also lost their dominant vital market share in the U.S.S.R.," a market position that, "because the Russians fear becoming dependent upon U.S. producers subject to the political whims of the U.S. government," "they were never able to recapture."[41] Hufbauer, Schott, and Elliott estimate a success rate of about one-third in achieving desired ends; and, in the case of those imposed by the United States, the authors conclude that sanctions were more successful between 1945 and 1969 than they were after 1970. It is not, however, clear whether it was the severity of the sanction or the extent of the level of enforcement that has shifted over time. The success rates were higher when there were more imposing nations – the more countries in the coalition, the fewer nations there were outside to circumvent the sanctions. As we have seen, almost all the sanctions were deployed by large nations and aimed at small

---

40 Hufbauer, Schott, and Elliott, *Economic Sanctions Reconsidered*, 33, 92–93. Elliott and Hufbauer, "Same Song, Same Refrain?" 404–405.
41 William H. Lash III, "An Overview of the Economic Costs of Unilateral Trade Sanctions," in Singleton and Griswold, *Economic Casualties*, 14.

nations; and, because the costs were relatively larger and more important to the target nation and relatively smaller to the imposing nations, nations that lost less as the sanctions were extended in time, the controls were generally more successful the larger the income disparity between targeting and targeted nations.

Among the types of sanctions, financial controls were used increasingly more frequently and those financial sanctions were relatively more successful than were the restrictions on trade – the result, presumably, of the fact that it is difficult to control trade flows in an expanding globalized world. Whatever the reason, the evidence clearly indicates that, at least in the U.S. case, trade sanctions have become less effective over time. "Trade sanctions have become ever more difficult to enforce in the world's huge and fluid marketplace."[42] By contrast, whereas the world market has become more global, the relative position of the United States in the world economy has declined.[43] In the decades immediately following World War II, the United States was both an economic hegemon and military superpower. Although it may still be a military superpower, since the 1970s it can no longer claim to be a hegemon in the world market place. It is no longer the "reservoir for rebuilding war devastated countries"; it is no longer the "major if not sole supplier of a variety of goods and services; nor is it any longer the primary source of economic assistance for developing countries." First, the European economies recovered from the devastation of the war; then Japan reasserted itself as an economic force to be reckoned with; and, finally, the Asian NICS (South Korea, Taiwan, Singapore, Thailand, Indonesia, and Malaysia) became major competitors in the world market. As a result, the United States has lost much of its economic leverage in international trade.[44]

Although between the end of World War II and 1990 the United States was involved in targeting far more economic sanctions against foreign countries than any other nation in the world (they were a principal sender in 70 of the 107 cases reported by Hufbauer, Schott, and Elliott), none, including the embargo on grain sales to Russia – an embargo, as we have seen, that may have cost the U.S. government alone over $2.0 billion in farm subsidies and permanently cost American farmers a substantial fraction of what had been their total export market – probably had more impact on the American public than their government's response to Cuba's involvement in the "missile crisis" of 1962. For almost a century and a half, the United States had

---

42 Uchitelle, "Whose Punishing Whom?", D1.
43 Hufbauer, Schott, and Elliott, *Economic Sanctions Reconsidered*, 110.
44 Hufbauer, Schott, and Elliott, *Economic Sanctions Reconsidered*, 107–109.

held that the entire Western Hemisphere was within its sphere of influence; and, in addition, since 1945, the geographic "containment of communist influence had emerged as the single most important touchstone of American policy. A successful communist government with ties to the Soviet Union established 'just offshore' of the American mainland by a charismatic leader with expansive aspirations constituted first and foremost an important *symbolic* threat to the Monroe Doctrine and American anti-communism." In addition, "Castro's defiant taunts and dares placed the American reputation for action at stake regardless of the desires of U.S. policy makers." In the words of Secretary of State Dean Rusk, the U.S. deployment of sanctions had four limited, but nonetheless substantial, objectives:

> "First, to reduce Castro's will and ability to export subversion and violence to other American states;
> "Second, to make plain to the people of Cuba that Castro's regime cannot serve their interests;
> "Third, to demonstrate to the people of the American Republics that communism had no future in the Western Hemisphere; and
> "Fourth, to increase the cost of the Soviet Union of maintaining a communist outpost in the Western Hemisphere."[45]

Despite many efforts, Castro remains in power. Thus, one might easily conclude that, despite their cost to the sender, the imposition of sanctions against Cuba could hardly be ruled a success in accomplishing the aims of the blockade.[46]

6. SANCTIONS BY THE UNITED NATIONS

The evidence indicates that sanctions have not always been successful in achieving the desired ends. At one extreme, sanctions may lead the target nation to undertake military or terrorist activities, activities that impose high costs to the targeting nation. It is clear that sanctions can produce wars, when the disparity in economic levels between the nations is relatively small; but, as Americans discovered on September 11, 2001, much more remains to be learned about a possible terrorist response to sanctions.

The case of the United Nations Security Council's deployment of an embargo against Iraq provides an excellent illustration of the problems

---

45 David A. Baldwin, *Economic Statecraft* (Princeton: Princeton University Press, 1985), 176. The statement by Dean Rusk is reported in U.S. Senate, Committee of Foreign Relations, *Hearings: East West Trade*, 88th Congress, 2nd session, 1964, 13.
46 Hufbauer, Schott, and Elliott, *Economic Sanctions Reconsidered: Supplemental Case Histories*, 194–197.

involved in effectively deploying commercial sanctions. In an attempt to force Saddam Hussein to withdraw Iraqi forces from Kuwait, an embargo was imposed in 1990. Because those forces were expelled by the American-led coalition before the embargo had had a serious impact on the state of the Iraqi economy, the focus of the sanctions was shifted to Hussein's stockpile of weapons of mass destruction. The original embargo banned all trade with Iraq, and it froze all Iraqi overseas assets. At one level, the sanctions were successful: by 1991 Iraq's economy had shrunk by nearly two-thirds; and it is estimated that, due to the Gulf War and sanctions, between 1991 and 1998 at least 100,000 (and probably as many as 227,000) children under the age of five had died.

This led to pressure to permit Iraq to exchange oil for food and medicine, an idea the implementation of which was of uncertain success and led to oil-for-food scandals of the United Nations. Yet, twelve years into the embargo, in part because of loopholes in the control, but in even larger part, because of Hussein's political power, the dictator, as well as any stockpile of weapons, remained in place.[47] Over that time, the United States and Britain have attempted to innovate smart sanctions to replace those originally imposed; but, because of political problems within the UN (including the threat by Russia to veto the proposal), those modifications have not been deployed. Thus, in July 2001, the old "dumb" sanctions were extended again; and Iraq's only response was not to bring back the UN weapon's inspectors. Finally, the next spring, the Council, under pressure from the United States and Britain, in an attempt to ease the suffering of the people of Iraq, and to "to shift blame for the country's misery away from Iraq's besiegers to the man who holds the keys to the castle, Saddam Hussein," and in the hope that Iraq would allow the inspectors to return, the sanctions against imports of nonmilitary goods – goods such as food and medicine – were eased.[48] A similar failure can be seen in the attempts by the United States and the UN to sanction Liberia by banning sales of arms to the country, embargoing diamond exports, and banning travel by senior members of the nation's government.[49] An April 2002 report indicates that, despite the sanctions, Liberia continues to buy arms that it uses to support the rebels in Sierra Leone; and, although the ban on diamond exports reduced production and exchanges in the official markets, the blackmarket trade has probably expanded.[50]

47 *Economist* (April 8, 2000), 23–25.
48 *Economist* (May 26, 2001), 25–28; (July 7, 2001), 45–46; (May 18, 2002), 44–45. *New York Times* (May 9, 2002), A5.
49 *Economist* (May 12, 2001), 51–52.   50 *New York Times* (April 17, 2002), A4.

Sanctions have costs and benefits for the imposing nation, but, hopefully, only costs to the target nation. In both cases, however, these benefits and costs do not necessarily accrue to, or are not necessarily imposed on, the entire nation. Again, the case of Iraq is revealing. The impact of the UN sanctions on the civilian population was such that, in 2002, the UN, in the hope of reducing the impact on the general population, greatly broadened the list of products that Iraq can "legally" import.[51] Sanctions are, however, often directed at some specific group (or groups) or set of individuals. Thus, the sanctions' impact on decision makers and elites may be different from their impact on the rest of society. In terms of costs, the two key questions that must be answered when considering the deployment of sanctions are: first, how much will the target nation, or its elites, be willing to lose before conceding defeat; and, second, who in the targeted country will bear the costs. This double measure of success has, in turn, two further dimensions. First, do the sanctions impose perceived costs of sufficient magnitude that the target nation would be expected to respond appropriately and change its policies? This question concerns the effectiveness of the sanctions in achieving the expectations of the imposer, whether or not they lead the target nation to undertake a shift in policy. Second, do the sanctions actually make the target nation do what the imposer wants in terms of policy changes? The answer to that latter question involves both the costs that are actually imposed and their distribution and the targeted nation's, or its elites, response to the threat of higher costs in the future.

There are also, of course, the hoped-for benefits of changes in policy, whether in full or only in part; such benefits are, however, often difficult to quantify. The costs to the imposer include those due to trade and financial transactions foregone as a result of sanctions, and those costs could affect the structure of production and the revenues received by producers and transactors in the targeting nation. In terms of costs to the sender, it should be remembered that the direct per capita costs of sanctions imposed on individual industries are generally much larger than those imposed on the overall economy. "Despite being largely offset at the national level, those direct losses to an industry can provide a useful indicator of the social costs of adjusting to trade restrictions." The government sometimes attempts to design its sanctions to minimize such costs. In the case of the United States, for example, "the 1985 EAAA requires the president to dismantle national security and foreign policy controls," and raise any sanctions on domestic

---

51 *New York Times* (May 15, 2002), A1, A5.

exports when the commodities potentially effected by a ban on such exports are available from foreign sources. Again, governments often provide assistance to their injured residents in the form of unemployment insurance or job training. However, such actions almost never entirely eliminate the costs imposed on the sender country – even unemployment insurance or job training are often not fully acceptable as substitutes for lost employment opportunities. As a result, even if the sanctions prove overall profitable, as the domestic "winners" seldom fully compensate the domestic "losers" – and the "losers'" costs are often significant to the businesses, workers, and communities involved – the results of the deployment are seldom Pareto optimal.[52]

It is clear that, in many cases, the type of behavior that might induce the deployment of a sanction is only one of a number of potentially conflicting issues that confront a potential targeting country. Seldom is the potential for such domestic political conflict more forcibly underscored than in America's relations with India. In 1998, in response to India's tests of atomic weapons, the United States had imposed economic and military sanctions. However, as issues involving potential terrorists, possible political upheaval in Afghanistan and Southern Russia, and the increasing tension of this nation's relations with Pakistan and China emerged, the United States moved to accept India's atomic status and in hopes of building an alliance with that nation, ended its sanctions.[53]

Furthermore in terms of the efficiency of sanctions, the evidence suggests the existence of a paradox. The result was certainly not what the policy-makers had intended. Hardly surprisingly, faced with an "atomic neighbor," Pakistan chose to become a nuclear power; and, in 2002, the two subcontinent nations stood on the brink of war – a war that might well involve atomic weapons. By 2002, however, because of September 11, and problems with the Taliban and Bin Laden, it was Pakistan that had become the important American ally. On the one hand, because the deployment of economic sanctions is conditioned by expectations of future conflict between target and sender, they are imposed more often on adversaries than on allies – there is more to be gained from an adversary backing down. On the other hand, sanctions are often more effective when directed against allies rather than adversaries. First, because "adversaries are less likely to back down, because

---

52 Congressional Budget Office, *The Domestic Costs of Sanctions*, xiii; Hufbauer, Schott, and Elliott, *Economic Sanctions Reconsidered*, 78–79.
53 *Economist* (August 25, 2001), 13–14; *New York Times* (August 27, 2001), A1, A8; (September 6, 2001), A8.

they are more likely to be threatened again in the future."[54] And second, sanctions directed against targets that have little trade with the sender country are generally less successful than those directed at countries that have close economic relations with the sender. Allies tend to be much more closely connected to a potential sender than are the country's adversaries.[55]

There are two additional types of indirect costs that must be considered when a state decides upon a policy of deploying sanctions. First, is the need to consider the political effects of costs suffered by those third parties who are neither imposers nor targets and whose goodwill may be necessary for other dimensions of international policy. Second, are the effects of the cost of sanctions on the opinions of other nations. Third parties may question how high a price and what amount of suffering it is appropriate to impose on the citizens of another nation. Thus, world public opinion may raise the implicit costs of imposing sanctions. The benefits to the imposing nations are possibly even more complex and, thus, more difficult to measure. There may be some gain from the tax aspect of economic sanctions. That is, the sanctions may change trade flows in such a way as to reduce the price of imports to the targeting nation – however, such "tax" responses also often have associated costs.

In each country, the impact of sanctions on trade will depend on the value of trade in the Gross National Product (GNP) of each country and on the percent of GNP represented by the specific goods that are sanctioned. In addition, the importance of financial flows across international borders will affect the costs and benefits of financial restrictions. In both cases, a measurement of costs depends, as is to be expected, on the forces influencing supply and demand.

If, for example, the sanctions involve an embargo on goods previously sent by the imposing nation to the target nation, there will be a reduction in the target nation's imports. The difficulties to the target nation will vary with the availability and cost of increasing production of that good and of finding some domestic substitute. Similarly, it also may depend on the availability of the sanctioned goods in the world market, if some supplying nations do not choose to respect the sanctions. For this reason, we would generally expect sanctions introduced by several nations to be more effective than those imposed unilaterally, although, this need not be the case if the degree of enforcement is influenced.

---

54 David Williams, review of Donald W. Drezner, *The Sanctions Paradox*, *Times Literary Supplement* (October 29, 1999), 33.
55 Hufbauer, Schott, and Elliott, *Economic Sanctions Reconsidered*, 99.

There are analogous conditions when, in the interests of reducing the income earned in foreign trade by the target nation and, thus, its ability to acquire goods in the world market, an embargo limits the exports of the target nation to the targeting nation. The loss of one potential buyer, the imposing nation, could be offset by a shift in domestic consumption in favor of the embargoed good, a shifting of the resources that had previously gone into its production of other goods for either domestic consumption or export, or an increase in the sales of the embargoed good to a different set of nations in the world market.

The difficulties in enforcing financial and monetary controls resemble those of enforcing trade embargoes. Insofar as there are nations that are not part of the sanctions-imposing coalition, there may be opportunities for the target nation to borrow externally from other nations, if those "neutral countries" have the funds available and if they are willing to lend to the target.

Third-party nations play a crucial role in determining the effectiveness of sanctions. They may help to enforce the sanctions, they may serve to help the target nation to circumvent the sanctions, and they also may implement diplomatic negotiations to bring the possible conflict to a peaceful resolution. Or, of course, they may do nothing and let events take their own course.

9

Blockades, War, and International Law

What It All Means

1. DEFINITIONS AND LAWS

Naval blockades can be traced back at least to the end of the sixteenth century, when vessel design had improved sufficiently to permit Dutch war ships to conduct a "blockade-like" operation against Spanish ports in Flanders. In 1630, in a major proclamation, the Dutch extended "to the investment by sea of coast towns the principles applicable to a siege in land warfare," thus claiming a right to confiscate all neutral commerce.[1] The proclamation stated that all ships sailing to or from those enemy ports would be confiscated. Not surprisingly, the concept of a legal blockade – a deployment of vessels whose missions were supposedly governed by a set of legal rules that covered the maritime activities of the warring parties as well as those of any neutral countries that became involved – was not immediately accepted by all governments. However, the terminology contained in various treaties among the Dutch, English, French, and Swedes between 1674 and 1679, as well as in the Treaty of Whitehall of 1689 make it clear that, even then, a "blockade" was widely understood to refer to the lawful exclusion of all commerce from an invested port or coastline.

Since that time, the debate over the legal rules governing blockades has been almost continuous; while, at the same time, serious questions about the possible effectiveness of such naval deployments have been raised. In terms of international law, the first set of fundamental principles was formally set out in the 1856 Declaration of Paris – a document that was ultimately signed

---

1 C. John Colombos, *The International Law of the Sea*, 4th rev. ed. (London: Longmans, 1959), 650. For more extensive historical detail, see Philip C. Jessup and Francis Deak, *Neutrality: Its History, Economics, and Law*, 4 vols, *Vol. 1, The Origins* (New York: Columbia University Press, 1935), 20–49, 105–123.

by the representatives of most of the developed world.[2] Those principles were modified and extended in the final recommendations of the 1909 Conference of London – a conference attended by the representatives of ten major powers. Those recommendations included a set of laws that, although establishing the legal environment that was generally accepted by the major powers at the beginning of World War I, was never ratified by all the participants. At least two basic problems emerged in the attempts to enforce this part of international law. First, as the targeting power or coalition of powers had a clear self-interest in the nature and the extent of the blockade, there was the question of who was to enforce the law; and, second, there was the question of the definition of contraband, that is, precisely what commodities were covered by the blockade.

From the point of view of this study, the focus has been on the efficiency of blockades from the time of the British blockades of France during the more than century-long series of wars between those countries – wars that extended almost continuously from 1694 to 1815 – through the British blockade of the United States during the American Revolution, the Northern blockade of the South during the Civil War, the Allied blockades of Germany during the two world wars, Germany's World War I and World War II submarine blockades of Britain and the United States, the American blockade of Japan during World War II, to the postwar blockades that have been deployed as part of sanctions that have marked international commercial history since World War I.

In addition, this study has examined what was once considered the policy opposite of a blockade – the embargo (the legal prohibition of exports). The result was an economic disaster for the United States, in the years of increasing economic and political tension leading up to the War of 1812. In an attempt to influence the targeter (Britain), between late 1807 and early 1809, the United States, one of the neutral targets of the British and French blockades, deployed an embargo. More recently, as late as the 1980s, in an attempt to induce the Soviet Union to withdraw from Afghanistan, the United States employed a embargo against grain exports to that eastern nation; and, a decade later, in an attempt to force Iraq to withdraw its military forces from Kuwait, the European community and Japan embargoed oil

---

2 The four provisions that were, in large measure, to define the interests of neutrals included: (1) privateering was abolished; (2) neutral flags protect an enemy's goods, except for contraband of war; (3) neutral goods, except for contraband, were not to be captured even under the enemy's flag; and (4) blockades must be effective (i.e., based on a force sufficient to prevent access to the enemy's coast). See Chapter 1.

imports from that Middle Eastern country. In these latter cases, however, unlike the earlier American policy, the embargoes were not defensive in nature. Instead, they were part of an economic offensive against a nation that was perceived to be acting against the world community's standards of behavior. The embargo had become a weapon that was the complement to, as opposed to a response to, other types of economic sanctions.

2. CHANGES IN TECHNOLOGY AND CHANGES IN BLOCKADES

Although the tension between nations is currently the major cause for the deployment of blockades and embargoes, and, although the nature of the international legal environment is crucial to the choice of policy weapons, in the longer run, the changes in the nature of the tactics deployed has, as is true in the case of many other aspects of economic change, depended on the nature of the available technology, both technical and organizational.

Although convoys date back at least to Venetian times, from the point of view of the time covered here, it was the replacement of sail by steam that was probably the most important technological innovation. Overall, some 85 percent of all Southern attempts to run the Northern blockade were successful. Although steamships had been operating in the Atlantic since the 1830s, it was during the American Civil War that they first became important additions to the fleet of vessels attempting to run a major blockade. Over the course of the war, those vessels accounted for a fraction of all blockade-runners, but some 47 percent of all successful blockade-runners. That fraction had risen from 41 percent in 1861 to 79 percent in 1864–1865. Despite their dominance, during that war steam vessels still presented problems. Although the long and narrow runners – frequently loaded with luxury goods for the Southern civilian consumer market – often were successful at running the Northern blockade of the South, they were not well designed to carry bulky commodities such as bales of cotton. Thus, although from 1856 through 1860 an average of 79.4 percent of the South's cotton crop was exported, over the years 1861 through 1864 the figure averaged only 3.2 percent, and output was much lower than before the war. Cotton exports were the South's major source of foreign earnings, but the South had limited cotton production and embargoed cotton exports, and the Northern blockade also had proved to be effective in limiting exports in an indirect way. Needless to say, although American shipyards continued to build sailing ships into the early twentieth century, from the point of view of vessels involved in blockades – ships that were deployed as part of the blockading force or that were engaged in attempts to run the several blockades mounted by the warring powers during World Wars I and II – only coal, or, later, oil-fired steam vessels played any measurable role.

Next to the substitution of steam for sail, over the years from the eighteenth through the twentieth centuries, in terms of blockade or antiblockade technology, convoys were probably the second most important innovation. Although convoys were expensive – first, before any vessel could sail it was necessary to wait until the entire convoy had been assembled; second, the departure and arrival of a convoy tended to jam harbors and, third, the speed of the convoy was limited by the speed of the slowest vessel – as the technology deployed by the target improved, convoys proved increasingly efficient. During World War II, for example, although almost 70 percent of Allied shipping losses can be attributed to German submarines, the monthly losses per submarine declined from 1,635 tons in 1942, to 520 tons in 1943, and to about 150 tons in 1944–1945. The figures for losses per operational submarine display a similar pattern – a decline from 3,556 tons in 1942, to 1,052 tons in 1943, to about 400 tons over the last 16.3 months of the war.

The improvement in the efficiency of convoys can be traced to a series of innovations – innovations that were both organizational and technical. At the organizational level, the focus of the productivity increase lay both in the increasingly effective level of government control of the convoys (initially an organizational product of World War I) and in the increasingly effective integration of the inter-Allied naval organizations. There was, for example, a constant exchange of information between the Admiralty and the U.S. Navy. Furthermore, although initially there was a considerable international mixture of vessels in many Allied convoys, gradually more clearly defined areas of national responsibility were designated; and the respective fleets were deployed within those boundaries. Moreover, administrative control of antisubmarine activities continued to improve. For example, in the United States, in May 1943 the Tenth Fleet was organized to combine all existing antisubmarine activities. Although even at the end of the war there were still problems in effecting air/sea cooperation between the aircraft of the United States and those of British/Canadian coalition that were both supporting the allied convoys, within both the British-Canadian and the American fleets there was an ever-increasing level of cooperation.

In terms of the technical innovations, the most important was almost certainly the deployment of the small escort carriers as part of the convoys and, then, the organization of the carriers and their naval "chaperones" into hunter-killer groups operating near the convoys. The convoys, thus, became an offensive as well as a defensive weapon. The convoy acted as a magnet for the submarines; and, once drawn, attached hunter-killer groups were then able to sink many of those underwater vessels. There were, of course, also other technical innovations. Of those radar was almost certainly the most important, but it was not the only such innovation that helped increase antisubmarine productivity. That list should be expanded to include high frequency direction finders, more effective depth charges and new methods of deploying them, the development of antisubmarine bombs, the Leigh Light, the "Foxer", "Sono" buoys, and the new class of destroyer escorts.

From the Allied point of view, these organizational and technical improvements were crucial. The Germans, drawing on their experience in World War I, had made their submarine fleet the primary tool in their attempts to blockade the British Isles in World War II. That earlier (1915–1918) German effort is, in fact, best described as a counterblockade – a blockade deployed in response to the British attempt to cut off Germany's imports. That British blockade initially was aimed at preventing the flow of what international law termed "absolute contraband"; however, it was soon extended to include "conditional contraband" (such as oil and nitrates); and, by 1915, it had been extended to include foodstuffs. In World War I, the British also had deployed what might be termed an indirect blockade – a blockade that, by rationing neutral country imports of strategic materials to a level that did not exceed their normal peacetime domestic consumption – was aimed at preventing European neutrals from reexporting those imports to Germany. In response to the two British policies, after a failed attempt in November 1914, in February 1915, the Kaiser signed Germany's first declaration of submarine warfare; and the German navy launched an unrestricted submarine offensive against the commercial shipping that supported the United Kingdom. Initially, from the German point of view, the success of the "blockade" was significant, if not spectacular – total allied shipping losses rose from a monthly average of 65,000 tons in August 1914 to 125,000 in May 1915. In the longer term, however, the blockade should be viewed as a spectacular failure. Not only did it violate international law (in terms of history, that hardly made it a new policy innovation), but, within two years, that policy decision led to the American entry into the war. That entry, in turn, initially led to the deployment of the U.S. navy on antisubmarine patrol in the Atlantic, and, in the longer run, almost certainly to the ultimate defeat of the targeting nation.

Less than a quarter century later, the results of the German submarine blockade in World War II, a blockade aimed at cutting Britain off from the Americas – although not leading directly to the American entry into the war – did, despite its potential cost to the United States in terms of its

Pacific defenses, result in the president deploying a significant fraction of the world's first or second largest navy to antisubmarine patrols in the Atlantic. Although the United States did lose one destroyer (the *Rubin James*) to German submarine attack months before the actual declaration of war, the Germans were reluctant to meet the Americans head on; and the deployment was very successful. In hindsight, it is clear that this "peacetime" American participation as escorts to the merchant vessels crossing the Atlantic played a major role in breaking the German Atlantic submarine blockade.

However, with the official entry of the United States into the war, the Germans took the gloves off; and, despite their experience in both World War I and in the "phony" war, in the months leading up to December 7, 1941, private shipping companies, the U.S. navy, and state and local governments were slow to respond. During the first six months of the real war, the losses of U.S. merchant ships exceeded that country's total losses suffered during all of World War I. During that period, the Germans shifted the focus of their submarine attacks from the vessels sailing on transatlantic routes to coastal shipping operating from Bermuda to New England. During the first four months of 1941, a handful of German submarines (on average probably less than a dozen) sank 137 ships (a total of 816,000 tons). The United States was slow to deploy coastal convoys, and the merchant vessels continued to use their radios – radios that the Germans could track. Moreover, towns and cities located along the east coast refused to dim their lights; thus providing the Germans with excellent visual targets as the merchantmen passed between the waiting submarines and well-lighted coast. Gradually, however, better weapons and tactics were deployed, and by May 1944 losses on both the coastal and transatlantic routes had declined and the number of submarines sunk had risen sharply – the monthly "rate of exchange" had declined from over 100,000 tons of Allied tonnage lost per submarine sunk, to less than 5,000 tons per submarine. By then, hardly anyone was surprised that, despite the German attempts to deploy their submarines to prevent the landing at Normandy, not a single Allied vessel was lost.

If the United States was slow to respond to the German submarine blockade, the evidence suggests that, although it may have taken the Navy a long time to digest the lessons learned in the years leading up to December 7, they were not slow to use those lessons in their offense against the Japanese homeland in the last years of the war. As early as December 1941, the American president had endorsed a proposal that the navy begin unrestricted submarine warfare against Japan – warfare designed to simply effect the "strangulation of Japan – strangulation altogether." Given that Germany had, until June 1944, controlled most of the European continent and its resources, the British-American blockade in the Atlantic generated little benefit. However, as Japan was driven back from her outposts in the Pacific, she was increasingly forced to depend on the limited resource base of the Home Islands and Korea; and, by the end of 1943, the United States and its allies had sufficient naval and air power to enforce a blockade – a blockade first of the Home Islands and Korea and finally of the Home Islands alone. The major weapons deployed to enforce the blockade were submarines, aircraft, and a combination of both. Of the three, the submarines were initially by far the most effective. As Holger Herwig (see Chapter 7) has written, "U.S. submarines waged *and won* the war against Japanese commerce, in effect sundering Japan's sea lines of communication." Because of the destruction at Pearl Harbor, for the first two years of the war, submarines were almost the only offensive weapon that the U.S. Navy possessed; however, because of defects in their torpedoes, at first, that weapon was not particularly effective. The torpedo problem was largely solved by mid-1944; and the American victory in the Battle of the Philippine Sea coupled with the success of the island hopping Pacific offensive made it possible to base submarines on islands closer to the Japanese mainland. At the same time, the navy, copying the Germans, began to deploy its submarines in wolf-packs; and the wolf-pack proved very effective. However, because of MacArthur's promise "to return," direct assaults on the Home Islands remained "over the strategic horizon" until the victory in the Battle of the Philippine Sea in June 1944. From that time on, however, it was the Home Islands that were in the direct line of fire. Over the year 1944, 546 Japanese merchant vessels of some 2,500,000 tons fell victim to Allied submarine attack; and, of that total, some 263 vessels of some 1,183,373 tons were sunk in the home waters.

So effective was the U.S. blockade that, by the end of the year, submarines deployed in the "Yellow and East China Seas and off the coast of Japan were seldom encountering good targets." The "enemy ships that were left were forced to operate in the Sea of Japan or the Yellow Sea," where their tactics made it "almost impossible for submarines to get at them."[3] Thus, continued enforcement of the blockade (now termed operation "Starvation") was left largely in the hands of long-range bombers operating from the Marianas. During the last 142 days of the war, those bombers laid twelve thousand mines in the waters between the Inner Zone (Manchuria, Korea, and North China) and the Home Islands. Between April and August 1945, those mines

---

3 See Chapter 7.

accounted for 222 merchant vessels of some 512,000 tons – 45 percent of the vessels and 47 percent of the total Japanese tonnage lost. Although U.S. submarines continued to operate in the Sea of Japan, it was the mines dropped from aircraft that kept the blockade in place and that finally strangled Japan.

Clearly, the fifty thousand sailors and the number of submarines they manned had made a major contribution to the defeat of Japan; however, at least one major question remains to be answered. Hindsight suggests that, had U.S. forces bypassed the Philippines, they might well have saved ninety thousand casualties, and they almost certainly could have taken the Mariannas some months before they did. With planes based on those islands, they could have begun their aerial blitzkrieg of the Japanese home islands some months earlier and possibly have brought the war to a close well before August. Although the long-term question of the consequences from the atom bombing of Hiroshima and Nagasaki can still be argued – the deaths and damage wrought by those bombings has almost certainly acted to deter other nuclear powers from deploying them in the years since 1945 – in the short run, at least, they were very costly; and, had we moved earlier, the Japanese might have surrendered before our atomic technology had become fully operational.

3. INTERNATIONAL LAW AND ORGANIZATION

At this point, it appears reasonable to turn from this brief summary of the history of blockades to a brief examination of the efficiency of the rules of international law that have been written to govern the actions of belligerents and the rights of neutrals. In the late eighteenth century, Russia enunciated a set of four principles that defined the rights of neutral powers during the blockades; and a number of European countries joined to form the League of Armed Neutrality – an organization based on these principles. However, these principles were not universally recognized; even before 1815 British courts had recognized a similar, but different set of rules. In this case, the Americans objected to Britain's attempt to enforce those rules; and this disagreement ultimately led to the War of 1812. The Crimean War again raised questions of the legality of blockades; those questions were addressed in the 1856 Congress of Paris – a meeting that produced the first international declaration of the fundamental principles of international law on the question of blockades. Among the declaration's provisions was the rule that free ships make free goods. Although the declaration was ultimately signed by many nations and generally recognized as binding by most, the United States was at least a partial exception. During the Civil War, the Northern government enunciated and the blockading fleet expanded the 1756 rule that became known as the principle of the continuous voyage. No longer did the United States recognize that "neutral ships mean neutral goods." The American government took the position that, despite intermediate stops and the shift of cargo from one vessel to another, a voyage from an original port of departure to an ultimate destination in the Confederacy formed one continuous voyage, and the United States had the right to seize contraband articles that were obviously intended for an ultimate destination in the Confederacy, even though those goods had initially been consigned to an intervening neutral port. Thereafter, the Northern fleet enforced that decision.

There also were other unilateral amendments to the rule. In 1885, the French and British disagreed on the definition of contraband – the former country demanding that foodstuffs be included in the list of prohibited imports – and, over time, the list continued to be expanded. The Russians, for example, declared raw cotton to be contraband. During the Russo-Japanese War, the belligerent powers defined strategic areas on the high seas – areas from which neutral shipping were to be excluded – and many neutral vessels were sunk. Also, given the possibility that goods could be shipped overland and the innovation of long-range artillery, mines, and submarines, it became obvious that rules limiting blockades to an enemy's coast and that required a "close" blockade were no longer viable. Thus, in 1907, a new convention was signed at the second Hague Peace Conference. That document's twenty-six articles focused on the rights and duties of neutrals; and the Covenant of the League of Nations included the provision that "should any Member of the League resort to war in disregard of its covenants . . . it shall *ipso facto* be deemed to have committed an act of war against all other Members of the League." The proposal also called for the establishment of an international prize court; however, the British were concerned with the definition of the powers of that court. As a result, they invited delegates to a conference that met in London in 1908–1909. The outcome of that conference was the adoption of a "Declaration Concerning the Laws of Naval Warfare"; however, issues involving the definition of "absolute" and "conditional" contraband, the makeup of the prize court, and Article 49 – an article that allowed the destruction of neutral prizes if the captor's safety would be endangered by bringing those vessels into port – were all subjects of disagreement, and the Declaration was never ratified.

World War I saw major amendments to the *de facto* if not the *de jure* rules governing "legal" blockades. Despite meetings and drafts of documents, there had been no generally ratified agreement since the Paris Declaration of 1856. By 1914, however, it was clear that the previous half century had seen both a technical and an institutional revolution in the nature of naval warfare; and, as a result, the outbreak of what was to become World War I convinced the belligerents that an unprecedented effort to halt enemy shipping was desperately required. As a result, both sides moved in ways that greatly trespassed on what had, heretofore, been the rights of neutral powers. The definition of the belligerent power's right of blockade was carried to the utmost limit in terms of the rights of visit and search and the capture and confiscation of contraband of war. Both sides moved to innovate policies that would not only had been "illegal" but unthinkable only a few short months earlier. The Germans launched a full-scale submarine assault on all Allied and neutral shipping. The British deployed an undeclared distant blockade of Germany; and, by imposing import quotas on neutral nations – nations that could not be physically cut off from trade with Germany – prevented those countries from reexporting supplies. Although Britain turned to America for a large fraction of needed munitions and other supplies, their fleet prevented the Germans from exploiting the U.S. market. The American government strongly objected to both sets of the belligerents' policies; however, when, in 1917, they entered the war, that same government was quick to replicate the British actions.

Neither The Hague nor the London Conference had focused on the question of submarines. As World War I neared its end, the British displayed some concern; but neither the Americans nor the Dutch concluded that there was anything in the existing rules of international law inapplicable to them. A reading of the 1936 Protocol of London indicates that the general rule for ships applied to submarines as well; however, during World War II both sides violated this (as well as most other confining) protocols.

Overall, then one might well hope that the delegates to the 1856, 1907, and 1908–1909 conferences were entertained with good food, drink, and parties. Clearly, their efforts to provide a legal set of rules to govern blockades had come to naught; each side violated any rule with which it disagreed. It is a well-known fact that without an effective method of enforcement no law, domestic or international, has much chance of success. After the war, the League of Nations, through the imposition of sanctions, attempted to provide such a mechanism; but, as the sanctions leveled against Italy over its invasion of Abyssinia were to prove, the League was ineffectual, there was no effective way to hold their member in line. More recently, the United Nations has proved somewhat more effective; however, that goal has depended very heavily on American cooperation – to say nothing of the threat of American action, although sometimes requiring the help of other nations to accomplish American ends.

Conclusion

Blockades have been used primarily as wartime measures to reduce the military power of foes, and they have been employed by both sides of the conflict to seek an advantage. During the conflict, blockades tend to become more inclusive in terms of the definition of contraband, including attempts to limit foodstuffs in order to weaken civilian consumption. Nevertheless, their success rate does not seem very high, because of difficulties of enforcement, the willingness of neutrals to trade with belligerents, and the difficulties when land access to one of the belligerents would be possible. Military strength and productive capacity play a more important role in the outcome of war, and the blockade will end when the war is over.

More recently, blockades have been deployed in an attempt to substitute for war, to attempt to coerce certain nations to meet the behavioral requirements of other nations or groups of nations. Such peacetime, or Pacific, blockades, tended to be imposed by strong nations against weaker nations, and they tend to be more limited in the definition of contraband. Such blockades have ceased either when success was achieved, or when the imposing nations feel that little further is to be gained by continuing. These blockades, too, have not been overly successful, as trade with nations not involved in blockading often continues, and world public opinion may limit the effectiveness of the blockade because of the adverse impacts on the population. A limited number of peacetime blockades do expand into full warfare, but most have ended with some accommodations not requiring military actions.

The possible trade-offs between wars and blockades are not certain, as wars have remained a frequent occurrence, even while the number of blockades has increased. Given, however, that most blockades are imposed by powerful nations on weaker nations, and that the more powerful nation can maintain a blockade for long periods, it is expected that in some cases the powerful can obtain desired results with little or no military activity. By contrast, a failed blockade may generate a willingness of the blockaded power to become more aggressive and combative.

Given changes in the technology of warfare, the nature of the blockades has changed over time. The early, traditional close blockade of the coast gave way, due to aircraft, steamships, and long-distance cannons, to the long-distance blockade by ships far removed from coastal waters. Other technological changes permitting or requiring changing methods of organization of blockades include the development of the submarine and the various means of controlling it. Attempts to deal with new methods of blockades often have required new international agreements, but these, even if agreed on, have generally been not kept once any conflict begins. In the future, we will no doubt continue to see nations try to deploy blockades, but greater success than that which has occurred in the past should not be expected.

Index

429

Pacific bases, for US submarines, 338, 341, 343, 374, 375, 423
Pacific blockades, 3, 387–390, 427
  definition of, 387, 388
  enforcement mechanisms for, 388
  globalization and, 389
  goals of, 390
  history of, 389–390, 403–406
  legality of, 387, 388, 389, 403–406
  success of, 427
  vs military blockades, 386
Pacific commerce, Japanese failure to attack, 324
Pacific convoys
  Japanese, introduction of, 325
  lack of, 324
Pakistan, nuclear testing by, 413
paper blockade, 111
  Civil War blockade as, 117
Parmelee, Maurice, 211
passengers, on merchant vessels, safety of, 21
patrol craft, 276
Peace Establishment Act (1801), 72
Peace of Amiens, 25, 28
Peace of Paris (1763), 55
Pearson, Zachariah C., 131
Pearson and Company, 131
Pensacola (Florida), blockade of, 111
Peterhoff case, 120
Philadelphia (Pennsylvania)
  British blockade of, 64
  British occupation of, 59
  effect of Prohibitory Act on, 57, 60
  inland water route through, 59
  shipping data, 60, 61
Philippine Sea, Battle of, 423
Philippines, during World War II, 380, 424
Picuda (submarine), 374
Piece's Pole Cats (submarine pack), 376
Piedras Negras, 142
Piranha (submarine), 374
Poland, German invasion of, during World War II, 246
political scandal, over US torpedoes, 339–340
politics
  and blockade deployment, 3
  and blockade response during World War II, 317
  and end of German submarine blockade during World War I, 173
  during Napoleonic Wars, 34, 35–37
  and success of sanctions, 385, 386, 413
  and US failure to deploy convoys during World War II, 275–276, 319
  and US strategy during World War II, 381
Polly decision, 74, 75, 78
poor rate, British, effect of American embargo on, 86

port(s). *See also specific port*
  blockaded, legal definition of, during 18th century, 7
Port and Transit Executive Committee (Great Britain), 188
Portugal, British alliance with, 88
pressure-operated mines, 340, 341
private blockades, 239
privateering
  abolishment of, during 19th century, 8
  during American Revolution, 63
  during War of 1812, 100, 103
prize
  British captures of, post-American Revolution, 74
  fair, during Napoleonic Wars, 29
  French decree on, after Revolutionary War, 67
  international laws relating to, 9, 11
prize court, international
  establishment of, 11, 425
  rules governing, 11, 12, 13
Prize Court (Great Britain), 13, 18
productive capacity, and success of blockades, 427
Prohibitory Act, 57
propaganda, German, during World War I, 230
protectionism
  American legislation establishing, 66
  Continental System as, 45
Protocol of London (1936), 426
Prussia, blockade principles adopted by, during 18th century, 7
psychological warfare, 1
public opinion
  of Civil War blockades, 111, 124
  on cotton embargo, 125
  and Pacific blockades, 427
  of sanctions, 414
  of War of 1812, 97, 102, 103
  of World War I blockades, 176
  of World War II blockades, 274, 422

Quintero, Juan A., 142

radar
  centimetric (*See* centimetric radar)
  as countervailing policy, effectiveness of, 23
  miniaturization of, 256
  as technological innovation, 421
  during World War II, 255, 256
    countermeasures, 250, 255
    German analysis of, 252
radar deceivers, 254, 255
radar detectors, 255, 257
radar receivers, 256, 257
radio
  daily sub reports by, 257, 318

Lightning Source UK Ltd.
Milton Keynes UK
UKOW041457130613

212212UK00001B/20/P